Fruzsina Gárdos-Orosz | Kinga Zakariás (Eds.)

The main lines of the jurisprudence of the Hungarian Constitutional Court

30 case studies from the 30 years of the Constitutional Court (1990 to 2020)

Nomos

The publication was supported by
Center for Social Sciences, Eötvös Loránd Research Network

Centre for Social Sciences tk | ELKH | Eötvös Loránd Research Network

The Deutsche Nationalbibliothek lists this publication in the Deutsche Nationalbibliografie; detailed bibliographic data are available on the Internet at http://dnb.d-nb.de

ISBN 978-3-8487-8561-2 (Print)
978-3-7489-2982-6 (ePDF)

British Library Cataloguing-in-Publication Data
A catalogue record for this book is available from the British Library.

ISBN 978-3-8487-8561-2 (Print)
978-3-7489-2982-6 (ePDF)

Library of Congress Cataloging-in-Publication Data
Gárdos-Orosz, Fruzsina | Zakariás, Kinga
The main lines of the jurisprudence of
the Hungarian Constitutional Court
30 case studies from the 30 years of
the Constitutional Court (1990 to 2020)
Fruzsina Gárdos-Orosz | Kinga Zakariás (Eds.)
548 pp.
Includes bibliographic references.

ISBN 978-3-8487-8561-2 (Print)
978-3-7489-2982-6 (ePDF)

Onlineversion
Nomos eLibrary

1st Edition 2022

Preface

Both judicial review and constitutional interpretation have a vast and growing body of literature. Constitutional interpretation is one of the standard topics of constitutional scholarship.[1] However, even the most recent literature has not dealt extensively with a jurisprudence that has undergone two constitutional transitions in the last 30 years, as was the case with Hungary in 1989–1990 and 2010–2012.[2]

As regards the concrete past of the literature on constitutional jurisprudence, one only needs to mention Georg Brunner and László Sólyom (eds), *Verfassungsgerichtsbarkeit in Ungarn: Analysen und Entscheidungssammlung 1990–1993*.[3] This book includes an introduction that is still one of the main works which provide an understanding of the early development of democratic Hungary.[4]

When it comes to access to Hungarian constitutional case law in English, András Holló, one of the former presidents of the HCC and Árpád Erdei, one of the former vice-presidents of the HCC, has published a

1 Susan J. Brison and Walter Sinnott-Armstrong, *Contemporary Perspectives On Constitutional Interpretation* (Routledge, 2020); Erin Delaney and Rosalind Dixon (eds), *Comparative Judicial Review* (Edward Elgar, 2018); András Jakab, Arthur Dyevre, and Giulio Itzcovich (eds), *Comparative Constitutional Reasoning* (Cambridge University Press, 2017) or Zoltán Szente and Fruzsina Gárdos-Orosz (eds), *New Challenges to Constitutional Adjudication in Europe* (Routledge 2019).

2 Academic interest in Hungary, furthermore, has adjusted to the spread of populist politics in Europe and the wider world over recent decades. Tom Ginsburg and Aziz Z. Huq, *How to Save a Constitutional Democracy* (Chicago University Press, 2018), or Nadia Urbinati, *How Populism Transforms Democracy* (Harvard University Press, 2019) or Fruzsina Gárdos-Orosz, Zoltán Szente (eds.), *Populist Challenges to Constitutional Interpretation in Europe and Beyond* (Routledge, 2021).

3 Georg Brunner and László Sólyom (eds), *Verfassungsgerichtsbarkeit in Ungarn Analysen und Entscheidungssammlung 1990–1993* (Nomos Verlagsgesellschaft: Baden-Baden 1995).

4 Georg Brunner, 'Vier Jahre ungarische Verfassungsgerichtsbarkeit' in George Brunner and László Sólyom (eds), *Verfassungsgerichtsbarkeit in Ungarn* (Nomos: Baden-Baden 1995), 13; László Sólyom, 'Zum Geleit zu den Entscheidungen des Verfassungsgerichts der Republik Ungarn' in George Brunner and László Sólyom (eds), *Verfassungsgerichtsbarkeit in Ungarn* (Nomos: Baden-Baden 1995), 59.

collection of cases in English.[5] We must also mention the translations of HCC cases on the homepage of the HCC and the translations and briefs of the Codices, which are very useful but not part of the academic analysis.

The book in the reader's hands builds on a methodological innovation that allows the jurisprudence of the HCC to become visible through the headnotes and their explications. The emphasis we put on the crystallization of the legal principles in the headnotes is a unique approach in case analysis which we recommend is applied to other jurisprudence and comparative work in forthcoming similar projects.

It is to be noted, in sum, that our book follows a unique approach because it contains a methodologically well founded selection of case law.[6] It focuses on one of the most significant contemporary challenges to constitutional democracies, bringing together pre-eminent scholars of law from almost all Hungarian law schools to provide insights into the various doctrinal solutions applied by the HCC.

1. *The goals of the book*

The collection offers a retrospective presentation of the practice of the HCC since its foundation and over the past three decades, acknowledging that between 1990 and 2011 this practice was determined by the Constitution, while from 1 January 2012, it has been based on the FL (Fundamental Law).

An example of the genre that we present here is a review of the case law of the GFCC, Jörg Menzel and Ralf Müller-Terpitz (eds), *Verfassungsrechtsprechung: Ausgewählte Entscheidungen des Bundesverfassungsgerichts in Retrospektive*.[7]

The present collection features legal analyses of significant cases. After presenting the facts on which the decision is based, the authors provide a doctrinal analysis of the decision, including an explanation of the background of the case and its consequences. The primary purpose of this

5 András Holló and Árpád Erdei, *Selected decisionsof the Constitutional Court of Hungary (1998–2001)* (Akadémiai Kiadó: Budapest 2005).

6 Similarly to András Jakab and Sebastian Schmid, 'Die Rundfrage über die gelungensten und misslungensten Entscheidungen des VfGH seit 1920' (2021) 76 *Zeitschrift für öffentliches Recht,* 1.

7 Jörg Menzel and Ralf Müller-Terpitz (eds), *Verfassungsrechtsprechung Ausgewählte Entscheidungen des Bundesverfassungsgerichts in Retrospektive* (3nd ed., Mohr Siebeck: Thübingen 2017).

collection of analyses is to present the relevant content of the Constitution, and the FL as explored by the HCC in the specific case. Accordingly, the authors highlight the reasoning behind the decision and recognise the new legal principles, introduced as a Headnote (in Hungarian case law this is not provided by the HCC itself),[8] and provide a thorough doctrinal analysis. Our ultimate aim is to record the milestones of the 30 years of practice of the HCC and to describe the main tendencies in its decision-making. We suggest that what we might term the 'landmark decisions' of the HCC mirror the constitutional change that is at the heart of the current debate in international scholarship.

2. *A Detailed Synopsis*

2.1. *Synopsis*

The English-language collection is based on the volume entitled "Constitutional Jurisprudence: 100 Landmark Decisions of the Constitutional Court 1990–2020",[9] which contains the 100 HCC decisions that are the most significant according to the majority of Hungarian full professors of constitutional law (i.e. the majority of expert opinion). The editors narrowed this selection down to 30 decisions of international interest, selected to explain the main lines and the main turns and shifts in the jurisprudence, and the different legal character of the jurisprudence at different points in time. According to our legal approach, a decision by the HCC can be considered a 'landmark decision' if it introduced or further developed a new doctrinal standard, or expanded or transformed the meaning of the relevant provision of the Constitution or the FL. The collection, therefore, places particular emphasis on highlighting the relevant headnotes when analysing each decision.

The headnotes highlighted in the analyses of the decisions are interwoven through the collection, so—it is hoped—the individual examples of case law deriving from the different eras of the institution will eventually paint a valuable picture of the practice of the last thirty years. To make

---

8 Kinga Zakariás, 'Az elvi tételek kiemelésének kérdése az alkotmánybírósági gyakorlatban' [Underlining the Headnotes in the Constitutional Court Jurisprudence] (2019) 10 *Pázmány Law Working Papers*, 1.

9 Fruzsina Gárdos-Orosz and Kinga (eds), *Az alkotmánybírósági gyakorlat: Az Alkotmánybíróság 100 elvi jelentőségű határozata 1990–2020. I-II.* (Társadalomtudományi Kutatóközpont – HVG-ORAC: Budapest 2021).

this picture as nuanced as possible, within the scope of the Background and the Aftermath part of the case study, each analysis also includes both the previous and the new constitutional court practice relevant to the constitutional issue under discussion.

2.2. *Basic structure of the case studies*

The analyses of the decisions not only examine a particular decision in a narrow sense, but also previous decisions and the general background and the aftermath of the judgment in a broad sense. The analysis of a decision in a narrow sense focuses on the interpretation of the decision itself. The task of the decision analysis in a broad sense is to create a more comprehensive legal context, to place the analysed judgment in the context of the practice of the HCC. Decision analysis, in a broader sense, provides a framework for the analysis. Accordingly, the chapters follow the following structural scheme: title, a summary of the significance of the decision, presentation of the background (including the legal context and the previous decisions), presentation of the motion, description of the operative part and the reasoning, doctrinal analysis, aftermath (both the legal context and later decisions), and bibliography. Each structural element (except for the significance of the decision) is separated under a distinct subheading, and these subheadings are highlighted in bold.

The main title contains the number of the HCC decision and the name given by the editors, and the subheading contains the key phrase of the unofficial headnotes.

The aim of the analysis of the decision—to describe the 'landmark decisions' and the most important tendencies of the 30-year practice of the HCC—is facilitated by emphasizing the significance of the decision at the beginning of the chapter. This places the decision in the context of the practice of the HCC.

The analysis of the decision in the broadest sense begins with the presentation of the previous decisions related to it. Based on the significance of the decision—in the spirit of a retrospective approach—it is necessary to look back at the antecedents of the HCC decision: the Hungarian and international legal environment, and the economic, social, and legal historical background.

The analysis of the decision in the narrow sense begins with a brief description of the motion, which shows the jurisdiction of the HCC, the reasons for initiating the proceedings, and the legal provisions or judicial decisions that the petitioner is challenging.

The decision of the HCC is separated from its reasoning. Therefore the decision is worded clearly in the first paragraph of this part.

The most important part of this subsection is the reasoning (*ratio decidendi*) supporting the operative part of the decision in order to reconstruct the content of the referred provision of the Constitution or the FL. This section presents the majority position, starting from a broad interpretation of the concept of *ratio decidendi* (all the legal principles that contribute to the substantiation of the operative part are included here).

The emphasis on the headnotes given separately at the beginning of each part helps the reader to recognize the new content. The interpreted provision of the Constitution or the FL is always indicated in parentheses at the end of the headnote. The headnote indicates the content of the interpreted provision and what requirement arises from it in the specific case. Headnotes are highlighted as subheadings, and their content is explained in detail during the reconstruction of the decision's reasoning. The location of the statement of the HCC is cited carefully in order to provide guidance for foreign readers, judges and the academic community, including students.

This section contains a doctrinal analysis of the reasoning supporting the decision, taking into account the dissenting and parallel opinions and the positions in the literature, the main task of which is to assess the solutions developed in the decision. The emphasis is on conflicting positions, so the names and sources of the representatives of the different views appear only in footnotes.

This section contributes most to achieving the aims of the collection of analyses, which is to present the impact of the HCC decision on the change in legal doctrine; consequently, it deals with it in great depth, with each headnote being covered.

The aftermath of the decision is the counterpart to the background section insofar as it provides an overview of the impact of the decision on the economic, social and regulatory environment (e.g. legislative amendments). It also serves as an apex stone, completing the analysis by providing feedback on the significance of the decision.

The Hungarian and English language sources are indicated in the bibliography, which will help those interested in getting to know the broader context of the topic and delving into specific details.

For the sake of better understanding we have simplified some legal terms throughout the book. Every legal provision is referred to as an "article" no matter what appears in the official translation. We have also made a list of abbreviations, including the most frequently used legal documents. In some cases we have simplified the legal references in the doctrinal explanation—for which we accept full responsibility—so as to provide the reader with a comprehensive explanation in English.

3. Acknowledgements

We owe special thanks to Csilla Fedinec who helped us with all this and other preparatory work. We would also like to thank Bálint Gárdos, George Seel and Michael Webb for the language review of the English texts. Special thanks goes to the reviewer of the Hungarian book that forms the basis of this collection, Prof. Dr. Peter Paczolay, former president of the HCC, current Hungarian national judge of the ECtHR. We would like to thank the Constitutional Court of Hungary for providing us with important statistical accounts on the examined period. Last but not least, we thank the Center for Social Sciences, Budapest for its generous support.

Budapest, 2021 October

The Editors

Table of contents

List of Abbreviations

CJEU
Court of Justice of the European Union

old Civil Code
Act IV of 1959 on the Civil Code

Civil Code
Act V of 2013 on the Civil Code

old Criminal Code
Act IV of 1978 on the Criminal Code

Criminal Code
Act C of 2012 on the Criminal Code

old Civil Procedure
Act III of 1952 on Civil Procedure

Civil Procedure
Act CXXX of 2016 on Civil Procedure

Criminal Procedure
Act XC of 2017 on Criminal Procedure

Constitution
Act XX of 1949 on the Constitution of the Republic of Hungary

EU
European Union

FL
Fundamental Law of Hungary

GFCC
German Federal Constitutional Court

HCC
Hungarian Constitutional Court

ECHR
European Convention on Human Rights

ECtHR
European Court of Human Rights

old HCC Act
Act XXXII of 1989 on the Constitutional Court

HCC Act
Act CLI of 2011 on the Constitutional Court

ICCPR
International Covenant on Civil and Political Rights

TEU
Treaty on European Union

TP
transitional provisions of the Fundamental Law

Organisational, functional and procedural changes of the Hungarian Constitutional Court 1990–2020

Fruzsina Gárdos-Orosz and Kinga Zakariás***

1. Introduction

During the democratic transition in Hungary constitutional aspirations gave birth to the institution of the Constitutional Court (HCC).[1] The last Socialist Parliament following the draft regulation accepted by the National Round Table adopted Act XXXI of 1989 on the amendment of the Act XX of 1949 on the Constitution and Act XXXII of 1989 on the Constitutional Court.[2] The HCC started its work on 1 January 1990 by making decisions of fundamental importance to establish and protect the rule of law, liberal, western type constitutionalism.[3] The Kelsen model constitutional court was a separate and independent constitutional institution created by Article 32/A of the Constitution, finally consisting of 11 judges to decide on matters of constitutionality. The old HCC Act created a unique solution, termed *actio popularis*, which meant that anyone could turn to the HCC to claim a piece of legislation was unconstitutional, without any personal involvement or interest, and could request its annulment. The HCC became an institution of the utmost importance, making decisions about the character of the new legal order. Although a complete revision of the former Socialist Constitution took place, the democratic transition operated in a situation of legal continuity. This meant that all legal provisions which were not against the new democratic legal order

* PhD, Senior research fellow, Centre for Social Sciences Institute for Legal Studies (Budapest), and Associate professor, Eötvös Loránd University Faculty of Law (Budapest).

** PhD, Associate professor, Pázmány Péter Catholic University Faculty of Law and Political Sciences (Budapest).

1 Sólyom and Brunner, *Constitutional Judiciary in a New Democracy*, (2000); Vincze et al. (eds), 'Az Alkotmánybíróság' in Jakab (ed), *Az Alkotmány kommentárja I.* (2009) 1099 (1103 ff.).

2 Halmai, 'Grundlagen und Grundzüge staatlichen Verfassungsrecht: Ungarn' in von Bogdandy et al. (eds), *Handbuch Ius Publicum Europaeum, Band I.* (2007).

3 Spencer 'Hungary's Remarkable, Radical, Constitutional Court' (1996), 1.

remained in force, while all those contrary to it were removed. In many ambiguous cases the final decision on the constitutionality of a given piece of law was decided by the HCC. As a primarily non-political institution, the HCC became a judge in law in many politically sensitive matters, as well as in its ex post facto review procedures.[4]

The Hungarian Constitutional Court was an activist institution,[5] especially in its first nine years, when László Sólyom was the head of the court.[6] Besides the many competences the HCC was given, which we will discuss later, the posterior norm control gave rise to a series of decisions creating an important role for the HCC, because decisions on constitutionality are essential in building a new democratic legal order. The political significance of the legal decisions was high, due to the independence and primarily non-political nature of the institution responsible for rule of law as the final arbitrator in questions of constitutionality. This might have occurred because of the consent and trust around the institution. Favourable and non-favourable decisions were easier to accept for politics and society when made by a quasi academic, knowledgeable body and formulated in normative legal terms.

In 2010 the two thirds majority in Parliament amended the Constitution by restricting the competence of the HCC,[7] withdrawing its power to review legislation related to the central budget, and increasing the number of judges from 11 to 15. In 2011, through its constitution making power, the parliamentary majority adopted a new constitution called the Fundamental Law (FL) that entered into force on 1 January 2012.[8] The FL was contested from the outset as being a non-consensual document,[9] but was also regarded by many eminent scholars at that time as a consolidated version of the former Constitution with modifications of minor relevance.[10]

---

4 Jakab and Fröhlich, 'The Constitutional Court of Hungary' in Jakab et al. (eds), *Comparative Constitutional Reasoning* (2017).

5 Halmai, 'The Hungarian Approach to Constitutional Review' in Sadurski (ed), *Constitutional Justice, East and West* (2002).

6 Jakab and Kazai, 'A Sólyom-bíróság hatása a magyar alkotmányjogi gondolkodásra' in Győrfi et al. (eds), *Kontextus által világosan: a Sólyom-bíróság antiformalista elemzése.*

7 Vincze, 'Wrestling with Constitutionalism: the supermajority and the Hungarian Constitutional Court' (2013), 86.

8 Schanda et al. (eds), *The basic law of Hungary: A First Commentary* (2012).

9 Tóth (ed), *A Disunited nation: On Hungary's 2011 Constitution* (2012); Kovács and Tóth, 'Hungary's Constitutional Transformation' (2011), 16.

10 Jakab, *Az új Alaptörvény keletkezése és gyakorlati következménye* (2012); Csink and Fröhlich, Egy alkotmány margójára (2012).

After nine subsequent amendments,[11] however, it is commonly accepted that the FL is one important and distinctive pillar of the new constitutional regime in Hungary,[12] where the Constitutional Court is responsible for its protection.[13]

In this introductory chapter, the authors will focus on describing the constitutional and legislative environment of the HCC in order to understand its role through the analysis of cases. This case analysis will draw out the prevailing tendencies in constitutional jurisprudence as the authors interpret them. The structure of the case studies as explained in the preface of this book allows both authors and readers to explain and understand the story of the last 30 years in the given field of jurisprudence. The case studies also show the prevailing tendencies, not only in the substantive matters of constitutionality but also in the competence and procedural matters of constitutional adjudication.

We expect that the applied methodology makes it possible to obtain a wider understanding of substance and procedure and overall, of thechangeof the HCC.

The final goal of this collection is to contribute to an understanding of the role of the HCC's decisions in the shaping of the constitutional order in the different periods of Hungarian democracy after the democratic transition of 1989. The first years were the period of activism which was followed by the consolidation period. Considering the constitutional changes that occurred in 1989–1990 and in 2010 and 2012, the case studies explain the situation of the HCC under the Constitution and the FL. The analysis of landmark cases can illustrate the main features of constitutional adjudication with regard to organisation, competence and procedure, and the tendencies of constitutional design by interpretation. The conscious and well-designed match between the periods and their landmark decisions will highlight the nature of the changes in the case law and in the role of the HCC.

---

11 Drinóczi, Gárdos-Orosz and Pozsár-Szentmiklósy, 'Formal and informal constitutional amendments in Hungary' (2019), 1.

12 Sonnevend et al. (eds), 'The Constitution in Everyday's Party Politics' in von Bogdandy and Sonnevend (eds), *Constitutional Crises in the European Constitutional Area. Theory* (2015).

13 Gárdos-Orosz, 'Challenges to Constitutional Adjudication in Hungary since 2010' in Belov (ed), *The Role of Courts in Contemporary Legal Orders* (2019), 321.

2. The constitutional regulation of the HCC in the Constitution and the Fundamental Law

Article 32/A of the Constitution stated that (1) The Constitutional Court shall review the constitutionality of laws and attend to the duties assigned to its jurisdiction by law; (2) The Constitutional Court shall annul any laws and other statutes that it finds to be unconstitutional; (3) Everyone has the right to initiate proceedings at the Constitutional Court in the cases specified by law; (4) The Constitutional Court shall consist of eleven members who are elected by the Parliament. Members of the Constitutional Court shall be nominated by the Nominating Committee which shall consist of one member of each political party represented in the Parliament. A majority of two-thirds of the votes of the Members of Parliament is required to elect a member of the Constitutional Court; (5) Members of the Constitutional Court may not be members of a political party and may not engage in any political activities outside of the responsibilities arising from the Constitutional Court's sphere of jurisdiction; (6) A majority of two-thirds of the votes of the Members of Parliament present is required to pass the law regulating the organization and operation of the Constitutional Court.

Article 24 of the FL establishes that the Constitutional Court shall be the principal organ in the protection of the Fundamental Law. (2) The Constitutional Court a) shall examine adopted Acts not yet promulgated for conformity with the Fundamental Law; b) shall, at the initiative of a judge, review the conformity with the Fundamental Law of any law applicable in a particular case as a priority but within no more than ninety days; c) shall, on the basis of a constitutional complaint, review the conformity with the Fundamental Law of any law applied in a particular case; d) shall, on the basis of a constitutional complaint, review the conformity with the Fundamental Law of any judicial decision; e) shall, at the initiative of the Government, one quarter of the Members of the National Assembly, the President of the Curia, the Prosecutor General or the Commissioner for Fundamental Rights, review the conformity with the Fundamental Law of any law; f) shall examine any law for conflict with any international treaties; g) shall exercise further functions and powers as laid down in the Fundamental Law and in a cardinal Act. According to the text, the HCC shall annul pieces of legislation and judicial decisions that are not in conformity with the Fundamental aw.

Before discussing the details of this constitutional framework of the operation of the HCC, we draw attention to one major change. While the HCC was originally charged with the review of constitutionality according to the Constitution, since 2012 it has been charged with the protection of the FL. In spite of the fact that the organisation, the competence and the procedure were more or less continuous in the first 30 years of constitutional jurisprudence (this is true in general terms even if significant changes were introduced that we take into account below), the subject of the protection changed.

We have described the goals of the book and the methodology we use in the preface. Here we explain why we believe that it is informative to view the 30 years of the HCC as one corpus of constitutional jurisprudence. In what follows we will carefully describe the important substantive changes that have affected the HCC. We draw attention to the fact that—in spite of this—it not so much the character and the task of the HCC which has changed but rather the content of the constitution itself and the political environment. Therefore, in our assessment it is valid to view the formal operation of the HCC as an important state institution involved in the protection of the Constitution and the Fundamental Law. Below, we will consider the most important differences between the different periods of the HCC. However, we first attempt to obtain an overall picture of the activity of the court, both in numbers through a statistical approach and by referring back and forth between decisions of both constitutional periods in the individual case analysis. Our final goal here is to make the change both in competence and procedure visible for the reader by the exemplary case analysis. As we have emphasised in the preface, the importance of this approach for comparative scholars lies—at least in part—in the exceptional nature of the Hungarian constitutional changes which have occurred with the cooperation of the HCC.

3. *Organisation of the HCC*

The Constitution originally set the number of members of the HCC at fifteen,[14] later reduced to eleven in 1994.[15] The 2011 amendment to the

14 Article 17 of the Constitution.

15 Article 1 of Act LXXIV of 1994 Amending Act XX of 1949 on the Constitution of the Republic of Hungary.

Constitution[16] and the old HCC Act re-established the number of members at fifteen,[17] which was incorporated into the HCC Act.

Article 8 (3) of the old HCC Act originally set the term of office of a Constitutional Judge at nine years and allowed for the possibility of re-election. Any Hungarian citizen with a law degree and no criminal record, who was 45 years of age or older, and who had outstanding theoretical knowledge or at least 20 years of professional experience could be elected as a member of the HCC [Article 5 (1)–(2) of the old HCC Act]. Membership of the HCC ceased, inter alia, at the age of 70.

Under Article 24 (8) of the FL, the HCC is a body of fifteen members elected for a term of twelve years by Parliament by a two-thirds majority of its members. Members of the HCC may continue to be elected from among lawyers with outstanding theoretical knowledge or with at least twenty years of professional experience in the field of law [Article 6 (1) of the HCC Act]. The change is that members of the HCC may not be re-elected [Article 6 (3) of the HCC Act] and that membership of the HCC does not cease on reaching the age of 70.[18]

Pursuant to Article 32/A (4) of the Constitution, the members of the HCC were proposed by a nomination committee composed of one member from each of the parties represented in Parliament. Following the amendment of the Constitution in 2011, the members of the HCC were proposed by a nominating committee composed of members of the parties represented in Parliament, taking into account the proportions of the MPs. The HCC Act maintained this rule.[19] According to this provision, the members of the HCC are proposed by a nominating committee consisting of at least nine and no more than fifteen members nominated by the MPs of the parties represented in Parliament. At least one representative of each party must sit on the committee [Article 7 (1) of the HCC Act].

---

16 Article 3 and 5 of Act LXI of 2011 on the amendment to Act XX of 1949 on the Constitution of the Republic of Hungary required for the adoption of certain temporary provisions related to the Fundamental Law.

17 Article 1 of Act LXII of 2011 on the amendment to Act XXXII. According to Article 2 (3), this law had no effect on the Constitutional Court Justices already in office.

18 Article 42(1) of Act CCVII of 2013 on the amendment of certain regulations in connection to the Fifth Amendment to the Fundamental Law annulled the upper age limit.

19 Article 3 and 5 of Act LXI of 2011 on the amendment to Act XX of 1949 on the Constitution of the Republic of Hungary required for the adoption of certain temporary provisions related to the Fundamental Law.

The HCC shall be presided over by the President of the HCC,[20] who, in addition to convening and presiding over the plenary sessions of the HCC, shall determine the order of the plenary sessions, the agenda, the management of the HCC's Office, the exercise of the rights of employment of the civil servants of the HCC's Office, the appointment of the rapporteur judge [Article 17 (1) of the HCC Act] and in the event of a tie vote, he or she shall have the casting vote [Article 30 (3) of the old HCC Act, 48 (5) of the HCC Act]. In addition to the previous tasks, the HCC Act also stipulates that the President shall contribute to ensure uniform jurisprudence.

Originally, the President and the Vice-President were elected by the members of the HCC from among themselves for a term of three years and were eligible for re-election. Under Article 24 (8) of the FL, the President of the HCC is elected by Parliament from among the members of the HCC by a two-thirds majority of its members. The term of office of the President shall last until the expiry of the term of office of the HCC judge.

The President of the HCC was replaced, in the event of his or her being prevented from attending, by the Vice President, who was also elected by the plenary session from among the judges of the HCC for a term of three years [Article 17 (2) of the old HCC Act]. According to the HCC Act, the President is assisted by a Vice President, who is elected from among the members of the HCC by the plenary session of the HCC on the proposal of the President [Article 21 (1)–(2) of the HCC Act].

From the outset, the administration and preparation of the proceedings shall be carried out by the HCC's Office, headed by the Secretary General elected by the Plenary Session. The Secretary General shall contribute to the preparation of the decisions of the HCC and shall work under the direction of the President of the HCC [Article 22 (3) to (4) of the HCC Act]. In addition to the Secretary General, the HCC Act also provides for civil servants to be employed in the Office of the HCC, who work on the judges' staff, prepare decisions and perform other professional duties as determined by the judge or the President.[21]

---

20 Presidents of the HCC: László Sólyom (July 1990—November 1998), János Németh (November 1998—August 2003), András Holló (August 2003—November 2005), Mihály Bihari (November 2005—July 2008), Péter Paczolay (July 2008 —February 2015), Barnabás Lenkovics (February 2015—April 2016), Tamás Sulyok (November 2016—).

21 Orbán and Zakariás, 'Az alkotmánybírósági érdemi munkatársak szerepe Magyarországon' (2016) 2 *Alkotmánybírósági Szemle*, 108, (110 ff.); Orbán and Zakariás, 'Are Law Clerks a Latent Chamber of the Constitutional Court?' in Zegre-

The HCC shall make its decisions in plenary session, in panels or as a single judge [Article 47 (1) of the HCC Act]. The HCC used to act in plenary session or in a three-member panel [Article 25 (1) of the old HCC Act]. The main body of the HCC is still the plenary session [Article 47 (2) of the HCC Act], but a significant number of cases are concluded in the procedure of single judges[22] or in the procedure of five-member permanent panels.[23] The panel may conduct proceedings in all cases that are not assigned to the plenary session's competence by this Act or by the Rules of Procedure of the HCC [Article 50 (1) of the HCC Act]. The plenary session of the HCC shall decide on preliminary norm control, on the removal from office of the President of the Republic, on the interpretation of the FL, on the annulment of a law that is contrary to the FL or an international treaty, and on all cases in which the decision of the plenary session is justified by the social or constitutional significance of the case, its complexity, the preservation of the unity of constitutional jurisprudence or other important reasons [Article 50 (2) (a), (b) and (f) of the HCC Act], if the majority of the members of the panel or five Members of the HCC who are not members of the given panel initiate it or if the President orders it [Article 49 (6) (b) of the HCC Act].

4. *Procedures falling within the powers of the HCC and legal consequences*

4.1. *Certain procedures*

4.1.1. *Preliminary and posterior norm control*

There were three types of preliminary norm control under the Constitution. The HCC had jurisdiction to examine in advance the unconstitutionality of laws already adopted but not yet promulgated, of the Parliament's

---

an and Costinescu (eds), *The role of Assistant-Magistrates in the jurisdiction of Constitutional Courts* (2016), (79 ff.).

22 According to HCC Act Article 55 (5), the HCC made its ruling on the rejection of the petition without further investigation, following the Secretary General's advice, in a single judge procedure. Single judges are elected on the President's recommendation by the plenary session, on one-year mandates (Rules of Procedure, Article 11).

23 According to Article 49 (1) of the HCC Act, the number and composition of panels, as well as the chair are decided on the President's recommendation by a full board. Panels are re-elected every three years, the chair every year.

Rules of Procedure and of certain provisions of international treaties [Article 1 (a)].[24]

Since 2012 the HCC Act distinguishes between four types of preliminary review: the preliminary review of a law that has been adopted but not promulgated [Article 24 (2) (a) of the FL], an international treaty before its binding force is recognised, the preliminary review of the provisions of the rules of the Parliament [Article 23 of the HCC Act] and the formal review of a law amending the Fundamental Law [Article 23/A of the HCC Act].

A typical form of preliminary norm control under both the old and the new HCC Act is the preliminary examination of the unconstitutionality of a law initiated by the President of the Republic and already adopted by Parliament but not yet promulgated.[25] Several controversial provisions of the 1989 regime change (e.g. the statute of limitations on criminal liability) were decided under this power (See Decisions No. 3 and No. 4). Even after the entry into force of the FL and the HCC Act, the preliminary norm control initiated by the President of the Republic is still the dominant procedure, and—although not a significant number—politically contentious issues are still submitted to the HCC in this procedure (See Decision No. 13.).

The main task of the HCC—and the only one enshrined in the Constitution—was the ex-post control of the constitutionality of laws, with particular reference to the protection of fundamental rights. The Constitution also provided that the ex post review procedure of the HCC may be initiated by any person in the cases provided for by law [Article 32/A (3)].

According to the HCC, the only power that followed from the Constitution was the power of ex post review, and this power was compulsory and complete.[26] In the practice of the HCC, plenary power meant that this power applied to all the rules of law, in addition to the legislation expressly mentioned in Article 1 (b) of the Constitution and other legal instruments of state administration. It was through the interpretation of plenary jurisdiction that the HCC made the law promulgating the international treaty subject to constitutional review,[27] and this is also the legal

---

24 The original text of the old HCC Act also referred the preliminary examination of the bill to the competence of the HCC, but this was repealed by paragraph 1 of the 1998 Act amending Act XXXII of 1989 on the Constitutional Court.

25 The Parliament and the President of the Republic have the right to initiate a preliminary review procedure in respect of a law adopted but not promulgated, pursuant to Article 6 (2) and (4) of the FL.

26 Decision 4/1997. (I. 22.) AB, ABH 1997, 41, 49.

27 Decision 4/1997. (I. 22.) AB, ABH 1997, 41.

basis for the review of the decisions of the Supreme Court, to which the HCC has extended its jurisdiction to ensure legal unity.[28] This is also the legal basis for the review of the decisions of the Supreme Court on the uniform application of the law.[29]

The primary function of abstract norm control is the objective protection of the constitutional legal order, which has made the HCC the guardian of the hierarchical legal order.[30] The HCC, in its ex post abstract review of norms, has examined the conformity of the 'old system' with the constitutional system of the rule of law (See Decisions No. 1 and No. 2), and in its examination of the new system, it has determined the content of the new constitutional system; for example, it has unpacked the content of the laconic and concise provisions of fundamental rights (See Decisions No. 5, No. 6 and No. 7). The power of ex post abstract review of norms was also the dominant power of the Constitutional Court in terms of the volume of cases.[31]

With the entry into force of the FL, the possibility for anyone to submit a petition for an ex post abstract review of the law was abolished, and pursuant to Article 24 (2) (e) of the FL, the HCC reviews the conformity of legislation with the FL at the initiative of a defined group of petitioners, the Government, a quarter of the members of Parliament, the President of the Curia, the Prosecutor General or the Commissioner for Fundamental Rights.

Another change is that the review of the constitutionality of legislation is not comprehensive, and the review of financial legislation is only possible in the case of infringement of specific fundamental rights [Article 37 (4) of the FL, Article 41 (2) of the HCC Act] (See Decision No. 8).[32] Moreover, the Fourth Amendment to the Fundamental Law expressly excluded a review of the content of the Fundamental Law or of the amendment to the Fundamental Law by only allowing examination in relation to the

---

28 Decision 42/2005. (XI. 4.) AB, ABH 2005, 514–515.

29 The HCC established a separate panel for the adjudication of municipal affairs and recommended reallocating municipal cases to ordinary courts. Sólyom, *Az alkotmánybíráskodás kezdetei Magyarországon* (2001), 91.

30 Sólyom, *Az alkotmánybíráskodás kezdetei Magyarországon* (2001), 29.

31 Gárdos-Orosz, 'Alkotmánybíróság 2010–2015' in Jakab and Gajduschek (eds), *A magyar jogrendszer állapota* (2016), 442 (451).

32 Act CXIX of 2010 amending Act XX of 1949 on the Constitution of the Republic of Hungary exempted financial legislation from full review, and the HCC could only review and annul it in cases of violation of certain fundamental rights [Article 32/A (1)–(3) of the Constitution]. This provision was introduced into the FL.

procedural requirements laid down in the FL for making and promulgating it [Article 24 (5) of the FL]. At the same time, Article 37 of the HCC Act extends the review of legislation beyond the public law organizational instruments to decisions on the uniform application of the law.

Since 2012, it has been the Commissioner for Fundamental Rights who has—almost exclusively—initiated ex post abstract review procedures. On this basis, the HCC has ruled on important issues, including the rights of homeless persons (See Decision No. 11),[33] the examination of the TP (See Decision No. 12) and the status of churches (See Decision No. 15). The practice of the Commissioner for Fundamental Rights in relation to his or her role as a petitioner depends to a large extent on role perception,[34] and as a result the number of ex-post abstract normative review petitions has decreased significantly since 2015.[35] The HCC has ruled on environmental issues within this power (See Decision No. 26).

4.1.2. The judicial initiative and the constitutional complaint

The legal institution of the judicial initiative for norm control in concrete cases was already recognised in the old HCC Act, but was rarely used by the courts.[36] The FL reorganised the relationship between the HCC and the ordinary courts by introducing the constitutional complaint against a judicial decision, and in this context the role of this power has increased significantly since the entry into force of the FL, although the rules have not fundamentally changed.

Pursuant to Article 24 (2) (b) of the FL, the HCC shall, on the initiative of a judge, review the conformity of the law applicable to an individual

33 In the field of ex-post abstract review of norms, the HCC ruled on the constitutionality of the Law on the Protection of Families (See Decision No. 7. Aftermath) and the provision of the Civil Code on the criticism of public figures (See Decision No. 20. Background).

34 Csink, 'Ombudsmani alapjogvédelem a gyakorlatban' in Jakab and Gajduschek (eds), *A magyar jogrendszer állapota* (2016), 600 (605).

35 Hence the necessity of broadening the range of possible petitioners, according to some experts. Gárdos-Orosz, 'Alkotmánybíróság 2010–2015' in Jakab and Gajduschek (eds), *A magyar jogrendszer állapota* (2016), 445 (451).

36 In 2010–2011 the number of judicial initiatives jumped due to parking cases: the HCC had previously ruled that the capital's parking regulations were unconstitutional, but annulled them *pro futuro*, so judges began to suspend their parking cases and appealed to the HCC on the grounds that they did not want to apply unconstitutional legislation.

case with the FL, in exceptional cases and within ninety days at the latest.[37] Pursuant to Article 25 (1) of the HCC Act, if a judge, in the course of the adjudication of a concrete case in progress, is bound to apply a legal regulation that he or she perceives to be contrary to the FL, or which has already been declared to be contrary to the FL by the HCC, the judge shall suspend the judicial proceedings and submit a petition for a declaration that the legal regulation or a provision thereof is contrary to the FL, and/or the exclusion of the application of the legal regulation contrary to the FL. According to the HCC, it is a constitutional requirement that a judge must decide the dispute before him or her on the basis of constitutional law, and therefore, where a judge finds that the law applicable to the case at hand is unconstitutional, he or she is obliged, in the absence of the power to disapply the unconstitutional law, to bring the case before the HCC.[38]

Since 2012, many important cases have been brought before the HCC for judicial initiative, such as the constitutionality of the mandatory life imprisonment regime (See Decision No. 19), the regulation of the conditions of detainees' accommodation (See Decision No. 21), foreign currency loan contracts (See Decision No. 22) and the regulation of the rights of persons with reduced working capacity (See Decision No. 29).

The old HCC Act recognised the legal institution of the constitutional complaint, but that type of constitutional complaint could only be directed against the norm applied in an individual case. Thus, the constitutional complaint was only a type of ex post review of a norm, which differed only in that it alleged a violation of a right of the petitioner guaranteed by the Constitution and was linked to a case that had been concluded by a final decision.

While before 2012 anyone could bring an ex post review of an abstract rule without having to justify a legal interest, even 'because of concern about the inconsistency of the legal order',[39] a constitutional complaint for violation of a right guaranteed by the Constitution could be brought before the HCC by a person whose rights had been violated by the application of an unconstitutional law and who had exhausted his or her other remedies or had no other remedy. The constitutional complaint could be

---

37 After the fourth amendment to the Fundamental Law, Article 24 (2) (b) of the FL contains a deadline of 1 April 2013. According to this, the challenged legislation had to be reviewed without delay, but within 30 days at the latest. This deadline was increased to ninety days from 1 October 2013 by the Fifth Amendment to the Fundamental Law.

38 Decision 35/2011. (V. 6.) AB, Operative part. Point 1.

39 Paczolay, 'Megváltozott hangsúlyok az Alkotmánybíróság' (2012), 67 (67).

submitted in writing within sixty days of the notification of the final decision [Article 48 (1)–(2) of the old HCC Act]. The constitutional complaint procedure thus imposed additional conditions on the ex post review of the norms, but the legal consequences of the procedure only provided a narrow scope of remedies for individual violations of fundamental rights. As a consequence, the constitutional complaint was not a decisive instrument of legal protection.

The FL—following the German model—redefined the powers of the HCC, which many considered to be 'one-sided': it introduced the constitutional complaint against a judicial decision [Article 24 (2) (d)]. The FL has retained, and at the same time incorporated into the Constitution, the old constitutional complaint for review of the law applied in an individual case [Article 24 (2) (c)]. In addition, the FL has created the possibility of an exceptional constitutional complaint directly against a statute [Article 26 (2)]. In contrast to *actio popularis*, the HCC Act made the substantive adjudication of all three types of complaint conditional on the person concerned being affected [Article 56 (2) of the HCC Act]

In addition to the other substantive conditions that require consideration,[40] the HCC examines whether the petitioner is affected in the admissibility procedure.[41] The significance of the admissibility conditions varies for the different types of constitutional complaint.

The FL has made the constitutional complaint against a judicial decision the most important competence of the HCC. According to Article 27 of the HCC Act, persons or organisations affected by judicial decisions contrary to the FL may submit a constitutional complaint to the HCC if the decision made concerns the merits of the case or another decision terminating the judicial proceedings, within sixty days of the notification of the decision complained of, provided that he or she has already exhausted all remedies. Article 27 of the HCC Act originally consisted of a single Article, to which the legislator added the words 'or limits its powers in a manner contrary to the Fundamental Law', which, in addition to the possibility of challenging a violation of the rights laid down in the FL,

40 Further substantive conditions are the exhaustion of the legal remedy [Article 27 (1) (b) of the HCC Act], the fundamental constitutional question and the fundamental law violation materially affecting the judicial decision [Article 29 of the HCC Act], the time limit [Article 30 of the HCC Act] and the matter adjudicated [Article 31 of the HCC Act].

41 Prior to the admission procedure, the Secretary-General examines, in the preparatory procedure, whether the application complies with the formal and substantive requirements laid down by law [Article 55. § (2)-(3) of the HCC Act].

also provides for the possibility of asserting a violation of powers. In addition, the legislator has inserted paragraphs (2) and (3), which provide the petitioner exercising public authority with the possibility to assert the rights conferred on them by the Fundamental Law.[42]

The HCC Act limits the scope of review of judicial decisions to the examination of violations of the rights laid down in the FL. In line with this, Article 29 of the HCC Act allows for the admission of a constitutional complaint if two substantive conditions are met: if a conflict with the FL significantly affects the judicial decision, or the case raises constitutional law issues of fundamental importance. In developing the concept of a question of fundamental constitutional importance, the HCC has developed a formula, modelled on the formula for the infringement of 'specific constitutional law' (*spezifisches Verfassungsrecht*) developed in the practice of the GFCC, which defines the scope of the review, according to which the HCC examines the infringement of the range of interpretation of the FL.[43]

The basis for the substantive review of judicial decisions is the obligation to interpret them in conformity with the Constitution, which is laid down in the FL itself. Under Article 28 of the FL, the courts, in the application of the law, shall interpret the text of legislation primarily in accordance with its purpose and in conformity with the FL.[44] In practice, the examination of the conformity of the interpretation of the law

---

42 The eligibility of petitioners exercising public authority has been disputed in the practice of the HCC. The HCC has attached importance to whether the petitioner acted as a subordinate legal entity or as an exerciser of public power in the dispute underlying the constitutional complaint, and has recognised the petitioner's entitlement in the former case {Decision 3091/2016. (V. 12.) AB, Reasoning [16]}. In the post-amendment practice, the HCC has recognised the right of a municipality to complain with regard to the fundamental right to a fair trial [Article XXVIII (1) of the FL] {Decision 3030/2020. (II. 24.) AB, Reasoning [21]}. In another decision, the HCC held that the right to a fair trial and the right to legal remedy invoked by the Metropolitan Court of Appeal [Articles XXVIII (1) and (7) of the FL] are rights laid down in the FL which, by their nature, do not apply only to human beings {Decision 3303/2020. (VII. 24.) AB, Reasoning [39]–[40]}.

43 Zakariás, 'A bírói döntések alkotmánybírósági felülvizsgálatának terjedelme a német és magyar gyakorlatban' (2019) 2 *Alkotmánybírósági Szemle,* 21.

44 The Seventh Amendment to the FL (in effect since 1 January 2019): 'In the course of the application of law, courts shall interpret the text of laws primarily in accordance with their purpose and with the Fundamental Law. In the course of ascertaining the purpose of a law, consideration shall be given primarily to the preamble of that law and the justification of the proposal for, or for amending, the law. When interpreting the Fundamental Law or laws, it shall be presumed

contained in a judicial decision with the FL primarily means examining whether the courts have taken into account the scope of protection of the fundamental rights concerned (See Decision No. 18), but the body also reviews the courts' discretion in cases of a conflict of fundamental rights in administrative law (See Decision No. 24), criminal law and misdemeanour (See Decision No. 27) and civil law cases (See Decision No. 20).

Article 26 (2) of the HCC Act also created the possibility of a constitutional complaint in cases where the violation of rights occurs directly, without a judicial decision, as a result of the application or the entry into force of a provision of a statute that is contrary to the FL. In such a case, the petition may be filed within one hundred and eighty days of the entry into force of the unconstitutional law.[45]

This type of exceptional complaint is distinguished from the ex post, abstract review of the law, which is merely aimed at defending the constitutionality of an objective legal order, by the need to remedy an individual violation of rights. The HCC has therefore established a threefold system of requirements of relevance, modelled on the German system: it requires personal, direct and actual involvement *(érintettség)*, which it examines separately for each petitioner and for each provision of law (See Decisions No. 10 and No. 16).

Although it is disputed in the literature whether this type of constitutional complaint is capable of filling the void left by the disappearance of the *actio popularis* in the protection of fundamental rights,[46] several

---

that they serve moral and economic purposes which are in accordance with common sense and the public good.'

45 However, the dissenting opinion attached to the order rejecting the constitutional complaint for exceeding the time limit drew attention to the fact that the strict grammatical interpretation of the time limit calculation in Article 30 (1) HCC Act and the narrow interpretation of the criterion of involvement (which requires the occurrence of a violation of rights for involvement) together lead to the result that a constitutional complaint cannot be admitted within one hundred and eighty days of the entry into force of the legislation due to the absence of actual involvement (i.e. because of premature filing), and beyond one hundred and eighty days – even if the petitioner is already involved – due to the fact that the time limit has been exceeded. Dissenting opinion by Judge István Stumpf. Order 3264/2012. (X. 4.) AB, Reasoning [12].

46 Chronowski Nóra, 'Alkotmányjogi panasz és alkotmányvédelem' (2014), 95; Gárdos-Orosz, 'Alkotmánybíróság 2010–2015' in Jakab and Gajduschek (eds), *A magyar jogrendszer állapota* (2016), 442 (459).

important cases have been brought before the HCC under Article 26 (2) of the HCC Act (See Decisions No. 10, 16, 23, 28 and 30).[47]

4.1.3. Interpretation of the FL and other competences

The Constitution already included the power of the HCC to interpret the Constitution, which the legislator—together with the practice of the HCC, which gave concrete form to this power[48]—incorporated into Article 38 of the HCC Act.

The HCC interpreted the Constitution not only in the procedure expressly designed for this purpose,[49] but in all procedures for examining the constitutionality of legislation, but this power differed from the interpretation of the Constitution in the exercise of other powers in that the interpretation is placed in the operative part of the decision and the abstract interpretation of the Constitution inevitably borders on constitutionalism.[50]

In this competence, the HCC does not interpret the FL in relation to an individual case or a specific legal provision, but in relation to a specific constitutional problem, if the interpretation can be directly deduced from the FL. The Parliament or its Standing Committee, the President of the Republic, the Government or the Commissioner for Fundamental Rights are entitled to submit a petition for the interpretation of the Fundamental Law.

Although the scope of those entitled to propose abstract constitutional interpretation was very narrow under the Constitution,[51] it was regularly on the agenda of the HCC and was used mainly for the interpretation of powers directly based on the Constitution (e.g. the powers of the President

47 The number of these cases was remarkably high in 2012–13, as the petitioners of previous ex-post norm control cases were able to bring their cases back under Article 26 (2) of the HCC Act if they were involved/affected.

48 Decision 21/2012. (IV. 21.) AB, Reasoning [24].

49 Decision 36/1992. (VI. 10.) AB, ABH 1992, 207, 210.

50 Sólyom, '*Az Alkotmánybíráskodás kezdetei Magyarországon*' (2001), 308.

51 The Parliament or its standing committee, the President of the Republic, the Government or a member thereof, the President of the State Audit Office, the President of the Supreme Court and the Attorney General may submit a petition for the interpretation of the provisions of the Constitution, according to the Article 21 (6) of the old HCC Act.

of the Republic),[52] but it was also a 'catch-all' for all kinds of concrete constitutional problems outside the scope of norm control.[53] After 2012, in only a few—but important—cases, the HCC decided under Article 38 of the HCC Act. The majority of cases[54] concerned the interpretation of the European clause [Article E of the FL] (See Decision No. 25).

The old HCC already regulated the examination of the conflict of laws with international treaties *ex officio* and on the initiative of specific petitioners,[55] and this was maintained in Article 32 of the HCC Act, with the right of petition being granted to one quarter of the members of Parliament, the Government, the President of the Curia, the Attorney General, and the Commissioner for Fundamental Rights. What is new is that, according to the HCC Act, judges may also initiate this procedure—in addition to suspending the court proceedings—if, in the course of the adjudication of a concrete case, they are bound to apply a legal regulation that they perceive to be contrary to an international treaty. In the latter case, the HCC acts within the scope of its jurisdiction under Article 25 of the HCC Act, the yardstick for its examination being, according to the content of the petition, the FL and the international treaty referred to (See Decision No 21) or the international treaty alone (See Decision No. 29).

Article 33 of the HCC Act provides for the HCC to examine a decision of the Parliament in connection with the ordering of a referendum. Under the current rules, the HCC, unlike in the previous rules,[56] does not examine the merits of a petition in which the petitioner invokes constitutional

52 Decision 48/1991. (IX. 26.) AB, ABH 1991, 217.; Decision 8/1992. (I. 30.) AB, ABH 1992, 51.; Decision 26/1992. (VI. 16. AB), ABH 1992, 207.

53 Sólyom, *'Az Alkotmánybíráskodás kezdetei Magyarországon'* (2001), 312.

54 Decision 22/2012. (V. 11.) AB; Decision 22/2016. (XII. 5.) AB; Decision 9/2018. (VII. 9.) AB; Decision 2/2019. (III. 5.) AB.

55 The Parliament or its standing committee, the President of the Republic, the Government or a member thereof, the President of the State Audit Office, the President of the Supreme Court and the Attorney General may submit a petition for conflict with an international treaty, according to Article 21 (3) of the old HCC Act.

56 On the basis of Act III of 1998 on National Referendums and Popular Initiatives and of Article 130 of the Act C of 1997 on Electoral Procedure, an objection could be lodged against the decision of the National Election Committee (OVB) by the Constitutional Court. According to Act CCXXXVIII of 2013 on the Initiative of Referendum, the European Citizens' Initiative and the Referendum Procedure, the substantive examination of the decision of the National Election Committee (NEC) is the responsibility of the Curia (Articles 29–30).

concerns regarding the content of the referendum question or the authentication of the referendum.[57]

The Constitution also contained a rule on conflicts of jurisdiction,[58] which has been taken over in substance by Article 36 of the HCC Act. According to this provision, if a conflict of jurisdiction arises between state bodies—with the exception of courts and administrative authorities—or between state and local government bodies, the body concerned may petition the HCC to eliminate the conflict of jurisdiction on the basis of an interpretation of the FL. The HCC decides which body has jurisdiction in the dispute and designates the body to be prosecuted.

The HCC has ruled on conflicts of jurisdiction in several cases under the Constitution, but has not ruled on the merits under the FL.[59] However, Article 27 (1) of the HCC Act also provides for the possibility to challenge a limitation of jurisdiction in violation of the FL in connection with the challenged judicial decision, so the competence to lodge a constitutional complaint may include the competence to resolve a conflict of jurisdiction.

Finally, the HCC has the competence to deprive the President of the Republic of his office (Article 13 of the FL, Article 35 of the HCC Act), to dissolve a body of representatives that is operating in violation of the FL (Article 34 of the HCC Act), or to issue an opinion on the unconstitutional operation of a religious community with legal personality (Article 34/A of the HCC Act).

57 The HCC, however, also reviews these judicial decisions under Article 27 of HCC Act {Decision 28/2015. (IX. 24.) AB, Reasoning [18]}. Pursuant to Act XXXVI of 2013 on Electoral Procedure, a constitutional complaint may also be initiated against a judicial decision taken in a legal remedy procedure in relation to a decision of an electoral body within three days of the notification of the decision challenged.

58 If a conflict of jurisdiction arises between state bodies, with the exception of courts, and between municipalities, or between municipalities and state bodies, with the exception of courts, these bodies may petition the Constitutional Court to eliminate the conflict of jurisdiction. The Constitutional Court decides, without hearing the petitioner, which body has jurisdiction in the dispute and appoints the party responsible for the proceedings (Article 50 of the old HCC Act].

59 Decision 3001/2012. (VI. 21.) AB is the only case examined in this jurisdiction in which the HCC found that the jurisdictional dispute detailed in the petition could not be decided by interpreting the FL, and therefore does not constitute a conflict of jurisdiction as defined in Article 36 (1) of the HCC Act (Reasoning [8]).

4.2. Legal consequences

Pursuant to Article 39 of the HCC Act, the decision of the HCC is binding on everyone and is not subject to appeal.

The legal consequence of the preliminary norm control is that the law may not be promulgated if the provisions challenged are contrary to the FL (See Decisions No. 3, 4 and 13) [Article 35 (2) of the old HCC Act, Article 40 (1) of the HCC Act]. The legal consequence of ex post norm control in the event of an infringement of the FL is the annulment of the statute or statutory provision [Constitution Article 32/A (2), old HCC Act Article 40, Article 24 (3) (a) FL, Article 41 (1) HCC Act]. The annulment of a statute does not affect legal relationships previously established, except in certain cases of review of criminal proceedings concluded by a final decision.[60] Accordingly, the HCC, as a general rule, annuls legislation that is contrary to the FL with *ex nunc* effect.[61] Thereafter, the annulled legislation may not be applied [Article 43 (1) of the old HCC Act, Article 45 (1) of the HCC Act].

Article 43 (4) of the old HCC Act already provided for the possibility to derogate from the general rule of *ex nunc* annulment: the HCC could determine the repeal of an unconstitutional law or its applicability in a specific case at another time, if this was justified by legal certainty or the particularly important interest of the initiator of the proceedings. These grounds are supplemented by the protection of the FL in Article 45 (4) of the HCC Act. The HCC has made use of the possibility of *ex tunc* (See Decisions No. 8, 10, 12, 15, and 19) and *pro futuro* annulment (See Decisions No. 14 and 21) in a number of cases.

The inapplicability of the annulled legal regulation does not in itself provide the complainant with a specific remedy. Decision 23/1998. (VI. 9.) AB gave the HCC the opportunity to declare an unconstitutional omission, since the legislator had not regulated the procedural consequences of the exclusion of the applicability in a specific case of a law declared uncon-

---

60 The HCC may order a review of criminal proceedings concluded by a final decision if the nullity of the law or legal provision applied in the proceedings would result in a reduction or omission of the penalty or measure, or in an exemption from or limitation of criminal liability or liability for a misdemeanour [Article 45 (6) of the HCC Act; Article 43 (3) of the old HCC Act] (See Decisions No. 11 and 19).

61 According to the old HCC Act, the law expired on the day of the publication of the decision [Article 42 (1)], and according to the current legislation it expires on the day following the publication of the decision [Article 45 (1) of the HCC Act].

stitutional by the panel in non-criminal proceedings.[62] Subsequently, the Parliament established the procedural rules for the redress of constitutional complaints, leaving the method of redress to the Supreme Court.[63] The HCC Act expressly states that, if the HCC annuls a legal regulation applied in a concrete case, the annulled legal regulation shall not be applied in the case that led to the proceedings of the HCC, and also provides for the possibility for the HCC to declare a general prohibition of application [Article 45 (2) and (4)]. The consequences of the annulment of a law applied in an individual case are determined by the ordinary courts on the basis of procedural law.[64]

In addition, the HCC Act contains the possibility of establishing as a legal consequence the constitutional requirement established in the practice of the HCC. Instead of the institution of reviewing the constitutionality of the application of the law, which was lacking in the Hungarian legal system, the HCC developed the doctrine of 'living law',[65] which it used to justify the annulment of a legal provision that could otherwise be interpreted constitutionally but which was consistently applied in judicial practice with unconstitutional content. The special opinion accompanying the decision already highlighted the need to force the law-enforcing bodies to interpret legislation constitutionally by using appropriate legal means, and not to 'punish' the legislator for unconstitutional interpretation of the law, and the HCC therefore sought other solutions to remedy individual violations of fundamental rights. One of the solutions for the review of the interpretation of the law that is still in force today was found in the constitutional requirement laid down in the operative part of the decision. In the absence of competence to review the application of the law, the

---

62 Decision 23/1998. (VI. 9.) AB, ABH 1998, 182.

63 Act LXV of 1999 on the establishment of a procedure for the retroactive exclusion of the applicability in a specific case of a legislative act declared unconstitutional on the basis of a constitutional complaint.

64 In the case of a successful constitutional complaint, the Civil Procedure provides for the application of the rules on the renewal of proceedings (Article 396), while the Criminal Procedure provides for the possibility of review. [Article 648 c)].

65 The HCC stated that the application of the law cannot be the subject of the HCC's proceedings in the absence of such competence, but 'the Constitutional Court must compare not the text of the norm as such, but the norm in force, the norm that is in force and is implemented, i.e. the 'living law', with the content of the provisions of the Constitution and the constitutional values. In the view of the Constitutional Court, 'living law' must be understood in conjunction with the content of the law as interpreted and applied.' Decision 57/1991. (XI. 8.) AB, ABH 1991, 272, 276.

HCC, taking the Constitution as a starting point, designated the scope of the constitutional interpretation of the law with *erga omnes* effect. In so doing, it effectively reversed the obligation to interpret the law in conformity with the Constitution.

This constitutional requirement is also preceded by the headnotes highlighted in the practice of the HCC. In its early practice, the HCC highlighted in the grounds of its decisions the principles which had served as the basis for its decisions and which it intended to follow in the future. The *ratio decidendi* was first separated at the end of the decision under three stars, and later placed in the operative part of the decision (See Decision No. 3).[66] Following the consolidation of the practice of the HCC, the *ratio decidendi*, with reference to settled practice, remained in the reasoning of the decisions even in the event of further development of the practice, and the practice of including the *ratio decidendi* in the operative part of the decision was merged with the institution of the constitutional requirement (See Decision No. 4),[67] which also fulfils the function of official headnotes.[68]

The HCC does not highlight headnotes in its current praxis, but often makes use of the possibility of establishing a constitutional requirement (See Decisions No. 16, 28, 29 and 30).

After the entry into force of the HCC Act, the independent power to declare an unconstitutional omission and to call on the legislator to fulfil its duties (See Decision No. 7)[69] ceased to exist and can only be used as an *ex officio* legal consequence. This legal consequence is also frequently invoked by the Court (See Decision No. 26), although legislation cannot be enforced.

Article 39 (3) of the HCC Act gives the HCC great freedom by stating that the HCC shall determine the legal consequences applied within the framework of the FL and this Act. Moreover, the HCC Act leaves it to the HCC to decide whether it considers it necessary to annul the legislation or

---

66 Sólyom, 'Alkotmányértelmezés az új alkotmánybíróságok gyakorlatában' (2002), (19).

67 Sólyom, *Az alkotmánybíráskodás kezdetei Magyarországon* (2001), 352 ff.

68 Zakariás, 'Az elvi tételek kiemelésének kérdése az alkotmánybírósági gyakorlatban' (2019), 1; Zakariás, 'Verfassungsmäßige Erfordernisse der Gesetzesauslegung als amtliche Leitsätze in der Praxis des ungarischen Verfassungsgerichts' in Darák et al. (eds), *Rechtswege – Urteilswirkungen* (2020), 154.

69 The HCC rejects the constitutional complaint alleging unconstitutional failure to act on the ground that the petitioner does not have the right to submit the petition. Order 3210/2014. (VII. 21.) AB, Reasoning [3].

whether it considers it sufficient to declare a constitutional requirement or to declare an unconstitutional omission. However, the choice of a lenient approach to the law in the case of a constitutional complaint procedure may jeopardise the subjective protection of rights, since in such cases the HCC rejects the complaint challenging the law (See Decisions No. 16, 28 and 30).

On the other hand, the HCC is obliged to annul a judicial decision if it is contrary to the FL [43 (1) of the HCC Act]. In this case, annulment is not a discretionary legal consequence and has no alternative. The procedural consequences of a decision of the HCC Act annulling a judicial decision are governed by the provisions of the laws containing the rules of judicial procedure. In court proceedings that must be conducted as a consequence of the annulment of a judicial decision by the HCC, constitutional issues must be dealt with in accordance with the decision of the HCC [Article 43 (2)–(3) of the HCC Act]. If the court in the repeated proceedings does not respect the authentic interpretation of the FL as contained in the decision of the HCC, it shall review the decision on the basis of Article 24 (1) of the FL and Article 39 (1) of the HCC Act and, if necessary, annul it (See Decision No. 20).

5. *Epilogue*

The HCC was a brand new institution in the Hungarian legal order in 1990 when it started its operation, there was no tradition of this type of constitutional review in Hungary, the idea was borrowed from western type constitutionalism. However, the history of the constitutional adjudication of the past 30 years was exceptionally rich from several aspects.[70] In the first years it took the eminent role in building the new rule of law democracy, and in European comparative context it was seen as an activist court, mostly in fundamental rights matters. Its attitude to the politically sensitive issues was very changeable during the 30 years, therefore its central role in the Hungarian constitutional system was questioned after

70 Sólyom, 'Das ungarische Verfassungsgericht' in von Bogdandy et al. (eds), *Ius Publicum Europaeum. Vol. VI. Verfassungsbarkeit in Europa. Institutionen* (2016), 705 (790).

2010.[71] Even after 30 years of continuous operation, the position of the body is still in constant change.[72]

The jurisprudence of the HCC may also be of interest to foreign scholars, because during these 30 years, as this collection shows, it extended to almost all substantive problems of constitutional law from abortion cases to judicial independence. The HCC has used actively almost all methods of interpretation[73], many well known doctrinal concepts as the volume describes. We can also observe the use and the misuse of certain theoretical designs and extremely rich material to study success and failure in constitutional justice. When the case studies follow the backgrounds and the aftermath of the decisions we not only give an insider scholarly view about the context but in many cases relate to the foreign and international legal experiments with a legal doctrinal focus to see their interrelated nature in constitutional justice.[74]

The institution of the Constitutional Court was borrowed from western type liberal democracies with all the doctrinal constraints that this idea offers. The HCC after the democratic regime change was a pioneer to do its best in adapting and developing doctrine especially favouring the GFCC jurisprudence.

The 30 case analysis included in this volume gives an exemplary occasion to follow a post-Socialist state that struggles to establish the rule of law[75] with the extensive contribution of the HCC,[76] sometimes hand in hand with political efforts and sometimes against them.[77] The HCC has operated together with different governments, contributed to the constitutional environment in different ways and to different extents. This all hap-

71 Gárdos-Orosz, 'The Hungarian Constitutional Court in transition: from actio popularis to constitutional complaint' (2012), 4.

72 Uitz, 'The illusion of a constitution in Europe', in Bell and Paris (eds), *Rights-Based Constitutional Review* (2016).

73 Szente, 'The Interpretative Practice of the Hungarian Constitutional Court: A Critical View' (2013),186.

74 Fazekas, 'EU law and Hungarian Constitutional Court' in Varju and Várnay (eds), *European Union Law in Hungary* (2014).

75 Sólyom, 'The Rise and Decline of Constitutional Culture of Hungary' in von Bogdandy and Sonnevend (eds), *Constitutional Crises in the European Constitutional Area* (2015).

76 Schanda, 'Az alkotmánybíráskodás új szerepe az Alaptörvény első évtizedében' (2021), 117 (117 ff.); Varga Zs, 'Az alkotmánybíróságok szerepe a nemzeti/alkotmányos önazonosság védelmében' (2018), 21 (27 f.).

77 Schwartz, *The Struggle for Constitutional Justice in Post-Communist Europe* (2000).

pened with focus on competence, procedure and doctrinal requirements that we highlight and expect in this volume.

The HCC has gone through more changes than most of the other European institutions and this transformation and the central role, the examination of diverse issues give floor to make an in depth study of doctrine that makes constitutional adjudication a legal effort.

Bibliography

Nóra Chronowski, 'Alkotmányjogi panasz és alkotmányvédelem' [The Constitutional Complaint and the Protection of the Constitution] (2014) 1–2 *Fundamentum*, 95.

Lóránt Csink and Johanna Fröchlich, *Egy alkotmány margójára: Alkotmányelméleti és értelmezési kérdések az Alaptörvényről* [Comments on a Constitution: Questions o Theory and Interpretation of the Fundamentlal Law] (Gondolat: Budapest 2012).

Tímea Drinóczi, Fruzsina Gárdos-Orosz, Zoltán Pozsár-Szentmiklósy, 'Formal and Informal Constitutional Amendments in Hungary' (2019) 18 *MTA Law Working Papers*, 1.

Lóránt Csink, 'Ombudsmani alapjogvédelem a gyakorlatban – az alapvető jogok biztosának működése' [Fundamental Rights Protection by the Ombudsman in Practice – the Operation of the Ombudsman] in András Jakab and György Gajduschek (eds), *A magyar jogrendszer állapota* [The Status of the Hungarian Legal System] (MTA JTI: Budapest 2016), 600.

Flóra Fazekas, 'EU law and Hungarian Constitutional Court', in Márton Varju and Ernő Várnay (eds), *European Union Law in Hungary: Institutions, Processes and the Law* (HVG-ORAC: Budapest 2014).

Fruzsina Gárdos-Orosz, 'Alkotmánybíróság 2010–2015' [Constitutional Court] in *A magyar jogrendszer állapota* [The Status of the Hungarian Legal System] (MTA JTI: Budapest 2016), 445.

Fruzsina Gárdos-Orosz 'The Hungarian constitutional court in transition: from actio popularis to constitutional complaint' (2012) 53 *Acta Juridica Hungarica, The Hungarian Jorunal of Legal Studies*, 4.

Fruzsina Gárdos-Orosz, 'Challenges to Constitutional Adjudication in Hungary since 2010' in Martin Belov (ed), *The Role of Courts in Contemporary Legal Orders* (Eleven Publishing 2019), 321.

Gábor Halmai, 'Grundlagen und Grundzüge staatlichen Verfassungsrecht: Ungarn' in Armin von Bogdandy, Pedro Cruz Villalón, and Peter M. Huber (eds), *Handbuch Ius Publicum Europaeum, Band I.* (C. F. Müller 2007).

Gábor Halmai, 'The Hungarian Approach to Constitutional Review: The End of Activism? The First Decade of the Hungarian Constitutional Court' in Wojciek Sadurski (ed), *Constitutional Justice, East and West. Democratic Legitimacy and Constitutional Courts in Post-Communist Europe in a Comparative Perspective* (Kluwer International Law 2002).

András Jakab and Johanna Fröhlich, 'The Constitutional Court of Hungary' in András Jakab, Arthur Dyevre, and Giulio Itzcovich (eds), *Comparative Constitutional Reasoning* (Cambridge University Press 2017).

András Jakab and Viktor Kazai, 'A Sólyom-bíróság hatása a magyar alkotmányjogi gondolkodásra' [The Effect of the Sólyom Court ont he Hungarian Constitutional Thinking] in Tamás Győrfi, Viktor Zoltán Kazai, and Endre Orbán (eds), *Kontextus által világosan: a Sólyom-bíróság antiformalista elemzés* [To see clear by context: The Antiformalistic Analysis of the Sólyom Courte] (L'Harmattan: Budapest [awaiting publication]).

András Jakab, *Az új Alaptörvény keletkezése és gyakorlati következménye* [The Birth of the New Fundamental Law and its Consequences] (HVG-ORAC: Budapest 2012).

Kriszta Kovács and Gábor Attila Tóth, 'Hungary's Constitutional Transformation' (2011) 7 *European Constitutional Law Review*, 16.

Endre Orbán and Kinga Zakariás, Az alkotmánybírósági érdemi munkatársak szerepe Magyarországon [The role of the legal clerks of the Constitutional Court in Hungary], (2016) 2 *Alkotmánybírósági Szemle*, 108.

Endre Orbán and Kinga Zakariás, Are Law Clerks a Latent Chamber of the Constitutional Court? in Zegrean Augustin and Costinescu Mihaela-Senia (eds), *The role of Assistant-Magistrates in the jurisdiction of Constitutional Courts Bucharest* (Universul Juridic: Bucharest 2016), 79.

Péter Paczolay: *Megváltozott hangsúlyok az Alkotmánybíróság hatásköreiben* [Changed Emphasis in the Practice of the Constitutional Court] (2012) 1 *Alkotmánybírósági Szemle*, 67.

Balázs Schanda, András Varga Zs., Lóránt Csink: *The Basic Law of Hungary: A First Commentary* (Clarus Press: Dublin 2012).

Balázs Schanda, 'Az alkotmánybíráskodás új szerepe az Alaptörvény első évtizedében. Kompromisszumok, identitás és jogfejlesztés' [The New Role of Constitutional Justice in the first Decade of the Basic Law. Compromises, Identity and Legal Development] (2021) 2 *Acta Humana*, 117.

Herman Schwartz, *The Struggle for Constitutional Justice in Post-Communist Europe* (The University of Chicago Press 2000).

László Sólyom, 'Die Ungarische Verfassungsgericht', in Armin von Bogdandy, Sabino Cassese, and Peter M. Huber (eds), *Handbuch* Ius *Publicum* Europaeum. *Band VI. Verfassungsbarkeit in Europa. Institutionen* (Müller, 2016), 705.

László Sólyom, *Az Alkotmánybíráskodás kezdetei Magyarországon* [The Beginning of Constitutional Adjudication in Hungary] (Osiris: Budapest 2001).

László Sólyom, 'Alkotmányértelmezés az új alkotmánybíróságok gyakorlatában' [Constitutional Interpretation in the Practice of the New Constitutional Courts] (2002) 2 *Fundamentum*, 18.

László Sólyom, 'The Rise and Decline of Constitutional Culture of Hungary' in Armin von Bogdandy, Pál Sonnevend (eds), *Constitutional Crises in the European Constitutional Area. Theory, Law and Politica in Hungary and Romania* (Hart 2015).

László Sólyom and Georg Brunner, *Constitutional Judiciary in a New Democracy: The Hungarian Constitutional Court* (University of Michigan Press 2000).

Pál Sonnevend, András Jakab, and Lóránt Csink, 'The Constitution in Everyday's Party Politics: The Basic Law of Hungary' in Armin von Bogdandy and Pál Sonnevend (eds), *Constitutional Crises in the European Constitutional Area. Theory, Law and Politica in Hungary and Romania* (Hart 2015).

Zoltán Szente, 'The Interpretative Practice of the Hungarian Constitutional Court: A Critical View' (2013) 14 *German Law Journal*, 186.

Gábor Attila Tóth (ed), *A Disunited Nation: On Hungary's 2011 Constitution* (CEU Press 2012).

Renáta Uitz, 'The illusion of a constitution in Europe: the Hungarian Constitutional Court after the Fifth Amendment of the Fundamental Law', in John Bell and Marie-Luce Paris (eds), *Rights-Based Constitutional Review. Constitutional Courts in a Changing Landscape* (Edward Elgar, 2016).

András Varga Zs, 'Az alkotmánybíróságok szerepe a nemzeti/alkotmányos önazonosság védelmében' [The Role of Constitutional Courts in Protecting National/Constitutional Identity] (2018) 2 *Iustum Aequum Salutare*, 21.

Attila Vincze, Péter Csuhány, Pál Sonnevend, and András Jakab, 'Az Alkotmánybíróság' [The Constitutional Corut] in András Jakab (ed), *Az alkotmány kommentárja* [Commentary ont he Constitution] (Századvég: Budapest 2009), 239.

Attila Vincze, 'Wrestling with Constitutionalism: the supermajority and the Hungarian Constitutional Court' (2013) *ICL Journal – Vienna Journal on International Constitutional Law*, 4.

Kinga Zakariás, 'A bírói döntések alkotmánybírósági felülvizsgálatának terjedelme a német és magyar gyakorlatban' [The Scope of the Constitutional Review of Judicial Decisions in the Practice of German and Hungarian Jurisprudence] (2019) 2 *Alkotmánybírósági Szemle*, 21.

Kinga Zakariás, 'Az elvi tételek kiemelésének kérdése az alkotmánybírósági gyakorlatban' [Defining the Leitsatz in the Constitutional Court Jurisprudence] (2019) 10 *Pázmány Law Working Papers*, 1.

Kinga Zakariás, ‚Verfassungsmäßige Erfordernisse der Gesetzesauslegung als amtliche Leitsätze in der Praxis des ungarischen Verfassungsgerichts', in Péter Darák, Hanno Kube, Fruzsina Molnár-Gábor, and Ekkehart Raimer (eds), *Rechtswege – Urteilswirkungen. Deutsch-ungarischer Verfassungsdialog* (Winter Universitätsverlag: Heidelberg 2020), 154.

Spencer Zifcak, 'Hungary's Remarkable, Radical, Constitutional Court' (1996) 1 *Journal of Constitutional Law in Eastern and Central Europe*, 1.

1. Decision 23/1990. (X. 31.) AB – Death Penalty

Zoltán Tóth J.[*]

The death penalty violates the right(s) to life and human dignity; these interrelated constitutional rights and fundamental values define the bases of human life, and no one can be deprived of them by the state.

In its decision on the death penalty, the HCC established the principle that human life and human dignity are fundamental values providing a prerequisite to the recognition and protection of human legal status, and, as guardians of such status, the rights to human life and human dignity may only be construed in unity, i.e., the right to human life and human dignity constitutes a single, indivisible right that cannot be restricted. This single right not only serves as a limit to the coercive power of the state by rendering the death penalty unconstitutional, but also allows for the recognition, and thus for the constitutional protection of fundamental rights not expressly specified in the Constitution.

1. *Background*

The death penalty was applied as a so-called ordinary punishment (*poena ordinaria*) from the outset of the Hungarian state until 1990; however, there were significant changes in the extent of the application and implementation of capital punishment during that period.[1]

The regime change, Act XVI of 1989 eliminated the possibility of imposing the death penalty for political crimes, i.e., crimes against the state.

In October 1990, when the HCC made its decision on the unconstitutionality of the death penalty, Hungary was not party to any international treaties that banned capital punishment. This legal institution still existed

---

* PhD, Professor, Károli Gáspár University of the Reformed Church in Hungary, Faculty of Law (Budapest).

1 On the history of the death penalty in Hungary, see the following monograph: Tóth, *A halálbüntetés intézményének egyetemes és magyarországi jogtörténete* (2010), 385.

in most European countries; however, the number of states where death sentences were executed was decreasing. This period was characterised by the so-called abolitionist process, due to which it became recognised (in Europe at least) that life is a quality to be valued in itself by any state committed to human rights, and an unrestrainable right that lacks exceptions must be guaranteed to protect it. The deprivation of human life in order to pursue any external goals (e.g., to achieve the effects of general or special prevention) is incompatible with the philosophical essence of human quality.

Certain international legal documents on human rights that also included provisions on the death penalty nonetheless existed in 1990, even though Hungary was not yet party to any of them.

In 1983, Protocol no. 6 to the ECHR 'concerning the abolition of the death penalty' was adopted, Article 1 of which established the following: 'The death penalty shall be abolished. No one shall be condemned to such penalty or executed.' Hungary joined the ECHR and its Protocol no. 6 only after the HCC had made its decision on the death penalty.

The only international convention that regulated the death penalty (and actually did so in a permissive manner) in 1990 and to which Hungary was a party at the time the decision on capital punishment was made by the HCC, was the International Covenant on Civil and Political Rights. The Covenant was adopted in the framework of the UN in 1966, took effect in 1976, and was ratified by Hungary with Law Decree 8 of 1976. Although the Covenant banned the arbitrary deprivation of life, expressly allowed for the application of the death penalty in countries where it had not yet been abolished (merely formulating some additional safeguards in terms of the imposition and execution of the death sentence). And even though the possibility of imposing capital punishment was restricted to the 'the most serious crimes' by Article 6 (2), each UN Member State had (and still has today) the discretion to determine the scope of those crimes.

2. *Petition*

In January 1990, immediately after the HCC commenced its operation, Tibor Horváth, a professor of criminal law filed a petition seeking the abolition of the death penalty in the name of the Anti-Death Penalty League which was established at the beginning of 1989. The petition requested that the HCC declare the unconstitutionality of the laws regulating the death penalty and annul them. The petition itself was not even a full page, but the study attached to it, presenting the history of the abolitionist process and outlining the legal, moral and practical arguments against capital punishment, was approximately seventy pages long.[2]

The petition, dated 17 January 1990, was worded as follows: 'Honorable Constitutional Court, In the name of the Anti-Death Penalty League, I make a constitutional complaint against the criminal law imposing the death penalty and I ask for the subsequent declaration of the unconstitutionality of these laws. Article 54 (1) of the Constitution, amended by Act XXXI of 1989, provides that »In the Hungarian Republic, every person has the inherent right to life and human dignity« [...] and that »No one can be subjected to torture, cruel, inhuman and humiliating treatment or punishment [...]« [The latter was actually set forth by Article 54 (2) – added by the author.] The League considers that the provisions on the death penalty of the effective criminal legislation do not comply with the above quoted provisions of the Constitution as they violate human rights. The death penalty as the remainder of the principle of ius talionis cannot be justified ethically, it is incompatible with human rights, irredeemable and irreversible, and an unsuitable and impractical means of punishment for preventing serious crimes or deterring others from committing crimes punishable by death. Instead of the death penalty, the protection of society can be adequately served by imposing life imprisonment or imprisonment for a definite long term—twenty or twenty-five years—for any crime committed. The detailed reasoning of the position of the League can be found in the attached specialist document.'[3]

The arguments intended to serve as grounds for the declaration of unconstitutionality were mostly moral and pragmatic, and, to a lesser extent, criminal law arguments; the constitutional argumentation was limited to the indication of the relevant provisions of the Constitution. The enumeration of the provisions to be abolished was also absent. Yet, the petition was sufficiently definite, which gave the HCC the opportunity to rule on whether the death penalty was compatible with the Constitution. The decision was finally rendered in the framework of subsequent abstract norm control, instead of the constitutional complaint filed in the petition (due to the lack of direct and individual concern).

2 See the whole text in: Horváth (ed), *A halálbüntetés megszüntetése Magyarországon* (1991), 17–68.

3 See Horváth (ed), *A halálbüntetés megszüntetése Magyarországon* (1991), 15.

3. Decision and its reasoning

The HCC found that the death penalty was incompatible with the Constitution and annulled, with *ex nunc* effect, all provisions in the field of criminal law, criminal procedural law and the law covering the execution of penalties effective at the time the decision was rendered.

3.1. In Hungary, every human being, regardless of their citizenship, has the inherent, inviolable and inalienable fundamental right to life and human dignity. Since the essential content of fundamental rights may not be restricted even by law, and the right to life and human dignity is a fundamental right, the maintenance and application of the death penalty conflicts with the Constitution due to the obligation of the state to respect and protect the right to life and human dignity [Articles 8 (1), 8 (2), 8 (4), 54 (1) of the Constitution].

To establish the unconstitutionality of the death penalty, it is necessary to read Articles 8 and 54 of the Constitution together, and construe them with regard to one another. Article 8 (1) of the Constitution prescribes the following: 'The Republic of Hungary recognizes inviolable and inalienable fundamental human rights. The respect and protection of these rights is a primary obligation of the State.' This provision considers the fundamental rights of 'humans' not as rights provided by the state but as factors inherent in the human status; consequently, the state may only recognise and protect them. Also, the state may not violate the said rights, because it has no power of disposal over them. The normative consequences of this concept are specified by Article 8 (2) of the Constitution: 'In the Republic of Hungary regulations pertaining to fundamental rights and duties are determined by law; such law, however, may not restrict the essential content of fundamental rights.' Article 8 (4) includes a definition of such rights: these are the rights that shall not be suspended or restricted even if an extraordinary legal order is introduced, which means that they are completely exempt from the state's power of disposal. These (with a term borrowed from legal dogmatics: 'absolute') rights include those set forth in Article 54 (1) [and also para. (2)] of the Constitution. Thus, the rights to life and human dignity are considered by the Constitution as fundamental rights which, in accordance with the foregoing, shall not be suspended or restricted (even if an extraordinary legal order is introduced). And if a right may not be suspended or restricted even in the event of an extraordinary legal order, then, *a fortiori*, it is not possible under the ordinary legal order either. Also, applying the same formula, if restriction of such rights is prohibited, then full deprivation must also be considered prohibited. Consequently, the arbitrary deprivation of the right to life and human dignity is prohibited.

Although 'non-arbitrary deprivation' is constitutionally possible, the death penalty does not fall within that scope, for the following reason. Article 54 (1) of the Constitution would not lead to the unconstitutionality of the death penalty in itself, since it allows for non-arbitrary deprivation; nonetheless, Article 8 (2) excludes the interpretation which would construe the death penalty as constitutional, i.e., the non-arbitrary taking of a person's life (ABH 1990, 89, 92.). It is clear that the right to life, based on the foregoing, qualifies as a fundamental right, pursuant to Article 8 (4) of the Constitution, whose exercise shall not be suspended or restricted even if an extraordinary legal order is introduced, and it is also clear that if restriction is prohibited, full deprivation shall also be deemed prohibited; consequently, the right to life and the right to human dignity are considered as unrestrainable rights by Article 8 (2) with a view to Article 8 (4) of the Constitution. Thus, Article 8—when construed in itself—renders all forms of deprivation of life unconstitutional, and Article 54—when construed also in itself—considers only the arbitrary taking of a person's life unconstitutional. When resolving the collision of two seemingly inconsistent provisions (in this case, when deciding whether Article 8 or Article 54 is 'stronger' in terms of the death penalty, i.e., which provision should be construed in the light of the other), the norm adopted later shall be governing (*lex posterior derogate legi priori*), as clearly, although not explicitly, recalled by the HCC. Since the text of Article 54 effective at the time the HCC rendered its decision on the death penalty was determined by Act XXXI of 1989, and the then effective text of Article 8 was determined by Act XL of 1990, the latter provision shall be deemed governing.

Consequently, as found by the HCC: 'the provisions of the [old] Criminal Code on the death penalty [...] conflict with the prohibition on restricting the essential content of the right to life and human dignity. That is because the provisions prescribing the death penalty, as a means of the deprivation of life and human dignity, not only restrict the essential content of the fundamental right to life and human dignity, but actually allow for the full and irreparable termination of life and human dignity, as well as the right ensuring them. Thus, the Constitutional Court found those provisions unconstitutional and annulled them.' (ABH 1990, 89, 92.).

3.2. *Human life and human dignity are values preceding the law that can only be construed in unity: one is a condition for the other. The protection of these values, which are untouchable for the law, are ensured by the rights to human life and human dignity on the level of constitutional law, which are rights which cannot be construed separately, either. This 'right to human life and human dignity' is uniform, indivisible, unrestrainable, and, as such, superior to all other constitutional rights, qualifying also as the origin and essential definitive factor thereto [Articles 8 (1), 8 (2), 8 (4), and 54 (1) of the Constitution].*

The so-called doctrine of indivisibility was formulated by the HCC in no more than two sentences, not in the *stricto sensu* reasoning of the decision but included in the *obiter dicta*. The doctrine was worded as follows: 'Human life and human dignity form an inseparable unity and have a greater value than anything else. The rights to human life and human dignity form an indivisible and unrestrainable fundamental right which is the source of and the condition for several additional fundamental rights.' (ABH 1990, 89, 93.). The details of this concept were explained partially in the concurring opinions (particularly in the concurring opinion of President of HCC László Sólyom), and partially in subsequent decisions of the HCC which applied the same doctrine (particularly in Decision Abortion I.). All in all, the following consensual standpoint emerges from the said opinions and decisions.

As mentioned above, the concurring opinion of László Sólyom provided, in several aspects, details and conceptual grounds for the rather concise decision. Legal literature and the HCC itself also considered Sólyom's opinion as such, thus, analysing it is essential when overviewing the reasoning of the decision. According to the concurring opinion of the then President of the HCC, the reason why the right to life can only be construed in unity with the right to human dignity (and not separately, i.e., in itself) is that dignity is a specific attribute of human life, distinguishing it from the life of animals. While animals do not have dignity, and so the life of the specimens of animals cannot be considered as values to be protected for themselves, humans have dignity which renders not only human life (in general) a value to be protected but also the life of each human being (as a unique, single and unrepeatable life). Moreover, this is true regardless of any other attributes (viability, mental status, sensibility, consciousness of the self, morals, etc.) or acts (e.g., crimes committed) of the given person. Thus, it is dignity that renders the life of humans something to be protected individually, and it is dignity that provides each human being with the right to life individually, rendering the right to life an individual right of humans. Since the dignity of each human being is complete and equal as such, each human has an equally inviolable and inalienable right to life which may not be violated by the state (the right to life of a human being who has inherent dignity means that he/she has the right to life and dignity as a uniform, indivisible and unrestrainable right).

From the doctrine of indivisibility, and from the fact that this uniform right is 'the source of and the condition for' all other fundamental rights, and that life and dignity is 'a greater value than anything else', it follows that the right to life and human dignity is superior to any other rights. Consequently, it affects the content of all other rights and, ultimately, serves—in itself—as grounds for decisions where no other constitutional right can provide governance in terms of the constitutionality of a certain piece of law. That line of argument was, again, presented comprehensively by László Sólyom who formulated the concept of the so-called 'invisible Constitution'. Although (with only one exception) this concept has never appeared in any decision (neither in the operative part nor in the reasoning),[4] it had a significant effect on the caselaw of the first fifteen years of the HCC. According to the original wording of the concept: 'The Constitutional Court must continue its effort to explain the theoretical bases of the Constitution and the rights included in it and to form a coherent system with its decisions providing a reliable standard of constitutionality—an 'invisible Constitution'—beyond the Constitution, which is often amended nowadays by current political interests; and which probably will not conflict with the new Constitution to be established or with future Constitutions.' (ABH 1990, 89, 97–98.).

4. *Doctrinal analysis*

4.1. *Clash of the deontologist and utilitarian concepts of the unconstitutionality of the death penalty in the concurring opinions*

Finding the grounds for establishing the unconstitutionality of the death penalty was one of the key issues in the decision of the HCC. None of the members of the body disputed that capital punishment is an improper penalty (Judge Péter Schmidt, who attached the only dissenting opinion to the decision adopted with 9 votes in favour and 1 vote against it, only

4 The above-mentioned exception was Decision 61/2011. (VII. 13.) AB whose reasoning included the said term.

voted against the decision because he believed that Parliament had the discretion to resolve the inconsistency between Article 8 and Article 54 of the Constitution, and, in the absence of the relevant powers, the HCC was not entitled to make a decision on the issue at hand). However, there were strong disagreements on whether to apply moral-theoretical—i.e., deontological—or pragmatic—i.e., utilitarian—argumentation (such as its practical lack of necessity or its incompatibility with the objectives of penalties) when formulating the grounds for the decision.

Most of the judges providing concurring opinions called for a theoretical justification based on fundamental rights,[5] while one judge stood up for a utilitarian argument based on criminal law.[6]

According to one leading opinion, as outlined above, life and human dignity are inseparable: life is inviolable due to the human dignity of each human individual of which no one can be deprived. Since dignity is 'indivisible and irreducible', each human being possesses it in its entirety, and the taking of one's life not only reduces one's dignity, but completely deprives the person of it and of the right ensuring it. Thus, the taking of a person's life by the state is necessarily unconstitutional. The rights to life and human dignity are unrestrainable by definition, and by virtue of these two inseparable rights 'human beings may remain individuals instead of being turned into objects or tools.' (ABH 1990, 88, 103.).

Another starting point was that human life and human dignity are not merely (fundamental) rights but also 'sources of rights' and 'values beyond the reach of law', thus, inviolable and inalienable by definition. The sphere of human life and human dignity is untouchable by the law, and the only role of the state is to recognise them as rights and protect them. Consequently, the death penalty is necessarily unconstitutional, due to the fact that it violates the supreme human values.

A distinctive view addressed the objectives of penalties and the role of the death penalty in this sense; however, it concluded that these issues bear no significance when assessing the constitutionality of the question at hand. According to Judge András Szabó, it is not the failure to fulfil the requirements of prevention that renders the death penalty unconstitutional, since those are not the requirements it should fulfil: the objective of penalties is not the prevention of criminal offences or crime in general. 'The aim of punishment is within itself: in the public declaration of

5 Judges László Sólyom, András Szabó, as well as Tamás Lábady and Ödön Tersztyánszky who provided a common concurring opinion.

6 Judge János Zlinszky.

the soundness of law, in the reprisal that does not consider the purpose' (ABH 1990, 88, 110.). Yet, such reprisal may only be proportionate, since only proportionate penalties can fulfil the requirements of constitutional criminal law. The death penalty, however, cannot be proportionate to any criminal act, because no crime deserves the deprivation of life; and that is what renders the death penalty unconstitutional.

Contrary to the above opinion, a strong utilitarian standpoint was represented as well in the debates. According to this a punishment can be constitutional only if it fulfils its objective, at the expense of causing a less serious injury than that caused by the crime committed. The death penalty is unconstitutional because, in terms of certain crimes, it has no preventive effect at all, and, in other cases, such a preventive effect cannot be scientifically justified. And, even in the latter case, capital punishment would only have a preventive effect if the imposition of the penalty could be taken for granted. At present, however (and also in general due to the characteristics of law enforcement), criminal acts often remain unpunished; thus, the general preventive effect of the death penalty cannot be justified. Although it is undoubtedly suitable for the prevention of repeated crime, such an objective can also be achieved by other, less serious means of punishment; thus, the application of the death penalty cannot be justified by the purposes of special prevention either. A further pragmatic risk of applying capital punishment may be that it diverts the attention of society from identifying the root causes of crime and from the importance of the prevention of criminal acts. Thus, the death penalty is basically counterproductive, since 'it disguises the delay in absolutely necessary steps to be taken by the state.' (ABH 1990, 88, 113.).

All in all, the deontological attempts to justify the unconstitutionality of the death penalty appear to be more persuasive, since the starting point of the assessments based on criminal law (i.e., those that remain below the level of the Constitution) is the effectiveness of law itself, or the lack of it. This, however, is a rather situational approach (and relative, even from a criminal law perspective). Conversely, the exploration of the fundamental moral factors that define human quality and the moral-legal grounds ensuring their protection seem quite stable, even if the assessment of such arguments may differ in every era; the least that can be said is that those factors are not dependant on aspects of efficiency or pragmatism which fall outside the scope of constitutional law. Finally, it should also be remembered that the HCC had to present such arguments in terms of fundamental rights that provide grounds for the interpretation of the Constitution, i.e., the constitutionality of the death penalty had to be evaluated on the basis of theoretical (or, according to Dworkin's definition:

constitutive)[7] reasoning (instead of a reasoning rooted in instrumentalism or consequentialism).

This debate on the fundamental approach to the question led to further disagreements on the evaluation of arbitrariness in terms of the prohibition of the deprivation of life and human dignity. Two strong standpoints collided: according to one of them, the deprivation of life (and of human dignity) is necessarily, *ab ovo* arbitrary, while those holding the other viewpoint believed that there are non-arbitrary cases of taking a life, although the death penalty is not one of them (i.e., it is not an exception to the prohibition). One concurring opinion to the decision stressed the following: 'the deprivation of the right to life and dignity is conceptually arbitrary' (ABH 1990, 88, 99.). This view covers all cases of the deprivation of life, including the taking of a person's life due to justifiable defence, distress or superiors' orders. Accordingly, a situation beyond the reach of law occurs—controlled by the 'state of nature'—each time a choice between lives is required. In these cases, the law may only evaluate whether or not a situation (e.g., justifiable defence) qualifies as being in the 'state of nature', can determine its limitation in time (the starting point and endpoint), and can examine whether other required conditions were present, 'without assessing what happened there' (ABH 1990, 88, 108.).

The other strong standpoint (which later became the predominant view) was that there are non-arbitrary cases of the deprivation of life (and dignity). For example, it argued that even though the death penalty does not fall within the scope of non-arbitrary cases of the taking of a life—since this would arbitrarily restructure the rights to life and human dignity that each human being has, as well as the ultimate values serving as the basis of such rights, and therefore capital punishment would be unconstitutional—nonetheless, 'it may not be stated that every deprivation of an individual's life is illegitimate or arbitrary' (ABH 1990, 88, 96.). Inter alia, the situations qualifying as justifiable defence are to be considered non-arbitrary, but the legal regulation of other situations may also be considered as such, including those where a choice between the lives and dignities of different persons is necessary. According to a third view, not even the death penalty may be deemed arbitrary by definition, since it is prescribed by law. As a complementary argument to this, although on different grounds, that the death penalty can be considered arbitrary only because it fails to fulfil its legal objectives as a punishment. According

7 Dworkin, *Freedom's Law: The Moral Reading of the American Constitution* (1996), 201.

to the one dissenting opinion opinion (which was the only dissenting opinion written to the decision) went even further: in his opinion, the death penalty cannot be considered the arbitrary taking of a person's life by definition; however, there are other aspects that render capital punishment inapplicable as a sanction, although—according to Schmidt—such a finding would fall outside the scope of the power of the HCC.

4.2. The role of the right to dignity—the joint conception of the life and dignity

From the outset, two distinct functions of the right to dignity have been present in the caselaw of the HCC of Hungary. On the one hand, there is 1) a right to dignity that is separate and stands in itself (as an individual, subjective right), construed independently from the right to life, and, on the other hand 2) the right to dignity as a fundamental right is present, which is absolute (indivisible) and unrestrainable (by definition), construed in unity with the right to life.[8]

In its latter function, the right to dignity is not independent, but prevails in an inseparable unity with the right to life. This function can be fulfilled by the indivisible and unrestrainable fundamental right to life and human dignity because, as a fundamental right at the top of the hierarchy of constitutional rights, it not only protects certain aspects of human beings but human quality, and the human status as a whole.

Thus, it is clear that the HCC applied the right to dignity in at least two [in fact three, since the interpretation under point 1) above was applied in at least two[9] further ways] dogmatically different functions which became a cause of continuous confusion related to the constitutional content of the concept. One of the reasons for voicing criticism as regards the dogmatic solution applied in the decision on the death penalty in relation to the right to dignity (and as regards the chosen interpretation of arbitrariness in terms of the right to life), is that establishing the unconstitutionality of the death penalty would also have been possible without addressing these issues. The decision could have been simply based on the constitutional protection of personality, by relying on the prohibition of torture, cruel, inhuman or degrading treatment or punishment regulated

8 Cf. e.g., Tóth, 'Egy nehéz eset: a könnyű halál' (1996), 77 (79).

9 On the differentiation between the non-comparative (with the purpose of the protection of personality) requirements stemming from the right to dignity construed in itself and the comparative requirements see, for example, Halmai and Tóth (eds), *Emberi jogok* (2003), 263–264.

in Article 54 (2) of the Constitution—as an imminent element of human dignity (on the negative side)—without recognising the conflict between Article 8 (2) and Article 54 (2) of the Constitution.[10]

According to the doctrine of indivisibility developed in this decision, the values of human life and human dignity, and the rights to human life and human dignity not only take the highest position in the hierarchy of fundamental rights and serve as a source of any other fundamental rights (regardless of whether or not the given fundamental right is expressly included in the Constitution), but also form an inseparable, i.e., single and indivisible unity. Therefore, the right to life and the right to human dignity do not constitute two separate rights but are two interdependent aspects of the same right. Ultimately, this concept of indivisibility serves the purpose of rendering the life and dignity of humans (legally) indispensable, and of rendering the (arbitrary) deprivation of life—due to the imminent dignity that characterises all human beings (and that all human beings have)—prohibited, so that it does not become a tool for achieving a state objective (such as the reduction of crime).

The starting point of the doctrine of indivisibility is the so-called monist concept of human quality, according to which the spiritual-mental integrity of humans can only be protected by physical integrity, and the latter is only worthy of protection due to the existence of the former which is the unique quality of human beings, absent in all other living creatures. The followers of the monist approach believe in the unity of body and soul; the physical and spiritual aspects of humans are interdependent, and neither dignity nor life can exist separately, without the other. Nonetheless, the case-law of the German Constitutional Court (*Bundesverfassungsgericht*)—which represents a model in many aspects—(and the German *Grundgesetz* itself), the ECtHR (and the ECHR), as well as several other legal systems embrace the so-called dualist concept that separates human life from human dignity, and the right to human life from the right to human dignity. The reason behind this is the recognition that the two said rights can conflict: borderline situations may occur where a choice must be made whether to preserve life or preserve dignity. Examples include situations where soldiers, police officers or firefighters sacrifice their lives for their country or fellow human beings, an act of sacrifice which leads to certain death. In systems embracing the dualist concept, similar borderline situations may be recognised in relation to euthanasia or assisted suicide.

---

10 Cf. for example, Kis, *Alkotmányos demokrácia. Régebbi és újabb közelítések* (2019), 237–244.

The primary reason why criticism has been voiced in legal literature against the doctrine of indivisibility is not related to the issue of the death penalty but the applicability of the doctrine in, and the potential implications of, borderline situations.

The starting point for criticism may also be that the merging of the two rights is incompatible with the wording of Article 54 (1) of the Constitution: it is clear from the syntactic interpretation that the text of the said paragraph refers to at least two rights, since the term 'these rights' [in Hungarian: 'amelyek'] is in the plural form. The text reveals the intent of the legislature as well, which rather clearly aimed at formulating two separate rights—with a view also to the fact that the constitutional process of 1989 in Hungary primarily used the German model where the two concerned rights are construed separately. (Nonetheless, according to some opinions, it is not the syntactic level that matters but the context. For example, the Commentary to the Constitution said that 'it follows from the joint reference made to the right to life and the right to dignity that these two rights form a unity'.)[11]

Another point of dispute was the finding of the HCC that one can only be deprived of dignity in an absolute sense, and only if one is also deprived of one's life. According to the opposite view, dignity can also be restrained, i.e., humans cannot only be deprived of their dignity but there are different degrees of the impairment of dignity.[12]

A further problem may be that if the inevitable inseparability of life and dignity is assumed, then—in situations where an actual choice would occur between the two rights—the ideological neutrality of the state may

---

11 Zakariás, 'Az élethez és az emberi méltósághoz való jog' in Jakab (ed), *Az Alkotmány kommentárja. II.* (2009), 1899 (1915).

12 According to the famous example brought by János Kis: 'it violates the dignity of a human being if, as someone who is said to belong to a lower species, he is banned from the places reserved for the race declared higher; an even more serious violation is if the specimens of the latter may beat him and mug him unpunished; and a violation even more serious than that is if he is obliged to obey any random order given by the species declared higher' [Kis, 'Az Alkotmánybíróság az élethez való jogról' (1992), 118 (121)]. Tamás Győrfi also believes that the violation of human dignity has different degrees, since if it could only be taken away (along with taking the given person's life) but not violated partially, then the right to dignity 'would not protect us from any mistreatment'—with the exception, of course, of taking our life [Győrfi, 'A tulajdonságok nélküli ember elmélete' (1998), 23 (24)]. Ildikó Kmetty and Albert Takács also argue for the divisibility of life and dignity, and for the recognition of the possibility of the restriction of dignity [cf. Kmetty and Takács, 'Az eutanáziához való jog' (2003), 125 (128, 131)].

be impaired. According to this latter concept, no difference should be made between individual world-views on an ideological basis; yet, the indivisibility of life and dignity is grounded in the ideological premise that the maintenance of one's dignity is only possible by maintaining one's life in all circumstances, since life is sacred.[13] It is plain to see that the significance of dignity in relation to life, and—as the ultimate grounds thereof—the recognition of the possibility of the restriction of dignity is highly dependent on the definition chosen for dignity. It is no coincidence that neither the Constitution (and neither the FL replacing it) nor the HCC has made any attempt to define dignity,[14] and even the scope of protection of the right to dignity was only determined negatively and by examples, outlining the essential aspects (the prohibition of torture and slavery, etc.). (In addition, the FL declared that human dignity—despite remaining undefined—is 'inviolable'.) Moreover, the HCC furthered the conceptual confusion by outlining three different aspects of the right to dignity, as presented above (firstly, as a definitive factor of human status in unity with the right to life, secondly, as grounds for the protection of human personality and the source of personality rights, and thirdly, as the origin of equal rights and non-discrimination).

13 Cf. e.g., Kmetty and Takács, 'Az eutanáziához való jog' (2003), 125 (130).

14 As Gergely Deli and István Kukorelli expressly found in their analysis: the HCC 'construed human dignity as a concept untouchable and undefinable in itself' [Deli and Kukorelli, 'Az emberi méltóság alapjoga Magyarországon' (2015), 337 (347)]. In its interpretation, the Constitutional Court provided further details to this untouchable 'first level' by defining certain aspects of the personality [the so called 'contact points' (in Hungarian: 'beszámítási pontok')] in the 'second level', and by defining the specific fundamental rights related to the 'contact points' on the 'third level' [Deli and Kukorelli, 'Az emberi méltóság alapjoga Magyarországon' (2015), 337 (341–342)]. Kinga Zakariás took an opposing position, naming autonomy and self-determination—which she considered positive, substantive elements recognised also by the Constitutional Court—as the specific content of the absolute right to dignity [Zakariás, 'Az emberi méltóság védelme' in: Csink, Schanda, and Varga (eds), *A magyar közjog alapintézményei* (2020), 550 (551)].

5. Aftermath of the Decision

The doctrine of indivisibility appeared in a total of 15 decisions of the HCC between 1990 and 2020.[15] The first was the decision on the death penalty itself, and the second was Decision Abortion I., which is analysed separately in the present volume. The doctrine was applied as substantial grounds for reasoning also in Decision 9/2004. (III. 30.) AB on the right of a police officer to use firearms, where it was found that the use of a firearm to capture or to prevent the escape of a perpetrator who has intentionally killed someone is constitutional, since such a perpetrator has him/herself previously violated the right to life. Although in these cases there is no immediate risk to life (which would render the addressing of the issue of constitutionality unnecessary), still—as a measure of last resort—the possibility to use firearms, which does not necessarily lead to the perpetrator's death but only to endangering his life, must also be ensured. Moreover, the HCC found that the provision in Act XXXIV of 1994 on the Police, prescribing that a police officer 'shall protect public safety and domestic order even at the risk of his or her life, if necessary' is not unconstitutional due to the fact that it does not necessarily entail the sacrifice of a life but the mere risk of it.[16]

Apart from the first decision on abortion, the first decision on euthanasia, i.e., Decision 22/2003. (IV. 28.) AB—which is also analysed separately in this book—was beyond doubt the most important in this regard. It was in this decision that the problems of the doctrine of indivisibility were revealed most apparently: while the HCC expressly maintained the doctrine of indivisibility, in its interpretation it weighed the right to self-determination as a measure to ensure the freedom of choice of individuals on the one side, against the obligation of the state to protect lives (as the objective side of the right to life) on the other. Thus, we do not find the right to dignity itself on one side but one of its—deduced—subsidiary rights which, as such, may be restricted, and on the other side there is the obligation of the state to protect life as a value, which is also relative and can also be restricted. The HCC found that the restriction of the

15 It was present merely as 'decoration' in most of these decisions, not playing any role in the substantial grounds thereof.

16 Decision 46/1994. (X. 21.) AB, which found the wording of the military oath constitutional, had been made on similar grounds earlier; however, that decision relied on the right to life and dignity only in general, and deduced the findings of the HCC mostly from the right to life, and did not expressly include the doctrine of indivisibility.

right to self-determination to an extent that deprives the given person of that right and renders it meaningless is unconstitutional[17] in the case of passive euthanasia (as worded by the Health Act: 'the right to refuse medical treatment'); however, in the case of active euthanasia, not even a restriction that renders the right to self-determination completely meaningless in order to fulfil the obligation to protect life can be considered unconstitutional.

Bibliography

Gergely Deli and István Kukorelli, 'Az emberi méltóság alapjoga Magyarországon' [The Fundamental Right to Human Dignity in Hungary] (2015) 7–8, *Jogtudományi Közlöny*, 337.

Ronald Dworkin, *Freedom's Law: The Moral Reading of the American Constitution* (Oxford University Press: Oxford – New York 1996)

Tamás Győrfi, 'A tulajdonságok nélküli ember elmélete: Az Alkotmánybíróság oszthatatlansági doktrínája és ami abból (nem) következik' [The Theory of Man Without Attributes: The Doctrine of Indivisibility of the Constitutional Court and What (Not) Follows Therefrom] (1998) 3, *Fundamentum*, 23.

Tibor Horváth (ed), *A halálbüntetés megszüntetése Magyarországon. Dokumentumgyűjtemény* [The Abolition of the Death Penalty in Hungary. Documents] (Halálbüntetést Ellenzők Ligája: Miskolc 1991)

János Kis, 'Az Alkotmánybíróság az élethez való jogról' [The Constitutional Court on the Right to Life] (1992) 3–4, *Jogtudományi Közlöny*, 118.

János Kis, *Alkotmányos demokrácia. Régebbi és újabb közelítések* [Constitutional Democracy. Older and Newer Approaches] (Kalligram: Budapest 2019)

Ildikó Kmetty and Albert Takács, 'Az eutanáziához való jog' [The Right to Euthanasia] (2003) 1, *Fundamentum*, 125.

Gábor Attila Tóth, 'Egy nehéz eset: a könnyű halál' [A Hard Case: Easy Death] (1996) 6–7, *Beszélő*, 77.

Zoltán J. Tóth, *A halálbüntetés intézményének egyetemes és magyarországi jogtörténete* [The General and Hungarian History of the Institution of Capital Punishment] (Századvég Kiadó: Budapest 2010)

Zoltan J. Tóth, *Changing Attitudes Towards the Death Penalty: Hungary's Renewed Support for Capital Punishment* (Palgrave Macmillan: Cham 2020)

17 In fact, the HCC primarily came to the opposite conclusion to the one above, i.e., that making such a regulation possible is not unconstitutional.

Kinga Zakariás, 'Az emberi méltóság védelme' [The Protection of Human Dignity] in Lóránt Csink, Balázs Schanda, and Zs. András Varga (eds), *A magyar közjog alapintézményei* [The Fundamental Institutions of Hungarian Public Law] (Pázmány Press: Budapest 2020), 550.

Kinga Zakariás, 'Az élethez és az emberi méltósághoz való jog' [The Right to Life and Human Dignity] in András Jakab (ed.), *Az Alkotmány kommentárja. II.* [Commentary on the Constitution. II.] (Századvég Kiadó: Budapest 2009), 1899.

2. Decision 64/1991. (XII. 17.) AB – Abortion I.

Kinga Zakariás[*]

The interrelation of the right to life and the right to human dignity with abortion requires that abortion be regulated by statute.

Decision Abortion I. was the first decision to distinguish the objective from the subjective legal side of fundamental rights, and the HCC extended the State's objective, institutional duty to protect life to the human life that is being created. In addition, Decision Abortion I. elaborated in detail the interpretation of the right to life and human dignity contained in Decision 23/1990. (X. 31.) AB (analysis of Decision Death Penalty see in this volume). Decision Abortion I. was the first to define the relationship of legal capacity to the right to life and human dignity, the concept of the right to human dignity and to reveal its essential relationship to the right to life.

1. Background

In Decision Abortion I., the HCC examined the conformity of the Soviet-style dictatorship's abortion legislation with the constitution of a state based on the rule of law. The regulation of abortion in the 'past regime' was based on the communist conception, which broke with the bourgeois conception of human rights and introduced the positivist conception of citizens' rights. The communist Constitution did not mention the right to life, and Article 47 only stated the protection of health for workers, which it sought to achieve by organising medical care.

It was in the context of the organisation of medical care that the Minister of Health of the Rákosi Era,[1] Anna Ratkó, issued Directive no.

* PhD, Associate professor, Pázmány Péter Catholic University Faculty of Law and Political Sciences (Budapest).

1 We can differentiate three eras within socialist legislation: 1. the Rákosi Era (1950–1972), 2. the Kádár Era (1973–1988), and 3. the Grósz Era (1988–1990). Jobbágyi, *Az élet joga* (2004), 148 ff.

81/34/1952 of the Ministry of Health, which regulated the termination of pregnancy with reference to the protection of women's life, health and working capacity and the increase in population growth. The order laid down exceptions to the prohibition of abortion contained in the official compilation of the criminal law in force. This marked the beginning of a decades-long practice of establishing exceptions to regulation by decree. The exceptions were not intended to protect the life of the foetus, but to promote the economic system of the one-party state, reflected in the propaganda against abortion: the publication of brochures, the showing of the propaganda film *Semmelweis* (1952, directed by Frigyes Bán), educational lectures, and public trials of 'abortionists'.

Decision 1047/1956. (VI. 3.) MT brought about a significant change by relaxing the rules on abortion. In addition to the illness of the pregnant woman, it allowed abortions to be granted up to the first 12 weeks of pregnancy in the case of 'reasonable personal and family circumstances' and also, if the applicant insisted on the abortion despite having been informed of its adverse health effects.

The above two new grounds were incorporated in Decree 2/1956. (VI. 24.) EüM of the Ministry of Health on the regulation of the procedure for termination of pregnancy.[2]

The change in the Soviet position and the development of the 'socialist concept of human rights' in the early 1970s brought about a new theoretical understanding of civil rights in Hungary, according to which civil rights are objective requirements of the communist state. This ideological change was intended to be signalled by the 1972 constitutional amendment. The new text of the communist Constitution declared in Article 57 the institutional protection of the life, physical integrity and health of citizens, but did not guarantee the subjective right to life, and the state sought to fulfil its duty to protect life by linking it to social rights (for example, the organisation of health institutions and medical care), but these too remained at the level of state objectives.

It was in this legal context that the basis for the Kádár Era regulation of abortion was laid by Resolution 1040/1973. (X. 18.) MT on the tasks of population policy, which, in addition to improving the population situ-

2 Act V of 1961 on the Penal Code of the Hungarian People's Republic, following the statutory elements defining abortion, specifically provided that a person who performs or has performed the termination of pregnancy in accordance with the permit issued by the legal authority shall not be punished for abortion [Article 256 (5)]. Act IV of 1978 on the Penal Code no longer contained a ground for excluding abortion from criminal liability. Authorised abortions excluded the unlawfulness.

ation, allowed abortion in certain cases specified by law, with reference to the protection of the health of women and unborn children. This principle was also declared in the first sentence of Article 29 (4) of Act II of 1972 on Health Care (old Health Care Act), thus explicitly allowing the grounds for abortion to be included in lower-level legislation. The grounds for authorising abortion were regulated by Decree 4/1973. (XII. 1.) EüM of the Ministry of Health on the examination of applications for abortion.

In the Grósz Era, abortion was regulated by Decree 76/1988. (XI. 3.) MT on abortion (MT Decree) and its implementing Decree 15/1988. (XII. 15.) SZEM (SZEM Decree), which again relaxed the conditions for authorising abortion. It allowed the termination of pregnancy for ten reasons: (1) health of the pregnant woman; (2) serious disability of the foetus; (3) absence of marriage or continuous separation of the pregnant woman for six months; (4) pregnancy as a result of a criminal offence; (5) lack of owner-occupied or rental housing; (6) the pregnant woman is over 35 years of age; (7) the pregnant woman has two living children; (8) the pregnant woman or her spouse is serving a prison sentence; (9) the pregnant woman's spouse is serving in the military; (10) other social reasons strongly justify it.

In Europe after the Second World War there was no agreement in principle on the legal regulation of abortion similar to that on the death penalty. Two equally strong human rights convictions were in conflict. The pro-choice movements give priority to the woman's right to self-determination, while the pro-life movements give priority to the right to life of the foetus.

Two models of compromise prevail in European abortion regulation because of the differences in principle. The deadline model or system of time limits allows a woman to decide freely to terminate a pregnancy in the first stage of pregnancy (usually 10–12 weeks after conception) on the basis of her right to self-determination. After this time, the pregnancy is usually terminated only for a specific indication.[3] The indication model essentially means that termination of pregnancy can only take place for a legally defined reason. Such reasons may include: endangering the life and health of the pregnant woman (medical indication), birth of a handicapped child (genetic indication), rape (criminological indication), and the

3 This regulatory model is in force in Austria, France, Greece, the Netherlands, Norway, Romania, Sweden, Switzerland, and Turkey.

emergency situation of the pregnant woman (social indication). However, the choice of grounds varies from one country to another.[4]

The ECtHR has not explicity taken a position on the question of whether the right to life of the foetus is protected vis-à-vis the mother, but has merely stated that the right to life of the foetus would be limited, where appropriate, by the mother's right to life and privacy. The ECtHR has previously, in view of the divergent approaches, outlined three options on the status of the foetus: (1) Article 2 of the ECHR does not apply to the foetus; (2) it recognises the right to life with the limitations set out therein; (3) the foetus has an absolute right to life. The latter option was rejected, primarily in view of the mother's right to life, but it did not consider it necessary to choose between the remaining options.[5] According to the ECtHR, the term 'everyone' does not exclude the protection of the right to life to the unborn human life,[6] but, citing the lack of European consensus, it left the assessment of the beginning of the right to life to the discretion of the Member States (margin of appreciation).[7]

The ECtHR, on the other hand, did not recognise the right of a pregnant woman to terminate her pregnancy, but in its subsequent jurisprudence it has held that the prohibition of abortion in certain cases (e.g. for health or welfare reasons) falls within the scope of the right to privacy guaranteed by Article 8 ECHR.[8] The positive obligation of the State therefore implies the enactment of relevant legislation and the enforcement of the protection of individual rights, even by specific measures.[9]

2. *Petition*

The HCC received several petitions in which the petitioners—on the basis of Article 37 of the old HCC Act—alleged the unconstitutionality of the legislation on abortion: Article 29 (4) of old Health Care Act, the MT Decree and the SZEM Decree and requested the annulment of the contested

---

4 The countries that follow the system of indications include United Kingdom, Belgium, Denmark, Finland, Ireland, Luxembourg, Hungary, and Germany.

5 *X v. the United Kingdom*, Appl. no. 8416/79, Admissibility decision of 13 May 1980.

6 Fenwick 'Abortion jurisprudence at Strasbourg: deferential, avoidant and normatively neutral?' (2014), 214 (216).

7 *Vo v. France*, no. 53824/00, judgment of 9 July 2004, paras. 82, 84.; *Evans v. United Kingdom*, no. 6339/05, judgment of 10 April 2007, para. 54.

8 *A, B and C v. Ireland*, no. 25579/05, judgment of 16 December 2010, para. 214.

9 *Tysiąc v. Poland*, no. 5410/03, judgment of 20 March 2007, para. 110.

legislation. The petitions presented two conflicting views on human rights, represented by the organisations that emerged after the regime change: the Pacem in Utero Association and the Feminist Network.

The 'pro-life' argument was based on the premise that 'human life begins at conception' and that the foetus is a full human being (ABH 1991, 297, 298.). In their view, regulation at the level of decrees is in itself a violation of Article 8(2) of the Constitution, which provides that the rules governing fundamental rights must be laid down by law. Moreover, the regulation of abortion allows abortion in an unconstitutionally broad scope and therefore violates the right to life and human dignity guaranteed by Article 54 (1) of the Constitution and Article 56 'guaranteeing human legal capacity'. Finally, they also complained that the legislation does not provide for the possibility for the doctor and other medical personnel to refuse to intervene and therefore violates the freedom of conscience guaranteed by Article 60 of the Constitution.

The 'pro-choice' advocates, on the other hand, argued that 'the decision to terminate a pregnancy is a matter of conscience for women', which derives from the right to human dignity, and that therefore the regulation of legislation interfering with this decision at the level of a decree was unconstitutional (ABI I 1991, 297, 298.).

3. *Decision and its reasoning*

In the operative part of Decision Abortion I., the HCC held that the laying down of rules on abortion by decree was unconstitutional. Therefore, it annulled, with effect from 31 December 1992, the contested provision of the old Health Care Act and the contested regulations. It found that the abortion regulation was unconstitutional from a formal point of view, but also pointed out the constitutional framework which limits the possibilities for constitutional regulation of abortion.

3.1. The interrelation of the right to life and the right to dignity (self-determination) with abortion requires that abortion be provided for by law. On the one hand, the exclusion of abortion directly and substantially affects the mother's right to self-determination. On the other hand, the State's objective, institutional duty to protect life extends to the human life that is being created. This obligation is not absolute, and it is therefore possible that other rights may be weighed against it [Articles 8 (2) and 54 (1) of the Constitution].

In the reasoning of Decision Abortion I., the HCC started from the premise that not all the connections with fundamental rights require the statutory regulation provided for in Article 8 (2) of the Constitution, but only the definition of the content of the fundamental right and the direct and significant restriction of the fundamental right. The HCC then went on to state that the regulation of abortion affects a number of fundamental rights, but the connection between the right to life and the right to dignity (self-determination) and abortion certainly requires that abortion be provided for by law (ABH 1991, 297, 301.).

According to the HCC, Article 54 (1) of the Constitution guarantees to 'every human being' the subjective right to life, which is the right of each individual to his or her own life. The state's obligation to 'respect and protect' fundamental rights—as a consequence of Article 8 (1) of the Constitution—is not limited to refraining from infringing subjective fundamental rights, but also includes the obligation to ensure the conditions necessary for their exercise. The subjective and objective aspects of a fundamental right do not necessarily overlap because of the different aspects of the right holder and the State.

Accordingly, from the objective aspect of the right to life, the State is under an obligation not only not to infringe the individual's fundamental right to life and to protect it through legislation and organisational measures, but also to do more, since it is human life as a value that is the object of protection. In view of this, the HCC extended the objective, institutional duty of the State to protect life to the human life that is being created and to ensure the conditions of life for future generations (ABH 1991, 297, 303.). According to the HCC, this obligation, unlike the subjective right to life, is not absolute. It is therefore possible to weigh against it the mother's right to health or her right to self-determination.

On the basis of the foregoing, the HCC held that the rules on termination of pregnancy laid down in the ordinance were unconstitutional and annulled, *pro futuro*, the MT Decree, the SZEM Decree and the provision of the old Health Care Act authorising legislation at the level of ordinances.

3.2. *The legal status of the human being includes two fundamental rights of substance which fill the formal category of legal capacity and express the human quality of the person: the right to life and the right to human dignity. The right to human dignity implies that there is a core of the autonomy of the individual outside the control of all others, whereby the human person remains a subject and cannot become an instrument or an object. Dignity is an inherent quality of human life, indivisible and unrestrictable, and therefore equal for all human beings [Articles 54 (1) and 56 of the Constitution].*

The HCC has stated that it will not examine the substantive unconstitutionality of the legislation on abortion, but it has examined the meaning of the term 'human being' in the Constitution. The HCC started from the premise that the Constitution, in accordance with international human rights conventions,[10] recognised the legal capacity of all human beings, i.e. their legal personality, and their being a person in the legal sense, thus making 'human being' a normative concept. At the same time, it established that legal capacity is a legal abstraction in which there is nothing human. It therefore held that 'the basic legal status of a human being also includes two 'substantive' fundamental rights which fill the formal category of legal capacity and express the human quality of the 'person': the right to life and the right to human dignity' (ABH 1991, 297, 308.).

The HCC then went on to define what the concept of the right to human dignity means: 'The right to human dignity means that there is a core of autonomy and self-determination of the individual, outside the control of all others, whereby, in the classical formulation, the human being remains a subject and cannot become an instrument or an object. It is this conception of the right to dignity which distinguishes a human from legal persons, which are entirely subject to regulation, having no »untouchable« essence' (ABH 1991, 297, 308.). It further pointed out the link between human dignity and the right to life by stating that 'dignity is a quality inherent in human life'. This ensures that no distinction can be made in law between the value of human lives: 'The dignity and life

10 Article 6 of the Universal Declaration of Human Rights; Article 16 of the International Covenant on Civil and Political Rights.

of every human being is inviolable, regardless of physical and mental development or condition, and regardless of how much human potential they have realised and why' (ABH 1991, 297, 309.).

By interpreting the right to life and human dignity, the HCC made abstract equality the most important substantive element of the legal concept of a human being, in relation to which it regarded the beginning of legal personality as a secondary issue. The HCC then stated that another element of the concept of a human is that legal personality begins at birth. The conclusion was that 'it does not follow from the Constitution that the legal personality of the foetus must be recognised, nor that the foetus cannot be regarded as a human being in law' (ABH 1991, 297, 312–313.).

3.3. *The protection of the life of the foetus is the state's duty from the moment of conception. It follows from the state's objective, institutional duty to protect life that the State cannot constitutionally permit unjustified abortion [Article 54 (1) of the Constitution].*

The HCC went on to point out the constitutional framework which, depending on the legislature's decision on the legal status of the foetus, limits the possibilities for regulating abortion.

If the legislator considers the foetus to be legally human, the foetus has a substantive right to life, which extinguishes the woman's right to self-determination. Thus, the mother's right to self-determination is not exercised as a rule, but only in a few exceptional borderline cases. If the legislature decides that the foetus is not legally human, the Parliament must weigh the mother's right to self-determination against the state's duty to protect life, which flows from the right to life and extends to the foetus. The protection of the life of the foetus is a state obligation from conception, and therefore the right to self-determination cannot be the sole rule in the early stages of pregnancy. 'It follows from the State's objective duty to protect life that the State cannot constitutionally permit unjustified abortion' (ABH 1991, 297, 316.). The HCC has emphasised that the existence of a reason is particularly necessary because abortion involves the deliberate destruction of an 'individual human foetus'.

3.4. The right of freedom of conscience in the context of abortion means that the State may not force anyone into a situation which is incompatible with an essential conviction which defines his or her personality. The State has a duty not only to refrain from such coercion, but also to allow, within reasonable limits, alternative conduct [Article 60 of the Constitution].

The HCC examined the relationship between freedom of conscience and abortion and held that the State may not force any person into a situation which would bring him or her into conflict with him/herself. The State has a duty not only to refrain from such coercion, but also to make possible, within reasonable limits, alternative conduct (ABH 1991, 297, 314.). After examining the legislation in force, the HCC held that the State fulfils its obligation under the right to freedom of conscience in relation to doctors who oppose abortion because the Labour Code allows exemption from the obligation to work or allows the creation of workplaces where doctors are not forced to perform an abortion against their convictions. Therefore, the HCC rejected the application for unconstitutionality by omission.

4. Doctrinal analysis

4.1. Formal unconstitutionality with substantive findings: right of self-determination versus the objective, institutional duty of the state to protect

The HCC found the regulation of abortion to be unconstitutional from a formal point of view, and elaborated in detail on the context which requires regulation at the level of a statute under Article 8 (2) of the Constitution. In the process of unravelling the context, it elaborated the doctrinal framework which provided the basis for the constitutionality of the abortion regulation.

The abortion problem is based on the conflict between the mother's right to self-determination and the state's duty to protect life. In its decision identifying the right to self-determination with the right to human dignity, the HCC has already identified the right to self-determination as a substantive element of the general right to personality[11] and has in its settled case-law given broad protection to the right of a person capable of making a free, informed and responsible decision to control his or

11 Decision 8/1990. (IV. 23.) AB, ABH 1990, 42, 45.

her own body and destiny.[12] In Decision Abortion I., the HCC included the decision to terminate a pregnancy, i.e. the disposition of foetal life, within the scope of protection of the right to self-determination, and also considered its narrow exclusion under the existing legislation as a restriction of the right to self-determination. As for the protection of the foetus, the HCC has developed a doctrinal construction of the State's objective, institutional duty to protect life.

It is a commonplace in the literature that the HCC in Decision Abortion I. derived the objective institutional obligation of the state to protect (in this case, life) from the term 'protection' in Article 8 (1) of the Constitution, following the German model.[13] In essence, the Hungarian practice followed the first abortion decision of the GFCC[14] by establishing in Decision Abortion I. the positive, active obligation of the state to protect life as a value, and by distinguishing between the subjective and objective content of fundamental rights.

The State's protection of foetal life in the practice of both bodies is to protect it from unlawful interference by others.[15] A significant difference is that in German practice the duty to protect is based on the assumption that fundamental rights apply in legal relations between individuals: fundamental rights include a prohibition on infringing the value they protect in respect of everyone.[16] In contrast, in Decision Abortion I., the objective aspect of the fundamental right was completely separated from its subject-matter and was exclusively directed at the objective protection of the legal institution which manifests the fundamental right as a constitutional value.[17] The HCC thus obscured the difference between the two forms of

12 Decision 21/1996. (V. 17.) AB, ABH 1996, 74, 80.

13 According to Gárdos-Orosz, the obligation to protect has two parts: on the one hand, the state actively ensures the exercise of the fundamental subjective right, and on the other hand, the state protects the legal institution manifesting the exercise of the fundamental right as a constitutional value. Gárdos-Orosz, *Alkotmányos polgári jog?* (2011), 82.

14 For a description of the decision, see Dederer, 'BVerfGE 39, 1 – Schwangerschaftsabbruch I' in Menzel and Müller-Terpitz (eds), *Verfassungsrechtsprechung* (2017), 264 ff.

15 BVerfGE 39, 1 (42).

16 The obligation to protect is based on human dignity, which defines the scope of protection of the substantive aspect of fundamental rights as the basis of the objective system of values constituted by fundamental rights, but the scope of the protection derived from it is determined by the specific value it is aimed at protecting. Zakariás, *Az emberi méltósághoz való alapjog* (2019), 53.

17 The concept of objective institutional duty of the state to protect life derives from Häberle's 'institutional conception' developed in the 1960s, in which he distin-

positive state obligations: the objective, institutional protection of fundamental rights through the operation of legal institutions (e.g. marriage, the health care network), which protects the individual in an impersonal way, through the agency of the institution, and the direct individual protection of fundamental rights against private individuals.

The strict separation in Decision Abortion I. is understandable, since the HCC has explicitly elaborated the State's objective duty to protect life in the event that Parliament does not recognise the legal personality of the foetus. Thus, by taking the impersonality of abortion to the extreme, the HCC resolved the contradiction between the general, impersonal duty to protect life under Article 54 and the individuality of abortion. In so doing, the HCC sought to uphold the inalienability of the right to life as elaborated in the death penalty decision.

On the other hand, it may be argued that the State's duty to protect life cannot be extended beyond the protection of a subjective right, since a fundamental right may only be restricted in order to protect another more important fundamental right.

4.2. The preliminary question of the legal status of the foetus

The HCC did not examine the substantive unconstitutionality of the legislation on abortion on the grounds that the question of the legal personality of the foetus could not be decided by interpreting the Constitution. However, it did examine the various concepts of a human person and took a position on the constitutional conditions for extending the legal personality concept. In doing so, it linked the concept of the person in the legal sense with the content of the right to life and human dignity, and it was here, in Decision Abortion I., that the concept of human dignity was first defined.[18]

The right to human dignity has appeared in the practice of the HCC in two forms: in a broader sense, as a relative right protecting the development of the personality (general right to personality), and in a narrower sense, as an absolute right (together with the right to life) protecting the

guished between the subjective and objective institutional protection aspects of fundamental rights. However, the HCC, in contrast, ignored the distinction between the 'institutional side' of fundamental rights and institutional guarantees. Zakariás, *Az emberi méltósághoz való alapjog* (2019), 70 f.

18 The concept of human dignity was previously defined in the concurring opinion of Judge László Sólyom to Decision 23/1990. (X. 31.) AB, ABH 1990, 88, 103.

fundamental conditions of human existence, which underpins the system of fundamental rights. The body has used the right to human dignity, first and foremost, not as an absolute right, but as a manifestation of the general right to personality, by identifying its constituent elements and reading from them various specific rights. The absolute right to human dignity is not, however, an empty one, contrary to the positions taken in the literature.[19]

Two approaches to the right to human dignity can be detected in Decision Abortion I.: a negative approach, based on the violations of human dignity that have occurred in history, and a positive approach, based on the philosophical concept of human dignity.

The decision, despite the phrase 'classical formulation', clearly takes the prohibition of objectification from GFCC practice in order to define the content of human dignity.[20] Whereas the application of the principle of objectification in the practice of the GFCC leads to a finding of an infringement of human dignity,[21] in abortion I it is merely a 'decorative element'.

In addition to the possibility of a negative definition, the decision also contains a positive element of human dignity, which points the way to an understanding of the relationship between the legal status of the foetus and the right to human dignity: autonomy and self-determination. The value protected by the right to dignity is therefore self-determination.

The right to self-determination, which is an integral part of the general right to personality in Decision Abortion I., is the right of the mother to control her own body and destiny, which may be restricted in order to protect the life of the foetus. The different structure of the two forms of the right to human dignity (unrestrictable—restrictable) leads to the conclusion that the scopes of protection of the two aspects of the right to human dignity are not identical.

19 Deli and Kukorelli, 'Human Dignity in Hungary' in Becchi and Mathis (eds), *Handbook of human dignity in Europe* (2019), 393 (401).

20 The formula for objectification *(Objektformel)* was developed by the GFCC: 'It is contrary […] to human dignity to make man a mere instrument of the state […]. The sentence that 'man must always remain an end' applies without limitation to all areas of law.' BVerfGE 45, 187 (228).

21 The prohibition of objectification is aimed at defining the restrictive conduct, so the finding of violation of human dignity is manifested through examples and depends on the circumstances of the specific case. BVerfGE 30, 1 (25); BVerfGE 115, 118 (153).

The meaning of the self-worth protected by the right is brought closer to the meaning of the right to life and the right to dignity: 'Dignity is a quality inherent in human life.' Thus, dignity and the self-worth it protects is a quality inherent in human life. In this way, the HCC has moved towards a biological conception of a human being, according to which a human person is every individual belonging genetically to the species *homo sapiens*.[22] The moral concept of a human being, on the other hand, refers to a person capable of autonomous action who, as a member of a moral community, makes a moral judgment of his or her life situation and adapts his or her conduct accordingly. This concept is narrower than the biological concept, since it requires a minimum of the qualities that constitute a person.[23]

It follows from the biological concept of a human that the preservation of the potential for individual self-determination is the object of protection. From the moral concept of a human, it follows that the development of individual self-determination in the moral community is a value protected by law. The two conceptions are mixed in the HCC's practice, which is why the right to human dignity appears in the two forms indicated above.

In the context of abortion, the question arises as to whether the foetus is entitled to the right to human dignity (and life) in the strict sense. Although the HCC has held that the biological concept of human being is extensive, it has stated that another element of the legal concept of the human being, in addition to equality in the abstract, is that its legal personhood begins at birth. The HCC thus identified the question of whether the foetus has the right to life and dignity with the question of whether the foetus is a legal subject.

The constitutional obstacle to deciding on the legal personality of the foetus—in addition to the dispute over the concept of the human person—was the various interpretations of the concept of 'congenital' in Article 54 (1) of the Constitution. According to one view, by using the term 'innate' the Constitution intended to draw a line between 'born human being', human life and so-called 'potential life' (foetal life), and only provided for

22 An example is the practice of the GFCC. In its first abortion decision, it clearly took the biological concept of the human person as its starting point in defining the right to human dignity when it stated: 'Where there is human life, it is entitled to human dignity; it is of no importance whether the bearer is aware of its dignity or is able to protect it. From the beginning, the potentialities inherent in human existence are sufficient to establish human dignity.' BVerfGE 39, 1 (41).

23 Kis, *Az abortuszról* (1992), 110 f.

the former.[24] It follows from this position that the existence of the legal personality of the foetus is conditional on the adoption of a legislative decision at the constitutional level. According to a position close to this, the Hungarian legal order treats foetal life as a value to be protected, but does not consider the foetus as a legal entity, a human being in the legal sense, but as a separate, specific subject of public law. A human being is a born human being, separated from the mother's body, who has legal capacity under the law in force. The concept of congenital is linked by the law in force to the moment of separation from the mother and not to the moment of conception in the mother's body.[25] In sharp contrast to this view, congenitality is not a right acquired by birth, but an inalienable right that is 'born with humans', i.e. one that derives from being alive and being human. Accordingly, there is nothing in the Constitution to justify the claim that the unborn have no right to life and human dignity.[26]

The division of the body led to the statement that 'it does not follow from the Constitution that the legal personality of the foetus must be recognised, nor that the foetus cannot be regarded as a human being in law' (ABH 1991, 297, 312–313.). The HCC thus made it the task of the legislator to regulate the legal status of the foetus and bypassed the question of whether the foetus is entitled to the fundamental right to life and human dignity. Given that the HCC is not bound by 'ordinary law' but is bound by its own case law, it would have been more appropriate to decide whether the foetus has a right to life and dignity.[27]

4.3. *Additional substantive findings*

Although the HCC has declared that it will not conduct a substantive examination of abortion legislation, it has nevertheless made further substan-

24 This position already appeared in the concurring opinion of Judge Géza Kilényi in Decision 64/1991. (XII. 17.) AB: 'the legislator does not contradict the Constitution in force even if it links legal personality to live birth' (ABH 1991, 297, 322.). The above position is explicitly expressed in the parallel reasoning of András Holló, in his interpretation of the concept of 'congenital' in the parallel reasoning to Decision 48/1998. (XI. 23.) AB, ABH 1998, 333, 368–369.

25 The concurring opinion of Judge János Zlinszky to Decision 64/1991. (XII. 17.) AB, ABH 1991, 297, 331–332.

26 Concurring opinion of Judge Tamás Lábady to Decision 64/1991. (XII. 17.) AB, ABH 1991, 297, 325.; dissenting opinion of Judge Tamás Lábady to Decision 48/1998. (XI. 23.) AB, ABH 1998, 333, 363 f.

27 BVerfGE 39, 1 (41).

tive findings which set out the constitutional framework for the regulation of abortion. The HCC outlined two scenarios with regard to the legislature's discretion as to the legal status of the foetus. According to the HCC, if the foetus is recognised as a legal entity, the foetus has a substantive right to life, which extinguishes the woman's right to self-determination. Therefore, the mother's right to self-determination does not apply as a rule, but only in a few exceptional borderline cases. It gave as an example only the case where an abortion becomes necessary in order to save the life of the mother.

In doing so, the panel left open the question of pregnancy resulting from rape. However, a parallel opinion offered a solution to the problem. It held that a mother has a free choice, based on her right to self-determination, as to whether she wishes to have a child, but that it is the mother's human and moral obligation to carry her foetus to term. However, this obligation only exists if the foetus is conceived by a free act. It is up to the legislator to decide whether to make this moral obligation a legal obligation.[28]

According to the HCC, the right to life is therefore a stronger fundamental right than the right to self-determination. The opposing view is that the right to self-determination of a pregnant woman does not compete with the foetus' fundamental right to life. The obligation to carry a pregnancy to term exists only if the mother has voluntarily participated in the creation of the pregnancy. The voluntary establishment of the pregnancy is a precondition for the right of the foetus to be born.

Although the HCC did not decide whether the foetus has a substantive right to life and dignity, it did set out the minimum protection which follows from the objective aspect of the right to life even in the event of the non-recognition of the foetus' legal status. On the one hand, it laid down that the protection of the life of the foetus is a duty of the State from the moment of conception. On the other hand, it deduced from the objective duty of the State that the State cannot constitutionally permit unjustified abortion.[29]

---

28 Concurring opinion of Judge János Zlinszky, Decision 64/1991. (XII. 17.) AB, ABH 1991, 258, 290.

29 Judge Antal Ádám was not looking for a solution to the protection of foetal life within the objective obligation of the state to protect life, but on the objective side of the right to life. In his view, a foetus has the right to be born even if the legislator does not classify it as a human being in the legal sense. However, this right is not an absolute but a derivative right, not identical to the right to life and

Decision Abortion I. thus took a position on the alternatives to the two known models of abortion regulation, the time-limited model and the indication model, and considered only abortion subject to a proper justification from the beginning of pregnancy to be constitutional.[30] In so doing, it went far beyond the limits of the exploration of formal unconstitutionality and the relationship with fundamental rights. The further substantive findings are in fact a judgment on the merits.

4.4. The relationship between freedom of conscience and abortion

The relationship between freedom of conscience and termination of pregnancy can be examined from different perspectives: the mother, the father and the doctor. The petitioners invoked the freedom of conscience of doctors, and therefore Decision Abortion I. states that the state cannot force obstetricians/gynaecologists into a situation that is incompatible with their personal convictions. In the HCC's interpretation, freedom of conscience is seen as a right to the integrity of the person, which as a 'secularised belief' avoids church membership becoming legally relevant.[31] Refusal to perform abortions is therefore not only a right for doctors belonging to a particular denomination, but also for anyone who invokes this conscientious objection.

5. Aftermath of the decision

5.1. Decision 48/1998. (XI. 23.) AB – Abortion II.

One year after the promulgation of Decision Abortion I., the Parliament enacted Act LXXIX of 1992 on the Protection of Foetal Life (Foetus Protection Act). The Foetus Protection Act did not extend the legal personality of the human being to the pre-natal period, but its preamble declares that 'foetal life, which begins at conception, deserves respect and protection'.

---

dignity of a human being in the legal sense. Concurring opinion of Antal Ádám, Decision 64/1991. (XII. 17.) AB, ABH 1991, 258, 275.

30 Sólyom, *Az alkotmánybíráskodás kezdetei Magyarországon* (2001), 96.

31 Schanda, '60. §. Lelkiismereti és vallásszabadság' in Jakab (ed), *Az Alkotmány kommentárja II.* (2009), 2194 (2200).

The Foetus Protection Act introduced a system of indications and accepted as an indication the woman's grave crisis.[32]

In the operative part of Decision Abortion I., the HCC held that it was not unconstitutional for the law to allow termination of pregnancy in the case of a pregnant woman in a serious crisis.[33] At the same time, it stated as a constitutional requirement,[34] and also stated in the operative part, that the definition of the concept of a serious crisis and the conditions for its application may only be defined by law [Article 8 (2), Article 54 (1) of the Constitution]. It therefore annulled the definition of a serious crisis as defined by law[35] and the provision of the Decree implementing the law which gives concrete form to that definition.[36] Thus, the institution of a serious crisis remained undefined.

The HCC also included the following principle in the operative part of its decision: the legislature may constitutionally waive the test of a serious crisis only if it also lays down provisions to protect foetal life which constitute an appropriate counterweight [Article 54 (1) of the Constitution]. The HCC, however, rejected the motions which claimed the unconstitutionality of the Foetus Protection Act as a whole on the basis that the Act did not explicitly define the legal status of the foetus, and rejected the motion for the body to determine whether the foetus is a human being.

---

32 Article 6(1) d) of the Foetus Protection Act.

33 In his dissenting opinion Judge Tamás Lábady rejects the whole concept of the decision. He reiterates the line of reasoning of his parallel opinion attached to Decision Abortion I., according to which the foetus is considered a person without legal capacity under the Constitution, and thus has an absolute right to life. Lábady also considers the level of protection introduced by the State's objective obligation to protect life to be insufficient within the concept of the decision (ABH 1998, 333, 346.). In the dissenting opinion of Judge Ödön Tersztyánszky the serious crisis situation should have been annulled as a ground for termination of pregnancy (ABH 1998, 333, 346.).

34 For the reasons of establishing the constitutional requirements, see Decision 48/1998. (XI. 23.) AB, ABH 1998, 333, 358–359.

35 Article 12 (6) of the Foetus Protection Act: 'A serious crisis is a situation that causes physical or mental distress or social impossibility, and thereby endangers the healthy development of the foetus. The pregnant woman shall certify the existence of a serious crisis by signing the application form.'

36 Article 9 (3) of the Decree 32/1997. (XII. 23.) NM: 'The woman requesting the termination of her pregnancy shall prove the existence of the condition by a declaration, and the staff member shall have no discretion as to the content or the authenticity of the declaration.' (The staff member here means the staff member of the Family Protection Service.)

In the reasoning of Decision Abortion II. stated that the Parliament had formally complied with the requirements set out in the earlier decision by enacting the foetus Protection Act. The legislature did not expressly provide for the legal personality of the foetus, and by regulating abortion in this law, Parliament implicitly expressed that the foetus is not legally human and has no rights. The HCC ruled, with reference to Decision Abortion I., that the failure to recognise the legal personality of the foetus does not mean that foetal life is not constitutionally protected. The legislator must balance the objective obligation to protect life, which includes foetal life, against the mother's right to self-determination (ABH 1998, 333, 339.).

According to the HCC, the serious crisis situation is a concretisation of the proportionality criterion applied to the specific facts of abortion. The restriction on the protection of the life of the foetus by the mother's right is rendered proportionate by the fact that the enforcement of the protection of the foetus would impose a burden on the pregnant woman which is significantly greater than normal. In a broader sense, all classically recognised indications are serious crisis situations, but in a narrower sense, social indications covered the term serious crisis situation. As a separate indication, a woman's serious crisis must always be qualified by the condition of the pregnant woman whose condition may justify abandonment of the protection of the foetus. The Foetus Protection Act, however, contradicts the nature and function of the indication and thus fails to meet the State's obligation to protect foetal life. The problem of constitutionality is further compounded by the fact that the woman's declaration of grave distress cannot be examined. The effect of the general indication of crisis and the waiver of the right to be examined is tantamount to a time-limited solution.

The at least symbolic maintenance of the indication is of great importance in principle, as it is intended to express that the state does not allow abortion without restrictions, at least in principle and for constitutional reasons. Therefore, if the controllability of the crisis situation is abandoned by the law, the protection thus lost must be made up for elsewhere. In Decision Abortion II., the HCC therefore also outlined two options for restoring constitutionality. One option is to check the indication of a crisis situation, the other is to ensure the protection of the foetus by other means.[37]

---

37 In a concurring opinion András Holló warns that making the crisis situation checkable would violate women's right to self-determination and privacy, there-

In Decision Abortion II., the HCC thus confirmed the principles developed in the Decision Abortion I. and made them more concrete with regard to the indication of a serious crisis situation by developing new principles.

Based on the decision of the HCC, the Parliament amended the Foetal Protection Act by Act LXXXVII of 2000 amending Act LXXIX of 1992 on the Protection of Foetal Life. The legislator still did not allow for any checking of the indication of a serious crisis situation, but strengthened the obligation to protect the life of the foetus by new means (psychological, medical, material assistance).

5.2. Protection of the foetus in the FL

After the entry into force of the FL, the HCC did not have to face the question of the constitutionality of the regulation of abortion. In Order 3112/2021. (IV. 14.) AB, the HCC rejected a judicial initiative against Article 6 (3) of the Foetus Protection Act,[38] which challenged the regulation of a case of genetic indication.

Contrary to the conceptual draft prepared by the ad hoc committee preparing the Constitution, which would have meant a radical change by stating the inviolability of life,[39] the text of the FL leads to the conclusion that no significant change in the constitutional understanding of abortion could be expected: the protection of the foetus from conception is an objective, institutional obligation of the state.

Although Article II of the FL left open the debate on the concept of the human person (the FL, unlike the Constitution, does not contain the concept of 'congenital'), the concept of the protection of foetal life—in the light of the dogmatic construction of the objective duty to protect life developed in Decision Abortion I.—may suggest that the second element

---

fore the state must introduce new legal institutions to protect foetal life and develop an institutional network to assist pregnant women (ABH 1998, 333, 370).

38 Pregnancy can be terminated up to 20 weeks – 24 weeks if the diagnostic procedure is delayed – if the probability of genetic, teratological harm to the foetus reaches 50%.

39 In 2010, the Parliament decided to set up an ad hoc committee to draft a new constitution by Parliament Resolution 47/2010. (29. VI.). The constitutional concept, by providing for the protection of life from conception in the same way as the FL, but with the declaration not only of dignity but also of the inviolability of life and dignity, would have meant a total ban on abortion, except in the case of the life-threatening condition of the pregnant woman.

of the legal concept of the human person remains that legal personhood begins at birth.[40] However, already in Decision Abortion I., the HCC moved towards a biological concept of human beings, which the FL fulfilled by declaring the protection of life 'from conception'.[41]

Moreover, the protection provided in the FL from 'conception', in accordance with the values it represents,[42] may mean more than an impersonal, objective obligation to protect foetal life competing with the mother's right to self-determination, which may in the future result in a change in the content of the state's obligation to protect life. This is also referred to in the dissenting opinions to Order 3112/2021. (IV. 14.) AB. According to one of the dissenting opinions, the overly broad possibility of terminating a pregnancy on the basis of the challenged provision renders the taking of foetal life unconstitutional.[43] The other dissenting opinion held that the provision governing termination of pregnancy, which contradicts the assessment of teratological harm, serious disability and other damage, should have been examined in the light of Articles II, XV and, where applicable, Article O of the FL, which establishes personal liability, and that the leaps in medical diagnostics and premature infant care which

40 According to Balázs Schanda, while the constitutional concept made it clear that the human being conceived has the right to protection, the duality of the words human/foetus in the final text of the FL expresses that the foetus to be protected is not considered a subject of human rights. Schanda, 'Keresztény vagy semleges?' (2015), 129 (133 f.)

41 In contrast, Balázs Schanda believes that in this respect the FL takes a step backwards compared to the constitutional concept. The appearance of the concept of the foetus weakens the unified concept of man, in which the biological and legal concepts of man coincide. Schanda, 'Élet és értékek az új Alaptörvényben' in Csehi et al. (eds), *(L)ex cathedra et praxis* (2014), 505 (508 ff.).

42 Catherine Dupré concluded from a combined reading of Article II and Article R (3) of the FL that the framers of the FL had chosen a so-called deterministic approach to dignity. This, in her view, renders the protection of the foetus from conception particularly problematic, because it allows for a particularly restrictive approach to abortion, 'paints a highly questionable picture of the dignity of the woman' and, by protecting the embryo, 'ignores the biological reality of the development of prenatal life at its various stages'. Dupré, 'Human Dignity: Rhetoric, Protection and Instrumentalisation' in Tóth (ed), *Constitution for a Disunited Nation* (2012), 143 (145–146, 152–156).

43 In his dissenting opinion Judge Béla Pokol also proposed a constitutional requirement: 'The HCC states, on the basis of Article II of the FL, that if the negative teratological effect does not constitute a complex developmental disorder and thus does not appear as a possibility of systemic damage, then termination of pregnancy is not eligible.' Reasoning [18]–[19].

have occurred in the decades since the adoption of the foetus protection act should have been given due weight and significance.[44]

Bibliography

Gergely Deli and István Kukorelli, 'Human Dignity in Hungary' in Paolo Becchi and Klaus Mathis (eds), *Handbook of Human Dignity in Europe* (Springer, Cham 2019), 393.

Catherine Dupré, 'Human Dignity: Rhetoric, Protection and Instrumentalisation' in Gábor Attila Tóth (ed), *Constitution for a Disunited Nation – On Hungary's 2011 Fundamental Law* (Central European University Press, Budapest – New York 2012), 143.

Daniel Fenwick, '»Abortion Jurisprudence« at Strasbourg: Deferential, Avoidant and Normatively Neutral?'(2014) 2 *Legal Studies*, 214.

Gábor Jobbágyi, '*Az élet joga. Abortusz, eutanázia, művi megtermékenyítés*' [The Right to Life. Abortion, Euthanasia, Artificial Insemination] (Szent István Társulat, Budapest 2004)

János Kis, *Az abortuszról. Érvek és ellenérvek* [On Abortion. Arguments For and Against] (Cserépfalvi, Budapest 1992)

Fruzsina Orosz-Gárdos, *Alkotmányos polgári jog? Az alapvető jogok alkalmazása a magánjogi jogvitákban* [Constitutional Civil Law? The Application of Fundamental Rights in Private Law Disputes] (Dialóg Campus, Budapest–Pécs, 2011)

Balázs Schanda, '60. §. Lelkiismereti és vallásszabadság' [Freedom of Conscience and Freedom of Religion] in András Jakab (ed), *Az Alkotmány kommentárja II.* [Commentary on the Constitution II.] (Századvég, Budapest 2009), 2194.

Balázs Schanda, ‚Keresztény vagy semleges? Az Alaptörvény identitásának kérdése' [Christian or Neutral. The Question of the Fundamental Law's Identity] (2015) 3 *Magyar Jog*, 129.

Balázs Schanda, ‚Élet és értékek az új Alaptörvényben' [Life and Values in the New Fundamental Law] in Zoltán Csehi, András Koltay, Balázs Landi, and Anett Pogácsás (eds), *(L)ex cathedra et praxis. Ünnepi kötet Lábady Tamás 70. születésnapja alkalmából* [(L)ex cathedra et praxis. A Celebratory Volume Presented to Tamás Lábady on his 70th Birthday] (Pázmány Press, Budapest 2014), 505.

44 Dissenting opinion of Judge Balázs Schanda, Reasoning [23]. The dissenting opinion was joined by Judges Ildikó Hörcherné Marosi and Marcel Szabó. In his dissenting opinion, Marcel Szabó also stressed that 'I would have considered it necessary to examine whether the yes-or-no level of certainty in the case of foetuses that are already viable outside the womb is constitutionally acceptable for the purpose of authorising and carrying out medical intervention to terminate pregnancy.' Reasoning [27].

László Sólyom, *Az alkotmánybíráskodás kezdetei Magyarországon* [The Beginnings of Constitutional Adjudication in Hungary] (Osiris, Budapest 2001)

Kinga Zakariás, *Az emberi méltósághoz való alapjog. Összehasonlító jogi elemzés a német és magyar alkotmánybírósági gyakorlat tükrében* [The Fundamental Right to Human Dignity. Comparative Legal Analysis in the Light of German and Hungarian Constitutional Court Practice] (Pázmány Press, Budapest 2019)

3. Decision 11/1992. (III. 5.) AB – Retroactive Transitional Justice

András Jakab[*]

Regime change cannot lead to an exception to the prohibition of retroactive criminal laws.

Decision Retroactive Transitional Justice was a key doctrinal decision, because it defined the constitutional framework of transitional justice (especially with regard to retroactivity) and the legal nature of regime change on the basis of legal continuity. In essence, the decision condenses all the methodological and substantive dilemmas that arose in connection with the first HCC.

1. Background

On the basis of a motion by Zsolt Zétényi and Péter Takács, MDF MPs, the Parliament adopted a law related to transitional justice on 4 November 1991,[1] which aimed to ensure the punishability of certain crimes commit-

* DSc, Professor, University of Salzburg; honorary researcher, Pázmány Péter Catholic University Faculty of Law and Political Sciences (Budapest); external researcher, Centre for Social Sciences Institute for Legal Studies (Budapest).
I am grateful to Miklós Kelemen for his help in obtaining the relevant literature and to Tamás Ádány, Eszter Bodnár, Johanna Fröhlich, Fruzsina Gárdos-Orosz, Viktor Kazai, Endre Orbán, Csaba Tordai, Bernát Török, Kinga Zakariás and Edvin Zukic for their critical comments on the manuscript. Chapters 4.2. and 4.3. are based on the commentary on Article 2 of the Constitution, written jointly by Tamás Győrfi and András Jakab (with the consent of Tamás Győrfi), cf. Jakab (ed), *Az Alkotmány kommentárja* (2009), 113–123, 130–131.

1 Zsolt Zétényi reports that Péter Takács contributed nothing of significance and was only formally a co-presenter. However Imre Békés and Katalin Kutrucz (Mrs Kónya), both criminal lawyers, helped a lot. See, Zétényi, 'Néhány őszinte szó az igazságtételről, avagy megtettünk-e mindent, ami tőlünk tellett?' (2017), December *Hitel*, 36 (40). Several legal scholars supported the contents of the law at the time, See, ibid. 50; Békés et al., 'Szakértői vélemények az »igazságtételről«. – I. Szakvélemény' (1992), 1 *Társadalmi Szemle*, 70.

ted before the change of regime but not prosecuted for political reasons.[2] The text of the law read as follows: 'Article 1 (1) On 2 May 1990, the statute of limitations shall begin to run again for the punishment of crimes committed between 21 December 1944 and 2 May 1990 and defined in the laws in force at the time of their commission, which were punishable under the Act IV of 1978 on the Criminal Code. In accordance with Article 144 (2), Article 166 (1) and (2) and Article 170 (5) of Act IV of 1978, the statute of limitations for the offences of treason, which are defined as treason, if the State has not asserted its criminal claim for political reasons, will be terminated as of 1 January 1990. (2) A sentence imposed pursuant to subsection (1) may be subject to unlimited mitigation. Article 2. This Act shall enter into force on the day of its promulgation.'

The Act was the subject of a heated debate in Hungarian public life, and its adoption gave rise to a politically historic debate between Iván Pető (SZDSZ) and Imre Kónya (MDF) on 16 November 1991 on the general question of transitional justice.

Internationally, a wide variety of solutions for dealing with the past (transitional justice) after the end of dictatorships or wars have been developed. In some countries, ex post prosecutions have been based on natural law (e.g. Germany); in others, the issue has been left to international law (Yugoslavia), and yet further cases, such procedures have been explicitly avoided (Spain).[3] At the time of the decision, there was no clear European trend in this respect. There was a clear international legal obligation to prosecute only in cases of aggression, genocide, apartheid and war crimes at the time of the HCC decision in question.[4]

---

2 The official explanatory notes to the bill have been published in: *Magyarország politikai évkönyve 1992* (1992), 525–527.

3 See, e.g., Werle and Vormbaum, *Transitional Justice. Vergangenheitsbewältigung durch Recht* (2018); Vassalli, *Radbruchsche Formel und Strafrecht* (2010) with further references.

4 See, e.g., Tomuschat, 'The Duty to Prosecute International Crimes Committed by Individuals' in Cremer et al. (eds), *Festschrift für Helmut Steinberger* (2002), 315–349; Orentlicher, 'The Duty to Prosecute Human Rights Violations of a Prior Regime' (1991), *Yale Law Journal*, 2537.

2. *Petition*

The President of the Republic, Árpád Göncz, did not promulgate the Act, but requested a constitutional review in his petition of 16 November 1991. The text of the petition was as follows:

'The essence of the (constitutional) concern is whether Article 1 of the Act does not violate the principle of the rule of law contained in Article 2 (1) of the Constitution or whether it does not conflict with Article 57 (4) of the Constitution. In detail:

Whether the provision of the Act providing for the resumption of the limitation period does not conflict with the fundamental constitutional principle enshrined in Article 2 (1) of the Constitution, according to which the Republic of Hungary is a state governed by the rule of law. Legal certainty is an indispensable component of the rule of law, without the maintenance of which there can be no question of the rule of law.

Does the wording of Article 1 not constitute unconstitutional retroactive criminal legislation, does it not infringe the principle of *nullum crimen sine lege*, a legal principle which has been established historically and made part of human rights by international conventions, particularly in view of the fact that the acts made punishable by Article 1 may already be time-barred under the criminal laws in force at the time of their commission?

Is the »reopening« of the entire limitation period after the expiry of the limitation period compatible with the principles of the rule of law? Does that provision not conflict with the rule of law requirement that, once the limitation period has expired, the State promises everyone immunity from punishment and does the withdrawal of that promise not infringe the fundamental principle of the rule of law that every citizen may rely on the credibility of the State and the law?

Does the law not infringe the rule of law principle of legal certainty by including completely general or vague concepts and provisions, such as »the State did not assert its claim to punishment for political reasons«; by defining treason and assault as qualifying offences without referring to the definition of the basic offence; and by providing for unlimited mitigation of punishment for these offences »in all cases«. Lastly, can the principle of the statute of limitations in criminal law, which is not known in the Criminal Code, i.e. in substantive criminal law, be applied by analogy in criminal law?

It is questionable whether the law does not make an unjustified and arbitrary distinction between the perpetrators of the same offences on the basis of the grounds on which the State has acted against them. Is that provision not contrary to the prohibition of arbitrariness laid down in

Article 54 (1) of the Constitution and to the rule of equality of citizens laid down in Article 70/A (1)?'

3. Decision and its reasoning

The HCC declared the Act unconstitutional[5] by ordering that 'The Constitutional Court declares that the Law on the Prosecution of Serious Crimes Committed between 21 December 1944 and 2 May 1990 and not Prosecuted for Political Reasons, adopted by the Parliament in session on 4 November 1991, is unconstitutional.'

3.1. The rule of law cannot be established against the rule of law (and in particular against legal certainty). It is also part of the constitutional principle of the rule of law that the limits and conditions of the criminal power of the State, as defined by law, cannot be altered to the detriment of the person whose acts are being criminally judged [Article 2 (1) of the Constitution].

In point III of the reasoning of the decision, the HCC includes general reflections on its own role, on the concepts of the rule of law and democracy, and on the constitutional framework of transitional justice. In this context, it notes that the constitutional amendment promulgated on 23 October 1989 effectively brought into force a new Constitution. It also established the, since then, oft-quoted thesis 'that Hungary is a state governed by the rule of law is both a statement of fact and a programme' (ABH 1992, 77, 80.). Implicitly, the HCC refers to the Western mainstream as an example to be followed (democracies in the plural: 'the requirements of the rule of law historically established in constitutional democracies and also used as a basis for the 1989 Hungarian constitutional revision').

The HCC states that 'the conceptual culture and values of the Constitution must permeate the whole of society. It is the rule of law that makes the Constitution a reality.' (ABH 1992, 77, 80.). Accordingly, 'any political

5 The HCC made its ruling unanimously, based on a motion by László Sólyom and András Szabó on 5 March 1992. The statements offered as *ratio decidendi* by the HCC (statements of principle, *Leitsätze*) were also placed in the binding operative part of the decision. See further, Zakariás, 'Az elvi tételek kiemelésének kérdése az Alkotmánybíróság gyakorlatában' (2009) 10 *Pázmány Law Working Papers*.

aspiration can only be realised within the framework of the Constitution' (ABH 1992, 77, 81.). The HCC emphasises that 'the enforcement of the constitutional norms applicable to the legal system—the observance of the rules of the legal system as they apply to the legal system itself—is a fundamental criterion of the rule of law' (ABH 1992, 77, 84.). Accordingly, 'a constitutional state governed by the rule of law can only react to violations of the rule of law' (ABH 1992, 77, 84.). Furthermore, the principle of the rule of law is not a subsidiary, secondary rule to these specific constitutional rules, and is not a mere declaration, but an independent constitutional norm, the violation of which in itself establishes the unconstitutionality of a statute [Decision 11/1992. (III. 5.) AB, ABH 1992, 77, 84.].

Within the principle of the rule of law, the HCC strongly emphasises a formal aspect of what it calls 'legality'. 'The principle of legality imposes on the rule of law the requirement that the rules of the legal system as they apply to itself must be unconditionally respected.' (ABH 1992, 77, 81.). It explicitly excludes the question of legitimacy (in a moral, not sociological sense) from the assessment of the validity of legislation (i.e. the invalidity of old legislation may only result from a contradiction with the new constitutional rules, not from a lack of legitimacy).

According to the HCC, exceptions to the general principle of legal certainty may be allowed on the basis of the principle of proportionality, but in doing so, injustice 'is not in itself an argument' against legal certainty (ABH 1992, 77, 81.). Accordingly, the fundamental (formal) safeguards of the rule of law cannot be set aside on the grounds of historical (regime change) circumstances and justice. In other words, 'The rule of law cannot be implemented against the rule of law.' (ABH 1992, 77, 82.). Moreover, as a statement of legal philosophy, the HCC also states that 'legal certainty based on objective and formal principles takes precedence over justice, which is always partial and subjective' (ABH 1992, 77, 82.). With regard to the constitutional guarantees of criminal law, the HCC establishes absolute protection, in relation to which no proportionality test is applicable. According to the HCC, 'an exception to the guarantees of criminal law would conceptually be possible only by an open setting aside of the guarantees, but this is precluded by the principle of the rule of law' (ABH 1992, 77, 83.).

It then contrasts the values embodied in the law with mere arguments of justice, judging the former to be more authoritative: 'On the basis of the value system of the rule of law, even a just claim cannot be asserted if it contradicts the guarantees of the rule of law.' (ABH 1992, 77, 84.). As regards its own task, the HCC states that 'the interpretation of the concept of the rule of law is also an important task of the Constitutional Court'

(ABH 1992, 77, 84.). Among the elements of the concept of the rule of law, the HCC specifically emphasises the prohibition of retroactivity (ABH 1992, 77, 85.).

In sum, the HCC held that the provisions of the Act were partly ambiguous (indefinite), partly they violated the prohibition of retroactive legislation [rule of law, Article 2 (1) of the Constitution] and specifically the principles of *nullum crimen* and *nulla poena* under Article 57 (4) of the Constitution.

The HCC emphasises that 'the constitutional principle which gives substance to the rule of law is also that the limits and conditions of the criminal power of the State, as defined by law, cannot be altered to the detriment of the person whose acts are the subject of a criminal judgment. Neither changes in criminal policy nor omissions or errors on the part of the authorities acting in the matter may be imputed to the offender.' (ABH 1992, 77, 88.). The HCC draws specific consequences from the general findings of the previous parts of the decision in point V of the reasoning of the decision. Accordingly, it states that the principle of legality (that includes the principle of non-retroactivity) requires that 'the law in force at the time of the commission of the offence must also apply to the limitation of criminal liability' (ABH 1992, 77, 88.).

3.2. *The re-criminalisation of offences for which the statute of limitations has already expired, the extension of the statutory limitation period for offences not yet statute-barred, the interruption of the statute of limitations for offences not yet statute-barred by a law, and the establishment of a reason for suspension or interruption by a retroactive law are unconstitutional [Articles 2 (1), 57 (4) of the Constitution].*

According to the HCC, 'the statute of limitations permanently extinguishes the criminal liability of the perpetrator of the offence. [...] Once the limitation period has expired, the offender has a substantive right not to be punished. [...] The principle of trust in the law necessarily requires that, once a ground for the removal of criminal liability has been established, the offence cannot be made punishable again by a new law.' (ABH 1992, 77, 88–89.). It also states that 'the limitation period for an offence which has already lapsed may not be resumed' (ABH 1992, 77, 89.), as it would be contrary to both Article 2 (1) of the Constitution (legal certainty) and Article 57 (4) (*nullum crimen* and *nulla poena*).

The statutory extension of the statute of limitations for an offence that has not yet expired raises somewhat different questions of constitutionality than the re-criminalisation of an offence that has already expired. According to the HCC, 'the institution of limitation does not guarantee that the criminal liability will actually cease within a predetermined period, but it does ensure that the rules for calculating the limitation period do not change to the detriment of the offender during the limitation period' (ABH 1992, 77, 90.). Thus, 'from the point of view of the guarantee, there is no difference between a law extending the limitation period for certain offences by increasing the normal limitation period and a law ordering that it be restarted' (ABH 1992, 77, 91.).

According to the HCC, the assessment of the limitation period, and in particular the determination of whether it has been suspended or interrupted, is a matter for the law enforcement authorities alone and ultimately for the courts. The legislator cannot decide on this issue ex post: 'This would mean that the law would extend the limitation period ex post, which, as explained above, is unconstitutional.' (ABH 1992, 77, 91.).

3.3. From the point of view of the limitation period, no constitutional distinction can be drawn between political and other reasons why the State has not asserted its criminal claim. Because of its indeterminacy, it is a violation of legal certainty and therefore unconstitutional to declare that 'the State has not asserted its criminal claim for political reasons' as a ground for the statute of limitations. It is unconstitutional for the law to include the crime of treason in its scope without taking into account the repeated changes in the legal subject matter protected by the offence under different political regimes [Articles 2 (1), 57 (4) and 70/A of the Constitution].

Even taking into account the specific purpose of the law, it is not possible to determine with sufficient certainty what is meant by the non-enforcement of a criminal claim for 'political reasons' (non-initiation, termination, ending with an unlawfully light sentence, and the very concept of 'political reason' is uncertain, especially in view of the numerous legislative and political changes during the period in question). This vagueness in itself renders the law unconstitutional.

The legal subject matter protected by the concept of 'treason' changes with the changes in political regimes and takes on different political connotations. Therefore, treason, despite its textual identity, is treated as a different offence under different political systems, and its omission for 'political reasons' is an ex post facto qualification which 'reclassifies the offence itself with retroactive effect' (ABH 1992, 77, 93.).

3.4. Excluding the possibility of a full pardon (and limiting it to mitigation of the punishment) is unconstitutional [Article 30/A (1) (k) of the Constitution].

According to the HCC, the text of the Act as adopted 'does not contain a provision on the imposition of punishment, but a provision on clemency. [...] The power of the President of the Republic to grant pardons, as guaranteed by the Constitution, cannot be limited. However, the present Act limits this power of pardon to a partial remission of the sentence and is therefore unconstitutional.' (ABH 1992, 77, 94.).

4. Doctrinal analysis

The decision is a small model of all the methodological features and content for which the HCC has been praised by some and criticised by others.

4.1. Objective-teleological reasoning vs. natural law

Objective-teleological arguments play a key role in the reasoning of the decision, most notably in the form of the 'Values of the Constitution' as a reference. The HCC makes it clear that it takes precedence over mere arguments of justice (ABH 1992, 77, 84.). This means that the HCC, while rejecting the earlier socialist literal interpretation,[6] also rejects natural law arguments. Instead, it considers values (in accordance with German constitutional doctrinal patterns) as a means of interpretation (and not as a matter of validity like natural law theories).[7] That is, values affect the validity of laws only through constitutional interpretation.

---

6 In the same way, it also rejects socialism's instrumentalist conception of law: 'In a constitutional state governed by the rule of law, criminal law is not merely an instrument, but protects a value and itself carries values: the constitutional principles and guarantees of criminal law. Criminal law is both the legal basis for the exercise of criminal power and a charter of freedom for the protection of individual rights. Although criminal law is the protector of values, it cannot be a means of moral cleansing in the context of the protection of moral values.' (ABH 1992, 77, 86.).

7 For further references and more on the rejection of the socialist tradition of interpretation and the German objective-teleological model, see Jakab and Kazai, 'A

4.2. The self-regulatory nature of the legal system

The judgment also concerns theoretical questions about the binding power of rules, especially about the extent to which the legislator is bound by and complies with the legal rules of law-making, or, to put it another way, the extent to which the legal system satisfies the requirement of legality.

This problem leads to the question of the identity of the legal system. The legal system can be thought of in a certain context as nothing more than an ordered set of legal norms. Intuitively, we think that if, for example, a particular norm of the Hungarian legal system is changed, this does not create a new legal system, but merely a change within the existing legal system.[8] However, if this intuition is correct, and I believe that it is, the question arises: when can we say that a new legal system has been created, instead of simply changing the content of the existing one? For how long can we claim that the legal system existing at time t1 is identical to the substantively changed legal system existing at time t2? Applying this conceptual framework to the history of the Hungarian regime change, the question is whether or not the post-change legal system is identical to the pre-change legal system. The thesis that answers the former question in the affirmative will be called the continuity thesis, while the one that answers the question in the negative will be called the discontinuity thesis.

If the question of the identity of the legal system cannot be answered on the basis of the content of each norm, and it is in principle possible that all the rules of conduct of the legal system could change between t1 and t2 and still be the same legal system, then we must conclude that, in the question of the identity of the legal system, the rule which is the ultimate criterion of validity of the system, which, to use Hans Kelsen's expression, can be called the basic norm of the legal system, plays a crucial role.[9] According to this view, the norms in force at t1 and t2 constitute

---

Sólyom-bíróság hatása a magyar alkotmányjogi gondolkodásra' in Győrfi, Kazai, and Orbán (eds), *Kontextus által világosan: a Sólyom-bíróság antiformalista elemzése* (2021), 115.

8 The problem has been compared in legal literature to the ship of Theseus (of which Theseus gradually replaced all the pieces one by one, and the question was whether it was still the same ship), see Sajó and Uitz: *The Constitution of Freedom* (2017), 67.

9 Here I adopt Kelsen's terminology, which is widely known to Hungarian lawyers. For my arguments though, it is not necessary to accept Kelsen's theory of validity. It is sufficient for the position taken here that the necessary condition for the identity of the legal system is compliance with the rules of legality. It is possible, however, that these conditions are not sufficient to regard two momentary legal

two different legal systems if the basic norms of the two systems differ at the two points in time. If, on the other hand, the basic norms of the two systems are identical, the identity of the legal system has not changed, irrespective of the fact that all the rules (except the basic norm) may have been exchanged between the two dates.[10]

In the case of a revolution that creates a new legal system and changes the basic norm of the previous system, the rules of the new system can be considered legitimate in a moral sense, but they cannot be considered legal in the sense that they themselves were created by adhering to the basic norm of the older legal system. Of course, the rules of the new legal system (which may be almost identical in content to the rules of the old legal system) can be considered legal on the basis of the newly established legal system's own criteria of legality.

In the decision under discussion here, the HCC, in characterising the nature of the regime change, clearly took the view that the political regime change had taken place while maintaining the continuity of the legal system. The HCC uses the term 'revolution according to the rule of law' to describe this nature of the transition. However, the question may be raised whether this legally continuous transition can subsequently be made (retrospectively) discontinuous without another revolution. If so, a new meaning is given to the proposition 'that Hungary is a state governed by the rule of law is both a statement of fact and a programme' (ABH 1992, 77, 80.). If the legal transition can subsequently become discontinuous, it may follow that the HCC's statements on the legality of the transition are not simply statements of fact about the past, but also normative statements formulating a programme for the future: the HCC must ensure that the legality of the transition is not compromised, because the principle of the rule of law requires that the rule-bound nature of the legal system must also extend to its criteria of legality.

---

systems as identical. Such a position is expressed in relation to the Hungarian regime change in e.g. Kis, 'Reform és forradalom között' (1993), 11 *Világosság*, 5. It also complicates the picture if we assume not the identity of the basic norm, but only its continuity. In Herbert Hart's doctrine of the legal system, for example, the basic norm, or, to use Hart's terminology, the rule of recognition, is a rule of customary law and therefore subject to continuous change. Hart, *The Concept of Law* (1961), 95.

10 This also shows, of course, that theoretically these questions cannot be answered satisfactorily without touching on the question of the legal theory of the ultimate validity criterion of the legal system.

If the rules on legislation are respected, how can the legality of the transition be affected at all? Two arguments are worth considering in this respect. As is widely known, the German courts, both after the fall of the Nazi regime and after German reunification, repeatedly used the arguments of legal philosopher Gustav Radbruch.[11] The essence of Radbruch's argument, the so-called Radbruch formula, states that a rule established by a formally correct procedure may be so intolerably unjust that it lacks legal status. Such a rule must be regarded not simply as a bad or immoral rule of law, but as a rule without legal validity.[12] The practical consequence of this understanding is that we must regard such rules as invalid at the time of their creation. In other words, courts arguing the Radbruch formula could, without the intervention of the legislator and in the absence of retroactive rules, attach different legal consequences to a particular act than the rule itself did.[13] In our view, it is a debatable question of legal theory whether such a practice of the courts in itself justifies the discontinuity doctrine.

A related problem is whether the laws of justice, including retroactive criminal prosecution, presuppose a discontinuity in the legal system.[14] Since the HCC has been confronted with the problem of retroactive justice on several occasions, we cannot avoid this question of principle. This argument seems tempting because, if it stands, we do not have to engage in complex moral debates in which the prospects for consensus are rather limited. This elegant strategy of argumentation requires only that one wishes to remain grounded in the legitimacy of the legal system, and as a lawyer one can hardly do otherwise. In this case, we would only have to show that the so-called laws of justice presuppose the discontinuity of the legal system.

---

11 See, e.g. BVerfGE 3, 225, 232 (1953).

12 Radbruch, 'Gesetzliches Unrecht und übergesetzliches Recht' (1946), *Süddeutsche Juristenzeitung*, 105–108.

13 The Radbruch formula should be broken down into two components. A procedurally correct rule has no legal quality if (a) it is intolerably unjust, or (b) the rule-maker has made no effort to respect the equality that is at the heart of justice. Since the latter criterion (b) is linked to the subjective intention of the legislator, the German courts have tended to use the first criterion (a) in their reasoning. See Alexy, 'A Defence of Radbruch's Formula' in Dyzenhaus (ed), *Recrafting the Rule of Law* (1999), 16.

14 '[T]he doctrine of justice cannot stand as a legally tenable claim unless the thesis of the discontinuity of the legal system is accepted with all its consequences.' Bragyova, 'Az igazságtétel legalitása' in Lamm and Bragyova (eds), *Visszamenőleges igazságszolgáltatás* (1992), 73.

We ourselves believe that this thesis is untenable. Retrospective legislation does not presuppose the truth of the discontinuity thesis, so, unfortunately, we do not consider such an elegant solution based on formal arguments for the retroactive judgement of justice to be possible. The author of a retroactivity rule does not claim that a rule was inherently without legal quality because of its substantive defects. It considers that this earlier rule, because it was established in accordance with the criteria of legality of the legal system, had legal status. However, the new rule, which was created in accordance with the same basic rule, attaches different legal consequences to certain conducts from the date of its entry into force than the earlier rules of the legal system did, but with retroactive effect.[15] The question of retroactive legislation, therefore, does not affect the legality of the legal system or the identity of the legal system and the legal continuity of the transformation. However, the decision's reasoning is based on the contrary.

4.3. *Conflict between legal certainty and justice in the specific historical context of the transition to the rule of law*

The duality of normality and exceptionalism, or the denial of it, plays a very important role in the reasoning of the present decision.[16] A situation cannot be exceptional (extraordinary, emergency, etc.) only because there is an imminent threat to the state. The special case of exceptionalism,

---

15 Bragyova writes: 'Retrospective legislation can add new legal consequences to previous facts, but it cannot declare illegal or unlawful what was lawful in the legal system in the conditions that can be traced back to the previous one.' Bragyova, 'Az igazságtétel legalitása' in Lamm and Bragyova (eds), *Visszamenőleges igazságszolgáltatás* (1992), 87. The first part of the sentence may give the impression that Bragyova's position does not radically differ from the view expressed here, and thus our criticism misses the point. If this were so, however, Bragyova's thesis that the laws of justice violate the legitimacy of the legal system would in any case not be generally tenable. The second part of the sentence again makes clear the difference between the two positions. A rule that criminalises conduct that was not previously punishable implies, according to Bragyova, the discontinuity thesis, whereas the position expressed here is compatible with the continuity thesis.

16 Cf. Sólyom, *Az alkotmánybíráskodás kezdetei Magyarországon* (2001), 693.This differs, for example, from the approach of the ECtHR, which accepts the role of special historical circumstances in the field of fundamental rights restrictions, see e.g. *Rekvényi v Hungary*, no 25390/94, judgment of 20 May 1999 [ECtHR], para. 48.

which cannot be covered by the usual legal concepts of state of war and state of emergency, is in contrast to the case of states aspiring to the status of a state governed by the rule of law, where the new political establishment has been created on the ruins of a former dictatorial or totalitarian political system. The basic question here is whether the principles of the rule of law can be applied immediately when the new political system is established, or whether, exceptionally, for a certain period of time, for certain cases or for certain groups, different rules can still be applied. These questions were raised in the present decision in relation to the non-retroactivity principle.

As indicated above, in our view, the heart of the theoretical problem of retroactive legislation is not the conceptual question of whether the rules of the legal system as such have been respected, or, to put it another way, whether the legality of the legal system has been violated—in our view, it has not—but the question of how we view the sometimes conflicting values of the rule of law and substantive justice, which presupposes a choice of values.[17]

This question would not have arisen so sharply if the unconstitutionality of the so-called statute of limitations law had been compellingly inferred from Article 57 (4) of the Constitution. In that case, the court would have indeed been only able to give way to the requirements of substantive justice by setting aside the text of the Constitution. However, the statutory provision in question allows for various interpretations, and the interpretation of the HCC on this point is also open to strong dispute.[18] Nor would this question arise if the requirements of the rule of law were always to be applied in an absolute, non-discretionary manner. An important element of the HCC's reasoning was that it sought to present the guarantees of criminal procedure as just such.

While it is conceivable that there may be some procedural guarantees for which this argument is convincing (e.g. the presumption of innocence), this is certainly not the case for all requirements arising from the rule of law. Therefore, we believe that the interpretation of the HCC, which also understood the rules on limitation as discretionary guarantees, is not a kind of conceptual necessity, but itself the consequence of a prior value choice.

17 For a classic formulation of the conflict between legal certainty and justice, see Radbruch, *Vorschule der Rechtsphilosophie* (1959), 33–34.

18 Hollán et al., '57. § – Bírósági eljárási garanciák' in Jakab (ed), *Az Alkotmány kommentárja* (2009), 289.

In the dilemma of formal legality and substantive justice—at least as it appeared in the context of the assessment of the Limitation Act—the HCC essentially took the side of the formal rule of law. In the event of conflict, the formal rule of law should be preferred to justice. 'The unjust result of legal relations [...] is not in itself an argument against legal certainty. [...] Legal certainty based on objective and formal principles takes precedence over justice, which is always partial and subjective' (ABH 1992, 77, 82).

However, we must add that, according to the retrospective interpretation, in this case there was in fact no 'compulsion of final choice', because the court did not argue against substantive justice, but only wanted to impose those notions of substantive justice which were compatible with the rule of law, since the HCC had subsequently opened up the possibility of prosecuting certain crimes through international law.[19] This does not, however, make it unnecessary to comment on the reasons for this choice of values as expressed in the limitation decision itself.

First of all, it is worth pointing out that the above-mentioned dilemma of legal certainty and justice was not only faced by the HCC. Many courts in several countries that have been confronted with this dilemma have reached a different conclusion from the HCC on the interpretation of the concept of the rule of law (indeed, the HCC's position has subsequently proved to be a distinct minority position in international comparison).[20] This at least confirms that even if the HCC's interpretation of the rule of law is defensible, this reading does not follow compellingly from the concept of the rule of law in any way.[21]

Secondly, an important element of the HCC's reasoning was the thesis that it is essentially 'indifferent' by which legal techniques the legislator makes a conduct punishable in this case (ABH 1992, 77, 89.). However, it is in fact a debatable question of criminal law doctrine whether the prohibition in Article 57 (4) of the Constitution extends to altering the rules of limitation.[22] It must be seen that these legal techniques affect the

---

19 Sólyom, *Az alkotmánybíráskodás kezdetei Magyarországon* (2001), 699, 705.

20 László Sólyom refers to Check, Polish and German examples: Sólyom, *Az alkotmánybíráskodás kezdetei Magyarországon* (2001), 699. See further, Varga (ed), *Igazságtétel jogállamban* (1995); Sadurski, *Rights Before Courts* (2005), 223–263.

21 In fact, some readings suggest that part of the rule of law is to hold accountable those who avoided punishment in previous dictatorships by the means of dictatorship in the new regime. For an example from South America, see Sampford: *Retrospectivity and the Rule of Law* (2006), 250, 253, 261.

22 For the conceptual separation of prohibition and its condition (i.e. nullum crimen/nulla poena must be distinguished from the limitation of the statute of

principles embraced by the rule of law to varying degrees, so that from the point of view of the underlying values, these legal techniques are by no means indifferent. While the ex post criminalisation of an act is problematic because we cannot adapt our behaviour to a rule introduced later, the most compelling argument in favour of a prohibition on changing the conditions of the statute of limitations is that such changes violate the perpetrator(s)' expectations of the law. In the former case, the choice between lawful and unlawful conduct is impossible to make, since the offender cannot know what is unlawful and what is not. In the latter case, the perpetrator may be aware that the act is unlawful, but the expectations as to how far the perpetrator can be held liable as a consequence of the unlawful conduct are violated. While it may be argued that this expectation is worth protecting, it is hardly a defensible position that arguments of equal weight should be required in the two cases.

As already mentioned, in the present decision the HCC contrasts formal legal certainty with subjective justice. This contrast suggests that legal certainty should be preferred to justice because it is formal and therefore objective, whereas justice is purely subjective. However, it must be seen that the interpretation of legal certainty given by the HCC is itself open to discussion, i.e. it is in a sense subjective. This concept of legal certainty was contrasted not simply with a subjective conception of justice, but with a conception of justice that was also debatable and, to that extent, truly subjective, but which was nevertheless the result of democratic decision-making.[23] The formality of legal certainty is not more 'objective', but merely protects different values. Or, to put it another way, the adoption of a more concrete concept of the rule of law (apart from its very broad conceptual framework, which denies the arbitrary nature of the state) is always the result of a conscious reflection and reflection on a specific historical situation, and has the character of a response.

limitations), see the critique of Miklós Hollán: Hollán et al., '57. § – Bírósági eljárási garanciák' in Jakab (ed), *Az Alkotmány kommentárja* (2009), 289.

23 Hence the criticism of the HCC's decision that the court has thus taken the task of shaping the conditions for regime change out of the hands of the legislature by overriding the legislature's different assessment of the balance between the rule of law and justice with its own debatable interpretation of the rule of law. See Sadurski, *Rights Before Courts* (2005), 256.

4.4. Doctrinal maximalism

The decision explicitly indicates that it does not intend to resolve the specific case alone, but also to build a conceptual system and set detailed benchmarks for the future legislator: 'The Constitutional Court examined the constitutionality problems of the law separately and independently of the fact that a position on one question might render the answer to the other superfluous or even exclude its premise.' (ABH 1992, 77, 87.). Moreover, at several points in the argument he sees his own value choices as conceptual necessities. These are all features of the style of argumentation that was characteristic of the German Federal Constitutional Court at the time and has been characteristic ever since. In Hungarian legal (especially constitutional) culture, this style of argumentation represented a radical change, which was mostly criticised as 'activism' in the debates of the time.

5. Aftermath of the Decision

In September 1992, Zsolt Zétényi and others submitted a new draft law with a similar judicial aim. The Parliament adopted it on 16 February 1993, but President of the Republic Árpád Göncz initiated a preliminary constitutional review again, and on 30 June 1993, the HCC again ruled it unconstitutional.

It is also an afterthought of the decision that the preamble of the new constitution (the FL) adopted in 2011 explicitly states: 'We deny the statute of limitations for the inhuman crimes committed against the Hungarian nation and its citizens under the National Socialist and Communist dictatorships.' Article U), on the other hand, contains detailed provisions on the statute of limitations for the crimes in question, denying at the constitutional level the main theses of the Decision 11/1992. (III. 5.) AB on transitional justice.

Finally, the last chapter in the aftermath of the decision is the fact that during the term of office of the second Orbán government, MP Gergely Gulyás (Fidesz) submitted a bill invoking international law to criminalise the perpetrators of the post-1956 repression and certain members of the judiciary of the time, which was adopted in 2011. Act CCX of 2011 on the criminalization and exclusion of statute of limitations for crimes against humanity and the prosecution of certain crimes committed under the communist dictatorship ('lex Biszku').

Bibliography

Robert Alexy, 'A Defence of Radbruch's Formula' in David Dyzenhaus (ed), *Recrafting the Rule of Law: The Limits of Legal Order* (Hart Publishing: Oxford, Portland Oregon 1999)

Imre Békés, Mihály Bihari, Tibor Király, István Schlett, Csaba Varga and Lajos Vékás, 'Szakértői vélemények az »igazságtételről«. – I. Szakvélemény' [Expert Opinions on Transitional Justice – Expert Opinion I.] (1992) 1 *Társadalmi Szemle*, 70.

András Bragyova 'Az igazságtétel legalitása' [The Legality of Doing Justic] in Vanda Lamm and András Bragyova (eds), *Visszamenőleges igazságszolgáltatás* [Retrospective Administration of Justice] (MTA Állam- és Jogtudományi Intézet: Budapest 1992)

H. L. A. Hart: *The Concept of Law* (Oxford University Press: New York 1961)

Miklós Hollán, József Lőrik, András Osztovits, István Varga, and Réka Végvári, '57. § – Bírósági eljárási garanciák' [Article 57 – Procedural Guarantees in Judicial Procedure] in András Jakab (ed) *Az Alkotmány kommentárja* [Commentary on the Constitution] (2nd ed., Századvég: Budapest 2009) 289.

András Jakab (ed), *Az Alkotmány kommentárja* [Commentary on the Constitution] (Századvég, Budapest 2009)

András Jakab and Viktor Kazai, 'A Sólyom bíróság hatása a magyar alkotmányjogi gondolkodásra' [The Effect of the Sólyom Court on the Hungarian Constitutional Thinking] in Tamás Győrfi, Viktor Zoltán Kazai, and Endre Orbán (eds), *Kontextus által világosan: a Sólyom-bíróság antiformalista elemzése* [To see Clear by Context: the Anti-formalistic Analysis of the Sólyom Court] (L'Harmattan: Budapest 2021) 115.

János Kis, 'Reform és forradalom között. Három hipotézis a rendszerváltás természetéről' [Between Reform and Revolution: Three Hypothesis about the Nature of the Democratic Transition] (1993) 11 *Világosság*, 5.

Magyarország politikai évkönyve 1992 [Political Yearbook of Hungary 1992] (Economix: Budapest 1992)

Diane F. Orentlicher, 'The Duty to Prosecute Human Rights Violations of a Prior Regime' (1991) *Yale Law Journal*, 2537.

Gustav Radbruch, 'Gesetzliches Unrecht und übergesetzliches Recht' (1946) *Süddeutsche Juristenzeitung*, 105.

Gustav Radbruch: *Vorschule der Rechtsphilosophie* (2nd ed., Vandenhoeck & Ruprecht: Göttingen 1959)

Wojciech Sadurski: *Rights Before Courts: A Study of Constitutional Courts in Postcommunist States of Central and Eastern Europe* (Springer: Dordrecht 2005)

András Sajó and Renáta Uitz, *The Constitution of Freedom. An Introduction to Legal Constitutionalism* (Oxford University Press: Oxford 2017)

Charles Sampford: *Retrospectivity and the Rule of Law* (Oxford University Press: Oxford 2006)

László Sólyom: *Az alkotmánybíráskodás kezdetei Magyarországon* [The beginnings of constitutional adjudication in Hungary] (Osiris: Budapest 2001)

Christian Tomuschat, 'The Duty to Prosecute International Crimes Committed by Individuals' in Hans-Joachim Cremer, Thomas Giegerich, Dagmar Richter, and Andreas Zimmermann (eds), *Festschrift für Helmut Steinberger* (Springer: Berlin 2002) 315.

Csaba Varga (ed), *Igazságtétel jogállamban. Német és cseh dokumentumok* [Lustration in a Rule of Law State: German and Czech Documents] (Budapest: Windsor Klub 1995)

Giuliano Vassalli, *Radbruchsche Formel und Strafrecht: Zur Bestrafung der 'Staatsverbrechen' im postnazistischen und postkommunistischen Deutschland* (De Gruyter: Berlin 2010)

Gerhard Werle and Moritz Vormbaum, *Transitional Justice. Vergangenheitsbewältigung durch Recht* (Springer: Berlin, Heidelberg 2018)

Kinga Zakariás, 'Az elvi tételek kiemelésének kérdése az Alkotmánybíróság gyakorlatában' [Underlining the leitsatz in the Constitutional Court Jurisprudence] (2009) 10 *Pázmány Law Working Papers,* 1.

Zsolt Zétényi, 'Néhány őszinte szó az igazságtételről, avagy megtettünk-e mindent, ami tőlünk tellett?' [Honest words about transitional justice, or have we done all we could?] (2017) December *Hitel,* 36.

4. Decision 53/1993. (X. 13.) AB – International Crimes

Tamás Ádány[*] – *Réka Varga*[**]

Generally recognised norms of international law become parts of Hungarian law by means of general transformation, while international treaties do so by means of specific transformation [through promulgation]. The harmony between international and domestic law must be ensured without prejudice to the hierarchy among the Constitution, international law and domestic law.

International law provides the conditions for the punishment of crimes to be prosecuted under international law. Therefore, the Constitution is not violated if an act of the Parliament stipulates—even retrospectively—that crimes against humanity and war crimes are not subject to statutory limitations. Nevertheless, this only holds true for offences where punishment is prescribed by international law.

The novelty of the Decision International Crimes, analysing the relation between international and domestic rules and crimes that are not subject to statutory limitations, was the HCC establishing well-known international legal theorems for the Hungarian legislation and for the domestic legal praxis. International law renders certain conducts punishable, therefore the *nullum crimen sine lege* maxim is to be applied in this case with regards to international law, and not domestic law. If international law rules out statutory limitations, then that should be respected regardless of domestic rules. The provisions of Art 7 (1) of the Constitution mean, therefore, that the relevant rules of international criminal law are to be applied through general transformation by force of the Constitution. Nevertheless, constitutionalism demands that such international rules can only apply through general transformation for offences defined by international law.

* PhD, Associate professor, Pázmány Péter Catholic University Faculty of Law and Political Sciences (Budapest).

** PhD, Associate professor, Pázmány Péter Catholic University Faculty of Law and Political Sciences (Budapest).

1. Background

1.1. Domestic legal background

Transitional justice was a core issue during the political transition of the early 1990s in Hungary. 'Historical justice'—as it was often termed in the contemporary media—encompassed individual responsibility for the crimes committed during the 20th-century totalitarian regimes. Not every model of the transitional justice solutions garnered legislative interest: there were neither clear lustration rules, nor did declared, public amnesties take place.[1] Fact-finding remained unfinished—the question of the identities of the agents and partners of the Communist secret services haunts Hungarian politics to this day.[2] A particular emphasis in this public discussion was placed on the atrocities committed in and after the 1956 revolution. The discussion was around to have or not to have criminal proceedings, without intermediary alternatives ever being on the public table for long.[3]

The most frequent argument[4] in support of the omission of criminal proceedings was the considerable lapse of time.[5] Against this background it is hardly surprising that the first major legislative attempt tried to cut this Gordian knot of time. A bill drafted by majority MPs Mr. Zsolt Zétényi and Mr. Péter Takács proposed restarting the relevant period for

---

1 Zalaquett, 'Confronting Human Rights Violations Committed by Former Governments: Principles Applicable and Political Constraints' in Kritz (ed), *Transitional Justice. Vol. 1. General Practices* (1995), 10–11.

2 See for example Máthé (ed), *Az nem lehet, hogy súlyos bűntett ne legyen büntethető* (2016), 369.

3 Péter Mádai (SZDSZ [Alliance of Free Democrats]) MP's first speech at the plenary session of the Hungarian Parliament on 2 February 1993: 'Hungarian society does not think about serving justice for the past but thinks about the present and the future'. Contemporary press reported in only one short paragraph about the suggestion of Professor Imre Békés about the setting up of a commission akin to Truth and Reconciliation Commissions. See Balázs Stépán, 'Változatok igazságtételre' [Variations for justice] *Magyar Hírlap*, 3 February 1993.

4 See especially the session of the Parliament of 2 February 1993 with respect to the debate around the law on international crimes where statutory limitations do not apply, that resulted in the HCC decision under present discussion (*Országgyűlési Napló*, https://bit.ly/3bIpFca) and plenary session of 2 February 1993 (*Országgyűlési Napló*, https://bit.ly/3fz7WFj).

5 See the Parliamentary debate on amendment of Act IV of 1978 on the Criminal Code of the Republic of Hungary. *Országgyűlési Napló*, 4 November 1991. https://bit.ly/3ywsc36

statutory limitations on a symbolic date of the political transition, notably 2 May 1990. This solution was deemed a violation of Constitutional guarantees in Decision 11/1992. (III. 5.) AB (for an analysis of Decision on Retroactive Transitional Justice see our volume).[6]

After few months, Mr. Zétényi and Mr. Zimányi drafted a new bill, which became the subject of the Decision International Crimes, enacted by the Parliament on 16 February 1993.[7] This avoided the radical efficiency of restarting the limitations period, rather it relied on exceptions from a general rule. In itself this solution was nothing new, because Hungarian criminal law is based on the general rule of statutory limitations; however, exceptions had been listed exhaustively by Article 33 (2) of the then relevant old Criminal Code.[8]

The novelty of this new act of 1993 would have been an extension of this closed list of exceptions to cover 'offences committed during the 1956 October revolution'. The offences were listed according to either Article 13 (7) of Act VII of 1945 or certain articles of the 1949 Geneva Conventions.

The former consists of the remnants of a controversial Hungarian law used to prosecute crimes committed during World War II. The source of this controversy is the lack of many fair trial guarantees at the so-called People's Courts that ruled over genuine war criminals but also held Communist backed show trials—sometimes even mixing the two aspects in the same procedure. This act created legal categories termed 'war crimes' and 'crimes against the people', not necessarily corresponding to the definitions of war crimes in international law.

---

6 The Constitutional Court decision on the law submitted by MPs Zétényi and Takács concerning statute of limitations established the unconstitutionality of a previously unpromulgated law. The law declared the re-commencement of the statute of limitations for three crimes (treason, intentional homicide, and fatal bodily harm) if the state did not enforce its criminal claim for political reasons. This HCC stated that any statutory provision relating to the statute of limitations is unconstitutional. Hence, the decision on the Zétényi–Takács act on statutory limitations cannot be considered as the antecedent of the Decision on international crimes because they are based on completely different legal bases: the decision on the Zétényi–Takács act on statute of limitations examines the nature of statute of limitations, while the Decision on international crimes deals with the domestic projection and application of the principle of *nullum crimen sine lege* applicable in international.

7 First speech of MP Zimányi Tibor on the plenary session of the Parliament on 2 February 1992. Országgyűlési Napló, https://bit.ly/3vamjXf

8 Mohácsi and Szeder, 'Büntethetőséget megszüntető okok' in Györgyi and Wiener (eds), *A Büntető törvénykönyv magyarázata – Általános rész* (1996), 80.

While there is an apparent semantic resemblance to international legal categories, the elements of the respective crimes evidently show that there are major, conceptual and contextual differences between them. These discrepancies existed not only in 1993 but also back in 1956. For various reasons the Hungarian legal system treated this international legal framework with so many and such grave conceptual mistakes that one may even conclude that the bulk of the relevant international legal materials remained unavailable to Hungarian legal praxis.[9] For this reason it was indeed an important observation in the Decision International Crimes that the provisions of international law regulating international crimes were to be considered, without a doubt, 'generally recognised rules', hence, making the relevant international standards applicable to domestic prosecutors and courts through the general transformation of the Constitution. Due to the wording of Article 7 of the Constitution, the next major question therefore emerged: how precisely shall such rules of international law be applied in Hungary?

1.2. International legal background

Article 1 of Act XC of 1993 on exceptions from statute of limitations exempted 'war crimes'—as defined by the background regulation of Act VII of 1945 on People's Courts—from statutory limitations. This definition had always been broader, or rather significantly different from the international legal definition of war crimes.

This difference is a major terminological discrepancy between war criminals and their crimes. According to the International Military Tribunal (IMT) Statute a 'war criminal' is nonetheless not equivalent to the person who committed 'war crimes'—as this category is only one of the three

9 Hungarian legal academics tried to remedy this situation. See Kovács, 'Alkotmányosság és nemzetközi jog' in Bánrévy, Jobbágyi, and Varga (eds), *Iustum, aequum, salutare* (1998), 186–203.; Hoffmann, 'A nemzetközi szokásjog szerepe a magyar büntetőbíróságok joggyakorlatának tükrében' (2011); Ádány, A Nemzetközi Büntetőbíróság joghatósága (2014); Varga, 'Biszku-Case Reloaded: International Law Obligations and Lacuna in Compliance with Respect to Communist Crimes' (2015); Ádám Gellért, 'Büntetlen bűnösök' [Unpunished criminals] *Index.hu*, 16 September 2017.

crimes prosecuted at the trials of 'war criminals'.[10] International law has omitted 'war criminal' as a legal term ever since the late 1940s.

Articles 11 and 13 of Act VII of 1945 reflect the use of 'war criminal' as a similarly embracing term. It is in itself noteworthy that the Act defines a 'war criminal' and not 'war crimes' as such. Consequently, while 'war crimes' as defined by international law cover 'violations of the laws and customs of war' and 'crimes committed by war criminals' in the meaning of Act VII of 1945 are distantly related, these are very far from bearing the same meaning.[11]

The offences listed in Act VII of 1945—as cited in the subject matter legislative acts from 1993—encompassed *inter alia* conducts related to starting or planning a war (by 'disrupting the peace among nations'), therefore treated by international law as 'crimes against peace'.[12]

Article 2 of Act XC of 1993 consisted of actual war crimes as per international law, defined along the relevant provisions on grave breaches of the 1949 Geneva Conventions. Such offences were e.g., grave breaches committed against prisoners of war or the civilian population.[13] The wording of this Article makes it clear that grave breaches are used in the international legal meaning as a technical term of the Geneva Conventions and its Protocols. All four Geneva Conventions set a clear list of grave breaches, the relevant Hungarian act clearly reflects articles 130 and 147 of the third and the fourth Geneva Conventions, respectively.

Notwithstanding the aforementioned international law considerations, the 1993 text of the Criminal Code only exempted 'war crimes' as defined by Act VII of 1945 from the statutory limitations. By disregarding international law, this list lacked crucial contextual elements of war crimes but consisted of quite a few elements that did not correspond to international law. First, the existence of any armed conflict was not stipulated as a legal prerequisite of war crimes in the Hungarian law. However, without a war

10 The other two would be crimes against peace and crimes against humanity. See: Annex to the Article 6 of the Agreement by the Government of the United States of America, the Provisional Government of the French Republic, the Government of the United Kingdom of Great Britain and Northern Ireland and the Government of the Union of Soviet Socialist Republics for the prosecution and punishment of the major war criminals of the European Axis (London Agreement).

11 Wright, 'War Criminals' (1945), 261.

12 See Gellér, *Nemzetközi büntetőjog Magyarországon, adalékok egy vitához* (2009), 16–17.

13 Ref. to the scope of application of the Third and Fourth Geneva Conventions.

(or an armed conflict after 1949),[14] violations of the rules and customs of war become a legal impossibility. The importance of the contextual armed conflict is even greater because the text of Act XC of 1993 did not refer to the grave breaches of the third and fourth Geneva Conventions, but it established a connection to common Article 3 thereof. As this is the only article from the 1949 Conventions applicable also in a non-international armed conflict, the classification of the contextual armed conflict as international or non-international became a central issue of the judicial treatment of the 1956 atrocities.

Furthermore, tying the notion of war crimes to pre-1949 legal concepts created an unresolvable anachronism. The 1949 Geneva Conventions were binding international legal obligations for both Hungary and the Soviet Union in 1956.[15] While both states have consented to the treaties, the promulgation in the USSR was delayed for decades, and the Hungarian promulgation was also troubled. Formally, Hungary promulgated the 1949 Geneva Conventions,[16] but only the titles appeared in the national legislation, the actual normative text was omitted. This fundamentally fraudulent promulgation could not but fail to perform its single most important task of specific transformation into domestic law and obviously lacked accessibility. As state consent had been previously expressed in due form, the 1949 Geneva Conventions were clearly and obviously opposable for Hungary in 1956.

The above considerations in themselves would already create a closer-than-usual knot between international rules and Hungarian legislative acts. All these above concepts about war crimes, war criminals, crimes of war criminals or grave breaches could have been irrelevant, if none of them had been subject to statutory limitations in the 1993 Act. However only one of these, 'crimes of war criminals' as defined by a controversial and anachronistic law was recognised as an exception from the general rule of limitations.

14 After the prohibition of war as a legal term with a well-established, i.e., legally defined concept and consequences in 1945, the concept of 'armed conflict' was used instead of 'war' in international law.

15 The Soviet Union ratified the Geneva Conventions on 10 May 1954, Hungary ratified the Conventions on 3 August 1954. https://bit.ly/3oPosFz

16 Decree law 32 of 1954 on the statutory force in the Republic of Hungary of the international conventions adopted on 12 August 1949 in Geneva on the protection of war victims.

It is therefore crucially significant how international law has regulated the effect of time lapse on the punishment of these crimes in 1956, in 1993 or today.

The UN General Assembly adopted a convention in 1968 about 'the Non-Applicability of Statutory Limitations to War Crimes and Crimes Against Humanity'.[17] Unsurprisingly enough, this text defines war crimes and crimes against humanity in line with the Nuremberg regulations. From these, the Hungarian Act XC of 1993 only used war crimes, combined with the concept of grave breaches. The 1968 Convention however does not mention crimes against peace, meaning that international law left the regulation of this particular issue to state competence; and national legislations actually did show a wide variance in this matter.[18] Considering this divergent state practice it is hardly possible to argue that the general rule of statutory limitations to all or certain crimes would be a *sine qua non* condition of rule of law systems[19] as it was commonly understood in Hungary in the early 1990s. On the contrary: there are some conceptual differences in common law and civil law countries in this matter. So much so that statutory limitations as such cannot be considered a rule generally recognised by civilised nations. Common law countries seem to prefer the general rule of no limitations based on the lapse of time, and these legal systems use the legislation to create exceptions where time actually becomes an issue for the enforcement of the law.

The divergent approach by states to statutory limitations may have had some contribution to the relatively low number of ratifications to the 1968 Convention.

The mandatory application of statutory limitations, particularly as a general rule is not supported by state practice.[20] As such, it cannot become customary law. Customary exceptions cannot develop either because of the missing general rule. War crimes and crimes against humanity are therefore not subject to statutory limitations under customary internation-

---

17 Convention on the Non-Applicability of Statutory Limitations to War Crimes and Crimes Against Humanity GA Res. 2391(XXIII) 23 UN GAOR p. 40. UNGA 16; A/RES/2391 (XXIII) (25 November 1968).

18 Question of the non-applicability of statutory limitation to war crimes and crimes against humanity. Study submitted by the Secretary General. E/C4.N/1966. 86. 105–106.

19 Question of the non-applicability of statutory limitation, E/C4.N/1966. 86. 103.

20 Question of the non-applicability of statutory limitation to war crimes and crimes against humanity. Study submitted by the Secretary General. E/C4.N/1966, 86. 103, 105–106.

al law: either because the general rule of statutory limitations is missing altogether, or because there is a general understanding that whatever the general rule may be, statutory limitations shall not apply to war crimes and crimes against humanity.[21]

3. *Petition*

The case was referred to the HCC by the President of the Republic. The President asked the HCC to examine the compatibility of the Act with the *nullum crimen sine lege* principle recognised by the ICCPR, the ECHR, the respective articles of the Constitution and with the legal requirements set out by the HCC in its earlier decision (Decision 11/1992, see analysis on the Decision on Retroactive Transitional Justice) on the Act on re-commencement of statute of limitations submitted by MPs Zétényi and Takács, because the President was of the view that the matter at hand deals with the same subject.

4. *Decision and its reasoning*

The HCC would not have found it intrinsically unconstitutional if the Act XC of 1993 had retrospectively exempted the 1956 atrocities from statutory limitations if it had been done along the conditions set out in its earlier decision, namely that such exceptions could have been provided by either international or by Hungarian national law. The HCC established a multiple prong test to decide if non-application of statutory limitations under international law would be possible: (1) The offence must be based on international law rule opposable to Hungary, (2) It must be classified as either a war crime or a crime against humanity, (3) International law renders non-application of statutory limitation either mandatory or at least possible for Hungarian law, (4) Were all these criteria to be met, it would be constitutional if the conditions of prosecution of the crimes defined by international law were applied according to conditions prescribed by international law, regardless of the statute of limitations in Hungarian law in force at the time of the commission of the offence.

---

21 Henckaerts and Doswald-Beck, *Customary International Humanitarian Law* (2009), 614–618. Analysing when this rule has become customary reaches beyond the scope of the present work.

4.1. Generally recognised norms of international law become parts of Hungarian law by means of general transformation, international treaties do so by means of a specific transformation, through promulgation. The harmony between international and domestic law must be ensured, without prejudice to the hierarchy among the Constitution, international law and domestic law [Article 7 (1) of the Constitution].

In this landmark decision laying the foundations of the relation between international law and Hungarian law the HCC observed that the first provision of Article 7 (1) of the Constitution stating that '[t]he legal system of the Republic of Hungary accepts generally recognised rules of international law' results in such rules becoming parts of Hungarian law without specific transformation. Transformation in these cases is achieved by the Constitution itself. The Constitution and domestic laws must therefore be interpreted in such a way as to make the application of generally recognised international rules possible. 'Undertaken international legal obligations' mentioned in the second provision of Article 7 (1) are subject to specific transformation. The same provision creates an obligation to ensure harmony, which applies to every kind of international legal obligation: generally recognised obligations and specifically undertaken obligations as well.[22] However, this is without prejudice to the hierarchy among the Constitution, international law and domestic law.

Next, the HCC examined the relation between international and domestic Hungarian law. As a first step, it clarified the consequences of the phrase 'generally recognised rules of international law'. The HCC did examine in detail what rules would be fitting in this category. As examples, it noted that the UN Charter and the 1949 Geneva Conventions do contain such provisions. The decision also noted that general transformation by means of the Constitution does not preclude the possibility of such norms being parts of specific treaties, whereby specific transformation is also possible [ABH, 1993, 327, 323–339.].

22 In practice, 'generally recognised obligations' encompass general rules accepted by civilized nations and customary international law. 'Specifically undertaken obligations' mean international treaties and decisions of international organizations.

4.2. The constitutionality of a rule connected to international law must be scrutinized from additional perspectives compared to a rule related exclusively to Hungarian law [Article 7 (1) of the Constitution].

The HCC found it important to specify the standard used in the constitutional review in the reasoning of the decision. This standard could not neglect international law and consequently Article 7 of the Constitution. Following a general inquiry into international law, the decision analysed war crimes and 'crimes against humanity' and found that the international community considers them criminal offences and defines their elements. While the difference between grave breaches and war crimes is not mentioned expressly, their dual legal consequences are present in the finding: 'War crimes and crimes against humanity are prosecuted and punished by the international community by means of international tribunals and also by obligating the states wishing to be members of this community to prosecute such crimes.' [ABH, 1993, 328, 323–339.].

The decision also cites a 1993 UN Secretary General's report on the establishment of the would-be International Criminal Tribunal for the former Yugoslavia (ICTY).[23] This report was found to 'specify and contain substantive international law, rules that are without a doubt customary in nature, therefore the problematic that not every state has become a party to certain treaties does not even emerge' [ABH, 1993, 329, 323–339.]. This report clearly identifies the relevant part of the Nuremberg legal materials to be part of international customary law. Building on these arguments on the customary character of international crimes, the HCC delivered yet another important *dictum:* 'the guarantee of *nullum crimen sine lege* in international law is meant to apply to itself and not to the domestic law' [ABH, 1993, 330, 323–339.]. Therefore, the criminality of a conduct must be examined in light of the sources of public international law.

4.3. Exclusion of statutory limitations may happen either according to Hungarian law, or by international law if there is an international legal obligation binding for Hungary [Article 7 (1) of the Constitution].

'In the application of Article 33 (2) of the [old] Criminal Code, a constitutional requirement is that non-limitation of criminal liability may be

23 Report of the Secretary-General pursuant to paragraph 2 of Security Council resolution 808 (1993) (S/25704).

established only in respect of the offences excluded from statutory limitations under Hungarian law in force at the time of the commission; unless the facts are classified as war crimes or crimes against humanity under international law, where exclusion from limitations is mandatory or possible under international law and there is an international obligation on Hungary to exclude limitations' [ABH, 1993, 323, 323–339.]. The merits of the decision found Article 1 of Act XC of 1993 (containing conducts deemed internationally crimes against peace) to be unconstitutional, but with regard to war crimes, the HCC found the rules allowing criminal proceedings (accepting an exception from statute of limitations) based on international law to be constitutional.

4.4. *The rules on the punishment of war crimes and crimes against humanity, as they fundamentally endanger humanity and international coexistence, are peremptory rules of international law [Article 7 (1) of the Constitution].*

Finding that the relevant rules are customary would have been sufficient in itself to establish their classification as generally recognised rules of international law. The HCC went even further and observed that these rules are part of international *jus cogens*.[24] The HCC summarised its most important findings as follows: 'The rules governing war crimes and crimes against humanity are undoubtedly part of customary international law; they are principles generally recognised by the international community, or in the wording of the Hungarian Constitution, they are among the 'generally recognized rules of international law.' These rules are 'accepted' by Hungarian law according to the first indent of Article 7 (1) of the Constitution; and are therefore, without any specific transformation or adaptation, among the 'international obligations undertaken' whose harmony with domestic law is also provided for in the second paragraph of the cited Article of the Constitution' (ABH, 1993, 332–333, 323–339.). It follows from this that it was not contrary to the principle of the *nullum crimen sine lege* principle at that time[25] that an act was punished in Hungary according to these rules of international law. The finding is therefore that

24 Amnesty International: Universal Jurisdiction: The duty of states to enact and enforce legislation. Chapter 3. 1.; Dörr and Schmalenbach (eds), *Vienna Convention on the Law of Treaties: A Commentary* (2018), 932; Berdud, 'El jus cogens, ¿Salió del garaje?' (2015), 116.

25 Article 57 (4) of the Constitution.

'the principle of nullum crimen does not break here, but its restriction to domestic law'.

5. *Doctrinal analysis*

5.1. *The relation between international law and domestic law*

This decision was the first to offer a dogmatic interpretation of the relationship between international law and domestic law in Hungary, by clarifying the somewhat ambiguous provisions of the Constitution.[26] Although a rigid divide between monistic and dualistic legal systems seems today rather artificial and impractical,[27] elucidation of the issue was crucial to strengthening Constitutional and other public law institutions in the early 1990s in Hungary.

The Decision International Crimes[28] laid the foundations for the essentially dualistic, but inherently mixed system of Hungarian law. A dualistic system of specific transformation applied to treaties, while 'generally recognised rules' were treated in a monistic way through a general transformation[29] by the Constitution itself. The HCC also declared that interpretation of the Constitution itself must be done with due regard to international law as well.[30] Meanwhile a well-known dilemma for so many countries emerged, namely the inherent difference between constitutional and international legal perspectives. As the former suggests that no rule of law may be of a higher standing than the Constitution,[31] the later finds

26 Molnár, 'A nemzetközi jog és a magyar jog viszonya' (Relations between international law and Hungarian law') in Jakab and Fekete (eds), *Internetes Jogtudományi Enciklopédia* (2018).

27 Ádány, 'A nemzetközi jog és a belső jog kapcsolata' in Csink, Schanda, and Varga Zs. (eds), *A magyar közjog alapintézményei* (2020), 194.

28 After the adoption of this decision, among others, Decision 4/1997. (I. 22.) AB and Decision 30/1998. (VI. 30.) AB dealt with this question.

29 According to Tamás Molnár the term 'general transformation' is incompatible with international law, because there is no existing body of international law in the case of customary international law that could be transformed. See Molnár, 'A nemzetközi jog és a magyar jog viszonya' in Jakab and Fekete (eds), *Internetes Jogtudományi Enciklopédia* (2018).

30 For an analysis of the decision see for example Blutman, 'A nemzetközi jog joghatásai az alkotmánybírósági eljárásokban' (2013), 10–13, 30–31, 35.

31 'However, the Constitutional Court gives a special place to the generally recognized rules of international law. These are made part of the Hungarian legal

that no state can rely on any of its own national rules to invalidate or terminate an international legal obligation it has previously consented to.

This decision of the Court also noted that the participation of Hungary in the international community is a constitutional command; and that this leads to a mandatory objective of interpretation in order to make actual applicability of international rules of law possible [ABH, 1993, 327, 323–339.]. In László Sólyom's interpretation this meant that even though the constitution must be interpreted in compliance with international law, international law is not of a higher hierarchical standing than the Constitution—this is why the HCC has the mandate for the constitutional review of domestic rules that transformed international law into national law.[32]

5.2. Constitutional review of norms deriving from international law

International law offers a choice for states to either make new treaty obligations compatible with their domestic legal systems or not to consent to be bound by such new treaties at all. Of course, such a simplistic approach is not feasible in the case of other sources of international law: these other sources typically are prone to a more dynamic evolution, sometimes even overriding the more static constitutional rules. Therefore, the HCC interpreted that the wording on accepting 'generally recognised rules of international law' as meaning that such rules are not part of the Constitution but are also 'obligations undertaken' and as such are part of domestic law that have to be applied [ABH, 1993, 327, 323–339.]. The above cited arguments from László Sólyom may still lead to a case where a HCC finds an international rule transformed into domestic law to be unconstitutional. A subsequent decision of the Court, however, clarified that such a finding would be irrelevant for the purposes of responsibility of a state

system through Article 7 (1) of the Constitution itself, and they are undoubtedly above the domestic laws in the hierarchy. But not over the Constitution. Whatever special status the Constitutional Court granted to the generally recognized rules, and actually »opened« the Hungarian legal order to the direct enforcement of these rules by para. 7, and even prescribed that even the Constitution should be interpreted to allow the application of the generally recognized rule of international law, it expressly maintained that the Constitution is superior to them and that the Constitutional Court is therefore entitled to examine the constitutionality of all international norms that have become domestic law.' Sólyom, *Az alkotmánybíráskodás kezdetei Magyarországon* (2001), 438.

32 Sólyom, *Az alkotmánybíráskodás kezdetei Magyarországon* (2001), 438.

under international law and would have no bearing on the existence of the international obligation.[33]

The HCC interpreted Articles 7 and 57 of the Constitution together—therefore the provisions of international law and the Constitutional rule of the *nullum crimen sine lege* principle jointly set up the minimum threshold of constitutionality.[34] By this solution of inserting international law into the constitutional review the Court effectively avoided the necessity of resolving a conflict between international and domestic law.[35]

5.3. *The assessment of the findings on statute of limitations*

The HCC noted that based upon the general rule of statutory limitations in the Criminal Code any exceptions thereto are constitutional only if those exceptions existed at the time of the commission of the crime—except for cases where such exceptions derive from international law, along with the elements of the crime itself. Thus, the decision follows the reasoning it had already presented with regards to the *nullum crimen sine lege* principle: it prescribes the application of domestic laws on statutory limitations in compliance with international law in force at the time of the commission of the act. An international obligation not to apply statutory limitations this way substitutes an explicit exception from this general rule under Hungarian law.

5.4. *Classification of international crimes*

The decision did not stop at examining the connection between international and domestic law, but it relied on substantive international legal arguments to decide the merits of the case. It was the only way to find that 'the Act interconnects various elements of personal and subject matter scope of the Geneva Conventions and creates a connection among them that is not present in the Conventions themselves. A domestic rule of law cannot change the content of an international treaty.' [ABH, 1993, 337, 323–339.].

---

33 Decision 4/1997. (I. 22.) AB.

34 Reference made in Decision 2/1994. (I. 14.) AB, point II/B.1.2.

35 Blutman, 'A nemzetközi jog joghatásai az alkotmánybírósági eljárásokban' (2013).

6. *Aftermaths of the Decision*

The decision became a standard reference point in discussing the relation of international and Hungarian law, and also for the domestic application of rules on international crimes. Therefore, the decision has remained an authority for many scholarly writings.

The system of international crimes subject to no statutory limitations has been reiterated by a number of subsequent decisions. Historical justice was revisited again in resolution 36/1996. (IX. 4.) AB. In its Decision 2/1994. (I. 14.) AB—reflecting on its Decision 66/1992. (XII. 17.) AB—the HCC upheld its findings from the present decision about generally recognised rules of international law becoming part of Hungarian law without a specific transformation.[36]

Decision 30/1998. (VI. 25.) AB further refined the hierarchy among international law—the Constitution—and domestic laws.

The new Hungarian constitution, the FL regulates the relation between international and domestic law in Article Q. It bears a significant resemblance to the former text of Article 7 of the former Constitution.[37]

Actual prosecution of international crimes did not take place in Hungary for quite a while. With a few notable exceptions (volley-cases, Képíró[38] and Biszku[39] cases) there were no genuine domestic criminal proceedings taking place. There would have been an applicable legal framework for such procedures: the very decision examined in this chapter clarified this legal framework, based on international law. That is one particular point of importance in the understanding of the effects of this decision: it made palpable that the provisions of international criminal law are to be applied in Hungarian law, regardless of any domestic rules on the punishment of such offences. All in all, the HCC established that there are no obstacles to prosecute and punish internationally defined crimes, regardless of the *lacunae* of Hungarian criminal law.

---

36 Decision 2/1994. (I. 14.) AB, ABH 1994, 52, 41–58.

37 The obligation to cooperate stipulated in Article Q) (1) of the FL was included in Article 6 (2) of the Constitution.

38 Budapest-Capital Regional Court, 10.B.155/2011.; Military Chamber of Budapest-Capital Regional Court, K. 35/2006. See also: Várady, 'Restitution of Hatred or of Mutual Understanding?' (2011).

39 Budapest-Capital Regional Court, 41.B.2158/2013. In a repeated procedure: Budapest-Capital Regional Court, 25.B.766/2015.

Bibliography

Tamás Ádány, 'A nemzetközi jog és a belső jog kapcsolata' [Relations of International Law and National Law] in Lóránt Csink – Balázs Schanda – András Varga Zs. (eds.), *A magyar közjog alapintézményei* [Basic Institutions of Hungarian Public Law] (Pázmány Press: Budapest 2020), 194.

Tamás Vince Ádány: 'A Nemzetközi Büntetőbíróság joghatósága' [Jurisdiction of the International Criminal Court] (Pázmány Press: Budapest 2014)

Carlos Espaliú Berdud, 'El jus cogens, ¿Salió del garaje?' (2015) 1 *Revista Española De Derecho Internacional,* 116.

László Blutman, 'A nemzetközi jog joghatásai az alkotmánybírósági eljárásokban' [Legal Effects of International Law in Constitutional Court Procedures] (2013) 4 *Jogelméleti Szemle,* 2.

Oliver Dörr and Kirsten Schmalenbach (eds), *Vienna Convention on the Law of Treaties, A Commentary* (Springer: Berlin and Heidelberg 2018)

Balázs Gellér, *Nemzetközi büntetőjog Magyarországon, adalékok egy vitához* [International Criminal Law in Hungary, Additions to a Debate] (Tullius: Budapest 2009)

Péter Kovács: 'Alkotmányosság és nemzetközi jog' [Constitutionality and International Law] in Gábor Bánrévy, Gábor Jobbágyi, and Csaba Varga (eds), *Iustum, aequum, salutare – Emlékkönyv Zlinszky János tiszteletére* [Iustum, aequum, salutare – Festschrift in Honour of Professor János Zlinszky] (Osiris: Budapest 1998), 186.

Jean-Marie Henckaerts and Louise Doswald-Beck, *Customary International Humanitarian Law* (Cambridge University Press: Cambridge 2009)

Tamás Hoffmann, 'A nemzetközi szokásjog szerepe a magyar büntetőbíróságok joggyakorlatának tükrében' [Role of International Customary Law in View of the Jurisprudence of Hungarian Criminal Courts] (2011) 4 *Jogelméleti Szemle,* 29.

Áron Máthé (ed), *Az nem lehet, hogy súlyos bűntett ne legyen büntethető – Jogi fejezetek a magyarországi igazságtétel és kárpótlás történetéből* [It Cannot Be That Serious Crimes Cannot Be Punished Legal Elements from the History of Transitional Justice and Reparations in Hungary] (NEB: Budapest 2016)

Péter Mohácsi and Gyula Szeder, 'Büntethetőséget megszüntető okok' [Grounds for Preclusion of Punishability] in Kálmán Györgyi and Imre Wiener A. (eds), *A Büntető törvénykönyv magyarázata – Általános rész* [Commentary to the Criminal Code – General Part] (KJK: Budapest 1996)

Tamás Molnár, 'A nemzetközi jog és a magyar jog viszonya' [Relations Between International Law and Hungarian Law] in András Jakab and Balázs Fekete (eds), *Internetes Jogtudományi Enciklopédia* [Internet Encyclopedia of Legal Scholarship] (2018) https,//bit.ly/2SlkCI4

László Sólyom, *Az alkotmánybíráskodás kezdetei Magyarországon* [The Beginnings of Constitutional Adjudication in Hungary] (Osiris: Budapest 2001)

Tibor Várady, 'Restitution of Hatred or of Mutual Understanding? On the 2011 Serbian Act on Restitution – from the Angle of History of my Home Town' (2011) 6 *Hungarian Review*, 20.

Quincy Wright, 'War Criminals' (1945) 2 *The American Journal of International Law*, 257.

Réka Varga, 'Biszku-Case Reloaded: International Law Obligations and Lacuna in Compliance with Respect to Communist Crimes' in Petra Lea Láncos, Marcel Szabó, and Réka Varga (eds), *Hungarian Yearbook of International and European Law* (Eleven: The Hague, 2015)

5. Decision 60/1994. (XII. 24.) AB – Lustration

Miklós Könczöl[*]

Data and records on individuals holding positions of public authority in a State governed by the rule of law, who have previously pursued activities contrary to the principles of the rule of law are information of public interest. Every person concerned by those data can practice their right to informational self-determination, i.e. to know and have access to their own personal data.

The importance of the decision[1] lies in the fact that it distinguishes, within the category of personal data, which generally enjoy constitutional protection, those whose disclosure is required by a fundamental right, constitutional principle or institution. It considers the freedom of information and data protection as mutually restrictive fundamental rights, the balancing of which therefore requires proportionality on both sides.[2]

1. *Background*

A direct precursor to the decision is the legislative efforts after the democratic transition to make public life more transparent by revealing the collaboration of individuals in certain positions with the intelligence agencies of the pre-1990 party-state regime. These efforts have led to several legislative proposals. Of these, only a Government bill was discussed in Parliament, which the Government then withdrew for revision in 1992. These were followed in 1993 by the Government's submission of a new bill, adopted by Parliament in 1994 as Act XXIII of 1994 on the back-

* PhD, Research fellow, Centre for Social Sciences Institute for Legal Studies (Budapest), and Associate professor, Pázmány Péter Catholic University Faculty of Law and Political Sciences (Budapest).

1 A partial English translation of the decision, followed in several passages of this chapter, is available in Sólyom and Brunner, *Constitutional Judiciary in a New Democracy* (2000), 309 ff.

2 For the significance of the decision, see Sólyom, *Az alkotmánybíráskodás kezdetei Magyarországon* (2001), 472 f.

ground checks for individuals holding certain key positions (Background Checks Act).[3]

Background checks covered the examination of whether the persons concerned had served in or cooperated with the former state security organs (Department III/III of the Ministry of Interior, or its predecessors), served in the armed forces in 1956–57, held political or administrative posts where they had received information from these authorities and, finally, whether they had been members of the (Nazi) Arrow Cross Party. The members of the 'screening' committees were appointed by Parliament from among the judiciary, with the consent of the President of the Supreme Court, on a proposal from the National Security Committee of Parliament, for a fixed term. 'Screening judges' were not allowed to sit in judgement during their term of office in the committees. If the committee found that the person under scrutiny has done any of the above, they were called to resign within 30 days, and warned that if they did not do so, the committee would publish the decision.

In the case of persons holding a church office, the Minister of the Interior or the Minister of Defence had to carry out the screening, upon request from the representatives of the churches concerned, and provide information on their findings, exclusively to the person or body making the request.

The documents serving as the basis of the background check (primarily the documents of the former Department III/III of the Ministry of Interior) should have been placed in the archives according to the decision of the Council of Ministers no. 3039/1990 Mt. on the restructuring of secret services, which did not happen. The Historical Archives of the Ministry of the Interior were established in May 1990, and the newly formed government's Minister of the Interior, Balázs Horváth, ordered access to the documents to be restricted.[4] The activities of Department III/III were reviewed in the report of the National Security Committee of the Parliament of October 1991 (Document no. 03236), which included material on and from persons within the network of the secret services.

As the decision indicates, the regulation of background checks was a typical problem of regime changes and especially of democratic transitions at the end of the 20th century. The purpose of the lustration laws was

3 Köbel, 'Áttekintés a volt állambiztonsági szervekkel kapcsolatban a rendszerváltás után keletkezett törvényekről, törvényjavaslatokról' in *A Szakértői Bizottság jelentése* (2008), 19.

4 Ripp, 'A jogi szabályozás változásai' in *A Szakértői Bizottság jelentése* (2008), 26.

partly to 'clean up' public life and partly to create the conditions for coming to terms with the past. The former was primarily based on incompatibility rules,[5] the latter on 'a genuine public disclosure of the nature of the previous regime […] through revealing the activities of the secret services' (ABH 1994, 349).[6]

2. *Petition*

The HCC received several petitions regarding the unconstitutionality of certain provisions of the Act, and a constitutional omission by the Parliament. The decision on these joint cases summarises the constitutional concerns of the petitions in eleven points (ABH 1994, 345–349.). Some of these related to the violation of constitutional rights of the persons concerned. According to these, the provisions of the Act restrict the right to privacy and the protection of personal data without this being necessary or even proportionate. According to the petitioners, the procedure provided for in the Act allowed persons to be exposed on the basis of unproven facts, and thus the human dignity (Article 54 of the Constitution) and reputation (Article 59 of the Constitution) of the persons under background check may be unjustly and unduly violated, even in case they were not in fact agents. With regard to Members of Parliament, the Act unconstitutionally restricted the right to stand as a candidate [Article 70 (1) of the Constitution], as it made it impossible for a person elected to complete their term. At the same time, it also prevented those under review from practising several other professions listed in Article 2, thereby violating the fundamental right to participate in public affairs, to hold public office [Article 70 (4) of the Constitution] and to choose one's occupation [Article 70/B (1) of the Constitution]. It also unconstitutionally restricted the right to judicial appeal.

The second group of concerns focused on the commissions and their procedure. According to the petitioners, the fact that judges were appointed members of the commissions violated the independence of the judiciary [Article 50 (3) of the Constitution] and the procedure was incompatible

---

5 For a comprehensive overview of Czech (and Polish) lustration laws, which focused on incompatibility rules, see David, 'Lustration Laws in Action: The Motives and Evaluation of Lustration Policy in the Czech Republic and Poland (1989–2001)' (2003), 387.

6 On the German example, see Miller, 'Settling Accounts with a Secret Police: The German Law on the Stasi Records' (1998), 305.

with the rule of law and legal certainty [Article 2 (1) of the Constitution]. A panel of judges acted without the safeguards of judicial procedure, with the Act suspending the judicial status of the members of the committee, placing them under the Civil Servants Act, while still granting them a status and immunity similar to that of judges.

The latter group also included concerns about the 'unprofessional and imprecise' drafting of the text, allegedly violating the rule of law. This also included uncertainties in terms of procedure (ABH 1994, 347–348.). On the other hand, and also in connection with the former group, one petitioner claimed that 'the principle of presumption of innocence [Article 57 (4) of the Constitution] cannot prevail in the proceedings. The person under review can only plead their »innocence« when presenting their point of view, as proving what they did not do or what they were not is conceptually impossible. Moreover, the Act does not impose any obligation on the Commission to provide evidence, nor does it require them to verify the information found in the register' (ABH 1994, 348.). Lastly, there were objections as to the format (a committee instead of a court) and the lack of transparency and adequate legal remedies.

The third group of objections was directed against unconstitutional discrimination (Article 70/A of the Constitution). According to these, Article 2 of the Act 'arbitrarily selects the activities and occupations' which determined the category of persons to be checked. It was further limiting the equality of rights and freedom of religion (Article 60 of the Constitution) by not imposing control on all persons holding church office (ABH 1994, 347).

3. Decision and its reasoning

The HCC upheld the petitions in part. It held that parts of Article 2, and Article 8, as well as Article 4 of the Act were unconstitutional, as well as Order no. 13/1994 of the Ministry of the Interior on the implementation of the Act within the Ministry. The HCC annulled Articles 2 and 4 of the Act, and the above-mentioned part of Article 8, as well as the Order (ABH 1994, 342–343.).

The HCC also held that, with regard to the functioning of the background check committees, it was a constitutional requirement that these must act in accordance with the provisions of Act IV of 1957 on the General Rules of State Administrative Procedure. In the application of Article 17, it was a constitutional requirement that the procedural rules of the committee may not establish rights and obligations for persons outside the committee (ABH 1994, 343.).

As a result of its *ex officio* proceedings, the HCC found that the Parliament had created an unconstitutional situation by failing to legislate on the exercise of the right to informational self-determination, in particular the rights of those concerned by the data collected to access these, or have these destroyed. The Parliament further committed an omission with regard to Article 9 of the Act by not making it mandatory for all authorities keeping public records, including the minister without portfolio supervising the secret services, to make the inspection of the records possible. The HCC therefore called on the Parliament to fulfil its legislative task by 30 September 1995 (ABH 1994, 344.).

3.1. *Information on persons exercising public authority or participating in political life, related to the fact that they were previously engaged in activities, or were members of an organization engaged in activities contrary to the rule of law, is information of public interest (Article 61 of the Constitution).*

The HCC pointed out at the very beginning of its reasoning that the constitutional problem underlying the case can be approached from two different angles: on the one hand, from the perspective of informational self-determination and, on the other, from the perspective of the disclosure of data of public interest. 'Both approaches, however, lead to the same crucial question: which data in the public records can nevertheless be treated as personal data; and which personal data can be classified as being of public interest?' (ABH 1994, 352.). It is in light of this question, i.e. the balance between self-determination and public interest, that the reasoning finally addressed the issue of discrimination.

The HCC held that it did not follow from the declassification of the records concerned that the data contained in these had to be made accessible to everyone, i.e. that the data automatically became data of public interest. The abolition of secrecy in itself had the effect that the right of informational self-determination [Article 59 (1) of the Constitution] could be exercised by all data subjects, i.e. they could access and dispose of their own personal data. Otherwise, however, it was the public position held by the persons under review that made their data of public interest according to Article 61 (1) of the Constitution: 'Data relating to the fact that persons exercising public authority in a state under the rule of law or participating in political life were previously engaged in activities contrary to the rule of law, or have been members of an organisation previously engaged in activities contrary to the rule of law, are data of public interest under Article 61 of the Constitution.' (ABH 1994, 342.).

Explaining that latter, the reasoning made it clear that '[t]he Constitutional Court in this decision thus uses the term »data of public interest« with reference to Article 61 (1) of the Constitution, rather than in the sense defined in Article 2 (3) of Act LXIII of 1992 on the protection of personal data and the disclosure of data of public interest (Data Protection Act), or as provided for in Article 19 (3) of the Data Protection Act' (ABH 1994, 352.). In addition to Article 61 (1) of the Constitution, para. (3) of the same Article, cited elsewhere in the decision, helps to clarify the concept: being of public interest means that the right to know these data is constitutionally protected as a basis for forming opinions on public issues.

Regarding the scope of the data covered, the HCC first dealt with the nature of the records of Department III/III, stating that '[t]hese records are contrary to the Constitution in terms of their creation, purpose, use and maintenance. In so far as they contain the data of persons under surveillance, they are contrary to the right to the inviolability of the private home, to privacy and to the protection of personal data—to informational self-determination—under Article 59 of the Constitution' (ABH 1994, 353.). According to the reasoning, two things follow from that: on the one hand, an obstacle to the full disclosure of the records and, on the other hand, the right of the persons on whom data had been collected, and of third persons included in the reports, to know and have access to the data concerning them, including the right to have these destroyed.

The HCC thus followed the principle of protecting personal data. Given that processing these data was unlawful from the outset in relation to the subjects of the files and third parties, unrestricted disclosure would have constituted a further violation of their right to informational self-determination. However, it is important that this is complemented, in the case of the persons concerned, by the right to be informed: 'the right to (informational) self-determination requires that each individual has access to the intelligence data collected on themselves, that they can understand the influence of the past regime on their personal fate and at least thereby mitigate the damage done to their human dignity' (ABH 1994, 353).

The very act of scrutinising the past of an individual necessarily involves identifying the persons who collected the data, and their activities. This brings us to the question that is in fact the subject of the legislation reviewed, and at the heart of the decision: to what extent the latter group, i.e. 'the agents', are entitled to data protection.

Disclosure without the consent of the subjects undoubtedly violates the constitutional principle of the protection of personal data. In relation to its acceptability, the HCC stated that in order to prove that the data are 'of public interest', it is not sufficient to state in the Act that their disclosure is 'in public interest', and hence the review of such legislation cannot be limited to the examination of whether there is such public interest.[7] 'It is therefore decisive to identify the fundamental right or constitutional principle or institution that requires the disclosure of personal data, and to examine whether the mutual limitations of the fundamental rights, those of freedom of information and data protection are proportionate to the aim of each' (ABH 1994, 354.).

As we have seen, the HCC sees the public interest as being connected to the freedom of expression and 'democratic public opinion',[8] and does not attribute any 'retributive' function to the Act. Dealing with the past, which necessarily takes place in the present, is nevertheless an aspect of the justification: 'Just as the violation of the right to (informational) self-determination requires that each individual has access to the intelligence data collected about them, that the influence of the past regime on ther personal fate be clarified and that the violation of their human dignity at least be mitigated [...] Similarly, it is necessary to come to terms with the past so that the secrecy of the former secret services does not persist' (ABH 1994, 353.).

After examining the constitutional context of the objective, the reasoning set out the standard to be applied in assessing the provisions of the Act. In so doing, it pointed out that, in the context of access to data of public interest and informational self-determination, the legislator has a margin of discretion, which results in a political decision not predetermined by the Constitution. The question to be answered by the HCC was therefore

7 In contrast to the case of expropriation examined in Decision 64/1993. (XII. 22.) AB. There, in accordance with Article 13(2) of the Constitution, the HCC ruled that '[a] constitutional court's examination of »public interest« served by a law [...] is not focusing on the absolute necessity of the legislator's decision, but—even if it is not formally directed to the existence of any »public interest«, but applies the standards of »necessity and proportionality«—must be limited to the question whether the reference to the public interest is justified, and whether the solution that is in the »public interest« does not in itself violate another constitutional right (for example, the prohibition of discrimination)' (ABH 1993, 382.).

8 On the relationship between freedom of information and democracy, see the reasoning of Decision 34/1994. (VI. 24.) AB. Cf. Koltay, '61. § A véleménynyilvánítás szabadsága, a sajtószabadság és a közérdekű adatok nyilvánossága' in Jakab (ed), *Az Alkotmány kommentárja. II.* (2009), esp. 2274.

twofold: on the one hand, whether the political decision remained within the said limits and, on the other hand, whether the standard established was applied through the legal provisions in accordance with the requirements of legal certainty and, in particular, in an equal manner, i.e. without discrimination. 'This political decision, i.e. the exact definition of the data to be examined and the circle of persons to be reviewed, cannot be inferred from the Constitution, but rather the requirement that the data cannot be kept secret, but cannot be disclosed in full either, and that—once the political decision has been taken—the Parliament must define the circle of persons to be reviewed as well as the data of public interest in an uniform manner, according to the stadard that it used—within its constitutional possibilities—to draw the mutual limits of Articles 61 and 59 of the Constitution' (ABH 1994, 357.).

As the decision shows, the HCC found unconstitutional provisions from both perspectives. With regard to the former, the list of categories of persons in Article 2 went beyond 'the constitutional possibilities of the legislator's political discretion,' as it included groups 'not only outside the scope of exercising public authority, but also outside the scope of political life.' With regard to the latter, the legislator was not consistent in applying 'the same criterion of delimitation between data of public interest and personal data' within the scope of political discretion, nor in drawing the line 'with regard to the exercise of public authority' (ABH 1994, 357.).

The HCC linked the concepts of the exercise of public authority and political life to that of public opinion, when it stated that 'past political activity is data of public interest in relation to persons whose current activity also influences public opinion, either by exercising public authority, by assuming a political role or by operating the channels and means of forming public opinion and thus being directly capable of shaping political opinion,' adding that the concept of shaping public opinion is limited to those who carry out such activities 'as their responsibility' (ABH 1994, 364.).

The HCC therefore did not wish to go beyond the issue of discrimination, and take position on a matter of political discretion, i.e. the narrow or broad definition of the persons to be checked. It partly also approached the question of the accessibility of data, on which the committees' decisions are based, from the point of view of discrimination.

Achieving the constitutional objective therefore required that the committees be given the widest possible opportunity to explore and consider the evidence. The provisions limiting that were annulled by the HCC as unconstitutional. The resulting text provided that 'the commission may examine or obtain any document from any record.' However, as the obligation to ensure the conditions of access did not extend to 'all the authorities keeping records' according to the wording of the Act, the HCC found a violation of the Constitution by omission (ABH 1994, 360.).

3.2. *Maintaining the confidentiality of political police records generated under a non-rule-of-law regime shall not restrict the right to informational self-determination of data subjects and other rights of interested parties with regard to data not declared to be of public interest [Article 59 (1) of the Constitution].*

According to the second fundamental principle of the decision, '[k]eeping the secrecy of political police records created in a non-rule-of-law regime may not restrict the right of informational self-determination of the persons concerned or other rights of parties concerned with regard to data not declared to be of public interest' (ABH 1994, 342.). The right to informational self-determination under Article 59 of the Constitution 'includes the right of each person to decide for himself whether to disclose and use his personal data [ABH 1990, 70.; ABH 1991, 42.; Article 1 (1) of the Data Protection Act]' (ABH 1994, 368.).

The HCC also found an unconstitutional omission in connection with the fact that '[the] Act only contains the further secrecy of the data of the persons to be reviewed (Article 25), it does not provide for the rights of those on whom files were kept, the »victims«'. In addition to the persons reported on, other persons included in the reports have a constitutional right to know and have access to their data. This right of disposal includes the right to have the data destroyed. Citing the principle laid down in Decision 22/1990. (X. 16.) AB, the reasoning states that 'the legislature has a duty to fulfil its legislative obligation even without a specific legislative mandate if the need for legislation has arisen as a result of the State's interference by means of law with certain relations, which deprived a group of citizens of the practical possibility of exercising their constitutional right (ABH 1990, 83, 86.)' (ABH 1994, 369.). Ensuring the protection of the rights of third parties is also part of the legislative obligation, and not a reason to exclude the informational self-determination of those concerned.

4. Doctrinal analysis

4.1. Data protection and data of public interest

The fundamental doctrinal question of the decision is where the limits for the protection of personal data should be drawn, and on the basis of what considerations this fundamental right, first formulated at the time of the change of regime, and a prominent point of reference in the practice of the first HCC, can be restricted.[9] The HCC approached the question through the historical context of legislation. That made it necessary to define the political function of the legislation: not to do justice, nor to investigate the past, but to provide information as a condition for a democratic public life. Apparently, the interpretation of the HCC appears to be the result of an interpretive choice itself, since the investigative and (partly) lustrational purpose of certain provisions of the Act would be difficult to deny (the former is explicitly mentioned in the reasoning). Thus, the HCC ultimately linked the limits of data protection to the freedom of expression. Although in contemporary (and later) policy debates the aspects of truth and memory are considered with at least equal weight, this choice has not been questioned by subsequent jurisprudence or scholarship.[10]

The existence of the legislature's margin of appreciation, albeit within constitutional limits, is explicitly acknowledged in the reasoning, indicating that a constitutionally acceptable objective can be achieved by a variety of means. The requirement derived from legal certainty is therefore simply the clarity and consistent application of the criterion, or criteria, of grouping. It is ultimately on this point that the decision finds shortcomings in the Act and declares certain provisions unconstitutional. As the later amendments to the Act show, the legislator had considered both broadening and narrowing the group of those under review.

---

9 For a comprehensive overview, see Koltay, '61. § A véleménynyilvánítás szabadsága, a sajtószabadság és a közérdekű adatok nyilvánossága' in Jakab (ed), *Az Alkotmány kommentárja. II.* (2009), 2274 f.

10 See Sólyom, *Az alkotmánybíráskodás kezdetei Magyarországon* (2001), 471. Although the concept of freedom of information as part of the right to freedom of expression is understood in a very positive way, cf. Kerekes, 'Törvényen innen és túl. Az információszabadság az Alkotmánybíróság első tíz évének gyakorlatában' (1999), 44 f. 'The Constitutional Court can be criticised mainly for having approved the legislators' acceptance of the very burdensome legacy of the party-state secret service into the rule of law at the sacrifice of the III/III department.' Majtényi, 'Az információs jogok' in Halmai and Tóth (eds), *Emberi jogok* (2003), 632. This was confirmed by Decision 23/1999. (VI. 30.) AB, ABH 1999, 213.

What provoked criticism was the HCC's move to depart from the definition of data of public interest as laid out in the Data Protection Act. According to the latter, data of public interest is 'data held by an organisation performing a state or local government function, which does not fall under the concept of personal data, and which does not fall among the exceptions provided for by law' [Article 2 (3) of the Data Protection Act]. Thus, after rejecting the possibility of referring to a mere public interest, the HCC has classified the personal data concerned *contra legem* as data of public interest, so that access to these can be considered a constitutional right, by virtue of the freedom of information.[11]

In addition to declaring the possibility of limiting the protection of personal data, and setting the constitutional standards for such restrictions, the decision explicitly points out the link between constitutional limits and the scope for political discretion. The majority reasoning shows the caution of the decision—criticised in the concurring opinion of Judge Imre Vörös—as regards the legal consequences, and the HCC's willingness to give guidance on legislative duties.

4.2. Informational self-determination: rights of persons under surveillance

The need for provisions to ensure the informational self-determination of the persons monitored by the services concerned by the intelligence reports is reflected in the decision as a 'contribution' of the HCC. This move, which is not new from a doctrinal point of view, shows both the continuity of the HCC's data protection agenda, and the activism of the first HCC in developing the law.

5. Aftermath of the Decision

A further petition challenged the constitutionality of the last sentence of Article 5 (5), according to which 'the President of Parliament shall exercise the rights of employer in relation to the members of the committee

11 Cf. Kerekes, 'Törvényen innen és túl. Az információszabadság az Alkotmánybíróság első tíz évének gyakorlatában' (1999), 46; Majtényi, 'Az »első« Alkotmánybíróság és az információs szabadságok (méltatás–bírálat)' in Halmai (ed), *A megtalált Alkotmány? A magyar alapjogi bíráskodás kilenc éve* (2000), 321 f.

carrying out the review.' However, that concern was found unfounded in Decision 18/1997. (III. 19.) AB.

An amendment of the Act soon followed (Act LXVII of 1996), which primarily defined the groups to be reviewed and the conditions for exercising the right of informational self-determination. In connection with the latter, the Act established the Historical Office (HO). That amendment was also challenged before the HCC, which was dealt with in Decision 23/1999. (VI. 30.) AB. In particular, the petitions objected to the narrowing of the scope of the persons to be reviewed (excluding judges, prosecutors, ambassadors and military generals) and to the 'failure to extend the scope of state security activities to be considered beyond those of Department III/III, to other Departments of the Ministry of Interior'. The decision upheld the petitions in part only, but annulled the provision on the background check of HO staff [second sentence of Article 2 (4) of the Data Protection Act], as well as the restriction on the research of personal data 'containing the names and natural identifying data of »strictly secret« officers and collaborators of former state security organisations and their predecessors' [Article 25/G (4) (c) of the Data Protection Act].

Following another amendment to the Act (Act XCIII of 2000), this time slightly extending the scope of persons to be reviewed, the HCC dealt once again with its constitutionality. As a result, Decision 31/2003. (VI. 4.) AB found, citing Decision Lustration, that the reference to the indirect shaping of public opinion in Article 2 (3) (16)–(18) of the Data Protection Act was unconstitutional.

These decisions unanimously consider the lustration decision as a foundational one, accept and apply the points made in it as a basis for constitutional review.[12] Criticism of the decision is rarely found in scholarship.[13]

---

12 Even though it does not appear among the most frequent references of ordinary courts, see Ződi and Lőrincz, 'Bezüge auf das Grundgesetz und die Rechtsprechung des Verfassungsgerichts in der Praxis der ordentlichen Gerichte, 2012–2016' in Darák et al. (eds), *Rechtsprechung im Dialog der Gerichte auf innerstaatlicher und europarechtlicher Ebene am Beispiel Ungarns und Deutschlands* (2020), 17 f.

13 See Majtényi, *Az információs szabadságok. Adatvédelem és a közérdekű adatok nyilvánossága* (2006), 174 f.

Bibliography

Roman David, 'Lustration Laws in Action: The Motives and Evaluation of Lustration Policy in the Czech Republic and Poland (1989–2001)' (2003) 28 *Law & Social Inquiry*, 387.

Zsuzsa Kerekes, 'Törvényen innen és túl. Az információszabadság az Alkotmánybíróság első tíz évének gyakorlatában' [Within and Beyond the Law: Freedom of Information in the Practice of the Constitutional Court during its First Ten Years] (1999) 3 *Fundamentum*, 42.

András Koltay, '61. § A véleménynyilvánítás szabadsága, a sajtószabadság és a közérdekű adatok nyilvánossága' [§ 61: Freedom of Expression, Freedom of the Press and Access to Data of Public Interest] in András Jakab (ed), *Az Alkotmány kommentárja. II.* [Commentary on the Constitution] (Századvég: Budapest 2009), 2219.

Szilvia Köbel, 'Áttekintés a volt állambiztonsági szervekkel kapcsolatban a rend-szerváltás után keletkezett törvényekről, törvényjavaslatokról' [Overview of the Laws and Bills Proposed since the Transition in Connection with Former Organs of State Security] in *A Szakértői Bizottság jelentése 2007–2008* [Report of the Committee of Experts, 2007–2008] (Budapest 2008), 19–24. https://bit.ly/3xP2llp

László Majtényi, *Az információs szabadságok. Adatvédelem és a közérdekű adatok nyil-vánossága* [Freedom of Information: Data Protection and Access to Data of Public Interest] (Complex: Budapest 2006)

László Majtényi, 'Az információs jogok' [Information Rights] in Gábor Halmai and Attila Tóth Gábor (eds), *Emberi jogok* [Human Rights] (Osiris: Budapest 2003), 577.

László Majtényi, 'Az »első« Alkotmánybíróság és az információs szabadságok (méltatás–bírálat)' [The 'First' Constitutional Court and the Freedom of Information (Assessment and Criticism)] in Gábor Halmai (ed), *A megtalált Alkotmány? A magyar alapjogi bíráskodás kilenc éve* [The Constitution Found? The First Nine Years of Hungarian Constitutional Review on Fundamental Rights] (INDOK: Budapest 2000), 312.

John Miller, 'Settling Accounts with a Secret Police: The German Law on the Stasi Records' (1998) 50 *Europe-Asia Studies*, 305.

Zoltán Ripp, 'A jogi szabályozás változásai' [Changes in Legal Regulation] in *A Szakértői Bizottság jelentése 2007–2008* [Report of the Committee of Experts, 2007–2008] (Budapest 2008), 26–40. https://bit.ly/3xP2llp

László Sólyom, *Az alkotmánybíráskodás kezdetei Magyarországon* [The Beginnings of Constitutional Adjudication in Hungary] (Osiris: Budapest 2001).

László Sólyom and Georg Brunner, *Constitutional Judiciary in a New Democracy: The Hungarian Constitutional Court* (The University of Michigan Press, Ann Arbor 2000).

Zsolt Ződi and Viktor Lőrincz, 'Bezüge auf das Grundgesetz und die Rechtsprechung des Verfassungsgerichts in der Praxis der ordentlichen Gerichte, 2012–2016' in Péter Darák, Hanno Kube, Fruzsina Molnár-Gábor, and Ekkehart Reimer (eds), *Rechtsprechung im Dialog der Gerichte auf innerstaatlicher und europarechtlicher Ebene am Beispiel Ungarns und Deutschlands* (Curia: Budapest 2020), 17.

6. Decision 22/2003. (IV. 28.) AB – Euthanasia I.

Mihály Filó[*] *– Máté Jenő Kiss*[**]

The decision of a terminally ill patient not to live until the natural end of his/her life when it is filled with suffering is part of the patient's right to self-determination.

In Decision Euthanasia I., the HCC determined that the decision of a terminally ill patient not to live until the natural end of his/her life when it is filled with suffering is part of the patient's right to self-determination. This right, however, can be restricted within the scope of the protection of the right to human life and the state's related objective obligation to provide institutional protection. The HCC determined that voluntary passive euthanasia falls within the protection of the right of self-determination, and declared it to be constitutional, provided that statutory guarantees related to the refusal of treatment do not constitute any disproportionate restriction of the right to self-determination. The other forms of end-of-life decision (and physician-assisted suicide) were found constitutionally justifiable by the HCC; however, the relationship between such end-of-life decisions and the right to self-determination was not clarified appropriately.

1. Background

Decision Euthanasia I. examined the constitutionality of the rules Act CLIV of 1997 on the Healthcare (Healthcare Act) and the related implementation decree applicable to refusing life-supporting or life-saving medical intervention. In connection with this, the decision declared an opinion on the constitutionality of the prohibition of other acts which can be included within the concept of euthanasia.

According to our understanding, the concept of euthanasia includes all wilful acts of the physician through which the physician—within the

* PhD, Assistant professor, Eötvös Loránd University Faculty of Law (Budapest).

** Doctoral student, Eötvös Loránd University Faculty of Law (Budapest), and Assistant Judge at the Pest District Court (Budapest).

scope of his/her occupation—ends or shortens the patient's life, with the explicit or presumed consent of the patient.[1] This definition takes into account the results of the European legal literature, as well as the ethics definitions of the medical profession.[2]

In Hungarian law, the shortening of the life of a terminally patient (including by a physician) has been evaluated as the criminal act of homicide since the first Hungarian Penal Code (1878). Homicide was punishable by law, regardless of whether it was committed by a physician at the request of a terminally ill patient. Act II of 1972 on the Healthcare (old Healthcare Act) prescribed that physicians provide the most diligent medical treatment for a patient, even if they deemed that patient to be terminally ill, and the Act did not allow a terminally ill patient to refuse any life-sustaining or life-saving treatment.

In an effort to strengthen patients' rights, the Healthcare Act which was promulgated in 1997 had already determined that the patient—in exercising his/her right to self-determination—has the right to decide whether he/she wishes to receive care, and for which treatment he/she gives his/her consent and which he/she refuses to receive. The law in force regulates in detail the patient's right to self-determination, as well as the right to refuse treatment (Article 20). In our opinion, the established system of rules legalises acts falling under the concept of passive euthanasia in Hungary—without the rules using the word 'euthanasia' itself. The right of a patient to refuse medical treatment—except for a few exceptions—even if it leads to his/her death, can be deduced from the law. The Healthcare Act stipulates the guarantee rule that refusal of treatments that would result in serious or permanent health damage can take place only in an authentic instrument or in a private document of full probative value, or if the patient has completely lost his/her ability to write, then in the presence of two witnesses. The Healthcare Act also allows the patient to decline life-sustaining or life-saving treatments, in order to thereby ensure

1 Filó, *Az eutanázia a büntetőjogi gondolkodásban* (2009), 43.

2 We can distinguish several types of acts within the designated concept. According to the systematization of Attila Gábor Tóth, there is (1a) voluntary euthanasia at the patient's request (1b) and non-voluntary euthanasia without the patient's consent; (2a) passive euthanasia, which occurs when a physician allows death to occur naturally in the absence or cessation of treatment; or (3a) direct euthanasia, where the patient's death is covered by the physician's intent, and (3b) indirect euthanasia, in which case the patient's death is a foreseeable but unintended consequence of the physician's activity. Tóth: 'Az emberi méltósághoz való jog és az élethez való jog' in Halmai and Tóth (eds), *Emberi jogok* (2003), 255 (347–348).

the illness takes its natural course. This is allowed only in case of illnesses which cause death within a short period of time—even if appropriate medical care is provided—and which are incurable.

Therefore, the intention of the legislature was, without doubt, to provide an appropriate legal foundation for terminally ill patients' choice of a natural, dignified death. Persons of legal incapacity or restricted legal capacity do not have the right to validly refuse those treatments the lack of which would lead to serious or permanent health damage. The Healthcare Act also stipulated that a person of legal capacity—taking into consideration the possibility that he/she would later become incapable of making decisions—has the right to decide on the refusal of life-saving or life-sustaining treatments in advance, subject to strict formalities, in the framework of a so-called living will.[3]

The attention of the general public was directed to the issue of euthanasia by a tragic case that received significant media coverage: the criminal case of Györgyi Binder[4] shocked the country, and it eventually led to the adoption of Decision Euthanasia I.

The defendant had a seriously ill child named Andrea; several times Andrea expressed her wish to die. The eleven-year-old girl suffered from incurable collagen disease (LED) that causes severe pain. Both the subsequent victim and her mother were consumed by the disease that entailed severe suffering and frequent hospitalisations. In September 1993, they were at home when the little girl begged the defendant to end her suffering, and to throw her from the tenth floor. Then, when her mother denied that request, she mentioned a film in which one of the characters received a fatal electric shock from a hairdryer dropped in the bathwater. Having heard this, the mother undressed her child, placed her in the bathtub, and put the hairdryer, which she had turned on, into the water. However, the expected effect did not occur – the hairdryer turned off automatically. The defendant then pressed a scarf on the child's face and pressed her head under the water. The girl drowned after a few minutes. Criminal proceedings for felony homicide were initiated in the case.[5] The Budapest Metropolitan Court sentenced the defendant to two years imprisonment suspended for five years, and in its judgment the court explained that the

3 Vissy, 'Méltatlan figyelem a méltó halál kérdésének' (2016), 56.
4 Filó, *Az eutanázia a büntetőjogi gondolkodásban* (2009), 50 f.
5 Tóth, 'Pulpitus és katedra' (2007), 251 (258).

defendant had committed 'active euthanasia'. 'It was a rare paradoxical situation where she killed out of love.'[6]

The Supreme Court (Kúria), however, did not deem that it was justified to suspend the imprisonment.[7] In our opinion, this was correct, as the supreme judicial forum held that the law in force did not recognise the privileged case of homicide upon request, and that an eleven-year-old child's wish to die cannot be considered serious and should not be fulfilled. However, one of the most important findings of the judgment is the determination that the act 'cannot be classified as »active euthanasia« because this term is to be understood first and foremost—and specifically—as a doctor-patient relationship. No other person—an external person—can perform this duty. For this reason, the criminal case already cannot be about euthanasia.'[8] Györgyi Binder was later granted clemency by the President of the Republic.

Although the right of a terminally ill patient to refuse life-sustaining or life-saving treatments was explicitly addressed by the HCC for the first time in Decision Euthanasia I., the issue of the enforcement of the right to self-determination in cases involving end-of-life decisions had already appeared in the case-law of the court. In Decision 36/2000. (X. 27.) AB, the HCC declared that 'the right of self-determination is attached to the person as the manifestation of the autonomy to act originating from human dignity'. Based on this, the HCC concluded that when the law institutionalises the action of another person in the scope of an individual's autonomy to act, the right of self-determination is not being 'transferred' to anyone. 'Exercising one's rights in his/her stead' empowers the other person to make a decision and, at the same time, restricts the right of self-determination; 'exercising one's right of self-determination in his/her stead' is not possible theoretically, as the right of self-determination is inseparable from the individual's personality.[9]

Speaking of the international background of the constitutionality of euthanasia, we have to mention that the right to refuse a life-sustaining or life-saving treatment was acknowledged by many countries by the end of the 20th century, deriving from the right to self-determination. In the Netherlands, in the 1970s, judicial practice began to decriminalize the assistance of a physician to lead the terminally ill patient to his/her death.

6 Budapest Metropolitan Court judgement, no. 9.B.855/1994/4.
7 Supreme Court (Kúria) judgment, no. Bf. IV. 220/1995/10.
8 Tóth, 'Pulpitus és katedra' (2007), 251 (254).
9 Decision 36/2000. (X. 27.) AB, ABH 2000, 241, 255–256.

The national legislation also reflected on this process and gradually relaxed the relevant prohibitions. The regulation was introduced in 2001, which—under exceedingly strict conditions—provides the following: a complete impunity for the doctor for the crimes of homicide and assisted suicide.[10] A somewhat similar law was passed in Belgium in 2002. Judicial practice in the United States has also moved forward in the euthanasia debate. This debate's major milestone was that the Federal Court declared the patients' right to decide on the refusal of life-sustaining treatments.[11] The decisions – which have been made in the cases *Washington v. Glucksberg*[12] and *Vacco v. Quill*[13]—declare that the regulations relating to these questions are completely up to the individual Member States.[14]

In parallel with the rapid evolution of judicial practice, referenda were organised in several Member States in connection with the matter of legalising euthanasia. The first state where liberalisation efforts led to success was Oregon. Here, medical assistance for the suicide of terminally ill patients was legalized and allowed in 1997.[15] Since this time, the number of dignified deaths which are legalised by the Death with Dignity Act—which actually falls within the concept of physician-assisted suicide—has increased continuously. In 1998, 24 prescriptions were issued, of which 16 deaths were registered, while in 2018 there were already 249 prescriptions and 168 deaths.[16]

There is no doubt that the issue of euthanasia repeatedly appears on the agenda in the international system for the protection of fundamental rights, and consequently the issue has also led to important findings in the forum of the European Council.[17] In 1996, the Parliamentary Assembly

---

10 The Dutch example of liberalization was highlighted by József Kovács, Head of Department at Semmelweis University in his lecture at the conference 'Suicide and Jurisprudence' at ELTE School of Law, 18 November 2011. It is also worth noting that the Dutch example is also presented by the HCC in the reasoning of the Decision Euthanasia I.

11 US Supreme Court, 497. U.S. 261 Cruzan v. Director, Missouri Department of Health.

12 US Supreme Court 521. U.S. 702 Washington v. Glucksberg.

13 US Supreme Court 521 U.S. 793 Vacco v. Quill.

14 Kőműves, 'Életvégi döntéshelyzetek' (2016), 303.

15 Kőműves, 'Életvégi döntéshelyzetek' (2016), 303.

16 Public Health Division Center for Health Statistics, *Oregon Death with Dignity Act 2018 Data Summary* (2019).

17 The practice of the Parliamentary Assembly of the Council of Europe is also described in the reasoning of the Decision 22/2003. (IV. 28.) AB, ABH 2003, 235, 258.

formulated a recommendation that the aim of medicine is not exclusively the prolongation of life, but also to alleviate severe suffering.[18] The General Assembly comprehensively addressed the issue of euthanasia in its 1999 recommendation. The recommendation proposed that states take comprehensive action in order to achieve the reduction of terminally ill patients' physical and mental suffering.[19]

One of the most important judgements of the ECtHR on euthanasia was made in the *Pretty v. The United Kingdom* case, in which the Court noted that Article 2 of the Convention, which confers the right to life, 'does not permit any right to death, neither with the help of another person nor with the help of the State'.[20] The right to life in this respect does not include the right to death; therefore in this sense, the right to life cannot be attributed to the right to death. The ECtHR's decision specifically referred to the fact that the member states have wide discretion in the protection of life, and they are, therefore, able to follow their own path in connection with the judgement of end-of-life medical decisions.

2. *Petition*

The previously mentioned provisions of the Healthcare Act and the relevant implementing regulations were challenged by Ildikó Kmetty, a lawyer, and Albert Takács, a college teacher, before the HCC in an abstract norm control procedure.[21] One of the reasons for the motion was the *Binder* case, which has already been analysed in detail.

The petition of 25 November 1995 was filed under the old Healthcare Act. On the one hand, petitioners alleged that one sentence of the law was unconstitutional, according to which 'the doctor is obliged to treat the patient whom he/she considers to be incurable with the utmost care'.[22] In addition, petitioners also alleged that the HCC should declare unconstitutionality manifested in omission, in view of the fact that the legislator failed to bring the Criminal Code's challenged provisions (homicide, assisted suicide) into conformity with the Article 54 (1) of the Constitution.

18 Parliamentary Assembly of the Council of Europe, resolution no. 779 (1996).
19 Parliamentary Assembly of the Council of Europe, resolution no. 1418 (1999).
20 *Pretty v. The United Kingdom,* no. 2346/02, judgement of 29 April 2002, ECHR, para. 19.
21 Kmetty and Takács, 'Az eutanáziához való jog' (2003), 125 (125).
22 Article 43 (2) of the old Healthcare Act.

For a long time, the HCC did not really deal with the motion in connection with the liberalisation of all forms of euthanasia, but waited for the legislators' answer before responding to particular questions.[23] László Sólyom, then President of the HCC, gave an interview in 1997 in which he noted the Body's failure to take a decision: 'According to the motion, our obligation would be to give a response—in all of its complexity—about euthanasia. We are almost expected to give a model law, which Parliament can later—based on our decision—accept without any concerns.'[24]

The HCC's tactic of waiting finally proved successful, because in 1997 the legislature enacted a new health law. The petitioners amended their motion in 2001 in view of the new regulation on euthanasia, stating that the right to human dignity is still unconstitutionally restricted by the new regulation.

The theoretical starting point of the motion is to examine the extent to which restrictions are conceptually compatible with the right to human dignity. 'This motion attempts to articulate an essential right of human dignity that is not simply a personal right but a human freedom, and that neither fair nor erroneous restriction is possible, precisely because it is a matter of human freedom. Our motion does not measure the permissibility of certain legal regulations in relation to a sub-requirement of human dignity, but asks whether human dignity has a domain whose essential content cannot be the subject of any legislative intervention.'[25]

The motion[26] stated that the normative range of the right to life and the constitutional principle of human dignity includes the right to a death worthy of a human being. The unconstitutionality of the regulation was ultimately identified by the petitioners as follows: the Healthcare Act's system of conditions imply an unconstitutional restriction of the right to self-determination based on human dignity [Article 54 (1) of the Constitution]. Firstly, it restricts the right to refuse life-sustaining and life-saving treatments to strict formalities. Also, the law is only available to those who are suffering from a disease that leads to death and whose illness is incurable in the short term. And last but not least, the criminal prohibition of active euthanasia should also be expressly mentioned.

The petitioners interpret the state's obligation to protect institutions in a new way: according to them, the state's obligation can be nothing more

23 Vissy, 'Méltatlan figyelem a méltó halál kérdésének' (2016), 56 (57).

24 Tóth 'A »nehéz eseteknél« a bíró erkölcsi felfogása jut szerephez' (1997), 31 (39 f.).

25 Kmetty and Takács, 'Az eutanáziához való jog' (2003), 125 (127).

26 The motion is introduced in detail by Filó, *Az eutanázia a büntetőjogi gondolkodásban* (2009), 185 f.

than to ensure the self-determination which arises from human dignity. All other state obligations already infringe the essence of the fundamental right to human dignity: i.e. personal self-determination. Human dignity cannot be protected against the right to self-determination, which is its essential content.

The petitioners also explain that the rules of the Criminal Code are not sufficient to validate human dignity. They also point out that the current privileged circumstances do not take into account such dramatic borderline situations of human dignity as occur in the Binder case, and therefore—in their view—the criminal law legislator does not regulate with due diligence regarding the possible cases of conflict between the right to life (which can be traced back to Article 54 (1) of the Constitution) and the right to human dignity. Regarding Articles 166–168 of the Criminal Code, the unconstitutionality manifested in omission is contained in this.

On the subject of the motion, Kis and Sajó—following the American example—turned to the HCC in the form of *amicus curiae*. It should be noted from what they write that the unrestricted right to life does not mean that life cannot be shortened by the will of an incurable patient in his/her interest. However, from the right to life this would only follow if the HCC decides that he/she is the subject of that right, so that under no circumstances can he/she decide on the end of his/her own life. However, if we assume that the right to life means that no one else is entitled to decide on a human being's life, the unrestricted right to life does not preclude the constitutionality of 'active euthanasia'.[27]

3. *Decision and its reasoning*

On 28 April 2003, the HCC fulfilled its long overdue obligation[28] and pronounced its Decision Euthanasia I. The verdict declared passive euthanasia—specifically, the regulations set forth in the Healthcare Act—to be constitutional, and active euthanasia—which had never been allowed in Hungary—to be unconstitutional.[29]

Given that the HCC found the regulations on the right of incurable patients to refuse life-sustaining or life-saving intervention to be in accor-

27 Kis and Sajó, 'Amicus curiae az Alkotmánybírósághoz' (2003), 134 (135 ff.).
28 Győrfy, 'A tulajdonságok nélküli ember elmélete' (1998), 23.
29 Tóth J., '»Oszthatatlan és korlátozhatatlan?«' (2005), [without page numbers].

dance with the Constitution, it rejected the related petition which aimed to determine that there had been an unconstitutionality manifested in omission because the legislature had failed to create consistency between Article 54 (1) of the Constitution and the rules of the Criminal Code on crimes such as homicide, voluntary manslaughter and aiding and abetting suicide.

3.1. The decision of a terminally ill patient not to live until the natural end of his/her life when it is filled with suffering is part of the patient's right to self-determination. This right can be restricted but should never be withdrawn. It derives from the state's positive obligation to protect human life that the law only allows this right to be exercised if certain preconditions are met [Articles 8 (2) and 54 (1) of the Constitution].

It is the foremost principle of Decision Euthanasia I. that everyone has the right to decide upon their own death. A legal system that has a secular constitutional basis should not take a stand regarding a person's decision on ending their life, whether supportive or not. This is a sphere that the state, in general, should stay away from. The state, in this respect, may only intervene to the extent that is necessary to fulfil its positive obligations imposed by the right to life.

From this we can conclude that the terminally ill patient's decision not to live until the natural end of his/her life when it is filled with suffering, and thus refusing life-sustaining treatment is part of their right to self-determination, a part that can be restricted, to the extent that is absolutely necessary to protect another human right, but should never be withdrawn. The subject of a constitutional assessment may, at most, be the justification of the restriction of the right to self-determination, for example, the fact that the law only allows patients to exercise this right if certain procedural requirements are met. On this basis, all forms of non-voluntary euthanasia are considered to be unconstitutional. Namely, if in the absence of an incurable patient's consent, the doctor or another person ends their life without their wish, even if they intend to do so in order to protect the patient's human dignity, there is no direct constitutional connection with the incurable patient's right to self-determination, because it is their consent that will be excluded from the decision concerning their life.

Decision Euthanasia I. based its reasoning on the general right of personality which had been derived from the right to human dignity by the HCC with Decision 8/1990. (IV. 23.) AB. 'The general right to personality is a »mother right«, that is to say, a subsidiary fundamental right which both the HCC and the courts may call on for the protection of the autonomy of the individual in all cases where none of the specific fundamental rights named apply.'[30] The HCC also referred to Decision 23/1990. (X. 31.) AB (analysis of Decision Death Penalty see in this volume), according to which the right to life and human dignity is the highest value, standing above all else, a fundamental right that shall not be restricted, protecting two values forming an inseparable unit.[31] However, although human dignity is only considered to be absolute and is not to be restricted in its unity with life,[32] certain sub-rights derived from it as a mother right (e.g. the right to self-determination) can be restricted.

Human dignity in its unity with life shall not be restricted by others. The right to a dignified death, however, does not arise in the context of the deprivation of life by others, but in the context of the termination of life of one's own volition, so the right to a dignified death and human dignity does not appear in its unity with the right to life. The violation of human dignity occurs for the very reason that life does not end at the point where pain and vulnerability put the patient's life and dignity in conflict. Therefore, in this case, unlike the cases of the death penalty and abortion, the right to life and the right to human dignity do not manifest themselves in unity; on the contrary, with the enforcement of one right, the other may be pushed into the background. Consequently, the right to human dignity and the right to self-determination which is derived from it, may be restricted.

The HCC has pointed out that if the legislator allows the right to a dignified death to be exercised without providing adequate guarantees, this could become a source of the arbitrary deprivation of life, creating an unconstitutional situation. It is essential to ensure that the decision embodies the patient's own, genuine and unaffected will. According to the forum, the system of preconditions for exercising the right to refuse a life-sustaining treatment (e.g. examination by a medical committee), as well as additional requirements for incapacitated persons, serve the fulfilment of positive obligations of the state imposed by the right to life and constitute a proportionate, and therefore constitutional, restriction of the right to self-determination.

---

30 Decision 8/1990. (IV. 23.) AB, ABH 1990, 42, 44–45.

31 Decision 23/1990. (X. 31.) AB, ABH 1990, 88, 93.

32 Decision 64/1991. (XII. 17.) AB, ABH 1991, 297, 308, 312.

3.2. *The desire of a terminally ill patient to end their life with the active help of a physician cannot be regarded as such part of their right to self-determination that cannot be withdrawn, even in its entirety, by law [Article 54 (1) of the Constitution].*

The desire of the incurable patient to end their life not merely by refusing a life-sustaining, life-saving medical intervention, but with the active help of a physician, was approached by the HCC from a somewhat different point of view. The forum found the criminalisation of active euthanasia constitutional for two reasons.[33] On the one hand, because in this case the right of a patient to self-determination is in conflict with the doctor's freedom of conscience, since in this case the doctor's active participation is required to bring about death, and no one can be obliged to do this. On the other hand, because the right to self-determination is opposed to the absolute nature of the right to life, which imposes a positive obligation on the state to protect human life and living conditions in general. The prohibition of active euthanasia reflects the state's obligation to protect these values. The above restriction of self-determination is necessary for the exercise of the right to life, and since the restriction is not unreasonably wide, it can be considered proportionate.

The desire of the incurable patient to have his/her doctor actively end his/her life is already a part of the right to self-determination which may even be completely withdrawn by law in order to protect other fundamental rights (ABH 2003, 235, 262.). Therefore, inducing the death of a patient upon their own wish but with the active help of a doctor cannot be considered to be part of the patient's right to self-determination.

The temporary or permanent nature of the decision is not a secondary issue in relation to the constitutional prohibition of active euthanasia. To answer this question, the HCC mentions that it has already occurred—also in the practice of the ECtHR—that changes in circumstances and the development of scientific knowledge have taken the debate beyond the previously justified restrictions on certain human rights. The line between the still constitutional and the already unconstitutional regulation regarding the right to self-determination of an incurable patient cannot therefore be considered a given once and for all, since it can be influenced by several factors (e.g. the level of knowledge, the state of health care institutions).

33 Tóth J., '»Oszthatatlan és korlátozhatatlan?«' (2005), [without page numbers].

4. Doctrinal analysis

4.1. The doctrine of indivisibility and the doctrine of 'living law'

As the HCC did not deal in detail with the interpretation of the right to human dignity in relation to euthanasia, but merely referred back to its previous decisions,[34] the panel's findings on passive euthanasia were fundamentally criticized in the constitutional literature, from two perspectives. Anomalies were drawn up related to the errors of the doctrine of indivisibility and the related problems of constitutional jurisprudence on the one hand, and related to the application of the regulation declared to be constitutional in practice (or rather the lack thereof) on the other.

The doctrine of indivisibility as established by the HCC in Decision 23/1990. (X. 31.) AB, is based on the monistic approach to human beings. The doctrine states that the life and dignity of human beings and the rights protecting these values are inseparable.[35] According to its classical interpretation, the unity of the right to human dignity and the right to life is indivisible; a conflict between human life and dignity is conceptually impossible. However, critics of the doctrine state that life and human dignity, as well as the rights that protect these values, can be separated, interpreted, and enforced separately. There is also at least one situation where life and dignity are clearly separable, and that is euthanasia itself,[36] but there can also be other situations in which they come into conflict.[37]

Nevertheless, the decision did not satisfy those who adhered to the classical interpretation of the doctrine of indivisibility. According to this view, the unity of the right to human dignity and the right to life is absolute and inseparable. Any wording that raises the possibility of a conflict between life and dignity, including the reasoning of Decision Euthanasia I., refers to a misinterpretation of the concept of human dignity. The right to decide one's own death does not derive from the right to human dignity. This decision (e.g. suicide, euthanasia) is of a non-legal nature.[38]

---

34 Filó, *Az eutanázia a büntetőjogi gondolkodásban* (2009), 187.

35 Győrfy, 'A tulajdonságok nélküli ember elmélete' (1998), 23.

36 Tóth J. 'Élethez való jog és életvédelem pro futuro' (2011), 1 (7).

37 Tóth J. cites several examples of conflicts between life and human dignity. Tóth J., '»Oszthatatlan és korlátozhatatlan?«' (2005), [without page numbers].

38 Judge Éva Tersztyánszkyné Vasadi, in her parallel reasoning on Decision Euthanasia I., commits herself to the classical interpretation of the indivisibility doctrine, which was explained in detail in Decision 23/1990. (X. 31.) AB.

In addition to the aforementioned systematic criticisms, it should be emphasized that the legal literature did not accept with unanimous enthusiasm that the HCC considered the strict preconditions surrounding passive euthanasia to be a necessary and proportionate restriction of the right to self-determination. The *amicus curiae* argues that the actual implementation (or rather, non-implementation) of healthcare legislation limits the essential content of a fundamental right.[39] With regard to the system of strict preconditions, it was also formulated that although the HCC is not a court that could take evidence, it can still examine how certain legal provisions are implemented and enforced in reality. As a result, in the 1990s, the forum had developed the doctrine of 'living law', according to which not only the formal law, but also its actual enforcement or lack thereof can be a ground for annulling laws.

However, in this respect, the decision and the regulations it declares constitutional raise serious concerns. The verdict's reasoning simply explains the strict conditions of passive euthanasia (e.g. examination by a medical committee, a three-day waiting period) and the regulation that does not treat terminally ill patients initiating the discontinuation of the life-sustaining treatment as capable persons with the positive obligation of the state imposed by the right to life.[40]

The nature of the conditions for the refusal of life-sustaining, life-saving care does not allow the decision-making right of terminally ill patients to be effectively exercised in medical practice. Thus, it is the very guarantees which are intended to ensure the patient's right to self-determination that nullify it.[41]

4.2. Active euthanasia: an eternal dream?

As we have seen, the HCC found voluntary passive euthanasia to be compatible with the right to self-determination and declared the prohibition of active euthanasia constitutional. In the reasoning to the decision, the panel states that the wish of an incurable patient that a physician bring about their death, for example by providing or administering a suitable drug,

39 Kis and Sajó, 'Amicus curiae az Alkotmánybírósághoz' (2003), 134 (137).

40 Otherwise, it would not order a psychiatric examination of all patients requesting euthanasia. Vissy, 'Méltatlan figyelem a méltó halál kérdésének' (2016), 56 (66).

41 Vissy draws attention to this in connection with the motion of Gábor Vadász which resulted in the second euthanasia verdict. Vissy, 'Méltatlan figyelem a méltó halál kérdésének' (2016), 56 (60).

cannot be considered such a part of their right to self-determination that could not be withdrawn by law, even in its entirety, in order to protect another fundamental right (ABH 2003, 235, 262.). However, the decision also concludes that inducing the death of an incurable patient through active medical help does not derive from the general right to self-determination held by all patients (ABH 2003, 235, 266.). It is therefore not clear whether the panel 'referred voluntary active euthanasia to the scope of the right to self-determination, or considered its limitation to be necessary and proportionate in view of the state's positive obligation to protect life'.[42]

Nevertheless, the decision of the HCC on active euthanasia came as no surprise to the legal literature. As the reasoning points out, the patient is extremely vulnerable to the influence of the environment, but also to the state of the healthcare system, in the decision between life and death. Medical experience also shows that active euthanasia can only be turned to responsibly in a society if the health care system is highly developed and the terminal patient has access to all medical care available at the given level of scientific progress. The real danger is that in an underdeveloped healthcare system, people would choose medical help to die instead of accepting unprofessional decisions and inadequate care, even though active euthanasia cannot replace, but only complement, advanced healthcare.[43]

The HCC, reflecting on the above experiences, left open the possibility of a future reassessment of the line between the still constitutional and already unconstitutional restriction of the right to self-determination.[44] Although some argue that the delicate line between constitutional and unconstitutional is clear in this regard once and for all, and that making such a reassessment possible means the relativization of the right to life,[45] references to the possibility of reviewing the prohibition and a broader

---

42 Zakariás, *Az emberi méltósághoz való alapjog* (2019), 198.

43 József Kovács, Head of Department at Semmelweis University, highlighted the above connections in his lecture at the conference 'Suicide and Jurisprudence' at ELTE School of Law, 18 November 2011.

44 The issue of res judicata was dealt with in detail by the HCC in Decision 4/2013. (II. 21.) AB, ABH 2013, 128, 133.

45 Parallel reasoning to the decision by Judge Éva Tersztyánszkyné Vasadi: 'A regulation that provides an informed, personal, free decision on rejection, free from all external coercion and influence, is constitutional. Such refusal of treatment does not cause death, but accepts that it cannot prevent it. What is more than that in the circle under review is unconstitutional because the Constitution excludes restrictions on the right to life.'

interpretation of the right to self-determination are to be found in several minority reports on the decision.[46]

5. *Aftermath of the Decision*

The decision has preserved the Hungarian regulation on euthanasia for a long period of time, and its essential elements have remained intact to this day. The approach to the issue was not changed by the perspective taken in the Fundamental Law, which entered into force in 2012, and the HCC was not forced to review the doctrine of indivisibility based on the monistic approach to human beings in any other context. Meanwhile, in the healthcare system, due to the cumbersome, uneasy regulation, terminally ill patients still cannot properly exercise their right to a dignified death.

In 2012, the HCC was forced to reopen the euthanasia file by a motion filed by a retired chief physician who was thoroughly acquainted with the practical problems of the regulation. The new motion did not aim to have the forum completely review Decision Euthanasia I. Instead, it sought to ensure that the right of terminally ill patients to a dignified end to life, as recognized in Decision Euthanasia I., was enforced. The motion presented the practical experiences of the regulation and the fact that the strict preconditions of refusing life-saving or life-sustaining intervention have in practice rendered the right to self-determination empty.[47]

The motion resulted in Decision Euthanasia II. [Decision 24/2014. (VII. 22.) AB].[48] The HCC only decided in favour of the motion within a very narrow frame of reference, within the conditions of the so called 'living will'. Otherwise, it did not loosen the conditions of passive euthanasia, although it ignored one of the dogmatic foundations of the first decision, stating that the state's obligation to protect the right to life was unrelated to the guarantees ensuring the patient's free choice.[49]

However, the panel progressively set free the 'living will' from its previous limitations when it considered unconstitutional the requirement for it to be renewed every two years, as well as the psychiatrist's opinion required for it. This has led to the fact that today it is practically easier to refuse life-saving intervention in the framework of a 'living will', in

46 Dissenting oppinions by Judges András Holló and Mihály Bihari.

47 Vissy, 'Méltatlan figyelem a méltó halál kérdésének' (2016), 56 (59).

48 ABH 2014, 1128.

49 Vissy, 'Méltatlan figyelem a méltó halál kérdésének' (2016), 56 (72); Zakariás, *Az emberi méltósághoz való alapjog* (2019), 315.

advance and conditionally, than in the absence of it if the patient enters a terminal state.[50]

Bibliography

Mihály Filó, *Az eutanázia a büntetőjogi gondolkodásban* [Eutanasia in the Criminal Legal Thinking] (ELTE Eötvös, Budapest 2009)

Tamás Győrfy, 'A tulajdonságok nélküli ember elmélete: az Alkotmánybíróság oszthatatlansági doktrínája és ami abból (nem) következik' [The Concept of the Man Without Qualities: the Non-divisibility Approach of the Constitutional Court and What Follows from It] (1998) 3 *Fundamentum*, 23.

János Kis and András Sajó, 'Amicus curiae az Alkotmánybírósághoz' [Amicus Curie to the Constitutional Court] (2003) 1 *Fundamentum*, 134.

Ildikó Kmetty and Albert Takács, 'Az eutanáziához való jog: indítvány az Alkotmánybírósághoz' [The Right to Euthanasia: Petition to the Constitutional Court] (2003) 1 *Fundamentum*, 125.

Sándor Kőműves, 'Életvégi döntéshelyzetek. Orvos által asszisztált öngyilkosság: Amerikai Egyesült Államok' [Decision at the End of the Life. Doctor Assisted Suicide: the United States] (2016) 5–6 *Lege Artis Medicinae*, 303.

Gábor Attila Tóth: 'A »nehéz eseteknél« a bíró erkölcsi felfogása jut szerephez. Interjú Sólyom Lászlóval, az Alkotmánybíróság elnökével' [It is the Moral Consideration that Decides in the Hard Cases. Interview with Judge László Sólyom] (1997) 1 *Fundamentum*, 31.

Gábor Attila Tóth: Az emberi méltósághoz való jog és az élethez való jog' [The Right to Human Dignity and the Right to Life] in Gábor Halmai and Gábor Attila Tóth (eds), *Emberi jogok* [Human Rights] (Osiris, Budapest 2003), 255

Mihály Tóth, 'Pulpitus és katedra. Emléktöredékek Pálinkás Györgyről' [Fragments of memory about György Pálinkás] (2007) 4 *Iustum Aequum Salutare*, 251.

Zoltán Tóth J., '»Oszthatatlan és korlátozhatatlan?« Gondolatok az emberi élethez és méltósághoz való jogról az eutanáziahatározat kapcsán' [»Indivisible and Unlimited?« Some Thoughts About the Right to Life and Human Dignity in Relation to the Decision on Euthanasia] (2005) 1 *Jogelméleti Szemle*, [without page numbers].

Zoltán Tóth J. 'Élethez való jog és életvédelem pro futuro' [The Right to Life and the Protection of Life pro futuro] (2011) 12 *Pázmány Law Working Papers*, 1.

Beatrix Vissy, 'Méltatlan figyelem a méltó halál kérdésének – széljegyzetek az Alkotmánybíróság második eutanáziahatározatához' [Undeserving Attention to the Deserved Death – Comments on the Second HCC Decision on Euthanasia] (2016) 4 *Állam- és Jogtudomány*, 56.

50 Vissy, 'Méltatlan figyelem a méltó halál kérdésének' (2016), 56 (73).

Kinga Zakariás, *Az emberi méltósághoz való alapjog – Összehasonlító elemzés a német és magyar alkotmánybírósági gyakorlat tükrében* [The Right to Human Dignity – Comparative Study in the Light of the German and the Hungarian Constitutional Jurisprudence] (Pázmány Press, Budapest 2019)

7. Decision 154/2008. (XII. 17.) AB – Registered Partnership I.

*Orsolya Szeibert**

The registered partnership is not unconstitutional for same-sex partners. However, the registered partnership should not be available for different-sex partners if the registered partnership is interchangeable with marriage (which is open only to different sex partners).

The Act No CLXXXIV of 2007 on registered partnerships (Registered Partnerships Act I) was accepted on 17 December 2007 by the Hungarian Parliament. It was the first attempt[1] to introduce the registered partnership into the Hungarian legal order, and the HCC dealt for the first time with the registered partnership and the Registered Partnerships Act I in Decision Registered Partnership I. It compared the registered partnership to marriage and dealt with the exact rules of the registered partnership. In fact, the registered partnership which was to be introduced at that time in Hungary was planned to be open both to same-sex partners and different-sex partners, and the definite name of this partnership was—translated literally—not 'registered partnership' but 'registered cohabitation'. However, I refer to it as registered partnership because it followed the model of registered partnerships[2] current in Europe at that time. The HCC evaluated the relationship between marriage and the registered partnership for same-sex partners and also between marriage and the registered partnership for different sex partners. Furthermore, the protection of the institution of marriage was also scrutinized in Decision Registered Partnership I.

---

* PhD, Professor, Eötvös Loránd University Faculty of Law (Budapest).

1 This Act did not enter into force as consequence of Decision Registered Partnership I.

2 Agell, 'The legal status of same-sex couples in Europe. a critical analysis', in Boele-Woelki and Fuchs (eds), *Legal Recognition of Same-Sex Couples in Europe* (2002), 124; Boele-Woelki, 'What comparative family law should entail' in Boele-Woelki (ed), *Debates in Family Law around the Globe at the Dawn of the 21st Century* (2009), 27.

1. Background

1.1. Registered Partnerships Act I

Although same-sex partners had been able to live in an informal cohabitation since 1996 in Hungary,[3] Registered Partnerships Act I was the first attempt to recognize the partnership of same-sex partners on a higher level.[4] The Act was to become law in January 2009. The reasoning of Registered Partnerships Act I referred to the increasing number of cohabitations and to the fact that a demand on the part of same-sex partners to live in a legally accepted relationship had emerged. This was the result of the fact that marriage was traditionally maintained for a man and a woman in Hungary and the informal cohabitation provided only very limited rights (and obligations) for the cohabitants. Registered Partnerships Act I affected two principal issues: the legal meaning and importance of marriage, and the legal recognition of a same-sex partnership.

Registered Partnerships Act I itself was a compact one, including only sixteen articles. Article 1 contained the rule on the establishment of the registered partnership, and Article 2 the legal consequences, while the remaining articles dealt with the termination of registered partnerships and the rules of certain acts which were to be modified according to the planned new form of partnership. The aim of the planned new legal institution was to make a third model of partnership available for both different-sex and same-sex partners besides marriage—available for one man and one woman—and informal cohabitation, which was open to both heterosexual and homosexual partners but with very minor rights and obligations.

Although there were some differences between the regulation of marriage and registered partnership, Registered Partnerships Act I ordered the application of rules regarding marriage to apply correspondingly to registered partnerships, at least as a main rule and as regards the relationship between the partners. The Act principally linked the same legal consequences to the registered partnerships between same-sex and different-sex persons. Nevertheless, their function was not identical, because same-sex

---

3 Szeibert-Erdős, 'Same-sex Partners in Hungary. Cohabitation and Registered Partnership' in Boele-Woelki (ed), *Debates in Family Law around the Globe at the Dawn of the 21st Century* (2009), 305.

4 See: Weiss, 'Gesetz über die registrierte Partnerschaft in Ungarn' (2008), 1724.

couples had the possibility to cohabit, while a man and a woman could also marry.

Registered Partnerships Act I ordered that in questions not regulated by this Act, the rules of Act IV of 1952 then in force on the marriage, family and guardianship (Family Act) were to be applied in an analogous way. The property consequences were to be entirely the same and for maintenance of the registered partner and for the use of the common house or flat the rules to be applied for marriage and registered partnership were to be identical, as well. The rules regarding personal legal effects were also planned to be the same as the main rule, but the Registered Partnerships Act I contained two exceptions, as registered partners could not, though this legal status, use their partner's surname, nor could they adopt a child together. While a child over 16 can marry with the permission of the public guardianship authority, this possibility would not be available for future registered partners. An extra method for the termination of registered partnership beside divorce before a court was planned to be introduced, namely the termination by public notary. This would create a difference between marriage and the registered partnership, as a marriage between living persons can only be terminated by judicial divorce.

It is worth mentioning that the personal consequences of same-sex registered and of different-sex partnerships could differ in terms of the possibility of having paternal status. While joint adoption was planned to be prohibited regardless of the gender of the registered partners, the paternal presumption would have been statutorily established in a registered partnership between different sex partners, just as in marriage. This statutory presumption of paternity would have been excluded in a same-sex registered partnership.

1.2. The notion of marriage in the Hungarian legal order and according to the interpretation of the HCC

Marriage is one of the main institutions of civil law and family law; however, its essential nature was defined neither in the Family Act effective at the time of Decision Registered Partnership I., nor by other legal sources. The issue of the approaches to marriage had already emerged in the context of constitutional law before 2007.[5] However, those did not deal

5 The family law perspective of marriage was not debated and did not play any role in the reasoning of this Decision.

with the sexual identity or orientation of the spouses. Some decisions of the HCC affected marital issues. The HCC's decision of 1990 stated that the regulations concerning marriage and family concerned fundamental rights and obligations.[6] Later the necessity of the constitutional and legal protection of marriage as an institution came to the fore. In 1992 the HCC referred to the conclusion that the right to human dignity also included the right to freedom of autonomy, and the right to the freedom to marry is a part of the right to autonomy,[7] while in 2006 the state was deemed to be obliged to protect marriage as an institution of society.[8]

The connection between marriage and the same-sex registered partnership had been discussed in only one previous decision of the Constitutional Court. The starting point of the decision[9] of 1995 was a petition in which the HCC was requested to declare two rules unconstitutional. According to the petitioner, both the rule in the then effective Family Act stating that only a man and a woman can marry and the rule in the then effective Civil Code, namely old Civil Code, stating that only a man and a woman can cohabit, gave rise to discrimination on the basis of sexual identity. In its decision the HCC drew a clear distinction between marriage and cohabitation, making it clear that marriage and cohabitation must be conceptualised on a different basis.

According to the reasoning of the decision, the aims of marriage are typically the birth of common children and their upbringing within the family; at the same time marriage provides a framework for the spouses to support and to take care of each other and therefore the heterosexuality of the spouses is one of the terms of a marriage. The reasoning emphasized that no discrimination can be alleged if there is different regulation between a same-sex and a different-sex partnership and this difference is based upon whether or not a child is affected by the partnership because the equal rights of the two sexes do not mean that the natural difference between them can be ignored.[10] Furthermore, the reasoning underlined that both women and men constitute separate groups which have to be handled in a special way with the aim of avoiding discrimination.[11] While the HCC investigated the purpose of marriage and the possibility of discrimination on the basis of sexual identity, it did not deal with the

---

6 Decision 4/1990. (III. 4.) AB, ABH 1990, 28, 30.
7 Decision 22/1992. (IV. 10.) AB, ABH 1992, 122, 123.
8 Decision 7/2006. (II. 22.) AB.
9 Decision 14/1995. (III. 13.) AB.
10 Decision 14/1995. (III. 13.) AB, ABH 1995, 82, 86.
11 Decision 14/1995. (III. 13.) AB, ABH 1995, 82, 84.

function and purpose of cohabitation. Instead, it examined which legal rules contain rights and obligations for cohabitants. The HCC stated that the legal recognition of cohabitation has a remarkably shorter history than that of marriage. However, a stable partnership between two same-sex persons may realize values which may be the basis of the conclusion that the human dignity of same-sex partners living in an informal partnership can successfully make a claim for legal recognition. The HCC stayed its proceedings in 1995, with the intention that the legislator could put an end to this unconstitutional situation and extend the definition of an unmarried partnership to cover same-sex partners.

2. *Petition*

The HCC had to deal with six petitions in this proceeding, and all petitions held the introduction of the registered partnership to be an offence (ABH 2008, 1203–1207.). Some of them referred to the fact that the Act was contrary to Article 15 of the Constitution, so the whole Act or some of its provisions were unconstitutional. According to Article 15 of the Constitution, the Republic of Hungary shall protect the institutions of marriage and the family. The petitioners emphasized that the institution of marriage and its significance would be destroyed through the establishment of a partnership for same-sex partners which is very similar to marriage. They agreed upon the fact that the registered partnership was not a new institution, but was identical to marriage with regard to its establishment, legal consequences and termination. According to the arguments of the petitioners, the introduction of the registered partnership offended legal certainty because its exclusive aim was to create an institution which was practically identical to marriage for same-sex partners, but it implicitly recognized same-sex marriage. Some petitions referred not only to the violation of Article 15 of the Constitution but also of Article 16 of the Universal Declaration of Human Rights, which states that men and women of full age, without any limitation due to race, nationality or religion, have the right to marry and to found a family, and Article 12 of the ECHR (men and women of marriageable age have the right to marry and to found a family, according to the national laws governing the exercise of this right).

3. Decision and its reasoning

The HCC reached the conclusion that the introduction of the registered partnership for same-sex partners was not unconstitutional, but that Articles 1 and 2 of the Act, which did not determine the exact nature of the registered partnership and created a new institution parallel with marriage for persons of different sexes, were contrary to the Constitution. The uncertain legal character of the registered partnership resulted in the inseparability of marriage and the registered partnership, and also on the inseparability of registered partnerships for same-sex partners and for different sex partners. The annulment of Articles 1 and 2 would have made the Act inapplicable, so the HCC declared the Act in its entirety as unconstitutional, and annulled it, so it could not enter into force in January 2009.

3.1. Marriage is protected as an institution by the state and this protection is to be maintained in the future (Article 15 of Constitution).

In Decision Registered Partnership I. the HCC confirmed the obligation to protect marriage as an institution, on the basis of the earlier approach to marriage of the HCC and the Hungarian constitutional history of the regulation of marriage. According to the HCC, the existence of this obligation is independent of whether there is any concrete instrument to protect marriage (ABH 2008, 1203, 1210.). The HCC emphasised that Article 15 of the Constitution—according to which Hungary should protect the institutions of marriage and the family—had to be interpreted in harmony with the aim of marriage, which had been determined in 1990 as the following: 'the aims of marriage are typically the birth of common children and their upbringing within the family and at the same time to provide a framework for the spouses to support and to take care of each other', although it was clearly stated that important changes had occurred in the traditional model of the family. The HCC underlined that the state was obliged to provide the right to marry (for heterosexual partners) in the framework of the obligation to protect marriage as an institution, which means that the state should not make marrying impossible or hinder it without any reason and should not put married persons at a disadvantage against non-married persons and persons cohabiting without marriage (ABH 2008, 1203, 1213.).

3.2. *The formation of a cohabitation is related to the right to self-autonomy [Article 54 (1) of the Constitution].*

The HCC connected not only the right to marry but also the right to establish a cohabitation to the right to self-autonomy. Article 54 (1) of the Constitution stated that in the Republic of Hungary everyone has the inherent right to life and to human dignity and no one shall be arbitrarily denied of these rights. It is worth mentioning that the phenomenon of 'cohabitation' was used as a category which embraced all non-marital partnerships, including both de facto cohabitation and the registered partnership. According to the conclusion of the HCC, marriage and other partnerships could be regulated in different ways and it was constitutionally allowed for the state to decide on the instruments used to protect marriage and decide on the legal consequences of a partnership other than marriage (ABH 2008, 1203, 1214.). Although marriage was held to be protected as an institution it was also emphasized that there was no obligation to protect any other extramarital partnership. While the state cannot hinder heterosexual partners marrying by superfluous obstacles, there is no such strict obligation in relation to any other partnership. At the same time, a stable partnership of same-sex partners should claim for recognition and protection based upon the right to human dignity, the right to self-autonomy, the right for freedom to action and right to the free evolution of personality (ABH 2008, 1203, 1224.).

3.3. *As same-sex persons cannot marry, their registered partnership does not hurt and endanger the protected heterosexual marriage (Article 15 of the Constitution).*

The HCC envisaged the institution of the registered partnership as being both for same-sex and heterosexual partners. At first the registered partnership was interpreted in connection with marriage and with special regard to the fact that it was available both for heterosexual and same-sex partners. The Constitutional Court made efforts to determine the main features of the new partnership and concluded that, from its name, it seemed to be a cohabitation, but in fact it was close to marriage with regard to its establishment, legal consequences and termination. This statement proved to be decisive, even though it was accepted that the legal aim was to create a new institution and there were slight differences between registered and other partnerships.

Secondly, the Constitutional Court investigated whether the new institution of registered partnership was contrary to the obligation contained in Article 15 of the Constitution on the obligation of the state to protect marriage. The state is obliged to protect the institution of marriage as a heterosexual, constitutionally protected and traditional partnership but this does not affect the partnership of same-sex persons who cannot marry. However, as the stable partnership of same-sex persons may claim for recognition upon the basis of the right to human dignity and self-autonomy, especially because they cannot live in marriage but only in de facto cohabitation, the registered partnership may have an extra importance for them. One of the most important statements of Decision Registered Partnership I. proved to be the fact that the registered partnership for same-sex partners was an institution independent of marriage as there was a clear distinction between (heterosexual and traditional) marriage and the registered partnership for same-sex persons (ABH 2008, 1203, 1225.). The parallel opinions questioned whether the legislator had such freedom in regulating same-sex partnership at all (ABH 2008, 1203, 1229 and 1233.).

3.4. *The registered partnership for heterosexual partners has factually the same legal consequences as marriage and this is contrary to Article 15 of the Constitution and it may empty the constitutional protection of marriage and cause legal uncertainty [Articles 2 (1) and 70/A (1) of the Constitution].*

The HCC investigated the differences and similarities between marriage and the registered partnership for heterosexual persons very thoroughly, with special regard to the fact that although the name used was 'partnership', it seemed to be very close to marriage in reality. All provisions and legal consequences were profoundly considered, taking into account whether the differences were only formal or substantial ones. Among others things, the lack of the possibility of joint adoption was analysed in depth. A difference between marriage and the registered partnership for heterosexual partners was that while spouses could adopt a child, this opportunity was not available for registered partners. Although the joint upbringing of heterosexual registered partners was not supported this way, this was not deemed to be a meaningful distinction according to the reasoning of the HCC, as heterosexual registered partners had other ways to have a common child. Another difference was the lack of a common family name for heterosexual registered partners; here, again, the HCC reached the same conclusion, namely the possibility of bearing a common family name did not affect the function nor the content of the partnership, so it did not constitute a clear distinction between marriage and the registered partnership, either (ABH 2008, 1203, 1221.).

The HCC summarized that as these partnerships proved to be very similar to each other, two similar partnerships would be available for different sex persons. As the state is obliged to support marriage it also obliged to provide different regulations for other partnerships. The HCC's unambiguous conclusion was that no partnership varying from marriage may enjoy the same protection as marriage because this could destroy its significance. The dissenting opinion held that the difference between marriage and the registered partnership for different sex persons was enough to define the latter as an independent institution (ABH 2008, 1203, 1239.).

4. Doctrinal analysis

4.1. The priority of the protection of marriage

The HCC upheld the approach which had been followed in the nineties in the sense that heterosexual marriage was not envisaged as one among several available partnerships but as a specially protected institution enjoying priority. Marriage was firstly accurately positioned in the Hungarian legal order and Hungarian society and all other partnerships were investigated afterwards in the light of national legal changes, such as international developments and tendencies. The nonmarital partnership as a category embracing all partnerships except for marriage, and the possibility of their protection was compared to marriage and the protection of marriage. It has to be emphasized that the social and traditional phenomena of marriage and especially its heterosexual character were taken for granted and not questioned, or at least circumvented. The possibilities of same-sex partnerships were surveyed only in the context of the history of their international development. Two separate opinions were connected to the decision and these lacked a stricter argument for an even stronger protection of marriage.[12] The one dissenting opinion underlined the changes concerning the notion of marriage and consequently disagreed with the

12 These are the separate opinions of Judges Elemér Balogh and László Kiss. Decision 154/2008. (XII. 17.) AB, ABH 2008, 1203, 1227–1229 and 1230–1234, respectively.

overwhelming majority opinion about preferring marriage over any other partnership[13] because of the requirement to protect marriage.[14]

4.2. *The merging of the definition of cohabitation and registered partnership into each other and the protection of cohabitation*

Decision Registered Partnership I. did not always use the phrases 'cohabitation' and 'registered partnership' ('registered cohabitation') clearly enough. Although the planned new Hungarian institution—the registered partnership—was the focal point of the petitions, the HCC did not sufficiently concentrate on comparing the registered partnership to marriage but endeavoured to denote the exact rank of the registered partnership in the order of the different extramarital partnerships. While searching for this rank the HCC changed the notion of 'cohabitation' and 'registered partnership' several times. The registered partnership—registered cohabitation according to the word-by-word Hungarian translation—was mentioned in the reasoning as one stage on the continuum of the legal recognition of cohabitation, and the registered partnership (registered cohabitation) was held to be one type of cohabitation which is 'established by registration'. The reasoning considered the registration a constitutive act. On the other hand, the relatively long reasoning in other cases referred to the registered partnership as a 'third type' of partnership and also as a partnership independent of cohabitation.

4.3. *The registered partnership as an independent legal institution*

The reasoning concluded in its summary that the registered partnership seemed to be closer to marriage than to cohabitation, and even the registration as a constitutive act was mentioned. Although the Hungarian term used for registered partnership—'registered cohabitation'—could have led to the conclusion that the registered partnership was one form of cohabitation, I must emphasize that the common feature between the two institutions is that neither of them were marriage. Their establishment, legal

13 The dissenting opinion of Judge András Bragyova. Decision 154/2008. (XII. 17.) AB, ABH 2008, 1203, 1234–1239.

14 Jakab, 'Az Alkotmánybíróság első határozata a bejegyzett élettársi kapcsolatról' (2010), 9.

consequences and termination made it impossible to consider either of them a type of the other. As far as the act of registration is concerned, it was a clearly declarative act as the registered partnership would have been established by the consent of the parties (just as in the case of marriage).

4.4. The registered partnership for different-sex partners

When the registered partnership was compared to marriage the decisive factor was whether the registered partnership could be established between same-sex or different-sex partners. Although it was determined that there were some differences between marriage and a heterosexual registered partnership, the HCC reached the conclusion that the latter is almost identical to marriage. The significance of the diversions would have been mitigated by the fact that a child could be born from the registered partnership of a man and a woman in a natural way which would have made the main paternal presumption just as applicable as in the case of spouses. The HCC did not discuss the issue of whether there would be any social group or aim—such as the avoidance of serial polygamy—for which the introduction of registered partnership between persons of different sexes would be used.

5. Aftermath of the Decision

5.1. Registered partnerships Act II

Registered Partnerships Act I did not become law. Parliament accepted Act XXIX of 2009 on the registered partnerships and the modifications made to it in connection with registered partnerships and the facilitation of the proof of cohabitation on 20 April 2009 (Registered Partnerships Act II). This Act, which is still in force, introduced the institution of registered partnership (according to the literal translation 'registered co-habitation') only for same-sex partners, maintaining all regulations which had been contained in the earlier, nullified Registered Partnerships Act I. The registered partnership, which was a new institution for same-sex partners beside de facto cohabitation, and established significantly more legal consequences for the partners was established on 1 July 2009. The Registered Partnerships Act II also contained rules on cohabitation which entered into force on 1 January 2010.

According to the Registered Partnerships Act II, which is now law in Hungary, registered partners may establish their relationship by a declaration before the registrar, and this creates a personal status.[15] In issues not regulated in this Act the rules applicable to spouses and marriage—i.e. among others, the rules of the Family Law Book of the Civil Code and other related provisions of the Civil Code—are to be applied analogously. The regulations related to property are the same in their entirety. Although the personal legal consequences are also the same as with the main rule, there are some exceptions. Registered partners cannot use their partner's surname, cannot adopt a child together—which means that step-parent adoption is also excluded—and cannot take part in a medically assisted reproduction process. The extra nonjudicial method of terminating their partnership has also been maintained.[16]

It must be mentioned that some further restrictions regarding adoption were made during 2020 and 2021 which affected same-sex partners, including registered partners. Previously, only spouses could adopt a child together, but adoption by a single parent was also possible, even though spouses were to be preferred as adoptive parents. A new rule of the Civil Code entered into force on 1 March 2021 which prescribes that only spouses can adopt a child and only the minister responsible for family affairs may approve adoption by a single parent in cases requiring special consideration [Article 4:121].

5.2. Decision 32/2010. (III. 25.) AB – Registered Partnership II.

Eight petitions were lodged referring to the unconstitutional character of the Registered Partnerships Act II. The petitions which were unified and adjudged within one proceeding held that the Act was contrary to the Constitution by raising the registered partnership to the legal position of marriage. In their opinions the right to self-autonomy could not be applicable to same-sex partnerships and an objection was made against

15 See, Weiss, 'Neues zur Regelung der registrierten Partnerschaft' (2009), 1566–1567; Szeibert, 'Partnerships in Hungary in the Light of the New Legal Developments: Status or Contract?' in Atkin (ed), *The International Survey of Family Law* (2012), 115.

16 Szeibert 'The changing concept of 'family' and challenges for family law in Hungary' in Scherpe (ed), *European Family Law. Vol. II.* (2016), 110.

the regulation which made it obligatory for registrars to proceed by the establishment of a registered partnership.[17]

The petitions were dismissed by the HCC upon the ground of Decision Registered Partnership I., which stated that the establishment of a registered partnership by same-sex partners was not unconstitutional, as they could not marry each other. The HCC noted the extreme importance of marriage and the family and the fact that the constitutional protection of marriage did not mean the exclusive protection of marriage, a point which allowed the protection of other (extramarital) partnerships. The state is obliged to protect marriage for heterosexual partners which also means that a partnership very similar to heterosexual marriage cannot be created, but a legally recognized partnership within the constitutional framework and based on the right to human dignity has to be made available for same-sex partners who cannot marry. As those affected by these regulations are not identical, the same-sex registered partnership does not endanger the protection of marriage.[18]

5.3. *The registered partnership and the Act on the protection of the family in the decisions of the HCC*

The HCC brought two decisions in connection with Articles 7 and 8 of Act CCXI of 2011 on the protection of family. When the Act entered into force, Article 7 contained rules on the establishment of familial legal status. Article 7 (1) defined the notion of the family and listed the marriage of a man and a woman, and the lineal kin relationship or the guardianship by which the child is cared for in the guardian's family and household as the (exclusive) grounds of the family, while Article 7 (2) established that the lineal kin relationship arose from the bloodline or via adoption. Article 8 dealt with 'the right to succession' and contained the main rules on succession but without the inclusion of the surviving registered partner. Decision 32/2012. (VI. 29.) AB, which was the first on this subject, found that these regulations of the Act on the protection of the family were contrary to the related rules of the old Civil Code and therefore might cause legal uncertainty.[19] As discussed above Article 8 was to enter into force in July 2012, but the HCC suspended it. The HCC compared the rules on

17 Decision 32/2010. (III. 25.) AB, ABH 2010, 194, 195–199.

18 Decision 32/2010, (III. 25.) AB, ABH 2010, 194, 208.

19 Decision 31/2012. (VI. 29.) AB, ABH 2012, 63, 67.

the inheritance of the surviving registered partner of the old Civil Code to those of Article 8 of the Act which contained no right for the surviving registered partner to inherit in case of the death of the registered partner and dealt with the existing harmony between the related rules of the old Civil Code and its own judiciary. By referring to the possibility of legal uncertainty there was no need to discuss Decision Registered Partnership I. in detail.

The next related decision, namely Decision 43/2012. (XII. 20) of the Constitutional Court, laid down the unconstitutionality of both Articles 7 and 8 and annulled them. It underlined in its reasoning the significance and summarizing character of Decision Registered Partnership I. and referred to the statements of its decision concerning the protection of the institution of marriage, which meant that spouses should not be put at a disadvantage with non-married persons. The HCC noted the constitutional framework, namely that the state was allowed to decide freely within that framework on the available legal instruments,[20] and also noted the state's opportunity to recognize extramarital partnerships.[21]

5.4. *Decision 3003/2021. (I. 14.) AB on the close relative status of registered partners*

The HCC had to envisage whether Article 8:1 (1) 1 of the Civil Code, which defines which persons belong to the circle of close relatives for the purposes of the Civil Code, was contrary to the FL. In Hungary, the FL was passed in April 2011 and entered into force on 1 January 2012, and the Constitution was made ineffective. This regulation lists the spouse as a close relative but does not include the registered partner. The petitioner claimed that this rule be declared unconstitutional and annulled. The HCC dealt with the significance and interpretation of the regulation concerned and took into account the fact that the old Civil Code contained a reference to the registered partner as a close relative. It was taken into account as a decisive factor that Article 3 of Registered Partnerships Act II ordered the application of rules which are applicable to spouses to registered partners as a main rule, analogously. This analogous application

20 Decision 43/2012. (XII. 20.) AB, ABH 2012, 296, 308.

21 Lápossy and Szajbély, 'A család(fogalom) és más alapjogok – alkotmányjogi megközelítésből' (2013), 1; Lápossy, Szajbély, and Szabó-Tasi, 'A családban marad? Döntés után, avagy az Alkotmánybíróság családképe' (2013), 1.

of legal rules was not considered for debate by the HCC, but they considered it necessary to bring a clear decision to avoid other possible legal interpretations and legal uncertainty. Therefore the petition was dismissed in the decision.

Bibliography

Anders Agell, 'The legal status of same-sex couples in Europe. a critical analysis', in Katharina Boele-Woelki and Angelika Fuchs (eds), *Legal Recognition of Same-Sex Couples in Europe* (Intersentia, Antwerp – Oxford – New York 2002), 122.

Katharina Boele-Woelki, 'What comparative family law should entail' in Katharina Boele-Woelki (ed), *Debates in Family Law around the Globe at the Dawn of the 21st Century* (Intersentia, Antwerp – Oxford – Portland 2009), 3.

Attila Lápossy and Katalin Szajbély, 'A család(fogalom) és más alapjogok – alkotmányjogi megközelítésből' [The Family and Other Fundamental Rights – From a Constitutional Law Perspective] (2013) 1 *Családi Jog*, 1.

Attila Lápossy, Katalin Szajbély, and Katalin Szabó-Tasi, 'A családban marad? Döntés után, avagy az Alkotmánybíróság családképe' [Does it Remain Within the Family? After a Decision – the Notion of Family According to the Constitutional Court] (2013) 2 *Családi Jog*, 1.

Orsolya Szeibert-Erdős, 'Same-sex Partners in Hungary. Cohabitation and Registered Partnership' in Katharina Boele-Woelki (ed), *Debates in Family Law around the Globe at the Dawn of the 21st Century* (Intersentia, Antwerp – Oxford – Portland 2009), 305.

Orsolya Szeibert, 'Partnerships in Hungary in the Light of the New Legal Developments: Status or Contract?' in Bill Atkin (ed), *The International Survey of Family Law* (Jordan Publishing, Bristol 2012), 115.

Orsolya Szeibert, 'The changing concept of »family« and challenges for family law in Hungary' in Jens Scherpe (ed), *European Family Law. Vol. II. The Changing Concept of 'Family' and Challenges for Domestic Family Law* (Edward Elgar Publishing, Northampton–Cheltenham 2016), 108.

Emilia Weiss, 'Gesetz über die registrierte Partnerschaft in Ungarn' (2008) 18 *FamRZ*, 1724.

Emilia Weiss, 'Neues zur Regelung der registrierten Partnerschaft' (2009) 18 *FamRZ*, 1566.

8. Decision 37/2011. (V. 10.) AB – Special Tax II.

Bernadette Somody[*]

The retroactive taxation of income earned without abuse with effect on already closed tax years is an infringement of taxpayers' human dignity.

Decision Special Tax II. was the HCC's second decision concerning the special tax on severance pay, and was passed following the curtailment of the HCC's competences relating to public financial matters. Decision Special Tax I. annulled the former special tax rules in 2010. In response, Parliament adopted a constitutional amendment that, first, restricted the HCC's powers in reviewing budgetary and tax laws, and second, allowed any income from public funds to be taxed retroactively for a period of up to five years. Passing Decision Special Tax II., the HCC accepted both the curtailment of its competences and the breach of the prohibition of retroactive legislation. Thus it essentially acknowledged the Government's use of the constitutional amendment as an instrument to realize its political goals.[1]

The HCC reviewed the tax law falling under the restriction of its competences on the grounds of the right to human dignity and declared that special tax rules having a retroactive effect are unconstitutional in respect of closed tax years. However, it did not find the retrospective effect on a tax year that has not yet been closed by a tax return to be unconstitutional, which was a shift from its former practice, according to which the time when tax falls due was relevant with regard to retroactive effect. The constitutional authorization for taxation with a retroactive effect was not included in the FL. However, due to the HCC's decisions on the special tax, the possibility of a retrospective effect on tax years not yet closed is provided under the FL.

---

* PhD, Assistant professor, Eötvös Loránd University Faculty of Law (Budapest).

1 Chronowski, 'Az Alkotmánybíróság második határozata a 98 százalékos különadó ügyében' (2012), 3 (10).

1. Background

1.1. Decision 184/2010. (X. 28.) AB – Special Tax I.

Decision Special Tax II. was the second occasion on which the HCC dealt with the constitutionality of the 98 per cent special tax on severance pay having, in part, a retroactive effect. Decision Special Tax I. concerned the regulation according to which private individuals must pay a special tax on public sector severance pay above HUF 2 million. While the law was promulgated on 13 August 2010, and came into effect on 1 October 2010, it had to be applied to incomes derived from 1 January 2010.[2]

Decision Special Tax I. was determined by the fact that, in connection with the adoption of the Act XC of 2010 on the adoption and modification of certain economic and financial acts (Special Tax Act), the constitutional provision on public burdens was also amended. According to the HCC's interpretation, the constitutional amendment permitted the legislature to tax retroactively incomes received from public funds if the income was given 'contrary to good morals' by state organizations. In other words, if these conditions are met then the legislature is permitted to disregard the prohibition of retroactive legislation.[3] The explanatory memorandum to the constitutional amendment made it clear that the intention behind the modification was expressly to make it possible to diverge from the preceding practice of the HCC.

In the decision of 2010, based on the new constitutional provision, the HCC divided its argumentation regarding the temporal scope of the Special Tax Act. On the one hand, with respect to retroactive regulation, it stated that the retroactive effect of the Special Tax Act was not limited to income given contrary to good morals, but also affected incomes given by law as a legal right. However, the latter cannot be taxed retroactively even on the grounds of the new provision of the Constitution. On the other hand, regarding the rules for the future, the rate of the special tax was declared to be unconstitutional. The new provision of the Constitution permitted the introduction of a 'special tax rate'; however, the legislature overstepped its constitutional mandate since a tax rate of 98 per cent essentially means the withdrawal of the income in its entirety.

2 Articles 8–12 and 133 of the Special Tax Act.

3 Article 70/I (2) of the Constitution being in force between 19 August and 19 November 2010. ABH 2010, 900, 908–909, 911.

1.2. New constitutional framework and new special tax rules

Following Decision Special Tax I., the Parliament, besides passing new rules on special tax, also amended the Constitution again in two respects: it modified the provision on the HCC's competences and, for the second time, the provision on public burdens.[4] In Decision Special Tax II., the HCC reviewed the constitutionality of the new rules on special tax in the new constitutional framework.

The changes restricted the HCC's powers in budgetary and tax issues.[5] According to the new rules, the HCC was entitled to review and annul public finance laws only in connection with one of the four fundamental rights indicated in the Constitution (the rights to life and human dignity, the protection of personal data, the freedom of thought, conscience and religion, and the rights related to Hungarian citizenship). The same curtailment of the competences, with a slight modification, has been maintained in the FL, so it remains in force.[6] Professionals voiced strong criticism that constitutional adjudication restricted on the grounds of subject matter cannot be in harmony with the rule of law and the division of powers given that in this way public financial legislation became legally unlimited, fundamental rights were no longer protected and can essentially be infringed without any legal consequence.[7]

The constitutional amendment regarding public burdens allowed any income from public funds to be taxed retroactively for a maximum of five years up to a rate lower than the income. In comparison with the former text of the Constitution, the amendment introduced three changes that partly reacted to Decision Special Tax I. Beforehand, the HCC had disapproved of the special tax not being confined to remuneration against good morals; in response, the new text of the Constitution did not include the reference to good morals. Previously, the HCC declared the rate of the special tax unproportionate; for this reason, the constitutional amendment permitted a tax rate that did not reach the total sum of the income. Finally,

---

4 Sonnevend, Jakab, and Csink, 'The Constitution as an Instrument of Everyday Party Politics' in Bogdandy and Sonnevend (eds), *Constitutional Crisis in the European Constitutional Area* (2015), 33 (95); Szente and Gárdos-Orosz, 'Judicial deference or political loyalty?' in Szente and Gárdos-Orosz (eds), *New Challenges to Constitutional Adjudication in Europe* (2018), 89 (93).

5 Article 32/A (2)–(3) of the Constitution in force from 20 November 2010.

6 Article 37 (4)–(5) of the FL.

7 For concerns of the Venice Commission see Opinion no. 720/2013 on the Fourth Amendment to the FL, 17 June 2013, 109–114.

the amendment extended the possibility of retroactive taxation to the fifth tax year.

The Parliament also changed the Special Tax Act. The most significant element of the modification was the retroactive extension of the temporal scope: the new rules promulgated on 19 November 2010, entered into force on 30 December 2010, while they had to be applied to income earned after 1 January 2005.[8] In essence, the constitutional amendment allowed retroactive taxation of up to five years. Under this possibility, the new law established a tax liability not only for the given tax year, but for the preceding five tax years.

2. *Petition*

The motions for posterior norm control were based on the unconstitutionality of the new rules in the Special Tax Act (2010s modification of the Special Tax Act)[9] and their retroactive effect.[10] Since the rules concerned taxes, the HCC had to comply with the recently passed limitation on its powers that permitted the review of tax laws exclusively relating to the fundamental rights listed in the Constitution. That is why it was important that the HCC separated the motions aimed to review conflicts between the Special Tax Act and international treaties, as well as those that referred to provisions other than the fundamental rights indicated in the Constitution. The HCC found that the rules can be reviewed because the motions examined in Decision Special Tax II. were based on the indicated constitutional provisions, in particular the right to life and human dignity.

The motions were based on different aspects of the right to human dignity. They included the equality function of the right to human dignity and its role in securing minimum subsistence derived from the right to social security. Furthermore, the prohibition of retroactive legislation falling within legal certainty was also formulated in this context.

According to the petitioners, the following led to the infringement of the right to human dignity: public employees are treated in a discriminatory way by the law in comparison to private employees; the tax, which withdraws almost the entire income is punitive and creates the impression that the payment was received unlawfully; the regulation has a retroactive

8 Article 2 (1) of the Act CXXIV of 2010 on the modification of the Act XC of 2010.

9 Articles 8–12 of the Special Tax Act.

10 Article 2 (1) of the Act CXXIV of 2010.

effect; the conditions of tax liability are altered posteriorly; the retroactive repayment obligation may threaten the financial security of individuals concerned; individuals are exposed to the measures of the state; the special tax may reduce the pension fund, which threatens minimum subsistence for the individual.

Besides the right to human dignity, the motions referred to further fundamental rights also indicated in the constitutional provision limiting the HCC's powers. Some petitioners claimed that the law is against the constitutional right to reputation and the protection of personal data because those who are obliged to pay the special tax can be identified, and the obligation implies a negative perception of them. Others posited that the law infringed on the right to freedom of thought and conscience because some of those obliged to pay the special tax are treated worse due to the fact that they held a leading position during the term of a different government from the one introducing the special tax rules.

3. *Decision and its reasoning*

While it rejected the other motions, the HCC declared that the retroactive effect of the new rules on the special tax was unconstitutional. Therefore, the Court annulled, with an *ex tunc* effect, the provision on the application of the special tax to income earned after January 1st, 2005.

3.1. *According to the Constitutional Court's established case law, the tax's primary function is to make natural and legal persons contribute to public burdens. Secondarily, it is also the means of state economic policy which can be applied to secure the rational use of public funds. The legislature has a wide margin of discretion regarding the application of tax as a regulatory instrument [Article 70/I (2) of the Constitution].*

The HCC necessarily had to build its reasoning on a fundamental right in respect of which the constitutional review of tax laws was allowed after the curtailment of the HCC's powers. This right primarily was the right to human dignity and its different aspects; the special tax rules were assessed based on its different aspects.

In a manner resembling Decision Special Tax I., the HCC also divided its argumentation in this decision. First, the HCC examined the rules for the future; in other words, the case of taxation when the individuals concerned are able to adapt to the altered circumstances. Here the HCC dealt separately with the employment relationships, mainly falling under the Labour Code, in the framework of which employers and employees can significantly influence the amount of a payment related to the termination of employment, and those in which the special tax is applicable to payments that are obligatory under by law.

Regarding the former, the HCC's starting point was the reinforcement of its previous theses on the constitutionally acknowledged functions of tax. Tax is primarily the means of increasing state revenue. Its primary function is that natural and legal persons should contribute to public revenues based on their income and wealth to secure financial cover for the maintenance of state organs and the fulfilment of public tasks. Besides this, it is generally accepted that tax is the regulatory instrument of state economic policy by which the legislator can, directly or indirectly, influence economic operators by taxing certain things and activities or by granting tax advantage. In this respect, the legislature has a wide margin of discretion.[11]

The HCC qualified the non-retroactive special tax relating to employment relationships falling under the Labour Code as a type of regulatory instrument given that its function is to motivate those who decide about state resources to reconsider. The HCC accepted the application of the special tax as a regulatory instrument.

The state has a wide margin of discretion regarding the application of the special tax as a regulatory instrument. However, it is limited by the equality function of the right to human dignity, i.e., the requirement of equal treatment. It raised the question of whether it is permissible for the special tax to be applicable only to severance pay from public funds, and thus the legislature treats employers deciding on and taxpayers receiving income from state resources in a different way from those who do not decide on or receive payment from state resources. The HCC held that the discrimination between income from state resources and other ones is not arbitrary but an objective distinction that does not infringe the right to human dignity (ABH 2011, 225, 237–238.).

Following the above, the HCC separately examined the non-retroactive special tax rules on the relationships in which the special tax related to payments that are obligatory under law. In these cases, there is a contradiction between the laws: both the special tax and the incomes affected by the special tax are determined by law; in other words, different ceilings

11 Decision 31/1998. (VI. 25.) AB.

for payments follow from the law on public employees and the special tax rules.

This raises concerns about the protection of reputation as an aspect of the right to human dignity. However, the HCC stated that neither the law on the special tax nor the related constitutional amendment included a moral judgement; they did not condemn either the payments or the individuals concerned. Thus, there is no connection between the special tax and the right to reputation.

Finally, the HCC reviewed the constitutionality of the special tax for the future from the aspect of the right to human dignity which protects individuals against state interferences that seriously threaten the subsistence of individuals and their resident close relatives. Since the special tax affects only payments that are higher than a certain amount and non-recurring (relating to the termination of employment), it cannot be considered a severe threat to taxpayers and an unlawful state interference into the autonomy of individuals. Furthermore, neither did the HCC establish a connection to freedom of thought, conscience and religion. Accordingly, it did not find the Special Tax Act to be unconstitutional.

3.2. The retroactive taxation that applies to incomes given by law and earned without abuse in a tax year closed by a tax return violates the right to human dignity [Articles 54 (1) and 70/I (2) of the Constitution].

The HCC dealt separately with the constitutionality of the retroactive effect of the Special Tax Act, since according to the provision giving effect to the new special tax rules, the Special Tax Act also applied to the past.

The standard of the constitutional review was again the right to human dignity as another phrase for a 'general right to personhood' protecting the autonomy of individuals. The HCC acknowledged that the constitutional amendment connecting to the 2010s modification of the Special Tax Act allowed any income from public funds to be taxed retroactively, up to a rate lower than the income, even for a maximum of five years. The constitutional question was whether further constraints are deriving from the Constitution, i.e., if the right to human dignity limits the possibility of taxation with a retroactive effect.

The HCC ruled that the mentioned authorization cannot be regarded as making any tax law *ab ovo* constitutional. The HCC can review whether the law serves the goal of the constitutional authorization—namely the protection of state resources, the prevention and the remedy of abuses of power—to decide on state resources. Based on the constitutional authorization, payments that are a misuse of state resources can be subjected to the special tax even retroactively. However, conversely, it also follows that the HCC can review taxation that oversteps this goal.

According to Decision Special Tax II., retroactive taxation that applies to incomes given by law and earned without abuse in a tax year closed by a tax return is considered to be going beyond the constitutional goal. This state interference into the autonomy of individuals has no constitutional justification; thus it violates the taxpayers' right to human dignity. Although the special tax is an income tax, in this case it does not relate to the taxpayer's income to be taxed and affects their current income and living conditions. While the law disregards the individual circumstances and the objective economic difficulties, the 98 per cent rate and five-year-long retroactive effect of the special tax together seriously endangers the individuals' subsistence from current income in many cases, thus it is an unlawful state interference. With regard to this, the HCC abolished, with an *ex tunc* effect, the retroactive part of the provision giving effect to the 2010s modification of the Special Tax Act.

4. *Doctrinal analyses*

4.1. *Limits of tax as a regulatory instrument*

The importance Decision Special Tax II. is significant also from the viewpoint of competences since the HCC had to decide within the limits of its powers as defined within the Constitution as a reaction to Decision Special Tax I. The question has not lost its importance since the restriction of the HCC's powers in reviewing budgetary and tax laws are still in force in the FL in force. This is why it is crucial that the HCC based the argumentation on different aspects of the right to human dignity as a legitimate basis for the constitutional review. While one can criticize the HCC's unreserved acceptance of the constitutional amendment curtailing its powers in budgetary and tax issues,[12] in this framework, the HCC performed the constitutional review of the special tax rules and referred to several aspects of the right to human dignity.[13]

12 Chronowski, 'Az Alkotmánybíróság második határozata a 98 százalékos különadó ügyében' (2012), 3 (10).

13 See Deák, 'Pioneering Decision of the Constitutional Court of Hungary to Invoke the Protection of Human Dignity in Tax Matters' (2011), 534.

The HCC separated the analysis of the Special Tax Act for the past and the future in both decisions on special tax. In Decision Special Tax I., the constitutionality of the non-retroactive rules depended on the special tax rate. The HCC considered that the special tax was also to be applied to incomes that were compulsory to be paid by law. The HCC held that the 98 per cent tax rate is not a regulatory instrument and does not aim to prevent abusive payments. Its function is the almost entire withdrawal of payments above a certain amount. According to the HCC's case law, the tax rate can only be subjected to review and unconstitutional exceptionally; however, it found it to be such an exceptional case when the tax rate is confiscatory, essentially a total withdrawal, and obviously excessive and unjustified.

At the time of Decision Special Tax II., as a result of the constitutional amendment adopted together with the new special tax rules, the Constitution ruled on the tax rate differently: it allowed a tax rate that is less than the income. The HCC emphasized that the constitutional amendment is a change related to the first special tax decision, which was adopted as a response to the HCC finding the 98 per cent tax rate to be unproportionate.

Within the constitutional framework, the HCC accepted that the 98 per cent special tax rate could be a regulatory means of serving the protection of state resources. There continued to be a contradiction between the law on the status of public employees providing for compulsory payments and the special tax. The HCC, however, found that it can be solved. It interpreted the special tax as a means of establishing a ceiling for the incomes from state resources and returning the amounts above the ceiling to the central budget. Since the special tax relates to a single situation and there are income bands not subject to the tax, it does not make the taxpayers' subsistence impossible. With this interpretation, in the new constitutional framework, the HCC accepted the tax rate it had previously found to be unconstitutional.

Both concurring opinions questioned this approach. Following the logic of Decision Special Tax I., Judge László Kiss insisted that the 98 per cent tax rate created a punitive conclusive presumption that the taxpayers had received the payment subject to the special tax in an abusive way, which violates the right to human dignity.[14] Judge Miklós Lévay stated that the tax rate is stigmatizing and punitive, thus humiliating.[15]

14 ABH 2011, 225, 250–251.
15 ABH 2011, 225, 257.

4.2. *Limits of retroactive taxation*

A striking element of both special tax decisions is that the HCC accepted on both occasions that with regard to taxation, a constitutional amendment could establish an exception to the prohibition of retroactive legislation that is an essential criterion of the rule of law.

In Decision Special Tax II., the retroactive legislation was found to be unconstitutional because it violated the right to human dignity. However, this unconstitutionality related only to the tax years 2005–2009, but not to the current tax year of 2010. The basis of the distinction was that the tax years 2005–2009 were closed by a tax return, while that had not happened in relation to the tax year 2010. This differentiation deviated from the HCC's previous case law that considered the time when the tax becomes chargeable relevant from the viewpoint of retroactive effect. The background of the deviation is the constitutional amendment connected to the original Special Tax Act, which decidedly aimed for this change. In justification of the constitutionality of the retrospective legislation affecting the given tax year, the HCC also argues that the special tax applies only above a certain amount, and a relatively short period of time had elapsed since earning the income. Thus, the deterioration of individual circumstances and the violation of the right to human dignity cannot generally be established.

Logically, the first question is whether it is justified to treat differently the taxation that goes back only to the tax year that has not yet been closed. According to Judge László Kiss's concurring opinion, the modification of rules following the tax year or even during the tax year after earning the income is retrospective and not predictable for taxpayers. In the other concurring opinion, Judge Miklós Lévay finds it acceptable that a tax rule adopted in a not closed tax year can be applied from the beginning of the given tax year ('not real retroactive effect'). However, in this case, he misses that the HCC did not consider whether the conditions, such as the special tax rate and the promulgation date, justified the retrospective effect's constitutionality. He thinks that in the specific case the conditions also lead to the infringement of the right to human dignity regarding the not closed tax year.

5. *Aftermath of the Decision*

After Decision Special Tax II., Parliament again adopted the retroactive special tax rules that entered into force on 14 May 2011.[16] According to this modification of the original Special Tax Act, the special tax rules must be applied to incomes earned following 1 January 2010. Thereby the legislator maintained the retrospective effect of the special tax for the year not closed by a tax return which the HCC had found acceptable. The special tax, whose rate later changed to 75 per cent, was in force until 2018.[17]

During this time, the ECtHR dealt with the special tax on severance pay and found it violated the Convention. According to the Strasbourg Court, the special tax applied to the applicants violated the right to property guaranteed by Article 1 of Protocol no. 1.[18] The civil servant applicants were dismissed in 2011, so their severance pay was subsequently taxed at 98 per cent in its part exceeding 3.5 million HUF. This represented an overall tax burden of 52 and 60 per cent on the eternity of the severance. The tax rate itself did not make the interference unproportionate. However, the ECtHR considered that the tax rate was high in a European comparison and considerably exceeded the general personal income tax rate of 16 per cent. It was a decisive factor that the applicants were given their severance pay by law, and that they had acted in good faith had never been called into question. The applicants had to suffer a substantial withdrawal of income in a period of considerable personal difficulty, namely that of unemployment, by a modification of the tax system that they could not be prepared for. Furthermore, the measure only targeted a particular group of civil servants, and any individualized assessment of the applicants' situation was not allowed. The HCC concluded that taxation at a considerably higher tax rate than that in force when the revenue in question was generated was regarded as an unreasonable interference with the expectations protected by the right to property.

As a consequence of the ECtHR's decisions, the HCC had to deal with the special tax again since, referring to the decisions of the Strasbourg Court, judges initiated the review of Special Tax Act because of their

16 Articles 1 (2) and 3 of the Act XLVI of 2011 on the modification of the Special Tax Act.

17 Repealed by Article 42 of the Act XLI of 2018 on the modification of tax laws.

18 *N.K.M.* v *Hungary*, no. 66529/11, judgment of 14 May 2013; *Gáll* v *Hungary*, no. 49570/11, judgment of 25 June 2013; *R.Sz.* v *Hungary*, no. 41838/11, judgment of 2 July 2013.

conflicts with international treaties. The HCC stated that the provision on the 98 per cent special tax is contrary to an international treaty and generally excluded its application in specific cases.[19]

The FL entered into force half a year after Decision Special Tax II. and created a new framework for the regulation again: the provision limiting the HCC's powers has been maintained, but the constitutional authorization for taxation with a retroactive effect was not included in the FL. The question arises of how the thesis of Decision Special Tax II. operates under the FL.

Regarding tax rate, interpreting Article XXX (1) of the FL on public burdens, the HCC stated that the legislator has a wide margin of discretion in deciding on tax subjects, types and rates. However, it is a constitutional constraint that the state must consider taxpayers' financial capacity and participation in the economy; in other words, it cannot make their living impossible in financial terms.[20] The FL also provides that essential rules on public burdens shall be laid down in a cardinal act.[21] The specialty of the relevant rules of the Act CXCIV of 2011 on the economic stability of Hungary (Economic Stability Act) is that they expressly indicate the ceiling of public burdens on work income. According to the tax wedge rule, the state is allowed to withdraw not more than half of the total labour costs as fiscal revenue; in other words, the sum of the employees' and employers' public burden cannot exceed the net income.[22] However, the violation of this rule does not in itself result in unconstitutionality since there is no difference between cardinal and ordinary acts in hierarchical terms.

The HCC expressly dealt with the retroactive effect of the Special Tax Act following the FL's entry into force. The HCC examined how to assess the retroactive effect of the Special Tax Act in the partly altered constitutional environment where the FL no longer includes the provision about retroactive taxation. From its Decision Special Tax II., the HCC confirmed that the right to human dignity does not in itself grant protection against retrospective taxation. The mere fact that the law establishes a tax liability for the current tax year or the following declaration period, and does not consider relevant the time when the tax becomes chargeable, does not constitute an infringement of the right to human dignity.[23] The Economic Stability Act provides that tax liability shall not be increased, the subjects

19 Decision 6/2014. (II. 26.) AB.
20 Decision 3047/2016. (III. 22.) AB, Reasoning [38].
21 Article 40 of the FL; Act CXCIV of 2011 on the Economic Stability of Hungary.
22 Article 36 (2) of the Economic Stability Act.
23 Confirmed by Decision 3353/2012. (XII. 5.) AB, Reasoning [68].

of the liability shall not be extended, and tax advantages and exemptions shall not be abolished or restricted with a retroactive effect.[24] However, similarly to the tax wedge rule, the violation of this rule of a cardinal act does not in itself lead to unconstitutionality.

The constitutional rules adopted before Decision Special Tax II. partly survived: the rule restricting the HCC's competences is still in force; however, the authorization for retroactive taxation was not included in the FL. Nevertheless, developments show that the possibility of retrospective taxation to a tax year not yet closed by tax return continues to exist also in the absence of a provision on the FL. The previous amendments to the FL moved the HCC's practice towards considering relevant the time of tax return and not the time when the tax becomes chargeable with regard to retroactive effect. The HCC confirmed this interpretation also under the FL.

Bibliography

Nóra Chronowski, 'Az Alkotmánybíróság második határozata a 98 százalékos különadó ügyében: az emberi méltósághoz való jog és a visszamenőleges adóztatás' [The Constitutional Court's Second Decision on the 98 Per Cent Special Tax: Human Dignity and Retroactive Taxation] (2012) 3, *Jogesetek Magyarázata*, 3.

Pál Sonnevend, András Jakab, and Lóránt Csink, 'The Constitution as an Instrument of Everyday Party Politics: The Basic Law of Hungary' in Armin von Bogdandy and Pál Sonnevend (eds), *Constitutional Crisis in the European Constitutional Area: Theory, Law and Politics in Hungary and Romania* (Hart/Beck, London 2015), 33.

Zoltán Szente and Fruzsina Gárdos-Orosz, 'Judicial Deference or Political Loyalty? The Hungarian Constitutional Court's Role in Tackling Crisis Situations' in Zoltán Szente and Fruzsina Gárdos-Orosz (eds), *New Challenges to Constitutional Adjudication in Europe. A Comparative Perspective* (Routledge, Abingdon 2018), 89.

24 Article 31 (1) of the Economic Stability Act.

9. Decision 165/2011. (XII. 20) AB – Media Content

Gábor Polyák[*]

Print and internet media products may be subject to specific media law obligations concerning their content and may be supervised by a public authority. To be constitutional, the regulation must be a necessary and proportionate restriction on press freedom and there must be a possibility of judicial review of the authority's decision.

1. Background

On 2 November 2010, Parliament adopted Act CIV of 2010 on the Freedom of the Press and the Fundamental Rules of Media Content (Media Constitution), and on 21 December 2010, Act CLXXXV of 2010 on the Media Services and Mass Communications (Media Act).[1] Prior to that, on 22 July 2010, Parliament adopted an amendment to Act I of 1996 on the Radio and Television (Radio and Television Act), which created the Media Council to replace the former media authority, the National Radio and Television Board (ORTT), and which started the process of merging the institutions providing and controlling public service broadcasting. The Media Act completed this institutional restructuring. It created an integrated authority, the National Media and Infocommunications Authority (NMHH), which performs both telecommunications and media regulatory functions, with the Media Council as its independent decision-making body.[2] It also created a public service institutional system which, while preserving the formal legal autonomy of the public service media providers and the public service news agency until 2015, placed the Media Services

* PhD, Senior research fellow, Centre for Social Sciences Institute for Legal Studies (Budapest).

1 About the laws see Bayer, Urbán, and Polyák, *Media law in Hungary* (2019)

2 Polyák and Rozgonyi, 'Monitoring media regulators' independence – Evidence-based indicators, Hungarian experience' (2015), 257; Nagy, 'Abnehmende Vielfalt auf dem lokalen Radiomarkt', in Holznagel and Polyák (eds), *Medienfreiheit unter Druck: Medienregulierung und Medienpolitik in Ungarn* (2016), 108.

Support and Asset Management Fund at the centre of the public service institutional system, without an independent body to monitor its operation.[3] The provisions of the two new media laws that received most attention were aimed at directly regulating media content and, critics argue, disproportionately restricted journalistic freedom through overly vague wording that left room for arbitrary interpretation. At the same time, it was precisely these provisions that drew most heavily on the similar provisions of the Radio and Television Act.

2. *Petition*

The HCC has received several motions from Members of Parliament, civic organisations and private individuals, which have initiated an ex-post abstract review of the new media regulation. The motions were extremely wide-ranging and essentially challenged all relevant points of the two media laws.

The panel decided to group or separate the motions in thematic order, and examined the following petitions.

One group of petitioners claimed invalidity of public law in connection with the entry into force of the Media Act. In this context, the lack of preparation time, the lack of consultations and public debate prior to the submission of the draft law, and the fact that the wording of the draft law had been amended on several essential points immediately prior to the adoption of the Media Act were considered to be of concern under Article 2 (1) of the Constitution.

Other petitions criticised the provisions of the Media Constitution which, together with the electronic media, also subject print and internet press products and their producers to official supervision.

A further group of petitioners considered the rules of the Media Constitution and the Media Act concerning the registration of press products to be infringing the freedom of the press.

Several petitioners objected to the provisions of the Media Act on the protection of journalistic sources and the data reporting obligations of media service providers under the Media Act as infringing press freedom.

Finally, some petitioners requested the annulment of the regulation on the legal institution of the Media and Infocommunications Commissioner

3 Polyák and Urbán 'Funding of the Hungarian Public Service Media' in Biggam (ed), *Online activities of public service media: remit and financing* (2015), 65.

in the Media Act, as it violates the constitutional requirements governing the restriction of freedom of expression and freedom of the press.

3. *Decision and its reasoning*[4]

Print and internet media products may be subject to specific media law obligations concerning their content and may be supervised by a public authority. This solution is not inherently unconstitutional. Constitutionality is conditional on the regulation being a necessary and proportionate restriction on press freedom and on the possibility of judicial review of the authority's decision. The decisive criterion in assessing the proportionality of a restriction is the impact of the medium on the public, and therefore the constitutional extent of the restriction varies from medium to medium [Article 61 (2) of the Constitution].

In relation to the constitutionality of the control of media products by the media authorities, the HCC examined each media law case separately

4 This paper focuses on the parts of the Decision that set out the constitutional framework for the regulation of media content. However, the decision also contains additional provisions. Laws that enter into force quickly and do not provide the persons and organisations covered by them with sufficient time to prepare [a requirement deriving from the rule of law under Article 2 (1) of the Constitution] do not necessarily suffer from public law invalidity. Consideration must be given to the extent to which the law is beneficial or burdensome for those concerned and to the fact that provisions imposing new obligations may not be applied until after entry into force'—Adequate and detailed legal guarantees are needed for the protection of journalistic sources of information, subject to respect for the freedom of the press. The regulation is constitutional if there is prior judicial control, the journalist can only be obliged to disclose the source of the information for a sufficient reason, and the regulation respects the principles of proportionality and subsidiarity [Article 61 (2) of the Constitution]'—The protection of information covered by the lawyer's privilege must be guaranteed not only from the lawyer's side but also from the client's side (who is not protected by the professional privilege), taking into account the requirement of Article 59 (5) of the Constitution to have the right to appeal. This obligation extends to data, files and documents arising from confidential communications between the client and the legal representative. The obligation for the press to provide information for general and uncertain purposes outside the official procedure is unconstitutional in view of the requirement to respect the freedom of the press under Article 61 (2) of the Constitution'—The obligation to register press products does not infringe the freedom of the press, provided that adequate guarantees are given [Article 61]. The existence

whether its 'content and scope do not unnecessarily and disproportionately restrict the operation and conditions of the free press in a democratic society'. In general, the Decision Media Content did not consider the media law regulation of print and online press products and the control of media authorities to be unconstitutional. On the one hand, it stated that the HCC had not categorically ruled out the possibility of content-based restrictions triggering state action in the case of print media products, and on the other hand, it stated that the possibility of systematic ex post control and sanctions by the state, which can be initiated ex officio, does restrict press freedom, but the mere possibility of such a restriction—with effective and substantive judicial control as a guarantee—cannot be considered unconstitutional.

On the basis of this yardstick, the HCC found the extension of certain media content requirements to print and internet media products to be unconstitutional. With regard to the media law obligations concerning human dignity [Article 14 (1) of the Media Act], the rights of the person making a statement (Article 15 of the Media Act), human rights (Article 16, second sentence of the Media Act) and the protection of privacy (Article 18 of the Media Act), the decision found that they constituted a constitutional restriction for radio and television media services, but that they constituted an unnecessary and disproportionate restriction of press freedom for print and internet media products.

The HCC took into account the 'differences in the impact of each medium on human thought and society'. In examining the regulation of Internet press products, it took two aspects into account. On the one hand, it found that a distinction must be drawn between private publications, blogs and social networking sites and newspapers and news portals on the Internet for information or entertainment purposes. On the other hand, the grounds for regulating the audiovisual media cannot be used as a basis for restricting the freedom of Internet media products. In the case of press products, there is no question of scarcity of resources, and access to the content they offer requires much greater activity on the part of the public. In addition, the public has much greater scope for selecting content and avoiding unwanted elements.

---

of an institution or commissioner with 'quasi-authoritarian rights', albeit without official powers, able to act in relation to content affecting press and editorial freedom, is in itself an infringement of press freedom, in view of the requirement to respect press freedom laid down in Article 61 (2) of the Constitution.

Media Constitution have significantly increased the control of media content by the media authority. Ex-post ex officio control and, where appropriate, sanctioning constitutes a restriction of press freedom, but the possibility of such a restriction is not considered unconstitutional under effective and meaningful judicial control, provided that the restriction meets the test of necessity and proportionality. The examination of the Media Constitution and the Media Act shows that, in the case of printed and internet press products, the NMHH and its Media Council monitor compliance with the provisions of Articles 14–20 of the Media Constitution. The HCC has therefore examined in detail whether the restrictions contained in Articles 14–20 of the Media Constitution can be considered necessary and proportionate when applied to the press.

In its examination of the provisions on the prohibition of incitement to hatred and exclusion'—the first turn of Article 16 of the Media Constitution and Article 17 of the Media Constitution'—the HCC referred back to an earlier decision[5] in which it assessed the incitement to hatred as a constitutional limitation on the freedom of the press. The basis of this decision was that 'media content which denies the institutional fundamental values of democracy linked to fundamental rights is conceptually excluded as a means of building and maintaining democratic public opinion'.

Article 14 (1) and the second turn of Article 16 of the Media Constitution, i.e. action for the protection of human rights and human dignity, constitute a special institutional protection procedure of the media authority. The HCC referred back to its earlier decision,[6] which stated that in proceedings for the protection of human rights the media authority does not decide on individual rights, but examines whether the subject, nature and point of view of the programme does not generally violate human dignity. However, the impact of the print and online press on the public is substantially different from that of the audiovisual media, so that 'this possibility of action, in this form, which covers human rights in general, is already a disproportionate restriction', i.e. unconstitutional when applied to print and online media products.

However, the prohibition on the presentation of persons in a humiliating and vulnerable situation, as contained in Article 14 (2) of the Media Constitution, is based on a particularly overriding public interest and is sufficiently narrow to ensure that the press is also subject to official action. The lack of or limited capacity to protect the rights of the individual covers

5 Decision 1006/B/2001 AB, ABH 2007, 1366, 1376.

6 Decision 46/2007. (VI. 27.) AB, ABH 2007, 592, 606.

cases where official action is justified, so that the regulation cannot be considered a disproportionate restriction in this area.

With regard to the media law provisions on the rights of the person making a statement (Article 15 of the Media Constitution) and the protection of privacy (Article 18 of the Media Constitution), the HCC has held that in these situations the publisher of the press product is faced with a uniquely identifiable person who has clearly defined and enforceable subject rights. There is therefore no justification for a restriction which would allow action by public authorities in the event of infringement and enforceability of individual rights.

4. *Doctrinal analysis*

The part of the decision which is in the focus of this analysis that will have the greatest impact on media regulation in the long term examines the conditions under which administrative judicial control by the media authorities can be extended to non-audiovisual media services. The starting point of the constitutionality analysis is that, in principle, media law provisions which provide for the application of sanctions for the communication of specific media content, irrespective of the impact of the communication or the medium, and which may also be applied in administrative proceedings before media authorities, may be constitutional.

At the same time, the HCC ignored several important aspects in its assessment of the proportionality of media law restrictions.

When examining the proportionality of the control of the media authorities, the HCC did not take into account in any case that the media sanction is only one of the means of protecting the rights and values concerned. The HCC also failed to examine the possible extent and nature of media law sanctions, despite the fact that the restriction of press freedom is in fact achieved through the sanctions that can be imposed. Nor has it examined whether the definition of the subject matter of the regulation, the clarity and precision of the definitions underlying the scope of the regulation, ensure that the restrictions only affect those communications for which the HCC considers that the restriction is justified. Finally, it did not examine whether the institutional framework responsible for implementation guarantees that all actors in the media system are subject to the same assessment of their conduct.

As Decision Media Content itself points out in the individual provisions, the media law provisions under consideration all restrict conduct that may give rise to civil, criminal and other legal consequences, such as data protection. In addition to the general legal consequences, media law sanctions directly affect the media service provider, the publisher of the press product. The proportionality of a restriction on communication can hardly be assessed without taking into account all the legal consequences of the communication. The combination of parallel proceedings and sanctions that can be imposed simultaneously in different proceedings also constitute a very serious deterrent to freedom of expression. Their combined 'chilling effect'[7] can lead to the disappearance of certain issues or critical voices'—self-censorship'—even if the justification for each procedure could be justified separately. The HCC, in its Decision 57/2001. (XII. 5.) AB, referred to the disproportionate effect of the combined effect of the various restrictions precisely in relation to freedom of expression.

The severity of any restriction on the freedom of the press can only be determined by taking into account the level of sanctions that may be imposed and other general conditions for the application of sanctions. The sanctions that may be imposed on press products, the fines that may be imposed, are still capable of making the operation of the press product concerned impossible. The severity of the sanction is of course also influenced by the other conditions for imposing sanctions. In this respect, although the law contains soft guarantees such as the principles of gradualness and proportionality, the detailed rules are in many respects vague and imprecise. The concept of repetition, which is an important criterion for assessing the infringement, has been significantly narrowed down compared to the original text of the law, making it clear that only infringements that are not more than 365 days apart can be considered as repeated, while the definition of serious infringement is still missing. The possibility of co-regulation, while substantially reducing the scope for the application of sanctions by the authorities, does not cover all press products covered by the law. All these aspects were not assessed by the HCC, which ruled on the question of proportionality without actually examining the gravity of the interference.

Although the HCC stated that '[private] publications, websites, blogs, community portals, etc. cannot be treated in the same way as internet newspapers and news portals aimed at informing or entertaining the masses', it did not examine in detail, also taking into account the aspects of the application of the law, whether the current provision fulfils this condition in defining the subject matter of the regulation. The law does not define

---

7 Schauer, 'Fear, Risk and the First Amendment: Unraveling the Chilling Effect' (1978), 685.

the concept of a press product as a periodical, an internet newspaper or a news portal and, despite the amendments made since the adoption of the law, does not provide a clear answer as to the scope of media regulation. This not only violates the requirement of clarity, but also has the potential to restrict communications too broadly, beyond what is constitutionally justified. This could only have been remedied if either the legislator or the HCC had provided clear criteria for the interpretation of the legal definitions.

The proportionality of the restriction is also influenced by the institutional framework that determines the conditions for the implementation of each provision. The political and economic independence of the media authority in charge of enforcement is a fundamental guarantee that the media law requirements are the same for all actors in the media system and that they are equally likely to be subject to non-discriminatory sanctions in case of infringement. However, in the present decision, the HCC did not deal with the submissions challenging the independence of the media authority, so the predictability of the legislation as a whole and its ability to ensure equal opportunities could not be a criterion of proportionality.

The HCC examined the media law restriction on hate speech in a single paragraph. The HCC found the provision of the Act to be constitutional, but made a restriction on its interpretation, which is hardly noticeable in the text of the decision, but which is all the more significant. Decision 1006/B/2001 AB examined the constitutionality of a similar provision of the 1996 Media Act, and found the provisions of the Media Constitution to be constitutional, although they were broader than the provisions of the Media Constitution but applicable only to radio and television broadcasting.[8] The decision did not clearly clarify whether the prohibition of incitement to hatred was considered to be the same or a lower standard of intervention than the criminal offence of incitement to hatred.

Decision Media Content decided this issue and stated that 'in its decision 1006/B/2001 AB, the panel identified the offence of incitement to hatred under Article 3 (2) of the Media Act with incitement to hatred'. This cannot be interpreted in any other way than that the scope of application of the provision of the Media Constitution is exactly the same as that

---

8 Koltay, 'A médiahatóság döntései és azok bírósági felülvizsgálata a gyűlöletbeszéd tárgyában (2001–2013)' (2013), 59; Polyák, 'Fórum a gyűlöletbeszéd szabályozásáról' (2008), 29; Török, 'A gyűlöletbeszéd tilalmának médiajogi mércéi' (2013), 59.

of the criminal offence of incitement to hatred. This, on the one hand, makes the application of the Media Constitution provision very narrow, which is necessarily a favourable interpretation from the point of view of freedom of the press. On the other hand, however, it raises the question of what happens if the criminal court and the media authority reach opposite decisions in two parallel proceedings assessing the same conduct, or if no criminal proceedings are brought in addition to the media censure. Despite the obvious differences between media law and criminal law sanctions, the different assessment of the same conduct according to the same yardstick seriously jeopardises legal certainty. The fact that criminal proceedings and administrative proceedings do not have the same subject matter does not change this. Indeed, the media law sanction against a media service provider is based on the fact that the media service provider, by assuming 'editorial responsibility' under the law, becomes itself a party to the act committed directly by the journalist or editor.

However, this does not answer the question of why such restrictions on press freedom are constitutional. In practice, the HCC does not answer this question. Its only argument is that 'in its previous practice, the HCC has also regarded offences committed through the press as a necessary limitation in the case of the written press, and has therefore limited itself in the present decision to confirming its previous position'. In so doing, it avoids the very question of what justifies the maintenance of a media law restriction in addition to the criminal law restriction. It is not clear what the HCC's confirmation of its previous position is, and the fact that 'offences committed through the media' constitute a necessary restriction does not at all imply that the provision of the Media Act and the associated sanction are proportionate. In any event, the reasoning of the HCC is flawed in this respect.

With regard to the regulation of media content, the decision has a serious shortcoming in that it only examines the provision of Article 17 (1) of the Media Constitution Paragraph (2) is a separate provision, according to which media content must not be capable of excluding any nation, community, national, ethnic, linguistic or other minority or any majority, church or religious group. Although a similar provision of the previous Media Act was found to be constitutional in Decision 1006/B/2001 AB, the reasoning of the decision under examination does not mention this provision at all. As regards a similar provision in the old Media Law, Decision 1006/B/2001 AB states that 'in order to protect the dignity of individuals and communities', freedom of expression may be restricted by media law provisions even if the threat of criminal sanctions for the same conduct would be unconstitutional.

The HCC found the media authority's control of non-audiovisual content to be unconstitutional in one case: in the case of action against violations of human rights (Article 16 of the Media Constitution) and human dignity [Article 14 (1) of the Media Constitution]. According to the decision, in individual cases of violations of the institutional content of human rights and human dignity, the power generally granted to the Authority to take action is wide-ranging, taking into account the case-law. In the case of the print and internet press, this constitutes a disproportionate restriction on press freedom and is therefore unconstitutional.

The HCC examined these provisions in relation to television and radio broadcasting in its Decision 46/2007. (VI. 27.) AB and found them to be constitutional. The constitutional grounds for this decision are not clear from the decision, which merely states that the media legislation 'establishes an administrative procedure in addition to the judicial procedure', in which the media authority 'does not decide on the infringement of rights of individual legal entities', but 'has the power to determine whether the broadcaster is acting in compliance with human rights and whether the subject matter, nature and point of view of its programmes do not violate the fundamental value of human rights'.[9] The HCC makes no attempt in any of its decisions to clarify the relationship between the right of self-determination and the ex officio administrative procedure. The application of the provision in this case, following the adoption of Decision 46/2007. (VI. 27.) AB, demonstrates that the HCC did not and could not give clear guidance to the legislator because of the ambiguous content of the provision.[10]

In Decision Media Content, the HCC referred back to the Decision 46/2007. (27. VI.) AB. The main task of the current explanatory memorandum is to list the arguments in favour of allowing the exclusion of non-audiovisual press products from the scope of the legislation. According to the HCC, in the case of audiovisual services, 'the public authority's intervention in the interests of viewers and listeners constitutes a necessary and proportionate intervention in view of the particularly strong influence it exerts on the public'. It argued that, as a consequence, 'in the case of the print media and the internet, which are not of the same nature, this possibility of action, in this form, which covers human rights in general, already constitutes a disproportionate restriction'. Even if we fully agree

9 Decision 46/2007. (VI. 27.) AB ABH 2007, 592, 606.

10 Polyák, 'A Legfelsőbb Bíróság ítélete. Az igazság ára című televíziós műsorszámról. Az emberi méltóság védelme közigazgatási eljárásban' (2011), 35.

with the conclusion, the argument leaves a serious sense of incompleteness. This shortcoming is primarily due to Decision 46/2007. (VI. 27.) AB, which does not provide adequate arguments to support the proportionality of the control of human dignity by public authorities.[11]

The HCC concludes that, in the case of non-audiovisual media products, 'human dignity is adequately protected by the legislation guaranteeing the exercise of personal rights'. The reason for this is the greater impact of audiovisual media, the fact that '[t]he audiovisual media [...] can cause a significantly greater destruction of the culture of respect for human rights, in particular human dignity'. In other words, media with a greater impact also pose a greater threat to the public interest by exerting a greater influence on the public, and in the latter case there is therefore a need for action by the authorities.

However, apart from the reservations here about the media effect as an argument justifying the regulation, the decision does not make clear why, if this is a factor affecting the proportionality of the interference in relation to human dignity, this aspect was not raised in relation to constitutional order and hate speech, or in relation to the other contested provisions. The argument of media impact alone is not sufficient to justify a different constitutional assessment of the different media law situations. In relation to human dignity, an additional argument could have been the violation of the right to self-determination or the proportionality of the restriction of the right to self-determination. However, this does not arise in Decision Media Content, and Decision 46/2007. (VI. 27.) AB simply states that the official control 'does not decide on the violation of rights of individual persons'. Neither decision clarifies the relationship between the right of self-determination and official control.

5. *Aftermath of the Decision*

The Parliament fulfilled the legislative obligations set out in Decision Media Content in June 2012 by adopting Act LXVI of 2012 amending certain Acts related to media services and press products.

Constitutional considerations on the regulation of media content also directly influence the practice of the media authority and the courts in applying the law. While the decision's findings on the protection of hu-

11 For more details see Majtényi and Polyák, 'A szabadság hazai hagyományának megtagadása – új médiatörvények Magyarországon' (2011), 13.

man dignity in the media essentially confirmed previous practice by the authorities and the courts, the HCC's interpretation of the prohibition of incitement to hatred has led to a significant change in the previous practice of the media authorities. In contrast, the Media Council, while recording a change in the media law yardstick for the prohibition of hate speech, bypassed the HCC's guidance in its entirety. It stated that the assessment of content in media law and in criminal law proceedings 'is carried out according to the same yardstick. However, in view of the different doctrinal rules and liability rules in criminal law and administrative law, the conditions for establishing an infringement (offence) differ significantly. The prohibition of hate speech in criminal law and in administrative law therefore runs in parallel, but this does not mean that content which is unlawful under one jurisdiction will be unlawful under the other, and vice versa: the absence of an infringement in one jurisdiction does not automatically mean exemption from liability under the rules of the other.'[12] With this turn of events, the Authority has made it clear that it does not intend to change its previous practice of intervening more widely than criminal law.

Decision Media Content found constitutional violations on important points, which were contested by many. However, it did not end the debate on media laws. The HCC did not address the institutional issues of the Media Council or the independence of public service media providers. In principle, in both cases, there may be individual cases that justify a constitutional complaint, but proving that the grievance is due to political bias on the part of the authority or the public media service provider is always a difficult task. The decision also does not address the regulation of market entry and restrictions on media concentration. Shortcomings in the tendering rules can be examined by the HCC in a constitutional complaint lodged following a tender procedure. At most, a constitutional complaint against the media concentration rules'—possibly in the case of a conspicuous distortion of a local media market'—can be filed on the basis of Article 26 (2) of the HCC Act, in which case also on the grounds of violation of the right to information.

The many question marks surrounding Hungarian media regulation are well illustrated by the fact that in 2015 the Venice Commission published a very detailed analysis of the provisions of media laws that violate

12 Decision 802/2013. (V. 8.) of the Media Council.

press freedom.[13] The Venice Commission's recommendations partly cover the issues already reviewed by the HCC in the decision under review. According to the Venice Commission, the content of the media content provisions is therefore uncertain and the law does not guarantee that the state will only intervene in the development of media content in the most necessary cases. Some provisions should therefore be removed, while in other cases the Media Council should draw up guidelines to help interpret the law. The law should limit the applicability of the more severe media law sanctions to the most serious abuses, and if the content provider goes to court, the enforcement of sanctions should be suspended pending the outcome of the proceedings. The analysis clearly argues in favour of the lack of independence of the Media Council and also identifies some constitutional concerns in the regulation of public service media.

Bibliography

Judit Bayer, Ágnes Urbán, and Gábor Polyák, *Media Law in Hungary* (3rd ed., Kluwer Law International 2019)

András Koltay, 'A médiahatóság döntései és azok bírósági felülvizsgálata a gyűlöletbeszéd tárgyában (2001–2013)' [Decisions of the Media Authority and Their Judicial Review on Hate Speech (2001–2013)] (2013) 3 *Médiakutató*, 59.

László Majtényi and Gábor Polyák, 'A szabadság hazai hagyományának megtagadása – új médiatörvények Magyarországon' [Denying the Domestic Tradition of Freedom – New Media Laws in Hungary] (2011) 1 *Közjogi Szemle*, 13.

Krisztina Nagy, 'Abnehmende Vielfalt auf dem lokalen Radiomarkt', in Bernd Holznagel and Gábor Polyák (eds), *Medienfreiheit unter Druck: Medienregulierung und Medienpolitik in Ungarn* (B&S Siebenhaar Verlag: Berlin 2016) 108.

Krisztina Nagy and Gábor Polyák 'Hungarian HCC: New Media Regulation partly under Constitutional Scrutiny: 19 December 2011, Ruling No 165/2011 (XII 20) AB' (2013) 7 *Vienna Journal on International Constitutional Law*, 110.

Gábor Polyák and Ágnes Urbán 'Funding of the Hungarian Public Service Media', in *Online Activities of Public Service Media: Remit and Financing* (European Audiovisual Observatory: Strasbourg 2015) 65.

13 CDL-AD(2015)015-e: Opinion on Media Legislation (ACT CLXXXV on Media Services and on the Mass Media, Act CIV on the Freedom of the Press, and the Legislation on Taxation of Advertisement Revenues of Mass Media) of Hungary, adopted by the Venice Commission at its 103rd Plenary Session (Venice, 19–20 June 2015).

Gábor Polyák and Krisztina Rozgonyi 'Monitoring Media Regulators' Independence – Evidence-based Indicators, Hungarian Experience' (2015) 6 *International Journal of Digital Television*, 257.

Gábor Polyák, 'A Legfelsőbb Bíróság ítélete. Az igazság ára című televíziós műsorszámról. Az emberi méltóság védelme közigazgatási eljárásban' [Supreme Court Ruling on the Television Programme The Price of Truth. Protection of Human Dignity in Administrative Proceedings] (2011) 2 *Jogesetek Magyarázata*, 35.

Frederick Schauer, 'Fear, Risk and the First Amendment: Unraveling the Chilling Effect' (1978) 58 *Boston University Law Review*, 685.

Bernát Török, 'A gyűlöletbeszéd tilalmának médiajogi mércéi' [Media Law Standards for the Prohibition of Hate Speech] (2013) 68 *Jogtudományi Közlöny*, 59.

10. Decision 33/2012. (VII. 17.) AB – Forced Retirement of Judges

Lóránt Csink[*]

The legislator can only reduce the retirement age of judges gradually, in due time, with regard to the irremovability of judges.

Decision Forced Retirement of Judges is certainly a milestone in Hungarian constitutional adjudication. The decision was issued amidst a rapidly changing constitutional environment, which affected the organization and competences of the HCC itself and was reflected in the subject matter of the decision as well. It was the first published case to decide a constitutional complaint submitted on the basis of Article 26 (2) of the HCC Act – a newly established procedure, which in certain instances allows the HCC to review individual complaints, alleging the unconstitutionality of a legal regulation, without an previous judicial decision. It also examined the legal implementation of novel constitutional provisions, introduced by the FL and its TP in context with the age-old principles of judicial independence and the irremovability of judges—also incorporated in the FL.

1. *Background*

The complaints alleged the unconstitutionality of two articles of Act CLXII of 2011 on the legal status and remuneration of judges (ASJ Act). Article 90 ha) set out the procedure of the termination of judicial service, by declaring that judges shall be discharged, by a decree of the President of the Republic, when they reach the retirement age applicable to them. Moreover Article 230 of the ASJ Act established an extremely short timeframe for the discharge of judges already reaching the age of retirement at the entry into force of the ASJ Act (1 January 2012) or in the follow-

---

* PhD, Professor, Pázmány Péter Catholic University Faculty of Law and Political Sciences (Budapest).

ing year.[1] Therefore these Articles of the ASJ Act abruptly shortened the judicial career, affecting both individual judges, who were forced to retire almost overnight, and the system of the judiciary as a whole, bringing about the retirement of nearly ten percent of Hungarian judges.[2]

However, these Articles were implementing constitutional provisions. While the previous Constitution did not contain any reference pertaining to the maximum age limit of judicial service,[3] according to Article 26 (2) of the FL, the mandatory retirement age of a judge (except for the president of the Supreme Court (Kúria) and of the National Office for the Judiciary) is the general retirement age. With this provision the FL establishes a mandatory age limit of judicial service at the constitutional level. However this is only a general reference, and does not provide a precise age as the upper-limit.

Another important provision regulating the age of retirement of justices at the constitutional level was introduced by Article 12 of the TP.[4] Article 12 determined the exact date of the termination of service for justices reaching the age limit of general retirement before 1 January 2012[5] as 30 June 2012 and for justices reaching retirement age by the end of December 2012 as 31 December 2012, therefore setting a quite short timeframe as well.

---

1 Article 230 (2) of the ASJ Act: If the judge reached the upper age limit before 1 January 2012, the starting date of their discharge shall be 1 January 2012 and the closing date of it shall be 30 June 2012, with the judicial office terminating on 30 June 2012. The motion on discharge shall be made at a date allowing the passing of the decision on discharge not later than on 30 June 2012. (3) If the judge reached the upper age limit between 1 January 2012 and 31 December 2012, the starting date of their discharge shall be 1 July 2012 and the closing date of it shall be 31 December 2012, with the judicial office terminating on 31 December 2012. The motion on discharge shall be made at a date allowing the passing of the decision on discharge not later than on 31 December 2012.

2 Venice Commission: *Opinion on Act CLXII of 2011 on the Legal Status and Remuneration of Judges And Act CLXI of 2011 on the Organisation and Administration of Courts of Hungary*. Strasbourg, 19 March 2012. para. 105.

3 Judges could remain in office until the age of 70.

4 The function of these provisions was to repeal the previous Constitution and introduce provisions regulating the transitional period between the two constitutions. The status of the TP and their relationship with the FL were initially uncertain, although according to the 1st constitutional amendment, coming into force on 19 June 2012, they were part of the FL. See: Sonnevend, Jakab, and Csink, 'The Constitution as an Instrument of Everyday Party Politics: The Basic Law of Hungary' in Bogdandy and Sonnevend (eds), *Constitutional Crisis in the European Constitutional Area* (2015), 33 (46).

5 It was the date of entry into force of the FL.

2. Petition

Many of the judges affected submitted constitutional complaints claiming the unconstitutionality of these Articles of the ASJ Act on various grounds. Some complaints alleged age based discrimination, prohibited by the FL. Others claimed the violation of the right to public office, private life or private property. Moreover, some complains alleged the violation of the principle of judicial independence set out in Article 26 (2) of the FL. The HCC only examined the impugned Articles on this ground.

3. Decision and its reasoning

3.1. *If there is only a formal legal remedy against a provision of a statute, then this statute is a directly effective statute for the purposes of Article 26 (2) of the HCC Act, and there is a right to lodge a constitutional complaint against it.*

The constitutional complaints in the present case were submitted under Article 26 (2) of the HCC Act.[6] Under the previous legislation on the old HCC Act, due to the possibility of *actio popularis,* an abstract review of legislation could be initiated by anybody, without any real interest in the outcome of the proceedings. The new HCC Act, created in 2011 narrowed down the avenues of abstract constitutional review and emphasized the individual constitutional complaint. The new regime requires individual standing as a precondition to submit a constitutional complaint in most cases.[7] Individuals are usually affected by an unconstitutional legal norm when such a law is applied by a judicial decision. However, the HCC Act also allows the initiation of HCC proceedings without an existing case with a direct and 'exceptional'[8] constitutional complaint set out in Article 26 (2) of the HCC Act (direct complaint).

In the present case, the HCC found that although the applicants had the hypothetical opportunity to challenge the termination of their service before a court,[9] and therefore to seek legal remedy, the provision requiring

6 HCC Act entering into force on 1 January 2011.

7 Abstract review can be initiated only by certain groups and officials, such as the Commissioner of Human Rights or one quarter of the MPs.

8 Köblös, 'A kivételes panasz szerepe az alkotmányos jogok védelmében' (2015) 184.

9 While the requirement of the termination of judicial service by reaching the mandatory age of retirement is established in law, in individual cases, these pro-

the termination of judicial service at a certain age is a cogent rule, leaving no room for discretion. Therefore the judicial procedure would be a formal one, and as such, cannot be regarded as a legal remedy capable of effectively repairing the violation of rights (Reasoning [60]).

Moreover, in regards to the individual concern, pertaining to the contested legislation, the HCC established, that individuals must be directly and actually affected by the legislation in order to be entitled to initiate a direct constitutional complaint. When assessing whether the applicants were affected by the impugned legal provisions in the present case, the HCC considered not just judges who had already been discharged, but those who were going to be discharged by the end of 2012 as well (Reasoning [61]–[67]).

3.2. *The reference to the historical constitution in Article R (3) of the FL means that the historical background of each institution must be taken into account in its interpretation.*

To examine the content of the constitutional rule of judicial independence and its applicability in the present case, the HCC first invoked Article R (3) containing mandatory principles of interpretation for the FL[10] and particularly the requirement to take into account the 'achievements of the historical constitution'. The HCC noted that with this provision, the FL highlights the historical dimensions of Hungarian public law and mandates the examination of the historical background of the legal institutions in question. The HCC also emphasized its own role (and power) in discerning what constitutes an 'achievement of the historical constitution'.

In the present case, the subjects of this analysis were two statutes from 1869 and 1871—the first acts in Hungarian legal history regulating the judiciary. The analysis focused on the ways these statutes guaranteed judicial independence and the provisions setting an age of retirement for judges. Based on these pieces of legislation, the HCC concluded that judicial independence is not just a normative provision of the FL, but also an achievement of Hungary's historical constitution. Subsequently, it

visions are executed via a decree of the President of the Republic ordering the discharge of individual judges. This decree can be contested at a tribunal.

10 Article R (3) of the FL: The provisions of the Fundamental Law shall be interpreted in accordance with their purposes, the National Avowal contained therein and the achievements of our historic constitution.

represents a principle that must be taken into account when examining the meaning of other provisions of the FL as well.

Moreover, the HCC emphasized, invoking its previous jurisprudence, that the irremovability of judges is an element of judicial independence and characterized it as a personal guarantee, which secures the autonomy of judges in passing judgements by excluding the possibility of causing any disadvantage to them through their position. The principle of irremovability of judges is primarily realized in legislation pertaining to the stability of the legal status of judges, and—among these—the upper age limit of judicial service. The HCC also noted that an extra guarantee of irremovability is also set out in Article 26 (1) of the FL, requiring that the reasons of the termination of judicial service must be regulated in a Cardinal Act[11] (Reasoning [84]).

Additionally, the HCC noted that the guarantees of the irremovability of judges are also necessary to secure the right of the parties of the judicial procedure to an 'impartial judge', enshrined in Article XXVIII (1) of the FL.

3.3. *Article R (3) of the FL also implies that when interpreting constitutional provisions, not only the individual provisions must be examined, but also their context, so that the FL remains a unified and inconsistent whole.*

The HCC pointed out that the FL only establishes the most important principles in relation to the judiciary, and requires the detailed rules on the organization of courts and on the legal status of judges to be laid down in a Cardinal Act—a lower level of legislation.

However, two important requirements on the termination of judicial service are still set out in the FL. First, that judges may only be removed from office for the reasons and procedures specified in a Cardinal Act,[12] and second, that one of the cases of termination is when a judge reaches the 'general retirement age'.[13] In regards to this second provision, the HCC noted that the FL does not specify the actual age which would qualify as the exact age of retirement. The HCC also noted that while Article 12 of the TP utilizes the notion of 'general retirement age' as well, it does not

11 Cardinal Acts are a different from ordinary laws as passing them requires the vote of two-thirds of the MPs present

12 Article 26 (1) of the FL.

13 Article 26 (2) of the FL.

contain a clear indication on what exactly the general age of retirement is, either (Reasoning [89]).

Turning to the level of ordinary legislation, the HCC first established that the general retirement age is not a concept of normative law in the sense that there is no Act of Parliament that contains a concrete age limit under this name in the Hungarian legal system. The HCC examined two specific acts, the ASJ Act (specifically its impugned provisions, concerning this subject) and Act LXXXI of 1997 on social security and pensions (ASSP Act). In regards to the ASJ Act, the HCC found that similarly to the constitutional provisions, it does not contain a precise age of retirement applicable to judges either. In connection with the ASSP Act, the court drew attention to the fact that while this act contains an age of retirement, it is not a general one—due to changes in Hungarian pension policy over the previous decades, the age of retirement set out in this piece of legislation can vary based on the birth year of individuals (Reasoning [91]–[93]).

Based on the uncertainty of these notions and the difference between them, the HCC concluded that it will be the HCC's duty to define the framework of interpretation of the term 'general retirement age'. The HCC invoked the 'integrity of the constitution'. It explained that this principle considers the FL to be a closed system without contradictions. It also requires the provisions of the FL to be interpreted with due regard to each other.

In the present case, this meant that according to the HCC, the 'general retirement age' could have only been interpreted in a manner not resulting in the violation of the essential elements of judicial independence.

3.4. *The retirement age for judges cannot be deduced from Article 26 (1) of the FL (judicial independence and immovability). This is a matter for the legislature to decide, and there is no obstacle to lowering the retirement age. However, it follows from this article of the FL that the lowering of the retirement age can only be done gradually, with an appropriate transitional period, and not from one moment to the next.*

The HCC pointed out that to determine whether the principle of irremovability is respected, not just the precise age of the 'general retirement age' (i.e. to what extent it differs from the previous age of retirement of 70 years) but the length of the period of time open to implement it must be assessed simultaneously. The more significant the difference between the new age of retirement and the previous age limit, the longer the time period to fully introduce the new age limit must be. It was also considered that while neither the FL, nor its TP contained the precise number of years of service as an upper age-limit of judicial service, the TP contained a quite short time period of implementation—3 months meaning that the 'general age of retirement' cannot be significantly lower than 70 years.

The HCC noted that contrary to the FL, Article 90 (and consequently Article 230, i.e., the disputed Articles) of the ASJ Act uses the notion of 'retirement age applicable to [the individual judge]' instead of 'general retirement age'. This notion appears to be referring to the ASSP Act containing different ages of retirement according to the date of birth of individuals.

The HCC found this troublesome for two reasons. First, it claimed that since the age limits set out in the ASSP Act (62 and 65 years) are significantly lower than the previous age of retirement of judges (70 years) this change constitutes a violation of the irremovability of judges and thus the principle of judicial independence. However, in the end, the HCC declared the impugned Article of the ASJ Act for formal reasons. It found that since these Articles do not set out the precise number of years of the age of retirement, but are referring to the ASSP Act instead, which is not a Cardinal Act, they violate Article 26 (2) of the FL, requiring the reasons of termination of judicial service to be regulated by a Cardinal Act (para. 105). The HCC also noted that the legislator has a wide margin of appreciation to determine the age of retirement as no concrete age can be deduced from the FL. Nonetheless, if the new age of retirement were significantly different from the previous one, it would need an appropriate time period to introduce it (Reasoning [106]).

4. *Doctrinal analysis*

4.1. *The issues of admissibility*

As mentioned earlier, this was the first published decision of the HCC originating from a direct constitutional complaint.

This type of procedure stands at the crossroads of abstract constitutional review and constitutional complaint, and is considered to be the closest to the old *actio popularis*.[14] This poses interesting questions about its character, since these two procedures have different functions. While the

14 Somody and Vissy, 'Citizen's Role in Constitutional Adjudication in Hungary' (2012), 95 (100).

different forms of abstract constitutional review (such as actio popularis) primarily aim to root out unconstitutional legal norms and not to compensate for individual injuries, constitutional complaints seek to remedy violations of the rights of individuals caused by unconstitutional legal norms and therefore presuppose an underlying 'case' where such an injury could have occurred. The present decision seems to emphasize the abstract nature of the direct constitutional complaint in three ways; a) it considers the principle of judicial independence as the individual judges' right enshrined in the FL, b) it considers judges not yet subject to a presidential decree to be individually concerned by the impugned Articles of the ASJ Act, and c) it adopted a substantial rather than a formal approach concerning the requirement of the exhaustion of domestic remedies.

Article 26 (2) of the HCC Act requires the violation of 'rights enshrined in the Fundamental Law'. If this type of procedure is to be considered another form of traditional constitutional complaint, requiring an underlying case, a strong argument can be made that only individual constitutional rights, enshrined in the chapter 'Freedom and responsibility' of the FL, should be regarded as a proper basis for these complaints because these are the rights individuals can rely on. However, if we focus on the abstract review aspect of this procedure, it is reasonable to consider that should some kind of personal involvement be presented, other constitutional principles can serve as a basis of this review as well, since this would facilitate the annulment of unconstitutional legal norms on a broader basis.

This interpretation is also supported by the majority's decision to deem complaints from judges not yet discharged, to be admissible. Although due to Articles 90 and 230 of the ASJ Act, they were about to have their judicial service terminated by 31 December 1012, no presidential decree had yet been issued in their case, and consequently there was no underlying case.[15]

With regards to the exhaustion of legal remedies, the HCC in the present case adopted a substantial rather than a formal approach. It found that the court proceedings the applicants could initiate against their discharge did not qualify as an 'effective remedy' and therefore cannot inhibit the submission of the constitutional complaints. This is the most flexible interpretation of this legal provision, although it carries some uncertain-

15 Judge Mária Szívós also noted this in her dissenting opinion, claiming that since there was no presidential decree issued in the case of these judges, they could not be considered as 'directly affected' by the challenged legislation.

ty.[16] Judge Béla Pokol criticized this approach in his dissenting opinion. According to him, the function of the available legal remedies is to determine the legality of the contested provision (i.e. whether it was applied correctly in the individual case) and not to remedy the unconstitutionality itself. Examination of the latter represents a separate stage of adjudication, and the fact that the available legal remedies cannot compensate for the unconstitutionality of the legal provision does not mean that these procedures can be omitted. However, this theory does not reflect on the abstract review-aspect of this type of constitutional complaint—i.e. that it does not require an underlying case—but aims to facilitate the ex-post review of legislation. (Item b) also confirms this).

Moreover some of the concurring opinions asserted that the complaints should be regarded (and thus dismissed) as disputing constitutional provisions, since the impugned Articles of the ASJ Act only implemented Article 26 (2) of the FL and Article 12 of the TP. However since they were not self-executing provisions, the laws implementing the constitutional provisions are subject to constitutional review.

In conclusion, it can be established that in this decision the HCC gave a flexible interpretation of the provisions establishing the exceptional constitutional review, emphasizing its abstract review aspects.

4.2. The achievements of the historical constitution as a mean of interpretation

Decision Forced Retirement of Judges is also the first to apply the achievements of the historical constitution as a mean of interpretation, established by Article R (3) of the FL. The necessary means of interpretation listed in Article R (3) constitute yet another novelty in the text of the FL, compared to the previous constitution. The notion of the 'historical constitution of Hungary' refers to the pre-charter-constitution era of Hungarian legal history. Before 1949, Hungary's constitutional structure was similar to that of Great Britain as the constitution consisted of different organic laws, whose constitutional character was mostly determined by customary law.[17]

Many authors consider this Article to be a mere rhetorical tool, being practically unusable, as there is no clear understanding of what is to be

16 Balogh-Békesi, '»Marbury felmentése« Alkotmánybírósági hatáskör-elemzés a bírói korhatár ügyön keresztül' (2012), 420 (421).

17 Trócsányi and Sulyok, 'The Birth and Early Life of the Basic Law of Hungary' in Patyi, Schanda, and Varga Zs. (eds), *The Basic Law of Hungary – A first commentary* (2015), 1.

considered a part of the historical constitution, and thus the mere cherry-picking of certain old legal provisions that correspond to the ideals of a present-day modern democracy does not promise any substantial novelty in the field of constitutional interpretation.[18] However, it can also be regarded as an attempt to widen the horizon of constitutional continuity, in order to incorporate into its scope some of the still relevant values (achievements) of the Constitution.[19] Nevertheless, following the entry into force of the FL, it was widely recognized that it would be the role of the HCC to discern whether, and to what extent, this provision would have any legal relevance.

According to the present decision, this provision compels the HCC to examine the historical dimension of legal institutions in the course of examining a concrete case. The concrete 'achievements' in the present case were regarded as a principle of interpretation, obligatory to everybody, which must be applied when the content of other provisions of the FL are to be explored (Reasoning [80]). Nevertheless, it must be noted that the method of the HCC utilizing this principle in this decision is not quite novel in its jurisprudence—the HCC had referred to historic laws to support its arguments numerous times before.[20]

Therefore, while the HCC acknowledged the novelty of the role of the historical constitution in constitutional interpretation, and attached more emphasis to the findings based on this principle, the actual approach utilizing this means of interpretation does not carry with it significant novelty.

4.3. The content and scope of the principle of judicial independence

Perhaps the most important point of the majority decision was to consider the independence of the judiciary—and specifically the irremovability of justices—to be an important factor in deciding on the regulation of the retirement age of judges. It was also a significant point of contention between the opinion of the majority and the dissenting justices.

---

18 Sonnevend, Jakab, and Csink, 'The Constitution as an Instrument of Everyday Party Politics: The Basic Law of Hungary' in Bogdandy and Sonnevend (eds), *Constitutional Crisis in the European Constitutional Area* (2015), 33 (74).

19 Hörcher, 'The National Avowal' in Patyi, Schanda, and Varga Zs. (eds), *The Basic Law of Hungary – A first commentary* (2012), 25 (47).

20 For example: Decisions 30/1992. (V. 26.) AB; 2/1994. (I. 14.) AB.

As discussed earlier, the HCC considered the guarantees regulating the status of judges (and *inter alia* the narrowly determined conditions of the termination of judicial service) as parts of the irremovability of justices, and consequently as the guarantees of the personal aspects of judicial independence. The majority decision linked the retirement age to judicial independence.

According to Judge István Balsai, the irremovability of judges should only protect the judiciary from interference in individual cases and it cannot be invoked against legislation applicable to every judge indiscriminately. Judge Egon Dienes-Ohm claimed that the retirement age of judges cannot be regarded as part of the guarantees of the irremovability of judges, since Article 26 (2) mentions it separately, creating a *lex specialis* guiding the assessment of this question and removing it from the scope of the irremovability of judges.

Furthermore a number of dissenting opinion criticized the majority opinion's finding that the fact that the ASJ Act did not contain an exact age of retirement violated the requirement that the conditions of termination of judicial service must be established in a Cardinal Act.

4.4. The integrity of the FL—managing the tension between constitutional provisions

The main consequence of the applicability of the principle of judicial independence in the present case, is that it draws attention to the tension between the content of this principle, as discerned by the HCC, and the 'general retirement age' of judicial service set out in Article 26 (2) and Article 12 of the TP. The HCC tried to reconcile these two provisions by invoking the principle of the 'integrity of the constitution'.

Many dissenting opinions disagreed with this solution. Judge Barnabás Lenkovics, joined by Judge Péter Szalay, recognised the contradiction between the two constitutional provisions but claimed that the HCC has no power to resolve this issue as it is the duty of the constitution-making power of the Parliament. Judge István Stumpf pointed out that the solution reached by the majority decision imposes on the legislator a requirement it cannot possibly achieve since no law can respect both the requirement of gradual implementation of a new retirement age and the time limits set in the TP.

Indeed, the use of this principle can be regarded as a way of bypassing the constitutional provisions establishing the 'notion of general retirement age', and this solution carries the danger that it might incite the legislative (and constitutional-making) power to circumvent the decisions of the HCC, as well.[21]

5. Aftermath of the Decision

5.1. Influence on legislation

After Decision Forced Retirement of Judges, on 7 September 2012 the Government initiated an amendment to the FL, according to which no-one can serve as judge after the age of 65. However, the initiative was withdrawn on 9 October 2012. On 6 November 2012 the CJEU decided that the Hungarian regulation is discriminatory on age, and it is not proportionate to the targeted aims.[22] Finally, the Act CLXII of 2011 on the legal status and remuneration of judges stipulated that retirement age for judges cannot be lower than 65; yet the law introduced the new retirement age for a 12 years of transitory period.

5.2. Influence on the judges effected

Decision Forced Retirement of Judges declared that the statuses of the retired judges do not 'resurrect' automatically as a result of the decision. Their statuses must be handled separately. The reason is that the status terminated not because of the Act CLXII of 2011 but due to the president's decision on the termination of office. The president's decision were out of scope of the HCC's procedure.

Among scholars, there emerged a minority view according to which the president should withdraw his decisions,[23] yet it was not followed in practice. Consequently, judges had to request the renewal of their status individually at courts.

It was also questioned if administrative positions (head of panel etc.) of judges should also be renewed. I conclude that they should not. The reason for unconstitutionality was the independence of judges and admin-

21 Balogh-Békesi, '»Marbury felmentése« Alkotmánybírósági hatáskör-elemzés a bírói korhatár ügyön keresztül' (2012), 420 (424).

22 *European Comission v. Hungary*, no. C-286/12, judgment of 6 November 2012.

23 Halmai, 'Alkotmányvédelem jogvédelem nélkül?' (2012), 104 (106–107); Csink, 'Az Alkotmánybíróság határozata a bírói hivatás felső korhatárának szabályairól' (2012), 8 (17).

istrative leadership has only a weak connection with Article 26 (1) of the FL.

5.3. *Influence on the jurisprudence of the HCC*

Decision Forced Retirement of Judges made it clear that constitutional issues must be decided upon the entire constitution, instead of particular decisions. As a result, the decision strengthened the integrity of the constitution. It also has a message to the constitution-maker: placing particular political wills to the FL does not guarantee success.

The decision also clarified that the TP does not have a constitutional rank; the FL prevails over the TP.

Furthermore, the decision was the first one to interpret the 'achievements of historical constitution'. Last but not least, this was the first case upon 'direct' constitutional complaint upon which the HCC practically performed ex post law review.

Bibliography

Nóra Balogh-Békesi, '»Marbury felmentése« Alkotmánybírósági hatáskör-elemzés a bírói korhatár ügyön keresztül' [»Marbury's acquittal« Analysis of the Constitutional Court's Jurisdiction through the Case of the Age Limit for the Exercise of the Judicial Profession] (2012) 10 *Jogtudományi Közlöny*, 420.

Lóránt Csink, 'Az Alkotmánybíróság határozata a bírói hivatás felső korhatárának szabályairól' [Decision of the Constitutional Court on the Rules on the Upper Age Limit for the Exercise of the Judicial Profession] (2012) 4 *Jogesetek Magyarázata*, 9–18.

Gergely G. Karácsony, 'A közvetlen panasz a magyar jogrendszerben' [The Direct Complaint in the Hungarian Legal System] in *Az Alaptörvény érvényesülése a bírói gyakorlatban. II. Alkotmányjogi panasz – a hatáskörrel kapcsolatos kérdések* [The Application of the Constitution in Judicial Practice. II. Constitutional Complaint – Question of Competence] (HVG-ORAC, Budapest 2019) 188.

Gábor Halmai, 'Alkotmányvédelem jogvédelem nélkül? Konfliktuskerülő és lojális alkotmánybírák a bírói függetlenségről' [Constitutional Protection Without Legal Protection? Complacent and Loyal Constitutional Judges on Judicial Independence] (2012) 2 *Fundamentum*, 104.

Ferenc Horkay Hörcher, 'The National Avowal' in András Patyi, Balázs Schanda, and András Varga Zs. (eds), *The Basic Law of Hungary – A first commentary* (Clarus Press, Dublin 2012), 25 (47).

Adél Köblös, 'A kivételes alkotmányjogi panasz gyakorlata' [The Practice of Exceptional Constitutional Complaints] in Lilla Berkes Lilla and Lóránt Csink (eds), *Az ombudsmani rendszer és az alkotmánybíráskodás átalakulása* [The System of Ombudsperson and the Transformation of the Constitutional Jurisprudence] (Pázmány Press, Budapest 2015) 89.

Bernadette Somody and Beatrix Vissy, 'Citizen's Role in Constitutional Adjudication in Hungary' (2012) 5 *Annales Universitatis Scientiarum Budapestinensis de Rolando Eötvös Nominatae. Sectio iuridica,* 95.

Pál Sonnevend, András Jakab, and Lóránt Csink, 'The Constitution as an Instrument of Everyday Party Politics: The Basic Law of Hungary' in Armin von Bogdandy and Pál Sonnevend (eds) *Constitutional Crisis in the European Constitutional Area: Theory, Law and Politics in Hungary and Romania* (Nomos, Tübingen 2015)

11. Decision 38/2012. (XI. 14.) AB – Homelessness*

*Attila Lápossy*** – *István Ambrus****

It is incompatible with the protection of human dignity to classify as 'harmful to society' and criminalize the acts of people who have lost their home for some reason and are therefore compelled to live in a public area, if this does not infringe or endanger the rights of others.

Decision Homelessness is a significant milestone in legal protection, despite the fact that the subsequent amendments to the FL and the decisions tried to enclose its findings in brackets. It was made at a special moment in time, at the end of the year following the adoption of the FL. It is worth noting that its references formed a kind of bridge between the standards of the FL and the interpretation of the Constitution, as well as the HCC practice developed in connection with the rule of law and constitutional criminal law, the 'clarity of norms' and guarantees related to the restriction of fundamental rights.

Decision Homelessness was based on the limitation test developed by the practice of the HCC, the examination of the legitimate aim, and the guarantee of the rule of law in constitutional criminal law. The panel made it clear that it is not constitutionally acceptable to criminalize living in a public area, or homelessness itself as a status which is not based on a choice. The HCC examined the declared, abstract public order purpose of the rules, as well as the underlying intentions. In Decision Homelessness, they emphasized that the removal of the homeless from public areas could not be a legitimate goal, nor could there be a coercive incentive to use social benefits, the so-called 'social blackmail'. The HCC also stated that homelessness is a social problem that the state must address through the means of social administration and care, not punishment. Decision Home-

* The authors would like to express their special thanks to Liza Bukor, PhD student in constitutional studies at ELTE Law School for her help in translating the original Hungarian study into English.

** Assistant professor, Eötvös Loránd University Faculty of Law (Budapest).

*** PhD, Research fellow, Centre for Social Sciences Institute for Legal Studies (Budapest), and Associate professor, Eötvös Loránd University Faculty of Law (Budapest).

lessness also made it clear that the establishment of Act II of 2012 on the regulatory offences, the procedure of the regulatory offence and the registry system of regulatory offences (Regulatory Offences Act) is covered by the rule of law and the 'clarity of norms'.

1. Background

Decision Homelessness itself did not address the issue of what international human rights standards and practices apply to the criminalisation of homelessness and long-term living in public areas. The HCC only took a narrow international perspective when reviewing the case law of the ECtHR in relation to the imposition of administrative sanctions, including sanctions for regulatory offences.

With regard to action against homelessness and other serious existential statuses, it is difficult to make a comparison with international standards, because there are no really similar cases that have been discussed in European law enforcement forums and can therefore be mentioned as a reference. The primary reason for this shortcoming is that, even if there is such regulation or enforcement practice, it will be resolved within the Member States, as domestic courts and HCC's can deal with measures that go beyond the constitutional framework.[1]

Although not covered by the decision, the case law of the United States is instructive in terms of the issues raised, which commanded to stop the quality-of-life laws of the Member States, which became popular from time to time. The stated and emphasized aim of these regulations was to protect the cityscape and to 'protect' the local population from the mess, annoyance and inconvenience caused by the sight of homeless people living in poverty, living on the streets, sleeping and meeting their needs. As early as the 1960s and 1970s, the U.S. Supreme Court made it clear that no one could be punished, either directly or indirectly,—by listing the wide range of conducts to be sanctioned—, solely on the basis of their situation, status, or condition; moreover, the possibility of future crime cannot be accepted as an argument. In the 1990s, the U.S. Court of Appeals reaffirmed in a number of judgments that it is unconstitutional to order the detention of

1 See Lápossy and Szajbély, 'Korlátozott terek' (2014), 52 (55).

anyone who has nowhere to go for an otherwise harmless (public) act or merely because of homelessness.[2]

At the same time, there are many examples around the world of the criminalization of socially dangerous acts associated with homelessness. Under the regulations of England and Wales—the Vagrancy Act 1824 (5 Geo. IV. C. 83)—punishable acts directly affecting the homeless include sleeping in a public area, begging, drinking alcohol, etc. Under the Criminal Justice Act (1967 c 80), any person may be arrested in any public area in cases of disorderly behaviour while drunk. Dutch law does not directly penalize homelessness; however, some legislation may indirectly affect homeless people. This may include offences such as disorderly behaviour, or drinking alcohol in a public area. As far as administrative offences are concerned, the ordinance of the municipality of Amsterdam contains various provisions that could potentially affect homeless people (e.g. bans on the public consumption of alcohol and drugs, gambling, sleeping on the streets, and begging). Under Article 443 of the Dutch Penal Code (Wetboek van Strafrecht, 1881), a violation of municipal regulations may result in a custodial sentence or a fine. In Australia, the law (Homelessness Bill, 2013) allows authorities to relocate homeless people from their place of residence when their mere presence could cause anxiety to others or disrupt the undisturbed presence of others in the same area.

2. *Petition*

The HCC, acting on the basis of the motion of the Commissioner for Fundamental Rights, examined the constitutionality of the objected provisions, acting within the competence of posterior abstract norm control. In his original complaint and subsequent amendments, the Ombudsman argued that the classification of living permanently in a public area as a regulatory offence was in a violation of the rule of law enshrined in Article B (1) of the FL and the requirement of legal certainty, and also contrary to the right to human dignity enshrined in Article II of the FL. According to the Ombudsman, there was no constitutionally justifiable, real, substantive and legitimate reason for declaring that living permanently in a public area be classified as a regulatory offence. The disputed norm criminalized homelessness as a condition, a situation in life which is incompatible with

2 See Mitchell, *The Right to the City. Social Justice and the Fight for Public Space* (2003), 303.

the fundamental rights of the persons concerned, in particular their right to human dignity and—with regard to a potential custodial arrest (involving the deprivation of liberty)—their right to personal liberty. Subject to this, he requested that the act of the administrative criminal offence enshrined in Article 186 of the Regulatory Offences Act be reviewed and annulled. According to the Commissioner for Fundamental Rights, the provisions empowering local authorities are contrary to the rule of law and the requirement of legal certainty. In the motion, he emphasized that the—virtually unlimited—authority given to local authorities by the law violates the requirement of the subordination of public administration to the law, and the normative content included in the disputed rules does not meet the requirement of the 'clarity of norms', and thus is contrary to the principle of the rule of law. The Commissioner therefore also sought the annulment of these provisions of the law in the supplement to his motion.

3. *Decision and its reasoning*

In Decision Homelessness the HCC found that Article 186 of the Act II of 2012 on Regulatory Offences, the Procedure of the Regulatory Offences and the Registry System of Regulatory Offences (Regulatory Offences Act) and Articles 51 (4) and 143 (4) (e) of the Act CLXXXIX of 2011 on the Local Governments in Hungary (Local Governments Act) were unconstitutional and were therefore annulled the day after the publication of the decision.

3.1. *The declaration of a regulatory offence must also comply with the requirements of the rule of law in connection with the declaration of a criminal offence, the criminal law intervention and the conditions for the restriction of fundamental rights (Articles B (1) and I (3) of the FL).*

The HCC first examined the constitutionality of the impugned provision of the Regulatory Offences Act, i.e. the classification of living permanently in a public area as a regulatory offence. According to its previous practice, the rule of law requirements for criminalisation, which fall within the scope of constitutional criminal law, also apply to the declaration of a regulatory offence. In Decision Homelessness, the HCC held that this practice should be followed even after the entry into force of the FL and the Regulatory Offences Act. This was confirmed by the fact that the normative constitutional standards, namely the principle of the rule of law and the guarantees of the restriction of fundamental rights, are regulated by the FL with the same content as the Constitution, so there is no obstacle to referring and applying the previous principles.

The HCC drew attention to the fact that the Regulatory Offences Act fundamentally changed the function and place of the institution of regulatory offence in the legal system: compared to the previous code, it took a significant step towards the development of bagatelle criminal law, after the Regulatory Offences Act in its preamble described the regulatory offence as a crime, i.e. as a criminal offence.[3] All this only makes the enforcement of the constitutional guarantees applicable in the case of criminal law interventions even more justified. Decision Homelessness emphasized that, as in the case of criminalization, the legislature should not act arbitrarily in classifying an act as a regulatory offence, but—in accordance with the case law of the ECtHR on the imposition of sanctions—should strictly comply with the constitutional requirements of clarity and the necessary and proportionate restriction of fundamental rights (Reasoning [46]). According to the HCC, a constitutional requirement against all kinds of punishable act is to make clear the legislative will on the protected legal interest and conduct.

3.2. *By declaring the use of public areas for permanent living to be a regulatory offence, without a legitimate aim, the legislator criminalized a forced life situation threatening a serious crisis, essentially homelessness itself, which is incompatible with the guarantees related to the restriction of fundamental rights and human dignity [Articles B (1), I (3), and II of the FL].*

In Decision Homelessness, the HCC argued that neither the legitimate aim, the reason, nor the legal object intended to be protected by the legislator could be clearly established as a restriction of fundamental rights in connection with the criminalisation of homelessness. (Reasoning [49]). According to the HCC, the examined provision of the Regulatory Offences Act classified a life situation, living on the street, and the existence of homelessness itself as punishable. In its decision, the HCC also pointed out that this is, moreover, an extremely serious, forced crisis situation for

---

3 See Ambrus, 'A szabálysértési jog néhány aktuális kérdése – büntetőjogászi szemmel' (2014), 30. See also Hollán, 'A büntetőjogra vonatkozó alkotmányos garanciák és a szabálysértési jog' (2016), 65.

those affected, which is only rarely the result of a conscious, well-thought-out, free choice (Reasoning [50]).

The HCC was concerned that neither the regulation of the law nor its justification could be used to establish the reason for declaring homelessness—which is a life situation otherwise included in social benefits—to be criminal conduct. Although the protection of public order could arise as an issue in this context, according to the HCC, the connection here is too indirect: neither the proper use of public areas, nor public order is endangered by the fact that people live their lives in public areas. In this regard, the decision points out that the law in force at that time provided the possibility of penalizing genuinely unlawful conduct which may actually or directly infringe the rights of others, or cause public order issues related to using public areas (e.g. breaches of the peace, breaches of public cleanliness, alcohol consumption, violations of public morality). Homelessness does not provide an excuse in connection with these; a homeless person—like everyone else—can be punished if he or she commits the above or similar acts that endanger public order in a public area. However, purely preventive intervention—related to the presumption that living in a public area may involve the mere possibility of violating the rights of others and public order—cannot be considered a legitimate ground for criminalisation. Similarly, according to the HCC, the legitimate aim of the sanction is not to remove the homeless from public areas or to encourage them to use social benefits.

Consequently, the HCC stated that 'it is incompatible with the protection of human dignity regulated in Article II of the FL to classify as dangerous to society and punish those who have lost their home for some reason and therefore live in a public area out of compulsion, but do not violate the rights of others or cause other illegal acts' (Reasoning [53]).

The reasoning of Decision Homelessness also contained an important and much-quoted statement when, in response to the arguments set out in the motion, it pointed out that sanctioning homelessness as a social problem was not an appropriate tool, because those people who are affected cannot afford their housing in the absence of income and are therefore unable to pay the fine.

3.3. *Regulatory Offences Act does not meet the requirement of the 'clarity of norms' as an increased requirement against the norms establishing the punishment, if the act creates, in essence, practically objective responsibility independent of the subject side [Article B (1) of the FL].*

On the basis of the petition, the HCC also examined whether the wording of the contested provision of the Regulatory Offences Act complied with the requirement of 'legal clarity'. In the reasoning, the HCC pointed out that, according to the definition of the Regulatory Offences Act, the regulatory offence may be a harmful activity or a passive neglect of a social responsibility. The HCC concluded that the examined regulatory offence could not be included in the legal concept of regulatory offence: the conduct indicated does not in itself violate or endanger the state, the social or economic order of Hungary, nor the person and the rights of natural and legal persons. In their view, it is therefore not possible for law enforcement bodies to determine when living on a public ground is an act dangerous to society which justifies the imposition of a penalty for a regulatory offence (Reasoning [55]).

In Decision Homelessness, the HCC also emphasised that while liability for a regulatory offence is a subjective form of liability, the investigated Regulatory Offences Act orders the punishment of a life situation existing as an objective fact, thus essentially creating objective liability. It also pointed out that the principle of the 'clarity of norms' is violated in other ways, as the definition of the conduct is not clear either, so the meaning of the terms 'long-term living' and 'within a public area' cannot be determined (Reasoning [57]–[58]). All this leads to the fact that it is not clear to individuals concerned what the specific conduct is through which they are committing a regulatory offence, which implies the possibility of the arbitrary interpretation of the law. From the point of view of the rule of law, it is also uncertain whether the possible exemption from liability for a regulatory offence depends on an external, elusive factor, namely whether the municipalities fulfil their social welfare obligations in the municipal area. Thus, the HCC also established the unconstitutionality of the investigated Regulatory Offences Act on the basis of the violation of the principle of the 'clarity of norms'.

3.4. *The authorization given to the local authority to create sanctions (fines) meets the requirement of the rule of law only with the substantive legal guarantees and clear framework prescribed by law, and excludes the possibility of arbitrary regulation [Article B (1) of the FL].*

The HCC also examined the disputed enabling provisions of the Local Governments Act in the light of the requirements arising from the rule of law. The HCC found that the Local Governments Act empowered local governments without defining the legislative competence and scope —i.e. without sufficient guarantees—to prohibit and sanction conduct that would not otherwise be considered illegal. Referring to the requirement of the 'clarity of norms', the HCC came to the conclusion that 'anti-social conduct' and 'apparently anti-social conduct' used by the empowering provisions of the Local Governments Act are indefinite legal concepts that give local authorities an extremely wide discretionary power. The HCC was concerned about this form of empowerment, which allows the municipality to exercise public power arbitrarily, without the interests of the community being genuinely prejudiced, and to intervene in the lives of citizens living in its territory by coercive means (Reasoning [83]).

According to the HCC, the risk of the abuse of legislative power is also increased by the fact that fines create an economic interest for local authorities, since they increase their revenue in this way. The decision also pointed out the constitutional context that, in principle, local public affairs do not include the imposition of a sanction for an unlawful conduct which can also be enforced through state coercion.[4] Thus, the provision of this type of sanctioning option only fulfils the requirement of the rule of law with the substantive legal guarantees and clear authorization provided by law. In the present case, however, according to Decision Homelessness, the legal framework was incomplete and insufficient. On the basis of all this, the HCC, based on the violation of the principle of the rule of law, found that the empowering provisions of the Local Governments Act were unconstitutional.

4 Cf. Gellér, Ambrus, and Vaskuti: 'A magyar büntetőjog általános tanai II.' (2019), 20.

4. Doctrinal analysis

4.1. Rule of law requirements for constitutional law of regulatory offences

The reasoning of Decision Homelessness focused on the standards of constitutional criminal law, the requirements of the rule of law and the purpose and manner of the restriction of fundamental rights. It is remarkable how the HCC transferred principles developed under the Constitution in connection with the guarantees of the rule of law under the FL, and indicated its compliance with European fundamental rights standards.

In connection with the critical analysis, it cannot be separated from the fact that after the decision, the Parliament 'responded' to the reasoning of the decision by adopting the fourth amendment to the FL. Thus, with regard to the sanctionability of homelessness, the first criticisms from specialists focused more on the parliamentary reaction to the constitutional amendment and the new regulatory offence (the process) than on the content and reasoning of the decision to be 'overwritten'. Thus, the alternative positions expressed in the dissenting opinions attached to the decision may be relevant and interesting mainly from the point of view of legal dogmatics.

4.2. Fundamental issues of sanctioning the use of public areas for long-term living

The decision is narrowly based on the dogmatic argument of fundamental rights, the elaboration of the content elements of the right to human dignity, and the emphasis on preventive intervention. The HCC did not emphasize the specifics of the vulnerable situation of the homeless as members of a vulnerable group. However, the concise clauses and message of the decision are forward-looking: the sanctioning of living on public ground is the same as the sanctioning of homelessness, from the point of view of fundamental rights it is not permissible to force the use of assistance. Following the reasoning of the decision, it is not acceptable to restrict the rights of the homeless 'in their own interest', nor can the social need to act due to their disturbing presence be identified with the protection of public order.

Two characteristic trends in the criticisms of the decision can be distinguished, which have been echoed in the dissenting opinions and in the subsequent 'responses' of the legislator.

The first critical position recognizes that the threat of an infringement fine may be pointless, but argues that after the regulatory offence and the empowerment of the Local Governments Act, local authorities become ineffective when long-living in public areas is a real threat to human life, health, environmental protection and the security of property. In the interests of public order, local authorities should be empowered to determine those public areas where long-term living is illegal and prohibited.[5] In this argument, the lack of legal instruments is also debatable from the outset, but it is also problematic from a dogmatic point of view. It concretizes the purpose of public intervention, but still speaks of a danger-based preventive restriction: it automatically presumes that in some public areas, long-term living necessarily leads to an activity contrary to public order.

The second critical position challenges the findings of the decision on a principled basis: in its view, the premiss that homelessness and living in a public area are the same is unfounded. Homelessness does not reasonably lead to long-term living in a public area, so there is no sanctioning of an objective life situation. Coercion is not a concern, nor can human dignity be violated by a regulation that requires the use of means that allow for more dignified living conditions.[6]

However, the concept of human dignity[7] presented in the second critical position is incompatible with the system of criteria developed in the previous practice of the HCC. Especially not by the fact that the person—in this case the homeless person—is not merely the object of law, but the subject of it. The 'end sanctifies the means' argument feels as if dignity in the majority reasoning is equivalent to the 'right to freeze on the street', and forcing homeless people to use the care system,—even through sanctions—would be a compensatory measure. However, this argument is more than unwarranted paternalism, it does not take into account the perspectives of homeless people, but suggests that it is their individual decision, i.e. that this lifestyle—which is unworthy of human dignity—is ultimately their own fault, and can only be deterred by the threat of sanctions.[8] 'Persuading' people to use a social benefit or service through the threat of coercion or sanction implies a fundamental contradiction: the client has to realize by him/herself that he or she needs help, because without a real voluntary personal decision, these services will not work.

5 See dissenting opinions of Judge Egon Dienes-Oehm, Reasoning [103]–[106].

6 See dissenting opinion of Judge Mária Szívós, Reasoning [111]–[113].

7 See Zakariás, *Az emberi méltósághoz való alapjog* (2019)

8 See Gács, 'Lakhatás helyett börtön. A hajléktalanság kriminalizációjának alkotmányossági problémái' (2014), 22 (26).

Such interventions require a very strong constitutional justification, which is not the case with homeless people living in public areas.

4.3. The principle of the 'clarity of norms' and the question of strict liability

The opinion of the HCC regarding the lack of the 'clarity of norms' can be justified, as any argument mentioned by it can in itself justify the violation of the principle of *nullum crimen sine lege certa*. Indeed, the term 'within a public area' cannot be interpreted, nor is the term 'long-term living' sufficiently defined. Concerns may be raised about the possibility of being exempted from liability for a regulatory offence, as this provision makes the existence of a regulatory offence conditional on a fact (the performance or lack of performance of the social responsibilities of the local authorities) of which the offender is typically unaware.

At the same time, the argument of the HCC in which it states that the act does not violate or endanger the state order of Hungary or the person and rights of persons, is questionable, since this opinion would imply that the law enforcer cannot establish the existence of a social danger. According to the prevailing Hungarian criminal law literature, social danger means the violation or endangering of legal objects. And legal objects are the highly abstracted interests that the legislature defines as dangerous to society. Detecting them is a legislative competence in the same way as creating legal facts. Thus, no one disputes the danger to society of, for example, drink-driving as a result of which no one is injured or actually endangered, nor bribery where no unlawful advantage is passed on at all, only the promise that it will be.

The reasoning of the HCC regarding a crime committed intentionally or by negligence of an act is not without problems either. In Hungarian criminal law, the establishment of a possible intention cannot be ruled out if the realisation of the material side of the crime can be blamed on the perpetrator. Thus, for example, the perpetrator is liable for failure to pay maintenance even if he or she is unable to pay maintenance because, for example, he or she has been dismissed from work for misconduct, and thus his or her insolvency is due to his or her own fault. By analogy, an intentional perpetration cannot necessarily be ruled out in the context of the acts under investigation, since it is not uncommon for the life situation in question to have arisen as a result of the perpetrator's previous conduct or for the perpetrator to have at least acquiesced in it. Contrary to the reasoning of the HCC, on a purely criminal dogmatic basis, the possible intention can be established in such a case, and there is no question that objective liability can be established.

4.4. The basic conditions of the rule of law in the creation of local authority sanctions

In a state governed by the rule of law, the power to create administrative and regulatory offence sanctions at the local authority level can only be constitutional within a legal framework as a guarantee that excludes arbitrary solutions as far as possible. The question is where and in what way these guarantees should be established in order to prevent local authorities from criminalising conduct when criminalisation would violate the fundamental rights of members of the community.

Based on the principles of the rule of law, Decision Homelessness argued for a stricter and more preventive guarantee system and found the provisions of the Local Governments Act to be unconstitutional. The HCC pointed out that local authorities were empowered to impose local sanctions on anti-social and apparently anti-social conduct on the basis of indefinite legal concepts, without the legislator regulating the scope of competence and its framework. In other words, from the outset, from the content-normative point of view, the possibility of arbitrary legislation must be prevented.

According to another, less strict viewpoint, if the procedure itself has a satisfactory general legal framework the guarantees of the rule of law can be properly enforced in connection with this type of sanctioning by reactive, posterior control by the HCC. The legal concepts underlying the creation of sanctions, in this case 'anti-social conduct' and 'apparently anti-social conduct', do not require a more thorough definition of the legal content if there is an unbroken and clear explanatory case law.[9]

The minimums related to rule of law are the review of the unlawful municipal decree and the decision based on it, and the existence of essential procedural rules. However, among the constitutional guarantees of the legislation, the basic requirement is to define the subject and framework of the empowerment. Declaring an act illegal and sanctioning it is, as a general rule, a matter of law. And if this is done in lower-level legislation, then the exact nature of the delegation is crucial. In the present case, it cannot be ignored that, albeit in an unspoken way, the erroneous regula-

9 See dissenting opinions of Judge Mária Szívós, Reasoning [118]–[121].

tory offence facts have been replaced by the prohibited, anti-social conduct of the municipal decrees, and in fact, in this construction, the possibility of revenue from fines enhances the problem. In addition, the lack of a sufficient legal framework and definition is also problematic in relation to control: the lack of standards can worsen the strength and efficiency of judicial review of municipal decrees.

5. *Aftermath of the Decision*

The decision did not lead to a correction of the legal regulations, but to a transformation of the previous constitutional standard. The fourth amendment to the FL made it possible to criminalize homelessness under certain conditions. Under the new paragraph 3 of Article XXII of the FL, a law or a decree of a local authority may, in order to protect public order, public safety, public health and cultural values, declare a long-lasting public residence illegal for a certain part of the public area. With this constitutional authorization, the legislature has created an opportunity for local authorities to designate in a decree, following these objectives, the zones where long-term living in public areas is prohibited and thus punishable.

The fourth amendment to the FL, including the element related to homelessness and the prohibition and criminalization of living in a public area, was also debated at both domestic and international levels. The objections of the Venice Commission included—among other things—that such a restriction should be regulated by law, and that raising it to the constitutional level is problematic, because in this way the restriction is removed from the constitutional review and turns into the standard itself.[10]

At the same time, the consistent legal practice of the Supreme Court (Kúria)—which was based on the motions of the Commissioner for Fundamental Rights—prevented certain local authority efforts which, based on the provisions of the FL and the Regulatory Offence Act, sought to extend the prohibition. The Curia made it clear that the statutory rule authorizing long-term living in a public area must be interpreted strictly. It can only be prohibited in well-defined areas where the values to be protected—public

10 See CDL-AD(2013)012-e Opinion on the Fourth Amendment to the Fundamental Law of Hungary Adopted by the Venice Commission at its 95th Plenary Session, Venice, 14–15 June 2013.

order, public safety, public health, cultural values—require explicit, factually verifiable enforcement.[11]

On 1 January 2013, a new Section 8 of the Local Governments Act entered into force, which, like the previous rule on prohibited, anti-social conduct, did not give a definition of the basic rules of community coexistence, but left their definition to local authorities. Pursuant to Article 8 (2) of the Local Governments Act, the representative body of the local authority may determine the content of the basic rules of community coexistence and the legal consequences of the failure to comply with the rules. In connection with the new legal provisions, citing the violation of the rule of law, the Commissioner for Fundamental Rights and the Kúria appealed to the HCC. The HCC rejected the motions in Decision 29/2015. (X. 2.) AB.

From 15 October 2018, the seventh amendment to the FL rewrote Article XXII (3) of the FL and provided, in general terms, without any further conditions or restrictions, that residence in a public area was prohibited. As a result, Article 178/B of the Regulatory Offences Act was added in such a way that whoever lives for a long period in a public area commits an offence. It is only possible to refrain from initiating regulatory offence proceedings or to use an on-site warning under certain conditions. The constitutional amendment thus puts a whole new basis for the criminalization of long-term living in a public area. In its Decision 19/2019. (VI. 18.) AB,[12] the HCC ruled on the basis of the motions filed against this solution of Regulatory Offences Act, and the redefinition and tightening of the facts, and rejected them, also in the light of the seventh amendment to the FL. The provisions of Decision Homelessness cannot be considered authoritative in the current constitutional environment, but the significance of their specialist and dogmatic reasoning is indisputable and lasting.[13]

---

11 See the judgment of the Kúria Köf.5020/2014/6, Reasoning [22].

12 See this decision in english here: https://bit.ly/3otayum

13 See Lápossy, Burján, and Ambrus, 'Alkotmányos tilalmon alapuló szankcionálás és az alapjogvédelmi mércék konfliktusa' (2020), 5.

Bibliography

István Ambrus, 'A szabálysértési jog néhány aktuális kérdése – büntetőjogászi szemmel' [The Constitutional Guarantees Concerning the Penal Law and the Regulatory Offence Right Hungarian Law Enforcement] (2014) 4 *Közjogi Szemle*, 30.

Miklós Hollán, 'A büntetőjogra vonatkozó alkotmányos garanciák és a szabálysértési jog' [Some Current Issues of Regulatory Offence Law – The Criminal Lawyer's Perspective] (2016) 3 *Magyar Rendészet*, 65.

Katalin Gács, 'Lakhatás helyett börtön. A hajléktalanság kriminalizációjának alkotmányossági problémái' [Prison instead of housing. Constitutional Problems in the Criminalization of Homelessness] 2014 (3) *Fundamentum*. 22.

Balázs Gellér, István Ambrus, and András Vaskuti, *A magyar büntetőjog általános tanai II. A büntetőjogi jogkövetkezmények tana* [General Doctrines of Hungarian Criminal Law II. Doctrine of the Consequences of Criminal Law] (ELTE Eötvös, Budapest 2019)

Attila Lápossy and Katalin Szajbély, 'Korlátozott terek. Szociális jogok az érdemesség és a kriminalizáció árnyékában' [Limited Spaces – Social Rights in the Shadow of Worthiness and Criminalization] (2014) 3 *Fundamentum*, 52.

Attila Lápossy, Evelin Burján and István Ambrus, 'Alkotmányos tilalmon alapuló szankcionálás és az alapjogvédelmi mércék konfliktusa. Az Alkotmánybíróság határozata a közterület életvitelszerű használatának szankcionálásáról' [Conflict Between Sanctioning Based on Constitutional Prohibition and Standards of Protection of Fundamental Rights. Decision of the HCC on Aanctioning Long-term Living in a Public Area] (2020) 4 *Jogesetek Magyarázata*, 5.

Don Mitchell, *The Right to the City. Social Justice and the Fight for Public Space* (Guilford Press, New York 2003)

Kinga Zakariás, *Az emberi méltósághoz való alapjog. Összehasonlító jogi elemzés a német és magyar alkotmánybírósági gyakorlat tükrében* [Fundamental Right to Human Dignity. Comparative Legal Analysis in the Light of German and Hungarian Constitutional Court Practice] (Pázmány Press, Budapest 2019)

12. Decision 45/2012. (XII. 29.) AB – Transitory Provisions

Tímea Drinóczi[*]

The Transitory Provisions are not part of the FL, nor do they constitute constitutional amendments; therefore, they are unconstitutional because they represent a source of law of an uncertain nature and deprive the HCC of its review powers.

The importance of Decision Transitory Provisions[1] is manifold. Firstly, in the Decision, the HCC establishes that the TP are neither part of the FL nor constitute a constitutional amendment, but, as a 'source of law of an uncertain nature', they are capable of continuously depriving the HCC of its review powers. Secondly, it defines certain constitutional requirements (*alkotmányos követelmény*)[2] which a constitutional amendment needs to meet: the 'rule of incorporation', the requirement of 'coherency in content and structure', and that any legislative authorization must indicate the source of law in which the authorized content appears. Thirdly, it requires compliance from both the constitution-making and constitution-amending powers, i.e., following its previous case-law, the HCC does not distinguish between original and derived powers. The HCC also maintains its previous practice: it does not have the power to review a text that has already become the part of the constitution and the constitutional amendments, except in the case of invalidity under public law (*közjogi érvénytelenség*).[3] Finally, by setting these constitutional requirements and following its self-interpretation, as the main body for protecting the constitution, the HCC implicitly predicted that, if a future amendment did not meet the requirements, it could indeed review it.

---

* DSc, Visiting professor, Federal University of Minas Gerais (Brazil).

1 The Decision is available in English: https://bit.ly/3D8l12z

2 Determining constitutional requirements is one of the powers of the HCC under HCC Act (for the competences of the HCC, see the Introduction in this volume).

3 Invalidity under public law (*közjogi érvénytelenség*) describes a situation in which a piece of legislation has not been adopted by the competent authority, voted for by the described parliamentary majority, and published, and violates legal hierarchy.

1. Background

1.1. The previous practice of the HCC

Decision Transitory Provisions is based on the HCC's previous case law, including Decision 61/2011. (VII. 13.) AB on the constitutional review of the amendment to the FL.

The essence of the previous practice is that the HCC does not have the power to annul or review[4] provisions of the constitution, propose that the legislator supplement the current constitution by establishing a constitutional omission by legislation, or resolve a perceived or real contradiction within the constitution. Should the HCC act in this way, this body, which has been created for the protection of the constitution, would take over the constitution-making power and, in the course of the review, would not only interpret the provisions of the constitution but would necessarily determine/create them.[5] Furthermore, the HCC cannot annul any provision of the constitution, because once it has been incorporated into its text by the two-thirds majority of the Members of Parliament, it has already become the part of the constitution, which makes it impossible to declare it to be unconstitutional in any way.[6]

The HCC has developed this argument because the Constitution, similarly to the text of the originally adopted FL (prior to the Fourth Amendment) was silent about the possibility of reviewing constitutional amendments, nor did it contain eternity clauses. The importance of the eternity clauses is that their alleged violation could establish a basis for the substantive review and annulment of a particular constitutional amendment. In this case, the original constitution-making power, which establishes the constitution, is visibly separated from the derivative constitution-amending power. This distinction, however, had not developed in the HCC's ju-

4 Decisions 293/B/1994 AB and 23/1994. (IV. 29.) AB.

5 Decision 1260/B/1997 AB, ABH 816, 819.

6 Decision 293/B/1994 AB, ABH 1994, 862.

risprudence due to the Hungarian constitutional design until the Seventh Amendment (2018)[7] and constitutional politics until 2010.[8]

Decision 61/2011. (VII. 13.) AB went beyond the previous practice as it allowed the review of the Constitution and constitutional amendments. The petitioner of this case challenged the validity (közjogi érvénytelenség) of a constitutional amendment adopted in the autumn of 2010 (after the parliamentary election of spring 2010).

1.2. Legal background

On 30 December 2011, the Parliament adopted the TP, which were published on 31 December 2011[9] and entered into force on 1 January 2012. The TP contained, among others, Decision Transitory Provisions, which the Parliament adopted as a constitution-making power, on the basis of the authorization of Point 3 of the Final Provision to the FL. The text of the Final Provision to the FL in force at the time was as follows: '1. The Fundamental Law of Hungary enters into force on 1 January 2012. 2. This Fundamental Law shall be adopted by the Parliament in accordance with Articles 19 (3) (a) and 24 (3) of Act XX of 1949. 3. The transitory provisions attached to this Fundamental Law shall be adopted separately by the Parliament in the procedure referred to in point 2.'

Articles 19 (3) (a) and 24 (3) of the Constitution provided as follows: Article 19 (3) read as follows '[i]n its power, the Parliament (a) establishes the Constitution of the Republic of Hungary', while Article 24 (3) stated that '[t]o change the Constitution and to take certain decisions laid down in the Constitution, the votes of a two-thirds majority of the Members of Parliament are needed.'

According to the explanatory memorandum to the TP, the Parliament adopted them in accordance with the FL and the procedure laid down

7 Seventh Amendment introduced into the FL the concept of constitutional identity, which can be perceived as an eternity clause. The practical consequence of this, given the unchanged constitutional majority from 2010 to 2021, has not yet been seen.

8 Albert, *Constitutional Amendments: Making, Breaking, and Changing Constitutions* (2019); Roznai, *Unconstitutional Constitutional Amendments: The Limits of Amendment Powers* (2017)

9 The legal background and the points of presentation of the motion are based on the following article: Szente, 'Az Alkotmánybíróság döntése Magyarország Alaptörvényének Átmeneti rendelkezései alkotmányosságáról', (2013), 11.

in the previous Constitution for the adoption of the new constitution and constitutional amendments. The explanatory memorandum, referring to the actual text of the TP, explains that the TP form part of the FL and consist of two main parts: the first deals with the 'transition from a Communist dictatorship to democracy', and the second contains rules of a legal-technical nature about the usual transitory provisions relating to the entry into force of the FL.

2. *Petition*

In his submission to the HCC dated 13 March 2012, the Commissioner for Fundamental Rights (Ombudsman), Máté Szabó, requested the HCC to annul the TP in its ex-post constitutional review process. It also invited the HCC to annul only its specific provisions if it did not see an opportunity to annul the entire TP.

Following the submission of this motion, and, perhaps as a consequence of it,[10] Parliament adopted the First Amendment to the FL in 18 June 2012 and added a new Point 5 to its Final Provisions. As a result, this provision read as follows: '1 The Fundamental Law of Hungary enters into force on 1 January 2012. 2. This Fundamental Law shall be adopted by the Parliament in accordance with Articles 19 (3) (a) and 24 (3) of Act XX of 1949. 3. The Transitory provisions relating to this Fundamental Law shall be adopted separately by the Parliament in the procedure referred to in point 2. […] 5. The Transitory provisions to the Fundamental Law Hungary (31 December 2011) adopted pursuant to Point 3 are part of the Fundamental Law.'

The Ombudsman requested the annulment of the entire TP, or, if this was not possible, its certain provisions. He claimed that the TP were contrary to Article B (1) (the rule of law and the requirement of legal certainty) and Article S) FL (on the constitutional amendment rules). He argued that the TP had not become a part of the FL, despite the specific self-definition declaring the TP to be so, and cannot be regarded as its amendment either. Consequently, the HCC has the power to conduct a constitutional review, as it would be fully consistent with its practice.

---

10 Szente, 'Az Alkotmánybíróság döntése Magyarország Alaptörvényének Átmeneti rendelkezései alkotmányosságáról' (2013), 11; Drinóczi, 'Constitutional politics in contemporary Hungary' (2016), 63.

In the light of the new situation created by the First Amendment to the FL, the HCC invited the petitioner to make a statement, and he amended and supplemented his original petition in light of the changes. Although his original motion stated that the TP would have constituted a part of the FL if the FL had declared that the TP had been one of its parts, he maintained his motion even after the fulfillment of this condition.

3. *Decision and its reasoning*

The HCC established that several provisions of the FL are unconstitutional; therefore, it annulled them with a retroactive force as to the date of their promulgation, from 31 December 2011, and from 9 November 2012 with regard to certain paragraphs [Article 23 (3)–(5)].

First, it declared the part on the transition from communist dictatorship to democracy (preamble) unconstitutional.[11] Second, the following other provisions have been deemed to be unconstitutional: Articles 1–4,[12] 11 (3)

---

11 This first part makes the Hungarian Socialist Party liable for the sins of the communist dictatorship as the legal successor of the Hungarian Socialist Workers' Party.

12 The reduction of pensions and other payments to leaders of the communist dictatorship determined by Act; making the period of statutory limitation recommence for crimes related to communist dictatorship and have not been prosecuted due to political reasons, creation of a National Memorial Committee to preserve the memory of the communist dictatorship, restriction of privacy of the 'the holders of power under the communist dictatorship'.

(4),[13] 12 and 13,[14] 18,[15] 21,[16] 22,[17] 23 (1) and (3)–(5),[18] 27,[19] 28 (3),[20] 29,[21] 31 (2),[22] and 32.[23]

3.1. *The TP cannot be classified as any source of law in the Hungarian legal system. The TP act as a 'slide' capable of continuously depriving the HCC of its review powers [Articles R (1) and T) of the FL].*

The TP and the accompanying explanatory memorandum underline that Parliament adopted the TP as a constitution-making power. They, however, cannot declare themselves as a part of the FL, as the FL declares itself as a unified document. Moreover, they are not only in conflict with the unity of the constitution but also the principle of the coherence of the FL (Reasoning [71]).

Using the TP, as a 'slide', gives the opportunity for the lawmaker to provide constitutional protection to provisions that are not part of the unified and coherent FL. The lawmaker considers the TP as an endless possibility to widen the range of these kinds of provisions and narrow the review power of the HCC. Creating 'slide-laws' similar to the Transito-

13 The power of the President of the National Judicial Office and the Prosecutor General to assign a court and bring cases, respectively, outside the general territorial jurisdiction determined by law to proceed in any case; the prosecutor general or the competent prosecutor can make accusation in a court outside the general territorial jurisdiction determined by law This power of the Prosecutor General, by the way, contradicted Decision 1149/C/2011 AB.

14 The retirement age of judges and prosecutors.

15 The rule that the member of the Budget Council in office appointed by the President of the Republic becomes the President of the Budget Council.

16 Rules on churches.

17 Rules on constitutional complaint.

18 Rules on general election.

19 Restriction of the review competence of the HCC.

20 Rules on local governments (failure to act).

21 Rule on the fact that there is no state obligation to comply with deriving from a decision of the HCC, the CJEU or any other court or an organ as long as the state debt exceeds half of the Gross Domestic Product.

22 '(2) The Parliament shall adopt the Transitional Provisions under Article 19 para. (3) item a) and Article 24 para. (3) of Act XX of 1949 on the Constitution of the Republic of Hungary, in accordance with point 3 of the Closing Provisions of the Fundamental Law of Hungary. The Transitional Provisions shall form part of the Fundamental Law.'

23 Declaration of the Day of the FL.

ry Provisions and thereby generating endless constitutional debates and questioning the constitutional legality of the legal system is not allowed (Reasoning [111]).

3.2. *Transitory provisions cannot be regarded as amendments to the FL [Articles B) (1) and S) of the FL].*

The FL can only be amended under Article S). The TP were adopted on the basis of an authorization to adopt transitory provisions and not to adopt a constitutional amendment (Justification [68]). This is why the HCC has jurisdiction to review the formal constitutionality of TP (Justification [88]).

3.3. *It is a requirement stemming from the rule of law that the scope and content of the FL in force can be clearly found at any time. The amendments must be incorporated into the constitutional text (rule of incorporation) [Articles B) (1) and S) of the FL].*

The constitution-making power may only insert constitutionally important subject matter into the text of the FL. Amendments to the FL must be incorporated in a coherent way into its structural order and should not result in irresolvable contradictions in the FL. The coherence of content and structure is a rule of law requirement arising from Article B (1) of the FL, which the constitution-making power must ensure (Justification [86]).

3.4. *The legislature included non-transitory rules in the Transitory Provisions, thus exceeding the scope of the authorization granted by the FL [Articles B (1) and S) of the FL].*

The authorization to legislate shall include the holder, subject matter, and framework of the mandate. Exceeding the power given results in unconstitutionality; rules of the Transitory Provisions exceeding the mandate to adopt transitory-type provisions are therefore invalid under public law (Reasoning [107]).

Regardless of the content of the ombudsman's motion, the HCC examined all other provisions of the TP to declare their transitory nature. If a law had provisions valid under public law and others invalid under public law, the requirement of legal certainty would be violated if the parts that are invalid under public law were not annulled because there was no motion requesting their annulment. Provisions that are transitory/temporary in nature and relate to the entry into force of the FL, are of a legal-technical nature, traditionally considered temporary, or aim to avoid disputes of legal interpretation. The transitory/temporary nature of pieces of legislation must be interpreted narrowly (Reasoning [130]).

4. *Doctrinal analysis*

4.1. *The TP to the FL cannot be regarded as part of the FL*

The assessment of the Decision Transitory Provisions can be found in the concurrent and dissenting opinions attached to the Decision, the literature on this Decision, and unconstitutional constitutional amendments and constitutional powers to review them. There seems to be a consensus that the TP were adopted by the constitution-making power and are not a constitutional amendment.

Views diverge about the TP's position in the legal source system, their nature, and the constitutional consequences this difference in opinion entails. However, one can also argue that Article S) and Point 5 are in contradiction. Therefore, it cannot be stated with certainty that the constitution-making power adopted the TP. Consequently, the HCC would not have the power to review it.

There are many interpretations concerning the relationship between the TP and the FL:[24] 1) the TP and the FL share 'one nature',[25] 2) the TP are an independent source of law with constitutional rank, 3) the TP are an independent source of law with constitutional rank and, together with the FL, constitute the 'constitution', 4) the TP, together with cardinal laws, 'double' the FL; 5) the TP do not have any 'rank' in terms of constitutional law. The HCC has embraced this latter (5) interpretation by declaring the TP to be a source of law of uncertain nature. At the same time, the basic

24 Views under points 1, 2, and 5 are summarized in Csink and Fröhlich, *Egy alkotmány margójára. Alkotmányelméleti és értelmezési kérdések az Alaptörvényről* (2012), 146.

25 This suggests that the TP are the actual textual part of the FL, but this view is generally rejected due to the existence of two separate documents.

precondition for exercising constitutional review is to establish whether there is a legal source that the HCC has the power to review.

The TP were created on the basis of Point 5, and cannot be classified as a constitutional amendment, nor as a law. If a 'special' legal norm or a legal source of an uncertain legal status exists, this cannot be interpreted within the framework of Article T) of the FL, i.e., it is not a law, and therefore the HCC cannot examine it. It can similarly be deduced that the HCC has created a new type of source of law in Article T), namely the TP.[26] If we accept this position, we must also admit that HCC has made an informal constitutional amendment by naming the TP as an 'open door', 'slide-law' or a law 'withering away the powers of the Constitutional Court'.[27]

The 'one nature-ness' of the FL and the TP indicates that the TP are part of the FL. However, due to the existence of two documents, this view is generally rejected, except in some dissenting opinions, which state that the TP are 'arguably' part of the FL, especially since its First Amendment.[28]

The TP appear as an independent source of law with constitutional rank in other dissenting opinions that accuse the HCC of overstepping its powers. According to these opinions, the most the HCC could have done was to indicate the existence of the problem; it was up to the constitution-making power to resolve it.[29]

Others held[30] that both documents, i.e., the FL and the TP, were created by the constitution-making power (original power), which is, in theory, a power that cannot be constrained by legal means. This argument is based on the text of the FL, its First Amendment, the circumstances of the adoption of the TP, its structure, and the content of some of its rules supplementing some provisions in the FL.[31] Consequently, in a formal

26 Erdős, 'Kritikai megjegyzések az Alaptörvény jogszabály-fogalmával kapcsolatban' in Szoboszlai, Kiss, and Deli (eds), *Tanulmányok a 70 éves Bihari Mihály tiszteletére* (2013), 134 (137).

27 Drinóczi, *Informális alkotmánymódosítás alkotmányértelmezéssel. Az alkotmánybíráskodás és a kormányzás összehasonlító és alkotmánytani elemzése* (2020).

28 Dissenting opinion of Judges Egon Dienes-Oehm and Barnabás Lenkovics.

29 Concurring opinion of Judges Péter Szalay and Mária Szívós.

30 Drinóczi, 'Constitutional politics in contemporary Hungary' (2016), 63.

31 A significant part of these rules substantially degraded the content of the constitutional rules, i.e. it reduced the scope of protection of fundamental rights, made the operation of the system of institutions for the protection of fundamental rights more difficult, and so on. The FL—due to its specific, non-inclusive drafting and adoption, as well as its content (e.g., limiting the power of the HCC) —had already provoked significant criticism by 2012. The TP, in addition to

sense, Hungary had two 'constitutions', the combination of which, from a substantive point of view, meant the 'single/united Fundamental Law' (postambulum). As a result, the HCC would not have had jurisdiction to review the TP. This line of thinking links the legal analysis of Decision Transitory Provisions with the evaluation of the constitution-making process and the constitutional policy of the then two-thirds parliamentary majority.[32] As a result, it is claimed that with 'Decision 45/2012. (XII. 29.) AB, shows the effort of the majority of judges to become a real counterweight to political power; the crisis situation requiring a substantive review of unconstitutional constitutional amendments also seemed to be recognized by the HCC, but the reaction was too late, and the HCC's decision is not justified in essence from the perspective of constitutional law and constitutional theory. The right decision should have been taken by the HCC in 2011, based on the theoretical considerations indicated above. From then on, the HCC should have taken action against unconstitutional constitutional amendments. However, when assessing the conduct of the HCC, the constitution-making process cannot be ignored, nor can the danger posed by talks at that time suggesting that the new constitutional system would be constructed without the HCC. This possibility could have —by itself—been capable of leading to the self-restraint of the HCC. At the end of 2012, the HCC seemed to have »woken up« for a short time, giving its own opinion so that it could slip back into a state of inertia of its own choosing.'[33]

An assessment of Decision Transitory Provisions, which is free from an analysis of constitutional politics, views the possibilities of the HCC more broadly. According to this opinion, the HCC, first, could have set aside the TP. Then, it could have annulled the lower-level legislation based on the TP that was deemed contrary to the FL.[34] However, this would only have been a positive scenario if the TP was treated as an independent source of law with constitutional rank, i.e., within the meaning of Point 2).

---

such constitutional provisions, contained even more questionable rules, which, however, were in line with the content of the relevant articles of the FL.

32 From the point of view of reasoning, this is necessary because if we ignore the circumstances, it is not possible to obtain a clear picture of the practice of the HCC, especially between 2010 and 2015.

33 Drinóczi, 'Constitutional politics in contemporary Hungary' (2016), 63.

34 Csink and Fröhlich, *Egy alkotmány margójára. Alkotmányelméleti és értelmezési kérdések az Alaptörvényről* (2012), 154.

The FL can be seen as an open constitution from the bottom, from above, and from the side.[35] Openness from the side means that the TP and cardinal laws 'double' 'the constitution' and, perhaps, fills the 'available space' to an even greater extent than before [see Point 4) above].[36]

4.2. *Transitional Provisions cannot be considered as amendments to the FL*

Dissenting opinions argue that the HCC could not have annulled the TP based on the 'unity' of the FL, because the postambulum containing it had no normative power; it is merely 'a kind of ennobling constitutional self-reflection'. For example, while Article R (3) FL instructs that the preamble be applied during the interpretation of the FL, it does not attach such importance to the postambulum. Moreover, the 'rule of incorporation' does not follow from the term 'uniform'; the FL does not contain a warrant for incorporation in respect of constitutional amendments. If the constitution-making power had had such a purpose, it would have clearly expressed it. The 'uniformity' deduced from the postambulum of doubtful normative status cannot be contrasted with the 'clear, unambiguous and precise' rule in Point 5. The HCC simply ignored this provision while arbitrarily selecting from among other rules of the FL.[37]

Others argue that the word 'unified' in the postambulum should have been disregarded because the arbitrarily deduced 'rule of incorporation' is alien to the spirit and structure of the FL.[38]

4.3. *The 'coherency of substance and structure' of the FL is a requirement of the rule of law*

This rule of law requirement has been assessed in two contradictory ways.

One stressed the importance of the constitution's unity, closedness, and non-contradictory nature and stressed that the 'rule of incorporation' is a constitutional 'command' stemming from these principles. This, in turn, also imposes formal and substantive duties on the constitution-making power. Constitutional amendments must not result in an insoluble contra-

35 Rixer, *A magyar jogrendszer jellegzetességei 2010 után* (2012), 101.

36 Rixer, *A magyar jogrendszer jellegzetességei 2010 után* (2012), 102.

37 Dissenting opinion of Judge István Balsai.

38 Dissenting opinion of Judge Egon Dienes-Oehm.

diction in the coherent system of the FL because if this happens, the HCC would have to rule that it was unconstitutional. It would be justified, in particular, if the constitution-making power inserted a provision into the FL that the HCC had already declared unconstitutional. Extending the constitutional review in this direction could be a possible direction for constitutional development.[39]

However, on the basis of a different line of reasoning, the requirement of substantive and formal unity (the entire content of a constitution is recorded in a single document) and the requirement of coherency, logical closedness, and the internal non-contradictory nature of its provisions do not appear to be well justified. The reason for this is that comparative constitutional studies show that the written constitutions of many constitutional democracies are drafted not in a single document but in several separate ones. This drafting style threatens the uniform and non-contradictory nature of the FL only if there is an irreconcilable substantive-logical conflict between the parts of the constitution which appear in different texts.[40]

4.4. The rules of the TP exceeding the authorization are invalid under public law

Scholars have challenged the view that there is an authorizing-authorized relationship between the FL and its Final Provisions on the creation of the Transitory Provisions.

One opinion claims that the FL had not yet come into force when the TP were adopted. Therefore, no legal effect could have been attached to it.[41]

Others argue that the TP embody two different manifestations of the constitution-making power because the difference between the constitution-making and constitution-amending power cannot be deduced from the FL.[42] It is, thus, likely that the Final Provisions are a binding 'self-restraint' of the constitution-making power. 'The constitution-making power exceeded the procedural framework laid down in the Fundamental Law,

39 Concurring opinion of Judge István Stumpf.

40 Szente, 'Az Alkotmánybíróság döntése Magyarország Alaptörvényének Átmeneti rendelkezései alkotmányosságáról' (2013), 11; Drinóczi, 'Constitutional politics in contemporary Hungary' (2016), 17 f.

41 Dissenting opinion of Judge Mária Szívós.

42 Concurring opinion of Judge András Holló.

thereby violating the self-imposed procedural rules' in cases in which it did not create rules of a transitory nature but other subject matter that should have been adopted in the ordinary procedure for a constitutional amendment.

In this context, the so-called signalization power[43] as a tool of the HCC to protect the FL could play an important role if it could win academic support. It would mean that the HCC could draw the attention of the constitution-making power to possible contradictions and problems connected to the coherency in the text of the constitution and could even formulate certain requirements. For example, suppose the constitution-making power inserts a provision into the text that the HCC has previously declared unconstitutional. In that case, it will remain unconstitutional until the original text of the FL, based on which the HCC ruled the rule unconstitutional, is changed.

5. *Aftermath of the Decision*

'Since 2010, the Constitutional Court has consistently stressed the limitations of its powers in reviewing constitutional amendments, but in all its relevant decisions it has made far-reaching statements—obiter dictum—concerning the constitutional limitations of the constitution-making power, and, also, in order to emphasize its own competence and the importance of constitutional interpretation.'[44]

The formulation of the requirements for constitutional amendments, which bind both the constitution-making and amending power, and their implicit legal consequence, as expressly stated in the Decision, was hampered by the Fourth Amendment to the FL.[45] This explicitly established the powers of the HCC to formally review constitutional amendments, thus excluding the possibility of a substantive examination. The review of this Amendment was conducted in the Decision 12/2013. (V. 24.) AB.

43 Judge András Holló in Decision 61/2011 (VII. 13) AB summarizes his views on the signalizing power of the HCC. See also the concurring opinion of András Holló and the dissent of Barnabás Lenkovics on Decision Transitory Provisions.

44 Bragyova and Gárdos-Orosz, 'Vannak-e megváltoztathatatlan normák az Alaptörvényben? (2016), 58.

45 Opinion on the Fourth Amendment to the Fundamental Law of Hugary. Adopted by the Venice Commission at its 95th Plenary Session (Venice, 14–15 June 2013).

In Decision 12/2013. (V. 24.) AB, the HCC stated that in its constitutional review process, it would also take into account Hungary's obligations under international treaties, including those associated with EU membership, as well as the generally recognized rules of international law, and the fundamental principles and values which appear therein. All these rules constitute a single system (value system) which, particularly in the case of those values incorporated in the FL, cannot be disregarded, neither in the constitution-making nor in the legislative process, nor in the constitutional review conducted by the HCC.[46]

The new constitutional development appearing in this Decision, i.e., the substantive and formal limitation of the constitution-making and amending power, was interrupted by Decision 22/2016. (XII. 5.) AB on identity control (analysis of Decision Constitutional Self-identity of Hungary see in this volume).[47] This decision, followed by the Seventh Amendment to the FL,[48] ignored the previous commitment to European values and prioritized national sovereignty and its associated identity.

Bibliography

Richard Albert, *Constitutional Amendments: Making, Breaking, and Changing Constitutions* (Oxford University Press, 2019)

Lóránt Csink and Johanna Fröhlich, *Egy alkotmány margójára. Alkotmányelméleti és értelmezési kérdések az Alaptörvényről* [About the Fundamental Law: Questions of Constitutional Theory and Interpretation] (Gondolat: Budapest 2012)

András Bragyova and Fruzsina Gárdos-Orosz, 'Vannak-e megváltoztathatatlan normák az Alaptörvényben?' [Are there Immutable Standards in the Fundamental Law?] (2016) 3 *Állam- és Jogtudomány,* 35.

Tímea Drinóczi, 'Constitutional Politics in Contemporary Hungary' (2016) 1 *Vienna Journal on International Constitutional Law,* 63.

Tímea Drinóczi: *Informális alkotmánymódosítás alkotmányértelmezéssel. Az alkotmánybíráskodás és a kormányzás összehasonlító és alkotmánytani elemzése* [Informal Constitutional Amendment with Constitutional Interpretation: the Comparative and Theoretical Study to Constitutional Adjudication and Governence] (Ludovika: Budapest 2020)

46 Decision 12/2013. (V. 24.) AB, Reasoning [48].

47 For an analysis from a comparative perspective, see Drinóczi, 'Constitutional identity in Europe: the identity of the constitution. A regional approach' (2020), 105.

48 HCLU'S analysis of the Seventh Amendment of the Fundamental Law, https://bit.ly/2ZQmpbB

Csaba Erdős, 'Kritikai megjegyzések az Alaptörvény jogszabály-fogalmával kapcsolatban' [Critical Remarks on the Notion of Law in the Fundamental Law] in Katalin Szoboszlai-Kiss and Gergely Deli (eds), *Tanulmányok a 70 éves Bihari Mihály tiszteletére* [Studies in Honour of Mihály Bihari on His 70th Birthday] (Universitas-Győr: Győr 2013) 134.

Ádám Rixer, *A magyar jogrendszer jellegzetességei 2010 után* [Features of the Hungarian Legal System after 2010] (Patrocinium, Budapest 2012)

Yaniv Roznai, *Unconstitutional Constitutional Amendments: The Limits of Amendment Powers* (Oxford University Press, 2017)

Zoltán Szente, 'Az Alkotmánybíróság döntése Magyarország Alaptörvényének Átmeneti rendelkezései alkotmányosságáról. Az Alaptörvény integritása és az alkotmányozó hatalom korlátai: 45/2012. (XII. 29.) AB határozat' [Decision of the Constitutional Court on the Constitutionality of the Transitional Provisions to the Fundamental Law of Hungary: Integrity of the Fundamental Law and Limitations of Constitution-making Power: Decision 45/2012. (XII. 29.) AB] (2013) 2 *Jogesetek Magyarázata*, 11.

13. Decision 1/2013. (I. 7.) AB – Voter Registration*

*András László Pap*** – *Boldizsár Szentgáli-Tóth****

Registration as a general mandatory requirement of the exercise of the right to vote is an unnecessary and disproportionate restriction on the right to vote.

Following a referral by the head of state (a rare action), Decision Voter Registration invalidates legislation that restricts the right to vote by setting forth intricate registration requirements that create a burden for a certain group of voters. (The decision also strikes down restrictions on publishing survey results and other forms of political campaign in movie theatres and disparate regulations concerning public and private media outlets.) The main significance of the decision concerns the assessment of the institution of registration, where the HCC held that, in line with the case law of the ECtHR, requirements for prior registration are not inadmissible per se, but need to meet proportionality standards. (The decision also strengthened free political speech standards.)

1. Background

The following facts are important to understand Decision Voter Registration. In 2010 the FIDESZ–Christian Democratic coalition gained a two-

---

* This research is funded by project no. NKFIH 128397 of Hungarian National Research and Innovation Grants investigating investigating the normative content of the principle of democracy from EU- and constitutional law perspectives, and project no. 134962 of Hungarian National Research and Innovation Grants on operationalizing ethno-racial identity, and project no. NKFIH 134962 of Hungarian National Research and Innovation Grants on operationalizing ethno-racial identity.

** DSc, Research professor, Centre for Social Sciences Institute for Legal Studies (Budapest); Professor, Eötvös Loránd University and University of Public Service (Budapest).

*** PhD, Research fellow, Centre for Social Sciences Institute for Legal Studies (Budapest).

thirds majority in the parliamentary elections, allowing it to adopt a new constitution and amend laws requiring a qualified majority. Within a month, even prior to electing the new government, Parliament amended by Act XLIV of 2010 the Act LV of 1993 on Hungarian citizenship. Act XLIV of 2010 offering citizenship to persons who were previously citizens of Hungary, or whose ancestors were citizens of Hungary, or who are of Hungarian descent but are now foreign citizens. This law is primarily meant to offer citizenship to persons of ethnic Hungarian descent whose Hungarian ancestors were placed outside the Hungarian borders as a consequence of the Paris Peace Treaties following World War I. The new electoral law abolished residency requirements for the eligibility to vote, instituting a legal framework in which non-residents' votes are worth less than half than those of residents, as—since they do not have single member destricts (SMDs), and cannot vote for SMD candidates—their votes are counted only in the national list. Estimates of the size of the ethnic Hungarian communities across the border vary, ranging between 2.5 and 3 million. (By the next, 2014 parliamentary elections 600,000 non-resident Hungarians had acquired citizenship, and 193,793 had registered to vote, but as a result of a complicated voting procedure, 128,429 valid postal votes were cast, with FIDESZ receiving the overwhelming 95.4 percent of these.[1]) Hungarian residents who work or study abroad could not vote by mail but needed to travel to a Hungarian embassy or consulate, whereas non-resident citizens could cast their votes from home. The decision concerned a new comprehensive law on electoral procedure, adopted by Parliament on 26 November 2012, in regards to which the President of the Republic used his 'constitutional veto' powers, referring it to the HCC for a preliminary review before signing and promulgating it.

According to Article XXIII (1) of the FL, every adult Hungarian citizen shall have the right to vote and to stand as a candidate in elections for Members of Parliament, municipal representatives and mayors, and for Members of the European Parliament. The President's concerns thus pertained to provisions in the Act requiring the registration in the registry of constituents as a precondition of exercising one's right to vote in parliamentary elections. This was a novel feature of the law as neither the previous constitution (in force until 1 January 2012) nor the related electoral procedures set forth such a procedure although the old constitution restricted the right to vote on parliamentary elections to resident citizens. The President of the Republic also initiated the preliminary review of

1 Pogonyi, 'Transborder Kin-minority as Symbolic Resource in Hungary', 85.

some provisions related to the election campaign, concerning their compatibility with the FL.

The ruling itself provides an overview of international jurisprudence regarding the central issue of registration. It refers to the Code of Good Practice in Electoral Matters, adopted by the European Commission for Democracy through Law (aka Venice Commission),[2] a consultative body of the Council of Europe, which acknowledges that ex officio registration, does not exclude the possibility of registration upon request (Reasoning, [35], [36]).

In assessing the complaints, the ECtHR used a well-elaborated set of criteria, allowing a wide margin of appreciation in relation to the obligation of the State to guarantee the conditions for exercising the right to vote, and noting that the primary obligation in the field of Protocol 1 Article 3 is not one of abstention or non-interference, as with the majority of civil and political rights, but one of adoption by the State of positive measures to 'hold' democratic elections.[3] However, 'conditions imposed must not thwart the free expression of the people in the choice of the legislature—in other words, they must reflect, or not run counter to, the concern to maintain the integrity and effectiveness of an electoral procedure'.[4] In the case *Georgian Labour Party v. Georgia*,[5] recalling that features that would be unacceptable in the context of one system may be justified in the context of another, the Court acknowledged that the active registration system (where voters could register even on election day) may not impose an unacceptable restriction per se, but restrictions can only be justified for the purpose of achieving a legitimate aim and only a justification of due weight can legitimize such measures.

2. *Petition*

Before promulgation, the President of the Republic initiated the preliminary review of Articles 88, 92, 151, 152 (5), 154 (1) and 353 (4) of the Act of 2012 on the election procedure (Election Procedure Act) adopted by the Parliament in the session of 26 November 2012. The President also requested the review of provisions closely connected to the challenged

2 Opinion no. 190/2002, Strasbourg, 23 May 2003, CDL-AD(2002)23.

3 Mathieu Mohin and Clerfayt 2 March 1987, Appl. no. 9267/81, ca., para. 50.

4 *Hirst v. United Kingdom* (no. 2.), no. 74025/01, judgment of 6 October 2005, para. 62.

5 *Georgian Labour Party v. Georgia*, no. 9103/04, judgment of 8 October 2008.

articles, and also asked from the HCC to establish those constitutional requirements which enforce the provisions of the FL.

First, the President challenged two provisions of the Election Procedure Act related to the central registry of constituents (registry of constituents). In connection with Article 88 of the Election Procedure Act, he held it as a disproportionate restriction of the right to vote provided in Article XXIII of the FL, that constituents having an address in Hungary are bound to use this address during their registration to the registry of constituents. According to the presidential motion, narrowing down the possibility of voluntary registration is unjustified in view of the FL and it is disadvantageous for some groups of voters (e.g. long-distance commuters). Furthermore, he asserted that Article 92 of the act amounts to an unjustified discrimination, in violation of Article XV (2) of the FL, in that in comparison with citizens living in Hungary, voters living in Hungary without a registered address do not need to initiate registration personally and have the option to register via mail, something which is not allowed for the former group. Based on all the above, the President of the Republic requested the court to rule that Articles 88 and 92, as well as the other closely connected provisions of the act, are contrary to the FL (Reasoning [3]).

The President of the Republic also initiated the a priori constitutional review of some provisions related to the election campaign. He held that Article 151 of the Election Procedure Act, allowing the dissemination of political advertisements only through public service media providers, and Article 151 (3), prohibiting the dissemination of political advertisements even by public service media providers within the 48 hours preceding the voting, are restrictions contrary to the FL. Similarly, he argued that Article 152 (5) of the Election Procedure Act, prohibiting cinemas from showing political advertisements during the whole campaign period is contrary to the FL. In addition, he claimed that Article 154 (1) of the Election Procedure Act, prohibiting the publication of the results of opinion polls connected to the elections on the last six days of the campaign period—including the day of the voting until the closing of ballots—violate the freedom of press and the freedom of expression.

3. *Decision and its reasoning*

The HCC found most arguments of the presidential motion well-founded, and held that Articles 82 (2),[6] 88 (1),[7] 92[8] and 106[9] [along with Articles 151,[10] 152 (5),[11] and 154 (1)[12]] of the Election Procedure Act are contrary to the FL.

---

6 'The central registry of names shall contain the data of the citizens who have the right to vote and of the citizens who do not have the right to vote due to the lack of adult age, but who are older than the age of 17 (in this chapter hereinafter together: »constituent«), recorded in the central registry of names upon their request.'

7 'Constituents having an address in Hungary may request the recording in the registry of names at the notary competent in accordance with the constituent's address, or, in the case under Section 89 para. (2), with their place of residence a) personally, b) through the electronic gateway.'

8 'The provisions on constituents living abroad and not having an address in Hungary shall be applicable to the request for recording, and the recording, in the registry of names in the case of constituents living in Hungary, but not having an address here.'

9 '(1) At the elections, the registry of names in the constituencies shall contain the names of the constituents who are recorded in the central registry of names on the basis of their request submitted not later than on the fifteenth day preceding the day of the voting. (2) At the elections set on a day following 1 January of the year of the elections under Section 85 para. (1), the registry of names in the constituencies shall contain the names of the constituents who are recorded in the new central registry of names on the basis of their request submitted not later that on the fifteenth day preceding the day of the voting.'

10 '(1) In the campaign period, political advertisement can only be disseminated through the public service media, on the same conditions for the nominating organisations establishing a national list in the election of the members of the Parliament, and the nominating organisations establishing a list in the election of the members of the European Parliament. It is prohibited to attach any opinion or an evaluating comment to political advertisements. (2) The public service media provider may not ask and may not accept any consideration for disseminating a political advertisement.'

11 'The ordering party of a political advertisement to be aired in the audiovisual media shall provide for subtitling the advertisement or supplying it with sign language interpretation.'

12 'In the campaign period, political advertisement can only be disseminated through the public service media, under the same conditions for the nominating organisations establishing a national list in the election of the members of the Parliament, and the nominating organisations establishing a list in the election of the members of the European Parliament. It is prohibited to attach any opinion or an evaluating comment to political advertisements.'

3.1. Registration as a general mandatory requirement of the exercise of the right to vote is an unnecessary and disproportionate restriction on the right to vote; however, such a measure may be constitutionally justified for certain special groups of voters (citizens without permanent residence in the country, national minorities, persons with disabilities) [Article XXIII of the FL].

The registry of constituents contains not only the basic for the list of constituents for each voting district. According to the Election Procedure Act, registration is voluntary, and made upon the request of the voter; failure to register is not sanctioned. Moreover, registration is an extra-constitutional prerequisite to exercise the right to vote, which is provided only by statutory provisions.

The right to vote plays an important role in enforcing an effectively functioning democracy. Although the State enjoys a wide margin of appreciation regarding the specific regulations, general and equal suffrage must be considered as an indispensable precondition of democracy in order to guarantee the unquestionable legitimacy of the elected bodies[13].

A particular rule on elections or a specific provision of electoral law can be rarely regarded as an undue restriction on the democratic character of elections (Reasoning [58]). The entire electoral regulatory framework needs to meet the requirement of facilitating—above all—the free expression of constituents' opinion.

The FL explicitly sets forth the right to vote as a fundamental right, and also stipulates a narrow list of grounds for exclusion from the right to vote, and amongst these criteria the request for registration at the registry of constituents is not mentioned (Reasoning [54], [60].). Grounds for exclusion from the right to vote form a closed list, and each ground must be based on the suffrage clause of the constitution; statutory provisions cannot broaden the scope of constitutionally prescribed criterion for exercising the right to vote[14].

The essential content of the active and passive right to vote may not be restricted by a statute except from cases in compliance with constitutional regulations. Thus, according to Article I (3) of the FL, a fundamental right may only be restricted in order to allow the exercise of another fundamental right or to protect a constitutional value, to the extent that is absolutely necessary, proportionately to the objective pursued, and respecting the

13 63/B/1995 AB, ABH 1996, 509, 516.

14 ABH 1994, 79, 82.; 339/B/1994 AB ABH 1994, 707, 710.

essential content of such fundamental right. Therefore the HCC continued the review on the basis of the petition by examining whether the Election Procedure Act would restrict the right to vote under Article XXIII in a manner contrary to Article I (3) of the FL.

The Election Procedure Act introduces an active method of electoral registration; the request has to be submitted personally at the notary, by mail within a specific scope, or through the electronic gateway. However, in the case of resident Hungarian citizens (with an official, registered domicile in Hungary), there is no constitutionally justifiable reason for excluding from the exercising of the right to vote those who have not asked for registration in the registry of constituents. One may establish from the text of the Election Procedure Act itself that, even without individual requests, the State can obtain the data necessary for compiling the registry of constituents made up of resident citizens who have the right to vote (Reasoning [67]).

The request for registration shall basically contain the citizen's name, his/her mother's name and his/her personal identifier. These are all personal data that can be found in the registry of citizens' data and addresses (the registry of citizens). With regard to the vast majority of voters—the registry specified in the Election Procedure Act only contains data that can also be obtained from the registry of citizens—the request for registration in the registry of voters cannot be regarded as an absolutely necessary restriction for all constituents. Moreover, in the case of the registration requirement, another register is to be made of the voters entitled to be registered in the registry of voters (to be used, among other things, in the course of setting up the voting districts, in order to enable the National Election Office to inform the eligible voters on the conditions for exercising their rights and on the method of registration).

A further question emerged; whether requiring registration is an appropriate tool to ensure the equality of the right to vote. In the voting districts the aim is to ensure that the number of voters must be as similar as possible, and differences are only allowed on the basis of due constitutional grounds[15].

The HCC pointed out that, on the one hand, according to the Election Procedure Act, the proportionality of individual constituencies has to be made on the basis of the number of voters on the polling day of the previous general election for parliament, and not on the basis of the persons entered in the register for the given election. On the other hand,

15 ABH 2005, 246, 254.

it would not be possible to lawfully determine the proportionality of the constituencies on the basis of the number of persons entered for the current election, since the Election Procedure Act on elections establishes that the borders of the constituencies cannot be changed between the first day of the year preceding the general legislative election and the day of the legislative election.

Moreover, ever since the free parliamentary elections in 1990 resident voters have had the possibility to exercise their right to vote without the obligation to register. This way of voting has become a constant element of the election procedure. If—in Hungary in the past—there had been no registry of citizens, and therefore the exercise of the right to vote could only have been possible on the basis of advance voluntary registration, then the constitutionality of the regulations found in the Election Procedure Act could be evaluated differently even in the case of the subsequent introduction of the registry of citizens (Reasoning [73].).

In the above, the HCC established that requiring registration in the registry of constituents as a condition of exercising one's right to vote was contrary to the FL. However, the constitutional review was not extended to registration in general. The registration of voters may be justified on certain grounds, as the current voter registry (based on the general registry of citizens) does not contain all groups of voters. Thus, for a specific group of voters (non-resident citizens, members of national minorities, voters in need of assistance), pre-registration is indeed a legitimate tool for exercising and facilitating the right to vote.

The HCC declared it a constitutional requirement, that the rules of the election procedure should facilitate the exercise of the right to vote (Reasoning [81]). The necessary data of all persons with a right to vote according to the registry maintained by the State shall be entered into the registry of constituents, thus granting the equal exercising of the right to vote for all persons who have suffrage. Thus, in the case of voters with a Hungarian address, filing the request according to their addresses is no longer a general precondition of exercising the right to vote. At the same time, there will remain a specific scope of persons with regard to whom it will be necessary to require a request for registration to the registry of constituents.

Regarding the equality concerns of the presidential motion, the HCC established that there is no justification to exclude, by the Election Procedure Act, the possibility of personal registration by voters living in Hungary without an address, as compared with electors having a Hungarian address (Reasoning [90]). Taking this into account, it amounts to an unreasonable discrimination not to grant the possibility of personal registration, similarly for the voters living in Hungary and not having an address.

3.2. *The ban on publishing political advertisements during electoral campaign periods in certain branches of the media as well as the ban on publishing the results of political surveys during the last six days before polling day amount to unconstitutional limitations on freedom of expression and the freedom of the press [Article IX of the FL].*

The President of the Republic considered that certain provisions of the Election Procedure Act regulating the participation of the mass media in the election campaign were contrary to the FL. The petition argued that the ban on disseminating political advertisements during the campaign period by non-public service media represents a severe limitation on freedom of expression and the freedom of the press. The HCC considered that this prohibition would result in the elimination of the possibility of political advertising in the very forms of media that reach the widest layers in society. Therefore, the prohibition is a significant restriction on the expression of political opinion in the course of the election campaign. The HCC has already pointed out that 'the media has a particularly important role in influencing the opinion of the public, and it is of prominent importance that in the period of election campaigns the right to the freedom of expression and the right to have information on data of public interest should be enforced in the framework of broadcasting'.[16] The HCC also explained in its decisions interpreting the freedom of the press that—with regard to the predominant social effect and manipulating power of the media—special obligations can be imposed on the functioning of media services.[17]

Regarding the election campaign, the HCC acknowledged in its established practice specific reasons that may (also) restrict the functioning of the media. Examining the rules on election silence, it pointed out in Decision 39/2002. (IX. 25.) AB that restricting campaign activity actually serves the purpose of the free articulation of the voters' will and, in this way, the establishment of the representative body on the basis of free

16 Decision 60/2003. (XI. 26.) AB, ABH 2003, 620, 621.

17 Decision 165/2011. (XII. 20.) AB, ABH 2011, 478, 505–509.

will, necessitated by the right to vote as a fundamental right and the requirement of the rule of law.[18]

However, in the present case, the HCC took due account of the facts that the Election Procedure Act had eliminated the institution of election silence, and campaign activities can also be performed on the voting day, while the prohibition only applies to public areas located within 150 meters of the entrance of the polling station. Moreover, the act stipulates that posters and flyers can be prepared and distributed all through the campaign period, including the day of voting; direct political campaigning can be performed even on the day of voting, while the holding of election gatherings is permitted all through the campaign period, with the exception of polling day (Reasoning [96]).

As recalled by the HCC, the predominant influencing power of the media services may justify imposing certain extra obligations by legislation—with due respect to creating equal opportunities for the political parties running—even if campaign activities are not restricted in general. However, with regard to the aim of allowing the free formation and the expression of the voters' will, it is gravely disproportionate to ban political advertisements on the wide scale specified by the Election Procedure Act, especially when the legislator has significantly eliminated the restrictions applicable to campaign activities. In addition to this, the HCC established that this provision of the Election Procedure Act neither serves the purpose of providing balanced information, nor can be justified by the intent of reducing campaign costs.

Moreover, the HCC considered that it was not a disproportionate restriction in itself if the broadcasting of political advertisements was fully prohibited in the media within 48 hours prior to polling day (Reasoning [102]). Such a restriction can be justified with the aim of ensuring the uninfluenced expression of the voters' will. Nevertheless, the prohibition affecting non-public media was contrary to the FL. Therefore, the 48-hour ban is also in conflict with the FL due to the close connections of the contents of the provisions.

The HCC examined a further provision of the Election Procedure Act, prohibiting cinemas from showing political advertisements in the campaign period. The HCC established that in the case of movie theatres, there are no special reasons that might justify the particular restrictions applicable in the case of media services. Therefore, in this case,—also taking into account the fact that the legislator has abolished the general restriction on

18 ABH 2002, 273, 279.

campaign activities—there is no constitutional justification for the ban on political advertisements.

In relation to the prohibition on disclosing opinion poll results connected to the elections during the last six days of the campaign period, the HCC recalled that it has already established that '[t]he restriction of the freedom of expression and the freedom of the press to any extent other than the election silence—if it is necessary and proportionate on the basis of the HCC's decision [Decision 39/2002. (IX. 25.) AB, ABH 2002, 273, 279.] in the interest of the protection of the right to vote and on the basis of the requirement of a democratic State under the rule of law—cannot be constitutionally justified' (ABH 2007, 135, 141.). Thus, the HCC established that the restriction of six days contained in Article 154 (1) of the Election Procedure Act restricts the freedom of expression and the freedom of the press not unnecessarily, but disproportionately.

4. *Doctrinal analysis*

4.1. *Whether the justification of registration is convincing and whether the new constitutional context of fundamental rights is taken into account*

The in-depth reasoning of the unconstitutionality of registration was provided by a concurring opinion.[19] This argumentation opened up the international context of the ruling and provided a deeper understanding of the registration requirement for each citizen in the electoral district based on his/her domicile under Article 3 of the First Protocol of the ECHR. The concurring opinion argued that this measure lacks clear and convincing justification, but in the light of the governmental communications, the following targets may be identifiable as promoting the fairness of elections: eliminating the short-comings of the citizen's registry, and integrating citizens without residence in Hungary into the electoral system.[20] However, in the light of a broader international comparison regarding registration as a requirement of exercising the right to vote, the concurring opinion concluded that such measures are widespread around the world, but the

19 Concurring opinion by Judge Péter Kovács.

20 Pozsár-Szentmiklósy, 'Politikai részvételi jogok az Alaptörvényben' in Fazekas (ed), *Jogi tanulmányok* (2012), 187.

criteria are usually less onerous for voters than the particular method of registration in Hungary.[21]

Finally, due to the requirement to register, certain groups of voters may be prevented from registration despite their lawful behaviour[22] (for instance when many requests for registration are submitted on the last day of the deadline set), and in this case, these citizens would be deprived of their right to vote (Reasoning [126], [130], [138], [143]).

In his dissenting opinion,[23] a member of the HCC called also for a more complex, detailed analysis of the system introduced for electoral registration, to assess its constitutionality. The dissenting opinion considered that the legislation has a wide margin of appreciation within the constitutional standards which exist to elaborate the electoral system, as long as the electoral law does not exclude certain people from voting on statutory grounds, or would impose unreasonable additional requirements on voters (Reasoning [151]).

Another competing way of interpretation[24] opined that although the fact that the requirement to register serves the seriousness of the electoral decision, and is in harmony with the new constitutional approach of mainstreaming citizens' responsibility and duties, the additional burden imposed on citizens is uncertain, and the justification of the necessity of such a measure is not convincing; therefore it is contrary to the FL (Reasoning [174]–[179]).

An additional dissenting judge[25] added a further element which potentially justifies the necessity of electoral registration. The increased mobility of the population within and across the borders of Hungary may result in the registry of citizens containing invalid data regarding the constituents. In this view, the registration requirement would also be a proper tool to deal with this issue (Reasoning [183]–[185]).

According to a yet further dissenter judge,[26] a further aspect should be brought to the discussion, expecting that the registration would strengthen

---

21 For further details please see: Jakab, 'A külföldön élő magyar állampolgárok választójoga egyenlőségének kérdése a választási törvény koncepciójában' (2011), 1.

22 In more detail please see: Kurunczi, 'Előzetes választói regisztráció az alkotmányosság mérlegén' (2012), 1.

23 Dissenting opinion by Judge István Balsai.

24 Dissenting opinion by Judge Barnabás Lenkovits.

25 Dissenting opinion by Judge Béla Pokol.

26 Dissenting opinion by Judge Mária Szívós.

the interest of citizens in public affairs, and their participation in exercising public power (Reasoning [215]).

Several commentators held that the ruling lacks the consideration of the amended constitutional context with the adoption of the FL, which established an inherently new context for the interpretation of fundamental rights, especially the right to vote.

According to one of the dissents,[27] the constitutional framework of political rights had been amended considerably, and the constitutional review of electoral registration should reflect this. The conceptualization of the political community has been reframed, and constituency boundaries have been also extended remarkably. The approach of the FL differs significantly from the previous concept in regard of the responsibilities and duties of citizens. The dissent invoked clauses of the National Avowal and also two articles of the FL as the main novelties of the constitutional framework in this regard: 'Article D): Bearing in mind that there is one single Hungarian nation that belongs together, Hungary shall bear responsibility for the fate of Hungarians living beyond its borders, shall facilitate the survival and development of their communities, shall support their efforts to preserve their Hungarian identity, the effective use of their individual and collective rights, the establishment of their local governments, and their prosperity in their native lands, and shall promote their cooperation with each other and with Hungary. Article O): Everyone shall be responsible for him- or herself, and shall be obliged to contribute to the performance of state and community tasks according to his or her abilities and possibilities.'

Other dissenting opinions[28] also highlighted the importance of the new constitutional standards, the greater weight on the responsibility and the duties of individuals towards the community.

4.2. Whether advance electoral registration and the campaign-related restrictions amount to a limitation on exercising certain fundamental rights

The reasoning of the ruling was based on the assumption that the registration requirement constitutes a limitation on exercising the right to vote.[29]

27 Dissenting opinion by Judge István Balsai.

28 Dissenting opinions by Judges Egon Dienes-Oehm, Barnabás Lenkovits, Béla Pokol and Mária Szívós.

29 Bodnár, 'Alkotmányjogi dilemmák az új országgyűlési választási törvénnyel kapcsolatban' (2012), 40.

The main question was then whether this limitation was necessary and proportionate. However, some members of the HCC rejected this idea. Three approaches were presented by the dissenting opinions.

The dissenting views[30] clearly demonstrate an alternative interpretation of the pre-registration requirement, such as that registration is a mere technical and administrative prerequisite of exercising the right to vote, and does not amount to a limitation of this fundamental right at all. For the sake of the fairness of elections and the prevention of manipulation, it can be reasonably expected of citizens that in every electoral cycle they devote a short time to identify themselves according to the rules prescribing this duty.

A further view[31] also opposed the description of registration as a limitation on the exercise of the right to vote. This opinion considered electoral registration as an administrative prerequisite, but on other grounds than the previous one, as here the only measures which could represent a limitation on exercising a fundamental right are those which set requirements for citizens that are beyond their influence, or which absolutely or in their real effect prevent citizens from exercising a fundamental right. The dissent argued that electoral registration is not covered by this definition.

Another approach[32] saw electoral registration as a functional element of the system, since lists of voters are indispensable to hold elections. In his view, the functional elements of exercising fundamental rights shall be exempted from the constitutional review, and only the specific rules on these functional elements may be challenged. Consequently, the constitutionality of electoral registration itself should stand beyond doubt, although the constitutionality of certain rules on registration might be questionable.

Finally, some concerns were also raised regarding the constitutional review of the prohibitions on certain campaign activities.

An additional line of argumentation[33] read together the constitutionally provided special role of responsibilities and duties with the campaign-related restrictions, and noted that these rules serve the limitation of the uncontrolled power of non-transparent private entities in an election campaign. The legal framework of elections needs to protect voters not only from the undue influence of the state, but also from private entities; there-

30 For example by Judge Egon Dienes-Oehm.
31 Dissenting opinion by Judge Mária Szívós.
32 Dissenting opinion by Judge Béla Pokol.
33 Dissenting opinion by Judge Barnabás Lenkovics.

fore these rules are deemed to be constitutional. Another dissent[34] added that the ban on political campaigning in the commercial media diminishes the cost of the electoral campaign, which reduces corruption. Nevertheless, in line with the majority, this dissenting opinion found the restrictions on cinemas to be a severe restriction on freedom of expression. Another dissenting opinion[35] also upheld the constitutionality of campaign-related restrictions; moreover, she urged for a more detailed analysis of the prohibition on cinemas and opinion polls in the light of the special nature of these forms of communication.

5. Aftermath of the Decision

The dogmatic pillars of Decision Voter Registration were not changed or contested.[36] The HCC emphasized that the Hungarian electoral system always operated without pre-registration, and, in the light of the HCC's earlier practice, this constitutional tradition is relevant under the FL as well. It was a crucial step in the light of those views, that the conceptualization of political rights should be reconsidered, due to the significant changes in the constitutional context brought by the new constitution, the FL.

Since Decision Voter Registration, the substance of the electoral framework has been challenged only once, when a petitioner submitted a constitutional complaint arguing that the permission to vote by post for Hungarian citizens without a permanent residence in Hungary, and the exclusion from this opportunity of those Hungarian citizens who have permanent address in Hungary, and are only abroad on the day of the elections constitutes an unjustifiable differentiation between persons in comparable situations. The HCC upheld the constitutionality of the challenged rules as they were supposed to fall within the responsibility and the room for manoeuvre of parliament [Decision 3086/2016. (IV. 26.) AB].

Registration is still required for Hungarian citizens who do not have a permanent residence in Hungary; for voters who belong to a national minority and wish to cast their votes on the designated 'nationality lists'; and also for persons with disabilities to be eligible for voting assistance.

34 Dissenting opinion by Judge Béla Pokol.

35 Dissenting opinion by Judge Mária Szívós.

36 Unger, 'A demokratikus választások alkotmányos és politikai ismérvei és a magyar választási rendszer' (2014), 5.

In the past years two notable developments have surfaced in regard to electoral legislation and registration in Hungary: opposition parties introduced the pre-selection of candidates, and the prerequisite of participating in these procedures is to submit a request for registration, and this is also expected to be possible via electronic means in 2021.[37] Furthermore, the COVID-19 pandemic boosted electronic and postal voting globally, and probably this tendency will be also relevant for Hungary, which may provide new functions, and justifications to advance certain forms of electoral registration.[38]

Electoral and referenda campaigning has remained a highly debated issue, fuelled particularly by a 2016 referendum,[39] and the 2018 parliamentary elections. Act XXXVI of 2018 amended the Election Procedure Act, affecting technical rules on electoral registration for citizens without a permanent address in Hungary, for ethnic minorities and for voters with disabilities; banning campaign activities on the day of the elections in and around polling stations; and imposing an obligation on private media to inform the National Electoral Authority in advance if they wish to disseminate political advertisements during the campaign period; yet criticism points to a need for further regulation.[40]

Bibliography

Eszter Bodnár, 'Alkotmányjogi dilemmák az új országgyűlési választási törvénnyel kapcsolatban' [Constitutional Dilemmas Concerning the New Parliamentary Election Law] (2012) 1 *Közjogi Szemle*, 40.

Anika Eleni Heinmaa: *Special Voting Arrangements (SVAs) in Europe: In-Country Postal, Early, Mobile and Proxy Arrangements in Individual Countries* (International IDEA, 2020). https://bit.ly/3iSpiPM

András Jakab, 'A külföldön élő magyar állampolgárok választójoga egyenlőségének kérdése a választási törvény koncepciójában' [The Equal Right to Vote of Hungarian Citizens Living Abroad at the Concept of the New Electoral Act] (2011) 38 *Pázmány Law Working Papers*, 1.

---

37 Opposition Parties in Hungary Agree on Primaries selection Method, https://bit.ly/3iQsGdX

38 Heinmaa: *Special Voting Arrangements (SVAs) in Europe* (2020).

39 Andrew Macdowal, 'Voters back Viktor Orbán's rejection of the EU migrant quotas', https://politi.co/3Av3bVL

40 Tóth, 'Kampánytilalom és kampánykorlátozás alapjogi szemmel' (2014) 59.

Gábor Kurunczi, 'Előzetes választói regisztráció az alkotmányosság mérlegén' [The Constitutionality of a Priory Electoral Registration] (2012) 43 *Pázmány Law Working Papers*, 1.

Szabolcs Pogonyi, 'Transborder Kin-minority as Symbolic Resource in Hungary' (2015) 3 *Journal on Ethnopolitics and Minority Issues in Europe*, 73.

Zoltán Pozsár-Szentmiklósy, 'Politikai részvételi jogok az Alaptörvényben' [The Right to Political Participation in the Fundamental Law] in Marianna Fazekas (ed), *Jogi Tanulmányok* [Legal Treatises] (ELTE Állam- és Jogtudományi Kar: Budapest 2012), 187.

Balázs M. Tóth, 'Kampánytilalom és kampánykorlátozás alapjogi szemmel' [Ban and Campaign Restrictions from a Fundamental Rights Perspective] (2014) 4 *Fundamentum*, 59.

Anna Unger, 'A demokratikus választások alkotmányos és politikai ismérvei és a magyar választási rendszer' [Constitutional and Political Criterion of Democratic Elections and the Hungarian Electoral System] (2014) 4 *Fundamentum*, 5.

14. Decision 4/2013. (II. 21.) – Five-pointed Red Star

Gergely Deli[*]

A provision of the old Criminal Code generally prohibited the use of the five-pointed red star as a symbol, regardless of the aim, method or result of such use, thus violating the principle of freedom of expression.

The HCC in its first decision concerning the prohibited totalitarian symbols has already examined the norm regulating the use of symbols of totalitarian regimes and upheld it. In contrast to this, the Decision Five-pointed Red Star found the regulation of the Criminal Code which prohibited the use of the five-pointed red star as a symbol in a general manner, regardless of the aim, method or result of such use, to be unconstitutional.

1. Background

1.1. Legal background and the former praxis of the HCC

Article 269/B (1) of the old Criminal Code described the use of symbols of totalitarian regimes as a punishable misdemeanour. This point listed types of criminal conduct (distribution, use as publicity material, exhibition in public) related to the swastika, the SS sign, the arrow-cross, the hammer and sickle, the five-pointed red star and any other symbol depicting the symbols listed above. The use of these symbols for academic purposes or the purposes of education, science, or art, or with the purpose of enlightenment about the events of history or the present time were to be considered as exceptions. The provisions also did not apply to the official symbols of states currently in use.

The HCC examined this Article of the old Criminal Code in Decision 14/2000. (V. 12.) AB and found it to be constitutional. The reasoning listed five arguments supporting one another. First, the HCC argued that

* PhD, Professor, National University of Public Service Faculty of Law Enforcement (Budapest).

criminal conduct related to the use of prohibited totalitarian symbols violated public peace and the dignity of communities committed to the values of democracy. Second, the historical events related to these symbols still had an effect at the time of the decision. Third, the restrictions at issue responded to a pressing social need. Fourth, according to the HCC, there was no other efficient legal tool than the tools of criminal law to achieve the objective at issue through the repression of these symbols. Finally, as a country with a similar historical background to that of Hungary, Germany applied similar measures against the use of these symbols. The first three arguments aimed to support the idea that it was unavoidably necessary to restrict the freedom of expression, while the other two elaborated on the fact that the restriction complied with the requirement of proportionality.

According to the first decision on the use of symbols, the images of totalitarian regimes were still very vivid in the collective memory. Thus, interestingly, it was consistent with the narrative phrased in the FL: 'We deny any statute of limitations for the inhuman crimes committed against the Hungarian nation and its citizens under the national socialist and the communist dictatorship.' The majority opinion aimed to articulate the value judgment of each and every member of a community (committed to democratic values) when it established that 'allowing an unrestricted, open and public use of the symbols concerned would [...] seriously offend all persons committed to democracy, who respect the human dignity of persons, and would offend in particular those who were persecuted by Nazism and Communism'. The HCC supported this view besides the application of a majority principle by supposing a common system of values possessed by the community and the persecuted individuals.

1.2. International outlook

In the practice (case law) of the ECtHR, there is a wide range of approaches taken when deciding what can be considered a necessary restriction of the freedom of expression from a democratic point of view, because the historical contexts are diverse.

In its Decision in the case of *Rekvényi v. Hungary*[1] which dealt with the prohibition on membership of a political party by police officers as a restriction on the exercise of their right to freedom of association, the ECtHR expressed that 'the desire to ensure that the crucial role of the

1 *Rekvényi v. Hungary*, no. 25390/94, judgment of 20 May 1999.

police in society is not compromised through the corrosion of the political neutrality of its officers is one that is compatible with democratic principles. This objective takes on a special historical significance in Hungary because of that country's experience of a totalitarian regime which relied to a great extent on its police's direct commitment to the ruling party.'

In its Decision in the case *Vajnai v. Hungary*,[2] the ECtHR took the position that based on Article 10 (2) of the ECHR, the breach of the applicant's right to freedom of expression was not justifiable. Persecution of persons merely for wearing the red star cannot be considered a response to a 'pressing social need'. Furthermore, the imposed sanctioning measure (probation) was a relatively lenient one, but still within the scope of criminal law, resulting in the most severe consequences. Thus, the measure taken was disproportionate to the legitimate aims pursued. Somewhat contrary to the case *Rekvényi v. Hungary*,[3] the ECtHR considered Hungary a stable democracy, because two decades had passed since the transformation into a plural society. In the present situation, reference to the specific circumstances of the transition to democracy does not justify any restrictions on the freedom of expression. In the Court's opinion, the threat of the restoration of the communist dictatorship by any political movement or party is unlikely.[4]

The ECtHR's Decision in the case *Fratanoló v. Hungary*[5] and supported the statements made regarding the case *Vajnai*. The ECtHR's Decision in the case *Fáber v. Hungary*[6] also reinforced the position that in the case of symbols with multiple meanings, only a detailed examination can pinpoint the meanings that are enshrined in Article 10 of the ECHR, and that are tolerable in a democratic society.[7] In the case at issue, the Árpád-striped flag was discussed as a historical symbol on the one hand and as the symbol of the Arrow Cross Party on the other.

---

2 *Vajnai v. Hungary*, no. 33629/06, judgment of 8 July 2008.

3 *Rekvényi v. Hungary* [GC], no. 25390/94, judgment of 20 May 1999. paras. 44–50.

4 *Vajnai v. Hungary*, no. 33629/06, judgment of 8 July 2008, paras. 48–49.

5 *Fratanoló v. Hungary*, no. 29.459/10, judgment of 3 November 2011.

6 *Fáber v. Hungary*, no. 40.712/08, judgment of 24 July 2012.

7 *Fáber v. Hungary*, no. 40721/08, judgment of 24 July 2012, para. 54.

2. Petition

The applicant was convicted of the offence of having worn a totalitarian symbol in public by the Pest Central District Court,[8] the Budapest Regional Court[9] and the Supreme Court (Kúria).[10] The Kúria also referred to the fact that the Strasbourg decision had not annulled Article 269/B of the old Criminal Code, therefore it remained normative. Consequently, the applicant complained during the court proceedings that his right to freedom of expression enshrined in Article IX (1) of the FL had been violated. He also requested the posterior norm control of the criminal law provision at issue regarding the phrase 'five-pointed red star' and, at the same time, its deletion, as, in his opinion, it endangered his freedom of expression. He further argued that this criminal law provision prohibited the distribution, public use and public exhibition of only such symbols that represented political regimes violating fundamental human rights. In his opinion, the five-pointed red star is a complex symbol that has several meanings, including the ideas of the Labour Movement and the fight against Fascism. According to him, this is how the five-pointed red star can be contrasted with the swastika, because the latter is an unambiguous symbol of the Nazi ideology and regime. This is why the argument that 'the restriction of free political expression is necessary to consolidate and sustain democracy' cannot be upheld.

3. Decision and its reasoning

The HCC established that the provision criminalizing the use of the five-pointed red star in general was unconstitutional, therefore it annulled the provision *pro futuro* as of 30 April 2013.

---

8 Decision 16.B.21/571/2004/5.

9 Decision 25.Bf.7262/2007/6.

10 Decision Bfv.II.37/2011/5.

3.1. The decision of ECtHR containing statements regarding the legal provisions examined by the HCC was a substantial circumstance from a legal perspective that necessitated a second revision process on the part of the HCC [Article 31 (1) of the HCC Act].

In the practice of the HCC, the principle of *res judicata* or preclusion is applicable only if the application in question is submitted in relation to the same provision and for the same reason as previously.[11]

The *res judicata* principle, however, is only a relative barrier for the HCC. It is justifiable to leave the possibility of reassessment for the HCC regarding issues in which changing circumstances provide a new or a different reason to perform a repeated review in the same constitutional setting. Accordingly, legal regulations make this possible by providing for exceptions to the principle of preclusion if the circumstances (especially the facts and points of law) have fundamentally changed since the first decision.

The HCC had already made a decision on the constitutionality of Article 269/B of the old Criminal Code regarding freedom of expression. However, the ECtHR's above mentioned decision in the case *Vajnai v. Hungary* regarding the same provision of the old Criminal Code was made subsequent to the HCC's first decision about the use of symbols of totalitarian regimes.

ECtHR decisions are declarative, that is, they do not directly change any points of law. Nevertheless, the Court's practice may aid the interpretation of basic constitutional rights (enshrined in a constitution or an international agreement) and the definition of their content and scope. Taking all of this into account, the HCC found that the ECtHR decision made in the case *Vajnai v. Hungary*, containing observations on Article 269/B of the old Criminal Code constituted just such a legally significant new circumstance and perspective that necessitated posterior norm control.

11 Decision 1620/1991. (XII. 17.) AB, ABH 1991, 972, 973.

3.2. *The criminalization of the use of totalitarian symbols may be justified, because behaviours related to the symbols of 20th century extremist political dictatorships may violate human dignity and are contrary to the constitutional values deriving from the FL [Article II of the FL].*

The National Avowal of the FL introduced a new concept of dignity, establishing that human existence is based on human dignity; however, individual freedom can only be complete in cooperation with others.

The HCC did not react to this change in its decision expressly, but made its observations in this spirit when establishing that the criminalization of the use of totalitarian symbols may be justified, because behaviours related to the symbols of 20th century extremist political dictatorships may violate human dignity on the one hand and are contrary to the constitutional values deriving from the FL on the other.

The general prohibition of the use of these symbols, however, may lead to the criminalization of behaviours that can only be considered as criminal offences at the cost of a disproportionate restriction of the freedom of expression.

At the same time, the HCC argued that the state's obligation of institutional protection safeguarding fundamental rights can justify a proportionate (i.e. constitutionally validated) state intervention. The HCC considered it a legitimate purpose for the legislative authority to protect human dignity and the constitutional order and values by prohibiting behaviours contrary to them.

3.3. *A requirement resulting from the provisions of the FL is a clear expression of what the legislative authority considers to be the protected legal interest and punishable conduct. The phrasing must carry an unambiguous message of what exactly constitutes the criminally sanctioned infringement, and at the same time, the possibility of arbitrary interpretation on the part of enforcement authorities must be minimalized [Articles B) (1), IX (1), and XXVIII (4) of the FL].*

It may be acceptable from the constitutionality perspective to penalize conduct such as the public expression or distribution of views identifying with totalitarian systems if the related criminal legislation is precise, concrete and specific to the extent that would not result in disproportionate interventions restricting the freedom of expression. At the same time, the restrictions must be applied in the narrowest possible scope that is still necessary to reach the intended objective.

An important constitutional barrier of criminal law is the requirement of a definite, specific, clear disposition of what the legislative authority considers to be the prohibited, criminally punishable conduct. This requirement, which results from Articles B) (1) and XXVIII (4) of the FL, necessitates a clear expression of what the legislative authority considers to be the protected legal interest and punishable conduct. The phrasing must carry an unambiguous message of what exactly constitutes the criminally sanctioned infringement, and at the same time, the possibility of arbitrary interpretation from the part of enforcement bodies must be minimalized.[12]

In Decision Five-pointed Red Star, the HCC had to examine whether the old Criminal Code's provision regarding the use of totalitarian symbols was in accordance with the constitutional barriers of criminal law, that is, whether the provision in question defined the behaviours punishable under criminal law in a specific and clearly defined way. Lack of clarity in the statutory definition of the criminal offense could result in an arbitrary restriction of the freedom of expression.

When a provision involves a restriction of fundamental rights, the legislator's authority is required to protect the functioning of the legal institution in question by very precise definitions and legal guarantees against arbitrary enforcement.

The HCC established that Article 269/B (1) of the old Criminal Code defined the type of behaviour subject to criminal sanction too broadly, because it did not differentiate and it criminalized the use of totalitarian symbols in general, even though considerations of the intention, the modus operandi or the outcome may be crucial in the case of certain symbols. The general prohibition of the use of these symbols led to the criminalization of behaviours that can only be considered criminal offences at the cost of a disproportionate restriction of the freedom of expression.

A substantive requirement resulting from constitutional criminal law, or in other words, from barriers of the criminal law stemming from the FL, is that a legislative authority must not define the scope of criminally punishable behaviours arbitrarily. The question of whether any specific act should be criminally sanctioned or not must be judged against strict criteria.

Criminal law provisions that necessarily restrict fundamental human rights and freedoms to protect certain areas of life and various moral and

12 For the earlier practice of the HCC, see Decision 30/1992. (V. 26.) AB, ABH 1992, 167, 176; Decision 12/1999 (V. 21.) AB, ABH 1999, 106, 110–111.

legal norms are justified only when absolutely necessary and only in a proportionate manner, if the safeguarding of national, social or economic objectives and values deriving from the FL is not possible in any other way.

3.4. *The HCC attaches great importance to whether the issue under consideration is subject to an already established judicial practice (case law) which is absolutely necessary to aid the enforcement authorities in the assurance of legal certainty [Article B) (1) of the FL].*

In Decision Five-pointed Red Star, the HCC established that judicial practice related to Article 269/B of the old Criminal Code was limited and controversial. Some of the court decisions established that a criminal offence had taken place, because all the elements detailed in the statutory definition of the related provision were observed. However, in several other cases, even though the elements constituting the offense were present, the intention to propagate the ideology of totalitarian regimes was missing, therefore the court ruled that no proven criminal offense had occurred.

It is not only the overly general legal provisions which may violate the requirement of legal certainty, but also the possible circumstance that the legislator does not define a legislative framework within which the enforcement authority decides, or—if this framework is defined too broadly—does not provide almost exclusive and subjective authority for the enforcement authority in making decisions. Legal provisions which are too general in wording pave the way for subjective and arbitrary law enforcement just as much as legislative authorities phrasing applicable legal norms in a manner that violates the principle of normative clarity.[13]

4. *Doctrinal analysis*[14]

4.1. *On the necessity of repeated posterior norm control*

As seen above, the HCC considered the ECtHR's practice (especially regarding the case *Vajnai v. Hungary*) as one that weakened the certainty

13 Decision 109/2008 (IX. 26.) AB, ABH 2008, 886, 913.

14 The controversial nature of the decision is apparent in the fact that five of the judges attached a concurring opinion and five of them attached a dissenting opinion to the decision. The legal dogmatic evaluation is based on the examination of

in law enforcement practices that had not been uniform to begin with. The HCC saw this as an important change in the circumstances that made the principle of *res judicata* irrelevant here. The ECtHR's decisions contributed to the fact that the provision at issue could not be interpreted unambiguously, which violated the requirement of normative clarity. However, one of the dissenting opinions[15] pointed out that substantive examination should have not been conducted in this case, because the *ex post* review of conformity with the FL had already occurred regarding the criminal law provision debated by the applicant. The posterior norm control was conducted in relation to Decision 14/2000. (V. 12.) AB on the basis of the aspects suggested by the applicant, but other provisions of the FL were also taken into consideration, so the principle of *res judicata* should have been applied. The circumstance of how the ECtHR judges a specific case in relation to the ECHR has no such significance regarding a decisive judgement of the HCC on the permissibility and boundaries of certain fundamental human right restrictions that would justify the reconsideration of the judgement.

A constitutional lawyer, on the other hand, interpreted the passages of the decision referring to preclusion differently:[16] according to her, the Strasbourg decision which observed a breach of the ECHR by Hungary was sufficient to overrule the *res judicata* principle, and due to the practice of the ECtHR, the HCC could even depart from the earlier precedent. However, the Strasbourg decision on its own did not overwrite the practice of the HCC and the protective measures of the ECHR must be considered merely as a minimum standard that cannot erode higher-level member state protection.

4.2. *On the criminalization of the use of totalitarian symbols and the protection of human dignity*

When the first decision was made on the prohibited symbols, the Constitution then in effect applied a different concept of human dignity which was based on individual freedom. When Decision Five-pointed Red Star was made, the HCC ruled on the basis of the FL, which applies a concept

---

these opinions and on a brief description of the most important related literature along the lines of the theoretical principles.

15 Dissenting opinion by Judge Mária Szívós.

16 Chronowski, 'Az első átfogó kézikönyv a nemzetközi jog hatásairól Magyarországon' (2014), 66.

of dignity that is based on the community and its values. The former concept protected dignity as a form, while the latter highlights certain specific values as well.[17] Nevertheless, the restriction of the freedom of expression was considered constitutional on the basis of the freedom-minded Constitution, while it was declared unconstitutional on the basis of the value-minded FL. This contradiction may only be resolved if the two different historical narratives are taken into consideration.

Thus, surprisingly, the historical narrative of the first decision on the prohibited symbols was consistent with the philosophy of the FL, and it declared the restriction constitutional. By contrast, Decision Five-pointed Red Star was based on the FL, but still considered the provision unconstitutional on the basis of the freedom-minded dignity concept, which was more characteristic of the Constitution. The explanation of this surprising situation is that the historical narrative of the first decision on the prohibited symbols was not in accordance with the freedom-minded dignity concept and the more flexible historical narrative of the Constitution that was in effect at the time. The dignity concept of the decision on the five-pointed red star was in accordance with the Constitution and in conflict with the FL, and it was proven to be stronger when set against the disapproving historical narrative of the FL.[18]

According to one of the judges,[19] the FL laid new foundations for the content of fundamental rights guaranteed for the individual. The individual can only exist in a community, and for this reason, it is important to ensure not only their own personal fulfilment, but also the survival of their community and nation through the exercise of their individual human rights. Protection of fundamental rights can be guaranteed in the light of the actual state of the given social community. Consequently, changes in the state of the community may justify certain restrictions, and this cannot be denied by the HCC by a declaration of a non-reduction policy regarding the protection of fundamental rights.

One of the dissenting opinions[20] argued that Hungary had had her share of the terror caused by both fascist and the communist dictatorships. Therefore, the collective and effective legal protection of the dignity of

---

17 According to the opposing view, human dignity is not an empty concept. See for example Zakariás, 'Az emberi méltóság védelme' in Csink, Schanda, and Varga Zs. (eds), *A magyar közjog alapintézményei* (2020), 550; Zakariás: *Az emberi méltósághoz való alapjog* (2019), 115 ff.

18 Deli, *Az eleven jog fájáról* (2018) 99 ff.

19 Dissenting opinion by Judge Béla Pokol.

20 Dissenting opinion by Judge Barnabás Lenkovics.

the Hungarian nation, the dignity of the current social community, the dignity of each and every victim, the personal dignity of the surviving relatives and the dignity of future generations was more important than either individual human dignity in the narrow sense or the abstract dignity attached to an abstract concept of the human individual. From a constitutional point of view, Article 269/B of the old Criminal Code should not be viewed as a 'restriction', but as the 'definition of the constitutional scope'[21] of the given fundamental right (which is the freedom of expression in the current case). If any opinion is expressed in such a way that is against a provision of the Criminal Code, 'it cannot be shielded by the constitutional protection of the freedom of speech', since it is not only unlawful, but it also violates the dignity of communities, the human dignity of survivors and the dignity of victims.[22]

One of the concurring opinions[23] emphasized that the FL had replaced the Constitution (originally intended as temporary), which meant that the transformation process to a democratic and constitutional state was completed. The FL intends to proclaim on the constitutional level that the inhuman crimes committed during the national socialist and communist dictatorships are not time-barred, and this fact can be considered a moral satisfaction that exists for the benefit of the human dignity of the victims' descendants. More than two decades after the fall of the dictatorships, in an established democracy, it is questionable to consider the use of any symbol as a criminal offense, provided that it is not coupled with other criminally punishable and dangerous acts, and it is not intended to violate the dignity of others.

4.3. On the clear articulation of the legislative intention

Decision Five-pointed Red Star was essentially based on the principle of legal certainty, but as is quite apparent from the dissenting and concurring opinions, (at least) some of the judges voted guided by the new historical narrative created by the FL—even if their considerations and conclusions were not all identical. One of the judges justified the deviation from the historical narrative of the Constitution with the historical fact of the creation of the FL: 'The fact itself that the Fundamental Law is replacing

21 Decision 538/2006. (VI. 08.) AB, ABH 2009, 2876, 2883–2884.
22 Decision 538/2006. (VI. 08.) AB, ABH 2009, 2876, 2890.
23 Concurring opinion by Judge Egon Dienes-Oehm.

the Constitution that was intended as temporary is to be highlighted here, because at the same time it means that the transformation process to a democratic and constitutional state is complete.'[24]

Another judge[25] argued that the Opinion of the HCC on the annulment should have been based on the grounds that the overly broad definition of the use of prohibited symbols in Article 269/B of the old Criminal Code resulted in a disproportionate restriction of the freedom of expression. The constitutional authority had already expressed through the published draft of the 4th modification to the FL that it intends to punish the public popularization of totalitarian ideology, but this cannot be interpreted as meaning that the mere use of these symbols, without any criminal intention, results in the cessation of constitutional protection.

4.4. On judicial practice (case law)

In essence, Decision Five-pointed Red Star mentioned only one argument for the annulment: the provisions of the old Criminal Code were not clear enough, which had led to various enforcement practices that violated the principle of the rule of law.

One of the judges[26] submitted a concurring opinion to the decision, because he considered it desirable for the majority opinion to point out clearly that behaviour otherwise constituting the offense defined by the provision is to be criminally sanctioned only if the use of the symbol is related to and expresses identification with the relevant totalitarian ideology. This would be important for providing guidance in enforcement, especially in the practice of ordinary courts. According to him, except for extreme cases, only the enforcement authority can judge whether behaviour involving Fascist and Nazi symbols (or symbols reminiscent of them) is intended to breach public peace, to disturb the constitutional order or to violate the right to human dignity (see for example the Hungarian Guard Movement's[27] inauguration ceremony which took place in the square in front of the residence of the President of the Republic, in which even a 'flag lady'[28] participated).

24 Decision 4/2013. (II. 21.) AB, Reasoning [100].
25 Dissenting opinion by Judge Béla Pokol.
26 Concurring opinion by Judge László Kiss.
27 A Hungarian far-right paramilitary organization.
28 A traditional function carried out by women during official military inauguration ceremonies.

Finally, he called attention to the fact that because of the *pro futuro* annulment of the provision it is the legislative authority's right and responsibility to decide on the statutory definition and sanctioning of the use of totalitarian symbols.

The majority opinion was also challenged by one judge,[29] because in her opinion, as opposed to what the decision stated, appropriate case law did exist for Article 269/B of the old Criminal Code (meaning that the identification of the perpetrator with the ideology had been taken into consideration), thus it was completely unnecessary to annul the debated provision on the basis of the lack of this practice.

Another judge[30] disagreed with the fact that the operative part of the decision annulled Article 269/B of the old Criminal Code *pro futuro.* This legal consequence of the decision was based on the statement of reasons that examined the fulfilment of the democratic requirements of constitutional criminal law, derived from Article B) (1) of the FL. However, the HCC should have judged the constitutionality of the debated provision primarily on the basis of Article IX (1) of the FL, which deals with freedom of expression. Article 269/B of the old Criminal Code restricted freedom of expression in an unconstitutional manner; therefore it should have been annulled *ex nunc.*

5. Aftermath of the Decision

The applicant, Attila Vajnai, the president of the left-wing Workers' Party of Hungary 2006 said after the decision that in the twenty years that had passed since the adoption of the debated old Criminal Code provision (1993) certain worries had been confirmed: Hungarian society is seriously endangered by the earlier and currently ruling powers, who attempt to 'blur the lines between the ideology of liberating the working class and oppressed people and the ideology of Fascism and its symbols'.[31] Some commentators welcomed[32] the fact that the HCC rejected this approach,

29 Dissenting opinion by Judge Mária Szívós.

30 Dissenting opinion by Judge Péter Paczolay.

31 See *Az Ab megsemmisítette az önkényuralmi jelképek használatát tiltó Btk. rendelkezést* [The HCC annulled the norm of the Criminal Code forbidding the use of symbols of totalitarian regimes], https://bit.ly/3oCD5xz

32 See Bakó, *Hordható lesz a vörös csillag és a horogkereszt?* [Can the the five-pointed red star and the swastika be worn?], (2013), https://bit.ly/3mu6OGn

because in their opinion it applied a double standard, and under the new decision, other totalitarian symbols had to be treated the same way legally as the red star.

Not long after the adoption of the decision, the Parliament reworked the provision to comply with the constitutionality requirements. The new Article 269/B of the Criminal Code was codified by Article 1 (1) of the Act XLVIII of 2013 on the use of symbols of totalitarianism. The norm entered into force on 30 April 2013, with regard to the deadline of the *pro futuro* annulment. The provision was also preserved in the Criminal Code by Aticle 335.

According to this provision, the distribution, public use or public exhibition of the swastika, the SS sign, the arrow-cross, the hammer and sickle, the five-pointed red star and any other symbol depicting the listed symbols is a punishable misdemeanour only if it is done 'to breach public peace—specifically in such a way to offend the dignity of victims of totalitarian regimes and their right to sanctity'.

Bibliography

Nóra Chronowski, 'Az első átfogó kézikönyv a nemzetközi jog hatásairól Magyarországon' [The First Comprehensive Handbook on the Effects of International Law in Hungary] (2014) 4 *Közjogi Szemle*, 66.

Gergely Deli, *Az eleven jog fájáról. Elmélet és történet a természetjog védelmében* [From the Tree of Vivid Law. Theory and History in Defence of Natural Law] (Medium: Budapest 2018)

Kinga Zakariás: *Az emberi méltósághoz való alapjog. Összehasonlító jogi elemzés a német és magyar alkotmánybírósági gyakorlat tükrében* [The Right to Human Dignity. A Comparative Study in the Mirror of the German and Hungarian Constitutional Practice] (Pázmány Press: Budapest 2019)

Kinga Zakariás, 'Az emberi méltóság védelme' [The Defence of Human Dignity] in Lóránt Csink, Balázs Schanda, and András Varga Zs. (eds), *A magyar közjog alapintézményei* [The Basic Institutions of Hungarian Public Law] (Pázmány Press: Budapest 2020), 537.

15. Decision 6/2013. (III. 1.) AB – Legal Status of Churches

*Gábor Schweitzer**

The state must ensure a legal status for churches allowing the independent operation of religious communities and the acquisition of other rights available for churches and based on objective and reasonable criteria in harmony with the right to the freedom of religion and the requirement of fair proceedings with the possibility of legal remedy.

After the entry into force of the FL, the decision on the legal status of churches was the first comprehensive interpretation of the regulations on the legal status of churches, religious denominations and religious communities.

1. Background

Decision Legal Status of Churches was delivered following a motion to examine the anti-constitutional nature of Act CCVI of 2011 on the right to freedom of conscience and religion and the legal status of churches, religious denominations and religious communities (Church Act).[1] The history nevertheless reaches back to the period when the FL and Act C of 2011 on the right to consciousness and the freedom of religion and the legal status of churches, religious denominations and religious communities (Church Act1) was accepted. This provided a new basis for the relationship between the state and churches, religious denominations and religious communities.[2] Above all, the changes were introduced by the provisions of the National Avowal of the FL, which are committed in terms of religion and ideology to withdrawing from the principle of the neutral position of

---

* PhD, Senior research fellow, Centre for Social Sciences, Institute for Legal Studies (Budapest), Associate professor, National University of Public Service Faculty of Political Science and International Studies (Budapest).

1 For a description of the Church Act, see Uliz, '»Hogy ki egyház és ki nem«' (2011), 23.

2 For an assessment of the Church Act1, see Szathmáry, 'Fórum' (2011), 60.

the state in terms of religion and ideology. In the name of the constituents of the Hungarian nation, the constitutional power proudly recalled that St. Stephen 'Made our country part of Christian Europe', and recognised 'the role of Christianity in preserving nations', furthermore it expressed appreciation of the different 'religious traditions' of the county.

Parliament adopted the Church Act 1 on 12 July 2011 following an amendment proposed by the Parliamentary Constitutional, Justice and Agenda Committee before the final vote had amended the unified bill had passed through the relevant committee, as well as general and detailed debates. The institution of amendments before final vote primarily[3] aimed to eliminate coherence-disturbances according to the Rules of the House, i.e., that the amendment would ensure that the bill would be in line with the Constitution and other laws before the final vote. In the case of the Church Act1, however, the legislator did not consider the elimination of coherence-disturbance since the aim of the amendment was not to create harmony but rather to change the provisions of the proposal prior to the final vote.

The Church Act1 terminated the neutral registration proceedings in the county or metropolitan courts as set out in Act IV of 1990 and introduced a new registration procedure ending in a parliamentary vote (i.e., a political decision) following an assessment based on an application. The registration procedure was not applicable to the churches[4] *ex lege* recognised by the Annex to Church Act1 which was registered by the minister in charge to maintain contact with churches.

The Church Act1 provided a church registration procedure for those religious communities to which the act denied the status obtained based on Act IV of 1990 (or even earlier) and exercised under regular conditions. In the case of these religious communities, the legal provisions were applied retrospectively, the necessity of which is not founded.

3 Parliament Decision 46/1994. (IX. 30.).

4 Churches recognised by Act C of 2011: 1. Hungarian Catholic Church; 2. Reformed Church in Hungary; 3. Evangelical-Lutheran Church in Hungary; 4–6. Jewish religious denominations: Federation of Hungarian Jewish Communities, Uniform Israelite Community in Hungary (Statusquo Ante), Autonomous Orthodox Israelite Community in Hungary; 7–11. Orthodox Church: Serbian Orthodox Diocese, Universal Patriarchate of Constantinople – Orthodox Exarchate in Hungary, Bulgarian Orthodox Church in Hungary, Romanian Orthodox Diocese in Hungary, Hungarian Diocese of the Russian Orthodox Church (Moscow Patriarchate); 12. Hungarian Diocese of the Hungarian Unitarian Church; 13 Baptist Church of Hungary; 14 Faith Church.

The definition of religious activity was among the novelties of Church Act1. 'For the purpose of this Act, religious activity shall be any activity related to world-view that is directed to the supernatural, has systematised beliefs, is doctrinally oriented towards the totality of reality and comprehends the entirety of human personality through specific behavioural conditions which do not offend morals and human dignity.'

Following the adoption of Church Act1. several motions were made to the HCC. Decision 164/2011. (XII. 20.) AB abrogated the Church Act1 prior to the entry into force of its effective provisions on 1 January 2012 due to its invalidity under public law. The HCC did not express a detailed viewpoint on the provisions of the Church Act1, it did not examine them. Only the legislative process objected to by the parties taking action was examined, paying particular attention to the use of the institution of amendment prior to the final vote. The explanation of the decision pointed out that the above-mentioned institution of the Rules of the House 'qualifies as a guarantee of the exercise of democratic power and activity for MP-s on behalf of the public, therefore violating it must be seen as such a severe procedural irregularity that causes invalidity under public law of part or the whole of the Act'. Regarding Church Act1, according to the viewpoint of the HCC, acceptance of the amendment prior to the final vote that was disputed by the parties taking action 'did not contribute to the harmony of the uniform proposal with the Constitution but expressly led to a regulatory situation jeopardising legal safety.' Based on the foregoing, the amendment to the course of creating Church Act1 'contained conceptual change' when compared to the uniform proposal and was submitted and accepted in a manner that violated the Rules of the House, which also resulted in a violation of the Constitution. Due to these, the HCC decided that the public law was invalid and chose also to annul Church Act1.

Following the annulment of Church Act1 due to invalidity under public law, a new bill was submitted to Parliament. The bill on the right to freedom of conscience and freedom of religion and the legal status of churches, religious denominations and religious communities was submitted to the legislative body on 22 December 2011 as a Private Member's Bill.[5] Overlaps occur between the spirit and provisions of the Church Act

5 Bill No: T/5315. https://bit.ly/2Z6VRmm

accepted on 30 December 2011 and the Church Act1 annulled by the HCC.[6]

The continuity between the two 'church acts' is seen through the adoption of the concept of religious activity by the Church Act. According to this definition, religious activity shall be any activity related to world-view, which is directed to the supernatural, has systematised beliefs, is doctrinally oriented towards the totality of reality and comprehends the entirety of human personality through specific behavioural conditions that do not offend morals and human dignity [Article 6 (1)].

Nevertheless the Church Act had a new approach to the concept of churches in terms of public law. According to Act IV of 1990, people following the same religious principles may establish a church with self-government in order to exercise their religion [Article 8 (1)]. According to Church Act1, a church is an autonomous organisation with a self-government consisting of natural persons following the same religious principles, operating primarily in exercising religious activities [Article 7 (1)]. According to the provisions of the Church Act, however, a church is an autonomous organisation with self-government that is recognised by Parliament and consists of natural persons following the same religious principles, operating primarily in exercising religious activities (Article 7 (1)]. The most significant change was introducing the recognition by the Parliament which was not set out in the Church Act1 in this form.

The rules of recognition as a church were partly modified under the Church Act. According to one of the important changes, the recognition of an association conducting religious activity as a 'fundamental objective' of a church may be initiated in Parliament by the signature of one thousand persons under the rules on initiatives of citizens but not by the competent minister whose authority was in practice limited to registration in the new 'church act'. The prerequisites for recognition as a church were also modified. In addition to twenty years of operation in Hungary, at least one hundred years of international operation of associations conducting religious activity as a fundamental objective is also sufficient to initiate recognition as a church.

Based on the provisions of Church Act1 and the Church Act, 14 churches were permitted to retain their former legal status *ex lege*, while after 1 January 2012 approx. 300 religious communities lost their former legal sta-

6 Schweitzer, 'Az egyházak, vallásfelekezetek és vallási közösségek a 2011. évi C. törvény és a 2011. évi CCVI. törvény rendelkezései tükrében' in Drinóczi and Jakab (eds), Alkotmányozás Magyarországon 2010–2011. II. (2013), 239.

tus without any explanation or the possibility of legal remedy. Approx. 80 churches, religious denominations and religious communities applied for recognition by the Parliament in 2012 based on the changed criteria. Based on this, the Annex to Act VII of 2012 extended by 13 items the circle of churches, religious denominations and religious communities recognised by Parliament,[7] while Parliamentary Decision 8/2012. (II. 29.) rejected without any explanation the recognition by Parliament of 66 churches, religious denominations and religious communities operating in Hungary. These communities lost their former legal status by 29 February 2012.

2. *Petition*

The inspection of the Church Act1 was initiated by the ombudsman and 17 churches were deprived of their former status. The ombudsman addressed the HCC with a subsequent norm control initiative while the churches who had been deprived of their status submitted a complaint under constitutional law in which they requested the conclusion that the entirety or certain provisions of the Church Act were contrary to the FL and the annulment thereof and, in certain instances, the prohibition of application.

The ombudsman initiated the annulment of Article 7 (1) and (4) of the Church Act on recognition as a church on the one hand and Article 14 (5) as well as Article 14 (1), (3) and (4). According to his viewpoint, while the FL did not create a legal basis for anyone to exercise their religion within a church, the close relation to the freedom of religion requires that the decision related to the recognition of churches and the provision of legal status for churches must meet the guarantee requirements of fundamental rights. In the event, however, that when providing legal status for churches, the decision-maker has a right to judge, the law must ensure that the interpretation of the law does not become a means for voluntary, subjective decisions for law enforcement bodies. Furthermore, the decision must be explained and the opportunity for legal remedy against the decision

7 Churches recognised by Act VII of 2012: 1. Hungarian Methodist Church; 2. Hungarian Pentecostal Church; 3. Saint Margaret of Scotland Anglican Episcopal Church; 4. Transylvanian Congregation; 5. Seventh-day Adventist Church; 6. Coptic Orthodox Church in Hungary; 7. Muslim Council in Hungary; 8. Apostolic Christian Nazarene Church; 9. Society for Krishna Consciousness in Hungary; 10. Salvation Army in Hungary; 11. The Church of Jesus Christ of Latter-day Saints; 12. Jehovah's Witnesses Church in Hungary; 13. Buddhist Religious Communities.

must be provided (ABH 2013, 196.). According to the viewpoint of the proposing party, the Church Act lacked these guarantee requirements. Furthermore, the ombudsman's motion also pointed out that the provisions of the Church Act disputed by him also violate the principle of division of power set out in Article C (1) of the FL since Parliament must not fulfil any responsibility based on law that does not fit the fundamentally political character of the legislative body, and the decision on providing the legal status of a church cannot be seen as being a decision of a political nature (ABH 2013, 197.).

Proposing parties deprived of their church status complained and found the entirety or certain provisions of the Church Act to be violations of the constitution and the guarantees of the rule of law:

In a change from former regulations, churches obtain their legal status by the decision of Parliament not by court registration, which qualifies as a political decision. This regulation violates the freedom of religion, and in connection with that the freedom of association, as well as the right to legal remedy (ABH 2013, 198.).

The condition that the legal status of a church is terminated by other than court proceedings violates the right to a fair trial (ABH 2013, 198.).

Connecting the legal definition of religious activities to morality, and the political nature of the decision on the recognition of churches, results in an unpredictable and disproportionate limitation of the freedom of religion and, furthermore, it is also damaging that there is no legal remedy against the decision of Parliament rejecting applications for church status (ABH 2013, 199–200.).

3. Decision and its reasoning

The operative part of the decision consists of 10 points, in which the HCC found that several provisions of Act CCVI of 2011 on the right to freedom of conscience and religion and on the status of churches, religious associations and religious communities were found to be unconstitutional, the provisions in force were annulled and the application of the provisions that were no longer in force were prohibited. The HCC stated a constitutional requirement in point 5 of the operative part of its decision. In addition to this, the petition was rejected or dismissed.

3.1. *It is a constitutional requirement that the legislative procedure takes place in accordance with the provisions of the Rules of the House [Articles B, 4 (1) and 5 (7) of the FL]. However, granting church status through a parliamentary vote could result in a politically motivated decision.*

The HCC set out as a constitutional requirement that the legislative procedure must take place according to the Rules of the House, and that in any case of uncertainty in interpretation related to the provisions of the Rules of the House, sufficient time must be provided for careful examination of the bills and for their discussion at committee and plenary meetings.

The HCC rejected the proposals to conclude on the invalidity of the Church Act under public law considering its previous practice and the provisions of the Rules of the House.

The HCC removed the phrase 'as recognised by Parliament' from the definition of churches Article 7) (1), and the rules on initiating procedures and parliamentary procedural rules. Regarding the phrase 'related to recognition of a church by Parliament', the explanation of the decision highlighted that the delegation to Parliament of power to make decisions on recognition is particularly questionable from the perspective of harmony with the FL, freedom of religion, as well as the regulation defining the separate operation of the state and the churches. Recognising the status of churches by parliamentary votes and delegating the decision-making process to Parliament may lead to political decisions. Taking such decisions away from the court and delegating them to Parliament, which is political in character, cannot be harmonised with the separate operation of state and church or the neutrality of the state in terms of religion and ideology (Reasoning [203] and [205]).

3.2. *It is a constitutional requirement for the state to ensure the acquisition of church status, enabling religious communities to function independently and to acquire entitlements available to churches based on objective and reasonable conditions commensurate with the right to religious freedom and the entitlement in question, in accordance with due process and with the possibility of legal remedy (Articles XXIV and XXVIII of the FL).*

Non-applicability was retroactively asserted by the HCC, which terminated the temporary rules in effect between 1 January 2012 and 31 August 2012 [Article 34 (2) and (4)] and since 1 January 2012 that had been applicable on the qualification of not recognising churches as associations.

Regarding Article 14 (1) and (3)–(5), and Article 34 (2) and (4) of the Church Act, the HCC stated that since they do not meet the requirements of the right to fair process and legal remedy, and therefore result in damage to the freedom of religion and the prohibition of negative discrimination, they are against the FL (Reasoning [212], [215]). Consequently, the HCC restored the legal status of the churches submitting the motions, as well as the churches listed in Parliamentary Decision 8/2012. (II. 29.) retroactively entering to force on 1 January 2012.

In contrast to the one-level regulation of Act IV of 1990, the Church Act named two levels or types of religious organisation: on the one hand the churches (church) recognised by Parliament, and associations (association) conducting religious activity on the other hand. The status of association was mostly given to or obtained by religious organisations deprived of their church status by the Church Act.

Related to the freedom of religion and regarding the role of the state in individual and collective exercise of religion, the HCC highlighted that the state—as in the case of classic freedoms in general—is above all obliged to behave neutrally and to refrain from restricting individual rights. The HCC pointed out that religion can be exercised individually too: 'The rules of behaviour arising from the teaching of a religion are not necessarily connected to the institutionalised religious community or church' (Reasoning [125]). The freedom to exercise religion collectively is not bound to an organisational form. The right to exercise religion together with others provided for by article VII of the FL is a freedom for everyone, irrespective of whether the religion is exercised collectively under a legally regulated framework or not, or in whatever organisational form it takes place. Considering, however, that the 'church (religious community)' is the socially accepted institution of religious life 'the freedom of religion and exercising it in an institutionalised form constitute a special area of the freedom of religion' (Reasoning [126]).

3.3. *The Parliament may establish specific rules for the operation of religious communities that allow greater freedom of internal organisation and regulation than associations. However, it is not a constitutional requirement for all religious communities to have the same rights [Articles VII (2) and XV (1)–(2) of the FL].*

The concept of church was interpreted by the HCC with consideration of the religious neutrality of the state—derived from Articles VII and XV of the FL—as well as in accordance with its own previous legal practice [see e.g., Decision 4/1993. (II. 12.) AB]. The FL uses the term 'church' similarly to the Constitution in the sense of a religious community recognised in a special legal form compared to the organisational forms generally available based on the freedom of association (Reasoning [134]).

Having defined the concept of church, the HCC—considering the Constitution and the FL, as well as its own previous legal practice—searched for an answer to whether religious communities have a right to operate in the form of a church. According to Decision 8/1993. (II. 27.) AB, on the one hand, the separation of state and church 'does not mean that the state cannot take the special characteristics of churches into consideration, and it should regulate the legal status of »churches« identically with all other social organisations', and on the other hand it also declares that 'the state is not obliged to establish a special organisational form for religious organisations but it is not bound in what special form or forms it may establish, either'.[8] Nevertheless article VII of the FL expressly set out the independence of churches, from which the HCC concluded that 'Parliament must create such special rules of legal form for the operation of religious communities that provide greater internal freedom for change in the organisation and regulatory freedom compared to other democratic social organisations' (Reasoning [137]). Churches, therefore, are eligible to wider autonomy than social organisations. Article 7 (1) of the Church Act specified that the church is an expressly autonomous organisation. Based on all this, the HCC concluded that it would be against the FL were religious communities to be operated in the form of associations or any other generally available form, irrespective of the freedom of religion, and there were no special legal forms that provide additional autonomy due to the freedom of religion. Taking constitutional development into account as well, the HCC declared that Parliament would not be allowed to make a decision corresponding with the FL that does not form a special church legal status for the operation of religious communities in a legal form. It would be against the FL 'if religious communities operated in Hungary in the form of associations or any other generally available form irrespective of the freedom of religion, and there are no special legal forms providing additional autonomy due to the freedom of religion' (Reasoning [140]–[141]). From the separate operation and independence of churches, the HCC—also taking Article XV of the FL and its previous practice[9] into account—concluded that the state must not be institutional-

8 Decision 8/1993. (II. 27.) AB, ABH 1993, 99, 103. Quotes: Reasoning [137].
9 See Decision 4/1993. (II. 12.) AB.

ly interconnected with any church, nor must it identify with the teaching of any church or interfere with the internal affairs of churches, neither must it express views on religious truths. As a consequence of all this, the state must handle all churches equally. Through the neutral and general legal framework, according to the HCC, 'the separate operation of state and churches provides the most complete freedom of religion possible' (Reasoning [142]).

While the state must rely on the self-interpretation of religions and religious communities in issues of content, 'in terms of recognition as »church« in a special legal form' the legislator may establish objective and reasonable conditions. Amongst these are the stipulations on the minimum number of people and the time of operation (Reasoning [143]). In relation to the establishment of conditions, the HCC emphasises that the decision of the state to recognise a church may not be voluntary according to the provisions of the FL and the procedure serving as the basis of the decision must meet the requirements arising from the right to fair process. It means that the case must be settled without bias, in a fair manner, and within a reasonable term, the decision must be appropriately explained and the opportunity for legal remedy must be provided against the decision (or the lack thereof). The HCC found the fairness of the procedure particularly important 'so that there must be no doubt in terms that the state acted according to the principle of ideological neutrality without negative discrimination against the given religious community' (Reasoning [147]).

The HCC neither qualified as constitutional procedure that all churches should have identical rights, nor that the state should cooperate with all churches to the same extent in order to achieve community objectives. In the enforcement of rights related to the freedom of religion, practical differences remain within the constitutional framework provided they do not arise from discriminative legal regulations or discriminative practice (Reasoning [155]).

Decision Legal Status of Churches examined what differences exist between the legal status of the churches recognised under the Church Act and the associations conducting religious activity as their basic objective. As a result of the examination, the HCC concluded that 'the legal regulations in force provide extra rights compared to the religious associations which significantly help and provide advantages for the religious and financial operation of recognised churches and thus the right of the involved religious communities to exercise their religion'. Consequently, however, 'the decision on the recognition of church status must meet the requirements of right to fair process and the right to legal remedy' while the HCC did not find it to be against the FL that Parliament should also recognise churches in law if it does not result in a closed list (Reasoning [167]–[168]).

In the examination of the harmony of the regulation of recognition as a church with the FL, the HCC took the reasons for the change of regulations into account as well. In connection with this, the HCC requested information from the Chief Prosecutor, based on Act IV of 1990: 'what measures did the prosecutor's office take in relation with churches conducting activities violating the Constitution or against the law?' (Reasoning [176]). According to the information received from the Chief Prosecutor's Office, actions and applications related to the activity of 33 entities with church legal status were received by the prosecutor's offices (most of these are related to the operation of specific organisations). Action by the prosecutor to terminate church organisation status was filed in five cases, two of which were successful, and in one more case the court terminated an organisation's status due to action by the prosecutor. Only one small church was suspected to have been established for profiteering purposes in order to obtain the higher state normative based on a public interest report, but the inspection was terminated in the absence of any criminal offence (Reasoning [178]). The information received from the prosecutor's office may be seen as particularly important because the Church Act, as previously in Church Act1, justified the necessity of new regulations with the phenomenon of extensive church business. The system level operation of church business, however, was not supported by the information received from the Chief Prosecutor's Office.

The HCC concluded that while the provisions of Act IV of 1990 also allowed 'action to prevent the church registration of organisations to be established for spurious religious—in particular for business—purposes and to take action against violations of law', the HCC does not dispute the right of Parliament to further detail the content requirements of recognition as a church or to build further guarantees in the recognition procedure and to provide more effective legal means against violations of law (Reasoning [180]). Nevertheless, the HCC did not consider the former legal status to be an acquired right protected by the FL, 'in the sense that it could not be revised and withdrawn in certain cases if it is subsequently proved that the conditions for availability do not exist' (Reasoning [181]).

4. *Doctrinal analysis*

4.1. *Constitutional justification for terminating church legal status*

The question of justification is an important aspect in establishing any Act. The legislator must take into account all circumstances which legitimate and credibly support the necessity for legislation. The Church Act proposed as a Private Member's Bill placed the aspects of justification into a special context. The general explanation of the bill pointed out the following in addition to offering an historical reasoning: Act IV of 1990 'widely provided freedom of conscience and religion, as well as the establishment of churches. Later, however, it became obvious that the extraordinarily generous conditions of establishing churches provides opportunities for abusing this basic right, as well as for illegally using the state supports for churches and for registering organisations not actually conducting religious activities as churches'.[10] The abuses generally mentioned in the explanation may be related to the expression known in political discourse as a business church. According to this, the business churches are religious communities not directly named by the legislator that not only abuse the generous conditions of founding churches in Act IV of 1990 but also use state support illegally. The necessity of legislation to filter out business churches was caused by this phenomenon.

The legislator and the law enforcement organisations are not only entitled but also obliged to filter and sanction any abuse of such rights. This, however, was also provided for by the provisions of Act IV of 1990 since the court deleted the church or church legal entity from the records based on action by the prosecutor, such activity being against the constitution if it was not terminated upon notice being given. The explanation of the decision on church legal status also referred to the information received from the Chief Prosecutor, which did not support the presence of church business at system level; it did, however, list some cases when religious communities with church legal status were cancelled from the court records after a 'customised' procedure due to abuse of rights. This procedure would be the constitutional means of sanctioning any violation of rights.

The Church Act, however, used a simpler solution but a more worrying one from the constitutional and rule of law perspectives. It is simpler because—while 14 religious communities were qualified as 'churches' by

10 Bill No: T/5315. https://bit.ly/3lRmJzD

the force of law—it deprived hundreds of religious communities of the legal status they had enjoyed until then while simultaneously stigmatising them as 'business churches' in single move. It is more worrying because at the time of the legislative processes, the necessity of this severe legislative decision was not supported by any constitutionally justified aspect, e.g., reports of final court decisions judging serial abuse of rights.[11] The lack of legitimacy of the Church Act was not sufficiently emphasised in the decision on church status. The approximately 300 religious communities deprived of their legal status by the provisions of the Church Act were referred to by the first parallel explanation at least in this form. By accepting the Church Act '»the legislator amended in a moment« the regulation made in the course of Hungarian development of law and deprived more than 300 previously legally registered religious communities of their already existing rights'.[12] In connection with the recognition of churches by the legislative body, it declared that the competence of recognising religious communities by the state should be delegated to the courts—and more precisely to the Supreme Court (Kúria)—since this solution would meet the expectations of the rule of law (Reasoning [255]). All in all, the establishment of the Church Act represented a retrograde step in the development history of the constitution, since it is an essential element of the development of law that rights were extended in every age, 'and not deprivation of constitutionally obtained rights' (Reasoning [256]).

4.2. Dilemmas in the religious activity and public law definition of churches

It seems to be an exceptional solution that the public law definition of religious activity was declared by worldly legislation even if only in terms of the Church Act.[13] The definition of religious activities necessarily related to the transcendental must not belong to the competence of state (worldly) legislation. In terms of religion and religious activities, the definition of religious communities must be relied upon and not that of the state. Nevertheless, the legislative body may define negatively what is not in itself

---

11 Schweitzer, 'Becsüljük országunk különböző vallási hagyományait' in Patyi (ed), Rendhagyó kommentár egy rendhagyó preambulumról (2019), 113.

12 The first parallel explanation was given by Judge Elemér Balogh, Judge Miklós Lévay joined the parallel explanation.

13 For the concept of religion and religious activity, see Schlosser Czeiziné, *Az egyházi jogi személy a régi és az új egyházi törvényben* (2012) 35–38., and Rixer, 'A vallás fogalmáról' (2011), 1.

considered to be religious activity from the perspective of the application of the Act it took place on the Church Act. The definition of religious activity by the legislator, however, not only challenges the principle of separation and the separate operation of state and church but also the principle of the secularity of the state.

As a main rule, international conventions avoid the definition of religion in the sense of public law. This may be seen as accidental since positive law would not be able to define the concept of religion in a legal sense due to the variety of religions. The provisions of Directive 2011/95/EC of the European Parliament and of the Council are exceptions. Under Article 10 of the Directive on standards for the qualification of third-country nationals or stateless persons as beneficiaries of international protection, for a uniform status for refugees or for persons eligible for subsidiary protection, and for the content of the protection granted, regulating the reasons for persecution, 'the concept of religion shall in particular include the holding of theistic, non-theistic and atheistic beliefs'. In relation with the concept of religion, General Comment No. 22, interpreting Article 18 of the International Covenant on Civil and Political Rights refers to Article 18, protecting theistic, non-theistic and atheistic beliefs, as well as the right to not confess religion or beliefs.[14]

The first parallel explanation to reflect on the legal concept of religious activity pointed out the problematic elements of the definition. The definition may be seen as discriminative 'because it sets out criteria to be enforced against other religions based on the Christian religion' (Reasoning [246]). Furthermore, reference to the 'supernatural' is also a defective element in the definition since some of the religious communities recognised by the Church Act—e.g., Buddhist communities—do not focus on the supernatural (in the same place). Nevertheless 'human dignity' must not be listed either among the criteria of religious activities 'because the philosophical bases of that are such that religions other than the European religions rarely share' (Reasoning [247]). Among the conceptual elements, the 'systematic religious principles' are problematic because certain religions, such the Jewish religion named in the first parallel explanation, do not have 'dogmatics', i.e., systemic religious principles (Reasoning [248]).

14 Schweitzer, 'Lelkiismereti és vallásszabadság' in Lamm (ed), *Emberi jogi enciklopédia* (2018) 466–467.

4.3. Two-level regulation instead of one-level regulation

In contrast to the one-level regulation of Act IV of 1990, the Church Act created a two-level regulation of religious communities since there was differentiation between churches recognised by Parliament and associations conducting religious activity. Further refining the picture, two types of churches may be differentiated, since some of the churches received this legal status by the force of law (the Church Act) while some other churches received the legal status as a result of a recognition procedure initiated by an application and a decision of Parliament (Act VII of 2012). The manner in which the legal status of church is obtained does not affect the rights of churches, but churches provided with the legal status of churches *ex lege* clearly had a different social weight.

In addition to the transition to the multi-level regulatory system, the expectation set out by the HCC—that the state must treat religious communities equally—is difficult to enforce. Nevertheless, in the decision on the legal status of churches, the HCC neither qualified as constitutional procedure that all churches should have identical rights nor that the state should cooperate with all churches to the same extent.

The two-level regulation introduced by the Church Act represented a step back from the circumstances preceding 1 January 2012 for several reasons. Act IV of 1990 provided 'church' status for religious communities, religions and churches meeting the mostly formal and doubtlessly easily achievable criteria established by the legislator, while religious communities did operate in the period between 1990 and 2012 in different forms, e.g., associations, which were either unable or did not wish to use the church status provided or offered by Act IV of 1990. From the perspective of ideological neutrality, it is also problematic in the regulation of the Church Act that organisations conducting religious activity clearly could obtain the legal status of churches through a political decision by Parliament. The decision made by a Parliament as a typically party-based representative body can hardly be neutral. Based on neutrality, religious communities could have obtained the legal status of churches through registration based on uniform principles and uniform procedure, but not as a result of a recognition procedure including assessment and judgement. Registration is compatible with the idea of an ideologically neutral state but not a recognition process ending in a Parliamentary vote. The uniformity of registration may be ensured if the procedure is delegated to one single court or administrative body by the legislator.[15]

5. Aftermath of the Decision

The decision on churches was essentially not executed, since 'the churches involved were not placed »back« onto the records of churches', and still did not become eligible for identical treatment with other churches.[16] Nevertheless, the constitutional power modified the FL twice within a short period of time, including certain provisions of article VII as well. Under amendment 4 of the FL (25 March 2013) Parliament may recognise certain organisations conducting religious activity, in the relevant Act through which the state cooperates on community objectives. The constitutional power also provided the opportunity for constitutional complaint [Article VII (2)] against the relevant provisions of the law on the recognition of churches. Nevertheless, the relevant Act may require longer operation, social support and suitability for cooperation in order to achieve community objectives as a condition of recognising organisations that conduct religious activity as churches [Article VII (4)] Amendment five of the FL (26 September 2013) modified Article VII (4) too. Under the new text, the state and the religious communities [as in the new terminology introduced in Article VII (2)] may cooperate in order to achieve community objectives on which Parliament shall decide upon the request of the religious community. The state provides specific rights for religious communities that operate as recognised churches, taking part in the cooperation in order to achieve such community objectives.

Amendment of the Church Act by Act CXXXIII of 2013 did not implement conceptual changes, however, some procedural guarantees were established.[17] It maintained the institution of the recognition procedure by the legislative body, the two-level system, and made the conditions of recognition as a church stricter. However, the legislator regulated in detail the legal status of the organisation conducting religious activity

15 Schweitzer, 'A magyar állam vallási semlegessége', in Gárdos-Orosz and Halász (eds), *Bevezetés az alkotmányjogba* (2019) 252–253.

16 Mink, 'A vallásszabadság a vélt közérdek oltárán' (2014), 87.

17 Mink, 'A vallásszabadság a vélt közérdek oltárán' (2014), 87–88., and Zalahegyi, 'A lelkiismereti és vallásszabadság jogáról szóló 2011. évi CCVI. törvény megalkotásának kronológiája, értékelése és lehetséges jövője' (2019), 67–68.

operating as an association and modified the concept of such activity so that reference to moral and human dignity was omitted.[18]

Bibliography

Júlia Mink, 'A vallásszabadság a vélt közérdek oltárán' [Freedom of Religion on the Altar of Assumed Public Interest] (2014) 3 *Fundamentum*, 87.

Ádám Rixer, '*A vallás fogalmáról*' [On the Concept of Religion] (2011) 4 *Jogelméleti Szemle*, 1.

Annamária Schlosser Cziziné: *Az egyházi jogi személy a régi és az új egyházi törvényben* [The Legal Person of the Church in the Old and the New Church Act] L' Harmattan Kiadó, Sapientia Szerzetesi Hittudományi Főiskola: Budapest 2012), 35.

Gábor Schweitzer, 'Lelkiismereti és vallásszabadság' [Conscience and Freedom of Religion] in Vanda Lamm (ed), *Emberi jogi enciklopédia* [Encyclopaedia of Human Rights] (HVG-ORAC: Budapest 2018), 466.

Gábor Schweitzer, 'A magyar állam vallási semlegessége' [Religious Neutrality of the Hungarian State] in Fruzsina Gárdos-Orosz and Iván Halász (eds), *Bevezetés az alkotmányjogba: Alapfogalmak* [Introduction to Constitutional Law. Definitions] (Dialóg Campus Kiadó: Budapest 2019), 252.

Gábor Schweitzer, 'Az egyházak, vallásfelekezetek és vallási közösségek a 2011. évi C. törvény és a 2011. évi CCVI. törvény rendelkezései tükrében' [Churches, Religious Denominations and Religious Communities in the Light of the Provisions of Act C of 2011 and Act CCVI of 2011] in Tímea Drinóczi and András Jakab (eds), *Alkotmányozás Magyarországon 2010–2011. II.* [Constitution-Making in Hungary 2010–2011. II.] (PPKE JÁK – PTE ÁJK: Budapest, Pécs 2013), 239.

Gábor Schweitzer 'Becsüljük országunk különböző vallási hagyományait' [Let's *Appreciate the Varying Religious Traditions of our Country*] in András Patyi (ed), *Rendhagyó kommentár egy rendhagyó preambulumról. Magyarország Alaptörvénye, Nemzeti hitvallás* [Extraordinary Comments on and Extraordinary Preamble. The Fundamental Law of Hungary, National Avowal]. Dialóg Campus: Budapest 2019), 113.

Béla Szathmáry, 'Fórum' (2011) 3 *Fundamentum*, 60.

Renáta Uliz, '»Hogy ki egyház és ki nem«. Látlelet a magyar állam és az egyházak viszonyáról" [»Who is a Church and Who is not?« Report on the Relationship Between the State of Hungary and the Churches] (2011) 3 Fundamentum, 23.

18 'Religious activity shall be any activity related to world-view that is directed to the supernatural, has systematised beliefs, is doctrinally oriented towards the totality of reality and comprehends the entirety of human personality through specific behavioural conditions which do not offend morals and human dignity.'

Zoltán Zalahegyi, 'A lelkiismereti és vallásszabadság jogáról szóló 2011. évi CCVI. törvény megalkotásának kronológiája, értékelése és lehetséges jövője' [Chronology, Assessment and Potential Future of Act CCVI of 2011 on Freedom of Conscience and Religion] (2019) 3 *Jogelméleti Szemle,* 67.

16. Decision 32/2013. (IX. 22.) AB – Secret Intelligence Gathering

*Kinga Zakariás**

Secret intelligence gathering enables a forcible intrusion into every segment of private life (including the intimate ones) and might affect people other than the target of the observation; it is therefore imperative that the procedure guarantees the requisite protection of all areas of private life.

In the post-9/11 period secret intelligence gathering became a major instrument in the counter-terrorism measures of different states, whereby they invoked national security interests in order to limit the private sphere of certain individuals. It is well known that, after Edward Snowden divulged the mass surveillance practices in June 2013, the discussion on the conflict between the protection of private life and national security interests has gained a new impetus in Europe as well. The HCC adopted its Decision Secret Intelligence Gathering in that international context.

The ruling is significant as the first interpretation, with regard to the unusual nature of secret information gathering, of the so-called 'exceptional' constitutional complaint, which may be initiated if fundamental rights were violated directly, without a judicial decision. Moreover, this decision was the first to interpret the right to a private sphere in Article VI (1) of the FL. Nevertheless, while establishing a constitutional requirement, the decision failed to strike the right balance between the conflicting claims of the right to a private life and national security.

* PhD, Associate professor, Pázmány Péter Catholic University Faculty of Law and Political Sciences (Budapest).

1. Background

1.1. The regulation in Hungary

The Hungarian regulation recognises two types of secret intelligence gathering: secret surveillance in a criminal investigation and secret surveillance in a non-criminal case. The rules of secret data gathering in a criminal case were contained in Act XIX of 1998 on criminal proceedings, since those take place after an investigation has been opened. Secret intelligence gathering in a non-criminal case is regulated by Act CXXV of 1995 on the National Security Services (NS Act). This latter law distinguishes between secret intelligence gathering strictly for the purposes of a criminal investigation and for other issues of national security. With a view to this organisational principle, the law has created a divided external authorisation system. In cases of a criminal investigation, based on suspected criminal activity, secret intelligence gathering can be authorised by the judge designated for the task in other cases of general intelligence gathering that power falls upon the minister of justice. That is possible in the interests of stopping acts of terror, defending Hungary's national security interests or protecting Hungarian citizens from armed conflicts or acts of terror abroad.

Article 7/E (3) of the Act XXXIV of 1994 on the Police (Police Act) empowered Counter Terrorism Centre (CTC), a counterterrorism unit, working as part of the police force but enjoying institutional autonomy, to secretly collect information, as part of their national security operations, on the authorisation of the minister for justice. Article 7/E of the Police Act, with a reference to Article 56 a)–e) of the NS Act, grants the CTC such extraordinary powers that include secret house searches and surveillance, opening postal deliveries, and examining and recording electronic and computerised communications without the permission of the persons involved. Importantly, Article 58 of the NS Act states that the person concerned will be informed neither of the authorisation nor the fact of secret intelligence gathering and there may be no appeal against the decision of the minister for justice.

1.2. Practice of the HCC

Formerly, the HCC never examined secret surveillance in a non-criminal case. However, in Decision 2/2007. (I. 24.) AB it did elaborate on the constitutional guarantees of the tools and methods of the use of secret intelligence gathering and obtaining secret data in criminal cases. The HCC argued that the Constitution defines the right to private life as a component of the right to human dignity and, as such, as a general personality right, while certain of its elements, such as the right to housing, privacy, and the protection of personal information, under Article 59 (1) of the Constitution, are explicitly placed under constitutional protection. The use of secret intelligence gathering tools and methods necessarily places limitations on the domain of private life most strictly understood, including a private home life, that enables the realisation of personal autonomy, as well as the privacy pertaining to all activities conducted therein, which form a part of privacy that, in its turn, is an inalienable part of the right to human dignity. The right to an uninfringeable private home life is a specific concretization of the right to human dignity. The protection of this spatial sphere cannot be relativized precisely, because fundamental rights' protection, based on the right to human dignity, protects not the place itself, but the person involved. The right to privacy itself is a powerful fundamental right, inextricably bound to such fundamental rights as the general freedom of action (based as it is on the right to human dignity), personality rights, and the right to communicate (under the aspect of self-determination).[1] Thereafter, the HCC highlighted that law enforcers must not be given a universal mandate that would enable the limitation of fundamental rights, without ensuring that the conditions of necessity and proportionality are met and are controllable with respect to every condition of the mandate, both *in abstracto* and *in concreto*, not even with a view to the constitutional aim of the protection of public order and security. It also emphasised that, from the perspective of the regulation, it is essential that no external control is allowed over secret information gathering, which make effective legal remedies, in the case of harm caused by such tools, virtually impossible.[2]

1.3. *International outlook*

Both national constitutions in Europe and the ECHR have enshrined the right to private life and ensure a broad-reaching protection of privacy. In practice, however, the mass use of cutting edge technology has always presented a challenge to such protection.

1 ABH 2007, 65, 88.
2 ABH 2007, 65, 89.

Therefore, the Committee of Ministers adopted the 'Declaration on Risks to Fundamental Rights stemming from Digital Tracking and other Surveillance Technologies' on 11 June 2013. This declaration states that 'legislation allowing broad surveillance of citizens can be found contrary to the right to respect for private life. These capabilities and practices can have a chilling effect on citizen participation in social, cultural and political life and, in the longer term, could have damaging effects on democracy.' Consequently, the Venice Commission adopted the 'Update of the 2007 report on the democratic oversight of the security services and report on the democratic oversight of signals intelligence agencies' in March 2015. The novelty of the report is that it distinguishes between targeted surveillance and strategic surveillance, the latter of which does not necessarily start with a suspicion of certain crimes, and therefore it has to meet stricter requirements. The power to 'contact chain', i.e. to identify people in contact with each other, should be framed narrowly: it should normally only be possible for people suspected of 'actual involvement in particularly seriously offences', such as terrorism. The Parliamentary Assembly approved Resolution 2045 on mass surveillance in April 2015. The Assembly recognised the need for effective, targeted surveillance of suspected terrorists and other organised criminal groups, but it questioned whether mass surveillance would contribute to the prevention of terrorist attacks.

The ECtHR examines 'covered investigations' in the light of Article 8 of the ECHR. Under the right to respect for private and family life, that Article designates four protected areas (private life, family, home, correspondence) that amount to the framework of personality rights. The ECtHR gives a broad interpretation to these concepts, i.e. it does not see them as pertaining merely to the immediate private sphere. However, protection is limited to the behaviours that contribute to the development of a personality.[3] The strength of the protection depends on the connectedness of the protected behaviour to personal autonomy. The ECtHR recognises a most intimate core of private life where authorities must only interfere with very pressing reasons.[4] Interference, however, is only forbidden in cases where the level of physical or psychological harm would rise to a lev-

3 ECtHR excluded hunting from among the sphere of Article 8 protection on grounds that it falls too far from the area of personal autonomy. *Friend and Others v. The United Kingdom*, nos. 16072/06 and 27809/08, Decision on admissibility of 24 November 2009, para. 43.

4 *Dodgeon v. The United Kingdom*, no. 7525/76, judgment of 22 October 1981, para. 52.

el of seriousness that amounts to an Article 3 infringement, i.e. one against the protection of the right to human dignity with certain behaviours (including torture and inhumane, degrading treatment of punishment).

The right to respect for private and family life, as guaranteed by the ECHR, is also closely tied to the respect for human dignity. However, that right, contained in Article 8 (1), can be limited. The ECtHR pointed out that in a democratic society the freedom of private life can only be limited under the legal constraints stated in paragraph (2), and with the aims therein contained (national security, public safety or the economic well-being of the country, the prevention of disorder or crime, the protection of health or morals, and the protection of the rights and freedoms of others), if its necessity is proven.

The 'in accordance with the law' clause means that all regulations must conform to rule of law principles. As secret gathering of information necessarily gives no room to legal remedies, it is vital that the procedure enabling its application should provide adequate guarantees for the protection of the concerned individual's rights. As such, the application should be accompanied by a control process in three phases: when the interference is decided on, during its realisation, and after its completion. Monitoring should be undertaken by 'bodies' independent of the executive branch. This regular, continuous and compulsory control is the main guarantee that the expectation of proportionality is met in individual cases.[5]

2. *Petition*

The basis of the case is a so-called exceptional constitutional complaint filed by two representatives of the Eötvös Károly Institute, which carries out NGO monitoring of the government, on the basis of Article 26 (2) of the HCC Act. The petitioners complained against Article 7/E (3) of the Police Act, which gave the newly established anti-terror unit of the police force the competence to realise secret information gathering beyond the specific crimes listed in law in the interests of protecting national security. They argued that the law offers fewer guarantees of privacy and informational self-determination in the interests of human dignity and, in cases of secret surveillance, in the interests of national security, than in cases of the investigation specific crimes' investigations. Concerning the interference,

5 *Klass and Others v. Germany*, Series A no. 28, judgment of 6 September 1978, paras. 55 and 56.

the petitioners found the guarantees offered by the minister for justice's authorisation unsatisfactory, as there is no legal demand for an explanation for the request for authorisation. They also took exception to the data management that follows secret information gathering, arguing that NS Act does not contain the obligation of deleting all information that has no bearing on the given case or, indeed, that of personal information on individuals not concerned in the case.

3. *Decision and its reasoning*

The HCC rejected the petition to establish the unconstitutionality of and to cancel Article 7/E (3) of the Police Act, which empowers the CTC to carry out secret information gathering on the minister for justice's authorisation in pursuit of its duties in protecting national security. In the interests of effective external monitoring, the HCC did, however, create a constitutional requirement on the minister for justice to provide a sufficiently detailed explanation for the authorisation.

3.1. *In cases of exceptional constitutional complaint, which is directed at a norm, the examination of personal involvement is exceptionally important, since it is the personal, direct, and present harm of the petitioner that differentiates between constitutional complaint and actio popularis [Article 24 (2) c) of the FL, Article 26 (2) of the HCC Act].*

After its examination of acceptability criteria the HCC stated that 'in cases of exceptional constitutional complaint, which is directed at a norm, the examination of personal involvement is exceptionally important, since it is the personal, direct, and present harm of the petitioner that differentiates between constitutional complaint and *actio popularis*' (Reasoning [18]). The HCC examined whether the pool of individuals concerned in secret information gathering cases can be defined following the Police Act regulation in question. It found that, coherently with what the petition suggested, the regulation enables extending the circle of individuals under secret investigation to be extended to unidentified persons. Moreover, the tools and methods of secret information gathering make the surveillance of every aspect of a person's life possible and therefore inevitably affect other uninvolved people as well (anyone coming into contact with the target of the surveillance). The Court also considered that the NS Act makes post-facto communication with the targeted person impossible, therefore, the petitioners' cannot be expected to prove they were subjected to information gathering. In view of the foregoing, the HCC established the personal involvement of the petitioners (Reasoning [30]–[32]).

After examining direct involvement, the HCC established that an executive act of constitutive effect is necessary in the regulation in question (the order of the minister for justice as the authoriser of secret data gathering) and that the petitioners should first attack that unlawful act of state power, but also recognized that the secret nature of data collecting make it impossible for the petitioners to be advised of the procedure. Therefore, the Court regarded the law behind secret data gathering as one that is directly in effect, even with regard to the constitutional complaint as a final legal remedy (Reasoning [34]). As regards present involvement, the HCC found it impossible to interpret in the context of secret surveillance.

3.2. *The right to private life and the right to human dignity are tied to each other exceptionally closely. The right to human dignity forms the foundation of the protection of the inviolable sphere of private life, which is completely beyond the reach of any type of government interference. The protection of private life, however, is not limited to the protection of the inner or intimate sphere but it extends to private life more broadly understood (human connections, home, and a good name) [Articles II and VI (1) of the FL]. The right to informational self-determination is very closely linked to the right to private life and provides broad-ranging protection for an individual's personal data, independent of how they came to be owned by the data manager [Article VI (2) of the FL].*

In the main part of the examination, the HCC based its arguments on the insight that Article VI (1) of the FL, unlike Article 59 (1) of the Constitution, offers a comprehensive protection of private life, including a person's private and family life, home, human connections, and good name. In defining private life, it upheld its earlier concept of the essence of private life as an area that nobody can intrude into against the concerned person's will, or even observe.

Thereafter, the HCC stated that there is an especially strong bond between the right to private life, as provided for by Article VI (1) of the FL, and the right to human dignity as guaranteed by Article II of the FL. Article II of the FL provides the foundation for the protection of the inviolable sphere of private life, which is unavailable for any state interference and provides the basis of human dignity. The protection of private life, however, is not limited to the protection of the inner or intimate sphere (as specified in Article II of the FL) as well as the spatial domain where private and family life is lived (the home). Furthermore, the public perception of somebody's life also enjoys special protection (the right to a good name) (Reasoning [84]).

The HCC emphasised that the right to informational self-determination is closely connected to the right to private life. The Court upheld its practice of interpreting the right to the protection of personal information as informational self-determination and explained that informational self-determination involves the right of the individual to decide when and to what extent to disclose personal information. The HCC argued that its decision to uphold the interpretation of the right to the protection of personal information as informational self-determination is, besides the identical contents of the last expression of Article 59 (1) of the FL and the first expression of Article VI (2), based on 'the FL's definition of the relationship between the individual and society as one wherein the individual is tied to society, without, however, mentioning the value of the individual. This follows especially from Article O) and Article II.' It also declared that 'as a social being and one embedded in society an individual has to accept having to disclose certain pieces of personal information and their being used by the state' [Reasoning 88].

The HCC also highlighted the differences between informational self-determination and the right to private life. The limitation of informational self-determination is based not on the nature of the information involved but on its use. Informational self-determination protects an individual's personal data regardless of the ways they were collected [Reasoning 89].

3.3. Secret intelligence gathering enables a forcible intrusion into all segments of private life (including the intimate ones) and might affect people other than the target of the observation; therefore it is imperative that the procedure guarantees the requisite protection of all areas of private life, as well as limiting the use of the data obtained for a specified purpose [Article VI (2) of the FL].

In the given case, the HCC established that the types of secret information gathering listed in Article 56 of the NS Act (secret house search and surveillance, opening postal deliveries, examining and recording electronic and computerised communications and obtaining information stored on computers) enables forcible intrusions into all segments of private life (including intimate ones) and can affect people other than the target of the observation. The HCC said that while the different areas of private life need different levels of protection, since the surveillance is carried out in secret and thus gives unlimited powers to the authorities who realise it, it is imperative that the procedure guarantees the requisite protection of all areas of private life. The Court also declared that the limitations on state interference are contained in the formal (legal regulation) and substantial (necessity-proportionality) requirements of Article I (3) of the FL (Reasoning [85]).

The HCC also found that the storage and use of information obtained in secret information gathering constitutes a significant limitation of the right to informational self-determination. In its interpretation of the 'proportionate to the objective pursued' phrase in Article I (3) of the FL, the HCC reaffirmed the principle elaborated in its earlier practice that the condition of the right to informational self-determination, as well as its most important guarantee, is being tied to an objective (Reasoning [90]–[91]).

Thereafter, the HCC examined the constitutionality of the authorisation of secret information gathering by the minister for justice.

The HCC came to the conclusion that in cases related to national security events are not always judged upon their criminal law relevance, so they do not necessarily need to be connected to crimes. Moreover, NS Act enables the monitoring of the minister for justice's authorisation procedure by actors independent of the executive power. External monitoring is conducted by the Parliament's National Security Committee (which can request both a general and a specific report from the minister for justice on the authorisation) and the Ombudsman (Reasoning [122]–[123]).

The HCC noticed, however, that NS Act does not specifically make explanations of acts of authorisation mandatory. It established that while the decision on authorisation has to be based on the application, it necessarily remains one sided, since it only admits the interests of national security. Therefore, it is the authoriser's responsibility to balance the interests of national security and those of the individual(s) targeted by secret surveillance, taking into account the latter's right to private life and informational self-determination; to weigh not only the necessity of limitation but also its proportionality (Reasoning [130]–[134]).

The HCC, thereafter, examined data management by the counter-terror organisation after the completion of the secret information gathering operation and found that while, unlike Article 73 (3) of the Police Act, NS Act does not make the deletion of information not strictly relevant to the case mandatory *expressis verbis*, an interpretation of the cumulative effect of its regulations makes it clear that all information collected during the operation that is not strictly relevant to the purposes which legitimized information gathering in the first place need to be deleted ex officio, especially if it belongs to persons not involved in the investigation. The above regulation is, therefore, adequate to the principle of targeted data gathering and is well-suited to stopping generalised information gathering (Reasoning [138]).

4. *Doctrinal analysis*

4.1. *Differentiating between Exceptional Constitutional Complaint and Actio Popularis*

The new type of constitutional complaint appeared in the Hungarian legal system in Article 26 (2) of the HCC Act and replaced the former legal instrument of *actio popularis*, which amounted to an abstract norm control and could be initiated by anybody. In its practice the HCC generally refers to the 'exceptional quality'[6] of norm control based on Article 26 (2) of the HCC Act to differentiate it from abstract norm control and insists on examining personal involvement; as it did in the case on secret information gathering (Reasoning [18]).

Complaints against laws are distinguished from posterior abstract norm control with a view to preserving the constitutionality of the objective legal systems by personal injuria.[7] Without citing direct involvement any petition can only be regarded as an application for abstract posterior norm control, which however only certain bodies and persons are entitled to submit, as listed in Article 24 (2) e) of the FL {3025/2013. (II. 12.) AB, Reasoning [4]}.[8] Being affected is, therefore, the *differentia specifica* of direct constitutional complaint against a law, which separates it from abstract posterior norm control.

6 Decision 23/2019. (III. 7.) AB, Reasoning [32], [35], [44]; Decision 3154/2016. (VII. 22.) AB, Reasoning [11]; Decision 3198/2015. (X. 14.) AB, Reasoning [79]; Decision 3105/2012. (VII. 26.) AB, Reasoning [3].

7 Decision 3367/2012. (XII. 15.) AB, Reasoning [13].

8 This led some to question whether constitutional complaint as defined in Article 26 (2) of the HCC Act is an adequate replacement of *actio popularis*, since the conditions of admittance limit the HCC's possibilities in the objective defence of the law. Vissy, 'Az individuális alapjogvédelem kilátásai az alkotmánybíráskodásban' (2012), 28 (36).

Following German tradition the HCC established a threefold system of criteria for being personally affected. Decision 33/2012. (VII. 17.) AB (analysis of Decision Forced Retirement of Judges see in this volume) first published these criteria in the following words: 'being personally affected is a condition of the admissibility of the complaint, namely that the legal provision deemed by the complainant to be contrary to the FL shall provide a rule directly, factually and actually affecting the concrete legal relationship of the complainant in person, resulting in the violation of the complainant's fundamental rights' (Reasoning [61]). This decision elaborated on the concept of being actually affected [analysis of Decision Forced Retirement of Judges see in this volume). Decision 3110/2013. (VI. 4.) AB was the first interpretation of all three of the conditions of admissibility (Reasoning [27]). Therefore, with a view to the unusual qualities of secret information gathering, the HCC examined the three criteria in its decision on secret information gathering.

The petitioners based their argument for being personally affected on 'everyone being a potential victim', but they also claimed that as an NGO that monitors the activities of all governments their employees are even more likely to be targeted. The HCC accepted the petitioners' claim of being affected, since due to the special character of secret information gathering, the petitioners cannot be expected to prove that they have become targeted (Reasoning [32]). Due to such a broad interpretation of being personally affected, the HCC accepted the possibility of being personally affected as a criterion of admissibility, even without examining the relationship between the fundamental rights position of the petitioner and the potential violation of the norm. My belief is that, due to the exceptionality of constitutional complaint, the Court should have examined whether the complainants were in a position that put them at *risque sérieux/reasonable risk*[9] of being the targets of secret information gathering. Constitutional complaint as a subjective legal remedy can only ever be functional if it is realised on the basis of a threat of a real violation of the legal subjects' rights; otherwise it is the defence of the objective legal system's constitutionality.

Being directly affected' means, in the practice of the HCC, that the law in question leads directly to the violation of the complainant's rights; in other words, the law in question directly affects a fundamental right of the

9 *Klass and Others v. Germany*, Series A no. 28, judgment of 6 September 1978, para. 31.

complainant.[10] In specific cases, the minister for justice authorises secret information gathering, therefore, in principle there is 'an executive act of constitutive effect', which can result in immediate violation of fundamental rights. The petitioners, however, cannot be expected to attack that, since it is impossible for them to establish the authoriser's decision. The criterion of directness is tied to the criteria laid down in Article 26 (2) b) of the HCC Act, since the violation needs to occur directly, without court interference. There is no legal remedy against the legal violation caused by secret information gathering.

In the practice of the HCC, being actually affected refers to a violation that has actually taken place therefore, as a main rule, if it has not actually happened by the time the complaint is made, it is merely hypothetical or potential and not actual.[11] The HCC, nevertheless, with a view to the secret nature of surveillance, concluded that the petitioners were actually affected, since they could have no information on whether or not there were ongoing or finalised information gathering operations targeting them. Therefore, the statement that being actually affected cannot be interpreted in such a case is incorrect (Reasoning [35]). The petitioners cannot be expected to fulfil the criteria of either directness or being actually affected.

The HCC, therefore, made an exception to the threefold system of criteria in the secret information gathering case. Given the special character of information gathering, this can be accepted, but only if there is serious risk of surveillance that the petitioners are exposed to. Otherwise, the distinction between constitutional complaint and *actio popularis* becomes hopelessly blurred.

4.2. The Foundations of the Right to Private Life

The decision on secret information gathering is based on Article VI (1) of the FL, of which it was the HCC's first interpretation. Following the German model,[12] the HCC distinguished between different areas of private life, according to how strong a protection they need. A distinction was

10 Decision 3110/2013. (VI. 4.) AB, Reasoning [30].

11 E.g. Decision 3033/2014. (III. 3.) AB, Reasoning [20].

12 BVerfGE 6, 32 (41); 34, 238 (248); 65, 1 (46). Academic literature has also proposed the possibility of completely or partially abandoning the theory of spheres. Dreier, 'Art. 2 Abs. 1 Freie Entfaltung der Persönlichkeit' in Dreier (ed), *Grundgesetz Kommentar* (2004) 341; Desoi and Knierim, 'Intimsphäre und Kernbereichsschutz' (2011), 398 (401).

introduced between the inner core of private life, the intimate sphere, which enjoys absolute protection and the broader private sphere, which enjoys relative protection.

The most significant novelty of the decision is the introduction (once again, following German precedent[13]) of the concept of 'the inviolable sphere of private life'. The question then becomes whether this amounts to a reinterpretation of the connection between the right to private life and the right to human dignity.

After the coming into force of the FL, the HCC declaratively upheld the distinction between those two aspects of human dignity[14] however, in my opinion, the HCC went further than had been its general personality rights practice respecting the relationship between the right to human dignity and the right to private life. The former Constitution, in the absence of the explicitly named category of general personality rights, identified (following the German model[15]) the restrictable aspect of the right to human dignity with general personality rights. In the practice of the HCC, general personality rights were seen as comprehensive personality protection rights, which became suitable for the comprehensive protection of personality through naming its various contents, in cases when none of the named fundamental rights could be applied to the given case. The decision that identified the right to human dignity with general personality rights, as a component of general personality rights, named the right to a private sphere as one of its components.[16] At the same time, it tied the essential part of the right to private life to the unrestrictable aspect of the right to human dignity.[17] In other words, the HCC had in an earlier decision

13 BVerfGE 6, 32 (41); 27, 1 (7); 80, 367 (374). Some authors, however, argue for the relativity of the untouchable core of private life. Baldus, 'Der Kernbereich privater Lebensgestaltung' (2008), 218 (224); Teifke, *Das Prinzip der Menschenwürde* (2011), 23.

14 The right to the protection of human dignity is only unrestrictable as the legal determinant of human status, while as a general personality right and the resulting partial rights can be restricted. Decision 7/2014. (III. 7.) AB, Reasoning [43].

15 Dupré, *Importing the law in post-communist transitions* (2003), 75 ff.

16 Decision 8/1990. (IV. 23.) AB, ABH 1990, 42, 45.

17 '[…] the essential content of the right to human dignity granted under Article 54 (1) of the Constitution is affected if the regulation allowing the application of electronic surveillance systems fails to address the respect and protection of privacy […] there are problems of interpretation concerning the regulation and in some parts the regulation is incomplete, certain especially sensitive fields of privacy (intimate situations: e.g. being in fitting rooms, restrooms, changing-rooms, toilets) cannot be completely excluded from the scope of surveillance' Decision 36/2005. (X. 5.) AB, ABH 2005, 390, 401–402.

already differentiated the areas of the private sphere that are of especial sensitivity and constitute the intimate sphere, and specified it as the core component of human dignity, but it conducted a necessity-proportionality investigation, nevertheless.

One approach suggests that the essential part of fundamental rights can be identified during a necessity-proportionality investigation by the HCC (the relative approach). This approach does not differentiate between the examination of the fundamental right's area of objective protection and the examination of the restriction, thus relativizing the concept of essential content. The other approach separates the examination of essential content from the necessity-proportionality examination, because the essential content is seen as given (the absolute approach).[18]

Nor does HCC practice reveal the exact nature of the relationship between the right to private life and the right to human dignity. Is the essential part identical to the core of human rights or is the essential part broader than the core of human dignity, containing it merely as one of its component parts? The reason for this is that the argument from the essential part of human dignity has only emerged whenever general personality rights were affected and when the human dignity component of the broadly understood and relative fundamental right was the absolute manifestation of the same fundamental right, which obviously meant that the essential part and the human rights core were always the same. As a consequence, the two manifestations of the right to human dignity are seen as broader or narrower definitions of the same concept.

Irrespective of the above question, the value component of the right to human dignity is, in the interpretation of the HCC, inherent in all fundamental rights from the outset. This interpretation was constitutionalised by the HCC when declaring the inviolability of human dignity.[19]

---

18 Pozsár-Szentmiklósy differentiates four approaches to essential content: the first regards it as abstractly definable and absolute; the second defines it through certain given contents; the third defines it through the decision on the restrictability of the given fundamental right; while the fourth grants it a purely symbolic role. He concludes that the relative approach dominates in Hungary and the relative approach has enjoyed a boom with regard to rights under absolute protection. Pozsár-Szentmiklósy, 'Megismerhető-e az alapjogok lényeges tartalma?' (2013) 714 ff.

19 The Reasoning of the FL bill stated that 'before the regulations on individual fundamental rights, the FL declares the inviolability of human dignity as a basic principle, which emphatically, specifically, and with a strong effect on the interpretation of other FLs states the untouchability of the essential component of human dignity'.

In its decision on secret information gathering, the HCC, while interpreting Article VI (1) of the FL, reaffirmed the practice of separating the intimate sphere from the private sphere and declared its support for the absolute interpretation of human dignity, since it positioned its protection within the untouchable domain of the private sphere, one which is exempt from all state interference. The untouchable domain of the private sphere is the human dignity core of the right to private life, which guarantees the absolute protection of the intimate sphere. The HCC has not given a general definition of the intimate sphere, but has listed its component parts. In its practice to date, it has included sexuality, having one's own name, the right to know one's origins, freedom of conscience, and the wish to have children in the core or intimate sphere.[20] From this we can conclude that both the intimate sphere and the untouchable domain of private life are connected to the individual's behaviour in the inner sphere, which is connected to significant elements of the individual's self-identity. Therefore the contents of the two concepts coincide. One important difference, however, is that the HCC, in its earlier practice, defined the intimate sphere through a necessity-proportionality test (relative theory) the untouchable domain, however, is defined through a list of its components, which are seen as unrestrictable (absolute theory).

Relying on the practice of the GFCC,[21] the HCC has highlighted the connection between informational self-determination and the right to private life. Nevertheless, following the altered text of the FL, it also separated the spheres that the two fundamental rights defend. Accordingly, informational self-determination protects the use of an individual's personal information, irrespective of how that information was acquired. The private sphere is potentially violated when information was gathered through an invasion of one's privacy.

The HCC based the application of its former practice on the anthropology of the FL, which fills the legal concept of human dignity with positive content, defining a human as an autonomous social being endowed with self-worth but also responsibility.[22] Therefore, the right to human dignity, as part of the essential content of other fundamental rights (including the right to private life and the right to informational self-determination) provides special protection to the static elements of a personality.

---

20 Decision 17/2014. (V. 30.) AB, Reasoning [32].

21 BVerfGE 65, 1 (48).

22 Decision 3110/2013. (VI. 4.) AB, Reasoning [49]; Decision 3132/2013. (VII. 2.) AB, Reasoning [95]; Decision 32/2013. (XI. 22.) AB, Reasoning [88].

The absolute protection of the human personality in the untouchable area of private life involves the individual's right to experience inner psychological processes or express emotions and personal ideas without having to worry about observance on the part of state authorities. Therefore, in judging on secret information gathering, what needs primarily to be considered is whether the human quality is ignored (objectification). The untouchable domain of private life can, however, also be defined positively in specific cases (e.g. with regard to aspects of sexuality). Here, it is the personal quality that is decisive, which, depending on the nature of the relationship, can also be influenced by another person's private sphere, or by public interest.

So, the circle of rights protected by private life is marked out by human dignity; it protects those elements of a psychological and moral personality without which humans simply cannot develop. The right to private life, however, is broader than that and extends to the dynamic aspects of realising an individual's personality, i.e. every private life behaviour that might contribute to a person's mental or moral development and can be restricted, especially if they collide with other people's fundamental rights. In decisions on private sphere restrictions, as opposed to those in cases involving violations of human dignity, in which the individual sense of being violated is irrelevant, the subjective experience also needs to be considered.

4.3. The Conflict between the Right to Private Life and National Security

The right to private life, as we have seen, is strongly tied to the human quality, and is, therefore, entitled to special protection. However, citing threats to national security, the state can systematically interfere in a person's relationships, thus violating their private spheres, often citing reasons of protection. Therefore the two interests can only be interpreted in conjunction.

The HCC accepted that authorisation for secret information gathering by the minister for justice is a sufficient fundamental rights guarantee, because the NS Act creates a possibility for a monitoring of the process by bodies independent of the executive branch. According to the majority opinion, reconciling this conflict is the responsibility of the authoriser, whose evaluating process is overseen by the National Security Committee of the Parliament and the fundamental rights' ombudsman.

According to the dissenting opinion, however, the reconciliation of the conflict between the right to private life and national security should not be a matter of political consideration, but should rather be decided on an examination of the necessity and proportionality of the restriction of rights. The institutional guarantee for such an examination is a court.[23] The dissenting opinion points out that giving the power of authorisation to use the secret information gathering tools of a government-directed organisation to a representative of the executive branch is already unjustified since the minister is not part of an external monitoring organisation.[24] Moreover, the regulation under review offers no effective external control over the authorization of the minister, since there is no regulation to guarantee that each decision is reviewed by the Committee, not even in principle.[25] The subject of secret information gathering is not even given posterior notice of the procedure, making external control impossible in practice. Although the fundamental rights' ombudsman, as an independent actor, would be well-placed to exercise external control, they could only initiate such a procedure within the framework of an official examination, one that ensures court supervision of its decisions. The dissenting opinion especially highlighted the fact that the regulation does not conform to the norms established by the practice of the Strasbourg court. The dissenting opinion has proved to be correct since the ruling was made.

5. *Aftermath of the Decision*

After the decision on secret information gathering was made, the ECtHR made its ruling in *Szabó and Vissy v. Hungary* and found that the regulation violates Article 8 of the ECHR.

First, the ECtHR argued that the regulation contained in NS Act enable extensive, so-called strategic information-gathering, since there is no requirement of a direct connection between the subjects under surveillance and the threat of terrorism, meaning that practically anyone can be subjected to secret data gathering in Hungary.[26]

Second, the ECtHR stated that the regulation does not conform to 'the test of strict necessity'. Secret information gathering can only be in conformity with the ECHR if, as a general consideration, it is strictly necessary for the protection of the democratic institutions and, as a specific

23 Judge Péter Paczolay's dissenting opinion, Reasoning [155]. Judge András Bragyova joined the dissenting opinion.

24 Judge Péter Paczolay's dissenting opinion, Reasoning [153].

25 Judge Péter Paczolay's dissenting opinion, Reasoning [157].

26 *Szabó and Vissy v. Hungary*, no. 37138/14, judgment of 12 January 2016, para. 73.

consideration, it is necessary for obtaining cardinal pieces of information in a specific operation. The ECtHR took the position that the lack of court oversight in both the authorisation and the application phase of the surveillance creates a fundamental problem.[27] Authorisation of the procedure falls within the domain of the executive power, disregarding the principle of strict necessity. As regards the authorisation of surveillance, non-court authorisation of surveillance is not necessarily a violation of the ECHR, but in such cases the authorising body needs to be sufficiently independent of the executive power.[28] However, the very nature of the minister of justice's deliberation makes the evaluation of strict necessity impossible, especially since there are no legal guarantees that the CTC would be obliged to substantiate or factually demonstrate the need for secret information gathering.

Third, the ECtHR found that, not just courts, all other legal remedies are denied in such a case. The monitoring power of the Parliament's National Security Committee are limited, since it is very general and is restricted mostly to examining the minister of justice's authorisation reports and, therefore, can offer no legal remedies for the individual harms suffered because of secret information gathering.[29] Moreover, there are limited opportunities for complaint as well, since, the citizens involved are not informed about the information gathering they have been subjected to. The minister for justice, who judges about the complaints received, cannot be seen as sufficiently independent. Finally, the ECtHR has observed that the ombudsman has never examined a case related to secret information gathering.[30]

As a result, preparations to amend the legislation have started,[31] but have still not been completed.[32]

---

27 *Szabó and Vissy v. Hungary*, no. 37138/14, judgment of 12 January 2016, para. 75.

28 *Szabó and Vissy v. Hungary*, no. 37138/14, judgment of 12 January 2016, para. 73.

29 *Szabó and Vissy v. Hungary*, no. 37138/14, judgment of 12 January 2016, para. 82.

30 *Szabó and Vissy v. Hungary*, no. 37138/14, judgment of 12 January 2016, para. 84.

31 For a detailed analysis of the aftermath of *Szabó and Vissy v. Hungary*, see: Csink and Török, 'The collision of national security purpose secret information gathering and the right to privacy' in Bień-Kacała et al. (ed), *Liberal Constitutionalism* (2017), 171 ff.

32 The Criminal Procedure Act eliminated the dichotomy between secret information gathering and secret data gathering and introduced significant innovations in the process of secret information gathering for the purposes of a criminal investigation. However, the regulation of secret information gathering for national security purposes has not changed.

Bibliography

Manfred Baldus, 'Der Kernbereich privater Lebensgestaltung – absolut geschützt, aber abwägungsoffen' (2008) 5 *Juristen Zeitung*, 218.

Lóránt Csink and Réka Török, 'The Collision of National Security Purpose Secret Information Gathering and the Right to Privacy. The Present and Future of Hungarian Regulation' in Agnieszka Bień-Kacała, Lóránt Csink, Tomasz Milej, and Maciej Serowaniec (eds), *Liberal Constitutionalism – Between Individual and Collective Interests* (Uniwesytet Mikołaja Kopernika W Toruniu, Torun 2017), 171.

Monika Desoi and Antonie Knierim: 'Intimsphäre und Kernbereichsschutz. Ein unantastbarer Bereich privater Lebensgestaltung in der Rechtsprechung des Bundesverfassungsgerichts' (2011) 10 *Die Öffentliche Verwaltung*, 398.

Horst Dreier, 'Art. 2 Abs. 1 Freie Entfaltung der Persönlichkeit' in Horst Dreier (ed), *Grundgesetz Kommentar* (Mohr Siebeck, Tübingen 2004)

Catherine Dupré, *Importing the Law in Post-communist Transitions. The Hungarian Constitutional Court and the Right to Human Dignity* (Hart, Oxford – Portland Oregon 2003)

Zoltán Pozsár-Szentmiklósy, 'Megismerhető-e az alapjogok lényeges tartalma?' [Can the Essential Content of Fundamental Rights Be Known?] (2013) 12 *Magyar Jog*, 714.

Nils Teifke, '*Das Prinzip der Menschenwürde. Zur Abwägung des Höchstrangigen*' (Mohr Siebeck, Tübingen 2011)

Beatrix Vissy, 'Az individuális alapjogvédelem kilátásai az alkotmánybíráskodásban. Merre mutat az alkotmányjogi panasz iránytűje?' [The Future of Individual Fundamental Rights Protection in Constitutional Justice. Where Does the Compass of the Constitutional Complaint Point?] (2012) 2 *Magyar Közigazgatás*, 28.

17. Decision 36/2013. (XII. 5.) AB – Transfer of Cases

András Osztovits[*]

The designation of the acting court by a discretionary decision of the President of the National Office for the Judiciary leads to an infringement of the right of access to one's lawful judge which originates from the requirement of a fair process.

One of the most important structural changes of the 2011 judicial reform was the creation of a judicial management model based on individual decision-making instead of the earlier concept of the collective responsibility of the members of a judicial council.[1] The competencies of the President of the National Office for the Judiciary (NOJ) drew both international and domestic criticism, the direction of the structural changes was indicated by the modifications of the FL as well as of the relevant cardinal acts of law, and the debated issues were settled towards the end of 2013.[2] Decision Transfer of Cases forms part of the foregoing, as it declared, with effect from the date of its delivery, that the competence—that had since been repealed—of the President of the NOJ concerning the transfer of cases had been contrary to the FL and to the applicable international treaty.

1. *Background*

1.1. *Evolution of the Hungarian legislation*

The high number of incoming cases, the heavy case workload and, consequently, the excessive length (protraction) of proceedings have been the most characteristic problems of the Hungarian justice system since the 1990 change of regime. The peculiarity of the situation is that, in compar-

* PhD, Professor, Károli Gáspár University of the Reformed Church in Hungary Faculty of Legal Sciences (Budapest).

1 Osztovits, 'Az új magyar bírósági szervezetrendszer' in Rixer (ed), *Állam és közösség* (2012), 381 ff.

2 Balogh-Békesi, 'A bírói hatalmi ág az Alaptörvény rendszerében' (2016), 9.

ison to the courts in the countryside, the courts of the so-called central region (which includes the capital city of Budapest and the surrounding county of Pest) are forced to deal with a significantly larger number of cases that raise more complex legal issues and often are of greater interest for the media.[3] The National Council of Justice (NCJ), a judicial body responsible for the central administration of the courts between 1998 and 2011, had been unable to address the above situation at a systemic level, the main reason for which was probably that, unlike the presidents of the courts of the central region (the minority), the leaders of the courts in the countryside (the majority) had no interest in changing the *status quo*.

The systemic problem of the protraction of proceedings is justified by the fact that, during that time period, the ECtHR found against Hungary mostly due to the excessive length of court processes.[4] In the case of *Gazsó v. Hungary*,[5] the ECtHR ordered, based on Rule 61 of the Rules of Court, the carrying out of a pilot judgment procedure, and held that the violations, i.e. the protraction of proceedings in an individual labour lawsuit, originated in a practice incompatible with the ECHR, specifically, Hungary's recurrent failure to ensure that proceedings determining civil rights and obligations were completed within a reasonable time.

The poor 'medical condition' of the justice system was, in that regard, evident at the time of the 2010 change of government; the legislator's 'diagnosis', however, entailed an almost three-year-long series of debates. Prior to the adoption of the FL, the Parliament enacted Act CLXXXIII of 2010 on the modification of certain acts of law with the aim of ensuring the efficient functioning of the courts and accelerating court proceedings.

3 Örkényi, 'Arányos ügyteherelosztás az igazságszolgáltatásban – elvek és teendők' (2012), 13.

4 Between the date of Hungary's accession to the ECHR and 1 May 2015, more than 200 judgments were delivered in which the ECtHR found that Hungary had violated the provisions of the ECHR as a result of the excessive length of civil court proceedings. In addition, the Hungarian Government concluded friendly settlements and made unilateral declarations in a great number of cases related to the length of civil court proceedings, which resulted in the subsequent striking out of the cases concerned. On 1 May 2015, approximately 400 such cases against Hungary were pending before the various judicial formations of the ECtHR, and the number of applications based on the protraction of proceedings was still continuously increasing at that time. Having regard to the fact that the ECtHR's cited judgements were necessarily delivered only after the exhaustion of the available Hungarian remedies, the numbers indicated above refer to the proceedings initiated prior to 1 January 2012. These are examined in detail in the case *Gazsó v. Hungary*, no. 48322/12, judgment of 16 July 2015, paras. 34 and 36.

5 *Gazsó v. Hungary*, no. 48322/12, judgment of 16 July 2015.

Article 10 of the aforementioned Act, with effect from 7 January 2011, modified Act LXVI of 1997 on the organisation and administration of the courts (former Courts Act) and included Article 33/A therein. Pursuant to the latter Article, the Supreme Court was entitled—on a recommendation by the President of the NCJ—to reassign, in exceptional circumstances, certain cases from the court of original jurisdiction to another court of analogous jurisdiction, if providing a reasonable timeframe for hearing the case or a group of specific cases assigned to the court could not be otherwise ensured due to the extraordinary and disproportionate workload of the court, and if having additional cases assigned would not impose a disproportionate burden on the court affected.[6]

As regards criminal proceedings, Act LXXXIX of 2011 on the modification of certain acts of law of a procedural nature and touching upon the administration of justice went even further, and Article 2 thereof added a new Article 17 (9) of Act XIX of 1998 on the Code of Criminal Procedure (former Code of Criminal Procedure), which enabled the prosecutor—on the basis of the prosecutor general's decision—to bring charges before a court other than the competent one in priority cases as defined by Article 554/B of the former Code of Criminal Procedure if the conditions to conclude them within a reasonable time or subject them to priority treatment were guaranteed at that other court. In its Decision 166/2011. (XII. 20.) AB, the HCC found that the aforementioned provision was unconstitutional and contrary to international law (Article 6 of the ECHR), and so decided to annul it.[7] The reasoning of the decision made it clear that the HCC undertook to be bound by the ECtHR's case-law on the right to a fair trial as well as by the objective and subjective tests of the independence of the judiciary.[8] At its session held on 30 December 2011, the Parliament adopted the transitional provisions of the FL; Article 11 (3) thereof provided for the right of the President of the NOJ to transfer court cases, while Article 11 (4) thereof determined the right of the prosecutor general to 'transfer the bringing of charges', with the content explained above.

Against this background, the rules on the designation of the acting court were included in Chapter V of Act CLXI of 2011 on the organisation

6 Article 102 of the same piece of legislation supplemented Article 47 of the former Code of Civil Procedure and reiterated, in substance, the relevant provision of the former Courts Act.

7 It is interesting to note the broad range of motioners who included, *inter alia*, the President of the Supreme Court and the President of the Hungarian Bar Association.

8 See in particular part III of the reasoning.

and administration of the courts (Courts Act). Articles 62–63 of the Courts Act enabled the President of the NOJ to reassign, in exceptional circumstances, a case from the court of original jurisdiction to another court of analogous jurisdiction. By virtue of Article 62 (1), such reassignment necessitated the fulfilment of two conditions: i) the hearing of the case or a group of specific cases lodged with the court within a given period of time cannot be ensured otherwise within a reasonable timeframe due to the extraordinary and disproportionate workload of the court, and ii) the reassignment does not impose a disproportionate burden on the court affected. Pursuant to Article 63, the right of the President of the NOJ to reassign cases was limited in time; moreover, prior to the exercise of such right, the President of the NOJ was obliged to obtain information about the court's caseload statistics, employment details and other information, as well as about the specificities of the case to be reassigned in order to decide on the well-foundedness of the motion to reassign the case and, eventually, on the other court to be designated.

The unlimited nature of the above regulation drew criticism almost immediately.[9] In its opinion[10] adopted at its session held on 16–17 March 2012, the Venice Commission—with reference to the ECtHR's jurisprudence—clearly indicated that the Hungarian regulation, in the absence of objective criteria, infringed the right to a lawful judge—as part of the right to a fair trial—under Article 6 of the ECHR. Furthermore, it stressed that the requirement of the adjudication of cases within a reasonable period of time also formed part of Article 6 of the ECHR; however, such requirement should not be absolute and should not violate the other elements of the right to a fair trial (paras. 86–94).

As one of the results of the consultations, Article 3 (1) of Act CXI of 2012—which primarily rearranged the competencies of the NOJ and the National Judicial Council (NJC)—modified Article 63 (3) of the Courts Act (with effect from 17 July 2012) and provided for the right to a direct appeal against the decision designating another court to proceed.[11]

9 Zajcsek, 'A törvényes bíróhoz való jog az ügyáthelyezés jogintézményének tükrében' in Varga (ed), *Codificatio processualis civilis* (2013), 529.

10 Opinion on Act CLXII of 2011 on the legal status and remuneration of judges and Act CLXI of 2011 on the organisation and administration of courts of Hungary. CDL-AD (2012)001.

11 The first ruling delivered by the Curia of Hungary in an appellate procedure assigned to the supreme judicial forum was ruling no. Kpkf.I.37.589/2012/2 in which the Curia of Hungary laid down that the President of the NOJ exercised the right to reassign a court case within the framework of his/her administrative

After further consultations[12] the Parliament adopted, on 25 March 2013, the Fourth Amendment to the FL; Article 14 of the amendment inserted the right of the President of the NOJ to reassign court cases into Article 27 (4) of the FL. Nevertheless, it specified that the scope of the cases that could be subject to reassignment and the criteria for reassigning them would be regulated by a cardinal act of law. Subsequently, the Hungarian Government immediately submitted a bill on the modification of certain acts of law in connection with the Fourth Amendment to the FL.[13] During this period, the European Commission and the Hungarian Government were engaged in an intensive consultation on the Fourth Amendment to the FL, therefore the debates on the bill were suspended for a month and a half. As part of the compromise achieved, the Hungarian Government promised to remove the instrument of the transfer of court cases from the country's legal system.[14] As a first step, the Parliament adopted, at its session held on 5 July 2013, Act CXXXI of 2013 to repeal the right of the President of the NOJ to reassign cases from Act III of 1952 on the Code of Civil Procedure (the former Code of Civil Procedure), the former Code of Criminal Procedure and the Courts Act.[15] Finally, the Fifth Amendment to the FL (26 September 2013) repealed, as a final step, the relevant provision of Article 27 (4) of the FL.

All of this entailed that, at the time of the delivery of its decision, the HCC had to examine the unconstitutionality of various pieces of legislation which were no longer in force, and their conflict with an international treaty.

---

competencies. In the course of the adjudication of the appeal, the Curia of Hungary did not address any considerations of appropriateness, as it examined only the lawfulness of the impugned decision.

12 The parliamentary debates are described in detail by Bárándy, *Centralizált Magyarország – megtépázott jogvédelem* (2014), 257.

13 Bill no. T/10593.

14 The minutes of the Parliament's plenary session held on 11 June 2013 (session no. 288), contributions no. 114–131.

15 The original version of the bill aimed at reforming the rules on the right to reassign court cases. According to the original text, the President of the NOJ could not be allowed to reassign individual cases, as his/her right of reassignment should have covered specific groups of cases enumerated by the bill, with a reassignment applicable only for a predetermined period of time. Moreover, the reassignment should have been made only to those courts that had a workload below the national average based on the last six months' caseload statistics. In addition, the reassignment would have needed to be petitioned by the president of the high court or regional appellate court concerned or by the prosecutor general and to be agreed on by the NJC.

1.2. International outlook

The issue of the transfer of court cases is an administrative matter related to the courts' workload and the number of incoming judicial cases. The addressing thereof in an efficient manner and in conformity with the relevant constitutional principles is a recurring concern in almost every country. There are no substantial differences between the national laws of the EU's Member States in this regard, their common feature being that they seek to make the assignment of court cases transparent and predictable on the basis of strict rules of jurisdiction and territorial competence. In addition, the question of the allocation of cases within a given court is also related to the issue of the transfer of cases; the case allocation models vary from fully automated processes to case-by-case allocations depending on the specificities of the legal disputes concerned.[16] Their common objective is, among others, to provide a balanced distribution of court cases, thus ensuring the implementation of the right to have one's case adjudicated within a reasonable time. By examining the ECtHR's jurisprudence, the HCC referred to the Slovakian regulation that allowed, in the period under examination, for the reallocation of cases with the aim of alleviating the court's workload (Reasoning [48]). In another case involving Albania where military judges were reassigned to hear an ordinary criminal case within the framework of the reassignment of judges due to the courts' excessive workload, the ECtHR held that the mere fact that the judges had been reassigned from another level of the judiciary had raised no concerns, since the ECtHR's assessment was to focus on whether the method of the reassignment had been in compliance with the guarantees set forth in Article 6 of the ECHR (Reasoning [52]).

2. Petition

Multiple motions were lodged with the HCC. The motioners—all of them being accused persons in criminal proceedings—requested that the HCC, due to the transfer of their case to another court, find that Articles 62, 63 and 64 of the Courts Act, Article 20/A of the former Code of Criminal Procedure and Decision 22/2012. (II. 16.) OBHE of the President of the NOJ had been contrary to the FL and to the applicable international treaty, and

16 Osztovits, 'A törvényes bíróhoz való jog a német szövetségi és az osztrák alkotmánybíróságok joggyakorlatában' (2005), 420.

consequently to annul them. Some of the motioners argued that the above provisions had not complied with the requirement of a fair process under Article 6 (1) of the ECHR. In particular, they had infringed their right to a lawful judge and the principles of impartiality and equality of arms by enabling the President of the NOJ to decide, at his/her own discretion, on the designation of the acting court. Moreover, the total absence of a right of appeal against the decision of the President of the NOJ violates Article 13 of the ECHR.

Other motioners referred to Article XXVIII (1), (3) and (7) of the FL. They took the view that the impugned legal provisions were contrary to the requirement of a fair process and infringed their rights of defence, in connection with a total absence of the right of appeal. They also argued that the principle of the rule of law under Article B (1) of the FL and the requirement of legal certainty originating therefrom had been violated as well, because the impugned provisions had significantly differed from each other in respect of the regulation of the right of the President of the NOJ to transfer court cases. Their constitutional complaint was based on Article 26 (1) of the HCC Act in respect of the contested provisions of the Courts Act, and based on Article 27 of the HCC Act in connection with the impugned decision of the President of the NOJ, since the latter decision qualified—in their opinion—as an on-the-merits decision that was delivered in an individual case and terminated the proceedings.

3. *Decision and its reasoning*

In the operative part of its decision, the HCC found that the provisions of the Courts Act and of the former Code of Criminal Procedure, in effect between 1 January 2012 and 6 July 2012, which had provided the President of the NOJ with the power to reassign court cases, had been contrary to the FL and to the applicable international treaty. On the other hand, the HCC dismissed the motion for the annulment of the decision of the President of the NOJ, based on the latter allegedly being contrary to the FL and to the applicable international treaty, contested by the motioners' constitutional complaint.

3.1. *The designation of the acting court by a discretionary decision of the President of the NOJ violates the requirement of a fair process [Article XXVIII (1) of the FL].*

In the reasoning part of its Decision Transfer of Cases, the HCC recalled its earlier case-law on the right to a fair process. The starting point of its established jurisprudence is that the 'fair trial' is a quality factor that may only be judged by taking into account the whole of the procedure and all of its circumstances. Therefore, a procedure may be 'inequitable', 'unjust' or 'unfair' even despite lacking certain details or complying with all the detailed rules [Decision 6/1998. (III. 11.) AB, ABH 1998, 91, 95.].

The HCC pointed out that, among the requirements of due process, it had thus far dealt with the right to a lawful judge (the prohibition on having one's lawful judge removed) only in a small number of cases. Both Article XXVIII (1) of the FL and Article 6 (1) of the ECHR stipulate that everyone shall have to right to have his/her case heard by a court established by law. The right to a lawful judge implies that an individual case is to be heard by a judicial forum designated by the general rules of jurisdiction and territorial competence, as set forth by the relevant procedural laws. The case's lawful judge is therefore a judge who has been designated in advance by a predetermined case allocation order within the court which has earlier been given jurisdiction and territorial competence by the law to deal with the legal dispute concerned. It follows from the foregoing that the assignment of a judge to hear a specific case may be made in compliance with the constitutional provisions only if such assignment is based on a predetermined set of general rules and a number of objective criteria (Reasoning [32]).

The HCC established that the contested powers of the President of the NOJ to transfer cases under the provisions of the Courts Act and the former Code of Criminal Procedure had constituted an exception to the guarantees of the right to a lawful judge. The legislator, however, failed to determine the conditions of use of these extraordinary powers and the criteria for the transfer of cases. As a result of the regulatory shortcomings, the transfer of cases could be made on the basis of a fully discretionary decision of the President of the NOJ (Reasoning [34]). In this context, the HCC recalled its earlier case-law according to which the fundamental right to have one's case dealt with by a judicial decision within a reasonable time formed an integral part of the requirement of a fair process. Nevertheless, such right was only one of many other elements, and its enforcement should not be exaggerated to an extreme degree: it should not gain priority over the other aspects of a fair trial, and it should never violate another fundamental right.[17]

3.2. The power of the President of the NOJ to transfer court cases does not comply with the right to a lawful judge either [Article 6 (1) of the ECHR].

The HCC reviewed the criteria developed by the ECtHR's jurisprudence on the transfer of court cases. By examining the judgements delivered in the cases *Coëme and others v. Belgium,*[18] *Lavents v. Latvia,*[19] *Ullens de Schooten and Rezabek v. Belgium,*[20] and *Kaçiu and Kotorri v. Albania,*[21] the HCC concluded that the transfer of an individual case or a group of cases from the court acting under the general rules of territorial competence to another court could be made in accordance with the ECHR only if the relevant legislation regulated the substantive and procedural legal rules as well as the preconditions of such transfer by using transparent, predetermined, clear and objective parameters, leaving no (or only minimal) scope for the exercise of a discretionary power. According to the HCC, the examined provisions of the Courts Act and the former Code of Criminal Procedure did not comply with the requirement of impartiality—following from both the FL and the ECHR—nor the appearance of impartiality.

The HCC recalled the criteria established by the ECtHR's case-law on the requirements of the courts' impartiality. The latter constitutes, on one hand, an expectation of judges and of their conduct and attitude, and, on the other hand, an objective requirement in respect of the regulation of the courts' procedure. Judges should avoid any situation which may give rise to justifiable doubt as to their impartiality. In some of its earlier decisions, the HCC also referred to the so-called twofold test applied by the ECtHR.[22] The subjective test examines the personal conduct and the declarations made by the judge on the case, from which the absence of impartiality may be deduced. The objective test is to consider whether there

17 Decision 20/2005. (V. 26.) AB, ABH 2005, 202, 228.

18 *Coëme and others v. Belgium,* nos. 32492/96, 32547/96, 32548/96, 33209/96 and 33210/96, ECHR 2000-VII.

19 *Lavents v. Latvia,* no. 58442/00, judgement of 28 November 2002.

20 *Ullens de Schooten and Rezabek v. Belgium,* nos. 3989/07 and 38353/07, judgment of 20 September 2011.

21 *Kaçiu and Kotorri v. Albania,* nos. 33192/07 and 33194/07, judgment of 25 June 2013.

22 Decision 166/2011. (XII. 20.) AB, ABH 2011, 545, 558–559.

has been any objectively justified reason for the assumption of the absence of impartiality, i.e. whether the given legal rules ensure the effectiveness of the requirement of impartiality and whether the court's procedure, from the point of view of the persons seeking justice, may objectively give rise to doubts as to its impartiality.

3.3. *The definitive nature of the decision of the President of the NOJ violates the right to remedy [Article XXVIII (7) of the FL, Article 13 of the ECHR].*

The HCC has pointed out that the right to remedy concerns judicial and administrative decisions and it means, in substance, that the parties are given the opportunity to turn to another body or a higher instance forum to request the review of an on-the-merits decision. The right to remedy may be exercised as defined by law, hence, there may be diverging rules on the exercise thereof in the different procedural regimes.[23] The possibility of redress is an essential, immanent element of each legal remedy, which means that a legal remedy conceptually and substantially involves the remediability of the infringement suffered.[24] In the HCC's opinion, the fact that the legislator has failed to provide any means of legal remedy against the decision of the President of the NOJ to transfer a court case (regulatory failure) justifies a conclusion that the regulation in question is contrary to the FL and to the applicable international treaty.[25]

3.4. *The decision of the President of the NOJ to transfer a court case does not qualify as an on-the-merits decision (Article 27 of the HCC Act).*

The decision of the President of the NOJ, rendered on the basis of Article 62 of the Courts Act, is not an on-the-merits decision, but rather qualifies as a decision of an administrative nature, which is delivered as part of

---

23 Decision 5/1992. (I. 30.) AB, ABH 1992, 27, 31.; Decision 29/1999. (X. 6.) AB, ABH 1999, 294, 297–298.

24 Decision 23/1998. (VI. 9.) AB, ABH 1998, 182, 186.

25 The operative part of the decision precisely indicates that it concerned the provisions of Articles 62–63 of the Courts Act as in force between 1 January 2012 and 16 July 2012, since Article 3 (1) of Act CXI of 2012 had modified (with effect from 17 July 2012) Article 63 (3) of the Courts Act as a result of which the parties had been given a direct right of appeal against the decision designating another court to proceed.

the main proceedings but in a separate procedure; thus the issue of the designation of the court to proceed has no impact on the decision in the main proceedings. The decision of the President of the NOJ to transfer a court case, therefore, does not meet the conditions laid down in Article 27 of the Constitutional Court Act; consequently, it cannot be challenged by a constitutional complaint.[26]

4. *Doctrinal analysis*

4.1. *The so-called objective test of the impartial administration of justice as one of the assessment criteria of the right to a fair trial*

Almost throughout its decision, the HCC refers to both Article XXVIII (1) of the FL and Article 6 (1) of the ECHR in the course of the examination of the right to a fair trial. The HCC cited one of its earlier decisions[27] in which it had already applied the twofold, subjective and objective test of the requirement of impartiality, developed by the ECtHR's jurisprudence. In its present decision, the HCC did not supplement or develop the aforementioned finding, but rather reapplied the criteria thereof (a regulation that is based on transparent, predetermined, clear and objective parameters) to conclude that the examined provisions of the Courts Act and the former Code of Criminal Procedure did not comply with the requirement of impartiality and the appearances of impartiality, following from both the FL and the ECHR. It merely added that the objective requirement of impartiality could be fulfilled only if the regulation provided sufficient guarantees to exclude any doubts (Reasoning [55]).

Agreeing with the final conclusion, it is worth noting that, in the reasoning part, there is a lack of clear delineation between the requirement of impartiality and the right to a lawful judge: in essence, the HCC relies on the same arguments to find the violation of these two, doctrinally non-identical elements of the right to a fair trial. The argumentation according to which the rules of jurisdiction, territorial competence and case allocation should be based on objective and predictable regulations can primarily be attached to the right to a lawful judge and can be linked to the requirement of impartiality only in an indirect manner.

26 It has already been established in its earlier case-law, see Ruling 3102/2012. (VII. 26.) AB.

27 Decision 23/1998 (VI. 9.) AB.

4.2. The right to a lawful judge

Based on the high number and the content of the dissenting opinions, it can be stated that during the decision-making process the greatest debate among the members of the HCC's panel was primarily related to the diverging answers to the question of whether the non-compliance of the repealed Hungarian pieces of legislation with international law could be examined *ex officio*.

It is worth noting that several HCC judges referred to the issue of sovereignty on the basis of which the *ex officio* examination of international treaties, in particular the ECHR, is not possible or possible only to a very limited extent.[28] The discussions related thereto—particularly in respect of the fulfilment of the obligations arising from EU law—appeared more and more frequently in the HCC's decisions delivered in the subsequent years.[29] Those HCC judges with a dissenting opinion rightly pointed out that the majority decision had not added any new elements to the requirement of the examination of the criteria laid down by the Strasbourg Court's case-law, meaning that the HCC delivered a decision instead of the ECtHR. It is evident, however, that the HCC explored almost the entirety of the ECtHR's relevant jurisprudence on the right to a lawful judge, and it correctly and consistently applied the requirements originating therefrom.

In the reasoning part of its decision, the HCC suggests that, from among the elements of the right to a fair trial, the right to have one's case dealt with within a reasonable time cannot take priority over the other elements, in particular over the right to a lawful judge.[30] Nonetheless, the outcome of the decision, in a peculiar way, is that the right to a lawful

---

28 Dissenting opinion of Judge István Balsai, Reasoning [80]; dissenting opinion of Judge Egon Dienes-Oehm, Reasoning [88]. The latter dissenting opinion was endorsed by Judge Barnabás Lenkovics.

29 Decision 22/2016. (XII. 5.) AB, Decision 2/2019. (III. 5.) AB and Decision 3/2019. (III. 7.) AB.

30 The issue of the right to a 'lawful judge', a 'judge assigned by law' and a 'court established by law' has been addressed in a number of other decisions: Decision 33/2012. (VII. 17.) AB, Decision 3145/2015. (VII. 24.) AB and Ruling 3063/2015. (IV. 10.) AB. Moreover, in certain of its decisions, the HCC also covered the importance of the case allocation order; see, for instance, Decision 21/2014. (VII. 15.) AB, Decision 3357/2017. (XII. 22.) AB, Ruling 3290/2018. (VII. 20.) AB and Decision 3003/2019. (I. 7.) AB. Cited by Csink and Marosi, 'Az Emberi Jogok Európai Bíróságának ítélete a Guđmundur Andri Ástráđsson kontra Izland ügyben' (2019) 48.

judge under the objective rules of jurisdiction and territorial competence has taken precedence over the right to have one's case heard within a reasonable period of time. One of the dissenting opinions indicated that the prevention of the several-year-long protractions in criminal proceedings is not only of public interest, but serves the interests of the accused person as well.[31] It is also more beneficial for the accused if they are not subjected to criminal proceedings lasting for many years. The decision itself admits that the contested power of the President of the NOJ enabled the transfer of individual cases to another court but not to another specific judge. Overall, however, it found that the regulation in question had not complied with the objective criterion of the right to a lawful judge due to a lack of detailed rules. It would follow that a new set of rules on the reassignment of cases that is subject to objective conditions, is more detailed and is defined by a cardinal act of law could comply with the HCC's relevant jurisprudence. It is a known fact that, subsequently, the legislator made no attempt to adopt new legislation in this matter. Overall, nevertheless, it can be established that, in its decision, the HCC classified each of the various elements of the right to a fair trial as equal, but the right to a lawful judge as more equal than the rest of them.

4.3. *The qualification of the decision of the President of the NOJ and the right to remedy*

This part of the HCC's decision is the least elaborated; it merely records the fact that no legal remedy lies against the decision of the President of the NOJ. The lack of such remedy justifies, in itself, the establishment of the violation of the right to remedy, guaranteed by the FL and the ECHR. In comparison to the foregoing, it seems that there is a contradiction in that, in the context of the admissibility procedure, the majority decision found that the decision of the President of the NOJ to transfer a court case did not qualify as a decision subject to constitutional complaint under Article 27 of the Constitutional Court Act, thus the latter was not to be considered an on-the-merits decision or another decision terminating the court's proceedings. Many of the dissenting opinions suggested that the decision of the President of the NOJ to reassign a case could be challenged by a remedy petition submitted against the on-the-merits decision deliv-

31 Dissenting opinion of Judge Mária Szívós, Reasoning [160]. Dissenting opinion was endorsed by Judge Barnabás Lenkovics.

ered in the main proceedings.[32] Another dissenting opinion argued that the right to remedy could be interpreted only in relation to rulings and judgements delivered in the course of the courts' adjudicating activities, but it could by no means be extended to the decision of the President of the NOJ, which was to be qualified—as determined by the majority decision—as an act of a general administrative and organisational nature.[33]

These criticisms against the majority opinion seem to be justified: if such a decision cannot be challenged via a constitutional complaint, then why should the possibility of a direct appeal have been guaranteed? Under these circumstances, there is a hypothetical question to be raised: if the possibility of a direct appeal, as part of the right to remedy, had been provided by the contested provision of the Courts Act even before the 17 July 2012 entry into force of Act CXI of 2012, to what extent would it have changed the merits of the HCC's decision?

5. *Aftermath of the Decision*

Having regard to the fact that the legislator acted faster than the HCC and repealed the contested legal provisions before the delivery of the HCC's decision, the latter had a direct impact only regarding the court proceedings affected by the motion.[34] The HCC established the violation of the right to a fair trial on the basis of the standards elaborated and adopted by the ECtHR. According to the majority view, the right to have one's case concluded within a reasonable time cannot be given priority over the other elements of the right to a fair trial. Although the HCC noted that, at the time the legislation examined was in force, the backlog of court cases had constituted a problem at a national level, which needed a clear and quick solution, it failed to properly admit the importance of the timeliness of the administration of justice.

---

32 Dissenting opinion of Judge István Balsai, Reasoning [75]; dissenting opinion of Judge László Salamon, Reasoning [134].

33 The dissenting opinion of Judge Imre Juhász, Reasoning [101].

34 Following the HCC's decision, the reassigned court cases affected by the motions were not 'sent back' to the original court, but instead they were concluded by the other court designated to proceed. In this context, the absence of the presentation of the possible means for eliminating the infringement of the motioners' individual rights and the absence of any specific guidance were criticised by Miklós Lévay's concurring opinion and László Kiss's dissenting opinion.

The hectic nature of and the geographical differences in the evolution of the number of incoming court cases and backlogs, however, continue to exist, and the solution of these issues has become an objective laid down by the legislator in the new procedural codes (Code of Civil Procedure, Code of Criminal Procedure) which, in the meantime, were codified and entered into force. The difficulty of the situation is shown by the fact that there are still significant differences between the high courts and district courts of the central region and those in the countryside as regards the number and composition of their incoming cases. Despite the modifications made in the last couple of years, it is clear that changes in the number of the members of the judiciary in themselves are not sufficient to address this phenomenon. The 2009 reform of the order for payment procedure may be invoked as an efficient solution, as a result of which the carrying out of such procedures has become a competence of the public notaries. Prior to the above reform, when such procedures had fallen within the competence of the courts, the rules of jurisdiction and territorial competence of the Code of Civil Procedure had to be applied, which had resulted in important differences at national level as to the length of proceedings. Since 2009, the digitalization of the procedure and the set of changes in the rules of jurisdiction and territorial competence have jointly resulted in the order for payment procedure being able to fulfil its law enforcement function practically and significantly faster and more efficiently.[35]

In the legal literature, there is an increasing number of views according to which the very strictly limited guarantees of the right to a lawful judge, as part of the right to a fair trial, cannot take absolute priority over the other elements of the requirement of due process.[36] Hence, particularly due to the development of information technology and its impact on the time dimension of the administration of justice, it is highly probable that the legislator and the judiciary will have to rethink the issue of how to avoid, in a more efficient manner and at national level, any significant differences in the length of court proceedings.[37] As part of the foregoing, it also has to be realised that the guarantees should not become counter-

35 Molnár, 'A fizetési meghagyás kibocsátása iránti kérelmek feletti hatósági kontroll terjedelme a jogszabály változások tükrében' (2014), 239.; J. Molnár, 'Alternatívák most és a jövőben is?' (2016), 151.

36 The relevant debates are summarised by Susskind, 'Online Courts and the Future of Justice' (2019), 166–168.

37 Osztovits, 'Online bíróságok és az igazságszolgáltatáshoz való jog – esély vagy veszély?' (2020), 625.

productive: if the rules of jurisdiction and territorial competence do not ensure the effective enforcement of claims, then the parties to proceedings will eventually seek out-of-court procedures. The first step is to consider whether there are any (non-litigious) proceedings that may be conducted without the parties' personal presence and exclusively in an online system, so that any of the country's courts would be able to proceed on the basis of an automated case allocation regime.

Decision Transfer of Cases is the final act of the 2010–2013 debate on the aforementioned judicial reform. In line with its earlier case-law and the ECtHR's relevant jurisprudence, the HCC confirmed the guarantee nature of the right to a fair trial without formulating any new criteria or any criteria different from those developed by the ECtHR's case-law. The decision has, on the whole, a historical bearing, without any aftermath.

Bibliography

Nóra Balogh-Békesi, 'A bírói hatalmi ág az Alaptörvény rendszerében' [The Judicial Branch of Power in the System of the Fundamental Law] (2016) 4 *Iustum Aequum Salutare*, 9.

Gergely Bárándy, *Centralizált Magyarország – megtépázott jogvédelem* [Centralised Hungary – Manhandled Legal Protection] (Scolar: Budapest 2014), 257.

Lóránt Csink and Ildikó Marosi, 'Az Emberi Jogok Európai Bíróságának ítélete a Guðmundur Andri Ástráðsson kontra Izland ügyben' [The judgement of the European Court of Human Rights in the case of Guðmundur Andri Ástráðsson versus Iceland] in (2019) 2–3 *Jogesetek Magyarázata*, 48.

Judit Molnár, 'A fizetési meghagyás kibocsátása iránti kérelmek feletti hatósági kontroll terjedelme a jogszabály változások tükrében' [The Extent of the Authorities' Control Over the Applications For an Order For Payment in the Light of the Legislative Changes] (2014) 5 *Jogtudományi Közlöny*, 239.

Judit Molnár, 'Alternatívák most és a jövőben is? Az egymillió forintot meg nem haladó pénzkövetelések érvényesítése Magyarországon' [Alternatives Now and in the Future as Well? The Enforcement of Monetary Claims Not Exceeding One Million HUF in Hungary] (2016) 2 *Jog, Állam, Politika*, 151.

László Örkényi, 'Arányos ügyteherelosztás az igazságszolgáltatásban – elvek és teendők' [The Balanced Distribution of the Caseload in the Justice System – Principles and Actions to Take] (2012) 1 *Debreceni Jogi Műhely*, 13.

András Osztovits, 'A törvényes bíróhoz való jog a német szövetségi és az osztrák alkotmánybíróságok joggyakorlatában' [The Right to a Lawful Judge in the Case-law of the Federal Constitutional Court of Germany and the Constitutional Court of Austria] (2005) 10 *Jogtudományi Közlöny*, 420.

András Osztovits, 'Az új magyar bírósági szervezetrendszer' [Hungary's New Court System] in Ádám Rixer (ed), *Állam és közösség* [State and Community] (KRE ÁJK: Budapest 2012), 381.

András Osztovits, 'Online bíróságok és az igazságszolgáltatáshoz való jog – esély vagy veszély?' [Online Courts and Access to Justice – an Opportunity or a Threat?] (2020) 11 *Magyar Jog*, 625.

Richard Susskind, 'Online Courts and the Future of Justice' (Oxford University Press: Oxford 2019)

Károly Zajcsek, 'A törvényes bíróhoz való jog az ügyáthelyezés jogintézményének tükrében' [The Right to a Lawful Judge in the Light of the Legal Instrument of the Transfer of Court Cases] in István Varga (ed), *Codificatio processualis civilis. Studia in Honorem Németh János, II.* (ELTE Eötvös: Budapest 2013), 529.

18. Decision 3194/2014. (VII. 15.) AB – Tobacco Retail

Márton Varju[*]

The commercial retail of tobacco products under a license does not constitute constitutionally protected property or proprietary expectation. The state monopolisation of that economic activity does not entail a violation of the freedom of enterprise provided that the former licensee is—in principle—not prevented from continuing its activity.

Decision Tobacco Retail concerning the new regulation of the commercial retail of tobacco products in Hungary confirmed that the constitutional control of market regulation under the right to property and the freedom of enterprise gives a marked priority to the declared general interest objectives of state regulation over the position of the individuals affected and its protection. Decision Tobacco Retail narrowed down the possibility of constitutional protection for individuals under these fundamental rights against the state's direct interference in the market, even in cases when the interference—affecting a larger number of economic operators—fundamentally restructured the specific economic sector and reshaped the market position and the living conditions of individuals there. As a consequence, it recognised a privileged position and role of the state as an actor in the Hungarian (market) economy.

1. *Background*

Decision Tobacco Retail examined a main pillar of the Hungarian tobacco market's restructuring after 2010. The new legislative provisions first established the commercial retail of tobacco products as an exclusive economic activity of the state,[1] and then enabled the state to cede—in the framework of commercial concessions—the right to perform that activity

---

* PhD, Research professor, Centre for Social Sciences, Institute for Legal Studies (Budapest).

1 Act CXVI of 2011 on the national assets [Article 12 (1) l)].

to commercial operators.[2] Practically, the state monopolised an economic activity which economic operators had been able to carry out under a general commercial license granted under the general Act[3] on retail, and then distributed the right to carry out that activity among new licensees. In the newly structured market, the commercial sale of tobacco products may only be carried out under a title provided in a concessions contract and in possession of a special tobacco product commercial retail license. The general commercial licenses issued previously no longer cover tobacco products.

The right to (private) property and the freedom of enterprise acquired a distinguished position in Hungarian constitutionalism—as expressed in the Constitution—after the regime-change. By way of distinguishing the new regime from the system of socialist production and economic organisation, Article 9 (1) of the Constitution declared specifically that the Hungarian economy is a market economy. It also held that public ('social') and private property have equal value and are subject to equal protection. Article 13 (2) ordered that the expropriation of property may only take place exceptionally and in the public interest, in cases and according to conditions determined in legislation, and subject to the condition that the owner is provided complete, unconditional and instant compensation. Nevertheless, the constitutional provisions acknowledged the special place and role of the state in the national economy. They recognised the state as an (exclusive) owner, and preserved the right for the state to obtain exclusive presence and rights in specific economic sectors. As ruled by Article 10 (2), legislation can determine what economic activities are reserved exclusively for the state.

In the jurisprudence before the introduction of the FL, the HCC developed a considerably broad interpretation of the right to property.[4] In particular, it recognised a number of rights representing pecuniary value and public law entitlements as property.[5] In Decision 64/1993. (XII. 22.) AB, the HCC conceptualised the fundamental right to property as providing the material basis of the personal autonomy (freedom of action) of

2 Act CXXIV of 2012 on the commercial retail of tobacco products (Article 2).

3 Act CLXIV of 2005 on the Trade.

4 As a relevant principle, it established that the constitutional concept must be distinguished from the concept of property in civil law. Decision 64/1993. (XII. 22.) AB, ABH 1993, 373, 380.

5 See ABH 1993, 373, 380.

individuals,[6] which latter core value has to be afforded constitutional protection irrespective of the constantly changing role of property in society.[7] The constitutional protection afforded covered primarily the value of property.[8] The HCC was much more reluctant to offer protection to the condition of property, which entailed that interferences in the public interest with this aspect of ownership were controlled under the Constitution less rigorously.[9] As a core element of the jurisprudence, the right to property was held to protect—as a main rule—so-called acquired possessions alone; proprietary expectations may be protected in exceptional cases only.[10]

In regards the applicable constitutional test, Decision 64/1993. (XII. 22.) AB held that the constitutional protection of the right to property does not have a generally applicable standard ('scope'), and the intervention needs to be assessed in light of the circumstances of the given case. The HCC also observed that the intervention or restriction needs to be proportionate having regard to the public interest objective pursued as well as the disadvantages imposed on individuals. The examination of proportionality depends to a large extent on the accepted social and economic function of property, and—in case of market regulation—on the specific economic policy context of the measure.[11] This latter constitutional approach was premised on the principle that property entails inherent 'societal limitations' and that this social embeddedness of property 'enables the broad limitation of the personal autonomy of the individual affected as represented in his property and ownership rights'.[12] The decision also ruled that in case the restriction is based on a public interest ground, which is expressed in legislation and which follows from the economic and social context of property, the constitutional control exercised must be restrained covering only the justifiability of the general interest ground raised and the

6 ABH 1993, 373, 380. See in this regard, Menyhárd, 'A tulajdon alkotmányos védelme' (2004), 24 (24).

7 ABH 1993, 373, 380. See Sólyom, *Az alkotmánybíráskodás kezdetei Magyarországon* (2001), 627.

8 ABH 1993, 373, 380.

9 ABH 1993, 373, 380. See Sólyom, *Az alkotmánybíráskodás kezdetei Magyarországon* (2001), 627.

10 ABH 1993, 373, 380.

11 ABH 1993, 373, 381.

12 ABH 1993, 373, 380. See in this regard Sólyom, *Az alkotmánybíráskodás kezdetei Magyarországon* (2001), 627, and Menyhárd's analysis of the constitutional concept of property, Menyhárd, 'A tulajdon alkotmányos védelme' (2004), 24 (25).

potential violation of another fundamental right, and must not extend to examining the 'absolute necessity' of the regulatory intervention.[13]

However, the HCC did not leave the standard of constitutional protection completely dependent on the circumstances of the individual case. For this purpose, it identified a number of objective benchmarks. This choice was discussed by the HCC rather openly when it raised that by assessing the objective technical (regulatory) hiatuses of state intervention it is able to compensate the limitations 'forced' by the earlier mentioned reasoning of Decision 64/1993. (XII. 22.) AB on the constitutional protection of property. It has a mandate and a duty to strike down such technical errors of regulation; for example when the temporal scope of the restriction cannot be determined in advance, or when no compensation is provided for a serious restriction.[14] These points indicate that the protection of individuals enjoyed a certain relevance in the constitutional jurisprudence alongside the general interest rationales of the state's intervention.

Similar to the Constitution, the FL guarantees the protection of private property and the freedom of enterprise [Articles XIII (1) and XII (1)], and —in parallel—recognises the special position of the state in the national economy. Article M) states that the Hungarian economy is based on the freedom of enterprise, and the state is obliged to guarantee the conditions of economic competition. Article 38 regulates the role of the state as an owner, and holds that in this position it must act in the public interest and in the interest of satisfying common needs. The state can be exclusive owner of certain property, and—as determined in so-called cardinal laws —certain economic activities may be performed exclusively by the state. These latter activities can be performed directly by the state, or the state can decide to cede them to others (e.g., private economic operators).

Decision 26/2013. (X. 4.) AB laid down the cornerstones of the HCC's jurisprudence under the FL.[15] The HCC kept the earlier developed fundamental principle that the 'scope and mode' of protecting the fundamental right to property is independent from the protection of property in civil law, and that the content of the right to property and its protection can only be determined together with the 'applicable (constitutional) public and private law limitations'. Citing Decision 64/1993. (XII. 22.) AB, it declared that the right to property does not have a universal 'scope', its scope depends on 'the subject, object and function of property and ownership,

13 ABH 1993, 373, 381.

14 ABH 1993, 373, 381.

15 Decision 26/2013. (X. 4.) AB, ABH 2013, 972, Reasoning [161].

and on the mode of its restriction'; therefore 'the legitimate possibilities of imposing restrictions in the public interest differ having regard to the circumstances of the specific case'. The decision confirmed that restrictions need to be proportionate having regard to the objectives pursued and the means used, as well as the weight of the relevant public interest objectives and the nature of the restriction. However, the general and strict necessity of the restriction does not form part of the constitutional scrutiny. The prevailing priorities of national economic policy may—on their own—justify restrictions, in particular regulatory interventions by the state.

The freedom of enterprise has been continuously interpreted by the HCC as representing the right of individuals to pursue economic and business activities.[16] However, the jurisprudence also clarified that the fundamental freedom entails only the right to enter into a 'specific framework of legal and economic conditions' as created by the state for undertakings and their economic activities; in other words, the limited right to become an entrepreneur subject to the conditions prescribed in law by the state.[17] It does not guarantee a substantive right to pursue (and/or to continue to pursue) a specific economic activity or an economic activity in a specific form. Primarily, it guarantees an enforceable obligation of the State to refrain from preventing that individuals become entrepreneurs, or making it impossible.[18] Beyond this obligation, the state is entitled to regulate particular economic activities, or economic activities in general, or to modify the existing regulatory environment.[19] In Decision 4/1993. (X. 13.) AB, the HCC declared that the earlier mentioned 'framework of economic conditions' may only be subject to limited constitutional review.[20] In case the state introduces so-called 'subjective' conditions for the performance of an economic activity—which conditions are objective in their nature and can be met by any economic participant—the review of the court will be less strict. In contrast, 'objective' conditions, which can be met by certain individuals only, will be subject to more stringent controls.

16 ABH 2013, 972, Reasoning [176].

17 ABH 2013, 972, Reasoning [176].

18 ABH 2013, 972, Reasoning [176].

19 Decision 282/B/2007 AB, ABH 2007, 2168.

20 Decision 54/1993. (X. 13.) AB, ABH 1993, 340, 341.

2. Petition

The petitioner claimed that the loss of previously acquired entitlements to sell tobacco products constituted a violation of the right to property and the freedom of enterprise. The regulatory changes had led to a loss of income and a decrease of turnover and profits, which disadvantages were not compensated by the state. The motion raised that economic activities performed under a commercial license should benefit from the constitutional protection of property. The commercial license is itself an entitlement representing pecuniary value. The continuing of the commercial sale of tobacco products was a legitimate proprietary expectation, and was also covered by the freedom of enterprise. The challenged measures constituted a disproportionate restriction as their regulatory objectives could have been achieved within the regulatory framework previously in place. Although the petitioner recognised the state's prerogatives in the national economy and in its regulation, it argued that the state cannot exercise its powers in an arbitrary manner, nor may it undermine the constitutional aim of a market economy based on the freedom of enterprise.

3. Decision and its reasoning

In the operative part of Decision Tobacco Retail, the HCC rejected the motion and refrained from establishing the incompatibility of the challenged measures with the FL.

3.1. *The carrying out of the commercial sale of tobacco products—in itself—does not entail that the said economic activity would constitute an acquired possession or a constitutionally protected proprietary expectation, and would thus need to be protected under the FL. Commercial licenses covering specific activities and issued for indefinite duration do not constitute rights representing pecuniary value that would fall under the constitutional protection of private property [Article XIII (1) of the FL].*

Decision Tobacco Retail held that a commercial retail activity carried out under a license—even for a longer period—in the interest of securing a regular income for the licensee (more precisely: the right to carry out that activity) is not covered by the constitutional protection of private property (Reasoning [20]). It also pointed out that the petitioner's commercial license granted to carry out the activity in question was not withdrawn in the case, the contested measures merely introduced new regulatory conditions. The petitioner, whose original license no longer covered the said commercial activity, was not prevented from fulfilling the new conditions and from continuing the commercial activity on that basis.

The HCC also ruled that the commercial license held by the petitioner does not constitute a right representing pecuniary value protected under the FL. It merely provided the 'regulatory condition' for carrying out retail activities (Reasoning [22]). Nor did the HCC accept that the loss of value of the petitioner's commercial property was protected by Article XIII of the FL. It argued that Article XIII does not guarantee protection for the market value of assets and investments which are necessary for carrying out an economic activity. It also established that 'the expectation of future profits from an economic activity' is not a proprietary expectation protected under the fundamental right to property (Reasoning [24]).

3.2. The commercial retail of tobacco products carried out for a longer period is protected by the freedom of enterprise. The monopolisation of that activity by the state on general interest grounds does not entail the violation of the freedom of enterprise, provided that previous licensees may—in principle—be able to continue the economic activity in question and fulfil the newly introduced regulatory conditions [Articles M) (1) and XII (1) of the FL].

Decision Tobacco Retail first observed that Article 38 of the FL explicitly enables the state to declare specific economic activities as its exclusive activity. When such a choice is supported with sufficient reasons in the public interest, the state can make its decision without any further constraints. The measure contested in the case was adopted within this constitutional framework, therefore the state's decision to monopolise tobacco retail cannot be criticised.

Decision Tobacco Retail found further that the challenged measure, which admittedly excluded a specific economic activity from the class of economic activities pursued under a previously issued commercial license, did not prevent the petitioner from continuing to pursue an economic activity in general, and from continuing the commercial activity at issue (Reasoning [29]). In principle, previous licensees could obtain the newly introduced special commercial license and meet the other novel regulatory conditions. The new conditions were so-called 'subjective' conditions which any economic operator in the market could fulfil; this meant that the HCC's review of the conditions had to remain restrained.

The HCC noted that contested measure pursued legitimate aims in the public interest. These aims also corresponded with specific obligations of institutional protection of the state as established in the FL. This meant that the new market regulation was based both on public interest grounds and on 'constitutional (public) interests relating to the protection of fundamental rights' (Reasoning [30]). The restriction of the freedom of enterprise was justified by the necessity of ensuring the protection of these interests and the corresponding fundamental rights. Furthermore, the new regulation aimed to address the significant risks and social costs posed by the relevant product, and on that basis it legitimately introduced more stringent conditions than that laid down in the previous regulatory framework (Reasoning [31]).

4. *Doctrinal analysis*

4.1. *The constitutional protection of private property*

Decision Tobacco Retail declined that any of the claimed rights or legally protected expectations would constitute property protected under Article XIII of the FL. Arguably, this followed from the established legal position that the constitutional protection of property covers more concrete entitlements than the possibility for an undertaking to pursue a range of economic activities, or in fact a specific economic activity. In this regard, the decision appears to be a manifestation of the long-held, evidently functional conceptualisation of property in constitutional law, which—having been separated from the notion in private law—can be applied rather flexibly by the HCC. This flexibility of the constitutional concept is a highly problematic aspect of the jurisprudence. While it can enable the broadening of constitutional protection, it may also be used for the purpose of narrowing down its scope excluding certain circumstances and expectations of individuals from fundamental rights protection. Overall, this entails the risk that the protection available under the constitutional framework is uncertain and unpredictable.

As a more concrete issue, Decision Tobacco Retail can be criticised for failing to examine in a detailed manner what entitlements or legally protected expectations can be regarded—in a commercial-economic context and outside of that context—as property. It did not avoid this scrutiny completely. However, it missed addressing directly the issue that should be an essential component of the constitutional concept: the question of whether the entitlement was sufficiently 'acquired' to guarantee constitutional protection. The HCC's reasoning was somewhat confusing in this regard. It kicked off with the observation that the carrying out of an economic activity under a license issued for that purpose is not property in the meaning of Article XIII. However, its detailed reasoning can be read as actually implying that the possibility of performing the activity in question was near 'acquired' by the individual concerned. The HCC noted specifically that carrying out the economic activity was not subject to a temporal limitation, the individual engaged in that activity on the basis of a precise administrative license issued to him, and the licensee had been carrying out the activity for a longer period of time with the personal purpose of securing a regular income. These latter considerations did not change the decision's conclusion, which as a result missed examining more closely the impact of the regulatory change on the situation of the individual affected.

As observed earlier, the decision turned on the argument that the new regulation did not—in principle—prevent former licensees from re-entering the market and continuing the economic activity in question. It seems that the HCC considered that the regulatory change entailed only a necessary and not particularly significant break in the exercise of economic activities by the individuals affected. However, a hypothetical possibility that the individual may (eventually) overcome—based on its own and not the state's efforts—the disadvantages caused by the state—without assessing and understanding whether that is actually possible—is an insufficient assurance in (constitutional) law. The suffering of concrete losses and disadvantages by individuals should not be justified with reference to compensatory or similar possibilities, the availability of which for the individual is not tested. As assessed below, the ECtHR held that previous licensees should be afforded a real opportunity to be able to continue the economic activity which they could no longer carry out under their original license.

Decision Tobacco Retail also failed to address the issue of whether the violation of the right to property took place by way of restricting the personal autonomy of the individuals affected. As noted earlier, Decision 64/1993. (XII. 22.) AB had explicitly recognised the connection between property and personal autonomy (in the market economy), which meant that the protection of the individual and its position was (used to be) a central element of the constitutional notion of property. These conceptual premises of constitutional protection were not addressed by Decision Tobacco Retail. Its reasoning was not open to the interpretation that the constitutional protection of property should extend to the personal autonomy of action of individuals.[21] Quite obviously, a focus on the autonomy and freedom of individuals in a regulated market economy would have contradicted the evident determination of the decision to give priority to the tasks, roles and opportunities of the state in the constitutionally mandated regulation of the Hungarian economy.

The allegation in the case that the state withdrew the original licenses provided the background for the conclusion by the HCC that a license issued to carry out economic activities does not constitute a right representing pecuniary value and therefore property protected under constitutional law. As noted earlier, the HCC argued that the license provided only the 'regulatory condition' for pursuing an economic activity, and that in compliance with the applicable legal framework it can be withdrawn by the issuing public authority. As in other places in Decision Tobacco Retail, the reasoning of the HCC is rather difficult to follow. Although its aim was to establish the contingent nature of entitlements under a commercial license, the HCC's assessment suggested that the petitioner's license represented rights which have been sufficiently acquired. Decision Tobacco Retail noted that the license was issued specifically to the person of the petitioner and was not transferable to other individuals. As a more relevant hiatus of the reasoning, the decision failed to demonstrate the ground for distinguishing constitutionally protected rights representing pecuniary value on the one hand and long-term commercial licenses issued to a specific person and a specific premise on the other. Decision Tobacco Retail was silent on the actual reasons why licenses, which secure a precise entitlement to carry out economic activities, do not constitute rights afforded protection under the fundamental right to property.

These problems with the HCC's reasoning become more evident when it is contrasted with the assessment by the ECtHR of the same Hungarian measure. In case *Vékony v. Hungary*, the ECtHR established the violation of Article 1 Protocol 1 of the ECHR as the previously held licenses were abolished, and the individuals affected were not offered new licenses 'in exchange'. The original general commercial license was accepted as property falling under the protection of the ECHR, especially because

21 See in this regard Bratza, 'The Implication of the Human Rights Act 1998 for Commercial Practice' (2000), 6, and van Banning, *The Human Right to Property* (2002), 167. Uncovering the functions assigned to property in society and the economy bears central relevance in the constitutional protection of property and ownership. See Schermers, 'The International Protection of the Right to Property' in Matscher, Petzold, and Wiarda (eds), *Protecting Human Rights: The European Dimension* (1988), 565 (572–573).

it enabled the licensee to generate regular income.[22] When assessing the proportionality of the restriction, the court placed an evident emphasis on the disadvantages suffered by individuals and their weight. Its judgment—as opposed to the HCC's decision—made a distinct effort to measure the public interest objectives pursued by Hungary against the rights and the position of the individuals concerned. In this regard, it emphasised that the regulatory change caused automatic and significant economic disadvantages, which threatened the livelihood of the licensee, without providing for a sufficiently long transitional period.[23] Furthermore, the new rules did not guarantee with sufficient transparency and subject to genuine opportunities for legal protection a real possibility for the licensee to retain its property (i.e., to continue the commercial sale of tobacco products).[24] The ECtHR found that the operation of the concessions and licensing regime introduced by Hungary was nearly arbitrary, and that it did not offer a sufficient opportunity for previous licensees to continue their activities.[25]

4.2. *The constitutional protection of the freedom of enterprise*

Decision Tobacco Retail's assessment of the freedom of enterprise followed closely the structure of the relevant provisions of the FL. As mentioned earlier, in parallel with guaranteeing the freedom of enterprise the FL recognised the special position and role of the state in the Hungarian economy. There is only one constitutional limit to these particular activities of the Hungarian state: they need to be supported by legitimate reasons in the public interest. Based on these transparent constitutional premises, the HCC made the conclusion quite legitimately that the monopolisation decision by the state was not arbitrary and unlawful.

Although it was based on long-standing jurisprudence, the HCC's assessment of the other claimed violation of the freedom of enterprise is somewhat dubious. The decision recognised—quite rightly—that narrowing down the class of activities that can be pursued lawfully under a

22 *Vékony v. Hungary*, no. 65681/13, judgment of 13 January 2015, para. 29.

23 *Vékony v. Hungary*, no. 65681/13, judgment of 13 January 2015, paras. 34–35.

24 *Vékony v. Hungary*, no. 65681/13, judgment of 13 January 2015, paras. 34 and 36. This was a key point in the judgment and the decisions closing the related Hungarian cases. See for example *Angyal v. Hungary*, no. 44367/13, judgment of 3 July 2018, paras. 13–17.

25 *Vékony v. Hungary*, no. 65681/13, judgment of 13 January 2015, para. 36.

commercial license constitutes a restriction of the freedom of enterprise. However, it found that this restriction was justifiable because the new regulatory framework—in principle—did not prevent the licensee—having met the novel regulatory conditions—from continuing the economic activity in question. As explained earlier, the hypothetical availability of (economic) advantages should not be able to compensate concrete (economic) disadvantages suffered by individuals. This hiatus in the reasoning is not affected by the HCC subsequently observing that the previous licensee—presumably—would have been able to fulfil the new regulatory conditions.

The conditions laid down in the contested legislation (for market entry) were found as justifiable by the HCC. Relying on its previous jurisprudence, it set a low intensity for their review. Its reasoning accepted that the introduction of the new requirements was supported by significant public interest grounds as well as by constitutional interests and rights laying down institutional protection obligations for the state, the weight of which—having regard to the content of the rules in question—was able to support the proportionality of the new measures. Decision Tobacco Retail explicitly rejected to examine the expediency, effectiveness and fairness of the legislation. This approach can—in principle—be acceptable. However, it had the important consequence that the decision could overlook the disadvantages caused to individuals by the state and their weight, and that the decision missed examining whether the individuals were required to accommodate the disadvantages in a constitutionally appropriate regulatory and administrative environment. As raised earlier, Decision 64/1993. (XII. 22.) AB discussed explicitly that the low intensity of constitutional review of economic regulation which pursues significant public interest objectives needs to be compensated by the HCC scrutinising the potential technical and similar hiatuses and weaknesses of the regulatory measure. Evidently, the HCC in Decision Tobacco Retail was not prepared to follow this route.

As another problem, Decision Tobacco Retail refrained from examining in detail the relationship between the content of the new regulatory framework for the market in question and the original decision of the state to monopolise the retail of tobacco as its exclusive economic activity. This linkage should have been assessed by the HCC as it established the proportionality of the new statutory conditions with particular reference to the provision of the FL that empowers the state to determine its exclusive activities in the national economy. Furthermore, Article 38 of the FL provides that the exclusive economic activities of the state must be determined having regard to certain general interest objectives listed in the constitutional text, such as satisfying common societal needs, delivering public interest objectives, or protecting the interest of future generations. Arguably, this can be interpreted as enabling the constitutional review of the decision taken under Article 38 to cover the concrete objectives served by state monopolisation. In Decision Tobacco Retail, the HCC should have examined whether the withdrawing of the commercial sale of tobacco products from the market and its subsequent readmission under new conditions was justified by one of the constitutionally recognised general interest objectives and whether the intervention in the market was genuinely supported by that objective.

5. *Aftermath of the Decision*

In Decision 5/2021. (II. 9.) AB, the HCC examined whether the 2020 modification of Act CLXXXV of 2012 on the waste—in particular its provision in which the state monopolised a large segment of waste management activities and enabled the state to cede those activities in concessions contracts to economic operators—was constitutional. The decision's reasoning was similarly unstructured as that of the decision assessed in this chapter. The HCC observed that holders of waste—in particular the original producer of waste—were 'evidently' owners of the waste and their entitlement constituted property under Article XIII of the FL.[26] It completely ignored the question of whether the rights of holders of waste—having regard the extensive legislative provisions governing the position and the obligations of these operators which the state may freely amend in the general interest—were sufficiently 'acquired' so that they deserve constitutional protection as property. Interestingly, the decision established that the proportionality of the restriction required the payment of due compensation and the regulation of that compensation in legislation.[27] The overall proportionality of the new regulatory framework, which transformed the position of the relevant economic operators in the market quite fundamentally, was however not questioned. It was sufficient for the HCC that the state relied on significant and complex public interest grounds in support of its intervention.[28]

---

26 Decision 5/2021 (II. 9.) AB, ABH 2021, 269, Reasoning [27].
27 ABH 2021, 269, Reasoning [30]-[32].
28 See ABH 2021, 269, Reasoning [35].

Bibliography

Theo van Banning, *The Human Right to Property* (Intersentia, Antwerp 2002)

Nicholas Bratza, 'The Implication of the Human Rights Act 1998 for Commercial Practice' 2000 (1) *European Human Rights Law Review*, 6.

Attila Menyhárd, 'A tulajdon alkotmányos védelme' [The Constitutional Protection of Property] 2004 (5–6) *Polgári Jogi Kodifikáció*, 24.

Henry G. Schermers, 'The International Protection of the Right to Property' in Franz Matscher, Herbert Petzold, and Gerard J. Wiarda (eds), *Protecting Human Rights: The European Dimension. Studies in honour of G.J. Wiarda* (Car Heymanns Verlag, Köln 1988), 565.

László Sólyom, *Az alkotmánybíráskodás kezdetei Magyarországon* [The Beginnings of Constitutional Adjudication in Hungary] (Osiris, Budapest 2001)

19. Decision 23/2014 (VII. 15.) AB – Concurrent Three Strikes

*István Ambrus**

The prescription of mandatory imposition of life imprisonment for a special case of a concurrence of criminal offences infringes the principle of legal certainty.

Decision Concurrent Three Strikes annulling the rule of 'concurrent three strikes' the HCC removed a crucial sanctioning provision from the criminal codex(es) that was an emblematic element of the criminal justice policy shift in 2010. In addition, it expressed the constitutional requirement according to which it is almost impossible to transpose a legal institution of Anglo-Saxon origin, unfamiliar to the domestic criminal approach, into Hungarian criminal law without the new provision established in the wake of such implementation being in conflict with the constitutional requirements for criminal legislation and with the dogmatics of continental criminal law. Especially, if the legislation pursues an even stricter regulatory goal than the sample regulation.

The HCC consistently applied the findings of Decision 9/1992. (I. 30.) AB, analysing the constitutional principle of legal certainty for the first time in detail, when it declared that a criminal provision may not be regarded as foreseeable and therefore predictable under which it depends, in practice, on the procedural activities of criminal authorities—joining or separation of the cases—and thus being ultimately potential, whether mandatory life imprisonment or a much more lenient sanction, depending on the discretion of the court, shall be imposed on an offender.

* PhD, Research fellow, Centre for Social Sciences Institute for Legal Studies (Budapest), and Associate professor, Eötvös Loránd University Faculty of Law (Budapest).

1. Background

1.1. The regulation of concurrent three strikes

The regulation of concurrence of criminal offences known as the concurrent three strikes was introduced by Article 2 of the Act LVI of 2010 on the amendment of the 1978 Criminal Code in the wake of the criminal justice policy from 2010. It was developed in the context of strengthening and preferring the strictest possible sanctioning, especially against repeat offenders. This provision complemented Article 85 of the old Criminal Code with a new paragraph with effect from 23 July 2010. According to the substance of the provision, if at least three violent criminal offences against a person constituting concurrence are committed by the perpetrator, the maximum of the penalty range for the most serious criminal offence constituting concurrence will be doubled. If the increased maximum of the penalty range exceeded twenty years, or if the law stipulated that any criminal offences could also be punished with life imprisonment, life imprisonment had to be imposed on the offender [Article 85 (4) of the old Criminal Code]. While applying several important restrictions, the above provision was maintained by Article 81 (4) of the Criminal Code entered into force on the 1 July 2013. Thus, the rule on mandatory life imprisonment remained in the special cases of concurrence of violent criminal offences against a person having at least three-components, where all delicts constituting concurrence reached a completed stage and were committed at different times.

It needs to be highlighted that parallel to the concurrent three strikes a variant of three strikes rules, which also provides similarly for violent multiple recidivists, had already existed and is still extant. However, a significant difference lay in that it was possible to impose concurrent three strikes on offenders without a criminal record as a result of the regulation of concurrence of criminal offences and concurrent sentences [Articles 6 (1) and 81 (1)–(2) of the Criminal Code]; however, a violent multiple recidivist is, by definition, a person who has served at least two terms of imprisonment for the commission of violent criminal offences against a person and, as a main rule, committed (logically at least) his third delict within three years of serving the last punishment [Article 459 (1) (31) (c) of the Criminal Code].

With regard to the historical background to the issue, there had been a tradition of taking more stringent action against repeat offenders previously convicted by a final decision (recidivists) in Hungarian criminal law;[1] however, concurrent three strikes could clearly be considered to be a novelty.

During the four years the legislation (2010–2014) was in force, concurrent three strikes clearly became a living legal institution, several cases attracted greater media coverage where mandatory life imprisonment was imposed on a person whose criminal offences might have been proportionate only to an imprisonment not exceeding six to eight years under the previous rules. The application of these provisions was particularly blatant if none of the criminal offences of the offender—otherwise to be considered violent criminal offences against a person according to the criminal classification—resulted in death. A striking example of this was the case at Kiskunfélegyháza where the perpetrator wounded three people with a knife in his hand with a single movement. An act which was assessed by the court to be attempted homicide, causing bodily harm that endangers life and causes grievous bodily harm.[2] Such outstanding cases gave rise to narrowing the scope of concurrent three strikes in the Criminal Code by the legislature; however, causing thereby additional problems of dogma.[3]

The fact that the Supreme Curt (Kúria) specifically addressed in its Opinion 5/2013. (XII. 11.) BK the details of the interpretation of concurrent three strikes rules, contained in Article 81 (4) of the Criminal Code, indicates the practical relevance of the issue.

1.2. International outlook

The context of international regulations, primarily the 'three strikes' rules introduced by some member states of the USA should be taken into consideration. In the USA, so-called Sentencing Guidelines were in existence as early as the 1970s that defined in relation to certain crimes specifically and beforehand, on a mandatory basis, the sanction to be imposed (as a minimum) (*mandatory sentencing*).[4] At this time and on several occasions since then, the Supreme Court of the United States has addressed the issue of whether such mandatory sanctioning rules are detrimental to the Eighth

1 The HCC mentioned Act XXI of 1913 and Act X of 1928.

2 'Három embert késelt meg egy férfi Kiskunfélegyházán' [Three persons have been stabbed in Kiskunfélegyháza] *Index.hu*, 23 August 2011. https://bit.ly/3ubCuE5

3 Gellér and Ambrus, *A magyar büntetőjog általános tanai I.* (2019), 360, 469–470.

4 For an overview see Grey, 'Mandatory Sentencing Around the World and the Need for Reform' (2017), 392.

Amendment to the Constitution which prohibits the infliction of cruel and unusual punishments.[5]

The three strikes rules appeared for the first time in 1993 in the State of Washington as an extreme type of mandatory and very serious sanction. The substance of these provisions is, according to a metaphor borrowed from baseball game, that the court must impose much more serious imprisonment (often for at least up to 25 years or even for life) than previously against an offender who is on trial for the third time for a crime (*'Three strikes and you are out!'*). The 1994 legislation of the State of California became the most infamous example, according to which, although the preceding two crimes of the offender subject to final instance conviction had to be serious or violent, in the third case any minor misdemeanour was sufficient to trigger the three strikes (or more precisely the third strike).[6] Thus, a person with two previous convictions was sentenced to 25 years imprisonment in 1995 for the theft of a single slice of pizza.[7]

The Supreme Court of the United States examined the original relevant legislation of California in the *Ewing v. California* case in 2003, from which it established that it cannot be considered as cruel and unusual punishment, and thus is in accordance with the American Constitution. However, the implementation of the three strikes resulted in an extraordinary increase in the jail population, which circumstance significantly increased the costs of maintaining penal institutions, and in most cases because several decades of custodial penalty would be executed on offenders of minor, non-violent offences.[8] Ultimately, California's legislation was amended in the summer of 2016 so that nowadays the third commission only gives rise to the application of the three strikes rules if the perpetrator has committed a serious or violent felony in the third case also.[9]

The three strikes or similar constructions have also appeared in other countries. Thus, it was proposed in both Germany and Italy, while legislation similar to the US version was adopted in Slovakia. However, it can be concluded that only in cases, where the offender was previously convicted

---

5 *Roberts v. Louisiana,* 431 U.S. 633 (1977); *Solem v. Helm,* U.S. 277 (1983); *Miller v. Alabama,* 567 U.S. 460 (2012).

6 Assembly Bill 971 (March 1994) and Proposition 184 (November 1994).

7 See Vitiello, 'Three strikes: can we return to reality?' (1997), 395 (396).

8 For the problems see Zimring, Hawkins, and Kamin, *Three Strikes and You're Out in California* (2001). On the expansion of prison population see Stewart, 'The Wrong of Mass Punishment' (2018), 45.

9 Couzens and Bigelow, *The Amendment of the Three Strikes Sentencing Law* (2017)

at least twice.[10] Thus, the domestic version of concurrent three strikes, which was triggered even against a person with no criminal record, could be considered unique in this sense, in international comparison also.

2. *Petition*

Two judicial initiatives were brought to the HCC, which were joined by the Court. According to the substance of the initiatives, the contested provision is not in line with the FL in several respects.

In the case of the special concurrent sentence rule, the conditions for doubling the maximum of the penalty range and for mandatory life imprisonment are both unclear and not entirely predictable. The offender whose third violent criminal offence against a person [Article 459 (1) (26) of the Criminal Code] is litigated in a separate proceeding, may expect a more favourable judgement than the one whose criminal offences are adjudicated in a single proceeding and who must be sentenced therefore, if applicable, to life imprisonment without any discretion. The facts of a criminal proceeding may make it accidental and unpredictable as to whether the strict rule will apply to the offender.

The imposition of mandatory life imprisonment does not allow for examining and giving effect to sentencing criteria, which is contrary to the requirement arising from legal certainty, according to which criminal law as a whole, including the sentencing system, may not be inconsistent with itself.

To impose mandatory life imprisonment on a perpetrator who is committing, for the first time, criminal offences not punishable by life imprisonment, is not in line with the requirement of proportionality to be expected of constitutional criminal law.

Finally, the initiatives referred to the fact that the criticized concurrent sentencing rule is also contrary to the legal institution of accumulative sentence, as the rational for the latter is to allow the person convicted in different proceedings to obtain a more favourable position if all of their criminal offences are adjudicated in a single proceeding.

---

10 See Knauer: 'Die Verwertung jugendstrafrechtlicher Vorverurteilungen bei Sanktionierungen nach Erwachsenesrafrecht' (2012), 204; Della Bella, 'Three strikes and you're out' (2007), 832 (832–833, 858–859); Fábry, 'A »három csapás« büntetési elv bevezetése és ennek tapasztalatai Szlovákiában' (2010), 127.

3. Decision and its reasoning

The HCC establishes that the application of Article 85 (4) of the old Criminal Code effective from 23 July 2010 to 30 June 2013 is contrary to the FL, thus, it is not applicable in the pending cases no. 11.B.972/2011 before the Budapest-Capital Regional Court and no. 6.Bf.230/2012 before the Budapest-Capital Court of Appeal. Furthermore, the HCC establishes that Article 81 (4) of the Criminal Code is contrary to the FL, therefore the Court annulled it with retroactive effect as of 1 July 2013. The HCC orders under Article 45 (6) of the HCC Act the supervision of criminal proceedings closed by a final decision adopted pursuant to Article 85 (4) of the old Criminal Code and Article 81 (4) of the Criminal Code.

3.1. It is contrary to the requirement of legal certainty if it is unpredictable in which cases the stricter concurrent sentences—constituting even mandatory life imprisonment—may be imposed [Article B (1) of the FL].

First, the HCC reviewed provisions with content similar to the Hungarian legislation that had been introduced to improve public security in the United States of America and in Slovakia. In this context it establishes that it is common in all foreign legislation that the third 'strike' may only be activated in cases of a third final conviction, but a provision which allows for the application of the three strikes in a single proceeding, even against an offender with no criminal record, is not known anywhere else.

Afterwards, it examined the possible domestic background of the legal institution. Here, the Court refers to the Act XXI of 1913 on shirkers of public danger (Workhouse Act), the Act X of 1928 on the regulation of certain issues of criminal justice introducing the category of 'hardened criminals' and the Decree Law 9 of 1979 (on the enhanced protection of the society for more efficient action against repeat offenders extremely dangerous to public order and public security), briefly highlighting the main characteristics of the mentioned legal institutions.

Hereinafter, the HCC briefly summarized the new provisions introduced by the Act LVI of 2010. The Court noted in its Opinion 5/2013. (XII. 11.) BK, in which the Kúria compared in detail the related concurrent sentencing provisions of the old Criminal Code and the Criminal Code. It highlighted from the Opinion of the Penal Board that the provision contained in Article 81 (4) of the Criminal Code, according to which the more severe penalty shall not be applied unless the completed criminal offences were committed at different times, means, in contrast to the legislation of the old Criminal Code, that only real concurrence of offences gives rise to it. Hence, the more severe sentencing provisions on concurrent sentences shall not be applied if the acts of the defendant constitute a statutory or natural unit. Furthermore, the application of concurrent three strikes shall be excluded if any of the three violent criminal offences are stuck in the stage of an attempt or preparation. Thus, overall, the Criminal Code allowed for the application of the more severe concurrent provisions in a significantly narrower scope compared to the old Criminal Code.

The HCC also draws attention to report no. AJB-5138/2013 of the Commissioner for Fundamental Rights prepared in February 2014, which analysed the three strikes rules in detail as well. In conjunction with the concurrent three strikes contained in Article 81 (4) of the Criminal Code it established the breach of legal certainty and the right to a fair trial; therefore, it found it necessary to amend the provision in accordance with the FL.

It refers to Decision 9/1992. (I. 30.) AB, according to which legal certainty requires from the legislator that legislation shall be clear, unambiguous and, with regard to its effect, predictable, and that it shall also be foreseeable for the addressee of the norm (ABH 1992, 59, 65.). Thus, it ruled as incompatible with the constitutional requirement of legal certainty the possibility arising from the contested rules that the applicability of the more severe concurrent sentencing rules should depend on the fact whether multiple criminal offences of the perpetrator are adjudicated in one or more criminal proceedings. Indeed, it cannot be validly expected to act in accordance with the legal provisions, where the wording of the law is unclear and enables different interpretations. Since the rules of criminal proceedings do not contain objective provisions on the joining or separation of the cases, it basically depends on the discretion of the competent authorities as to whether the criminal offences are adjudicated in one or more proceedings.

Thus, overall, it can be seen that different procedural situations result in different sentencing with regard to perpetrators who have committed three violent criminal offences against a person. Indeed, when the three violent criminal offences against a person are adjudicated in one proceeding, the penalty shall be defined under the more stringent concurrent sentencing provisions. However, in so far as the same three criminal offences are not adjudicated in a single proceeding and the perpetrator committed all criminal offences prior to the announcement of the earliest first instance judgement, the punishment shall be imposed between the range of penalties defined in the Special Part of the Criminal Code according to the provisions on accumulative sentence, that will result in a different sentencing.

The HCC summarized the above thoughts that in connection with the norms related to concurrent three strikes, it is not foreseeable when the more stringent concurrent rules should be applied, and the controversial nature of the legislation cannot be remedied even by judicial interpretation (Reasoning [53]). Therefore, the HCC found that Article 81 (4) of the Criminal Code and Article 85 (4) of the old Criminal Code are not in line with the requirement of legal certainty arising from the rule of law covered by Article B (1) of the FL.

3.2. *The threat of similar punishment for criminal offences of different material gravity undermines legal certainty by breaching the principle of proportionality, besides, narrowing judicial discretion by creating mandatory sentencing rules, combined with further reasons, may be in conflict with the FL.*

The HCC highlights that the main element of the constitutional barriers of criminal law is that the individual is protected against the arbitrary use of means provided for by criminal law by the State. The Court therefore does not consider it constitutionally justified to lay down uniform sentencing rules for violent criminal offences of very different material gravity, which makes it impossible for the court to assess each criminal offence according to its actual gravity (Reasoning [62]).

The HCC records that it is not apparent from the constitutionally recognisable objectives of punishment that it would preclude legislation providing for mandatory rules within the scope of sentencing (Reasoning [60]). As an example, it refers to the penalty of expulsion [Article 59 (1) of the Criminal Code], to the secondary penalty of exclusion from participating in public affairs [Article 61 (1) of the Criminal Code] and to the mandatory imposition of probationary supervision [Article 119 of the Criminal Code]. Notwithstanding these theoretical considerations, it establishes in relation to the mandatory application of life imprisonment that it cannot be constitutionally justified even in cases of multiple offences in so far as its imposition is provided for by the act in relation to a limited range of criminal offences but of different material gravity (Reasoning [62]).

It establishes that a rule leaving no room for discretion is also contrary to Article B (1) of the FL, as it is not in line with the requirements arising from FL relating to a penalty system governed by the rule of law. Differentiated sentencing, in conformity with the fundamental legal criteria of the penalty system, could have been best served if the legislature provided the opportunity to exercise discretion between fixed-term and life imprisonment (Reasoning [63]).

As the HCC established under Article B (1) of the FL that Article 81 (4) of the Criminal Code and Article 85 (4) of the old Criminal Code is in conflict with the FL, it neglected further substantive assessment of the concerned provisions.

4. *Doctrinal analysis*

4.1. *Concurrent three strikes and the requirement of predictability arising from the requirement of legal certainty*

In the context of the comparative legal outlook in the introduction of Decision Concurrent Three Strikes, the HCC referred correctly to the fact that the provision on concurrent three strikes was essentially the peculiarity of Hungarian legislation.

It can be concluded from the findings of the HCC that a legislation providing for sanctions as strict as those applicable to violent multiple recidivists in cases of a 'simple' concurrence of three violent criminal offences against a person raise concerns. This is because violent multiple recidivists are a special group even among persons with a criminal record. People against whom final imprisonment has been imposed on several occasions for violent delicts against a person that, despite being (typically) enforced, apparently failed to achieve the special preventive purpose of the punishment given that the convicted person committed the same (or similar) criminal offence again for the third time,. Furthermore, the aspect taken from historical overview that a criminal provision which would impose a punishment of the same severity on repeat offenders, even those without a criminal record, as those applicable to multiple recidivists, largely applied at the time of the legally unsound criminal thinking (with regard to 'hardened criminals' in the 1930s, then repeat offenders of felonies against social property in the 1950s) that was grounded in the almost purely perpetrator-based criminal law, may support the correctness of this approach indirectly.

In our view, no meaning could be given to the rule on concurrent three strikes that would have conformed with the FL. In light of this, the position of the HCC, which found it unconstitutional, shall be deemed appropriate in all aspects. The legislation did not comply with and could not have complied with, the constitutional requirement of legal certainty.

This is because the applicability of more stringent concurrent sentences depended on the fact of whether the—at least three—violent criminal offences against a person committed by the perpetrator were adjudicated in the same or in different criminal proceedings.

According to the relevant literature, if 'the prosecutor did not file a single indictment, or in case the judge decided to separate the most severe criminal offence [...]', the perpetrator had to face an 'ordinary' and not an increased penalty; and later, provided that its statutory requirements were satisfied, they could even benefit from an accumulative sentence. Thus, in such a legal environment the regulation on concurrent three strikes was incompatible with the requirement of predictability. This is so despite the textbook and commentary literature analysing the rules on concurrent three strikes still in force at that time stating that if more than one proceeding is initiated, the cases shall be joined, or the separation of violent acts against a person involved in a single procedure might not be acceptable, otherwise the strictness of the act would not have prevailed according to the intention of the legislature. However, Article 72 of the old Criminal Procedure did not provide for a provision prescribing the joining as a mandatory rule and prohibiting the separation. It is easy to understand that beside the lack of practicability, other 'guidelines' on criminal procedures as popular today as strengthening, such as timeliness, also often undermine the non-joining or non-separation. Thus, assuming that the perpetrator committed two criminal offences, which may be straightforward, that is, robbery (Article 365 of the Criminal Code) and causing grievous bodily harm [Article 164 (3) of the Criminal Code] in respect of which a single criminal procedure was concluded. Nevertheless, the defendant was also involved in human trafficking (Article 192 of the Criminal Code), which was complex, difficult to detect and to prove, also considered to be a violent criminal offence against a person under Article 459 (1) (26) (d) of the Criminal Code, the investigation of which and the court procedure was expected to extend over many years. The court, which would have insisted on joining the two criminal cases only to 'strike' using the rule of concurrent three strikes, would have gone against the timeliness of the proceeding on robbery and causing grievous bodily harm to be resolved, even under a prosecution, by a final judgment in some weeks or months at the most.

4.2. *Concurrent three strikes and the constitutional criteria with respect to the penalty system governed by the rule of law*

A further circumstance may be mentioned with respect to concurrent three strikes also eroding the requirement of legal certainty beside the incidental joining/separation. A prosecutor is not obliged to bring an indictment in every case, neither is the criminal court obliged to pass a judgement establishing guilt with respect to all criminal offences, even when a single procedure is conducted for the (at least) three violent and proven criminal offences against a person, that is, the legal condition to impose the stricter concurrent sentence is, in principle, met. Indeed, a prerequisite of the legal consequence of concurrent sentencing is qualification of criminal offences as concurrence; and for qualification as a concurrence of criminal offences, both substantive and procedural conditions have to be met. Thus, it is a decision in a substantive (dogmatic) issue if the concurrence of the three criminal offences is not considered by the court as real, but merely unreal, thereby reducing it to a two-component concurrence or even to a unit of criminal offences. Based on that fact, the concurrent three strikes could not have been applied, because the criminal offence taking the second place in an unreal concurrence would no longer be deemed independent, therefore no criminal liability could be established for it (it could constitute an aggravating circumstance at most). It could have led to the same result if the court had regarded the three criminal offences of the perpetrator to be integrated into a statutory unit, for example in the unit of continuity. An example might be the case, otherwise quite difficult to judge, and far from being assessed uniformly in legal literature and in practice, where the perpetrator has committed robbery with a weapon in the branch of the same financial institution on three occasions [Article 365 (3) (a) of the Criminal Code].

The concurrent three strikes could become inapplicable due to procedural reasons as well. The typical case for this is when the prosecutor or the court has exercised its right as ensured by the act on criminal procedure and failed to conduct the procedure for the criminal offence(s) which was (were) irrelevant in order to establish liability in addition to the more severe criminal offence of the perpetrator. This case—which, if the partial omission concerned two from the three criminal offences constituting concurrence, could even be regarded as a special criminal procedure unit of criminal offences—has the consequence that the criminal offence, otherwise committed in the substantive sense, also falls out from the final decision, thus, the stringent concurrent sentence could not have been applied in this case either.

Prognostically, it can be mentioned that if the rule of concurrent three strikes had been preserved for some time, it could have even involved the return of the—arguably correct—judicial approach, known from the 1960s, restricting concurrence of criminal offences. Since in case-law life sentence may not be imposed automatically, for instance, even for (multiple) aggravated cases of homicide [Article 160 (2) of the Criminal Code], the judges were presumably averse to applying a mandatory life sentence, especially in case of three criminal offences not resulting in death but being violent criminal offences against a person according to the act. In light of this, it is conceivable that (old) new principles would have been laid down in judicial practice, by which the unreal concurrence of criminal offences could have been based and reasoned, to avoid the stringent concurrent sentence.

Finally, similarly to the USA, a further possibility could have arisen in our country as well. In this, the courts—as if exercising the power to grant 'pardons'—could have considered even a criminal offence as unproven that could otherwise be regarded as proven without concern, or the prosecutor could have filed a motion to dismiss in relation to an act to ensure that three criminal offences which give rise to the application of the concurrent three strikes rule do not constitute a concurrence in respect of a perpetrator who does not deserve such an excessive sentence according to their respect for legal principles. Finally, it might have been possible that the court (or the prosecutor in performing its tasks of preparing the indictment), for the same reason, might have interpreted the scope of a ground of impunity—for example of justifiable defence—going beyond the legal frameworks.

The existence of the above possibilities, and others similar to them, could have been capable of damaging legal certainty. This permits the conclusion that the rule on concurrent three strikes would not have met the requirement of predictability and, accordingly, of legal certainty, if the at least three violent criminal offences against a person had been adjudicated in a single procedure.

Therefore, all the HCC's findings that ruled the provision on concurrent three strikes to be unconstitutional, taking also into account that it made individualised sentencing impossible and excluded judicial discretion, can be approved unconditionally. However, the finding of the judicial body arguing that a statutory provision on mandatory sentencing rules may comply with the objectives of punishment, may require further support with regard to the disputable veracity of the cited examples. It is true, with respect to both expulsion and exclusion from participating in public affairs that they are represented in the Criminal Code by using the term 'shall', thus, in principle, they are legal consequences whose application is mandatory.

We cannot fail to consider that the statutory definition of both sanctions involves also components requiring discretion. Hence, expulsion shall be applied only against those non-Hungarian nationals whose staying in the country is undesirable [Article 59 (1) of the Criminal Code]. And any person unworthy of participating in public affairs, if further cumulative conditions are met, shall be liable to the secondary penalty of exclusion from participating in public affairs [Article 61 (1) of the Criminal Code]. It can be seen that both 'undesirable' and 'unworthy' characters are components left to judicial discretion. Based on the wording of the act, even though a rule is mandatory, if further conditions already requiring discretion are associated with it by the legislation, the outcome of the application of the given sanction is no longer mandatory but is rendered to the discretion of the judge. In the latest legal literature, these and other similar sanctioning rules are considered to be seemingly mandatory—consequently optional—rules, which are therefore, by their nature, less appropriate in supporting the argumentation in favour of the constitutionality of the exclusion of judicial discretion.

5. *Aftermath of the Decision*

In the wake of Decision Concurrent Three Strikes, with regard to the annulment *ex tunc*, the cases of the defendants falling within the scope of concurrent three strikes were subject to extraordinary appeal (review). However, the importance of the decision goes far beyond this circumstance. While the HCC highlighted on several occasions in its decision that its findings shall not affect the constitutionality of the similarly severe legal consequences relating to multiple violent recidivists, in fact, all that the judicial body expressed shows that mandatory statutory provisions, excluding judicial discretion, should be essentially avoided, as only the application of a sanction proportionate to the act and properly tailored to individual cases may be in conformity with the principles of sentencing and ultimately with the objective of punishment.

Bibliography

Richard Couzens and Tricia A. Bigelow, *The Amendment of the Three Strikes Sentencing Law* (2017) https://bit.ly/3ET3X2k

Angela Della Bella, 'Three strikes and you're out: la guerra al recidivo in California e i suoi echi in Italia' (2007) 2–3 *Rivista Italiana di Diritto e Procedura Penale*, 832.

Anton Fábry, 'A »három csapás« büntetési elv bevezetése és ennek tapasztalatai Szlovákiában' [The Introduction of the Concept of »Three Strikes« in Slovakia and Its Experience] (2010) 6 *Ügyészek Lapja*, 2010/6. 127.

Balázs Gellér and István Ambrus, *A magyar büntetőjog általános tanai I.* [The General Part of Hungarian Criminal Law I.] (2nd ed., ELTE Eötvös, Budapest 2019)

Anthony Grey, 'Mandatory Sentencing Around the World and the Need for Reform' (2017) 3 *New Criminal Law Review*, 391.

Florian Knauer: 'Die Verwertung jugendstrafrechtlicher Vorverurteilungen bei Sanktionierungen nach Erwachsenesrafrecht. Ein Rechtsvergleich zwischen den US-amerikanischen Three-Strikes-Gesetzen und der deutschen Sicherungsverwahrung' (2012) 1 *Zeitschrift für die gesamte Strafrechtswissenschaft*, 204.

Hamish Stewart 'The Wrong of Mass Punishment' (2018) 1 *Criminal Law and Philosophy*, 45.

Michael Vitiello, 'Three Strikes: Can We Return to Reality?' (1997) 2 *Journal of Criminal Law and Criminology*, 395.

Franklin E. Zimring, Gordon Hawkins, and Sam Kamin, *Three Strikes and You're Out in California. Punishment and Democracy* (Oxford University Press, New York 2001)

20. Decision 28/2014. (IX. 29.) AB – Police Image I.

Kinga Zakariás[*] – *Márton Sulyok*[**]

Images of police action can be published without the consent of police personnel appearing in them, and without violating human dignity.

In their Decision Police Image I., the HCC annulled a final judgment issued by the Budapest-Capital Regional Court of Appeals (Fővárosi Ítélőtábla[1]), which (based on unified judicial practice) stated that police officers exclusively carrying out tasks related to their service duties do not qualify as public figures, therefore the publication of images of them without their consent by the online news portal *Index.hu* had violated their image-rights-related personality rights. The HCC elevated the right to protect one's image to a constitutional level by establishing a fundamental right to an image, while holding that in the case of police officers ensuring the public safety and security of a demonstration, only human dignity may impose a limit on freedom of the press. The HCC did not examine the judgment of the Supreme Court (Kúria) maintaining the force and effect of the final judgment, and while it rejected[2] the constitutional complaint[3] against the uniformity decision of the Kúria,[4] the HCC did not avoid

---

* PhD, Associate professor, Pázmány Péter Catholic University Faculty of Law and Political Sciences (Budapest).

** Phd, Assistant professor, University of Szeged Institute of Public Law (Szeged).

1 In Hungary, the ordinary judicial courts are structured in a four-tier system: (i) the lowest, first-instance, 'municipal' level is the local court (járásbíróság) – also including district courts in the capital Budapest, followed by (ii) the first and second-instance 'county' courts (törvényszék) sitting as tribunals, above which (iii) the regional courts of appeal exercise appellate jurisdiction, to be eventually topped by (iv) the Supreme Court, i.e. the Kúria.

2 Through Order 3246/2014. (X. 3.) AB (in terms of the constitutional complaint filed against Uniformity Decision no. 1/2012. BKMPJE).

3 For a short summary on the new regime of constitutional complaint under the FL, see: T. Sulyok, Deli, and M. Sulyok, 'Constitutional Law' in Harmathy (ed), *Introduction to Hungarian Law* (2019), 15 ff.; M. Sulyok, 'The Hungarian Verfassungsbeschwerde' in Balogh et al. (eds), *Fundamental rights in Austria and Hungary* (2015), 24 ff.

4 Decisions on the uniformity of the law (judicial practice) can be issued by the Kúria to ensure the directionality of consistent judicial practice (and the harmo-

conflict with it. In the ensuing new proceedings due to the annulment, the Kúria established that image rights cannot solely be limited to the protection of human dignity on the grounds that police officers carry out their duties as part of the exercise of public power. In a more recent decision [Decision 3/2017. (II. 21.) AB], the HCC has annulled a Kúria judgment which restrictively interpreted the essential constitutional legal content of Decision Police Image I.

The competence dispute between the HCC and the ordinary courts has also been widely echoed in daily news media and the press, making the 'police image' decisions (as there were several) landmarks in focusing on the extent of the constitutional (judicial) review of ordinary courts' decisions through the new constitutional complaint procedure introduced by the FL.

1. Background

Human image rights are protected in Hungary by many branches of law, including substantive civil law. Articles 80 (1)–(2) of the old Civil Code understood any kind of abuse of one's image or recorded voice to be a violation of personality rights. This also required consent from those affected by any publication of the aforementioned, except for 'appearances in public life' (*nyilvános közszereplés*). However, the old Civil Code did not contain a definition of such 'appearances' (as a public figure). The above-referred uniformity decision of the Kúria (no. 1/2012 BKMPJE) has created a *sui generis* notion of 'appearance in public life', an important element of which is the freely made decision of the person concerned to act in front of the general public, with a motive to try and affect the life of the public. Based on the above, it was argued that merely being in a public space (carrying out public duties and exercising public power—whether in the line of duty or not—or an assignment based on an employment relationship,) obviously does not qualify as 'taking action', and thus does not fall under Article 80 (2) of the old Civil Code regarding 'appearances in public life'.

In this context, the new (effective) Civil Code entered into force on 15 March 2014 (under Civil Code), and while the courts proceeding in the review of the case underlying the constitutional complaint analyzed here

---

nized application of the law) and to prevent and reduce departure and divergence therefrom, if there is no good reason for this.

applied the old Civil Code to decide the case, we should not discard an analysis of the new Code, as it is invoked by Decision Police Image I. as well.

The Civil Code sets forth that everyone shall respect human dignity and the personality rights derived from it [Article 2:42 (2)],[5] and specifically enumerates violation(s) of the right to the protection of one's image and recorded voice [Article 2:43 g)]. Article 2:48 sets forth that recording a person's image or voice and using such a recording shall require the consent of the person concerned, except for 'recordings of a crowd' and 'appearances in public life'. The law here requires consent from those concerned for the making of the recording, and uses the term 'appearance in public life' (*közéleti szereplés*) instead of 'public appearance' (*közszereplés*), eventually stating that for 'recordings of a crowd' no consent is required for the recording to take place, nor for using the recording.[6] These differences are, however, only illusory as earlier judicial practice had already applied these rules. A more significant difference is that Article 2:44 of the Civil Code contains a provision on the exercise of fundamental rights ensuring a free discussion of public affairs, which 'may limit the personality rights of public figures to an extent that is necessary and proportionate and is without prejudice to human dignity'.

Then, in light of the Seventh Amendment of the FL (Am7)[7]—adding to the protection of Article VI (1) on the right to privacy, and Act LIII of 2018 on the protection of privacy[8] enacted under it—Article 2:44 of the Civil Code was amended, now declaring that the exercise of fundamental rights ensuring a free discussion of public affairs may limit the personality rights of public figures to an extent, without prejudice to human dignity, that is necessary and proportionate. However, it shall not violate their private and family life and home. Further protections involve provisions such as public figures' entitlement to the same protection as non-public figures with regard to communications or conduct falling outside the scope of

5 For the official translations of the relevant Civil Code articles, see the National Law Register (NJT) at https://bit.ly/39CbeoP (For relevant parts, see pages 12–13 of the law.)

6 Decision 28/2014. (IX. 29.) AB, Reasoning [32]–[34].

7 Please note that Am7 amended Article VI after Decision Police Image I. was published. Now, Article VI (2) guarantees state protections for the peace of the private home, and Article VI (3) includes protections regarding personal data. References in this paper refer to the earlier version of the text (in effect in 2014). For a brief summary of the constitutional background of the Amendment, see: Tribl and M. Sulyok, 'Constitutional Law 2018 Hungary' (2018), 1229 ff.

8 For the English text of the law see NJT at https://bit.ly/2XRQZRn

free discussion of public affairs, and 'public affairs' are defined to mean 'everything but' the activities and data related to the private or family life of public figures.

This part of the Civil Code entered into force with a text that was established by Decision 7/2014. (III. 7.) AB, noting that civil law liability may only be claimed in a restricted number of cases, where the opinions voiced appear as a complete, obvious and blatantly degrading denial of the human status of the person concerned, and as such do not violate personality rights enumerated under Article 2:43, but do violate the unrestrictable aspect of human dignity contained in Article 2:42. In this sense, this can only serve as an absolute limit to freedom of the press in a very limited number of cases in which someone is fundamentally denied their human status.[9]

Many European countries provide for the protection of public figures' image, and this 'public figure' quality generally amounts to an exception from the consent requirements necessary in terms of taking and using photographs. Especially the German practice influenced Decision Police Image I. The GFCC elaborated on the right to one's own image in their famous Caroline decision,[10] reaffirming individuals' rights to decide regarding the photos taken of them and then used (derived from the so-called *allgemenines Persönlichkeitsrecht*, i.e. the general right to personality).

In GFCC jurisprudence, the right to one's own image is bound to privacy, also concretizing the general right to personality. The protection of privacy, however, according to this body—in contrast to the protection of the right to one's own image—does not specifically protect against portrayal, but is to be adjudicated in respect of the topic and place of dissemination, or publication.[11] According to the Caroline decision, a fundamental condition of privacy protection is absent regarding public spaces: one's need to be secluded.

In the jurisprudence of the ECtHR, the publication of photographs—in connection with the protection of reputation—falls under Article 8 of the ECHR.

According to the ECtHR, the most important criterion in balancing privacy ('private life' in the ECHR's language) and freedom of expression (under Article 10 of the ECHR) is deciding to what extent any photos dis-

9 Decision 7/2014. (III. 7.) AB, Reasoning [60]–[62].

10 See: BVerfGE 101, 361 (381). In academic analysis: Fiedler, 'BVerfGE 101, 361/120, 180' in Menzel and Müller-Terpitz (eds), *Verfassungsrechtsprechung* (2017) 657 ff.

11 BVerfGE 101, 361 (382).

closed to the public might contribute to the creation of debate necessary to realize the public interest. In other words, they stress the 'informational value' of the broadcast.[12] In the landmark *von Hannover v. Germany* case, the ECtHR held that by publishing photos taken of the princess of Monaco without her consent, her Article 8 of the ECHR rights were violated, as the photos were of a private nature and did not contain any information of public interest.[13] Later ECtHR jurisprudence also reflects that in Europe—as opposed to the United States[14]—reputation is highly valued and interpreted in connection with human dignity, and freedom of speech does not enjoy *ab ovo* priority against it. Therefore, when they are in conflict, the competing interests need to be balanced. After *von Hannover*, in *Sciacca*[15] and *Hachette Filipacchi*,[16] the ECtHR also found violations of Article 8 of the ECHR resulting from press publications of photos taken without the consent of those appearing in them.

As for the United States, freedom of expression protected by the First Amendment is regarded as having more 'constitutional value' than reputation as a common law right, unprotected by the Constitution. However, the interests related to privacy are subject to protections of a different level, as the privacy interests of citizens directly implicate First Amendment rights.[17]

2. *Petition*

Index.hu Zrt. (Petitioner) filed a constitutional complaint under Article 27 of the HCC Act. Petitioner requested that the HCC declare the final decision of the Metropolitan Regional Court of Appeals unconstitutional and thus annul it due to a violation of the freedom of expression and the press, protected respectively under Article XI (1)–(2) of the FL. According to the facts underlying the constitutional complaint, Petitioner's online

12 *Von Hannover v. Germany*, no. 59320/00 (2005) EHRR 1, para. 60.

13 *Von Hannover v. Germany*, no. 59320/00 (2005) EHRR 1, para. 72.

14 In 38 US states, so-called 'one party consent' rules apply, and citizens have a statutory right to record police officers. 'All party consent' is required in further 10 states, but these do not include photos taken in public spaces and photos portraying police officers. For more detail, see e.g. Cope and Schwartz, *You Have First Amendment Rights to Record the Police* (2020)

15 *Sciacca v. Italy*, no. 50744/99, (2006) 43 EHRR 20.

16 *Couderc and Hachette Filipacchi Associés v. France*, no. 40454/07 (2015) ECHR 992.

17 For more detail, see Constitution Annotated, First Amendment or the life's work of William Prosser on torts of privacy, e.g. Prosser, 'Privacy' (1960), 383 ff.

news website published an article about a demonstration by a law enforcement trade union, with a photo gallery of pictures taken—without their consent—of police officers dispatched to the venue to ensure safety at the demonstration. The court of first instance declared in their judgment that the news website violated the personality rights of the officers to protect their image. On appeal, the court of second instance upheld the first instance decision, and pointed out that, based on its consistent practice, only those police officers are not to be regarded as public figures who carry out service-related duties, and as such, their image(s) can only be recorded and made public with their consent. Petitioner, in turn, argued that the civil court had not interpreted the applied provisions of the Civil Code in harmony with the FL. The Civil Code excluded public figures from the main rule regarding the protection of their image, and judicial practice interprets the concept of 'public figure' narrowly.

3. *Decision and its reasoning*

As for the operative part, the HCC concluded that the challenged final judgment of the Metropolitan Regional Court of Appeals is unconstitutional, and therefore, annulled it.

3.1. *It is the task of the HCC to examine whether the protection of human dignity justifies the restriction of the freedom of the press in the case at hand, i.e. whether the judgment complained of creates a balance between the different viewpoints of the unencumbered provision of information (szabad tájékoztatás) and the protection of image rights originating in human dignity [Articles 24 (2) d) and 28 of the FL].*

The HCC determined that it did not intend to decide the civil law dispute underlying the judicial decision subject to review, but anchor its inquiry to the provisions of the FL regarding freedom of the press and human dignity (Reasoning [27]).

The HCC saw their task in examining whether the protection of human dignity justified the restriction of the freedom of the press in the case at hand, i.e. whether the judgment complained against created a balance in the case between the different viewpoints of the unencumbered provision of information and the protection of image rights originating in human dignity (Reasoning [35]). In relation to the tasks of the ordinary courts, the decision also referred to Article 28 of the FL, which prescribes that, in applying the law, courts shall interpret the text of laws primarily in accordance with their purpose and with the FL (Reasoning [47]).

3.2. *Any reports of an assembly shall constitute a direct manifestation of the freedom of the press, the unencumbered provision of information, and of the role the press has in creating 'a democratic public opinion'. Thus, the contents of such reporting are justifiably protected to a greater extent [Article IX (2) of the FL].*

With regard to the fact that the coverage brought into question by the ordinary court was of a demonstration, the HCC examined the scope of 'the constitutionally understood right of assembly', and held that it shall include various, also irregular, forms of coverage, as long as they serve the formation or expression of opinions. The HCC also concluded that any reports of an assembly shall constitute a direct manifestation of the freedom of the press, the unencumbered provision of information, and of the role the press has in creating 'a democratic public opinion', therefore stating that the increased protection of such reporting is justified (Reasoning [37]–[38]).

3.3. *Image rights protect the external manifestation of the human personality and—broadcasting essential traits of personality—are indirectly used to identify it. Consequently, image rights are to be limited differently from other personality rights. (Article II of the FL).*

The HCC delineated the right to one's own image from Article VI (1) of the FL, considered in its essence a provision on 'protecting secrets', which is not relevant to the kind of individual activity which cannot be considered a part of private life. As the HCC put it, protections of privacy—as opposed to protection of one's own image—are not specifically directed at portrayal, but are to be adjudicated in respect of the topic and place of dissemination, or publication. In public spaces, the essential condition of any reference to the protection of privacy—one's need to seclude—is absent (Reasoning [24]–[26]).

To conclude this part, the HCC defined the essence of the right to image as follows: 'Image rights protect the external manifestation of human personality. Both images and voice recordings are indirectly used to identify personality, broadcasting essential traits of personality. Consequently, image rights are to be limited differently from other personality rights. Any unauthorized or interfering conduct shall be unlawful in terms of the image of others (Reasoning [39]).'

3.4. As long as certain ways of providing information do not abuse the freedom of the press, references to image rights might rarely serve as grounds to limit the exercise of the freedom of the press. Photographs of police actions without the consent of those in them may be published, if publication does not violate the human dignity of the police officers (photographed in action) [Article IX (2) of the FL].

The HCC specified their general comments regarding the scope of the freedom of the press and image rights, tailored to the civil law dispute giving rise to the constitutional complaint. Their starting point in adjudicating the conflict between these fundamental rights ensuring the free debate of public affairs and the protection of the personality of public figures, including those exercising public power, was Decision 7/2014. (III. 7.) AB, leading to the conclusion that 'as long as certain ways of providing information do not abuse the freedom of the press, references to image rights might rarely serve as grounds to limit the exercise of the freedom of the press. [...] The image of a person thrust into the public eye in connection with present events may generally be published—in connection with the event in question—without their consent (Reasoning [42]).'

According to the HCC, 'dispatching police forces to demonstrations shall always be considered a »present event«, even when the police officers are not actual 'participants' in what transpires' (Reasoning [44]). The reason for this is that reporting on an assembly regularly entails the publication of photos and video footage, and police officers present to ensure the safety of the event are most often visible on such recordings. The HCC held that any forcible inclination to change these recordings prior to publication—when they don't exceed the content necessary to illustrate the events with fidelity—would amount to a prior control of the information intended to be published (Reasoning [45]). Therefore, the HCC was of the opinion that any recordings of police action may be broadcasted to the public even without the consent of those present in the photos. An exception was specified, however; namely, if publication would 'violate the human dignity—considered as the protection unconditionally due to the internal essence of the human condition—of the police officer, for instance, by presenting the suffering of a police officer injured in the line of duty.'

In the case in question, the court only took into account whether a police officer carrying out service-related tasks in the line of duty is to be considered a public figure or not as a default (Reasoning [48]).

4. Doctrinal analysis

4.1. The extent of constitutional review of judicial decisions in civil law cases

By introducing constitutional complaints against judicial decisions, Article 24 (2) d) of the FL created a possibility for the HCC to review the judicial interpretation and application of the law, and to annul these decisions if found unconstitutional. This competence necessarily impinges on the relationship between the HCC and ordinary courts, and tensions first appeared in the so-called '*Police Image*' cases; thus it is important to clarify the extent of the constitutional review of the challenged judgment in Decision Police Image I.

The constitutional legal question arising in individual cases is the location of the threshold between the freedom of the press and the image rights of police officers. This, in turn, also raises the issue of enforcing fundamental rights in private legal relations (the horizontal effect or *Drittwirkung* problem),[18] which has long been one of the most important questions of constitutional legal discourse in Hungary. Starting from Article R (1)–(2) FL, the HCC settled for indirect horizontal effect, meaning that the FL shall permeate the entire legal system. In private law, this is realized indirectly through the fundamental rights contained in the FL 'beaming through' (based on the German theory of *Ausstrahlungswirkung*[19]) into its territory. The rights contained in the FL permeate the system of private law through the interpretation of private law rules.[20]

---

18 Drittwirkung problems construed as the 'horizontal effect' were first introduced in Hungarian legal terminology and dogmatics by Gárdos-Orosz, *Alkotmányos polgári jog?* (2011), 15 f.

19 Hungarian constitutional discourse was made aware of this theory by a former President of the Republic and the first President of the HCC, László Sólyom, in his seminal work on the theory of personality rights. Sólyom: *A személyiségi jogok elmélete* (1983) 42.

20 Decision 8/2014. (III. 20.) AB, Reasoning [54]–[56].

Ordinary courts' ties to the FL have been specified by Article 28 of the FL, also mentioned above, by stating that courts have an obligation to engage in interpretation that is in conformity with the FL. Courts are to apply the law to the individual cases before them by an interpretation that gives effect to the provisions of the FL. *Ausstrahlung* becomes significant through the opportunity of a constitutional complaint against a judicial decision, because this enables the HCC to examine whether in applying the law courts have actually enforced the rights contained in the FL.

Therefore, in controlling compliance with the obligation of interpretation in conformity with the FL, in Decision Police Image I., the HCC examined whether the courts had recognized the fundamental-rights-related aspects and interpreted Article 80 of the Civil Code enforcing the constitutional content of the fundamental right brought into question. However, the HCC—similarly to the jurisprudence of the ECtHR—did not satisfy with a unilateral examination of the enforcement of the fundamental rights brought into question, but also looked at whether the 'judgment complained against has created a balance in the current case between the different viewpoints of the unencumbered provision of information and the protection of image rights originating in human dignity (Reasoning [35])'. This wording indicates that the HCC extended their review to the discretion of the civil court, in addition to reviewing the enforcement of the fundamental right in question. The respective steps of this inquiry (review) are not unambiguous, as Decision Police Image I. examines the challenged judgment—following the abstract introduction of the scope of fundamental rights—by only referring to its actual content twice. In other words, a differentiated test aimed at justifying the constitutional review of judicial discretion cannot clearly be determined from the decision. At the same time, and as a matter of principle, we have already specified above that creating a balance between conflicting fundamental rights in private law relations falls within the courts' (enforceable) responsibilities and should be monitored. In horizontal legal relations, there is generally no exclusivity between conflicting fundamental rights, thus efforts to create a (fair) balance between them—construed as competing interests—should be justified.

4.2. The scope of the freedom of the press

In Decision Police Image I., the HCC established protections for the freedom of the press by including the right to assembly in its constitutional inquiry. Press protections have thus been created for all aspects of reporting on an assembly, as the broadcast brought into question by the ordinary court was one made of a demonstration (protest), which—in accordance with the decision—falls under the protection of the right of assembly as an expression of opinion. Therefore, reporting on an assembly—with regard to the role of the press in creating democratic public opinion—falls within the scope of the freedom of the press. The 'mother-right' of freedom of expression thus served as a foundation for the freedom of the press.

4.3. *The scope of the right to one's image*

In Decision Police Image I., the HCC expressly anchored the constitutional protection of one's own image rights to the guarantee of human dignity.[21] The scope of image rights—cf. GFCC practice[22]—primarily extends to the 'optical aspect' of self-portrayal, including a (freely made) individual decision on publication. Photos, however, are manifestations of an individual's identity, and image rights have two foundational elements: (i) a static one: identity, and (ii) a dynamic one: self-portrayal. It stands to reason that control over photographs that capture and broadcast the identity of an individual is an essential element of one's own image rights. This is why 'recognizability', or identifiability is of extraordinary importance when image rights are affected: if the person portrayed is not identifiable, identity remains unharmed, thus the right to self-determination also remains irrelevant.

The HCC further examined whether this scope is covered by the personality rights specifically enumerated in the FL. To do this, it distinguished the newly elaborated special personality rights from the right to privacy [Article VI (1) of the FL], based on criteria identical to those defined by the GFCC in the Caroline decision (above). The HCC also emphasized that the right to one's own image is more than the right to the protection of personal data under Article VI of the FL. At the same time—contrary to previous case-law—this distinction was based on the jurisprudence of the ECtHR. Since these fundamental rights were not found suitable to protect a person's image, human dignity was chosen as the pivot for protection. With this, the HCC elevated 'the protection of image rights tied to human dignity' to constitutional rank, making it the constitutional foundation of all civil-law image rights protection.

21 Zakariás, *Az emberi méltósághoz való alapjog* (2019), 239.
22 Dreier, 'Art. 2 Abs.' in Dreier (ed), *Grundgesetz Kommentar* (2004), 330.

Nevertheless, these foundations of the right to one's own image remained controversial within the HCC. According to one of the approaches, recordings suitable for individual identification were to be considered personal data under Article VI of the FL,[23] while others believed that the facial images of police officers published in media coverage and corresponding reports violated the officers' privacy rights, which they had a legal claim to, also while carrying out official police duties.[24] Consequently, the right to one's own image may fall within the scope of more specifically enumerated fundamental rights; it only seems to be a 'new' fundamental right. In this sense, Küpper differentiates between 'genuinely' new fundamental rights, put forward by a constitutional court beyond the constitutional text and 'non-genuinely' new ones, which only trace the change of the content of the fundamental rights in question, in line with newly arising problems and constitutional change (*Verfassungswandel*).[25]

Decision Police Image I. did not only define which enumerated fundamental right's protection extends to this newly deduced right, but also declared that it can be limited, thus placing it within the realm of the right to human dignity, which may be subject to limitations. This, in established HCC case-law, equals the general right to personality.[26] The decision generally refers to 'the right to one's own image being considered one of the manifestations of the general right to personality', but despite this 'generality', the decision unambiguously relies on German practice in this context again, linking the right to one's own image to the general right to personality (*allgemeines Persönlichkeitsrecht*).

Based on the above, we can conclude that in HCC practice, the right to one's own image is—at least implicitly—considered a special right originating from the right to self-determination (understood as a part of the general right to personality), and it may be subject to limitations as per the provisions of Article I (3) of the FL. With this, the decision disregards the fact that the text of the FL—compared to the Constitution[27]—has

23 Dissenting opinion of Judge Egon Dienes-Oehm, Reasoning [52].

24 Dissenting opinion of Judge Béla Pokol, Reasoning [59].

25 Küpper, 'IT-alapjog és elektronikus magánszféra' (2009), 2 f.

26 See the following quote from the above-mentioned Decision 7/2014. (III. 7.) AB, in relation to Article 54 (1) (right to life and human dignity): 'The right to human dignity may only be inviolable as a legal determinant of the human status, while as a general right to personality and all personality rights arising thereunder [it] may be subject to limitation.' (Reasoning [43]).

27 The former constitutional text of Article 54 of the Constitution made limitation of the right to human dignity possible, and the HCC has primarily made use of this right in the form of the general right to personality.

changed, now prescribing—in its Article II (1)—that human dignity shall be inviolable. Thus, in our view, this 'new' fundamental right should have been based—in addition to a dogmatically clear interpretation—on the mutually considered interpretation of Articles II and VI (1) of the FL. The reason for this is that this latter provision is directed at the increased protection of individual self-portrayal as a special case of the right to reputation expressly enumerated in the FL, as it is in close connection with the identity of the individual.

4.4. Limiting the scope of the freedom of the press in order to protect the right to human dignity

Decision Police Image I. examined whether the judicial decision brought into question created a balance between the different viewpoints of the unencumbered provision of information and the protection of image rights originating in human dignity. It acknowledged that police officers (carrying out tasks in the line of duty at a public event falling under the scope of the right of assembly) are entitled to—a narrowly tailored—protection of image rights,[28] possibly based on the limited nature (tied to the violation of human dignity) of personality protection established in earlier case-law in terms of those exercising public power (and public figure politicians).

What is unclear from Decision Police Image I. is the exact scope of the right to one's own image in terms of police officers in the line of duty. Two possible interpretations can be read from this decision: (i) one which supposes that the right to one's own image protects the persons concerned in a broader sense, and in addition to humiliating and degrading images, also protects against the publication of offensive, hurtful, or false publications (of these images), and those which might project a false impression

---

28 András Koltay is of a similar opinion in the leading Hungarian academic literature, believing that it is not acceptable to argue that personnel carrying out public tasks, or acting in connection with those public tasks, would not have personality rights. The solution is, he argues, that the freedom of the press and personality rights should be brought into a fair balance (*schonender Ausgleich*), which is a standard that oftentimes appears in the jurisprudence of the HCC based on the FL [e.g. Decision 13/2016. (VII. 18.) AB], especially in cases dealing with the right of assembly and the protection of privacy. Koltay also writes specifically on the topic of freedom of speech, personality rights and public figures, relevant to the topic of this paper, e.g. Koltay, 'The Freedom to Discuss Public Affairs and the Protection of Personality Rights in the Hungarian Legal System' (2019), 115 ff.

of those in them,[29] and (ii) one which considers the scope of image rights to be restricted to the protection of human dignity, i.e. 'to protection unconditionally due to the internal essence of the human condition'.

To sum up: the HCC tacitly considered police officers carrying out tasks in the line of duty as public figures in the cases at hand—contrary to 1/2012 BKMPJE—because it applied the stricter standard to protect their image rights, constructed by HCC jurisprudence. Although the judicial decisions serving as a basis for the constitutional complaint herein presented did not specifically refer to 1/2012 BKMPJE as a legal basis, they had—through the interpretation of Article 80(2) of the Civil Code, and its 'public appearance exception'—started from the interpretation of the concept of a 'public figure' under the uniformity decision 1/2012 BKMPJE. The HCC intended to avoid conflict with the Kúria when it disregarded a uniformity decision as the legal basis for the interpretation of the law, along with the judgment of the Kúria (reached in extraordinary judicial review proceedings), originally maintaining the final judgment in its effect.[30] Thereby, the HCC put aside the interpretation of the law contained in the judicial decision and replaced it with its own.

In this case as well, the starting point was Decision 7/2014. (III. 7) AB, according to which, 'from the point of view of the application of specific standards, it is not the status of the person concerned on its own, but the nature of the opinion tying the person to public affairs, that has a determinative role'.[31] This conclusion seems to be reflected in Decision Police Image I. and in the concurring opinions attached to Decision Police Image IV.[32] as well. It does not follow from the foregoing that the status of the person concerned would have no significance regarding the examination of the fundamental right to be protected in the constitutional complaint proceedings. On the contrary: it becomes relevant from the viewpoint of personality protection when in conflict with the freedom of the press. If the natural person concerned is not a public figure, then they are entitled—in general—to a broader protection of their own image.

29 Decision 28/2014. (IX. 29.) AB, Reasoning [41].

30 Béla Pokol has pointed out that the HCC, by ignoring the judgment of the Kúria and at the same time annulling the final judgment—created a 'controversy in the administration of justice'. Dissenting opinion of Judge Béla Pokol, Reasoning [60].

31 Reasoning [31], [47].

32 Decision 28/2014. (IX. 29.) AB, Reasoning [48]; Decision 3/2017. (II. 21.) AB, Concurring opinion of Judge Ildikó Hörcherné Marosi, Reasoning [41]; Concurring opinion of Judge Péter Szalay, Reasoning [45]–[49].

If they are public figures, however, then they can only claim narrower protection, extending to the protection of the core of human dignity.

In the case at hand, the HCC—similarly to the right to one's own image—needed to identify the scope of the freedom of the press in conflict with it. In doing so, the HCC complemented this scope with the publication of images or video recordings, also applying to the publication of images made of police officers participating in ensuring the safety of an assembly. The HCC, however, did so in a manner that was contingent on two alternative conditions: (i) publication of the image of the person needs to occur in the context of representing present events, (ii) which should fall within the scope of information subject to public interest in terms of the exercise of public power. Then, they also defined an exception: the violation of human dignity. In Decision Police Image I., the HCC considered the violation of police officers' human dignity an abuse of the freedom of the press, and therefore removed it from its scope. The decision unequivocally specified that the right to human dignity shall mean the unconditional protection of the internal essence of the human condition, i.e. inviolable human dignity. Consequently, the scope of the freedom of the press does not include the presentation of images that are in violation of the identity of police officers.

The HCC thus resolved the problem of conflicting fundamental rights on the level of defining their scope, amounting to a situation where the protection of human dignity will define the scope of the freedom of expression. Given that the right to human dignity shall be inviolable under the current constitutional framework, the restriction of the scope of the freedom of the press to protect human dignity is a dogmatically acceptable solution. It does, however, carry the risk that given the lack of a general definition for the scope of human dignity, the boundaries of protecting the freedom of the press will become blurred. An example of this could be Decision 1/2015. (I. 16.) AB, in which the majority opinion declared that the judicial decision acquitting the defendant violated the human dignity and reputation of the attorney for one of the parties,[33] because it unconstitutionally extended freedom of expression.[34] By mixing

33 In contrast, Sulyok wrote that human dignity was directly violated, i.e. the 'human condition' (the inviolable core of the fundamental right at issue). Concurring opinion of Judge Tamás Sulyok, Reasoning [94].

34 Decision 1/2015. (I. 16.) AB, Reasoning [39], [45]. In the same case, according to Paczolay, the decision should not have started from the status of the person affected by the expression of opinion, as such grounds will not directly decide the issue of which constitutional standards to apply, but the decision should have

together the absolute right to human dignity and the right to reputation arising thereunder (but itself subject to limitations) and by excluding the limitation of both from the scope of freedom of expression, this decision reduced the scope of the latter fundamental right in order to justify restriction. Contrary to the solution chosen at that time by the HCC, in our view the scope of freedom of expression should not be reduced or restricted. The delicate balancing of conflicting fundamental rights positions needs to be decided on the level of justifying the restriction of fundamental rights and not on the level of defining their scope.[35]

The judicial decision challenged in Decision Police Image I. narrowly interpreted the scope of the freedom of the press despite the court's failure to determine any circumstances pointing to the violation of human dignity. According to the final judgment of the Metropolitan Regional Court of Appeals, the representation of police officers carrying out their public duties together with their images does not fall under freedom of expression. Consequently, the HCC based the annulment of the final judgment on the fact that it intentionally disregarded the scope of freedom of the press and did not attribute any significance to the circumstances in which the recordings were made, nor to the purpose of their publication. In turn, the judgment only ascribed any importance to the sole factor that police officers are generally considered public figures when carrying out their service-related duties. It seems that the HCC only required the court to reevaluate their discretionary assessment regarding the scope of the freedom of the press, but in reality, it replaced the judicially omitted balancing of conflicting interests with its own discretionary assessment.

assessed whether (or not) the court had in fact examined that the expression of opinion is at all connected to debating public affairs. In this case, Paczolay erroneously extended the scope of freedom of expression, because in the case at hand, none of the facts suggested that the opinion expressed had anything to do with debating public affairs. Concurring opinion of Judge Péter Paczolay, Reasoning [69].

35 Bernát Török reaches a similar conclusion in analyzing the HCC's freedom of speech jurisprudence. Török, *Szabadon szólni, demokráciában* (2018)

5. Aftermath of the Decision

In accordance with Decision Police Image I., the HCC determined in all further 'police image cases'[36]—in addition to requiring a judicial re-assessment of balancing freedom of the press and the right to one's own image—that the judicial decisions challenged were based on the fundamentally flawed interpretation of freedom of the press. In other words: ordinary courts have either completely disregarded the scope of freedom of the press or have interpreted it overly narrowly and thereby unconstitutionally limited the right to freedom of the press.[37] In connection with the extraordinary judicial review judgment by the Kúria that gave rise to Decision Police Image III., it could also be added that the Kúria has overextended the scope of the right to human dignity when it declared that only one person being visible in the pictures does not affect human dignity.[38]

It is probable that the conflict between the Kúria and the HCC did not end with the conclusion of the 'police image cases'.[39] Nevertheless, the following results of this 'saga' may contribute to alleviating the tensions coded into the institution of constitutional complaints: (i) limiting the extent of constitutional review to examining the direct violation of rights contained in the FL;[40] (ii) the differentiated and consistent application of the test created to reassess judicial discretion in accordance with Decision Police Image I.

---

36 Decision Police Image II. [Decision 16/2016. (X. 20.) AB]; Decision Police Image III. [Decision 17/2016. (X. 20.) AB]; Decision Police Image IV. [Decision 3/2017. (II. 21.) AB].

37 Decision 28/2014. (IX. 29.) AB, Reasoning [48]; Decision 16/2016. (X. 20.) AB, Reasoning [23]; Decision 3/2017. (II. 21.) AB, Reasoning [22].

38 Decision 17/2016. (X. 20.) AB, Reasoning [29].

39 For instance, in Decision 3375/2018. (XII. 5.) AB, the HCC established that judicial decisions on the unlawful retention of a child were unconstitutional, and therefore annulled them. In Decision 3068/2020. (III. 9.) AB had annulled those decisions that have been reached in the new judicial proceedings as a result of the previous HCC decision – among others in reference to the 'police image cases'.

40 The violation is direct if by disregarding their obligation of interpretation in conformity with the FL, courts violate fundamental rights contained in the FL. The violation is indirect, if the judges' conduct—by disregarding their subordination to laws—realize a violation of the right to a fair trial. Zakariás, 'A bírói döntések alkotmánybírósági felülvizsgálatának terjedelme a német és magyar gyakorlatban' (2019), 34.

Bibliography

Fruzsina Orosz-Gárdos: *Alkotmányos polgári jog? Az alapvető jogok alkalmazása a magánjogi jogvitákban* [Constitutional Civil Law? The Application of Fundamental Rights in Private Law Disputes] (Dialóg Campus, Budapest–Pécs 2011)

Herbert Küpper: 'IT-alapjog és elektronikus magánszféra – az alkotmánybíróság legitim jogfejlesztése vagy tilos jogalkotása?' [Fundamental IT law and electronic privacy – legitimate development of law by the Constitutional Court or prohibited legislation?] (2009) 4 *Közjogi Szemle,* 2.

András Koltay, 'The Freedom to Discuss Public Affairs and the Protection of Personality Rights in the Hungarian Legal System' (2019) 1 *ELTE Law Journal,* 115.

William L. Prosser, 'Privacy' (1960) 3 *California Law Review,* 383.

László Sólyom: *A személyiségi jogok elmélete* [The Theory of Personality Rights] (Közgazdasági és Jogi Kiadó, Budapest 1983)

Tamás Sulyok, Gergely Deli, and Márton Sulyok, 'Constitutional Law' in Attila Harmathy (ed), *Introduction to Hungarian Law* (Wolters Kluwer International, The Hague 2019), 15.

Márton Sulyok, 'The Hungarian Verfassungsbeschwerde – a new regime for the constitutional complaint: something old, something new, something borrowed?' in Elemér Balogh and Márton Sulyok (eds), *Fundamental rights in Austria and Hungary: Research seminar, Vienna, 24–25. April 2015.* (Iurisperitus Bt., Szeged 2015), 24.

Bernát Török, *Szabadon szólni, demokráciákban. A szólásszabadság magyar doktrínája az amerikai jogirodalom tükrében* [Free Speech in Democracies. The Hungarian Doctrine of Freedom of Speech in the Light of American Legal Literature] (HVG-ORAC, Budapest 2018)

Norbert Tribl and Márton Sulyok, 'Constitutional Law 2018 Hungary' (2018) 4 *European Review of Public Law,* 1229.

Kinga Zakariás, 'A bírói döntések alkotmánybírósági felülvizsgálatának terjedelme a német és magyar gyakorlatban' [The Scope of the Constitutional Review of Judicial Decisions in the German and the Hungarian Practice] (2019) 2 *Alkotmánybírósági Szemle,* 21.

Kinga Zakariás, *Az emberi méltósághoz való alapjog. Összehasonlító jogi elemzés a német és magyar alkotmánybírósági gyakorlat tükrében* [The Fundamental Right to Human Dignity. Comparative Legal Analysis in the Light of German and Hungarian Constitutional Court Practice] (Pázmány Press, Budapest 2019)

21. Decision 32/2014. (XI. 3.) AB – Size of the Prison Cell

György Vókó†*

From the absolute prohibition of inhuman or degrading treatment, it follows that the space available to prisoners in multiple cells must in all cases be at least sufficient to ensure that they are accommodated in a prison without prejudice to their fundamental right to human dignity.

In Decision Size of the Prison Cell, the HCC collected and presented the cases in which the ECtHR had sanctioned Hungary for the size of prison cells and thus for the violation of the prohibition in Article 3 of the ECHR, promulgated by Act XXXI of 1993 on the Promulgation on the Convention for the Protection of Human Rights and Fundamental Freedom. It also described cases which may be taken as indicative of ECtHR practice.

1. Background

1.1. Introductory remarks

The housing of prisoners is a penitentiary task that entails the construction of premises of a size and standard of equipment appropriate to the operation of the prison, the provision of technical and other conditions necessary for the functioning of the prison, and is also part of the treatment of prisoners in the broader sense. The treatment of prisoners in each country is seen as an indicator of the quality of the rule of law in that country. The offender must be seen not only as an individual but also as a fellow human being.[1]

For the convicted person, criminal punishment is not only an obligation, but also a right, because the criminal has the moral right to atone for a crime in a penal setting. However, in a state governed by the rule of

* PhD, Director, National Institute of Criminology (Budapest).

1 Vókó, *Magyar büntetés-végrehajtási jog* (1999), 143.

law, these restrictions and their extent have to be strictly prescribed by law, since they are a restriction of fundamental rights.

The normative content of the FL is interpreted and explained in the decisions of the HCC.[2] In order of importance, the right to life and human dignity has been declared by the HCC to be the mother of certain other rights.[3] It also stated in principle, inter alia, that the State's power to impose punishment, including the execution of sentences, is not unlimited and cannot mean that the sentenced person is completely at its mercy. The legal safeguards for the execution of sentences have, therefore, been confirmed by the Constitution. The limits set by the FL cannot be exceeded even by the state's penal power, which the HCC monitors as a guarantee and a protection.

The fact of detention means that the detainee's necessities of life and other human needs must be provided for by the detainer by virtue of the latter's constitutional obligation. Treatment is the responsibility of the detainer, realised in a hierarchical relationship between a subordinate and a superior party. This area, which stems from the detention relationship, can be divided into two broad areas in terms of the content and scope of the treatment. The objective element of the treatment is, for example, the quality of accommodation and the hygienic conditions, while the subjective element is, among other things, the attitude of staff towards prisoners, the way in which they are treated, their relations with the prisoners, their work, etc.

It is clear from the practice of the ECtHR and the domestic courts, as well as from the legislation in force, that the overcrowded conditions of detention, which are contrary to the prohibition of torture, cruel, inhuman or degrading treatment, are a basis for compensation. When determining the extent of the damage, the sentencing judge takes into account the existence of other circumstances aggravating the damage resulting from the overcrowded accommodation, or the possible accumulation of such circumstances. The prisoners can also pursue their claims for compensation in civil proceedings.[4]

The legislative context on which the HCC proceedings are based focuses on the change in the regulation of Article 137 (1) of the Decree 6/1996. (VII. 12.) IM, which is relevant for the placement of a detainee in a multi-

---

2 Szabó: 'Büntetőjogi dogmatika – alkotmányjogi dogmatika' (1997), 293.

3 Decision 37/1992. (VI. 10.) AB, ABH 1992, 227–229.

4 Article 10/a. of the Act CCXL of 2013. on the execution of punishments, criminal measures, certain coercive measures and confinement for administrative offences (Prison Code).

ple-person prison cell, namely the insertion of the expressions, in 2010, 'as far as possible' in Article 1 and 'as far as possible' in Article 3. The number of persons who may be accommodated in a cell (living quarters) is to be determined in such a way that each prisoner has at least (the expression 'as far as possible' has been replaced by 'as much as possible') six square metres of air space and (the expression 'as far as possible' has been inserted) three square metres of space for male prisoners and three and a half square metres of space for juvenile and female prisoners [Article 137 (1)]. In determining the space available, the area of the floor space of the cell (living quarters) occupied by the fixtures and fittings that reduce it shall be disregarded.

1.2. International outlook

One of the objectives of prison systems throughout the world is to make them increasingly capable of facilitating the reintegration of prisoners by providing fair and humane treatment and an appropriate environment.

The prohibition of torture, inhuman or degrading treatment or punishment was first enshrined in the United Nations' Universal Declaration of Human Rights (UDHR, 1948) and the International Covenant on Civil and Political Rights (ICCPR, 1966). These were followed by the Convention against Torture and Other Cruel, Inhuman or Degrading Treatment or Punishment (UNCAT, 1984).[5] The latter is a widely accepted, legally binding international convention that defines torture and lists the measures required of states. To ensure compliance with the obligations laid down in UNCAT, the UN has also set up a body of independent experts in this field, the so-called Committee Against Torture (CAT), and on 18 December 2002 the UNCAT Additional Protocol was adopted. The prohibition of torture and inhuman or degrading treatment or punishment are *jus cogens*, i.e., rules that must be unconditionally enforced.[6]

The starting point among the Council of Europe's documents is the ECHR. In Europe, the Strasbourg system of human rights protection refers to Article 3 of the ECHR in relation to the assessment of overcrowding. This states that 'no one shall be subjected to torture or to inhuman or degrading treatment or punishment'. The ECHR does not define the con-

5 The UN Convention against Torture was promulgated in Hungary by Decree-Law no. 3 of 1988.

6 Rodley and Pollard, *The treatment of prisoners under international law* (2009), 65–66.

cept of torture or inhuman or degrading treatment or discrimination, so the ECtHR has given it substance. On 26 November 1987, the Council of Europe adopted the European Convention for the Prevention of Torture and Inhuman or Degrading Treatment or Punishment (European Convention for the Prevention of Torture), which came into force on 1 February 1989. This document, to which only Council of Europe member states may accede, like the ECHR, did not define any of the concepts in its title.

The implementation of the European Convention for the Prevention of Torture is also monitored by an international body of independent experts, the European Committee for the Prevention of Torture and Inhuman or Degrading Treatment or Punishment (CPT). The Council of Europe aims and expects Member States to take measures to combat overcrowding, but leaves the ways and means of doing so to governments and public authorities.

Recommendation no. 2 of 2006 of the Committee of Ministers of the Council of Europe on European Prison Rules 18.1 declares: 'The accommodation provided for prisoners, and in particular all sleeping accommodation, shall respect human dignity and, as far as possible, privacy, and meet the requirements of health and hygiene, due regard being paid to climatic conditions and especially to floor space, cubic content of air, lighting, heating and ventilation.'

The recommendation on European prison rules leaves it solely to the Member States to determine the minimum amount of personal space per prisoner. Paragraph 18 of the recommendation does not provide for a specific figure, which therefore varies from country to country. Currently, in Hungary, the legal requirement is 6 m^3 of air space and 4 m^2 of room for manoeuvre. For the purpose of defining the space available, the area occupied by furniture and equipment (bed, seat, cupboard, sink, ashtray, mirror, cleaning equipment, waste receptacle, washbasin, and toilet) should be disregarded.[7]

In ECtHR case-law, overcrowding of prisoners in a penitentiary clearly falls under Article 3, namely under the prohibition of inhuman or degrading treatment or punishment. An extreme level of overcrowding is in itself a violation of the Convention, while a less severe level, in general, combined with the negative effects of other circumstances existing during detention, amounts to a violation of Article 3, as referred to by Article 39 of the HCC of the reasoning of its decision.[8] Accordingly, one of the

7 Article 121 of the Decree 16/2014. (XII. 19.) IM.

8 *Kalashnikov v. Russia*, no. 47.095/99, judgment of 15 July 2002, para. 97.

objective, quantifiable elements of the ECtHR's yardstick for determining overcrowding is that, when examining cases of this kind, it takes account of the CPT's recommendation that the minimum living space for prisoners in multiple cells should be 4 m^2.[9] If the ECtHR finds that living space per person in the cell in the applicant's case reaches 4 m^2, it does not declare the conditions of detention to be in breach of the Convention.[10] Thus, the ECtHR's quantification is that if the available living space is less than 3 m^2, this constitutes, irrespective of the other circumstances, a case of serious overcrowding, which in itself constitutes a violation of Article 3.[11]

The ECtHR has ruled in four cases involving Hungary until the date of the HCC's decision, based on applications from prisoners who had complained about overcrowding in various penitentiary institutions in Hungary.

In *Szél v. Hungary*, the ECtHR found that the overcrowded conditions of detention did not respect fundamental human dignity and were, therefore, likely to have had a detrimental effect on the physical and mental well-being of the prisoner. In light of these factors, it concluded that the overcrowded and unhygienic conditions amounted to inhuman and degrading treatment.[12]

In *István Gábor Kovács v. Hungary*, it took into account the overcrowded accommodation together with the fact that the applicant had to spend almost the whole day in the cell, and therefore considered it a violation of fundamental human dignity, i.e., a violation of Article 3 ECHR.[13]

In *Hagyó v. Hungary*, the ECtHR considered that a prolonged stay in crowded conditions, together with the fact that the applicant was overweight and suffered from respiratory diseases, including asthma and chronic sinusitis, constituted a treatment which went beyond the suffering inevitably associated with lawful detention. It therefore found a violation of Article 3 ECHR in view of the cumulative effect on the applicant's physical well-being.[14]

In *Fehér v. Hungary*, the applicant was held for more than 2 years and 5 months in cells with an average floor area of 1.7 m^2 per person, which the ECtHR assessed as a living space so limited that it could not be considered

9 *Cenbauer v. Croatia*, no. 73.786/01, judgment of 9 March 2006, para. 46.

10 *Semic v. Slovenia*, no. 5741/10, judgment of 5 June 2014, para. 30.

11 *Tunnis v. Estonia*, no. 429/12, judgment of 19 December 2013, para. 44.

12 *Szél v. Hungary*, no. 30.221/06, judgment of 7 June 2011, para. 18.

13 *Kovács István Gábor v. Hungary*, no. 15.707/10, judgment of 17 January 2012, para. 26.

14 *Hagyó v. Hungary*, no. 52.624/10, judgment of 23 April 2013, paras. 45–47.

to be mitigated even by the 4 hours a day of time spent outside the cells for the greater part of the period in question.[15]

In *Varga and Others v. Hungary*, the ECtHR found that the space available to the detainees, together with other inappropriate conditions, caused the complainants suffering to an extent that exceeded the suffering necessarily entailed by detention. In this respect, there was a violation of the prohibition of inhuman and degrading treatment laid down in Article 3 ECHR. The Hungarian State has to pay a total of €73,900 to the six complainants who served their prison sentences in different prisons in the country.[16]

Finally, following the case of *Csaba Domján v. Hungary*, the ECtHR accepted in November 2017 that the domestic remedy introduced by the legislature complied with the requirement of Article 35 (1) of the Convention; therefore, Hungary had complied with Article 46 and 8,200 applications could be disposed of.

2. *Petition*

The petitioner judge initiated proceedings before the HCC in three pending cases in which he challenged Article 137 (1) of the Decree 6/1996. (VII. 12.) IM and Article 3 of the Decree 12/2010. (XI. 9.) KIM, amending it in accordance with Article 3 of the Decree XXXI of 1993, Article 31 of the ECHR, which prohibits torture and inhuman or degrading treatment or punishment, and Article III (1) of the FL. Referring to the relevant ECtHR case-law, it explained that the State must ensure respect for the human dignity of the detained person under conditions and circumstances which do not cause him 'anguish and hardship of a degree of severity which goes beyond the inevitable level of suffering necessarily entailed by detention'.

In addition to the decisions of the ECtHR, the petitioner also referred to the CPT's opinion, which considers a minimum of 4 m^2 of space per person to be acceptable for multiple-person cells. This was only an opinion of the CPT, a non-binding recommendation since the regulation of the amount of space in multiple occupancy cells has been—and still is—different in the various countries. During its visits and inspections in Hungary, the CPT did not criticise the existing regulation—which was

15 *Fehér v. Hungary*, no. 69.095/10, judgment of 2 July 2013, para. 20–21.

16 *Varga and Others v. Hungary*, nos. 14097/12 and 5 others, judgment of 10 March 2015

contained in Article 137 (1) of the Decree 6/1996. (VII. 12.) IM and in the previous regulation—but the failure to comply with the size of the cells. The petitioning judge saw an economic necessity, a scarcity of available prison space, in the amendment made to the provision in question, and his final conclusion is that a fundamental human right cannot be restricted for economic reasons. The author's uncertainty is expressed in the primary, secondary and tertiary motions. This hierarchy has repeatedly failed, or will fail, when, in the words of the proposer, the one nominated as the tertiary will be the primary.

3. *Decision and its reasoning*

In point 1 of the operative part of Decision Size of the Prison Cell on the finding and annulment of the infringement of an international treaty and the unconstitutionality of para. Article 137 (1) of the Decree 6/1996. (VII. 12.) IM on the rules for the execution of imprisonment and pre-trial detention, the HCC found that the above provision infringes an international treaty and the FL, and therefore annulled it with effect from 31 March 2015. In point 2 of the operative part, it annulled Article 3 (1) of the Decree 12/2010. (XI. 9.) KIM of the Administrative Court of the Capital City, incorporating Article 137 (1) of the Decree 6/1996. (VII. 12.) IM of the Administrative Court of the Capital City into that Decree, and rejected the initiative of a judge of the Metropolitan Court to suspend the proceedings in the three pending cases.

3.1. *According to the consistent practice of the HCC, if the petitioner claims that the content of a new provision is unconstitutional, the HCC does not examine the unconstitutionality of the law enacting the new provision, but the law incorporating the new provision as a result of the amendment.*

The HCC rejected the judicial initiative for annulment of Article 3 (1) of the Decree 12/2010. (XI. 9.) KIM, which replaced Article 137 (1) of the Decree 6/1996. (VII. 12.) IM, in force until then, by referring to its previous practice of examining the unconstitutionality of the legislation, which incorporates the new provision by means of an amendment, i.e., the legislation in force at the time of the examination, and annulled the amended basic provision.

3.2. The absolute prohibition of inhuman or degrading treatment laid down in the ECHR and the FL requires that the space for life and movement provided for prisoners in multiple-person cells must in all cases be at least sufficient to ensure that they are placed in a prison without prejudice to their fundamental right to human dignity. It follows that the minimum degree of freedom of movement to be granted to prisoners must be laid down by law in a cogent manner, excluding any derogation [Article III (1) of the FL].

The reasoning for the decision emphasises that the HCC's procedure is based on Articles Q (2) and (3) of the FL, according to which 'In order to comply with its obligations under international law, Hungary shall ensure that Hungarian law is in conformity with international law. Hungary shall accept the generally recognised rules of international law. Other sources of international law shall become part of the Hungarian legal system by promulgation in laws.'

The HCC also refers to the CPT's recommendations in its reasoning, and then describes a number of cases from the case-law of the ECtHR, including judgments against the United Kingdom, Ireland, Italy, Russia, Turkey, France, Finland, Greece, Poland, Belgium, Russia, Turkey, Finland, Poland and the United Kingdom in relation to complaints by prisoners of violations of Article 3 of the Convention. The ECtHR has consistently held that suffering and humiliation beyond certain forms of lawful punishment and treatment constitute a violation of the prohibition in Article 3 ECHR.[17] It considers overcrowding in a penitentiary as such, while less severe levels of overcrowding generally, together with the negative effects of other circumstances of detention, give rise to a violation of Article 3.

The decision of the HCC is supported by its previous decisions of principle,[18] which, in full accordance with the legal literature of the years of the regime change, have declared, inter alia, that interference with the fundamental rights of prisoners, the actual restriction of rights, takes place in the course of enforcement, and that the change in the legal situation of prisoners is triggered by the fact of enforcement. The limits of the constitutionality of the execution of sentences are defined by the right to human dignity and the right to security of person, on the one hand, and the prohibition of torture and cruel, inhuman or degrading treatment or

17 *Kudla v. Poland*, no. 30.210/96, judgment of 26 October 2000, paras. 92–94.

18 Decisions 5/1992. (I. 30.) AB; 13/2001. (V. 14.) AB; 30/2013. (X. 28.) AB.

punishment, on the other. The absolute nature of this right means that its enforcement must be guaranteed in all cases, including the execution of detention.

Since Hungary has submitted to the jurisdiction of the ECtHR,[19] which is competent to interpret the ECHR, the HCC has examined whether the contested provision is in conformity with the ECHR and the FL. In light of ECtHR case-law, it could not declare it to be in conformity.

However, the justification for *pro futuro* destruction is not entirely reassuring (Reasoning [60]–[61]). On the one hand, the period from 3 November to 31 March would have been acceptable (as the most obvious solution) for amending such a regulation, for example by repealing Article 3 of the Decree 12/2010. (XI. 9.) KIM of the Minister of Justice and Public Administration and replacing it by another regulation, or even by enacting or maintaining the former regulation. The time is too long and a regulation that is contrary to the FL and the Convention has remained in force for too long, giving the enforcement officials the opportunity to violate the FL for too long.

4. *Doctrinal analysis*

In Hungary, since its establishment, the HCC, as the main body for the protection of the FL,[20] has been dealing with the legal consequences of criminal law.[21] As a basic principle, it has emphasised that in a state governed by the rule of law, the state does not and cannot have unlimited penal powers, since public power itself is not unlimited. Because of the fundamental rights and freedoms protected by the constitution, public power may interfere with the rights and freedoms of the individual only with constitutional authority and on constitutional grounds. A further characteristic of the exercise of penal power under the rule of law, according to the practice of the HCC, is that the same constitutional principles and requirements apply to the whole process of criminal prosecution, including the enforcement phase.

In the first years after the change of regime, the HCC set out the criteria for the constitutionality of the execution of sentences in its decision on

19 Decision 3206/2014. (VII. 21.) AB, Reasoning [30].

20 Article 2 of the HCC Act.

21 Lukács, 'A szabadságvesztés büntetés kontrolljának modelljei és az alkotmánybírósági kontroll' in Szabó (ed), *Doktoranduszok Fóruma* (2017), 193–198.

the right of appeal against the decisions of the prison judge. Currently, Article III (1) of the Constitution provides that '[n]o one shall be subject to torture, inhuman or degrading treatment or punishment, or held in servitude. Trafficking in human beings shall be prohibited.' Act CCXL of 2013 on the execution of punishments, criminal measures, certain coercive measures and confinement for administrative offences states in its Preamble that Parliament had passed that law 'in order to protect the inviolable and inalienable fundamental rights of the human person, in particular the human dignity of convicted persons and persons detained on other grounds, to respect the prohibition of torture, cruel, inhuman or degrading treatment or punishment and the requirement of equal treatment, taking into account Hungary's obligations under international law and the law of the European Union, to enforce the penal powers of the State through enforcement [...]'.

According to Article Q (2) of the FL: 'In order to comply with its obligations under international law, Hungary shall ensure that Hungarian law is in conformity with international law.' Article T (3) provides that '[n]o law shall conflict with the Fundamental Law'. Article 24 (2) (f) of the FL empowers the HCC to examine the conflict with an international treaty. In the interpretation of the HCC, the prohibitions contained in Article III (1) are also separate, specific formulations of the prohibition of the violation of the right to life and dignity of the human person. This understanding is also in line with the content of Article 3 of the Convention, as developed by the ECtHR, according to which a violation of these prohibitions also constitutes a violation of human dignity.

The HCC has accepted, as a minimum standard for the realisation of fundamental rights, the level of legal protection set out in international treaties and the case-law relating to them.[22]

4.1. Examination of the legislation incorporating the new provision

In my view, in criminal cases, it is a questionable practice that in all cases the HCC examines the legislation incorporating the new provision as a result of the amendment and does not examine the constitutionality of the original legislation.

---

22 Decision 32/2012. (VII. 4.) AB, Reasoning [41]; last reconfirmed: Decision 3206/2014. (VII. 21.) AB, Reasoning [30].

This is not consistent with the principles and practice of the HCC in the various branches of law, nor with the depth of its intervention in the human and civil rights situation. It is no coincidence, for example, that the HCC first took this position in relation to old Code of Civil Procedure, i.e., on a civil law issue, where the principle is that of juxtaposition and not subordination. Punishment is the most serious interference in the legal situation of citizens, and it is during its execution that the deprivation of rights, or the restriction of rights, which it contains, is actually carried out, and for this very reason it is the area whose regulation and legality require immediate action. It is a matter of legal and logical necessity—and respect for the legislator's original intention—to restore the situation in criminal law and the law on the execution of sentences to that which existed before the amendment in such cases.

The practice of the HCC sets the course for the development of penitentiary law. Its task is to enforce sanctions, to enforce in practice the restrictions of rights that constitute their content, in accordance with the provisions of the FL and Act CCXL of 2013 on the Enforcement of Penalties, Measures, Certain Coercive Measures and Detention for Misdemeanours (Prison Code), taking into account the purposes of punishment. However, the HCC has a major role to play in this area.

4.2. Determination of the minimum amount of space to be provided for detainees

The problem of overcapacity and overcrowding in prisons is being tackled by several countries around the world that are trying to find alternative solutions to reduce it and to create more space. However, in the face of an increasingly brutal, cruel and violent criminality, society, other people and victims have a fundamental legal duty to protect their lives and dignity.

The extent to which the ECtHR's ad hoc ruling on such a technical matter should be considered a provision based on conventions from which no derogation is possible is questionable. Expectations and practice are not the same in each country. What seems clear, however, is the need for adequate staffing levels, sufficient professional knowledge, experience and expertise, the creation of an infrastructural and financial basis, active cooperation and joint work to ensure the success of the development of prison systems.[23] The HCC has considered it necessary to examine a technical norm containing data that can vary according to circumstances, as a norm that can, even if remotely, jeopardise the human dignity guaranteed by the Constitution.

Although the case-law of the ECtHR does not impose any legislative obligation, the question of the resulting changes to the law falls within the competence of the legislature.

The size of the detention facility is only one of the factors that determine the conditions of detention. The quality of the conditions is also affected by other factors, which the court is able to assess in a complex manner, as the basis for a possible claim for damages as a whole. The constitutional protection function of the HCC takes precedence over its power to examine whether a law is contrary to an international treaty. It would have been in accordance with the practice of the HCC to expressly refer in the grounds of its decision to the non-application of the prohibition of application.

However, neither the petitioner nor the HCC paid attention to the fact that Article 239 (1) of the Decree 6/1996. (VII. 12.) IM of the Ministry of Justice of the Republic of Hungary was amended by Article 6 of the Decree 12/2010. (XI. 9.) IM of the Ministry of Justice of the Republic of Hungary. In the last sentence of that regulation, the expression 'at least' was omitted, which was nevertheless an orientation to comply with a minimum value. In the original sentence, the following was stated: 'The number of persons accommodated in the cell (living quarters) shall be determined in such a way that, as far as possible, at least ten cubic metres of air space and four square metres of room for movement are provided per person.' The omission of the word 'at least' from this sentence also falls within this scope, not to mention the fact that this provision applied to the accommodation of a person 'previously' arrested who has not yet been convicted and who is still entitled to the presumption of innocence during the execution of the arrest.

It should also be stressed here that the relevant provisions of Decree 6/1996. (VII. 12.) IM have never been challenged for many years, in view of the large areas of movement and the provisions on the accommodation of free persons in common. According to Article 137 (1) of the said Regulation, the requirement was 3 m^2 for male prisoners and 3.5 m^2 for juveniles and women, and Article 239 (1) stipulated that each person

23 Pallo and Törőcsik, 'A magyar büntetés-végrehajtás szabályozási környezete az európai elvárások tükrében. 2. r.' (2011), 1 (12).

arrested (including persons not convicted by final judgment) should have, as far as possible, 10 m² of air space and 4 m² of room for movement. It is interesting to note that Article 6 of the Decree 12/2010. (XI. 9.) KIM has taken it out of Article 239 (1), but neither the petitioner nor the HCC paid attention to this, although it also opened the way to a narrower margin of manoeuvre. The legislator could, therefore, have solved the problem in a simpler way.

5. *Aftermath of the Decision*

Of the period since the HCC's decision, the so-called pilot judgment of 10 March 2015 in the case of *Varga and Others v. Hungary* deserves special attention.[24] In this judgment, the ECtHR held that the combination of the space available to detainees and other inadequate conditions caused the complainants suffering to an extent that exceeded the suffering necessarily entailed by detention.

In its judgment of 20 October 2016, the Grand Chamber of the ECtHR resolved the conflict between its own case-law and the values guided by the CPT.[25] It set out the principles and standards to be followed in assessing prison overcrowding in relation to multi-convict cells. It set a minimum of 3 m² of living space as a guideline, calculated by subtracting the area of the toilet and lavatory from the available space but not the furniture. It also considers this to be a guideline for prisoners and remand prisoners. Article 137 (1) of the Decree 6/1996. (VII. 12.) IM complied with this. The modification of the word 'at least' was unjustified in 2010 and subsequently in 2014 [Article 121 (1) of the Decree 16/2014. (XII. 19.) IM], until the text of Article 27 of the Decree 24/2016. (XII. 23.) IM, which entered into force on 1 January 2017.

Act CX of 2016, amending the Code of Criminal Procedure, which entered into force on 1 January 2017, introduced the current system of remedies for prisoners for any prejudice they may have suffered as a result of their placement conditions. In order to facilitate the procedure in such cases, a law adopted by Parliament in 2016 allowed for the possibility of appeals at the national level. Detainees dissatisfied with their detention conditions can now seek redress at the national level, without having to

24 *Varga and Others v. Hungary*, nos. 14.097/12, 45.135/12, 73.712/12, 34.001/13, 44.055/13, 64.586/13.

25 *Mursic v. Croatia*, no. 7334/13, judgment of 12 March 2015

go to the Strasbourg Court. Where conditions of detention are in breach of fundamental rights, the commanding officers will, on the basis of a complaint, take the necessary measures to improve or compensate for the conditions of detention, such as transferring the prisoner to another cell, allowing more time in the open air, or increasing the frequency or duration of certain forms of contact. Where appropriate, they may take the initiative of transferring the prisoner to a prison in which the living conditions provided for by law can be guaranteed.

'The challenge of how a society treats its offenders is a measure of its own humanity and dignity.'[26] There is a worldwide call for more modern and efficient prisons that serve humanity. The main elements of the new orientation are: increased demands for legality, equality and the rule of law in the whole process of sentencing.

Finally, it should be highlighted that the payment of reparation was suspended in January 2020 and the law introducing the new rules entered into force on 1 January 2021.

In addition to the conditions and forms of sanctioning, the enforcement of sentences is also important for the future of a people-centred justice system. The limits to freedom and the scope for protection that have been disturbed by the offence must be re-established quickly and publicly in order to be effective, in such a way as to set an example of compliance with the law and to encourage the offender to do the same.

Ensuring that fundamental human rights and humanism are upheld together with the protection of society is one of the most sensitive areas of the rule of law. This is where the optimum limit must be found: limiting rights only to the extent that the law allows.[27]

26 Vókó, *Magyar büntetés-végrehajtási jog* (1999), 121.

27 Vókó, 'Gondolatok a büntetés-végrehajtási jog szerepéről' (2020), 645 (648).

Bibliography

Krisztina Lukács, 'A szabadságvesztés büntetés kontrolljának modelljei és az alkotmánybírósági kontroll' [Models for the Review of the Liberty Taking Penalties with Special Regard to the Constitutional Review] in Miklós Szabó (ed), *Doktoranduszok Fóruma: Állam- és Jogtudományi Kar szekciókiadványa* [Forum of Doctoral Students] (Miskolci Egyetem, Miskolc 2017), 193.

József Pallo and Balázs Törőcsik, 'A magyar büntetés-végrehajtás szabályozási környezete az európai elvárások tükrében. 2. r.' [The Environment of the Hungarian State Penalty Execusion in Light of the European Standards] (2011) 3 *Börtönügyi Szemle*, 1.

Nigel Simon Rodley and Matt Pollard, *The treatment of prisoners under international law* (Oxford University Press, New York 2009)

András Szabó, 'Büntetőjogi dogmatika – alkotmányjogi dogmatika' [The Penal Law Doctrine – Constitutional Law Doctrine] (1997) 7–8 *Jogtudományi Közlöny*, 293.

György Vókó, *Magyar büntetés-végrehajtási jog* [The Law of the State Penalty Execusion in Hungary] (Dialóg Campus, Budapest–Pécs 1999)

György Vókó, 'Gondolatok a büntetés-végrehajtási jog szerepéről' [Ideas about the Role of Prison Law] (2020) 5 *Magyar Tudomány*, 645.

22. Decision 34/2014. (XI. 14.) – Foreign Currency Loan

Fruzsina Gárdos-Orosz[*] *– Péter Gárdos*[**]

In the enforcement of consumer protection, as defined by Article M of the FL, the State must take into account the aspects of the protection of human dignity, which allows for the application of different rule of law standards in a financial crisis situation.

The first decision of the HCC on the unilateral right to modify contracts in the consumer loan agreements of financial institutions, with its new, different interpretation of the FL, set new constitutional standards in the context of constitutional consumer protection in the broad sense, primarily with regard to the concepts of the rule of law and legal certainty, the right to a fair trial, its partial prerogatives and the prohibition of retroactive legislation. On several points, the new standards run counter to the theoretical and doctrinal foundations of constitutional law and to the previously settled practice in this area.

1. *Background*

On 4 July 2014, the Parliament adopted Act XXXVIII of 2014 on the Resolution of questions relating to the uniformity decision of the Supreme Court (Kúria) regarding consumer loan agreements of financial institutions (FCL Act[1]), which entered into force on 19 July 2014. The purpose of FCL Act, as indicated in its preamble, was to give effect to certain requirements stemming from the Kúria's Uniformity Decision 2/2014 PJE.

---

* PhD, Senior research fellow, Centre for Social Sciences Institute for Legal Studies (Budapest), and Associate professor, Eötvös Loránd University Faculty of Law (Budapest).

** PhD, Assistant professor, Eötvös Loránd University Faculty of Law (Budapest).

1 Foreign Currency Loan Act. The chapter is based on the authors former publications in Hungarian on this topic and especially, in English, on Fruzsina Gárdos-Orosz, 'Constitutional Justice in Credit Crises. The Hungarian Case' (2018) 1 *Südosteuropa: Journal for Politics and Society*, 94.

The economic crisis that started in 2008, and in particular the deterioration of the forint exchange rate, led to a significant deterioration of the situation of many debtors, as their debts were not in forint but in other currencies, typically Swiss francs. The adverse change has led to a number of lawsuits in which consumers challenged loan agreements with financial institutions on various grounds. The issues raised in these cases have been examined by the Kúria on several occasions.

As a result of the more favourable interest rates, foreign currency loans also became widespread in other countries in the region, such as Romania, Croatia, Poland and Slovenia. The depreciation of national currencies also caused serious problems in these countries, which national legislators tried to address through a number of instruments. In Poland, for example, the possibility of repayment in foreign currency was first introduced by a recommendation of supervision and then by law. In Romania, a law was passed to convert foreign currency loans into leu loans (although the Romanian Constitutional Court subsequently ruled this practice unconstitutional). In Croatia, the conversion law gave debtors the choice of converting the loan into euro or kuna.[2] In the course of crisis management, a number of courts referred questions to the CJEU for a preliminary ruling, which has interpreted Directive 93/13/EEC in a number of judgments.[3]

In order to address this problem, Hungary was the first country to set up a jurisprudence analysing working group at the Kúria to examine specific issues of unfairness. On the basis of the summary opinion[4] of the jurisprudence analysing working group as a type of contract as such, the Civil Chamber of the Kúria adopted the Civil Chamber's Opinion 2/2012. (XII. 10.) PK. Paragraph 6 of Opinion—fundamentally changing the previous court practice—set out the principles along which the unilateral right to modify a contract in consumer loan agreements can be fair.

Subsequently, the Kúria adopted PJE Decision 6/2013, which defined the civil law concept of foreign currency contracts and established that a foreign currency loan contract as a type of contract is not invalid per se because the exchange rate risk is borne by the debtor in exchange for a more favourable interest rate. However, the PJE Decision did not take a

---

2 Mańko, 'Unfair terms in Swiss franc loans' (2020)

3 See, e.g., C-26/13; C-186/16; C-483/16; C-51/17; C-118/17; C-38/17; C-260/17; C-511/17.

4 Summary opinion of the jurisprudence analysing working group 'set up to assess the unfairness of a unilateral contractual modification in the general terms and conditions applied by a financial institution in a consumer loan contract', https://bit.ly/2UDDmmX

position on the question of when a contractual term allowing unilateral modification of the contract meets the requirement of transparency. The decision on this issue was postponed until the CJEU has given its decision in the preliminary ruling procedure C-26/13.

Following the CJEU's decision, the Kúria issued PJE Decision 2/2014, which examined three questions. It held that the fairness of the imposition of the exchange rate risk on the consumer cannot be examined (point 1); it held that a contractual provision allowing for a unilateral modification of the contract is unfair if it does not comply with the principles listed in point 6 of the PK opinion (point 2); and it pointed out that the application of an exchange rate margin, i.e. the application of the buying rate at the time of disbursement and the selling rate at the time of repayment, as determined by the financial institution, is unfair (point 3).

It was against this background that the Parliament adopted the examined law, which basically regulated two issues: the nullity of the exchange rate margin (§ 3) and the unfairness of the unilateral right to modify a contract (§ 4).

The HCC issued its decision on 14 November 2014, a few days before the Kúria issued its judgment in the first review proceedings under the FCL Act, taking into account the available statutory time limit.

2. *Petition*

Three petitions against the FCL Act were submitted to the HCC by the Economic Chamber of the Metropolitan Court.[5] According to the petitions, the requirement of legal certainty derived from the rule of law [Article B (1) of the FL] is infringed by several provisions of the FCL Act, since, inter alia, the presumption laid down in Article 4 (1) of FCL Act introduces a presumption retroactively to 1 May 2004 which did not exist before the entry into force of the Act, and the legislature does so despite the fact that unilateral contract modification was regulated by several laws between 2004 and 2014. The legislator invokes the economic crisis of 2008 as a reason for the rules laid down in the FCL Act, but this cannot, by definition, legitimise the rules for the 2004–2008 period. Many provisions of the FCL Act do not meet the requirement of clarity; in particular, it is not clear which contractual constructions fall within its scope, what constitutes a contract term that has not been individually negotiated, what

5 Metropolitan Court 52.G.43.484/2014; 4.G.43.571/2014; 3.G.43.590/2014.

is meant by the phrase 'shall not apply' in Article 1 (2) of the FCL Act and who has the right to bring proceedings in the event of termination without succession.

By attaching the legal consequence of nullity to unfairness, the FCL Act overrides the rule in the 2004–2006 Civil Code that the consumer may challenge an unfair term. The FCL Act changes the statute of limitations rule in the Civil Code, thus making claims that are already time-barred enforceable. The enacting provisions of the FCL Act do not provide sufficient time for financial institutions and courts to prepare.

According to the petitioners, it is not clear to whom the judgment applies in the event of the plaintiff's default, and in the absence of an express statutory provision, the *erga omnes* effect of the judgment cannot be inferred. The applicants must decide to bring the action without being aware of the legal consequences of invalidity, since the law on settlement was only adopted in autumn 2014, after the deadline for bringing the action had already expired. Furthermore, the fact that the applicants must bring the action against the Hungarian State, which does not have a private law relationship with them, raises a constitutional problem for the application of the FCL Act.

Article C (1) of the FL is also infringed by the FCL Act, according to the petitioners, as its regulation violates the principle of separation of powers. Articles E and Q of the FL are infringed by the FCL Act, as its regulation is not in line with EU law, having been adopted without consultation of the European Central Bank (ECB). FCL Act violates the freedom to conduct a business [Article M of the FL].

According to the petitioners, the FCL Act also infringes the right to a fair trial (Article XXVIII of the FL), as it sets extremely tight deadlines for bringing and conducting proceedings, which makes the situation of the parties considerably more difficult, it also violates the principle of equality of arms and prevents the court from reaching an informed decision. For all these reasons, FCL Act also hinders the enforcement of substantive justice. The petitioners also invoked a violation of the right to judicial remedy, given that the FCL Act precludes the rebuttal of the presumption of service of the submissions, provides for a significantly shorter than average time limit for filing an appeal and request for extraordinary revision, and precludes the filing of a request for certification. The petitioners also invoked a violation of Article XXVIII of the FL in relation to the provisions of Act imposing a duty at a rate significantly higher than that provided for in Act XCIII of 1990 on fees. According to the petitioners, the FCL Act also infringes the principle of the independence of judges [Article 26 (1) of the FL].

3. *Decision and its reasoning*

The HCC dismissed the judicial initiatives seeking a declaration that the FCL Act in its entirety and Article 1 (1) to (3) and (6) to (7), Articles 4 to 15 and Article 19 thereof are unconstitutional and annulment thereof, and rejected the other judicial initiatives.

3.1. *In the event of a serious crisis affecting the fundamental rights of the masses of the weaker parties, the protection of consumers' rights and the duty to help the victims are the primary duty of all branches of government (Articles M and B of the FL).*

The starting point of Decision Foreign Currency Loan was the statement that the economic crisis of 2008 had led to many households being placed in a difficult situation due to foreign currency loan contracts, tens of thousands of families being threatened with eviction, etc. The negative consequences of the problem were borne by society and the national economy as a whole, and it was not possible to deal with them or remedy them through the courts (in the context of individual legal protection). The HCC concluded, on the basis of the substantive consistency of Article B (1) of the FL on legal certainty and Article 2 (1) of the Constitution, the contextual adequacy of the FL as a whole, and the rules of interpretation of the FL, that there was no obstacle to the applicability of its previous findings on the requirement of legal certainty. At the same time, in the context of this particular case, the serious and protracted social and economic consequences of hundreds of thousands of foreign currency loan contracts could not be ignored.

With regard to Article R (3) of the FL, the HCC started from the fact that the National Avowal states that '[w]e proclaim that we are duty-bound to help the vulnerable and the poor'. One such a duty of a democratic state governed by the rule of law under Article M (2) is to combat unfair competition, abuse of dominant position and to protect the rights of consumers. When the fundamental rights of the masses of weaker parties are threatened by a serious crisis, it is the primary duty of the State (and of all branches of government), both under the rule of law and under the principle of legal certainty, to protect them. In the absence of such an 'intervention' by the State, the fundamental rights of debtors in a vulnerable situation, and ultimately their right to human dignity, would be irreversibly undermined. The courts should have interpreted the legislation in this way under Article 28 of the FL even in the absence of the law under examination (Reasoning [51]).

3.2. When assessing whether the rule of law infringes legal certainty, the calculation of the sufficient period of preparation and the assessment of retroactivity may also take into account whether it was possible to obtain knowledge of the new legislation being prepared in advance, in particular because its content can be deduced from the general legal texts [Article B of the FL].

The HCC first examined the question of the time for preparation in relation to the breach of legal certainty. With regard to the preparation period, the HCC recalled that it was clearly known to the financial institutions 'from the time of the adoption of the PK opinion (or at the latest the PJE decision) onwards, which principles would—and must—be applied by the courts in the event of a dispute brought by consumers in order to determine the contractual terms in dispute'. According to the decision, there is no doubt that the FCL Act provides for a short preparation period, in particular given that it reversed the parties' litigation positions and that it applies for a relatively long period. However, according to the HCC, the statutory presumption concerns only a single issue, the identification of which should not pose a serious problem. Therefore, in view of the significant social problem caused by foreign currency lending, the HCC dismissed the petition (Reasoning [107]–[113]).

In the area of legal certainty, the HCC then went on to examine in detail whether the FCL Act violated the prohibition of retroactive legislation. To this end, Decision Foreign Currency Loan considered it necessary to examine whether the substantive provisions of FCL Act created a substantively new regulatory environment. In its analysis, the HCC started from the fact that Article 4 (1) of the Civil Code, which lays down the principles of good faith and fair dealing, Article 5 (1), which prohibits abuse of rights, and Article 200 (2), which penalises an infringement of good morals by nullity, have remained unchanged since 2004.[6] These rules are now enshrined as a constitutional value in Article M (2) of the FL.

6 In view of Article 50 (1) of Act CLXXVII of 2013 on the transitional and enabling provisions in connection with the entry into force of the Civil Code, Act IV of 1959 on the financial and certain personal relations of the citizenry shall apply to the general terms and conditions under review.

The provisions appearing in the sectoral laws did not override the Civil Code rule, they have always been in force as underlying law, therefore the FCL Act did not create a new legal environment. In the present case, the FCL Act has created a presumption of unfairness of contractual terms that did not previously comply with the general prohibition of general clauses. 'The content of the law is, therefore, nothing more than an authentic legislative interpretation of the law (in this case, the legislator), as deduced from the practice of the implementation of law.' In view of this, Decision Foreign Currency Loan also considered the petition to be unfounded in this respect (Reasoning [96]–[113]).

The HCC separately examined the question whether the fact that the Civil Code granted the consumer a right of action between 2004 and 2006, while FCL Act retroactively attributes nullity to unfairness, violated the prohibition of retroactivity. In this context, the HCC, referring to the position of the CJEU in the case *Océano Grupo* (C-240/98), pointed out that, also between 2004 and 2006, consumer relationships were subject to the legal consequence of nullity. It therefore considered the application to be unfounded.

3.3. The time limit for bringing an action and the length of the procedure are related to the fundamental right of access to a court, but do not violate the right to a fair trial [Articles XXVIII and C of the FL].

The motions concerning the short time limit for bringing an action were rejected by the HCC. As a starting point, the HCC held that the length of the time limit for bringing an action is related to the fundamental right of access to a court, but not to the right to a fair trial. As regards the necessity and proportionality of the limitation, Decision Foreign Currency Loan pointed out that 'it cannot be established that the law imposes time limits on the parties for bringing an action which are much shorter than those provided for in certain sectoral laws'. In this context, the HCC refers, inter alia, to the rules applicable to actions for annulment of decisions of legal persons, the actions for the exclusion of a member, the actions for review of decisions of the mountain region court, concluding that 'the imposition of a time limit of 30 days or even less for bringing an action in certain specific proceedings is not an unusual legal solution'. In the HCC's view, the constitutionality of the legislation requires an examination of whether 'the time limit for bringing an action open to financial institutions is sufficient to enable them to consider and decide realistically whether they wish to challenge the legal presumption of unfairness'. However, this was not only 30 days, as the bill was available on the Parliament's website, so that 'at the latest when the bill was voted [...] it became clear to financial institutions what the main issue in the civil litigation would be'. In this context, the HCC also pointed out that 'the legislative intentions of the Parliament on this subject were not without precedent. [...] The financial institutions [...] had good reason to expect a general legislative settlement' (Reasoning [156]).

After the time limit for bringing an action, the HCC examined the further procedural time limits. The decision quoted at length Decision 59/2003. (XI. 26.) AB on the constitutionality of the electoral procedure,[7] which stated that it was important that 'final decisions should be taken as soon as possible'. The importance of this cannot be questioned in the case of the legal relationships covered by the FCL Act. The HCC stressed that when considering time limits, it should also be borne in mind that the cases under consideration 'essentially concern the documentary proof of factual issues and the determination of related questions of law, which do not justify the involvement of experts'. The HCC also considered it unnecessary to call witnesses in order to decide the cases. It also pointed out that the plaintiff's electronic submission of the application to the court facilitates the decision. In view of the above, the HCC did not consider the procedural time limits laid down in the FCL Act unconstitutional. In support of this, the HCC also referred to the fact that 'a large number of cases have already been concluded with a decision on the merits' (Reasoning [165]).

3.4. *Although the set of special procedural rules creates a special procedural order which, due to the accumulation of legal restrictions, raises constitutional doubts as to the fairness of the procedure as a whole, this does not in itself constitute an unconstitutionality [Articles B and XXVIII of the FL].*

Decision Foreign Currency Loan also held that the application for a declaration that the presumption of service was not rebuttable was unfounded. Decision Foreign Currency Loan recalled in detail the findings of Decision 46/2003. (X. 16.) AB[8] on the presumption of service and then pointed out that the FCL Act does not provide for postal service in this context, but for

7 ABH 2003, 607.
8 ABH 2003, 488.

a special method of service which is faster and more efficient than postal service. The parties to the proceedings were aware of this method of service in advance, so that there is no disproportionate burden on them to ensure receipt. Decision Foreign Currency Loan also pointed out that irregular service is detected ex officio by the court of competent jurisdiction, so that in the case of irregular service the hearing cannot be held.

The HCC also rejected a claim that the higher than average amount of the procedural fee was unconstitutional, pointing out that the amount of the fee 'bears no direct material relation to the right to a remedy or to the right to a fair trial' (Reasoning [151]).

Decision Foreign Currency Loan also rejected the motion that the Act FCL Act violated Article XXVIII of the FL, as the suspension of pending cases would result in those cases being decided indirectly by other judges. The HCC held that the suspension of proceedings does not directly result in the suspended case being decided by another court or another judge (in the same way that the Kúria did not decide the case by issuing the PJE decision, even indirectly). Decision Foreign Currency Loan further pointed out that the suspension was necessary to ensure the unity of law (Reasoning [96]).

Decision Foreign Currency Loan then went on to consider whether, taken as a whole, the contested legislative provisions rendered FCL Act unfair. In this regard, the decision pointed out that '[t]he combination of special procedural rules [...] gives rise to a special procedural order which, by virtue of the cumulative effect of the legal restrictions, raises constitutional doubts as to the fairness of the proceedings as a whole'. Decision Foreign Currency Loan concludes, however, that 'the constitutional concerns about the procedural order as a whole do not rise to the level of an infringement of the FL in the present case' (Reasoning [201]).

Decision Foreign Currency Loan also found the application based on the infringement of judicial independence to be unfounded and rejected it. In this regard, the decision, citing in detail Decision 19/1999. (VI. 25.) AB,[9] pointed out that the essence of judicial independence is that judges are subject only to the law, i.e. they cannot be instructed. However, the fact that judges are not subject to instruction cannot, of course, mean that they are not subject to the law. Although the petition complained that the strict time-limits for the conclusion of the hearing prevented a complex assessment of the case, it is precisely the task of HCC judges to form their 'own internal conviction on the facts of the case before him, which will en-

9 ABH 1999, 150.

able him to take his decision on the basis of the relevant legislation [...]'. Invalidity must, therefore, be decided accordingly following the provisions of the law (Reasoning [208]–[210]).

3.5. *EU law is not international law, so the HCC has no jurisdiction to examine whether a law is in breach of EU law, or whether it has been adopted in conformity with EU law in form or substance [Article E of the FL].*

Lastly, Decision Foreign Currency Loan rejected the application for infringement of Articles XV (1), C (1) and M (2) of the FL for failure to state reasons. Decision Foreign Currency Loan also rejected the application for a declaration of an infringement of the FL by reason of the failure to act, since the applicant had no legal possibility of bringing such an application. Finally, the HCC also rejected the claim that FCL Act was invalid under public law on the ground that the ECB had not been consulted prior to its adoption. The HCC confirmed its consistent practice that EU law does not constitute international law, from which it concluded in Decision Foreign Currency Loan that the HCC 'has no jurisdiction to examine whether a law is contrary to European Union law' and whether 'the law has been adopted in conformity with European Union law in form or substance' (Reasoning [54]).

4. *Doctrinal analysis*

4.1. *Consumer protection in a financial crisis*

It is undeniable that the economic crisis placed debtors of foreign currency loan contracts in an extremely difficult position, as the exchange rate depreciation has led to a significant increase in the level of repayments in forint. However, the starting point of Decision Foreign Currency Loan is already wrong: that change, which is unfavourable to debtors, is not the result of the unilateral right to amend the contract, which is the subject of the application, but of the change in the exchange rate. As paragraph 1 of PJE 6/2013 points out: 'The parties had both fixed the monetary debt of the creditor and the debtor under the loan agreement in foreign currency (the issuing currency) and both parties were obliged to pay it in forints (the debtor currency). In this type of contract, the debtor is indebted in foreign currency at a more favourable interest rate than the forint loan prevailing at the time, and therefore bears the effects of the exchange rate fluctuations: a weakening forint leads to an increase in the debtor's payment burden, while a strengthening forint leads to a decrease.' The starting point is also wrong in that '[t]he so-called »hardship clause«, as it is known in international commercial practice, obliges the parties to renegotiate the contract if the circumstances specified in that clause (e.g. a significant change in the exchange rate) occur'.[10]

Decision Foreign Currency Loan is one of a series of decisions in which the HCC does not clearly interpret the rule of consumer protection enshrined in the FL as a state objective.[11] The summary statement in Decision Foreign Currency Loan that the courts should have acted in the same way as FCL Act in the absence of the Act with regard to Articles R (3) and M (2) of the FL is not clear in its content. Indeed, it is not clear whether this statement is derived from the provisions of the Civil Code subsequently examined by Decision Foreign Currency Loan or whether the HCC's assertion is that the system of requirements should have been directly enforced by the courts as a result of the FL.[12]

The finding is worrying because, according to both interpretations, the HCC uniformly and implicitly retroactively classifies as contrary to the FL those judgments of the HCC which did not examine the unfairness of the clauses in the lawsuit according to the seven principles laid down in the FCL Act, even if, taking into account the whole reasoning, it can be concluded that this legal effect was undoubtedly not intended by the HCC in this form.

Decision Foreign Currency Loan also gave an extended interpretation to the autonomy of property ownership and, in this context, to the right to human dignity, since the decision invoked as a final argument the inviolability of human dignity, which, as can be seen from the dissenting opinions, had not yet been used in this sense by the HCC. The right to

---

10 For details, see, von Bar and Clive (eds), *Principles, Definitions and Model Rules of European Private Law. Draft Common Frame of Reference (DCFR) Full Edition* (Sellier, München 2009) 710–715.

11 See, especially, the dissenting opinion of Judge Barnabás Lenkovics: Decision 8/2014. (III. 20.) AB, ABH 2014, 300, 312–313.; and subsequently, following the decision here discussed: Decision 2/2015. (II. 2.) AB, ABH 2015, 132, 138–139. For a brief overview of the relevant decisions, see: Téglási: 'A devizahitelezés problémája és kezelésének alkotmányos kérdései az Alkotmánybíróság gyakorlatának fényében' in Lenter (ed), *A devizahitelezés nagy kézikönyve* (2015), 315–334; Drinóczi, 'Az Alkotmánybíróság határozata a devizahitelekről' (2014) 3.

12 On the differences between the two interpretation, i.e. those between direct and indirect horizontal effect, see: Gárdos-Orosz, *Alkotmányos polgári jog?* (2011)

human dignity, even according to the doctrine of the FL, means that the essence of human personality, the human quality, cannot be taken away by legal regulation.[13]

Decision Foreign Currency Loan also opened up new avenues in terms of the proportionality test, when it stated that the HCC, in assessing the constitutionality, considered that the legislator, by adopting a solution in accordance with the FL, caused significantly less damage to the interests of financial institutions using unfair clauses than it would have caused to the unsuccessful debtors if the legal solution had not applied to all debtors in the same situation.

Furthermore, the role of reliance on legal certainty in the interpretation of legal certainty appears in the decision as an unusual explanation. Although the HCC refers here to the exceptional and unique nature of the solution, it is worth pointing out that the standard applied by the HCC is also exceptional and novel. Decision Foreign Currency Loan accepts that the original situation should be restored by the power of a law, even where there have already been final judicial decisions to remedy the situation, because the concept of legal certainty includes, in the interests of 'substantive justice', the ex post remedying of legal unfairness. This idea is certainly at odds with the foundations of the interpretation of the rule of law formulated by the HCC in the case *Zétényi–Takács*.[14]

4.2. Criteria for legal certainty

As regards the preparation time, the reasoning of the HCC is based on the fact that the principles along which the courts will examine the unfairness of the clauses were known from the adoption of a court opinion from December 2012. This statement is undoubtedly correct. However, the problem of preparation time, according to the petitions, is not primarily alleged to be related to the emergence of the seven principles, but rather to the fact that only a very short period of time was available to financial institutions after the entry into force of FCL Act to review dozens of

13 Kukorelli and Deli: 'Az emberi méltóság alapjoga Magyarországon' (2015) 337. See also Zakariás and Várszegi, 'Existenzminimum und würdiges Leben – die Menschenwürde als Grundlage des Sozialstaates: Eine ungarisch-deutsche Rechtsvergleichung' in Schubel et al. (eds), *Jahrbuch für Vergleichende Staats- und Rechtswissenschaften – 2018/2019* (2020). 47.

14 Decision 11/1992. (III. 5.) AB, ABH 1992. 77. For an analysis, see the relevant chapter in this book.

contracts over ten years in light of the changed litigation position, determine which clauses were covered by the FCL Act and decide whether to bring an action in the absence of knowledge of the legal consequences. In this respect, the court opinion and the uniformity decision are, by definition, irrelevant. However, in response to this argument, the decision merely states, in a very summary manner, that '[t]he identification of these elements, even over a contractual period of approximately 10 years, should not give rise to a problem that would make it impossible to meet the time limit for bringing an action' (Reasoning [65]).

A novel argument, pointing towards a change in the previous practice on the preparation period, is that the relevant date for the starting date of the preparation period would not be the date of publication of the legislation but an earlier date. In a number of decisions, the HCC has stressed the fundamental importance of a sufficient preparation period, but has always calculated it from the date of publication of the legislation and not from an earlier date, in accordance with the guarantees of the rule of law (publication in the official journal—*Magyar Közlöny* [Hungarian Gazette]—is a condition for the validity of the legislation).[15] The novel interpretation laid down in the decision is, therefore, contrary to the essence of the constitutional protection of the period of preparation.

Decision Foreign Currency Loan is extremely vague on the question of retroactivity. According to the decision, Articles 4–5 and 200 (2) of the Civil Code have always imposed the same requirement as 4 (1) of FCL Act with regard to Article M (2). In this respect, the majority reasoning does not address the question of how the general rules referred to have actually been applied in the settled practice of the ordinary court (living law) and how they have shaped the outcome of the specific litigation. The HCC therefore submits that the requirements laid down in paragraph 4 of FCL Act have not brought about any change in relation to the Civil Code, since the rules of the Civil Code have always had to be interpreted in this way. While the majority opinion does not refer to any judgments, one of the dissenting opinions[16] cites a number of court decisions which are to the contrary of this interpretation of the HCC.

---

15 See, e.g. Decision 28/1992. (IV. 30.) AB, ABH 1992, 155, 156–157. On the recent practice and the interpretation of the sufficient period of preparation by the Constitutional Court—which also demonstrates that the reference to well-known facts in this context has never appeared in domestic, foreign or international practice—see: Papp, 'A jogbiztonság formai eleme: A kellő felkészülési idő követelménye' (2013), 5.

16 Dissenting opinion of Judge László Kiss.

Decision Foreign Currency Loan also points out that, although the wording of the Civil Code between 2004 and 2006 did not add the legal consequence of nullity to the unfairness of consumer contracts, but of voidability, this in fact sanctioned unfair terms with nullity, in the light of the CJEU's judgment in Océano Grupo. This reasoning of the decision is based on the fact that the CJEU pointed out that the court's interpretation should follow the requirement of harmonious interpretation.

4.3. The content of the right to a fair trial

As regards the short time limit for bringing an action, the HCC uses three arguments: (a) there are similarly short time limits in other proceedings, (b) financial institutions were aware of the time limit for bringing an action before it was promulgated, as the adopted law was available on the website of the Parliament, and (c) the commencement of the proceedings and their conclusion by a decision on the merits also demonstrate that the time limit was appropriate.

One parallel reasoning[17] correctly points out that it is not permissible for the majority decision to refer to non-litigation procedural time limits in the case of litigation, since the fundamentally different purpose and different nature of the proceedings preclude comparability. We have also pointed out, in the context of the preparation period that the fundamental criterion of the rule of law is that no legal effect may be attached to legislation which has not been promulgated. It is logically flawed to argue that the actions brought prove that there was sufficient time to bring the action. The HCC did not examine either the extraordinary effort required of the applicants to bring the action, which would have been impossible for smaller financial institutions, or the extent to which the short time available contributed to the applicants' frustration. In that regard, the HCC should have laid down clear criteria on the basis of which the constitutionality of the time-limit could be decided on the basis of objective criteria. The HCC also fails to provide sufficient reasons as to why the time-limit for bringing proceedings does not fall within the scope of the protection of the right to a fair hearing.

17 Parallel reasoning of Judge Imre Juhász.

4.4. *Procedural obstacles—significant impediment to the exercise of fundamental rights*

The constitutionality of the short procedural time limits was justified by the HCC on the grounds that there was essentially no need for expert evidence in the proceedings. However, the allegation that an expert had been called is not only unsupported but also incorrect. In our view, the determination of whether the circumstances set out in the contract comply with the principles of factuality and objectivity may be a matter for the experts.

With regard to the equality of arms, the majority decision merely states that the application is erroneous because the defendant has a shorter time-limit for lodging a counterclaim than for lodging the application. A dissenting opinion correctly points out the inadequacy of the reasoning in this regard: the majority decision fails to address why the equality of arms is not violated by the fact that the plaintiff must respond to the counterclaim presented at trial immediately at trial, while the defendant is given at least three days by the FCL Act to respond to the action.[18]

The reasoning of Decision Foreign Currency Loan with regard to the presumption of service is also unconvincing. The HCC argues that as a result of the legislation under review, 'the possibility of improper service is unlikely', but supports this claim with the specific rules of the FCL Act to expedite the procedure. These provisions, however, bear no logical relation to the question of service.

The decision does not provide any explanation as to why the possibly excessive level of the fee is not related to the right to a fair trial and the right to a remedy. The lack of reasoning in the majority decision is particularly clear in the light of the fact that the level of the fee is of serious constitutional relevance in the context of the right to a fair trial if the purpose of a specific fee is to deter the pursuit of justice.[19]

Furthermore, paragraph 201 of the grounds of Decision Foreign Currency Loan examines whether—even if the individual provisions of FCL Act individually comply with the requirements of the FL—the procedure as a whole does not result in unfairness. In this respect, the decision states that the procedural order 'raises constitutional doubts as to the fairness of the procedure as a whole, in view of the cumulative effect of the restrictions on the rights'. The decision then summarises the procedural

18 Dissenting opinion of Judge Imre Juhász.

19 As emphasised in the dissenting opinion of Judge László Kiss as well.

rules of FCL Act, reiterating that 'the procedural order as a whole, as established by the special procedural rules, must be examined', despite the fact that '[t]he violation of the right to a fair trial cannot be established separately in relation to each element of the procedure established by the Act'. However, without any further examination, the HCC concludes that 'the constitutional concerns relating to the procedural system as a whole do not rise to the level of an infringement of fundamental law in the present case' (Reasoning [202]).

Decision Foreign Currency Loan 'sends a message' to the legislature, however, that 'such exceptional means may be used only in exceptional cases and to the narrowest possible extent' (Reasoning [203]). The reasoning of the HCC in this respect is not clear: from the reference to the cumulative effect of the restrictions on the right to a fair trial, it appears that the HCC has found that the FCL Act as a whole restricts the right to a fair trial, but that the HCC considers the fundamental restriction on the right to a fair trial to be constitutional on the basis of Article I (3) of the FL. However, the majority decision does not contain any information on the assessment made.

4.5. Relationship between EU law and domestic law

Decision Foreign Currency Loan also points out that, although the wording of the Civil Code between 2004 and 2006 did not add the legal consequence of nullity to the unfairness of consumer contracts, but the consequence of voidability, this in fact sanctioned unfair terms with nullity, in the light of the CJEU's judgment in *Océano Grupo*. This reasoning in Decision Foreign Currency Loan is based on the fact that the CJEU has pointed out that courts must interpret national legislation in conformity with the principles; an interpretation in conformity with principles requires that the right to challenge be interpreted as a nullity.

The reasoning of the decision is, in our view, wrong on this point. In the Océano Grupo case, the CJEU examined whether the national court was entitled to examine of its own motion the unfairness of a jurisdiction clause in a contract. In this context, the CJEU stated, referring to its previous judgments, that national law should be interpreted as far as possible in a manner consistent with principles. However, an interpretation in conformity with the Directive cannot lead to the national rule being set aside or changed. In the present case, however, the Civil Code has clearly established that unfairness is subject to the right of challenge and not to the consequence of nullity. Decision Foreign Currency Loan therefore does not provide any valid explanation as to why the rule of the FCL Act is not retroactive for the period 2004–2006.

5. *Aftermath of the Decision*

Against the FCL Act, the Metropolitan Court of Appeal also subsequently referred the matter to the HCC, requesting the HCC to declare that Articles 4(2)–(3), 6–15 of the Act infringe Articles B (1), C (1), XXVIII (1), 25 (1) and 26 (1) of the FL. This was the result of Decision 2/2015. (II. 2.) AB. In addition, several other constitutional complaints have been decided in the case, but these decisions have not determined new substantive claims.

In the operative part of Decision Foreign Currency Loan, the HCC dismissed the judicial initiatives to declare Article 6 of FCL Act unconstitutional and to annul it. According to the grounds of the decision, the position of the Hungarian State as defendant does not infringe the principle of the separation of powers, since the State is a legal person with legal capacity in the context of litigation, and its legitimacy in the context of litigation is exceptionally also preserved when, like the prosecutor, it does not act in the context of litigation as the subject of the property relations concerned. In the present case, its intervention was necessary in the public interest and the State's position in the proceedings is in accordance with Article M (2) of the FL. In this context, the HCC also pointed out that the State is not involved in the action as a legislator and that the legislation does not put the State in a more favourable position. According to the HCC, it can be clearly established by interpretation who is covered by the final judgment. Decision Foreign Currency Loan also held that the FCL Act does not violate the requirement of the immutability of closed legal relationships. This is because Articles I–II and M of the FL require a reassessment of the legal relationships that have already been adjudicated. The HCC considered the restriction of fundamental rights to be necessary and proportionate to the aim pursued.

In the Hungarian legal literature, András Téglási's paper[20] offers an overview of how the crisis situation as a legal ground appears in the case law of some EU Member States, the CJEU and the ECtHR in the field of social rights. Nóra Chronowski and Attila Vincze's study[21] has

20 Téglási, 'A szociális jogok (alapjog)védelmi szintjének csökkenése a gazdasági válság hatására' (2016) 141.

21 Chronowsi and Vincze, 'Alkotmánybíráskodás (gazdasági) válságban' (2014) 104.

shown when and how the 'crisis situation' appeared as a reference point in Hungarian constitutional jurisprudence since 1990. The reference to the crisis appears as an essential element in Decision Foreign Currency Loan and in Decision 2/2015. (II. 2.) AB.[22] In Decision Foreign Currency Loan, there is only a laconic justification that the economic crisis has had serious consequences in Hungary, after which the HCC, referring to its previous decisions, develops an interpretation different from those. On this basis, it is not possible to determine whether the HCC's decisions are only relevant during the economic crisis or whether the HCC intended to revise its previous position independently of the economic crisis.

Bibliography

Christian von Bar and Eric Clive (eds), *Principles, Definitions and Model Rules of European Private Law. Draft Common Frame of Reference (DCFR) Full Edition* (Sellier, München 2009)

Tímea Drinóczi, 'Az Alkotmánybíróság határozata a devizahitelekről. A szerződési szabadság régi-új korlátai" [The Decision of the Constitutional Court about Foreign Currency Loan. The Old and New Limits of Freedom of Contract] (2014) 2 *Jogesetek Magyarázata,* 3.

Fruzsina Gárdos-Orosz, 'Constitutional Justice in Credit Crises. The Hungarian Case' (2018) 1 *Südosteuropa: Journal for Politics and Society,* 94.

Fruzsina Gárdos-Orosz, *Alkotmányos polgári jog? Az alapvető jogok alkalmazása a magánjogi jogvitákban* [Constitutional Private Law? The Application of the Fundamental Rights in Private Relations] (Dialog Campus, Budapest 2011)

Fruzsina Gárdos-Orosz and Nóra Chronowski, 'The Hungarian Constitutional Court and the Financial Crisis' (2017) 2 *Hungarian Journal of Legal Studies,* 139.

Fruzsina Gárdos-Orosz and Péter Gárdos, 'Az Alkotmánybíróság első határozata a pénzügyi intézmények fogyasztói kölcsönszerződéseiben alkalmazott egyoldalú szerződésmódosítási jogra vonatkozó törvényi szabályozásról' [The First Decision of the Constitutional Court about the Unilateral Contract Amendments of Loan Contracts of Financial Institutions] (2015) 2 *Jogesetek Magyarázata,* 3.

Nóra Chronowsi and Attila Vincze: 'Alkotmánybíráskodás (gazdasági) válságban' [Constitutional Jurisprudence in Financial Crisis] (2014) 2 *Alkotmánybírósági Szemle,* 2014/2. 104.

István Kukorelli and Gergely Deli, 'Az emberi méltóság alapjoga Magyarországon' [The Fundamental Right to Human Dignity in Hungary] (2015) 7–8 *Jogtudományi Közlöny,* 337.

22 Decision 2/2015. (II. 2.) AB, Reasoning [64].

Rafał Mańko, 'Unfair Terms in Swiss Franc Loans. Overview of European Court of Justice Case Law' (March 2021) European Parliamentary Research Service, https://bit.ly/3yF4KzL

Imre Papp, 'A jogbiztonság formai eleme: A kellő felkészülési idő követelménye' [The Formal Element of the Rule of Law: the Proper Time to Prepare for the Implementation of the Law] (2013) 1 *Kodifikáció*, 5.

Kinga Zakariás and Márk Várszegi, 'Existenzminimum und würdiges Leben – die Menschenwürde als Grundlage des Sozialstaates: Eine ungarisch-deutsche Rechtsvergleichung' in Christian Schubel, Stephan Kirste, Peter-Christian Müller-Graff, Oliver Diggelmann, and Ulrich Hufeld (eds), *Jahrbuch für Vergleichende Staats- und Rechtswissenschaften – 2018/2019* (Nomos, Baden-Baden 2020) 47.

András Téglási, 'A szociális jogok (alapjog)védelmi szintjének csökkenése a gazdasági válság hatására' [The Reduction of the Level of Protection of Social rights in Time of Economic Crisis] (2015) 2 *Justum Aequum Salutare*, 141.

András Téglási, 'A devizahitelezés problémája és kezelésének alkotmányos kérdései az Alkotmánybíróság gyakorlatának fényében' [Tackling the Constitutional Problems of the Foreign Currency Loan in the Light of the Constitutional Court Jurisprudence] in Csaba Lenter (ed), *A devizahitelezés nagy kézikönyve* [The Comprehensive Handbook of Foreign Currency Lending] (Nemzeti Közszolgálati és Tankönyvkiadó, Budapest 2015) 315.

23. Decision 19/2014. (V. 30.) AB – Liability for Online Comments

András Koltay[*]

The internet service provider is liable to all rights infringing comments, even if the website is not moderated.

According to the Decision Liability for Online Comments, the operator of a website may be held liable for comments containing infringing content, even if it does not moderate users' content. The decision highlights the fact that the system of personality rights protection has difficulties in dealing with personal rights violations which occur as a result of online comments: civil law does not exclude or significantly limit the liability of content providers, even if it is difficult to justify why it holds the content provider (website operator) liable for an infringement which, although related to its conduct, is clearly separable from it and was committed by another person. Conversely, decisions which limit liability under the information society services regulations may appear to be favourable to content and hosting providers, but mean that they may also be liable for non-removal or late removal of infringing comments. It follows from the reasoning of the decision that the full release of content and hosting providers from liability is therefore not conceivable under any of the regulatory regimes.

1. Background

The main issue in the debate is whether it is Act CVIII of 2001 on the certain aspects of electronic commerce services and information society services (e-Commerce Act), or, alternatively, the general rules of civil law which apply to the liability of the platforms that provide an opportunity to comment, i.e. whether, on learning of a (personality rights) infringing comment, prompt removal leads to an exemption, or, in the event of

* PhD, Professor, University of Public Service (Budapest), and Pázmány Péter Catholic University Faculty of Law and Political Sciences (Budapest).

involvement in the publication of the infringing content, the fact of infringement leads to the establishment of liability.

Under the e-Commerce Act, the hosting provider is, in principle, liable for the infringing information. However, it is not required to verify the information which it merely transmits, stores or makes available, and, moreover, it is exempted from liability if certain conditions are satisfied. The hosting provider shall be released from liability if it was unaware of the infringing nature of the content and took action without delay to make such content inaccessible as soon as it became aware of it. (A content provider which also provides the opportunity to comment is theoretically allowed to be considered a hosting service according to the e-Commerce Act.)

In contrast, according to the relevant provisions of both the previous, repealed Civil Code and the recent one currently in effect (Civil Code), the mere fact of the publication of an item of content that infringes a personal right is a decisive factor, and any immediate removal upon being informed does not result in an exemption from the objective legal consequences.

A few months before the HCC's decision, the ECtHR adopted a first instance decision in *Delfi*,[1] which was the first comment case to come before the Strasbourg forum. According to the facts of the case, readers of *Delfi*, a popular news portal in Estonia, commented extensively on a company mentioned in an article. Although the Estonian court of first instance applied the legislation on e-commerce, classifying the news portal's service provider as a hosting provider, the Court of Appeal and the Supreme Court decided on the basis of the law on civil law obligations, establishing the violation of the rights of the applicant (the owner and supervisory panel member of the company concerned). The application by the service provider was turned down in 2013 by the Section I the ECtHR, and in 2015 by the Grand Chamber,[2] declaring that its call to account does not violate Article 10 of the ECHR.

The ECtHR's investigation focused primarily on the content of the objections which had been complained against, the identifiability of the commentator, the identity and conduct of the service provider concerned and, in addition to the (possible) impact of the comment on the person attacked, the form and extent of the sanction applied. It is worth mention-

1 *Delfi AS v. Estonia*, no. 64569/09, judgment of 10 October 2013. On the *Delfi* case, see Cheung, 'Liability of Internet Host Providers in Defamation Actions: From Gatekeepers to Identifiers' in Koltay (ed), *Media Freedom and Regulation in the New Media World* (2014), 289.

2 *Delfi AS v. Estonia*, no. 64569/09, judgment of 16 June 2015 [GC].

ing that, on the basis of the arguments appearing in subsequent judgments related to user comments,[3] it is not possible, for the time being, to draw up a uniform system of criteria, on the basis of which the contents in question can be clearly judged and the related system of liability can be clearly established. This implies that the ECtHR also considers it permissible for the courts of a State Party to apply civil law liability rules or special rules applicable to hosting providers or, in particular, to content providers, which provide them with a wider exemption.

2. *Petition*

According to the facts established in the court proceedings on which the constitutional complaint was based, the Association of Hungarian Content Providers (Magyar Tartalomszolgáltatók Egyesülete, or MTE), as a self-regulatory organisation of Internet content providers, published a decision on its website regarding the advertising practice of a real estate agency's website. The MTE investigated complaints it had received about the website and declared the contractual practices of the website unethical and unfair, without a court establishing that the website had acted unlawfully. In addition to publishing the decision, the MTE ensured that anyone could make comments on the website. Among the comments, several contained opinions and remarks that could have been offensive to the companies concerned.

The content provider of the real estate agency then filed a lawsuit against MTE (as well as the publisher of the *Zöld Újság*, the recipient of the notice, and *Index.hu*). In its opinion, the communication published on the website and its further communications, as well as the statements appearing in certain comments, were untrue, offensive in content and violated the personal right to reputation.[4] Judgment no. 19.P.21.022/2010/7

3 Decision Liability for Online Comments is the antecedent of *Magyar Tartalomszolgáltatók Egyesülete and Index.hu Zrt. v. Hungary*, no. 22947/13, judgment of 6 February 2016. Other EctHR cases related to online comments are: *Pihl v. Sweden*, no. 4742/14, judgment of 9 March 2017; *Tamiz v. the United Kingdom*, no. 3877/14, admissibility decision of 19 September 2017; *Høiness v. Norway*, no. 43624/14, judgment of 19 March 2019.

4 The three comments found to be unlawful were as follows: 'They have talked about these two rubbish real estate websites a thousand times already', 'Is this not that Benkő-Sándor-sort-of sly, rubbish, mug company again? I ran into it two years ago, since then they have kept sending me emails about my overdue debts and this and that. I am above 100,000 [Hungarian forints] now. I have not paid and I am

of the Budapest-Capital Regional Court, acting in the first instance, stated, in relation to the comments relating to the article, that these comments were subject to the same judgment as reader's letters to a newspaper and constituted edited content, and thus the MTE was liable for the content published in this form that violated the applicant's reputation.

In its judgment no. 8.Pf.21.129/2011/4, the Metropolitan Court of Appeal upheld the first instance judgment, stating that, while the decision published on the website was not infringing, the content in the comments led MTE to infringe the applicant's personal right to reputation. However, in the statement of reasons given by the panel, it reached a different conclusion regarding the assessment of the comments and stated that they did not constitute reader's letters. While anyone can express an opinion on a particular topic in the form of a comment, without editorial filtering, readers' letters are published only after editing. Nevertheless, the content provider of the website is equally liable for violations taking place in the posts.

However, the appellate court also found that the comments constituted private communication and therefore did not fall under the material scope of either the e-commerce services or the e-Commerce Act. By providing an opportunity for grossly offensive, demeaning posts to appear on its website, MTE committed defamation by making possible to distribute defamatory statements. In the Court's view, the fact that the owner of the website immediately deleted the infringing content cannot be assessed in the context of the objective determination of the infringement; it can only be taken into account in the context of the claim for damages or exculpation.

The Supreme Court (Kúria), in a judicial review procedure, upheld the challenged provisions of the final judgment in its judgement no. Pfv. IV.20.217/2012/5. In its statement of reasons, the Kúria explained that, by providing MTE with the opportunity to publish blog posts on its website, for the content displayed in this manner, the limited liability of the hosting provider specified in Section 2(l)(lc) of e-Commerce Act may not be applied to it. In view of this, the owner of the website cannot be exempted from the finding of an infringement as an objective legal consequence applied due to infringing communications, as—and here the Kúria referred to one of its earlier decisions—anyone providing others with the opportunity to comment on his/her website must keep in mind

not going to. That's it.' and 'People like this should go and shit a hedgehog and spend all their money on their mothers' tombs until they drop dead.'

that infringing comments may occur among them. The Kúria stated in its judgment that the violation of personal rights is an objective matter of fact.

MTE subsequently filed a constitutional complaint with the HCC, requesting the annulment of the judgment of the Kúria—and at the same time the judgments of the courts of first and second instance. According to the petitioner, the judicial interpretation of the law adopted in the judgments violates Article IX (1)–(2) of the FL (the freedom of expression clause).

3. *Decision and its reasoning*

The HCC rejected the constitutional complaint seeking to establish the unconstitutionality of the Kúria's judgment and to annul it.

3.1. *The Internet is not an area exempt from the law; the communication taking place there may be subject to legal regulation, and the enforcement of the rights and obligations enshrined in the FL is also required in this form of the communication of opinions (Articles VI and IX of the FL).*

Any statements appearing on the website in the form of a comment were considered by the final court judgment as upheld by the Kúria to be private expressions, and from this it was concluded that they should not, therefore, belong within the scope of the e-Commerce Act (Reasoning [40]), although the HCC did not agree with this. Private expressions (which, moreover, fall within the scope of the protection of privacy enshrined in Article VI of the FL) are fundamentally distinguished from communication, which is also protected by the freedom of expression, since the latter is intended for the public, that is to say, 'for everyone', irrespective of the fact that it involves only the private opinion of a single person (Reasoning [42]).

With regard to the issue of moderation, it was not disputed in the case under review that the website operator did not moderate the posts, so the author of the infringing comments was primarily responsible for them. However, if it is not possible to identify the infringer, (as was also the case for the posts in question), then the operator of the website is responsible for the posts (Reasoning [43]).

The HCC also examined whether the liability of the website operator for unmoderated, infringing comments constituted a proportionate restriction of a fundamental right (although it did not differentiate between comments from anonymous and identifiable authors). The HCC stated that since liability for infringing communication is based solely on the fact that the communication is infringing and does not depend on the existence of moderation, the situation of moderated and unmoderated comments after the infringement occurred is identical. Consequently, the panel concluded that it was not necessary to distinguish between moderated and non-moderated websites when examining the proportionality of a restriction on fundamental rights (Reasoning [64]–[65]).[5]

3.2. *The 'web 2.0' sites are outside the scope of the services examined in the case, as in the specific case typical private expressions were published, addressing communication to a specific stakeholder group (Articles VI and IX of the FL).*

In addition to drawing the above distinction between different types of service providers, the HCC also highlighted the differences between individual websites, distinguishing the specific characteristics of 'web 2.0' sites (interactive online services such as social media and blogs). The HCC stated that the characteristic feature of these pages is that they do not have an editor and do not act with the intention of informing the public; their purpose is to provide interfaces for public discourse. According to the panel, these sites provide access to content for users identified by the notifier (operator) and therefore they are not even considered to be identical to online press products and news portals that serve the purpose of informing and entertaining the wider public (Reasoning [61]).

5 On the issue of online anonymity, see Barendt, *Anonymous Speech. Literature, Law and Politics* (2016), and Coe, 'Anonymity and Pseudonymity: Free Speech's Problem Children' (2018), 173.

3.3. It constitutes a restriction of the freedom of the press if the operator of a website may be held liable for any post published without moderation that is otherwise infringing (Article IX of the FL).

According to the HCC, the liability of the website operator for infringing content constitutes a restriction on the freedom of the press if the existence of this possibility is capable of legally restricting its freedom of action. According to the HCC, there may be various effects of this restriction, such as increasing the cost of maintaining the site, or making it impossible to operate or inducing the site operator to behave in a way that it would not choose to in the absence of this responsibility, such as by deleting certain comments (Reasoning [59]).

3.4. The assessment of proportionality depends on the amount of damages awarded for the infringement (Article IX of the FL).

In addition to stating that it was not justified to distinguish between moderated and non-moderated comments in terms of the proportionality of the restriction of fundamental rights, that is that the establishment of an infringement against a non-moderating operator was not disproportionate, the HCC held that the assessment of proportionality depends on the amount of damages awarded for the infringement, and that no other circumstance creates a special situation. It is important to note that the proportionality of the amount of compensation may only be established by the HCC on a case-by-case basis (Reasoning [66]–[67]).

3.5. The liability of the website operator is based solely on the fact of the infringement and the moderation of comments or its absence is not a decisive factor; after the occurrence of the infringement, the legal liability of all websites and operators is identical (Article IX of the FL).

In the present case, the fact of the infringement was not disputed by either of the parties, nor was it disputed by the website operator (therefore the HCC did not conduct a substantive investigation in this respect), but it merely objected to be subject to any liability for third-party content, regardless of whether the entry had been removed without delay upon notification, relying on the e-Commerce Act in the arguments (Reasoning [56]). According to the Decision, the liability of the website operator is based solely on the fact of the infringement; other circumstances cannot be decisive. In the event of an infringement, no distinction can be made between different websites' and the operator's legal liability (Reasoning [64]).

4. *Doctrinal analysis*

4.1. *Regulation of Internet communication*

The majority reasoning assesses the nature of 'private expressions' and their relationship with the freedom of expression (Reasoning [42]): according to the text, these (private letter, telephone conversation, e-mail, private conversation, diary) 'do not fall within the protected scope of freedom of expression'. This statement is not supported by previous decisions of the HCC. While the presence of the public or its size may have significance in restricting speech, so far the panel has not explained how the logic can work the other way around, and the lack of publicity can lead to a lack of constitutional protection. Moreover, in the other part of the statement of reasons for the decision, the panel states exactly the opposite.

For our part, we agree with the latter of the two contradictory approaches that can be read from the Decision, because it seems unreasonable to exclude non-public speech altogether from the scope of freedom of expression as a whole, for which no theoretical justification is to be found, even if disputes usually start in connection with content made public, and it may be justified in some cases to provide additional protection to expressions intended for public consumption. The statement to the contrary in the Decision in Reasoning [42], which raises important questions of principle regarding the distinction between public and private communications, is therefore questionable.

As regards the role of moderation in determining liability, this is another point which can be criticised in the reasoning of the Decision, as it does not seek to clarify in principle the issue of comments and, in particular, what the HCC considers to be comments under the current legislation. The panel considered it to be within the scope of judicial interpretation of the law, so it does not consider it a constitutional issue to judge whether the content provider of the website does indeed spread rumours when providing an opportunity for users to comment. It is also unclear, for example, what importance the panel attaches to moderation. However, the finding in the statement of reasons that legal liability does not depend on moderation or the absence thereof, because it is based on the fact of the infringement (Reasoning [65]) may deter service providers from providing moderation of users' comments, as they may ultimately be held liable when they act in good faith or it may even motivate them to filter out any comments that are in the slightest way 'suspicious'.

According to the motion, the lack of moderation reduces the content provider's liability for infringing communications, because without moderation the content provider could not have been aware of the infringement or have made an informed decision to publish the comment (Reasoning [43]). While it is possible to agree with the reasoning of the Decision, it does not answer the question of whether the fact of moderation may in itself lead to the necessary differentiation in terms of legal liability.

I believe that the existence or non-existence of pre-moderation determines whether a comment falls within the scope of media regulation in the case of media (content) services.[6] This is because if there is pre-moderation, then that is a conscious decision made by the media service on whether or not to publish the certain comment, so it makes an editorial decision and, if it decides to publish (approve the publication of the comment), it makes the comment part of the edited content. In doing so, the comment published becomes media content, and thus covered by media regulation, if the service in question is under the scope of it. (In Hungary this is true for comments related to articles of an online press product. Furthermore, this conclusion is without prejudice to the application of the rules on the protection of personality rights.) To this extent, the petitioner's suggestion regarding more favourable treatment of unmoderated comments seems to be justified, even if it is true that he also wanted this distinction to be recognised by the panel with regard to the application of the Civil Code.

The HCC's decision also addresses the issues of editing and editorial responsibility, but in a different context, and includes content which is open to criticism, namely, Reasoning [61] states that web 2.0 services (social media sites, blogs) 'have no editor, and therefore are not intended for information or similar purposes'. In my view, this is a fundamental mistake. On the one hand, for single-person blogs, the blogger is both the author and the editor of their own blog, and on the other hand, multi-author blogs also have an editor, because someone always has to decide what

6 Of course, several methods of moderation are known. With regard to the scope of media regulation, what is pertinent here are the methods in which the content provider of a website makes a conscious decision, knowing the text of a comment, to publish or reject its publication.

content to display on the page. Furthermore, contrary to what the HCC claims, bloggers seek to inform (and argue, take a position, etc., or indeed to pursue 'similar purposes'). A blogger is not part of the 'media' and is not subject to media regulation because she does not primarily provide an economic service; rather, she seeks to participate in public life as an individual, instead of through an institution, as part of the professional media, hence, comments related to blog posts are not subject to media regulation either.

4.2. The need for differentiation between online content services

The Decision identifies a need to differentiate between different types of comments. Reasoning [61] distinguishes between 'edited content service' and 'web 2.0, that is social networking sites and purely opinion pages (for example, Facebook, blogging, etc.)'. The statement of reasons states that the latter are not covered by the decision as it covers only edited content services. It is striking, however, that in the specific case the statements that were challenged appeared on a blog on the MTE website, a fact that was not examined further by the HCC's majority reasoning.

In my opinion, the necessary demarcation did not properly take place. I have already explained above the criteria for classifying online content as a media service and how the comments appearing in these services can become media content and thus the subject of media regulation. Comments from social networking sites and private blogs are therefore left untouched by media regulation. However, this exemption does not apply to the application of civil and criminal law rules for the protection of personality, which are generally applicable and are not limited to certain types of online services. In the question under consideration, therefore, the nature of the website at issue in this case should not have been relevant to the HCC, at most only the issue of whether or not moderation took place.

4.3. Liability for the content of the comment

An important finding in the majority reasoning is that the liability of content providers for infringing comments constitutes a restriction on the freedom of the press (Reasoning [59]). It follows, as detailed in Judge Paczolay's concurring reasoning, that a constitutional balance must be struck between the need to protect freedom of expression, or the freedom of the press, and the protection of the personality (Reasoning [75]). While this may seem obvious, it is still important to declare it, because it also follows that neither aspect is inherently superior, that is, neither those in favour of the freedom of comments nor those concerned about personal rights are inherently correct when they make the case for the exclusive enforcement of the right they consider should take priority.[7]

4.4. *The question of proportionality*

It turns out from Reasoning [65] that the HCC considers the responsibility for moderated comments to be proportionate (with regard to moderation as an editorial decision), but does not consider it justified to treat non-moderated comments more lightly (the petitioner's suggestion in this regard). In my opinion, while pre-moderated comments do not necessarily warrant stricter judgment, editorial interference may result in the comment being subject to media regulation (if the website in question is included in the media), which is otherwise indifferent to the protection of personal rights, as media regulation does not directly protect personal rights, and the publication of a comment may be considered to be spreading false statements of facts, as known from civil defamation law. And even if media regulation does not deal with defamation, other restrictions may apply to the comment as 'edited' content (for example, the ban on hate speech known by the media act as well). Another possible interpretation, where pre-moderation may be relevant, is that if the possibility of commenting is considered to constitute a 'hosting service' then, in the absence of moderation, knowledge is gained of the infringing content only when attention is drawn to it and it is relevant to the determination of liability (although the HCC did not consider the activity under review to be a hosting service).

Proportionality must also be examined in terms of the sanctions and legal consequences applied. The HCC does not consider compensation to be constitutionally excluded in this respect either (Reasoning [66]). According to Judge Paczolay, the application of imputability-based legal sanctions should be narrowed in terms of proportionality and their appli-

7 On the alternative liability regimes applicable in comment cases see Angelopoulos and Smet, 'Notice-and-Fair-Balance: How to Reach a Compromise Between Fundamental Rights in European Intermediary Liability' (2016), 266.

cation should be excluded when the offending comment is removed upon request.

4.5. The importance of the infringing nature of the comment

The statement of reasons to the HCC's decision also notes that the infringing nature of the comment was not disputed in the case (Reasoning [56]). It is important to add that commenting as a specific *genre* of expression is not frustrated, even if the content provider may be held liable for a comment written by another, because in public debates, in relation to public figures, the infringing nature of a comment may only be established very narrowly. The constitutional principle and rules of freedom of public debate have been reaffirmed or enshrined in a number of HCC decisions and, based on this practice, the right to reputation and honour can only be protected to a much narrower extent than opinions in general cases.[8] This should in all events be the starting point in a case, and a decision on the infringing nature of a message precedes a decision on who is liable.

5. Aftermath of the Decision

The case on which the HCC decision is based has also been referred to the ECtHR. The Section IV of the ECtHR decided in favour of the applicants in *Magyar Tartalomszolgáltatók Egyesülete and Index.hu Zrt v. Hungary*.[9] The Strasbourg court found the decision of the Hungarian courts to be in breach of Article 10 of ECHR, mainly due to the less offensive nature of the comments compared to the comments in *Delfi*.[10] The *MTE* judgment sets out that the subject of the original article (about which comments were posted) concerned a public matter.[11] Increased protection of freedom of expression is essential for the discussion of matters of public interest. The ECtHR considered not only the articles concerned but also the comments made on them to be protected speech, due to their participation in a

8 See, for example, Decisions 36/1994. (VI. 24.) AB; 7/2014. (III. 7.) AB; 13/2014. (IV. 18.) AB.

9 *MTE* (n 3). On the MTE case, see Spano, 'Intermediary Liability for Online User Comments under the European Convention on Human Rights' (2017), 665.

10 *MTE* (n 3) paras. 76 and 91.

11 *MTE* (n 3) para. 72.

debate on public affairs, which accorded them high priority.[12] In *Delfi* and also in *MTE*, the target of the comments was a legal entity, the operation and criticism of which clearly qualified as a public matter. In any case, the protection of a legal entity's rights should be assessed differently than that of natural persons; the 'moral' rights of legal entities deserve less strict protection.[13] The ECtHR considers it necessary to make this distinction.[14]

The panel considered the consequences for content providers to be serious, even without an obligation to pay compensation. Although the Hungarian authorities, in addition to establishing the infringement, ordered payment of the not excessively high court fees, according to the ECtHR, the wider consequences of the decision must also be taken into account. For example, it may lead content providers to close down their interfaces for commenting in the future and not to provide this option to their readers.[15] Hungary has therefore infringed Article 10 of ECHR.[16]

Bibliography

Christina Angelopoulos and Stijn Smet, 'Notice-and-Fair-Balance: How to Reach a Compromise Between Fundamental Rights in European Intermediary Liability' (2016) 8 *Journal of Media Law*, 266.

Eric Barendt, *Anonymous Speech. Literature, Law and Politics* (Hart, Oxford 2016)

Anne SY Cheung, 'Liability of Internet Host Providers in Defamation Actions: From Gatekeepers to Identifiers' in András Koltay (ed), *Media Freedom and Regulation in the New Media World* (Wolters Kluwer, Budapest 2014), 289.

Peter Coe, 'Anonymity and Pseudonymity: Free Speech's Problem Children' (2018) 22 *Media & Arts Law Review*, 173.

András Koltay, *New Media and Freedom of Expression* (Hart, Oxford 2019)

Robert Spano, 'Intermediary Liability for Online User Comments under the European Convention on Human Rights' (2017) 17 *Human Rights Law Review*, 665.

12 *MTE* (n 3) para. 72.

13 See also: *Uj v. Hungary*, no. 23954/10, judgment of 19 July 2011, para. 22.

14 *MTE* (n 3) para. 65.

15 *MTE* (n 3) 86.

16 On the case law of the ECtHR related to online comments, see Koltay, *New Media and Freedom of Expression* (2019), ch. 6.

24. Decision 3/2015. (II. 2.) AB – Proportionality

*Zoltán Pozsár-Szentmiklósy**

Ordinary courts have to take into consideration the fundamental rights aspects of those cases which are relevant from the fundamental rights perspective, as well as the protected scope of the fundamental rights concerned. In the absence of this consideration, the judicial decision is unconstitutional.

In the case 'napi.hu' the HCC declared as a matter of principle, for the first time in the period since the FL entered into force, that the ordinary courts have to analyse the conflicts between fundamental rights in judicial disputes, as well as to interpret the concerned fundamental rights in accordance with the practice of the HCC; furthermore, courts also have to apply the principle of proportionality when examining the limitation of the fundamental rights concerned. This requirement is significant, taking into consideration that in the past the HCC did not examine the applicability of the proportionality test. Moreover, the requirement has the force of precedent for the consideration of future constitutional complaint cases, claiming the unconstitutionality of the judicial interpretation (based on Article 27 of the HCC Act).

1. Background

The principle of proportionality, as the basis of the method applied to the examination of the constitutionality of the limitation of fundamental rights, was expressly mentioned by the HCC right at the beginning of its activity.[1] The practice of the HCC based on the Constitution has usually

* PhD, Associate professor, Eötvös Loránd University Faculty of Law (Budapest).

1 The need for protection of other (concurring) fundamental rights, the necessity of the limitation and the extent of the limitation, as requirements related to limitation of fundamental rights, first appear in the dissenting opinion of Judge László Sólyom to the Decision 2/1990. (II. 18.) AB. [Dissenting opinion of László Sólyom, Decision 2/1990. (II. 18.) AB, ABH 1990, 18, 23.]. Later, in the reasoning of the Decision 20/1990. (X. 4.) AB it appeared that the balancing of the importance

referred in this regard to Decision 30/1992. (V. 26.) AB, which explains the steps in the examination of the proportionality test as a structured framework.[2] However, in its early practice the HCC did not explore in its decisions the constitutional organs which have to apply the proportionality test. Of course, when exercising its norm control-type powers in fundamental right-related constitutional disputes, the HCC has used the proportionality test—which implicitly indicates that the legislature is also bound by the requirements related to the limitation of fundamental rights and the duty to respect their core content.

The entering into force of the FL did not introduce a new standard for the examination of the constitutionality of the limitation of fundamental rights. However, it is a significant development that the text of the FL—contrary to the text of the Constitution—alongside the formal requirement of regulating fundamental rights in parliamentary acts and the requirement of full respect for the core content of fundamental rights, also includes the substantive standard of limitation, explicitly mentioning the requirements related to the proportionality test.[3] Since then, the HCC has interpreted Article I (3) of the FL in its Decision 30/2012. (VI. 27.) AB for the first time. The Court declared that these provisions are identical to Article 8 (1) of the Constitution taking into consideration the requirement of regulating fundamental rights in parliamentary acts, as well as the requirement of full respect for the core content of fundamental rights, while the proportionality test is identical to the standard elaborated in the previous practice of the HCC.[4] Later the HCC did not reformulate the proportionality test, rather it emphasized the link between the standard of the FL and the previous practice,[5] it reformulated the description of the test, identical to the Decision 30/1992. (V. 26.) AB.[6] Furthermore, the

---

of the legislative aim against the burden on the affected fundamental right, the requirement of choosing the least restrictive measure and the requirement of suitability [Decision 20/1990. (X. 4.) AB, ABH 1990, 69, 71.].

2 'The state may limit certain fundamental right when the protection of another fundamental right or the protection of another constitutional value is not possible with other means. […] It is also required to be in accordance with the requirement of proportionality: the importance of the legislative aim and the burden on the limited fundamental right have to be in proportion with each other. The legislature has to choose the least restrictive means which are suitable to support the legislative aim.' See Decision 30/1992. (V. 26.) AB, ABH 1992, 167, 180–181.

3 Article I (3) of the FL.

4 Decision 30/2012. (VI. 27.) AB, Reasoning [17].

5 Decision 5/2013. (II. 21.) AB, Reasoning [55].

6 Decision 3046/2013. (II. 28.) AB, Reasoning [38].

Court declared that—in accordance with its previous practice—the proportionality-based standard follows from the requirement of full respect for the core content of fundamental rights—a fact that was also recognized by the constituent power when formulating the text of the FL.[7]

Prior to the *napi.hu* case, the question had not arisen in the new practice of the HCC of which constitutional organs have to apply the proportionality test. This case demonstrated that the standard of proportionality binds the legislature when regulating certain fundamental rights, as well as the law-enforcement bodies and courts when examining fundamental rights-related legal disputes.

In the 'napi.hu' case analysed below, the provisions interpreted and applied by the ordinary court in the original case were included in Act CXX of 2001 on the Capital Market (CM Act) and related the prohibition of insider dealing and market manipulation,[8] as well as the definition of activities that can be considered to be market manipulation. Based on the latter, 'the notification, rumouring and publication of unfounded, misleading and false information can be considered as market manipulations in the case [when] the person who spreads the information is aware of the false or misleading nature of the information or should have been aware of it based on due care and diligence.'[9]

2. *Petition*

The basic question of the case was whether an article published on the napi.hu news site on the 16th of October 2013 had any effect of market manipulation. The article focused on the Norway Oil Fund, which had a 1.64% quota share in the Hungarian oil company, MOL Plc. At that time, a criminal procedure was in progress in Croatia against the CEO of MOL Plc. in relation to the acquisition of a company in Croatia, and an international arrest warrant had also been issued. According to the article published on the napi.hu site, the sale of the quota share of the Norway Oil Fund in MOL Plc. might have been a possibility due to the Ethical Code of the Norway Oil Fund, which prohibits acquisition in companies that could be linked to corruption. The article also dealt with the potential effects of the sale: the shares of MOL Plc. could be under significant

7 Decision 6/2013. (III. 1.) AB, Reasoning [128].
8 Article 200 of the CM Act.
9 Article 202 d) of the CM Act.

vendor pressure. In a different report related to this article, the news site announced that the chairman of the Supervisory Board of MOL Plc. partly sold his quota share.

After publishing this article on the napi.hu news site, the Hungarian Central Bank (HCB) started an *ex officio* market supervision procedure against the company that runs the news site. In its resolution, the HCB stated that by publishing the article concerned, the news site had violated the rules banning market manipulation stipulated in the CM Act. According to the HCB, the article was suitable to influence the attitude of investors, by suggesting the worst-case scenario from the point of view of MOL Plc. (the sale of the quota share of the Norway Oil Fund). In the HCB's view, the article was misleading as the probability of the worst-case scenario was uncertain. In a similar vein, it was misleading that the news site had published a related report that the chairman of the Supervisory Board of MOL Plc. had sold his quota share. According to the resolution of the HCB, the company that runs the napi.hu news site had to pay a market supervisory fine.

The suit against the HCB resolution was rejected by the Budapest-Capital Administrative and Labour Court in its judgment no. 26.K.33.829/2013/6. According to the court, the HCB interpreted properly the ban on market manipulation, furthermore, in the challenged resolution it was not the opinion of the journalist that was the basis of the supervision of the HCB, rather the unfounded nature of the published information. The court also emphasized that arguments related to fundamental rights-related issues (expressed in the petition) cannot be taken into consideration as 'fundamental rights are unenforceable before ordinary courts'.

The petitioner (the owner of the news site) turned to the HCC, claiming the unconstitutionality of the judgment in its constitutional complaint. The argumentation was built on the alleged violation of the freedom of speech and the freedom of press because in its resolution the HCB had not taken into consideration the constitutional requirements related to the limitation of fundamental rights, furthermore, the published information was directly related to the discourse on public affairs.

According to the arguments expressed in the petition, the public nature of information which is related to discourse on public affairs falls under the protection of the freedom of speech and freedom of press. The petition emphasized that 'the freedom of expression of those opinions which are related to public affairs is part of the inner circle of the freedom of speech'.[10] The petitioner also claimed that 'decisions of state organs can limit the freedom of speech regardless of the area of law these belong to. From the point of view of the limitation of the freedom of speech, the most important factor is the dissuasive effect of the decision of the public authority. The type and severity of the sanction typical to the related field of law have to be considered based on proportionality.' In the present case, imposing a fine and its confirmation was a disproportionate limitation of the freedom of speech, taking also into consideration the chilling effect of the sanction related to future cases on publishing information on public affairs.

3. Decision and its reasoning

The HCC declared that a legal interpretation that does not take into consideration the fundamental rights-aspects of a case that is otherwise relevant from the perspective of fundamental rights is unconstitutional. Consequently, the HCC annulled the judgment of the Budapest-Capital Administrative and Labour Court.

The test on the possible limitation of fundamental rights included in Article I (3) of the FL primarily binds the legislator, however, it also contains constitutional requirements addressed to law-enforcement bodies, related to their powers. Based on this requirement—taking also into consideration Article 28 of the FL—ordinary courts, when interpreting a legal provision that limits the exercise of a certain fundamental right, have to interpret the law in a way that results in the necessary and proportionate limitation of the fundamental right in question.

The HCC has built up its reasoning on Article 28 of the FL, which stipulates that ordinary courts shall interpret the text of laws primarily in accordance with their purpose and with the FL. According to the HCC, 'from this requirement it follows that the court—within the room of manoeuvre given by the law—has to identify the fundamental rights' aspects of the given case and has to interpret the relevant legal provisions by taking into consideration the constitutionally protected scope of the fundamental right in question.'[11] Accordingly, based on the constitutional complaint

10 Decision 7/2014. (III. 7.) AB, Reasoning [45].
11 Decision 7/2014. (III. 7.) AB, Reasoning [17].

submitted against a judicial decision,[12] the HCC has to examine, whether the ordinary court supported the fulfilment of the fundamental right in question.

When examining the relevant facts underlying the judgment, the HCC made the following statements. Questions related to the ownership and the shares of MOL Plc. are strongly related to the economic and fiscal interests of the country, therefore, the public discourse related to them is a public matter. The HCC cited the arguments expressed in Decision 7/2014. (III. 7.) AB related to the freedom of press: this fundamental right enjoys particular protection, and its function is the presentation of the relevant circumstances related to public affairs. The legal acts of law enforcement bodies that implement a legal provision (in this case, the ban on market manipulation) related to a statement published in the press can be considered to be limitations on the freedom of press.

Based on the above arguments, as well as the requirement of interpreting legal norms in compliance with the constitution expressed in Article 28 of the FL, the HCC reached the following conclusion. The court, when reviewing the resolution of the HCB, has to interpret the legal provision on the ban on market manipulation and apply it to the concrete case in a way that also takes into consideration the fulfilment of the freedom of press, based on the proportionality test. The HCC itself also examined this case from the point of view of proportionality. According to the HCC, the purpose of the legal provision on the ban of market manipulation (which in this case limits the freedom of press) is the protection of the proper functioning of capital markets, which can be considered to be a legitimate aim. When considering the proportionality of the limitation caused by this provision, the HCC declared that the freedom of speech and the freedom of press are in a prominent position within the system of fundamental rights. Therefore, in cases of conflict between fundamental rights, these rights prevail in most cases, and especially in cases that are related to public affairs. The HCC also examined the requirements related to the interpretation of the legal provision on the ban of market manipulation. In this regard, the HCC stated that the ban on the notification of 'unfounded, misleading and false information' has to be interpreted restrictively. In the HCC's view, in the case of statements which are supported by relevant facts, the 'unfounded, misleading' nature can be considered only in cases when the press has acted in an explicitly malicious manner. Even the HCC did not formulate its conclusion in an explicit manner, based on

---

12 Article 27 of the HCC Act.

the above arguments, it can be summarized that in the present case the severity of the limitation on the freedom of press was not outweighed by the importance of the concurring constitutional value (the protection of the proper functioning of the capital markets), therefore, the limitation is unproportionate.

Taking into consideration that the court did not evaluate the above-described constitutional aspects of the case, the HCC annulled the judgment.[13]

4. *Doctrinal analysis*

The requirement formulated by the HCC is convincing. Ordinary courts play the most important role in the protection of fundamental rights. For the effectiveness of that, it is crucial for the courts to take into consideration the fundamental rights standards when formulating their judgments in cases that are relevant from the fundamental rights' perspective. However, the reasoning of the HCC would be more convincing if it were to apply the proportionality test in the present case based on proper methodology. Detailed arguments are missing from the reasoning of the HCC related to the question of why law-enforcement bodies are also obliged to apply the proportionality test alongside the legislator. In a similar vein, a detailed methodological guide on how to apply the doctrine related to fundamental rights and the norms of the specific field of law in the same case would have been useful for the ordinary courts. The absence of the structured, detailed arguments related to the above-described aspects of the case is presumably caused by the partial disagreement between the justices. However, these statements and requirements can be highlighted based on the decision of the HCC and the literature. In the following parts I will analyse the decision based on these aspects.

The proportionality test is a permanent standard in the practice of the HCC; however, its application is inconsistent. The proportionality-based reasoning of the HCC in many cases is not sufficiently detailed—in this regard, the decision delivered in the present case is no exception. The practice of the HCC is coherent in accepting the protection of other fundamental rights or other constitutional values to be possibly legitimate aims (concurring with the concerned fundamental right). The suitability

13 However, the HCC did not annul the resolution of the HCB, because the repeated review of it is the competence of the ordinary court.

is rarely examined explicitly. The examination of necessity, measuring the means of the limitation is in most cases performed by referring to the formula of inevitability (whether the means used are inevitable in reaching the legislative purpose). The examination of necessity by focusing on the selection of the least restrictive means is rarely performed by the HCC. When focusing on proportionality in the strict sense, the HCC usually balances the importance of the legislative aim and the severity of the limitation of the concerned fundamental right; however, this balancing method is rarely presented explicitly in the reasoning. It often happens—as in the present case—that certain steps of examination are included under other subtests of proportionality.[14]

In the present case, the HCC identified the proper functioning of capital markets (free from undue external influence, smooth operation) as the legislative purpose of the related provisions of the CM Act, which in the present case were in conflict with the freedom of press. The HCC declared in a short sentence that this legislative purpose is legitimate, however, it did not explain the arguments that could support this statement. These arguments would have been especially relevant in the subtest of proportionality in the strict sense when the HCC had to balance the severity of the limitation of the concerned fundamental right against the importance of the concurring constitutional value.

An examination of suitability is entirely missing from the reasoning of the HCC. In many cases, courts implicitly refer to suitability within the subtest of necessity when comparing alternative measures that are all suitable to support the legislative purpose—however, in the present case the separate examination of necessity is also missing.

The HCC used the methodological standards related to the examination of limitations of fundamental rights properly when emphasizing the role of the freedom of press, the exceptional possibility of its limitation concerning public issues within the subtest of proportionality in the strict sense. These considerations supported the HCC in performing the weighing and balancing stage of its examination in a more precise manner. However, it would have been useful to explicitly examine the severity of the limitation in the present case, e.g., by focusing on the fact that the ownership structure of a company that has a strategic significance in the national economy could be considered to be a key topic in a disclosure on public affairs. In a similar vein, the HCC did not examine explicitly the

14 For a detailed analysis on the Hungarian doctrine on proportionality see Pozsár-Szentmiklósy, *Alapjogok mérlegen* (2016)

arguments that could support that importance of the legislative aim (the proper functioning of capital markets) concurred with the fundamental right. Instead of these considerations, the HCC examined the modality, that is, how the different formulas (e.g., on misleading information and diligence) of the CM Act shall be interpreted. Consequently, a balancing of the severity of the limitation of the concerned fundamental right against the importance of the legislative purpose is missing from the reasoning. Therefore, the examination of proportionality in the strict sense is not complete.

Nevertheless, the interpretation and the conclusion of the HCC is of course right. Due to the unambiguous basic question of the case, the absence of the transparent chain of arguments included in the steps of examination of the proportionality test does not significantly weaken the convincing nature of the conclusion. At the same time, the HCC would have been able to formulate the *ratio decidendi*, the requirement addressed to ordinary courts in a more authentic and justified manner if had itself structured its own arguments and considerations in the present case based on proper proportionality reasoning.

The reasoning of the decision, as well as the concurring and dissenting opinions delineate the contours of a debate on the question of whether, alongside the legislator, the law-enforcement bodies are also obliged to apply the proportionality test. It is noteworthy that in the previous practice of the HCC, this question did not arise explicitly. However, based on the literature[15] and the practice of other judicial fora,[16] it can be deduced that both the legislator and law-enforcement bodies (including ordinary courts) are the addressees of the proportionality requirement.

Based on the above cited majority opinion, it follows from Article 28 of the FL that the courts do have to identify the fundamental rights aspects of the case and have to interpret the relevant laws by taking into consider-

---

15 Aharon Barak differentiates the role of the legislator and the role of the judge related to the application of the proportionality test. While the legislator has to consider the requirement of proportionality when choosing the purpose and the means of the legislative acts, the role of the judge (in a broad sense) is to review these legislative acts and to take counteraction when these are not in accordance with the requirement of proportionality. See: Barak, *Proportionality. Constitutional Rights and their Limitations* (2012), 417.

16 In Canada, within the course of the preparatory phase of the parliamentary legislative process a formal proportionality-focused monitoring of draft laws is often performed in order to prevent the possible future unfavourable judicial decisions related to the concerned piece of legislation. See: Hogg, *Constitutional Law of Canada* (2009) 724.

ation the constitutionally protected scope of the concerned fundamental right.[17] Article 28 prescribes the teleological interpretation[18] and the requirement of interpretation of laws in accordance with the provisions of the FL ('the requirement of constitution-conform interpretation')[19] as a general interpretation rule. Despite the HCC does not offer a comprehensive interpretation of Article 28 of the FL, it can be deduced form the requirement of constitution-conform interpretation that the judge is also the addressee of Article I (3) of the FL. Accordingly, the judge may not set aside the fundamental rights aspects of the case even when certain pieces of legislation related to a specific field of law have to be applied.

The reasoning of the decision contains a general consideration: based on Article I (3) of the FL, the proportionality test 'pre-eminently binds the legislator and, on the other hand, by taking into consideration their powers, it also prescribes a constitutional requirement addressed to the law-enforcement bodies' (Reasoning [21]). Emphasizing the legislator who is in every case the addressee of Article I (3) is not a novelty. This kind of phrasing supposedly supports the second statement, according to which, under certain circumstances ('by taking into consideration their powers') the constitutional requirement also binds the law-enforcement bodies. The reasoning also specifies this requirement from the point of view of the applicable method: 'when interpreting a legal provision which limits the exercise of a certain fundamental right, the court—within the margin for the interpretation permitted by the law—has to restrict the limitation of the concerned fundamental right to a necessary and proportionate interference' (Reasoning [21]). In other words, the HCC calls upon the ordinary courts to apply the proportionality test—nevertheless, courts have to do so within the context of the legal acts applied in the concerned case.

In the HCC decisions delivered in the recent years (after the *napi.hu* case) the intensity of the debate on the addressee of the proportionality test (the legislator or the law-enforcement bodies and courts)[20] seems to

17 Decision 3/2015. (II. 2.) AB, Reasoning [17].

18 András Jakab draws the attention that this requirement applies to the objective teleological interpretation. See: Jakab, 'A bírói jogértelmezés az Alaptörvény tükrében' (2011), 86.

19 For a detailed analysis of the applicability of this requirement see: Chronowski, 'Az alkotmánykonform értelmezés és az Alaptörvény' (2017), 7.

20 The contours of this debate can be delineated based on the concurring and dissenting opinions related to the napi.hu case, as well as other decisions. E.g. concurring opinion of Judge Ágnes Czine, Decision 3/2015. (II. 2.) AB, Reasoning [35]; concurring opinion of Judge Mária Szívós, Decision 3/2015. (II. 2.) AB, Reasoning [84]; dissenting opinion of Judge András Varga Zs., Decision 3/2015. (II.

have toned down. However, it is important to emphasize a further theoretical argument which was not explicitly mentioned in the napi.hu case. It follows from the normative force of fundamental rights that the safeguards which aim at keeping their limitation within the framework prescribed by the constitution have to be applied in every situation where a limitation can occur.[21] The interpretation and the decisions of law-enforcement bodies and courts can also lead to limitation of fundamental rights; therefore, the requirement of proportionality which safeguards their core content, has to be applied both to the legislative powers and the powers that enforce the law. Therefore, the enforcement of the application of the proportionality test follows from the normative requirement of the protection of the constitution.

The reasoning of the decision did not offer a detailed methodological guide for the courts on how to apply in the same case the doctrine of fundamental rights (including proportionality) and the legal provisions of the specific field of law. To outline the basic elements of such methodological guide the following aspects must be taken into consideration.

The proportionality test can support its function related to the system of protection of fundamental rights as a framework of interpretation and reasoning. Within the framework of proportionality—based on the structure of the test described in the literature—it is possible to build up a reasoning which clarifies the permissibility and the justifiability of the limitation of fundamental rights in a structured manner in norm control cases. In this regard, there is no difference between the task of the legislator (e.g., in the preparation phase of the legislation) and of the implementation body (e.g., the court that initiates or performs norm control)—their examination can

2.) AB, Reasoning [53]–[53]; dissenting opinion of Judge Imre Juhász, Decision 3/2015. (II. 2.) AB, Reasoning [72], dissenting opinion of Judge Béla Pokol, Decision 3/2015. (II. 2.) AB, Reasoning [78]–[79]; dissenting opinion of Judge Mária Szívós, Decision 3/2015. (II. 2.) AB, Reasoning [86]–[87]; concurring opinion of Judge László Salamon, Decision 4/2015. (II. 13.) AB, Reasoning [59]; concurring opinion of Judge László Salamon, Decision 30/2015. (X. 15.) AB, Reasoning [62]; dissenting opinion of Judge László Salamon, Decision 13/2016. (VII. 18.) AB, Reasoning [89]; dissenting opinion of Judge István Stumpf, Decision 13/2016. (VII. 18.) AB, Reasoning [118].

21 It is noteworthy that the requirement of the application of the proportionality test is not linked to positive legal norms which prescribe its application. According to Robert Alexy's theory, the requirement of the application of the proportionality test follows from the particularity of fundamental rights as being optimalization requirements. See: Alexy, *A Theory of Constitutional Rights* (2010), 67.

be performed within the same framework of interpretation. If the activity of the court is not related to norm control, but rather requires the simultaneous application of fundamental rights doctrine and legal provisions related to a specific field of law (as in the napi.hu case) the task of the court is much more complex and requires a prudent approach.

Based on the requirement formulated in the napi.hu case, the modality of the simultaneous application of fundamental rights doctrine and legal provisions related to a specific field of law can be structured. First, the judge has to clearly identify the fundamental rights aspects of the case at hand: the concerned fundamental right, the fundamental right-based conflict and its context. In the next phase, the judge has to identify the constitutionally protected scope of the applicability of the concerned fundamental right within the context of the legal dispute by applying the proportionality test. In this phase, the structured steps of examination of the proportionality test have to be followed. After this examination, by taking into consideration the constitutionally protected scope of the concerned fundamental right, the room for manoeuvre of the judge in interpreting and applying the legal provisions related to the specific field of law related to the legal dispute at hand can be identified. Within this room for manoeuvre, the judge has to formulate the final decision of the case based on these, specific legal provisions. However, if the judge concludes that the legal provisions related to the specific field of law have no interpretation which would allow their application without limiting the core content of the concerned fundamental right, she has to initiate concrete norm control before the HCC.

If any of the above-described steps of examination are missing or the judge reaches the wrong conclusion related to these sub-questions, individuals and legal entities can turn in their cases to the HCC with a constitutional complaint. At that point, a declaration of the unconstitutionality of the judgment by the HCC is justifiable—this is the requirement formulated by the HCC, explained in detail. One can add that these mistakes in the legal interpretation and legal reasoning could uphold or a cause an unjustified limitation of fundamental rights.

5. Aftermath of the decision

The concerned legal provisions of the CM Act (applied in the market-supervisory procedure of the HCB and interpreted in the judgment which led to the constitutional complaint) later remained part of the Hungarian legal system in a different form. From the 3 July 2016, Regulation (EU) no.

596/2014 (on market abuse) became generally applicable. This Regulation also contains provisions related to the public disclosure of inside information.[22] Accordingly, the Hungarian legislature—alongside other financial laws—amended the CM Act.[23]

The Decision of the HCC received special attention in the Hungarian literature,[24] taking into consideration that in recent years the examination of constitutional complaints submitted against judicial interpretations became the most significant power of the HCC. Moreover, this was the first case in which the HCC formulated the requirement that in the practice of law enforcement bodies and courts the fundamental rights aspects of the concerned cases have to be taken into consideration. The formation of this requirement and the judicial practice related to that could also significantly influence the success of future constitutional complaints.

The significance of this decision is also marked by the fact that the requirement formulated in the napi.hu case was later supported by other HCC decisions. In two consecutive decisions, the HCC added a new element to the previously formulated requirement: ordinary courts, alongside the application of the proportionality test, also have to take into consideration the related interpretations of the HCC.[25]

It would be preferable if Decision Proportionality were to have a significant impact on the judicial practice. In 'clear', explicit fundamental rights-related cases (on the direct exercise of a certain fundamental right) judges do apply the proportionality test properly in most cases. However, the protection of fundamental rights is also essential in legal disputes that require the application of legal provisions related to a specific field of law, different from fundamental rights doctrine.

22 Regulation (EU) no. 596/2014, Article 17.

23 Act LIII of 2016 on the amendment of several fiscal acts. Promulgated on the 1 June 2016.

24 See: Hörcherné Marosi and Kormányos, 'Az Alkotmánybíróságnak a Fővárosi Közigazgatási és Munkaügyi Bíróság piacfelügyeleti bírsággal kapcsolatos ügyben hozott ítéletét megsemmisítő döntése' (2015) 5; Pozsár-Szentmiklósy, 'Az arányossági teszt a jogalkalmazásban' (2016); Szilágyi, 'Az Alkotmánybíróság az alkotmánykonform bírói jogértelmezésről – terítéken az Alaptörvény 28. cikke' (2015) 66; Török, 'Alkotmányjogi tesztek hálójában. A sajtószabadság esete a tőkepiaccal' in Fejes and Török (eds), *SUUM CUIQUE* (2016), 671.

25 Decision 16/2016. (X. 20.) AB, Reasoning [16], [23], [25], and Decision 17/2016. (X. 20.) AB, Reasoning [25], [29].

Bibliography

Robert Alexy, *A Theory of Constitutional Rights* (translated by Julian Rivers) (Oxford University Press, New York 2010)

Aharon Barak, *Proportionality. Constitutional Rights and their Limitations* (Cambridge University Press, Cambridge 2012)

Nóra Chronowski, 'Az alkotmánykonform értelmezés és az Alaptörvény' [The constitution-conform interpretation and the Fundamental Law] (2017) 4 *Közjogi Szemle,* 7.

Peter W. Hogg, *Constitutional Law of Canada* (Carswell, Toronto 2009)

Hörcherné Marosi Ildikó and Kormányos Zoltán, 'Az Alkotmánybíróságnak a Fővárosi Közigazgatási és Munkaügyi Bíróság piacfelügyeleti bírsággal kapcsolatos ügyben hozott ítéletét megsemmisítő döntése' [The decision of the Constitutional Court on the annulment of the judgment of the Budapest-Capital Administrative and Labour Court, related to the market supervisory fine case] (2015) 3 *Jogesetek Magyarázata,* 5.

András Jakab, 'A bírói jogértelmezés az Alaptörvény tükrében' [The judicial interpretation in the light of the Fundamental Law] (2011) 4 *Jogesetek Magyarázata,* 86.

Zoltán Pozsár-Szentmiklósy, *Alapjogok mérlegen. Az általános alapjogi tesztek dogmatikája [Fundamental right on scale. The doctrine of the proportionality test]* (HVG-ORAC, Budapest 2016)

Zoltán Pozsár-Szentmiklósy, 'Az arányossági teszt a jogalkalmazásban' [The proportionality test in the application of law] (2016) 2 *Alkotmánybírósági Szemle,* 97.

Emese Szilágyi, 'Az Alkotmánybíróság az alkotmánykonform bírói jogértelmezésről—terítéken az Alaptörvény 28. cikke' [The Constitutional Court on the constitution-conform interpretation—article 28. of the Fundamental Law in the focus] (2015) 1 *Közjogi Szemle*, 66.

Bernát Török, 'Alkotmányjogi tesztek hálójában. A sajtószabadság esete a tőkepiaccal' [In the net of tests of constitutional law. The case of the freedom of press with the capital market] in Fejes and Török (eds), *SUUM CUIQUE – Ünnepi tanulmányok Paczolay Péter 60. születésnapja tiszteletére [SUUM CIUQUE – Festschriften on the occasion of the 60th birthday of Péter Paczolay]* (Pólay Elemér Alapítvány, Szeged 2016), 671.

25. Decision 22/2016. (XII. 5.) AB – Constitutional Self-identity of Hungary

Nóra Chronowski[*] *– Boldizsár Szentgáli-Tóth*[**] *– Attila Vincze*[***]

The HCC may examine whether Hungary's joint exercise of competences with the EU infringes human dignity, other fundamental rights, the sovereignty of the country, or the self-identity of Hungary based on its historical constitution.

Upon the motion of the Commissioner for Fundamental Rights (Ombudsman), the HCC reviewed the relationship between EU law and the FL in the context of the planned relocation quota system for refugees in the EU. The HCC relied upon an extensive international comparison and attempted to identify the constitutional limitations of the primacy of EU law. The HCC has established three main constraints on the supremacy of EU law: fundamental rights, the sovereignty of member states, and the constitutional self-identity of Hungary. As long as Hungary is a sovereign country, its sovereignty and constitutional self-identity is primarily safeguarded by the HCC; nonetheless, all other state bodies also have the duty to protect these values. The HCC declared its power to examine whether the exercise of powers transferred to the EU violates human dignity, Hungary's sovereignty or its constitutional identity. In doing so, the Body opened a new chapter in the relationship between EU law and Hungarian domestic constitutional law.[1]

---

* PhD, Senior research fellow, Centre for Social Sciences Institute for Legal Studies (Budapest), and University of Public Service Faculty of Law Enforcement (Budapest).

** PhD, Research fellow, Centre for Social Sciences Institute for Legal Studies (Budapest).

*** PhD, Senior lecturer, Masaryk University Brno Judicial Studies Institute (Brno).
The research leading to this article has received funding from the European Research Council (ERC) under the European Union's Horizon 2020 research and innovation programme (INFINITY, grant agreement no. 101002660).

1 Mohay and Tóth, 'Decision 22/2016. (XII. 5.) AB on the Interpretation of Article E)(2) of the Fundamental Law' (2017), 468; Körtvélyesi and Majtényi, 'Game

1. Background

The decision was handed down during the escalation of the migration crisis, which significantly divided the Member States. In 2015, in order to alleviate the migratory pressure on Italy and Greece, the European Commission called on Member States to voluntarily accept those refugees from the Mediterranean region who really needed international protection, as an expression of solidarity among Member States. The European Council enacted a resolution by consensus on 20 July 2015, then adopted a decision by qualified majority on 22 September 2015 on the distribution within two years of 40 000 asylum seekers according to quotas in the various Member States of the EU.[2] Hungary and Slovakia sought legal remedy at the CJEU against the widely contested reallocation mechanism; this application was dismissed[3] and the Ombudsman raised almost the same questions in an internal constitutional context.

In this situation, an unsuccessful referendum was organised in Hungary about the quota-system on 2 October 2016,[4] but the government considered it as politically effective and a few days later, on 10 October 2016, a motion was submitted to amend the FL[5] with the aim of prohibiting 'resettlement of a foreign population in Hungary' and to protect 'our constitutional identity rooted in the historical constitution', and to restrict further the transfer of powers to the EU. According to this amendment, the joint exercise of powers 'must be in accordance with the fundamental rights and freedoms enshrined in the FL, it may not restrict the inalienable right of disposition on Hungary's territorial unit, population, form of government and state system'. During this period the government did not have a two-thirds parliamentary majority, and the amendment was not supported by Parliament. Nevertheless, the HCC used the essential elements of the considerations contained in the proposal in the interpretation of the Constitution, which can be assessed as an informal constitutional

of Values' (2017), 1721.; Bakó, 'The Zauberlehrling Unchained?' (2018), 863.; Halmai, 'Abuse of Constitutional Identity' (2018), 23.; Kelemen and Pech, 'The Uses and Abuses of Constitutional Pluralism' (2019), 59.

2 Council Decision (EU) no. 2015/1601 of 22 September 2015.

3 C-643/15. *Council v. Slovakia*; C-647/15. *Council v. Hungary*, judgment of 6 September 2017, ECLI:EU:C:2017:631.

4 Szente, 'The Controversial Anti-Migrant Referendum in Hungary is Invalid' https://bit.ly/3cs2Uca

5 Document no. T/12458. Submitted: 10. October 2016. https://bit.ly/3qKHrA4

amendment. This was a dramatic change in comparison with the earlier case law which dealt with EU law only tangentially.

2. *Petition*

On 3 December 2015, the Ombudsman requested from the HCC an interpretation of Articles E) and XIV of the FL, on the question of whether the implementation of EU decisions regarding the distribution of migrants and refugees would violate the constitutional prohibition on the collective expulsion of certain groups.[6]

Although the demand for an interpretation of Article E) was indeed logical, it is doubtful to what extent this issue is the Ombudsman's duty. The interpretation of Article XIV, i.e. the problem of the prohibition on collective expulsions, is more interesting, and an answer was sought to the question of whether the 'unconditional prohibition on group expulsion of foreigners' extends to the 'the instrument of execution carried out by the Hungarian state, which is indispensable for the implementation of an illegal group expulsion carried out by another state'. According to the Ombudsman, the asylum seekers in Italy and Greece have a right to remain in these countries, and their relocation is essentially an expulsion, an indispensable instrument. Consequently, the reception of these asylum seekers in Hungary would constitute such an action, which would be in conflict with the prohibition on collective expulsion.

A further peculiarity of the case was that the HCC did not answer the question of expulsion, which represented a concrete constitutional problem for the Ombudsman from the point of view of his motion. This is not a completely irrelevant issue, because pursuant to Article 38 (1) of the HCC Act, following a motion of the Commissioner for Fundamental Rights, the HCC interprets a provision of the FL in connection with a concrete constitutional problem. However, the HCC in the given case did not interpret Article XIV, but only Article E). Finding an adequate answer would not have been easy anyway, because the Council Decision EU, as the basis of the conflict, on the transfer of asylum procedures, is not a general rule, its implementation was faltering and its personal and temporal scope was limited: it was only valid until 26 September 2017, thus, without

6 The issue had already been raised in the context of the above-mentioned Council Decision of the EU.

the interpretation from the CJEU, it would have been problematic if the HCC had taken a position on it.

3. *Decision and its reasoning*

Based upon the petition of the Ombudsman the HCC stated that it has competence to review the constitutionality of the joint exercise of powers with the European Union and posited the aspects of this review.

3.1. *In exercising its powers, the HCC may examine whether the joint exercise of certain powers by the EU violates human dignity, other fundamental rights, Hungary's sovereignty or self-identity based on its historical constitution [Article E) (2) of the FL].*

After having declared the motion as admissible, the Court pointed out that the enforcement of fundamental rights and their adequate protection takes precedence over all other duties of the state, including those following from the primacy of EU law. No Member State may justify violations of fundamental rights by evoking duties based upon EU law, and the exercise of the powers of the EU must not result in a violation of human dignity.

If an EU legal instrument is deemed to be *ultra vires*, the Parliament or the Government of Hungary must take the necessary steps, and may file an action of annulment with the CJEU, alleging infringement of the principle of subsidiarity. The powers of the EU may therefore only be exercised within the constitutional framework of Hungary, which particularly requires the observance of Hungary's sovereignty and constitutional identity. The protection of Hungary's sovereignty and constitutional identity is the constitutional duty of the Parliament and the Government; however, pursuant to Article 24 (1) of the FL its principal guardian is the HCC. The subject of sovereignty and identity review is not directly the act of the EU act or its interpretation, hence the HCC does not judicate upon its validity or invalidity.

According to Article B) of the FL, the source of public power shall be the people in Hungary, and the exercise of powers by the EU cannot override this provision. By allowing the joint exercise of powers with the other Member States by the EU, Hungary did not relinquish its sovereignty, therefore the source of any powers of the EU is the sovereignty of Hungary (the presumption of reserved sovereignty). In the FL the sovereignty is the ultimate source of powers, and is not a competence in itself, so the joint exercise of powers by the EU and its Member States must not result in the people losing ultimate control over the exercise of public power, whether at level of the EU or its Member States. The HCC assessed this as a confirmatory argument for the ratification[7] of the international treaty enabling the joint action, the transfer of powers to the EU which required a two-thirds parliamentary majority, and the possibility of holding a referendum.[8]

Regarding constitutional identity, the HCC relied on Article 4 (2) of the TEU, according to which the EU shall respect the equality of Member States before the Treaties, as well as their national constitutional identities, which form an integral part of their fundamental political and constitutional order, including regional and local authorities. The protection of constitutional identity presupposes a cooperation between the CJEU and national constitutional courts based on the principles of equality and collegiality, as well as mutual respect. The constitutional identity of Hungary is not understood as a list of enumerated and static values, nonetheless several of its elements were highlighted by the HCC: the basic freedoms, the division of power, republicanism, respect for autonomy, freedom of religion, the exercise of legitimate power, parliamentarism, equality of rights, recognition of judicial power, and protection of nationalities. According to the reasoning of the HCC, Hungary's constitutional identity is a value that has not been established by the FL; the FL merely acknowledges its existence. Therefore Hungary cannot relinquish it as long as it has sovereignty, and up to this moment the HCC also remains obliged to protect this constitutional identity.

3.2. *The HCC attributes great importance to the constitutional dialogue within the EU [Article E) (2) of the FL].*

The reasoning outlines the aforementioned ambiguity of EU law as a legal source: the CJEU sees European law as an autonomous legal order, while the sovereignty-based interpretation describes the EU as a community based on the sovereign will of its member states, which can, in the final instance, decide on the limits of the supremacy of European legal in-

7 Article E (4) of the FL.

8 Article XXIII (7) of the FL.

struments. However this should happen through a constitutional dialogue between national constitutional courts and the CJEU.

Regarding ultra vires acts and the reservations in favour of fundamental rights, the HCC considered the practice of other member states as well, (e.g. the Czech Republic, Denmark, the UK, Estonia, France, the Republic of Ireland, Poland, Latvia, Italy, Germany, Spain, and Wales). It is noteworthy, that only such rulings were considered which supported the limitations of the transfer of powers to the EU.

4. Doctrinal analysis

The decision mostly follows the German case law regarding ultra vires and the constitutional self-identity as limits of European integration,[9] which has also been imitated by several national constitutional courts. The HCC literally copied several passages of the OMT Decision of the GFCC.[10]

By enacting this decision, the HCC established a new ground for constitutional review and stated, that 'by exercising its powers, the HCC may examine, on the basis of a motion to that effect', whether the joint exercise of competences with other Member States of the EU infringes certain specific constitutional provisions (fundamental rights, sovereignty), and a so far not only not concretely elaborated, but also almost completely unknown constitutional value, constitutional self-identity. According to paragraph 46 of the reasoning, that power is exercised by the HCC 'in exceptional cases and on an *ultima ratio* basis, i.e. while respecting constitutional dialogue between Member States'.

4.1. The new competence and the three tests

In a single sentence of the operative part, the HCC established at least three separate concepts: what does it mean to 'exercise its powers'; what is meant by 'joint exercise of powers' based on an EU empowering provision; and what exactly is the test it applies?

---

9 An instructive analysis is offered by Wendel, 'The Fog of Identity and Judicial Contestation' (2021), 465. For a broader overview see for instance Berger, *Anwendungsvorrang und nationale Verfassungsgerichte* (2016).

10 Some also suggest that the HCC misunderstood the German case-law, cf. Martinico, 'Taming National Identity' (2021), 447.

In the operative part of the ruling, the HCC stated, that 'in the exercise of its powers, the Constitutional Court may examine on the basis of a motion to that effect', whether the exercise of competences jointly with other Member States of the EU infringes certain specific constitutional provisions (fundamental rights, sovereignty), and a so far not only not concretely elaborated, but almost completely unknown constitutional value, identity. According to paragraph 46 of the reasoning, that power is exercised by the HCC 'in exceptional cases and on an *ultima ratio* basis, i.e. while respecting constitutional dialogue between Member States'.

The reasoning does not make clear exactly what kind of competence the HCC vested itself with in the operative part. In the context of EU law, starting from the current regulatory environment (the HCC Act), it would have a clear competence only for the preliminary constitutional review of the founding treaties.

For the time being, the consequence of stating this principle of the operative part, namely that 'it may examine [...] in the exercise of its powers' may be that the Court will use it as a 'bridge' or 'springboard' in a subsequent procedure, and will concretize in that particular procedure, whether, for example, in the case of the EU decision challenged at that time, or the Hungarian legal act adopted on the basis thereof, the fundamental rights, sovereignty and identity of Hungary are affected, and whether the HCC has jurisdiction in the specific case.

The aforementioned limitation on the exercise of powers is the requirement of exceptionality, the *ultima ratio* character and the requirement for 'constitutional dialogue'. In the decision, the HCC authorized itself to examine whether the exercise of joint competence based on Article E (2) infringes fundamental rights, sovereignty or constitutional identity. The various possibilities of interpretation also relativize the subject matter of the newly established review competence. It is not at all clear to what extent it is possible to examine whether the joint exercise of competence infringes the FL and constitutional identity.

What does the HCC mean by the joint exercise of competence underpinning participation in the EU? The joint exercise of competence can be approached partly on the basis of the way in which it is carried out and partly on the basis of its 'product'.

The way it is carried out can include the participation of Member States, mainly governments, in the EU decision-making process, in which case the actual implementation of the procedure—compliance with procedural rules—can be measured by EU law, and the CJEU can judge whether procedural rules for EU decision-making have been violated. Member States' constitutional law typically includes cooperation between parliament and government in EU affairs, based on the requirement of democratic legitimacy and control.

The latter, i.e. the 'product', raises a wide range of response options, because the joint exercise of competence may result in (i) an amendment of primary EU law through an amendment of the Treaty, (ii) the adoption of a secondary EU legal instrument or individual decision, (iii) a further EU or Member State decision implementing this, (iv) an EU judicial decision, or (v) ratification[11] of an international treaty concluded by the EU in the Council and before the national parliament, if necessary.

The HCC imposed two restrictions on the examination of EU legal acts. On the one hand, as mentioned several times above, the HCC explicitly stipulated, that 'the subject matter of sovereignty or identity control is not directly an EU act or its interpretation, thus, it does not declare its validity or invalidity or its priority in application' (Reasoning [56]). On the other hand, in the case of EU *ultra vires* acts, it referred the action based primarily on the founding treaty and the regulations of the Parliament to the responsibility of the Government and the Parliament (Reasoning [50]–[51]).

It follows that the HCC, in addition to the parliament and the government, may have an interest in the issue of exceeding its powers, and it does not wish to deal directly with EU legislation or its primacy. In this way, a conflict of competence with the CJEU can indeed be avoided. The question, however, is what the basis and legal consequences of a subsequent decision will be in a case such as *ultra vires* or identity violation. The optimistic scenario is that if such a motion arises in the future, the HCC will ask the CJEU for a preliminary ruling on the above issues, for otherwise it cannot justify a violation of the constitutionality of domestic law.

We face further problems when examining the 'joint exercise of competence', if we approach it from the point of view of what may be the subject of various constitutional court proceedings according to the Hungarian law in force. Exercising ex-post norm control—with the exception of the preliminary examination of compliance with the FL—the HCC may review legislation, normative decisions and orders or decisions on the uniform application of the law [see Articles 24–26, 32, 37 (2) of the HCC Act],

11 Grzeszick, 'Völkervertragsrecht in der parlamentarischen Demokratie' (2016), 1753.

and the standard may be the FL or an international treaty.[12] The individual German type constitutional complaint procedure (Article 27 of the HCC Act) examines whether the judicial decision violates the rights guaranteed in the FL.[13] In terms of reviewing other constitutional court proceedings, these—with the exception of the abstract interpretation—typically serve the powers of the HCC to give an opinion, review an individual decision, or establish public liability, i.e. they are not directly relevant from the aspect of the enforcement of EU law. Although German practice allows citizens themselves to lodge a constitutional complaint because of an alleged breach of competence or an alleged violation of their constitutional identity, as expressly permitted by the GFCC in the Maastricht decision (BVerfGE 89, 155.),[14] this results in an *actio popularis*, or at least a constitutional complaint that can be initiated without violating individual public law.[15] The recent case law of the HCC is precisely characterized by a miserliness against constitutional complaints, which would be difficult to reconcile with the intensive extension of the right to complain in a particular environment without the charge of constitutional court governance being dismissed.

The conflict of competence is only resolved (Article 36 of the HCC Act) in a procedure in which the HCC reveals to whom (which organ) the exercise or non-exercise of a given power can be attributed. This is the only procedure that directly deals with some kind of (negative or positive) 'exercise of power'. The decisions of the GFCC, which caused a great storm (Maastricht, Lisbon, OMT), also mentioned exactly the exercise of this kind of power, when the parliamentary minority, not necessarily the opposition, but representatives acting on behalf of the Bundestag as litigation

12 It is worth recalling here that in its practice prior to the introduction of the FL, the HCC expressly excluded the examination of a 'conflict with Community law' in the absence of jurisdiction, as it is a competence of the CJEU. Decision 61/B/2005. AB, ABH 2008, 2201.

13 It follows from the notion of an individual case and a judge that the proceedings are a judicial decision to be understood in accordance with Hungarian law, which was made on the merits of the case or closes the court proceedings, and there was no final or no legal remedy against it. Articles 27 and 1 of the HCC Act.

14 Subsequent practice also acknowledged this, cf. BVerfGE 97, 350 – Euro; 123, 267 – Lisbon; 129, 124 – EFS; 130, 318 – Stabilizerungsmechanismusgesetz. See, on the other hand, BVerfGE 1, 396 – Deutschlandvertrag.

15 Vincze, *Unionsrecht und Verwaltungsrecht* (2016), 218–219.

commissioners (Prozessstandschaft), appealed to the HCC alleging that the current government or the Bundesbank had exceeded its powers.[16]

Pursuant to Article 36 (1) of the HCC Act, in the interpretation of conflicts of jurisdiction between public bodies the HCC must be significantly more innovative, almost activist, if it wishes to include the exercise of powers under Article E (2) in this scope too. In these and only in these proceedings, the legal consequence is that the HCC decides which body has jurisdiction and designates the body obliged to conduct the proceedings. We have already mentioned that, from the point of view of the exercise of the newly interpreted competence of the HCC, it would be an interesting legal issue, whether it is possible to force Member State bodies to resist EU acts that violate identity. Failing this, the newly designated limit on the competence to prevent identity violations will be very narrow. Although the decision attracted attention primarily by the institutionalization of the topos of 'identity based on a historic constitution', the operative part itself sets three control mechanisms: the HCC may examine whether the joint exercise of competences under Article E (2) of the FL violates human dignity and other fundamental rights, or Hungary's sovereignty, or self-identity based on its historical constitution.

At first glance, these three areas of control seem to be a narrowing down within the FL, creating a kind of untouchable essence, which the HCC had already moved, implicitly, very close to in the case law process of 'unconstitutional constitutional amendments', although at that time it did not identify a specific standard against the constitutional power.[17]

However, in contrast to EU power, the test(s) acquired a name, and on closer inspection, it seems to be not so much moving towards a narrowing within the FL, but rather towards an extension through identity protection: in principle, any violation of any norms which relate to the designated control areas, even those outside the FL, may be considered. However, this is contradicted by the fact that the HCC, exercising its powers, can only act in the case of a violation of a specific provision of

16 Disputes between constitutional bodies are, in German law, a subjective procedure for the protection of the powers or prerogatives of a constitutional body, which may be brought not only by the body itself but also, in practice, by an autonomous part (e.g. a parliamentary group, a Member), or a lawful litigant. See, in detail, Hillgruber and Goos, *Verfassungsprozessrecht* (2006); Lechner and Zuck, *Bundesverfassungsgerichtsgesetz* (2011); BVerfGG para. 63, mn. 12.

17 Chronowski, 'The Fundamental Law Within the Network of Multilevel European Constitutionalism' in Szente, Mandák and Fejes (eds), *Challenges and Pitfalls in the Recent Hungarian Constitutional Development* (2015) 223.

the FL. Therefore, we take a closer look at what the standards outline, separately and in their contexts.

Although *ultra vires* was also not given much emphasis in the decision, it is made clear by the HCC that *ultra vires* and identity control are two different standards, and are connected to each other, so 'the two controls relating to them must in some cases be carried out with respect to each other' (Reasoning [67]).

The appearance of the *ultra vires* standard is relatively easy to explain, as it is the core of the German decision that strongly inspired the HCC ruling, precisely in the context of how these two constitutional standards (*ultra vires* and identity) can be separated. The Hungarian decision is therefore a borrowed one, but this, like all legal transplants,[18] also has unintended consequences.

The third standard introduced by the HCC is Hungary's constitutional self-identity. The HCC stated that 'it is a fundamental value not established but merely acknowledged by the Fundamental Law. Consequently, constitutional self-identity cannot be waived by way of an international treaty—Hungary can only be deprived of its constitutional identity through the final termination of its sovereignty, its independent statehood' (Reasoning [67]).

In this form, self-identity is a somewhat alterable standard which, at the time of the decision, had not, unlike the German Fundamental Law, yet been provided for expressly in the text of the Constitution, as Judge András Zs. Varga also pointed out in his concurring opinion.[19] However, according to the decision, the text does not even have to assume or refer to this, because the FL simply acknowledges this self-identity. It therefore, *ab ovo*, exists as an absolute, or as formulated by the HCC: Hungary can only be deprived of its constitutional identity 'through the final termination of its independent statehood' (Reasoning [67]).

However, it also follows from this, as Judge István Stumpf's concurring opinion points out, that there is a kind of norm above the FL, which is 'a kind of invisible Fundamental Law',[20] and just as it strains against the transfer of powers 'sanctified' by a two-thirds parliamentary majority, it may equally stand in the way of the constitutional or legislative power of a two-thirds parliamentary majority. With this limitation, which is not

18 Vincze, 'Ist die Rechtsübernahme gefährlich?' (2020), 193.; Teubner, 'Legal Irritants' (1998), 11.

19 Concurring opinion of Judge András Zs. Varga: the decision 'did not explain the legal basis for this finding' (Reasoning [111]).

20 Concurring opinion of Judge István Stumpf (Reasoning [109]).

included in the FL, the HCC gives itself a very wide authority with regard to—seceding from and independent of the text and content of the FL—deciding what is constitutional and what is not. 'The preference for starting from general formulas [...] inevitably results in the more specific provisions of the Fundamental Law slowly being relegated to the background and losing their significance. This, in turn, may create, to a degree, the rewriting of the Fundamental Law by constitutional court judges, and this means they occupy the place of the constituent power',[21] which is nothing but 'the imperialism of the constitutional judiciary'.[22]

4.2. The weaknesses of comparative analyses: constitutional dialogue in action

On the ground of the decision's reasoning, constitutional dialogue means on the one hand, that the CC examines the approach and the constitutional practice of other EU member states (Reasoning [33]–[43]); on the other hand, it implies cooperation with the CJEU based on collegiality, equality, and mutual respect. However, an exclusive institutional tool has been established for dialogue with the CJEU: the request for preliminary ruling.[23] Nevertheless, this procedure does not constitute a mechanism 'based on collegiality and equality'; instead of this, the CJEU provides a binding interpretation of the EU law, and the initiation of this proceeding is not only an option, or a form of politeness for national constitutional courts, but also a legal mandate. In contrast with other constitutional courts, the Hungarian Court has failed to comply with this duty in any of the cases heard so far.

The other interpretation—which may be also deduced from certain references provided by the ruling—is that the HCC shall conduct comparative legal analyses. According to Par. 43 of the reasoning: 'The Supreme Court of the United Kingdom in one of its decisions highlighted the significance of constitutional dialogue and called for a ruling of the GFCC. The question is whether the Hungarian decision has complied with this cited requirement. The comparative analysis shall not mean only the collection of case law and arguments in harmony with the already established

21 Decision 27/2015. (VII. 21.) AB. Concurring opinion of Judge Béla Pokol (Reasoning [64]).

22 Decision 988/B/2009. AB, ABH 2011, 2037. Concurring opinion of Judge Béla Pokol.

23 Kalbheim, *Über Reden und Überdenken* (2016) 52.

outcome.'[24] The colourful European overview may be convincing and presupposes reading and thorough knowledge,[25] but it should not be considered as a methodologically well-founded comparison. The decision simply copied some paragraphs from the OMT ruling of the GFCC.[26] Par. 142 of the German reasoning, and par. 34 of the Hungarian ruling are literally identical. The HCC even cited the non-German (for instance the Italian) case law on the basis of their translations published in the Europarecht, a German law journal.

Apart from the many mistakes in citing the referred cases properly, what is even harder to explain is the deeply cited *Thoburn v. Sunderland City Council [2002] EWHC 195 (Admin) (18 February 2002)* case (Reasoning [42]), which did not show any significant novelty by declaring that the supremacy of EU law shall be grounded on British law itself. That had been already concluded implicitly by Lord Bridge in the Factortame case,[27] a case which, however, was not mentioned by the HCC. The main novelty of the *Thoburn* case was rather to introduce the term 'constitutional statute', which may be close to the Hungarian category of cardinal law, which should not be repealed implicitly, but explicitly. In the meantime—and this should be taken into account during the comparative argumentation—in the light of the stare decisis doctrine, the judgement of the High Court is not binding for the Supreme Court and for the Court of Appeal. Furthermore, if the HCC had read with sufficient care the also cited Pham case,[28] which, according to the best of our knowledge, is the sole Supreme Court ruling which referred to the *Thoburn* case, it might have been clear that the arguments of Thoburn are interesting rather than binding for the

24 A critical approach of this kind was provided by Justice Scalia in the case *Roper v. Simmons*, 543 U.S. 551, 627 (2005). See also Kahn-Freud, 'On Use and Misuse of Comparative Law' (1974), 1; Saunders, 'The Use and Misuse of Comparative Constitutional Law' (2006), 37; Hirschl, 'The View from the Bench' in Hirschl, *Comparative Matters* (2016), 20.

25 For researchers interested in the topic the names and reference numbers of at least supposedly relevant cases provided in par. 34 of the reasoning should be a valuable orientation, but this is really far from a real comparative interpretation.

26 Here again the case of the GFCC on 21 June 2016 should be highlighted [BVerfG, 21.06.2016 – 2 BvR 2728/13; 2 BvR 2728/13; 2 BvR 2729/13; 2 BvR 2730/13; 2 BvR 2731/13; 2 BvE 13/13].

27 *R v. Secretary of State for Transport ex p Factortame Ltd (Interim Relief Order)* [1990] UKHL 7 (26 July 1990).

28 Pham v. Secretary of State for the Home Department [2015] UKSC 19 (25 March 2015), [2015] 3 All ER 1015, [2015] WLR(D) 166, [2015] UKSC 19, [2015] 2 CMLR 49, [2015] Imm AR 950, [2015] INLR 593, [2015] 1 WLR 1591, [2015] WLR 1591, paras. 207–208.

Supreme Court. These examples show that for the sake of constitutional dialogue, the HCC introduced an incautious and biased selection of the relevant case law that does not contribute much to the recognition of the importance of a substantial analysis of the indicative foreign case law in order to find the best constitutional solutions.

5. Aftermath of the Decision

It is a significant fact from the aftermath of the decision that the failed seventh amendment to the FL in 2016 was put back on the agenda in 2018, and this time its original goal was successfully achieved. The Seventh Amendment to the FL added the following to Article E (2) in 2018[29] in order to specify the necessary degree of the joint exercise of powers: 'The exercise of powers under this paragraph shall be in conformity with the fundamental rights and freedoms enshrined in the Fundamental Law, nor shall it restrict the inalienable right of disposition of the territorial unit, population, form of government and the form of the state of Hungary.'[30] With this, the duty of protecting fundamental rights and state sovereignty became part of the EU clause. Moreover, the protection of constitutional self-identity was included in Article R (4) as a general duty of all state bodies, while the *National Avowal* stated: 'We hold that the defence of our constitutional self-identity, which is rooted in our historical constitution, is the fundamental responsibility of the state.'

Despite the already clear authorisation in the FL, the HCC did not apply the control measures established in the decision analysed here against EU law until July 2021.

The topos of the 'European constitutional dialogue' has, however, become a recurring point of reference following this decision, making a number of cases more colourful. It was a reference, for example, in three

29 Seventh Amendment to the FL (28 June 2018) Article 2.

30 Explanatory memorandum to the proposal for a Seventh Amendment to the FL: 'The proposed addition to Article E would specify and fill with content the »as necessary« version of the current paragraph 2, which would essentially mean a clear clarification of the exercise of EU competence.' It is also clear from the explanatory memorandum that this is necessary in order to respect the national identity of the Member States as set out in Article 4 (2) TEU and to protect the constitutional self-identity.

suspension orders issued by the HCC on 4 June 2018.[31] The HCC suspended its proceedings in connection with the review of Act XXV of 2017 on the amendment of CCIV Act of 2011 on national higher education and Act LXXVI of 2017 on the transparency of organisations supported from abroad, i.e. in the Central European University (CEU) case and in the case of NGOs, because the European Commission initiated proceedings before the CJEU for the contested provisions. The reason for the suspension is the same in all three cases; it is sufficient to quote from one of the orders: in the decision relating to Hungary's self-identity the HCC stated, that: 'the European Union is able to ensure, through institutional reforms, the Charter of Fundamental Rights and the CJEU, that fundamental rights are largely or at least satisfactorily protected at the level guaranteed by national constitutions [...]. Consequently, the possibility of review reserved for the Constitutional Court should be applied in the light of the duty to cooperate, with a view to enforcing European law as far as possible'. On the basis of the above, the HCC concluded that, in view of the fundamental rights context specifically raised by the case under consideration and the obligation to cooperate within the EU, it is necessary to await the completion of the proceedings pending before the CJEU.[32] In 2020, the CJEU ruled in both proceedings before it, and stated that EU law, as well as the Charter of Fundamental Rights, had been violated.[33] However, the 'dialogue' did not appear to continue on the side of the HCC until the Government pushed through an amending bill in the CEU case. When the bill was adopted, the HCC noticed that the regulation has substantively changed and the applicants did not submit any supplementary petition, thus the HCC terminated its proceedings, although without any further 'European

31 Order 3198/2018. (VI. 21.) AB – Act LXXVI of 2017 on the transparency of foreign-supported organizations, Act CLXXXI of 2011 on the court register of non-governmental organizations and related procedural rules, ex-post norm control; Orders 3199/2018. (VI. 21.) AB and 3200/2018. (VI. 21.) AB – Act CCIV of 2011 on the National Higher Education, Act XXV of 2017 on the amendment to Act on the National Higher Education, ex-post norm control and constitutional complaint procedure against the law as a whole (invalidity under public law, right to academic freedom).

32 Order 3199/2018. (VI. 21.) AB, Reasoning [5].

33 C-78/18, *Commission v. Hungary*, judgment of 18 June 2020, ECLI:EU:C:2020:476 (foreign-supported NGOs); C-66/18, *Commission v. Hungary*, judgment of 18 June 2020; judgment of 6 October 2006, ECLI:EU:C:2020:792 (CEU case). To the CEU case, see Chronowski and Vincze, 'The Hungarian Constitutional Court and the CEU case' (2021), forthcoming.

judicial dialogue', because the subject matter had become obsolete and there was no need to adjudicate it.

Also in 2018, in a neutral area compared to the above, a HCC order[34] suspending proceedings in a tax case was also issued in the spirit of European judicial dialogue. The HCC suspended its procedure relating to the constitutional review of the Hungarian Supreme Court (Kúria) judgment, because it found that the Szeged Administrative and Labour Court had referred a question to the CJEU for a preliminary ruling, and it wished to await the result. The CJEU made a decision[35] in April 2020, which was then only formally referred to by the HCC in its February 2021 decision,[36] thus, instead of dialogue, parallel monologues took place.

Finally, it is worth mentioning the Decision 26/2020. (XII. 2.) AB which established that if the (ordinary) court initiates a preliminary ruling procedure, the CJEU is also a legitimate judge in terms of the procedure. This is a half-turn from the previous practice, as for a long time the position of the HCC was[37] that the initiation of a preliminary ruling procedure is a question of professional law or the interpretation of the law which the HCC has no jurisdiction to review. Subsequently, as a small shift, the HCC qualified it as constituting a grievance of the right to a fair trial, if the court rejects the party's request for a preliminary ruling without giving any substantive reasons. In the reasoning to its decision of December 2020, the HCC also called for a decision on the joint exercise of EU competence and concluded that only the mutual judicial dialogue open to each other's arguments is capable and fit for the purpose of striking a balance between 'the core of Member States' constitutional law untouchable by integration and European law with priority for application, developed by the European Court of Justice, because without such a dialogue 'neither the constitutional law of the Member States nor the sui generis nature

34 Order 3220/2018. (VII. 2.) AB – Act XCII of 2003 on the order of taxation, and judgment of the Supreme Court (Kúria) Kfv.V.35.729/2016/8. Constitutional complaint and reference for a preliminary ruling against the judgment of the Court of First Instance (refund of VAT, default interest, Community law).

35 C-13/18 and C-126/18, Sole-Mizo Zrt., and Dalmandi Mezőgazdasági Zrt. v. Appeals Directorate of the National Tax and Customs Administration (Reference for a preliminary ruling from the Szeged Administrative and Labor Court and Szekszárd Administrative and Labor Court), judgment of 23 April 2020, ECLI:EU:C:2020:292.

36 Decision 3040/2021. (II. 19.) AB.

37 Order 3110/2014. (IV. 17.) AB; Order 3165/2014. (V. 23.) AB; Order 3038/2015. (II. 20.) AB.

of European law can be guaranteed'.[38] The HCC has also stated that it cannot take a neutral position in this institutionalized cooperation either,[39] even noting that 'the Constitutional Court's right to initiate a preliminary ruling procedure may also be deduced from the Fundamental Law, thus, in particular, if in the case before it there would be a threat to compliance with fundamental rights and freedoms under Article E (2) of the Fundamental Law or to the restriction of Hungary's inalienable right to dispose of its territorial unit, population, form of state and state system.'[40] Although this is merely an *obiter dictum* remark in relation to the subject matter of the case, the HCC first referred as a matter of principle that it may itself initiate a preliminary ruling procedure too, within the framework of Article E (2), essentially to check that fundamental rights are upheld and to protect sovereignty.

Bibliography

Beáta Bakó, 'The Zauberlehrling Unchained?: The Recycling of the German Federal Constitutional Court's Case Law on Identity-, Ultra Vires- and Fundamental Rights Review in Hungary' (2018) 4 *ZaöRV*, 863.

Alina Berger, *Anwendungsvorrang und nationale Verfassungsgerichte* (Mohr Siebeck, Tübingen 2016)

Bernd Grzeszick, 'Völkervertragsrecht in der parlamentarischen Demokratie' (2016) *NVwZ*, 1753.

Nóra Chronowski, 'The Fundamental Law Within the Network of Multilevel European Constitutionalism' in Zoltán Szente, Fanni Mandák and Zsuzsanna Fejes (eds), *Challenges and Pitfalls in the Recent Hungarian Constitutional Development* (L'Harmattan, Paris 2015)

Nóra Chronowski and Attila Vincze, 'The Hungarian Constitutional Court and the CEU case: justice delayed is justice denied – Decision of the Hungarian Constitutional Court of 6 July 2021 and the Judgment of the ECJ of 6 October 2020, Case C-66/18.' (2021) 4 *European Constitutional Law Review*, forthcoming.

Gábor Halmai, 'Abuse of Constitutional Identity. The Hungarian Constitutional Court on Interpretation of Article E) (2) of the Fundamental Law' (2018) 1 *Review of Central and East European Law*, 23.

Christian Hillgruber and Christoph Goos, *Verfassungsprozessrecht* (2nd ed., C.F. Müller, Heidelberg 2006)

38 Decision 26/2020. (XII. 2.) AB, Reasoning [23].
39 Decision 26/2020. (XII. 2.) AB, Reasoning [24].
40 Decision 26/2020. (XII. 2.) AB, Reasoning [25].

Ran Hirschl, 'The View from the Bench' in Ran Hirschl, *Comparative Matters* (OUP, Oxford 2016) 20.

Otto Kahn-Freud, 'On Use and Misuse of Comparative Law' (1974) *Modern Law Review,* 1.

Jan Kalbheim, *Über Reden und Überdenken* (Mohr Siebeck, Tübingen 2016)

Daniel R. Kelemen and Laurent Pech, 'The Uses and Abuses of Constitutional Pluralism: Undermining the Rule of Law in the Name of Constitutional Identity in Hungary and Poland' (2019) *Cambridge Yearbook of European Legal Studies,* 59.

Zsolt Körtvélyesi and Balázs Majtényi, 'Game of Values: The Threat of Exclusive Constitutional Identity, the EU and Hungary' (2017) 7 *German Law Journal,* 1721.

Hans Lechner and Rüdiger Zuck, *Bundesverfassungsgerichtsgesetz* (6th ed., C.H. Beck, Münich 2011)

Giuseppe Martinico, 'Taming National Identity: A Systematic Understanding of Article 4.2 TEU' (2021) 3 *European Public Law,* 447.

Ágoston Mohay and Norbert Tóth, 'Decision 22/2016. (XII. 5.) AB on the Interpretation of Article E)(2) of the Fundamental Law' (2017) 2 *American Journal of International Law,* 468.

Gunther Teubner, 'Legal Irritants: Good Faith in British Law or How Unifying Law Ends up in New Divergences' (1998) 1 *The Modern Law Review,* 11.

Cheryl Saunders, 'The Use and Misuse of Comparative Constitutional Law' (2006) *Indiana Journal of Global Legal Studies,* 37.

Zoltán Szente, 'The Controversial Anti-Migrant Referendum in Hungary is Invalid' https://bit.ly/3cs2Uca

Attila Vincze, 'Ist die Rechtsübernahme gefährlich? Zur Rechtswirklichkeit und Tragfähigkeit des Konzepts eines Verfassungsgerichtsverbundes anhand des Beispiels der Verfassungsidentität' (2020) *Zeitschrift für öffentliches Recht,* 193.

Attila Vincze, *Unionsrecht und Verwaltungsrecht* (Baden-Baden, Nomos 2016)

Mattias Wendel, 'The Fog of Identity and Judicial Contestation: Preventive and Defensive Constitutional Identity Review in Germany' (2021) 3 *European Public Law,* 465.

26. Decision 28/2017. (X. 25.) AB – Natura 2000

Gyula Bándi[*]

The impact of the loss of biodiversity on mankind, particularly the rights of future generations, the duties of current generations, common heritage, precaution and thinking with a perspective.

The Decision Natura 2000 in question is an 'intermediate', but nevertheless important one. Intermediate, since the provisions of the FL and of the previous constitutional requirements had already introduced the essential elements of the right to environment, providing a solid basis for the stability of proper interpretation—by, amongst others, the HCC—while the new trends have also been presented: sustainable development, the rights of future generations, the precautionary principle with its full context all discussed later. Intermediate is taken as a significant distinction, a bridge between the more traditional and the improved concepts.

1. Background

The history of environmental rights in Hungary dates back to the Act II of 1976 on the protection of human environment. By Article 2 (2) the 'right to live in an environment, worthy of man'. Environmental rights were inserted into the amendment of the Constitution in 1989. This contained two provisions for environmental human rights: as a separate right in Articles 18 and as an instrument implementing the right to health in Article 70/D.

The cornerstone and the first product of the HCC in this area was Decision 28/1994. (V. 20.) AB, followed by many similar decisions. The decision asserts that the right to a healthy environment constitutes a state responsibility, secured by the establishment and maintenance of the specific system of institutions. From the point of view of non-retrogres-

* DSc, Professor, Pázmány Péter Catholic University Faculty of Law and Political Sciences (Budapest).

sion/non-derogation[1] the basis is the 'the unrestrictability of the current level of environmental protection', completed by point IV.1. with certain anticipated minimum levels of protection—'the state does not have the freedom to tolerate either the degradation, or the risk of degradation of the state of [the] environment'. The paramount answer is to use preventive measures. The HCC in case 1007/B/1994/12 extended these requirements to individual cases, too. Later the HCC declared that the implementation of the right to environment does not allow changes owing to economic and social explanations—which might occur in the case of social and cultural rights—as there is no chance of remediating the status quo later. Alongside prevention, the proportionality-necessity test has also been added: 'the state [...] may only make steps backwards in cases where there is likewise a room for limiting a substantial right [...] Any derogation shall be based on an unavoidable necessity and proportionally.'[2]

The FL even under the National avowal, has some vital messages in this respect, while the Article P of the Foundation is crucial in connection with the common heritage of the nation and the rights of future generations. In Freedom and Responsibility—the part on human rights—the following articles are the most important: human dignity (Article II), property (Article XIII), the right to healthy living conditions and in connection with it the instrumental role of environmental protection (Article XX) and the distinct environmental right (Article XXI). Articles P) and XXI shall form the essential basis of the Decision Nature 2000.

By accepting the obligations towards future generations, the previous concept of the right to a (healthy) environment has been topped, while both exist in complete harmony. Consequently, it is not a whole new set of obligations, but rather the enhancement of the existing one towards the equitable treatment of future generations as the elementary constituent of sustainable development.

The first overall interpretation of the environmental constituents of FL took place in Decision 16/2015. (VI. 5.) AB), elucidating continuity with the previous decisions of the HCC, interpreting for the first time the novel provisions of the FL, providing wider, stronger implications (Reasoning [91]). The decision encapsulated and reinforced the vital elements of previous—before 2011—HCC decisions, namely: the prohibition

1 The official translation of the HCC case-law uses the term 'non-derogation', while the international legal narrative prefers 'non-retrogression', therefore we rather use this term below.

2 Decision 48/1997. (X. 6.) AB.

of non-retrogression, covering similarly contextual, procedural, and institutional elements, the requirement to refer to the necessary guarantees, the importance of prevention (e.g., Reasoning [109]), the necessity of reasonable limitation of the freedom of property, also the need to establish the desirable proportionality between property rights and other rights (Reasoning [82]), integrating built environment and physical planning (Reasoning [83]) with reference also to proportionality, the duty to create institutions for the realization of the right to life (Reasoning [85]).

The different provisions of the FL mentioned: National avowal (Reasoning [88]), Foundations (Article P), Reasoning [53] and [89]), and the two human rights references (Articles XX and XXI, Reasoning ([90]).

The dual approach of the HCC might be noticed, on the one hand the will to save the previous elements of interpretation and on the other hand to present how the FL goes beyond the former system. The expansion of obligations to society as a whole is also stressed, but without further details. Still the three-fold set of duties—to protect, sustain and preserve for future generations—has also been articulated.

Decision 3223/2017. (IX. 25.) AB summarizes the major constituents and messages of the non-retrogression principle, shaping the foundations for interpretation. The most important message is that non-retrogression must cover the substantial, procedural, and institutional elements in their complexity, and more that the requirement is also obligatory for the individual decision of a public authority (Reasoning [28]–[29]).

Turning to the preliminary questions of the contested decision, it is worth mentioning that domestic nature protection and the Natura 2000 areas do not necessarily cover the same territory, also the features of protection are slightly different. It is also relevant that following the EU accession a new category was created, the Pannon biogeographical region, taking into consideration the peculiarities of the given area, which covers the Carpathian basin. The FL also emphasizes the importance of this region, definitely based on historical traditions.

It is also crucial that neither the domestic law, Act LIII of 1996 on the nature conservation, nor the special regulations on Natura 2000 areas contain any provision which might exclude a sort of economic use of these areas. Government Decree 275/2004. (X. 8.) on the management of the Natura 2000 areas clearly states that those activities which do not hurt or endanger the protective functions of the given areas may be undertaken. Of course, there are several regulatory limitations, among others, the need to require an authorization in most cases.

2. Petition

Two parallel claims have been presented to the HCC in connection with Act CVI of 2016 on the 'Land to Farmers' programme and with the use and property issues of arable lands, regulated by the Act LXXXVII of 2010 on the National Land Fund. Both in connection with—on the one hand—the protection, sustain and preservation of natural resources, primarily arable land, forest and water resources, biodiversity (and endemic flora and fauna in particular), and—on the other hand—the use and marketing of those Natura 2000 areas, which do not belong to the scope of protected areas, as delimited by domestic law.

In one of the two cases [Decision 27/2017. (X. 25.) AB], while rejecting the claim—addressing the regulatory procedure and not the substance—the HCC still declared a regulatory omission by its own motion, stating that this is contrary to the FL. The substantial problem was that in the case of Natura 2000, areas that do not belong to the system of domestic nature conservation areas, the given legislation infringed upon the objectives described by Article P) (1) of the FL; on the right to a healthy environment, as provided for in Article XXI, allowing the already available level of the nature protection system to deteriorate in such a way that the proper implementation of a diverse fundamental right or constitutional value would not be unavoidable. In the contested legislation—according to the claim—the only method of passing Natura 2000 sites into private ownership was through sale by auction, leaving no room for nature conservation aspects.

The HCC turned to the minister of agriculture, the commissioner of fundamental rights and the Hungarian Academy of Sciences for specialist assistance, while the Hungarian Birds' Society filed an *amicus curiae*.

3. Decision and its reasoning

The operative clause has three parts. First, the HCC stated that the Parliament caused an omission, contrary to the FL, since it had not defined those guarantees necessary for the proper implementation of nature conservation objectives in connection with the sale and utilization of Natura 2000 areas that do not belong to the scope of protected areas, as provided for in Article P) (1) of the FL. Consequently, the HCC invited the Parliament to meet its regulatory obligations by 30 July 2018.

Secondly, the HCC rejected a part of the claim, related to a particular point of National Land Fund regulations, as it is in line with the FL.

Finally, there is an official final statement that 'the other elements of the motion are rejected'.

3.1. The duty to preserve biodiversity has become a constitutional value, which should be taken into consideration when defining regulations within sectoral policies.

The main issue is how Natura 2000 areas might be taken into private ownership, with a special focus on areas that do not receive protected status under domestic law, consequently they do not receive satisfactory protection guarantees. According to the HCC, the objective of Directive 79/409/EEC on the conservation of wild birds, as the first legal bases of Natura 2000 legislation, is the conservation of all species of naturally occurring birds in their wild state in the European territory of the Member States, while the objective of Directive 43/92/EEC on the conservation of natural habitats and of wild fauna and flora is to promote the maintenance of biodiversity, the long term existence of species and habitat types, the conservation and improvement of their natural reproduction. 21.44% of Hungary is designated as a Natura 2000 area within the Pannonian biogeographical region, which comprises the whole area of the country (Reasoning [16]).

The basis of both EU and domestic protection is biodiversity, having a higher value. No wonder then that the HCC referred to the scientific value of the preservation of biodiversity, including its current status and trends. Knowing that the subject of the current case is to specify the possibility and the conditions of agricultural utilization of nature conservation areas, it is noteworthy that the HCC recognised that 'agriculture is responsible for two-thirds of the loss of biodiversity' (Reasoning [17]). The conclusion is: 'In Hungary the biggest threat to biodiversity is the intensification of agriculture.'

We must mention—proving the significance of the whole procedure—that the HCC was clear in respect of the unity of biodiversity, acknowledging that the burden on a single species might have a consequence on others and ultimately on the whole ecosystem. The entirety of environment regulations should serve the survival of biodiversity in Hungary, covering together Natura 2000 sites, nature conservation areas and those areas without any conservation status (Reasoning [18]). Also, the HCC notes that domestic and EU regulations mutually strengthen each other. Finally, the specific role of ecological corridors has also been underlined.

The HCC asserts, that 'the loss of biodiversity and the corresponding ecosystems have a direct impact on human life' (Reasoning [20)], plus the specific role of ecosystem services are also mentioned, listing the four types of such services: provisioning, such as the production of food and water; regulating, such as the control of climate and disease; supporting, such as nutrient cycles and oxygen production; and cultural, such as recreational benefits.

In this respect the HCC repeated an earlier message towards state conduct in general, demanding long-term thinking and regulation, which goes across government cycles (Reasoning [19]).

The most important conclusion and the assignment of corresponding responsibilities begins with a reference to Article P) of the FL, within which biodiversity—especially the native flora and fauna—is stressed as a part of a non-exhaustive list, covering selected items of environmental protection. This specific reference means that that duty to preserve 'biodiversity has become a constitutional asset the legislator must take into consideration when defining regulation in different sectoral policies. The preservation of diversity of species is not only essential because they might be utilized by human activities or might be understood as exploitable resources, but they are also valuable and deserve protection in their own [right]' (Reasoning [35]).

3.2. *When interpreting Article P) (1) of the FL, one should not forget the natural law foundations of biodiversity protection and the international commitments of Hungary.*

The HCC puts emphasis on envisioning the ethical—or natural law—basis, also to apply it as an ultimate argument. We may think of the Encyclical Letter Laudato Si' of Pope Francis, or the message of the ecumenical patriarch Bartholomew I. The ethical base is also taken care of in the latest decisions of HCC.

The crucial role of international commitments means the relevant treaties (Reasoning [37]), among others the Convention on Biological Diversity (CBD), which—according to the reasoning—became 'a common concern of mankind as an individual category of international law' (Reasoning [39]). And this leads to direct legal obligations. Likewise, the UN Sustainable Development Goals (SDGs) are mentioned, with the following concluding remarks: 'Hungary, while it has sovereign rights over its natural resources, should also take into consideration that this right is not absolute: the sustainable use of biological resources and the preservation of biodiversity should be taken care of, ensuing from Article P) (1) of

Fundamental Law, in harmony with the international commitments of Hungary' (Reasoning [43]).

The HCC—in line with its previous practice—refers to EU law: 'there is no obstacle to the Constitutional Court referring to the specific provisions of the European Union, even without providing or demanding an individual interpretation of it' (Reasoning [16]).

3.3. *In connection with the state of natural assets, an absolute contextual canon results from Article P) of FL (rights of future generations and the subsequent obligations, the importance of long-term thinking, also the precautionary principle), commencing objective requirements towards ordinary activities of the state.*

The HCC took as a primary focus of its procedure the provisions of the FL directly connected with future generations. Beside Article P) (1), there is Article 38 (1) related to the property of state and local governments as taking them to be national property, declaring also that their use and protection shall take into consideration the needs of future generations. According to the HCC, the obligations towards the protection of physical, biological, and cultural foundations as provided for in Article P) (1) is 'a structural principle infusing the whole spirituality of Fundamental Law, reflecting the commitment of Hungary towards the protection of natural values, for the interest of handing them over as well-preserved to the future generations' (Reasoning [25]).

The third conceptual reference appears in the National avowal, in two paragraphs. If we add to it the references to fundamental rights—mental and physical health in Article XX and the *expressis verbis* declaration of the right to a healthy environment in Article XXI (1)—we better understand the reference to a paragraph of a previous decision {Decision 16/2015. (VI. 5.) AB, Reasoning [91]}: 'Fundamental Law has not only preserved the level of constitutional protection of the fundamental right to a healthy environment, but also included much wider provisions in this respect.'

The inclusive understanding of responsibilities and the prohibition of non-retrogression—as being part of the decisions of the HCC since 1994—are also present: '[…] the will of the legislator stems directly from Article P) of Fundamental Law, that is to protect human life and living conditions, in particular arable land and, in connection with it, biodiversity in such a way to assure the prospects for life of future generations, and based on the generally accepted principle of non-retrogression (non-derogation) should by no means worsen it. Non-retrogression, being a supplementary obligation of the state, should cover contextual, procedural, and institutional regulations {3223/2017. (IX. 25.) AB, Reasoning [27]–[28]}.'

The comprehensive understanding of responsibilities also raises the question of whether it is possible to make a distinction according to the extent of such responsibilities. The HCC goes beyond the terms of Decision 16/2015. (VI. 5.) AB when defining the centre of gravity of responsibilities: 'While the duty to protect the environment is equally relevant to the state in its broadest meaning, the natural and legal persons, this duty might not be identical for the different entities. While we may not generally require that natural and legal persons should tailor their behaviour to an abstract objective, which has not been specified by the legislator and this also may not be enforced, it is required that the state should unequivocally define those legal obligations, which both the state and private persons should implement, for among other reasons to provide an effective protection for those interests, appraised in Article P) (1) of Fundamental Law [30].' (Reasoning [92]). Thus, the state has a special role and a special responsibility.

Furthermore, the decision also refers to the first decision of the HCC in 1994: 'all those duties, which the state might implement elsewhere with the protection of fundamental rights, here should be executed via the stipulation of legislative and institutional guarantees' (Reasoning [30]). This is the obligation to provide institutional protection.

In terms of future generations, the HCC definitely relies on the basis, that is the impact of international law—common heritage, common concern—covering two interrelated ideas: 'Article P) (1) of Fundamental Law commissions a hypothetical heritage for future generations. [...] According to this, the Hungarian citizens and the state accept that the state institutions guarantee the protection of those values, defined in a non-exhaustive way in Article P) (1). This might be taken, as compared with the »common concern of humanity« as a concretized obligation' (Reasoning [31].

According to this understanding, retrogression might risk this heritage, consequently Article P) designates direct obligations and not merely principles: 'An absolute, contextual canon originates from Article P) of Fundamental Law, in connection with the state of natural resources, which stipulates objective requirements towards the activities of the state at any point in time.' (Reasoning [32]).

A three-fold obligation is presented in the decision: 'According to Article P) (1) of the Fundamental Law the current generation has a three-fold obligation: to preserve the chance of choice, the quality and the access. The chance for choice [...] is the freedom of choice of future generations to solve their own problems, instead of forcing the coming generations by the current decisions onto an inescapable path. Preservation of quality means that we should hand over the natural environment in at least the same quality as we received it from the previous generations. Access to natural resources means that the current generation might have access to the available resources until they respect the equitable interests of future generations.' (Reasoning [33]).

According to the majority opinion, the best method would be to define the obligations of current generations and, more precisely, of the decision-makers, and less to think about the extent of conditions of how to specify the rights. Decision Natura 2000 also clearly requires—reinforcing a previous point of the decision that 'the legislator shall decide along the lines of a long-term thinking, make deliberations across government cycles' (Reasoning [34]).

The HCC also commenced an interpretation procedure in connection with the precautionary principle, among others, to urge the state to be more active: 'In order to protect the environment [...] legislator[s] shall take into consideration the precautionary principle, accordingly the state shall justify that—considering also scientific uncertainty—due to a given measure the deterioration of the state of the environment certainly does not happen.' (Reasoning [75]).

3.4. *The alienation of the state-owned nature conservation areas is possible, but along the lines of strict legal guarantees, which are capable for the qualitative and quantitative protection of the values itemised in Article P) of the FL. As these guarantees did not prevail the omission of legislator is detected.*

As one starting point the HCC underlines that while the utilization requirements of greens in Natura 2000 areas are regulated in specific legal regulations '[i]n [the] case of other land usage categories no similar requirements are in force' (Reasoning [49]). One other initial question is that under the 'Land to Farmers' programme the state-owned lands might be purchased, and only the forests and nature protection areas under domestic rules (the Natura 2000 sites do not belong to this category) are taken as exceptions. That is the reason why we focus on Natura 2000 areas that are not taken as protection areas under domestic law.

Although private ownership or purchase is not generally excluded, there are still many specific, strict guarantees in the case of protection areas under domestic law in a way that 'the entirety of guarantees is satisfactory in order to quantitatively and qualitatively protect the values specified under

Article P) of the Fundamental Law' (Reasoning [59]). This will be the first issue in the list of regulatory omissions. It is without doubt that '[w]hen selecting the areas for alienation there are no guarantees, which provide the quantitative and qualitative protection of state-owned areas, instead only the general land policy objectives of the Government are applicable' (Reasoning [60]).

The consequence is similar in that the first decision of the HCC (Decision 28/1994. (V. 20.) AB), namely in cases of environmental and nature conservation matters, 'such preliminary guarantees are needed, which might exclude the damages with such a probability as if the areas were in state ownership and in the management of nature conservation organs'. The result is clearly a regulatory omission (Reasoning [61]).

The HCC in chapter VI of the decision goes back to the major problem (Reasoning [62]), whether the relevant regulations on private purchase of Natura 2000 areas might not lead to the 'deterioration of the institutional level of nature protection'. The whole is very relevant from the point of view of the non-retrogression principle. In the case of state-owned Natura 2000 areas the 'nature protection requirements are guaranteed in case of utilization of areas within the system of nature conservation type of property management' (Reasoning [64]). Also, in the case of state-owned areas, utilized by private persons under a contract of lease, 'there is an obligatory and enforceable land utilization requirement, sometimes reinforced with individual contractual obligations. [...] in [the] case of purchase agreement of land, forming a part of a protected area, there is a catalogue of requirements, serving the conservation and improvement of natural conditions form an inseparable part of the contract' (Reasoning [65]).

Unfortunately, the same is not necessarily true in other cases—'in [the] case of Natura 2000 areas in private ownership a similar control and liability mechanism related to a catalogue of requirements does not exist,' and of course there is no regular supervision of the conditions. The only exception is the regulations of greens, as it has already been mentioned (Reasoning [66]–[68]).

The HCC takes into account that since the first decision (1994) the problem of lost guarantees 'in case of protected or would-be protected areas in private ownership even the regulation which is identical with the requirements related to state-owned areas is not sufficient: if these areas are in private ownership or managed by private owners, the obligations of users shall be made stricter in a way which does not allow the restriction of the level and of effectiveness of protection' (Reasoning [74]).

4. Doctrinal analysis

4.1. Rights of future generations and the associated obligations

It is of the utmost importance to clarify the legal approach related to future generations. Here the point of view of the HCC is progressive, based upon the FL, primarily upon Article P), while the traditional human right perspective in Article XXI is also present. Decision Natura 2000 forms the basis of further decision, giving life to the theoretical provisions of the FL—see, for example, 'the obligations towards the protection of physical, biological and cultural foundations of Article P) (1) construe a structural principle infusing the whole spirituality of the Fundamental Law, reflecting the commitment of Hungary towards the protection of natural values […]' (Reasoning [25])—having not only academic but also practical answers. There are contextual requirements which might be and are deducted from the given paragraph. The HCC also agrees with the most well-known scholar on the topic, Edith Brown Weiss.[3]

Article P) (1) provides a hypothetical heritage for the future generations. One constituent of it is the well-formulated prohibition on non-retrogression, covering substantive, procedural, and institutional aspects at the same time. This might be impaired if the state were to undertake this duty of protection without taking into consideration the condition of the heritage—even passing this heritage in a run-down state. The consequence is that there is an absolute, positive canon related to the state of natural assets, setting objective requirements towards everyday activities.

Article P) covers all environmental media and impact, although not providing a taxative list—using the term 'in particular'. The HCC was clear in the respect that we may not select from among the different environmental media, as they are equally important for current and future generations.

The message of FL in connection with future generations is not one of how to dedicate some concrete rights, but how to clarify that the best and most efficient method of generating a responsible conduct towards future generations is to *develop responsibilities for current generations*. Accepting the viewpoint of comparative legal literature, it means three set of obligations: to preserve the option of choice and to preserve quality and ensure access.

3 There is also a book by the author on this subject, for the shorter version see: Edith Brown Weiss: 'In Fairness to Future Generations and Sustainable Development' (1992) 1 *American University International Law Review*, 19.

4.2. Precautions and long-term thinking

Although non-retrogression is not a novel issue, still its value has been substantially raised, as the HCC directly attached it to the provisions of the FL, namely Articles P) (1) and XXI (1). Thus, the principle could receive a constitutional status.

In connection with the prohibition of non-retrogression, the HCC also added that the principles of prevention and precaution should also be taken into consideration, but not simply as it had been understood before—'the state shall guarantee that the deterioration of the state of environment should not happen as a consequence of a given measure', but as an even sharper condition, not being a novelty in the case of precaution, as the burden of proof is not only reversed in case of the user of environmental resources, but it is also extended to the state. 'Coming from the precautionary principle, if a regulation or measure might have an impact on the environment, the legislator shall justify that the given measure does not mean a retrogression and does not cause potentially irreversible damage or does not create even the likelihood of any such damage.' The relationship of prevention and precaution has also been clarified.

Sustainable development definitely covers at least inter- and intra-generational equity, and the precautionary principle, as it is globally accepted in Principle 15 of the Rio Declaration on Environment and Development. Also, the international, EU and domestic legal foundations in harmony provide a kind of list of the sources of this principle and underline its utmost importance (Reasoning [75]).

Decision Natura 2000 further underlines that the precautionary principle 'prevails as a stand-alone principle [...] when making decisions it is the constitutional obligation of the legislator to take into consideration in their appropriate weight the most likely or certain risks according to the scientific perception'. This provides the proper basis for the conclusion—delineated in the following decision—that precautionary principle, similar to the prohibition of non-retrogression must have a constitutional force with the content prescribed above in point 5 (Reasoning [62]).

These all reinforce again the proportionality-necessity test, 'also taking into consideration the precautionary principle the state should justify, along the lines of necessity and proportionality, the retrogression from the already accessible level of environmental protection, seriously compared with prevailing another fundamental right' (Reasoning [21]).

The best way for implementation is the long-term thinking, the deliberate decision-making, which also underlines the importance and the integral operability of planning, also being a basic principle of environmental law. This shall also be a direct part of following decisions.

4.3. Protecting biodiversity

Furthermore, we should not overlook that the unity of biodiversity is of the utmost importance for human life. We must also add to it the indispensable importance of ecological (ecosystem) services provided by biodiversity and particularly of the Natura 2000 protection and in a broader sense nature protection.

A short remark at the end: the references cover ethical (natural law), international and EU law consideration in harmony and jointly.

5. Aftermath of the Decision

While the direct topic of the current case is biodiversity, still the rights of future generations obligations of current generations proved to be the most significant question complemented by precautionary principle, long-term thinking or planning and all became a starting point for further decisions by the HCC; and all are supported by a robust ethical, international and EU law background.

First, Decision 13/2018. (IX. 4.) AB (well drilling) deserves attention, focusing on several fundamental issues and clarifying to a greater extent the content of the right to environment. The protection of future generations is the beginning, while non-retrogression and precautionary principles work in tandem. Precautionary principle receives an even greater constitutional mandate, resulting in direct and strict requirements (Reasoning [20] and [62]). 'One designated aim in the Fundamental Law is the responsible management of assets, belonging to the common heritage of the nation, which is not a political concern, and must be controlled in a scientifically backed manner, implementing also the principles of prevention and precaution.' A central problem is the focus on the specific role of authorization, which might not automatically be replaced with notification, as this may weaken the guarantees (Reasoning [15]).

A next key decision of the HCC—and by far the lengthiest—was issued in summer 2020, following a motion of the commissioner of fundamental rights, in connection with the amended forest legislation—it is Decision 14/2020. (VII. 6.) AB. The subject was the shrinking protection level due to forestry reasons, which could even reach 80–90% in some areas. Beside future generations, common heritage, precaution, long-term thinking, some new aspects have also been raised, such as: 'the state is acting as kind of trustee (fiduciary) of the natural and cultural assets, as a public trust commissioned by the future generations as beneficiaries, and as a consequence, the utilization and consumption of these assets by the current generations may only be possible to the extent it does not jeopardize the long-term subsistence of these natural and cultural values, as protected resources on their own right' (Reasoning [22]).

The public welfare status of forests, also their ecological services are discussed in detail. According to the HCC: 'In connection with forests, the »common national heritage status« means that the protection of forests passes obligations on the state, forest owners, forest users, or even on those, who might use forests freely' (Reasoning [23]).

The duty to protect future generations is stronger than ever before: 'Article P) (1) renders the protection of natural and cultural heritage on their own, also their safeguard for future generations, who do not have [a] legal personality, even against the (temporary economic) interests of current generations' (Reasoning [35]). Prevention, precaution, necessity-proportionality, non-retrogression is all referred to.

A characteristic example related to the core of the problem: 'the Constitutional Court affirms that the regulations should be taken as definite retrogression compared with the previous level of protection, in order to promote the economic interests of forest management' (Reasoning [154]).

Bibliography

Gyula Bándi, 'Interests of Future Generations, Environmental Protection and the Fundamental Law' (2020) 29 *Journal of Agricultural and Environmental Law*, 7.

Gyula Bándi, 'The Case of the Hungarian Constitutional Court with Environmental Principles' in Marcel Szabó, Laura Gyeney, and Petra Lea Láncos (eds), *Hungarian Yearbook of International Law and European Law* (Eleven International Publishing, Den Haag 2019) 49.

Edith Brown Weiss, 'In Fairness to Future Generations and Sustainable Development' (1992) 1 *American University International Law Review*, 19.

27. Decision 1/2019. (II. 13.) AB – Disfigurement of a Soviet War Memorial

*Bernát Török**

If the disfigurement of a monument is an act of expressing an opinion, both in terms of the communicative purpose of the person whose opinion is thus manifested and by an objective judgment, its lawfulness must be decided in accordance with the standards of freedom of expression.

The examination of the scope of freedom of expression is generally pushed into the background,[1] as courts take it for granted that standards of freedom of expression are taken into account when placing state restrictions on human communication. In most cases, this approach is permissible and even justified, but in certain situations the question of what the right to freedom of expression covers becomes more acute.

In case-law, symbolic speech acts, also known as non-verbal expressions or communicative conduct, make the issue of the scope of free speech especially pertinent. In such cases, courts must pay particular attention to the criteria which connect the relevant act to the fundamental right to freedom of expression. The significance of Decision Disfigurement of a Soviet War Memorial derives from the fact that the HCC, faced with a case of paint being poured over a monument, attempted for the first time to give doctrinal clarification of the factors which can be used to define the scope of freedom of speech in a particular case.

---

* PhD, Associate professor, University of Public Service Faculty of Public Governance and International Studies (Budapest).

1 The decisions of the HCC most often refer to the designation of situations related to certain fundamental rights as the 'scope of protection' of a fundamental right. In this case, we primarily use the term 'scope'. In the Anglophone literature that most explores the problem, a distinction is made between 'coverage' and 'protection', but in addition to 'coverage', the equivalent use of the term 'scope' is also present. For the former see e.g. Schauer, 'Categories and the First Amendment: A Play in Three Acts' (1981) 265 and Barendt, *Freedom of Speech* (2005), 74–78. For the latter see, for example, Post, 'Participatory Democracy as a Theory of Free Speech' (2011), 477.

1. Background

Among the more direct antecedents of this decision are the cases in which the HCC faced the issue of symbolic speech. These include Decision 13/2000. (V. 12.) AB, assessing various types of violations of a national symbol in the criminal law, including the possible act of burning the national flag. Similarly, Decision 14/2000. (V. 12.) AB on the criminalisation of the use of symbols of authoritarian regimes sought to identify the typical forms taken by symbolic expressions of opinion. The HCC considered both burning a flag and wearing a symbol to be manifestations of freedom of expression *per se*, and did not feel it necessary to justify their expressive nature in a doctrinal explanation. Decision 95/2008. (VII. 3.) AB treated it as settled case law that '[a] person expressing an opinion can share his thoughts with his surroundings not only in words, but also, for example, by using pictures and symbols or wearing an item of clothing'.[2] Wearing symbols of authoritarian regimes, as textbook examples of symbolic speech, became a central issue most recently in Decision 4/2013. (II. 21.) AB, but in the light of previous decisions, it did not provide a special justification as to why the HCC considers the arguments of freedom of speech relevant in this context.

The Act II of 2012 on infractions, infraction procedure and the infraction records system (Infractions Act) constituted the legislative starting point for the legal assessment of this case. According to the infraction form of public nuisance, anyone who engages in provocatively anti-communitarian behaviour that is likely to cause outrage or alarm in others commits an infraction, and the courts in this specific case classified the conduct of perpetrators disfiguring the Soviet monument as an infraction.

The HCC was able to draw on well-known international jurisprudence in the constitutional assessment of non-verbal expressions. The Supreme Court of the United States first pointed out that freedom of expression applies not only to verbal communications but also to all other cases where the perpetrator is motivated by the communication of a particular message and where the circumstances make it likely that the message can be interpreted by those encountering it.[3] Despite the fact that the so-called Spence test has been subject to serious theoretical criticism,[4] it continues

2 Decision 95/2008. (VIII. 3.) AB, ABH 2008, 782, 787.

3 *Spence v. Washington*, 418 US 405 (1974) 410–411.

4 Post, 'Recuperating First Amendment Doctrine' (1995), 1249.

to serve as a compass in case law when delineating the scope of freedom of speech.

The HCC also took into account the legal interpretation by the ECtHR. The ECtHR also summarised the arguments put forward for communicative conduct being included in freedom of expression when reviewing the sanctioning of a person who had poured paint over sculptures. In case *Murat Vural v. Turkey*, the Court broadly recognised the possibility of treating non-verbal acts as expressions of opinion, and it highlighted two main factors when assessing the nature of a particular act: on the one hand, the communicative nature of the act must be examined from an objective point of view, while the intention or purpose of the perpetrator must also be evaluated. In the Murat Vural judgment, the ECtHR considered the act of defiling sculptures using paint to be covered by freedom of speech, and found that the right to express an opinion had been violated, in view of the disproportionate nature of the sanction applied and the motivation of the authorities.[5]

2. *Petition*

In their constitutional complaint, the petitioners fined for the infraction requested that the HCC establish the unconstitutionality of the court decisions in their case. In their opinion, the court orders convicting them of public nuisance violated freedom of expression.

According to the facts contained in the order of the court of first instance, the petitioners flung a balloon containing orange paint at a Soviet war memorial in Budapest, leaving paint stains on the surface of the monument. In their testimony at the court hearing, the petitioners acknowledged the act detailed in the police report while asserting that they had not committed an infraction by this act. They said their act was meant to raise public awareness by expressing their critical views on the government's pro-Russian policy. The authority establishing the infraction confirmed the fact that the paint could be completely removed from the surface of the monument without rubbing it, using tap water.

The court of first instance did not accept the petitioners' defence and found that the petitioners had committed the infraction of public nuisance. According to the reasoning, it could be established beyond any

5 *Murat Vural v. Turkey*, no. 9540/07, judgment of 21 October 2014, paras. 54, 55, 65–68.

doubt that the petitioners' acts had violated and disregarded the norms of social coexistence, rules of conduct and expectations, and were of a provocatively anti-communitarian nature. In the court's view, the act was objectively capable, beyond any doubt, of provoking displeasure, resentment, and fear in those who perceived it. This fulfilled the conditions of the infraction; therefore the court ordered the petitioners to each pay a fine of 30,000 Hungarian forints (about €85).

The appellate court upheld the order. It shared the view that political opinion could not only be expressed verbally, but at the same time it held it absolutely necessary that it must be clear to those perceiving such an expression that the relevant act or protest is directed against a government measure. In the absence of this, the opinion of the perpetrators would not be conveyed, nor would the aim they intended to achieve be fulfilled. In the view of the appellate court, the motives of the petitioners in this case could not be interpreted by outsiders, pelting the monument in question with paint does not even indirectly indicate displeasure with the pro-Russian policy of the government as interpreted by the petitioners. In the opinion of the court, the petitioners' conduct was therefore nothing more than the disfigurement of a monument in a public space, which is defiantly anti-communitarian in nature, since everyone should be expected to respect either the creator or the memory represented by them to others. Furthermore, this lack of respect is likely to cause, and in this case in particular it did indeed cause, indignation in others, as this is the most likely explanation for the fact that a person reported this incident to the police. The court concluded that this act was dangerous to society, and thus an infraction had been committed.

In their constitutional complaint challenging the court decisions, the petitioners explained that the orders violated their right to freedom of expression as enshrined in the FL. According to the petitioners, their behaviour was an expression of a political opinion: they wanted to draw attention to a very dangerous foreign policy trend, of improving relations with Russia, particularly after past events when traditional forms of expression of opinion had not proved to be effective. This characteristic of their conduct, if interpreted correctly, precludes the realisation of conceptual elements of nuisance. The constitutional complaint also stated that the political nature of the speech precludes the act being dangerous to society even if it is otherwise disturbing, shocking or crude. In this case, however, their expression of opinion did not involve any violence or vandalism, and did not violate the rights of others, and the perpetrators even took deliberate care not to cause any lasting damage.

3. *Decision and its reasoning*

The HCC found that the challenged judicial decision was in line with the FL and therefore rejected the constitutional complaint.

3.1. *The scope of freedom of speech covers communicative acts which are part of the public social dialogue [Article IX (1) of the FL].*

In order to determine the scope of freedom of speech, the HCC first interpreted the notion of 'expression' enshrined in the FL. The HCC stated that the concept of 'expression' is normative in nature: its limits are not determined by speech in the ordinary sense *per se*, but by the acts related to the constitutional justification of free speech. On the one hand, the HCC pointed out that freedom of speech only applies to communications intended for the public, so private communications (private letters, telephone conversations, e-mails, private conversations, diaries, etc.) are not covered by freedom of expression, despite the fact that they are manifestations, and typically the most important manifestations, of our personal lives. On the other hand, and closely related to this, the HCC clarified that while its case law treats freedom of speech as a doubly-justified fundamental right that needs to be guaranteed to allow the democratic functioning of the political community and due to the need for individual self-expression, the main aid in determining the scope of freedom of expression is the aspect of participation in democratic social communication. Accordingly, communicative acts that constitute participation in the public social dialogue are associated with the right of expression.

3.2. *Freedom of speech may cover non-verbal expressions. A necessary but not sufficient condition to this is that the perpetrator acts with the aim of expressing his or her opinion. In addition, the application of freedom of speech also requires that the selected form of communication may be considered objectively as a suitable means to communicate thoughts [Article IX (1) of the FL].*

Confirming its earlier case law on symbolic speech, the HCC established that freedom of speech may extend to communicative acts not expressed verbally. The FL protects communication, i.e. the transmission of opinions to others, irrespective of its form of manifestation, so that the scope of freedom of expression is wider than that of verbal expressions.

According to the reasoning of the HCC, the question of whether a given communicative act indeed falls within the scope of freedom of speech may only be decided on the basis of a complex assessment of several factors. Courts must first of all examine the intention and motivation of the actor in the course of his action. However, the perpetrator's goal of expressing his or her opinion is only a necessary but not a sufficient condition for treating any act as an expression of opinion. In order to apply freedom of speech, it is also necessary that the chosen form of communication can be regarded as an objectively suitable means of conveying thoughts. On the one hand, members of society exclude certain actions from the scope of expression at the outset, regardless of their possible effect as communication of opinions. On the other hand, the act in question must be specifically capable, when assessed objectively, of communicating and being interpreted by the public—at least hypothetically. The HCC has pointed out that, when assessing the constitutional law position of communicative conduct, specific aspects become relevant compared to traditional forms of speech, as certain forms of expression may, by their nature, involve the consideration of additional special criteria.

3.3. A specific act of disfigurement of public works of art and monuments may be considered political speech, falling within the scope of freedom of expression, but in other cases it may qualify as barbarism, violating the rules of social coexistence. If the disfigurement of a monument is—according to both the communicative purpose of the person and objective consideration—an act of expression of opinion, its lawfulness must be decided by the standards of free speech [Article IX (1) of the FL].

When assessing the act of pouring paint over a monument, the HCC assumed that all public works of art convey a social message, and this is why they are exhibited. Public artworks and monuments thus become a self-evident part of the community dialogue, and expressions of opinion about them may also be important manifestations of social discussion.

The HCC explained that the special feature of any monument is that it expresses its message to the community in a physical form, and thus objections and protests to them may also tend to be in a form that can be interpreted physically. However, precisely because of the physical reality of the work, there may be unique limits to such negative statements of opinion that do not apply to purely verbal statements. The mutilation and demolition of a monument may be considered vandalism, and acts affecting works located in public spaces may also influence public order in other ways. Another particular consideration related to monuments is that, as works of art or memorials carrying a message, they are subject to different rules of social coexistence than other street objects.

On the basis of the above, the disfigurement of a monument may be regarded as symbolic speech within the scope of freedom of expression because, in addition to the personal intention to express one's opinion, such an act can be considered an objectively suitable means of, and mediator for, communicating thoughts. In the interpretation of the HCC, there is no objective criterion, based on social judgement, on the basis of which these acts should be excluded from the scope of freedom of speech from the outset, without examining any further circumstances. On the contrary, under certain circumstances, such an act may constitute an important expression of public opinion. The specific act of disfigurement and pouring paint or other substances over public works and monuments may, however, fall outside the acts protected by freedom of expression. According to the rules of social coexistence related to monuments, as works of art and memorials carrying a message, the disfigurement of a monument is in many cases an act of barbarism rather than an act covered by free speech.

The HCC emphasised that it is up to the courts to decide whether an act is a deed enjoying strong constitutional protection to be assessed under the scope of freedom of expression or an act of barbarism, based on the elements of the individual facts of the case. Amongst others, the place and time of the act, its connection with current events and the direct connection between the expression of opinion and the monument concerned must be taken into account.

On the basis of the above, the HCC finally established that the interpretation of the law of the court of second instance, which considered the aspects of freedom of speech to be applicable only under certain conditions in the case of pouring paint over a monument, is in line with the requirements arising from the FL. The HCC held that the court did not violate the constitutional criteria of the assessment of the facts presented to it when it excluded the specific conduct from the scope of freedom of speech.

4. Doctrinal analysis

4.1. Scope of freedom of speech

Defining the scope of freedom of speech seeks to answer the fundamental question of what exactly the rule of freedom of speech covers. The question may also be formulated as what precisely do we mean by 'speech'? Which types and cases of communication does it refer to? Freedom of speech does not protect 'speech as such'.[6] Numerous instances of speaking or writing have nothing to do with freedom of expression.[7] However, not only is certain speech excluded from freedom of speech, but also other actions are actively included, i.e. there are cases where a situation is covered by freedom of speech without anyone speaking. It is not speech in the ordinary sense, but certain characteristics of communication that make the guarantees of freedom of speech applicable. Some verbal actions do not have these characteristics, while some non-verbal actions explicitly do.[8]

Decision Disfigurement of a Soviet War Memorial serves to draw a fundamental dogmatic distinction, as it sheds light on which constitutional justification of the right to freedom of expression assists in defining the scope of free speech. Of the masses of communicative acts in the ordinary sense, only those that are related to the justification of freedom of speech are relevant. In the various possible theoretical justifications that have been identified many times in the literature, communications can basically represent three types of values: they can contribute to the common effort to seek the truth,[9] they can freely develop our personality,[10] and they can allow participation in democratic social life.[11]

The earlier case law of the HCC does not exclude the importance of any value from the domestic concept of free speech, and it presents all three

---

6 Post, 'Recuperating First Amendment Doctrine' (1995), 1249 (1250).

7 We do not apply the arguments of freedom of expression to words spoken when doctors or a lawyers advise their clients, or in the course of an argument at the dinner table at home. This list could be continued with a number of situations taken from everyday life, in which people speak but which are not classified as issues of freedom of speech.

8 Schauer, 'Categories and the First Amendment: A Play in Three Acts' (1981), 272.

9 Milton, *Areopagitica* (1644); Mill, *On Liberty* (1859).

10 Redish, 'The Value of Free Speech' (1982), 603; Dworkin, *Freedom's Law. The moral reading of the American constitution* (1996), 199–202.

11 Meiklejohn, *Free Speech and Its Relation to Self-Government* (1948); Post, *Democracy, Expertise, and Academic Freedom: a First Amendment Jurisprudence for the Modern State* (2012).

values within the framework of the right to freedom of expression.[12] However, dogmatic clarification of fundamental concepts such as the scope of a fundamental right requires us to distinguish between the justifying power of these values.

The decision of the HCC is in line with thirty years of case law when it designates the scope of freedom of speech on the basis of participation in social and public life. Hence, in the Hungarian concept of freedom of speech, the basic constitutional value of speech is determined by its participation in public social dialogue. Freedom of expression is particularly precious for a pluralistic, democratic society because, first of all, it enables the well-founded participation of the individual in social and political processes. Its special significance lies in the fact that the free expression of ideas and views, facilitating the informal development of democratic public opinion, is a basic condition for the existence of a society capable of development and vitality. Participation in public social dialogue is hence an important criterion for determining whether communicative acts fall within the scope of freedom of speech.

However, this does not preclude the existence of other arguments, which may even play a decisive role in the assessment of certain issues or cases.[13] It would be impossible to seek exclusivity amongst these arguments, simply because the justifications are correlated and complementary on important points.[14] All that can be stated is that the arguments of democratic justification are of most help in defining the scope of freedom of expression and in the comprehensive explanation of the doctrine.

4.2. *Non-verbal expression of opinion, symbolic speech*

Following earlier decisions on some of the most typical cases of symbolic expressions (for example the use of symbols and flags), the decision stated with general validity that freedom of speech applies not only to verbally expressed communications but also to non-verbal manifestations

12 The basic Decision 7/2014. (III. 7.) AB, for example, explicitly refers to all three justifications in the context of the possibility to criticise public actors. Decision 7/2014. (III. 7.) AB, Reasoning [9]–[13].

13 Robert Post similarly discusses the 'lexical priority' of justifications when analysing American practice. Post, 'Participatory Democracy as a Theory of Free Speech' (2011), 477 (489).

14 Lichtenberg, 'Foundations and limits of freedom of the press' in Lichtenberg (ed), *Democracy and the mass media* (1990), 334.

through which the perpetrators participate in social dialogue. Although it would have been difficult, considering the case law, to deny the existence of a category of non-verbal expressive statements, the general approach reflected in this decision should be regarded as an important theoretical clarification.

It is no accident, however, that non-verbal expression is one of the most challenging questions in the literature on freedom of speech:[15] compared to verbal expressions, special considerations must also be taken into account when evaluating these types of communicative acts. Decision Disfigurement of a Soviet War Memorial specifies these aspects, employing reasoning similar to the interpretations given by international judicial fora, in particular the US Supreme Court and the ECtHR. These agreed that the motives of the actor must be examined first of all, since, when it comes to communicative conduct, it may be less clear that an act has been committed with the intention of taking part in social dialogue.

A key dogmatic cornerstone of non-verbal expressions is that, in addition to the subjective motive, in order to be protected by freedom of speech it is necessary for the chosen form of communication to be an objectively suitable means of communicating thoughts. The scope of freedom of speech does not necessarily extend to every single act which might otherwise be linked to social communication in terms of its communicative nature, intention or effect. The role of objective assessment is twofold. On the one hand, the normative definition of 'speech' reserves the right to exclude from the scope of freedom of speech acts that are not acceptable by common sense or a constitutionally defensible public perception (at the abstract level of objective assessment). It cannot be questioned, for example, that although a political assassination or an act of violence against a person may carry a strong public 'message', if a perpetrator argued that this constituted free speech it would hardly matter. Similarly, it would be in vain to invoke the freedom to criticise the condition of the public transport system for anyone who carves his or her criticism into the upholstery of a bus seat with a knife.[16] Life, of course, tends to confront the courts with less clear questions than those in such extreme cases, as it did in connection with pouring paint over a public monument. Another aspect of objective assessment is that the specific act under review must be specifically capable of being, at least hypothetically, a communication

15 For a summary of this issue, see Barendt, *Freedom of Speech* (2005), 78–88.

16 Post, 'Recuperating First Amendment Doctrine' (1995), 1249 (1252).

to the public according to an objective assessment (at the specific level of objective assessment).

4.3. Pouring paint over a monument and freedom of speech

The HCC then examined whether the disfigurement of a statue or monument could fall within the scope of freedom of speech. The finding in this decision that such an act may be an act of freedom of speech is essential for the case-law on non-verbal expressions. I am convinced that the HCC could not have given any other guidance on the basis of either subjective or objective assessment. On the one hand, it may be considered natural that in many cases the motive of any physical manifestation targeting statues—as public works erected specifically with a social message—is the intention to participate in social dialogue. On the other hand, it is in line with social reality and public perception that there is no objective, socially-judged aspect on the basis of which these acts should or could be excluded from the outset without any further examination (i.e. at the abstract level of objective assessment) from the protection afforded by freedom of speech.

Another issue is that acts involving statues or other public monuments do not always fall within the scope of freedom of speech. The HCC rightly explains that monuments as works of art or memorials are subject to different rules of social coexistence than other street objects. On the basis of these, the act can be considered simple barbarism if the conditions for inclusion in the scope of freedom of speech are not met.

The HCC found that, in order for a specific act of disfigurement of a monument to be considered an expression of opinion, it is also necessary that the act be a communication that can be interpreted in public, at least hypothetically (at the specific level of objective assessment).

Concurring and dissenting opinions, with one exception, disagree with arguments that the decision should consider the possibility of treating the desecration of a monument as an expression of opinion. According to one debating argument, where an act constitutes an infraction (or a crime), it is no longer possible to consider whether it falls within the scope of freedom of expression. These opinions, however, can be said to 'depart' from the logic of decision and dogmatics. In this case, what is at stake in an assessment of a specific act of non-verbal expression committed against a Soviet heroic monument is precisely whether this actually constitutes an infraction. According to the logic of the fundamental rights assessment, it cannot be assumed that an act qualifying as an infraction cannot be prosecuted due to free speech concerns, but if the above considerations arising from free speech lead to this then a violation has not taken place to begin with. The Infractions Act itself provides a sufficient framework for this consideration, since, in addition to the factual nature of the act, the dangerousness of the act to society is also a conceptual element of the infraction. Arguments in favour of the protection of a specific speech act 'pull the rug from under the feet' of dangerousness to society, thus precluding the idea that an infraction has been committed.

Another argument which crops up in the concurring opinions is that the justification for an expression of opinion manifested in conduct can only be accepted in exceptional cases, in particular if the act also qualifies as an infraction. The decision views symbolic speech not as an exception to 'normal' expression, but as a communicative act that, in justified cases, deserves equally strong constitutional protection as its verbal counterparts. Although the opinions expressed non-verbally will always be in the minority in numbers, exceptional recognition is by no means the starting point of their constitutional assessment.

Finally, only a single dissenting opinion challenged the rejection of the constitutional complaint. This opinion asserted that the strong constitutional protection for political expression should have been granted to an act of disfiguring the Soviet monument, given that the act of expression that was committed against a public memorial of a historical event which has divided millions in Hungarian society did not reach the level of vandalism. In my view, one of the concurring opinions defends the decision in a well-founded manner on this point. On the one hand, this opinion admits that, given the condemnation of the Soviet occupation in the FL, the extent to which an expression of a negative opinion against a Soviet war memorial may be considered dangerous to society is 'highly thought-provoking'. On the other hand, the concurring opinion supports the reasoning of the decision that the HCC cannot deprive the courts of their power to assess the facts before them. Taking into account the case law of the HCC, it is worth noting that there have been cases in which the constitutional review boldly upbraids the courts for 'constitutional aspects of judicial deliberation'. However, under the circumstances of this case, the majority of the Court did not see this as an option.

5. *Aftermath of the Decision*

Shortly after Decision Disfigurement of a Soviet War Memorial a case arose in which, as a result of disregarding the constitutional arguments expressed in this decision, the HCC annulled the judicial decision under review. In the case leading to Decision 14/2019. (IV. 17.) AB, the act of expressing a non-verbal opinion was painting a section of a pavement, with the communicative aim of bringing to the attention of the authorities the intolerable state of the cracked pavement. In this case, the HCC treated the act of the perpetrators, who had been convicted of violating public sanitation rules, as an expression of opinion. The statement of reasons in this case reflected the differences from the facts examined in Decision 1/2019. (II. 13.) AB, pointing out that the cracked and painted pavement section was the direct carrier of the opinion: the petitioners painted the faulty parts of the pavement in protest against its neglected condition, thereby seeking to draw attention to the fact that the relevant section should be repaired. Consequently, in addition to the fact that painting a pavement is also a suitable means of conveying a message on the basis of an objective assessment (at the abstract level), the specific act itself was an interpretable communication to the public (at the specific level). Since the HCC had already established the scope of freedom of expression, in this case it proceeded to make a specific assessment of the conflict between freedom of expression and the right to property and, following a proportionality test, ruled in favour of free speech. Overall, it can be concluded that Decision 14/2019. (IV. 17.) AB applied the steps detailed in Decision Disfigurement of a Soviet War Memorial for the test and, by annulling the revised judicial decision, it also gave these steps sufficient weight to ensure a coherent constitutional assessment of non-verbal opinions in its future case law.

Bibliography

Eric Barendt, *Freedom of Speech* (Oxford University Press, Oxford-New York 2005)

Ronald Dworkin, *Freedom's Law. The Moral Reading of the American Constitution* (Oxford University Press, Oxford – New York, 1996)

Judith Lichtenberg, 'Foundations and Limits of Freedom of the Press' in Judith Lichtenberg (ed), *Democracy and the Mass Media* (Cambridge University Press, Cambridge 1990)

Alexander Meiklejohn, *Free Speech and Its Relation to Self-Government* (Harper Bros., New York 1948)

John Milton, *Areopagitica* (London 1644)

John Stuart Mill, *On Liberty* (John W. Parker and Son, London 1859)

Robert C. Post, *Democracy, Expertise, and Academic Freedom: a First Amendment Jurisprudence for the Modern State* (Yale University Press, New Haven – London 2012)

Robert C. Post, 'Recuperating First Amendment Doctrine' (1995) 47 *Stanford Law Review*, 1249.

Robert C. Post, 'Participatory Democracy as a Theory of Free Speech' (2011) 97 *Virginia Law Review*, 477.

Martin H. Redish, 'The Value of Free Speech' (1982) 130 *University of Pennsylvania Law Review*, 591.

Frederick Schauer, 'Categories and the First Amendment: A Play in Three Acts' (1981) *34 Vanderbilt Law Review*, 265.

28. Decision 3/2019 (III. 7.) AB – Illegal Immigration

Ádám Békés[*]

The relevant provision of the Criminal Code on supporting illegal immigration should not include altruistic conduct that fulfils the obligation to help the vulnerable and the poor, and which is not related to a prohibited aim.

Decision Illegal Immigration can be considered to be a cornerstone in two aspects. On the one hand, the constitutional complaint, which Amnesty International filed in the present case concerning a criminal offence under Article 353/A[1] of the Criminal Code established by Act

* PhD, Associate professor, Pázmány Péter Catholic University Faculty of Law and Political Sciences (Budapest).

1 Article 353/A (1) Anyone who carries out organizing activities in order to (a) to allow an asylum procedure to be initiated in Hungary for a person who, in his home country or in the country of habitual residence or in another country through which he has arrived, is not subject to persecution because of his or her race, nationality, membership of a particular social group, religious or political beliefs, or whose fear of direct persecution is unfounded, or (b) a person who enters Hungary unlawfully or is illegally residing in Hungary shall obtain a residence title, if a more serious offence is not committed, he or she is punishable by detention for a misdemeanor. (2) A person who provides material means or carries out the organizing activity regularly shall be punishable by imprisonment of up to one year. (3) A person who commits the offence referred to in paragraph (1) shall be punishable in accordance with paragraph (2) (a) for financial gain, (b) assisting more than one person, or (c) within a radius of 8 km from the boundary of the external border of the Hungary in accordance with Article 2 point (2) Regulation (EU) 2016/399 Of The European Parliament And Of The Council of 9 March 2016 on a Union Code on the rules governing the movement of persons across borders (Schengen Borders Code) (hereinafter referred to as the 'Schengen Borders Code') committed. (4) The sentence may be reduced indefinitely against the perpetrator of the offence referred to in paragraph 1, in cases of particular appreciation, if the offender reveals the circumstances of the offence until the charge is brought. (5) For the purposes of this Section, it shall be considered to be an organizing activity in particular where, for the purposes set out in paragraph 1, (a) organize border monitoring at the external border line or border mark of the territory of Hungary in accordance with Article 2 point (2) of the Schengen Borders Code, (b) prepares, disseminates or commissions information material, (c) build or operate a network.

VI of 2018, which became known as 'Stop Soros', has been extended by the HCC to new criminal facts which criminalize the conduct permitted before their entry into force.[2]

On the other hand, with regard to the interpretation of *nullum crimen sine lege* and the principle of the clarity of norms, the HCC waived the previously stricter constitutional court practice, and reference to decisions before 2012 is essentially omitted from the reasoning. However, it proactively corrects possible flaws in the clarity of norms by establishing a constitutional requirement for the interpretation of the criminal facts. The latter is interesting because there is no interpretation specifically from a constitutional point of view among the methods of interpretation of criminal law, the FL is a source of law, admittedly important and fundamental, used in the course of each method of interpretation, with which the result of the interpretation must be consistent. However, the application of the law and the judgments of the judges rarely trace the interpretation of the statutory facts back to the privileges of the FL, especially if it is a principle of legality as set out in Article 1 of the Criminal Code. In the decision under examination, however, the HCC, having regard to the provisions of the National Avowal, took the view that, in order to help the poor and the vulnerable, and in order to ensure the unconditional application of Articles I (3) and XXVIII (4) of the FL, it lays down new constitutional requirements as a condition for the application of Article 353/A of the Criminal Code in order to ensure legal certainty, while leaving it untouched.[3]

1. *Background*

On the 1 January 2019, the Seventh Amendment to the FL entered into force, which, among other things, supplemented Article XIV of the FL. Since then, under Article XIV (4) of the FL,[4] the granting of asylum is

---

2 The HCC did so by stipulating that the Article 26 (2) of HCC Act made the term 'exceptionally' a conjunctive condition. While this has taken a step towards broadening the applicability of constitutional complaints, the use of exceptionalism, which is the fight against illegal migration in relation to the decision, has also constituted a subjective barrier to avoiding excessive *actio popularis* character. However, the latter will make it more difficult in the future to attack a new legal situation with a constitutional complaint.

3 Belovics, *Büntetőjog I. Általános rész* (2017), 112–114.

4 Article XIV (4) Hungary, if neither their country of origin nor any other country provides protection, grant asylum on request to non-Hungarian citizens who are persecuted in their home country or in their country of habitual residence because

prohibited for people wishing to migrate through a safe country. However, the direct precursor of the decision to support illegal immigration was the amendment of Criminal Code with Act VI of 2018, based on the amendment of Article XIV (4) of the FL, on the 1 July 2018, which created the crime of facilitating and supporting illegal immigration as a new offence (Article 353/A of the Criminal Code).[5] The legal facts classify the organising activity related to illegal immigration as a misdemeanour and, by example, define the content of the organizing activity, which may mean organising border monitoring; preparing or disseminating information material or commissioning others to do it; or building or operating a network of it. The decision is an indirect political precedent to the European Commission's infringement proceedings against Hungary in 2018, as the Commission considered the 'Stop Soros' Act to be contrary to EU law.[6]

The HCC responded to this by issuing Decision 2/2019. (III. 5.) AB, stating in the context of the interpretation of Article XIV (4) of the FL, that, in view of its international obligations under Hungary, the granting of asylum 'cannot be regarded as a constitutional obligation of the Hungarian State to a non-Hungarian citizen who has arrived to Hungarian territory through a country where he has not been subjected to persecution or imminent threat of persecution'. It follows that the amendments introduced by Act VI of 2018 are in line with the FL, in particular regarding its Seventh Amendment.[7] Judge Béla Pokol points out in his dissenting opinion that the constitutional complaint and the government's request met exceptionally, creating an opportunity for the HCC to answer the constitutional questions of legislation on illegal migration two days apart (Reasoning [113]).

The decision is accompanied by two concurring reasonings and three dissenting opinions. With the exception of the concurring reasoning of

---

of their race, nationality, membership of a particular social group, religious or political beliefs, or who have a well-founded fear of direct persecution. A non-Hungarian citizen who has arrived in Hungary territory through a country where he or she has not been subjected to persecution or imminent danger of persecution shall not be entitled to asylum.

5 It should be noted that the European Union's objectives include combating illegal immigration. Directive 2002/90/EC (28 November 2002) of the European Council introduced the facts of assistance for unlawful entry, transit, and residence, so it has already laid down in Section 2 of its Preamble that measures should be taken to combat assistance to illegal immigration.

6 The Commission will open infringement proceedings against Hungary. Press release, 25 July 2019. https://bit.ly/38zjyW6

7 Decision 2/2019. (III. 5.) AB, Operative part.

Judge Mária Szívós, the dissenting opinions and concurring reasonings deal essentially with the admissibility of a constitutional complaint, although this is not at the heart of the examination of the decision, but rather the assessment of the protected legal subject matter and purpose of the criminal law, the meeting of *nullum crimen sine lege* and the clarity of norms, its interpretation of the constitutional court and the changes in interpretation.

Since the outset, the HCC has been examining and taking much-cited decisions on the requirement of the clarity of norms and the content of the *nullum crimen sine lege* principle[8] [Decision 11/1992. (III. 5.) AB; Decision 30/1992. (V. 26.) AB]. In the former, the HCC formulated a fundamental and future-determinative reasoning for extending the statute of limitations on criminality by substantive law and applying it retroactively.[9] He identified the *nullum crimen sine lege* principle as part of the constitutional requirement of legality, which not only represents the formal placement of the criminal norm, but also enshrines its predictability as a constitutional principle, the precondition of which is that the norm text is clear and unambiguous. Obviously, the constitutional principle of the legality of criminal law is more than that, as the explanatory memorandum points out since it also includes the principle of *ultima ratio* and the prohibition of retroactive effect.

The requirements of constitutional criminal law have been further extended by Decision 30/1992. (V. 26.) AB, according to which the disposition describing the conduct must be 'firm, delimited and clearly defined'.[10] A constitutional requirement is to clearly express the legislative will on protecting the protected legal subject and forbidding the conduct of the offender. It should contain a clear message as to when an individual commits a criminally-sanctioned offence. At the same time, it should limit the possibility of arbitrary interpretation of the legal practitioners. It is therefore necessary to examine whether the facts indicate the scope of the criminal behaviours very broadly and whether they are sufficiently firm.

This reasoning for the decision is also revived by Decision 481/B/1999. AB, taken in the course of subsequent norm control of the unconstitutionality of misappropriation. According to the petitioner, the undoubtedly abstract disposition of misappropriation did not meet the requirement of

---

8 Hollán, 'Büntetőbírói döntések az Alkotmánybíróság ítélőszéke előtt – a nullum crimen et nulla poena sine lege elv tükrében' in *Az Alaptörvény érvényesülése a bírói gyakorlatban* (2019), 79–80.

9 Decision 11/1992. (III. 5.) AB, ABH 1992, 77, 77 to 78.

10 Decision 30/1992. (V. 26.) AB, ABH 1992, 167, 176.

the clarity of norms since its concepts required further interpretation. On the question of the interpretation of the concepts, the HCC held that the interpretation of the elements contained in the legal facts of misappropriation has, on the one hand, a clear judicial practice that has been used for many years and, on the other hand, the related rules of the Criminal Code and 'other legal branches contain conceptual definitions relating to certain elements of the facts',[11] as a result of which the rule of law requirement is fully fulfilled.

This suggests that if the explanation of the concepts in the factual elements is not provided by the facts itself, but there is a long-standing judicial practice or other legislation explaining its meaning, then the rule of law requirement is fully complied with by that legal provision. In fact, the HCC said nothing more than an acknowledgement of the methods of interpreting criminal dogmatics and resolved a hypothetical problem: namely, how descriptive the criminal norm should be. Abstraction is a fundamental feature of the criminal law, as this is the only way to avoid casuistic criminal codification.[12] The necessary inherent part of abstraction is interpretation—of which there are a variety of known methods.

The significance of the decision is to draw the line between the interpretation that does not conform to the principles of the clarity of norms and legality, thus instructing the legislature on the framework within which abstraction and the use of concepts are possible in future legislation, allowing and assisting the judicial application of the law to compare historical and legal facts. It is clear that, in the field of legal certainty and the clarity of norms, the Constitutional Court has included an examination of the indecision of the legal facts by stating that the application of judicial law is in fact 'a comparison of historical and legal facts' and the interpretation of the concepts contained in the legal facts in relation to the law as a whole, jurisprudence and events that have taken place.[13] The interpretation and consideration of the judicial law, which entails the application of judicial law, is therefore the internal essence of judicial activity, which in no way constitutes a violation of the principle of *nullum crimen sine lege,* and this type of judicial interpretation does not result from legal uncertainty or shortcomings.

---

11 Decision 481/B/1999. AB, ABH 2002, 998, 1013.

12 Békés, 'A bűncselekmény tana' in Busch (ed), *Büntetőjog. Általános rész* (2006), 87–90.

13 Decision 167/B/2000. AB, ABH 2002, 1113, 1120.

The HCC found that the facts of abuse by a performance-enhancing agent or method were unconstitutional, since certain elements of the legal facts contain vague legal concepts, such as the term 'breach of the rules of an international organisation', the vague and multiple interpretation of which goes beyond the comparison of the judicial facts referred to above.[14]

Although not closely related to criminal material law, Decision 10/2003. (IV. 3.) AB analyses in detail the requirement of the clarity of norms, while referring to Decision 26/1992. (IV. 30.) AB and Decision 116/B/1992. AB. Accordingly, the clarity of norms assumes that the legislation is not too detailed, which would already impede free judicial discretion; at the same time, it is not very broad, abstract and general in order to create a lack of legal unity through a subjective enforcement decision. The decision established the latter quality in relation to the concept of 'internal struggle': although everyone uses and understands the concept in its context, it can be interpreted in too many ways to bring judicial judgment to the legal unity, so its outcome is uncertain.[15]

Decision 54/2004. (XII. 13.) AB almost bombarded the legal facts of the time on drug abuse, even if some of its elements showed the original 'good intentions' of the legislation. The reasoning underlines that in the case of the introduction of a concept which was not previously known by the Criminal Code, the use of clear concepts is particularly important. If it is not possible to establish the meaning of the factual element by scientifically known methods of interpretation, it may lead to an arbitrary judicial decision, which in one case may result in acquittal or in other cases conviction, thereby resulting in unwanted discrimination. 'Co-consumption' and 'occasion of use' are contrary to the principle of the clarity of norms precisely because of the possibility of multiple meanings, as they might be considered as subject of judicial fantasy.[16] It is important to refer here to Decision 571/D/2010. AB, which examined and established the constitutionality of BJE 1/2004. Recalling its earlier decisions, the HCC reiterated that the interpretation of the law of the judiciary and the interpretative function of the decision on the unity of law do not conflict with the principles of *nullum crimen sine lege* and legality. It is a necessary part of the judge's decision.[17] The constitutionality of the norm text is impaired

14 Decision 47/2000. (XII. 14.) AB, ABH 2000, 377, 380.

15 Decision 10/2003. (IV. 3.) AB, ABH 2003, 130, 136.

16 Decision 54/2004. (XII. 13.) AB, ABH 2004, 690, 741.

17 Decision 571/D/2010. AB, ABH 2011, 2141, 2147.

only if the text opens the door to the possibility of incomprehensible, uncertain, subjective interpretation.

However, with the entry into force of the FL, the question may arise as to the extent to which the previous practice of the HCC governs Article XXVIII (4) of the FL.[18] In Decision 16/2014. (V. 22.) AB, the HCC took the view that 'in addition to the wording of the Constitution and the Fundamental Law with retroactive criminal law, a substantial contextual derogation of the constitutional texts can be established', according to which the HCC 'uses the previously established constitutional court practice in its interpretation of the constitutional rule set out in Article XXVIII (4) of the Fundamental Law in the light of these provisions of principle'.[19] In this way, it continued to adopt the provisions of the previous decisions already referred to in *nullum crimen sine lege* as guiding principles, in the light of which the provisions of the FL must therefore be compared when examining the constitutionality of the criminal facts examined as a result of constitutional complaints.

2. *Petition*

According to the constitutional complaint received by the HCC, Article 353/A of the Criminal Code is contrary to the provisions of Article B (1) of the FL (principle of the rule of law, in particular the clarity of norms), Article I (3) (principle of necessity-proportionality), Article VIII (2) (right of association), Article IX (1) (freedom of speech) and Article XXVIII (4) (*nullum crimen sine lege*), and the requesting NGO therefore asked the HCC to declare the new legislative provision to be contrary to the FL and annul it.

Referring first to its involvement, the petitioner pointed out that—similarly to the findings stated in Decision 32/2013. (XI. 22.) AB—the definition of the criminal offence laid in the law is so wide and vague that practically anyone might be subject to it at any time. Accordingly, as per the opinion of the petitioner, the HCC must take a position on the constitutionality of similar, completely unforeseeable criminal law provisions, since, according to it, Article 353/A of the Criminal Code violates the clarity of norms and the expectation of a closed list of facts giving rise to

18 Bricks, 'The fundamental rights protection practice of the Constitutional Court after the entry into force of the Fundamental Law' (2015), 17–23.

19 Decision 16/2014. (V. 22.) AB, Reasoning [31].

the establishment of constitutional criminal liability. In this context, the petitioner complained that other norms of the legal system do not provide an explanation for what the 'organising border monitoring', 'prepares, disseminates information material or gives commission to do so', and the 'builds or operates a network' terms mean in the norm text.

Furthermore, according to the constitutional complaint, the petitioner was concerned that Article 353/A of the Criminal Code fails to comply with the *ultima ratio* character of criminal law, and deliberately uses vague, ambiguous terms that thus threaten completely legal activities such as the provision of legal representation or humanitarian services for asylum seekers in Hungary. The regulation therefore penalises, in the opinion of the petitioner, a criminal law instrument for speaking out in a high-priority public case in such a way that its applicability is unpredictable, in no way proportionate to the objective pursued, and the need for it is questionable, given the criminal law instruments already available to control illegal migration.

On this basis, according to the petitioner, it is a fundamental constitutional issue and therefore it is essential to examine whether the criminalisation of organising activities related to illegal immigration is in accordance with the FL in the light of the principle of *nullum crimen sine lege,* freedom of speech and freedom of association, in accordance with Article 353/A of the Criminal Code.

3. *Decision and its reasoning*

In the operative part of its decision, the HCC held that, in interpreting and applying Article 353/A (1) of the Criminal Code, it is a constitutional requirement, pursuant to Article XXVIII (4) of the FL, that it should not cover altruistic conduct that fulfils the obligation to help the vulnerable and the poor, which is not related to a prohibited aim in the facts, and has otherwise rejected the motion to declare and annul the legislation based on its unconstitutionality. The HCC has therefore held that the new facts of the Criminal Code punishing the support of illegal immigration are not against the FL but can only be applied in compliance with the constitutional interpretation requirements laid down by the HCC.

3.1. *The facts of each offence must be determined by law. There is insufficient basis for inference with regard to the new facts of this Article of the Criminal Code to conclude that certain decisions contained therein – organizing activities, organising border monitoring, building or operating a network – would be incomprehensible and therefore inapplicable [Article XXVIII (4) of the FL].*

In the reasoning of the decision, the HCC assumed that the legal facts of the Criminal Code not only require them not to be incomprehensible, but also that the question of constitutionality should include the fact that the criminalization of a 'conduct' within the meaning of Article XXVIII (4)[20] of the FL does not contain indefinite concepts of law. In this context, it explained that indefinite disposition is incompatible with the principle of *nullum crimen sine lege,* because in such a case the addressees of the legal facts cannot decide what kind of a conduct they should refrain from or what kind of conduct may result in penalties under the law.

According to the HCC, there is no adequate ground to conclude that the specific definitions of the new statutory fact—such as organising activities, organising of border monitoring, building or operating a network—are in themselves uninterpretable and therefore inapplicable, as opposed to the motion, other statutory definition of the Criminal Code contain elements referring to organisation and organising activities, to which related judicial practice might provide a bases for interpretation (Reasoning [71]). In this context, the HCC refers to recruitment or intermediation in human trafficking, as well as the perpetrators who facilitate illegal stay as examples. In the view of the HCC, the offences of supporting illegal immigration are 'in particular' organising activities due to the specificity of its facts—either by using information materials or by building or operating networks for the exploitation of people.

According to the reasoning of the decision, the facts do not prohibit the establishment of organisations or the right to join organisations, but rather organising activities for a precisely defined purpose. The order to punish this organizing activity is not against the FL in the light of the *nullum crimen sine lege* rule of the FL, neither because of the indecision of the elements of fact applied in the motion, nor because of the stated lack of a

20 Article XXVIII (4) No one shall be found guilty or punishable by an act which, at the time of the offence, was not a criminal offence under Hungarian law or, within the scope defined by an international treaty or by an act of the European Union, by the law of another State.

legitimate purpose of the facts, and does not restrict freedom of expression in accordance with Article 353/A of the Criminal Code.

Articles 3 (3) and 3 (4) of Act CLXXV of 2011 on the right of association, the status of public benefit and the operation and facilitation of civil society organisations state that the exercise of the right of association must not violate Article C (2) of the FL, it should not constitute a criminal offence or a call to commit a criminal offence or violate the rights and freedoms of others. On this basis, the HCC, in its decision on supporting illegal immigration, first pointed out that, under the right of association, all organisations can still be set up in accordance with the FL, and that Article 353/A of the Criminal Code is not incompatible with this basic principle. Since the right of association does not give the possibility of setting up an organisation for a purpose the pursuit of which is prohibited by law, the HCC has held that the rule under appeal does not conflict with the FL, since it does not conflict with the rights conferred by the right of association.

The HCC also pointed out that the facts do not restrict the activities of natural persons and legal persons to act to prevent violations of the rights stated in human rights conventions, to promote and ensure human rights. In this regard, the Decision Illegal Immigration cited as an example the fact that Article 1 (5) of Act LXXVIII of 2017 on the Activities of Lawyers states that the exercise of the activity of a lawyer shall not be aimed at circumventing the law, for illegal purposes or for participating in such a legal transaction, but neither Act LXXVIII of 2017, nor Article 353/A of the Criminal Code precludes the right of natural or legal persons to protect those people who are arriving in the territory of Hungary, fleeing their own country.

3.2. *The criminal facts of supporting illegal immigration should not include altruistic conduct which fulfils the obligation to help the vulnerable and the poor and which is not related to a prohibited aim [Article XXVIII (4) of the FL].*

According to the motion, the facts can be interpreted and extended to cases where humanitarian aid is the objective of the organising activity, despite its aim. Reflecting on this, the HCC interpreted the law when examining the law's unconstitutionality. However, as a new statutory fact, the HCC did not have the opportunity to examine judicial practice and could therefore rely only on its own interpretation. The HCC stressed that although the historical facts and the interdependence of the law fall within the competence of the general courts, it is the responsibility of the HCC to examine the interdependence of the law and the FL, so it was examined and interpreted exclusively from this point of view.

Since the National Avowal is a mandatory framework for the interpretation of the FL under Article R (3) of the FL, the HCC began its examination with that. The National Avowal states that 'we hold that we have a general duty to help the vulnerable and the poor'. In view of Article 28 of the FL and the Article referred to in the National Avowal, the HCC considers the threat of punishment for organizing activities fulfilling the obligation to help the vulnerable and poor to be incompatible with the objective laid down therein. However, since Article 353/A of the Criminal Code does not refer to this in the opinion of the HCC, nor can a general court reach such a conclusion in addition to the reasonable interpretation requirements demanded by Article 28 of the FL, the concerns raised in the motion are unfounded according to the decision of the HCC. Regarding the new rule, in line with the traditional interpretation of the law, it has been established that it shall be up to the judicial practice of general courts to determine the conditions under which an organising activity should be considered as humanitarian assistance and to state which forms of assistance are not punishable and when these limits are deemed to have been crossed.

The obligation to help the poor and the vulnerable is fulfilled in accordance with the National Avowal and the provisions of Article I (3) and Article XXVIII of the FL. Article 4 (4) shall be unconditionally enforced by the constitutional requirements set out in the operative part.

The HCC—pursuant to Article 46 (3) of HCC Act—acted ex officio and considered it necessary to interpret the facts in accordance with Article XXVIII (4) of the FL and to record it in the form of a constitutional requirement. A similar definition to the examined statutory definition could be found in France in Act no. 2012–1560 which deals with facilitating illegal entry, movement, and residence of a foreign person, in which, at the initiative of the penal panel of the Cour de Cassation, the Conseil Constitutionnel reached a similar conclusion to the HCC in several points. The HCC stressed that the Conseil Constitutionnel had annulled the French legislation in mosaics because it excluded voluntary humanitarian assistance, but that the Hungarian statutory definition under consideration did not contain such a broad wording and, as described by the HCC, could not even reasonably be interpreted that way.[21] Based on this, the HCC

21 Décision n° 2018–717/718 QPC du 6 juillet 2018 (M. Cédric H. et autre).

provided for this constitutional requirement only for the unconditional enforcement of the obligation to assist the vulnerable and poor laid down by both the National Avowal and Article I (3) and (4) of the FL—in the context of the application of Article 353/A of the Criminal Code.

4. Doctrinal analysis

4.1. Nullum crimen sine legerule

In the dogmatic evaluation of the decision, we focus essentially on its criminal law content in order to determine to what extent the HCC has changed or improved the principles of *nullum crimen sine lege* and the clarity of norms. The reasoning of the decision treats the previous decisions of the HCC on a similar subject with caution, so although it re-referred to Decision 35/1999. (XI. 26.) AB in paragraph 68, only the reasoning detailing the prohibition of retroactive criminal law and the application of the law was recalled from that decision. This reasoning tends to avoid the merits of the decisions presented in the historical part of this study.

In paragraph 70 of the reasoning, the *nullum crimen sine lege* principle was interpreted in a way that statutory facts and the penalty for the crime can only be established by law [Article XXVIII (4) of the FL]. Furthermore, the reasoning for the decision does not address in more detail the *nullum crimen sine lege* principle and its relationship with the clarity of norms but focuses rather on the analysis of the statutory facts. The HCC has basically built the basis for its decision rejecting the motion on two elements: the terms describing the conduct committed are clear in the system of the Criminal Code and in a grammatical sense; the purpose of the subjective side of the statutory facts sufficiently narrows the scope of the conducts potentially involved.

The HCC considered the concepts of facilitating and organizing activities to be of no concern, saying they also occur in other legal facts. Indeed, the verb 'organisation' occurs in the organisation of illicit gambling and pyramid schemes, but in the case of these offences, it is due to the nature of the activity, thus the general language meaning of the word 'organisation' can be used and that it why its interpretation is not necessary. In the case of human trafficking, which is exemplary by reasoning, the identity of the organiser is highlighted among the perpetrators, which is also understood in the general grammatical sense. The dogmatic problem arises by the fact that, in the case of Article 353/A, the legislature wanted to deviate from the general grammatical meaning and used the possibility of interpretative provision in paragraph 5. By interpreting the law, the legislature seeks to narrow down the applicability of the methods of interpretation of the legal practitioner and is rather restrictive in terms of the outcome of the interpretation.

As Judge Béla Pokol points out in his dissenting opinion, the deleting of the word 'especially' by mosaic-like annulment from the interpretative provision could probably have given a clearer result of interpretation. By the term 'in particular', the legislature gave only guidance on the direction in which the judge in the individual case tries to fill and apply the verb organization in substance but has expanded rather than narrowed down its limits. The extent to which the examples given for the understanding of the verb 'organization' correspond to the Hungarian language meaning of the verb, and how clear the verbs serving as examples are in themselves in interpreting the statutory facts raises a methodological problem. The preparation or assignment of information material does not fall within the narrower or broader meaning of the verb 'organising', nor does it include 'building or operating a network'. In the case of the latter, we understand from the direction of criminal policy what the term 'network' might mean, but this again does not bring us any closer to understanding the meaning of the verb 'organising' (Reasoning [114]).

The legal technical feature of the Criminal Code is that the statutory facts abstracted from individual cases necessarily require interpretation in the application of the law, and interpretation methods are available for this, which are an important part of the legal dogmatics. It is the judge's responsibility to determine which method of interpretation he uses in order to ensure that his decision corresponds to the intention which would also lead the legislature if he were to sit in the judicial pulpit when the individual case is delivered. Precisely due to the fact that this is impossible, criminal jurisprudence must be an intact system that fulfils both its theoretical and practical function. As Imre Békés said: 'Dogmatics are related to written law, in this sense dogma. Its aim is to explore the meaning of legal concepts and to build a logical system of these concepts without any contradictions. The exploration of the meaning of legal concepts [...] ensures the unity of the justice system in the territory of the state concerned, and the establishment of a logically uncontradictory conceptual order makes the material of the existing law manageable. Dogmatics seeks to develop thought-type solutions and bring them to justice. With these types of solutions, dogmatics removes the judgments from the circle of judicial improvisations, shares with the judge the burden of conscientious objection, and makes the legislation not only manageable, but also learnable.'[22]

With regards to the reasoning for the decision, the extent to which the activities and exemplary misconduct described in paragraph 5 can provide a solid basis for the judge sitting alone in the courtroom and their ability to share the responsibility for the decision may arise as a matter of control. The reasoning of the HCC does not promise much in this regard, when it states in Article 81 that 'it shall be up to the judicial practice to specify the conditions under which an organising activity should be considered as humanitarian assistance, to state which forms of assistance are not punishable and when these limits are deemed to be crossed'.

The HCC therefore did not bring the legal practitioner closer to determining the meaning of the verb 'organising', but entrusted the task to judicial practice; however, the HCC has mentioned that the verb 'organising' has been already interpreted in the past for other offences by judicial practice. However, by the means of the interpretative provision, the critical point of this idea is that the legislature itself diverted the possibility for the legal practitioner to turn to the jurisprudence of other offences.

4.2. *The constitutional requirement*

The other pillar of thought is the aim of the crime. It is true that the subjective aim greatly narrows the scope of the acts to be ponied up. The sharp line between civil breach of contract and the crime of fraud is precisely the perpetrators' purpose. It is likely that, without the interpretative provision in paragraph 5, the very existence of the purpose would have solved the problems of application of the law and would not raise the possibility of a misdemeanour. The purpose of the legislator is to impose on the prosecution the burden of demonstrating the consequences that the perpetrator would surely have foreseen, which shaped the intellectual side of the perpetrator's consciousness at the moment before they commence the act; and demonstrating the emotional charge of their desire for those consequences. In addition to this considerable narrowing, the constitutional court's conclusion and teleological interpretation derived from the National Avowal do not seem necessary.

22 Békés, 'A büntetőjog-tudomány módszertana. A dogmatika' in Busch (ed), *Büntetőjog. Általános rész* (2006), 31.

The HCC sought to put the application of the statutory facts in a safe zone, stressing that the interpretation and application of Article 353/A should be subject to the constitutional requirement that it should not cover altruistic conduct which fulfils the obligation to help the vulnerable and the poor and which is not related to a prohibited purpose in the facts. Paragraph 81 of the reasoning of the decision refers to this as evidence. However, if this is evidence, why should it be laid down in the operative part of the HCC's decision? In fact, the HCC repeated two existing dogmatic aspects with the operative part. The first is teleological interpretation of the law, which seeks to remove from the scope of crimes to which the legislature 'did not wish to shoot', but which, as a result of abstraction, may even fall within the scope of the statutory fact. It is obvious to the criminal law practitioner that the legal facts of child pornography are not intended originally for when the 18-and-a-half-year-old takes a picture with his phone of his 17-and-a-half-year-old girlfriend without clothes. The application of teleological interpretation of the law does not depend on the improvisation of the legal practitioner, but on the mandatory comparison of whether the individual case was infringed in relation to the dogmatic meaning of the protected legal subject set out in the statutory facts. If the answer is no, you must be convinced that the conduct under investigation is not a criminal offence. The mapping of this substantive rule is a reason for termination or acquittal, as set out in the Criminal Procedural Law.

The other dogmatic thesis is that all the statutory facts in the specific part of the Criminal Code are—*ipso iure*—potentially harmful to the society as a result of the concept of criminal offence. The concept of being potentially harmful to society itself refers to the FL by the fact that the conduct is harmful to society, which prejudices or presents a risk to the person or right of others, or the fundamental constitutional, economic or social structure of Hungary provided for in the FL. It follows, without further explanation, that conduct compatible with the FL or expected by the FL obviously cannot be harmful to society. Compared to old Criminal Code, the current Criminal Code 'plays safe': when applying the law, it does not wait for the conclusion that it is incomprehensible to establish the crime in the absence of it being harmful to society, but Article 24 gives a clear order: an act permitted by law or declared unpunished is not punishable. In view of all this, the message of the operative part intended for legal practitioners can be considered as a proactive activity of the HCC, without which the application of law could be clear. Our hypothesis that the HCC also perceived, in order to make entrusting the interpretation of concepts it considers to be a concern to the legal practitioner risk-free, made the decision aware of the limits of judicial interpretation that also result from criminal material and procedural rules.

It is interesting to ask whether the *nullum crimen sine lege* principle and the requirement of the clarity of norms should be considered as principles within or outside of criminal law. This unusual approach is based on the fact that with this decision and reasoning of the HCC, it may seem that a definite and unambiguous wording of the law (the clarity of norms) is a requirement which, if not provided by the Criminal Code, can be solved by interpreting the law based on other legislation. The decision clearly does not provide an answer to this dilemma—if it can be considered a real dilemma at all. Rather, its suggestion is merely interesting, since the principle of nullum *crimen sine lege* as a rule of criminal law derives from and affects the Criminal Code. This is not exceeded by the fact that this principle of the rule of law in criminal law is also included in the FL, as the reason for this is the representation of the rule of law value system in the FL, and in no way the replacement of the legal nature of the Criminal Code.

Constitutional judges István Stumpf and Mária Szívós also emphasize the function of purposefulness in defining the statutory facts. It must be agreed with Judge Mária Szívós that, in view of this, the need to interpret the constitutional requirement could have been omitted. Her opinion is strictly dogmatic.

5. *Aftermath of the Decision*

In view of the fact that the decision under consideration is among the most recent ones, there is no information available about its afterlife. However, since it has not taken any other position with regard to the *nullum crimen sine lege* principle and the need for the clarity of norms compared to the decisions described in the history part of this study, thus it has not broken with the idea of those decisions, it is not likely that this particular decision will be cited as a precedent. Given the 'evidence' explained earlier, it is also not expected that the HCC will subsequently add a constitutional interpretation to the new provisions of the criminal law. We do not consider these to be necessary since the application of judicial practice necessarily considers the specificities of the legal system and the content of superior norms in the hierarchy of the sources of law.[23]

We are sceptical whether the constitutional complaint as per Article 26 (2) of HCC Act will now also be opened with regards to the norm control of the legislation amending the Criminal Code, since the reference to or the absence of exceptionalism will constitute an obstacle to the reception of this constitutional complaint.

Bibliography

Imre Békés, 'A bűncselekmény tana' [The Concept of Crime] in Béla Busch (ed), *Büntetőjog. Általános rész* [Criminal Law. General Part] (Budapest: HVG-ORAC 2006), 87.

Imre Békés: 'A büntetőjog-tudomány módszertana. A dogmatika' [The Methodology of Criminal Legal Science: Doctrine] in Béla Busch (ed): *Büntetőjog. Általános rész* [Criminal Law. General Part] (Budapest: HVG-ORAC 2006), 31.

Ervin Belovics, *Büntetőjog I. Általános rész* [Criminal Law I: General Part] (Budapest: HVG-ORAC 2017)

Bricks Andrew, 'The Fundamental Rights Protection Practice of the Constitutional Court After the Entry Into Force of the Fundamental Law' (2015) 2 *Public Law Review*, 17.

Miklós Hollán, 'Büntetőbírói döntések az Alkotmánybíróság ítélőszéke előtt – a nullum crimen et nulla poena sine lege elv tükrében' [Criminal Court Decisions before the Constitutional Court – in Light of the Nullum Crimen Sine Lege] in *Az Alaptörvény érvényesülése a bírói gyakorlatban* [The Application of the Fundamental Law in Ordinary Jurisprudence] (Budapest: HVG-ORAC 2019), 79.

23 It should be noted that the HCC also established constitutional requirements in connection with Article 178/B of Act II of 2012 on the misdemeanor, the misdemeanor proceedings, and the misdemeanor registration system in Decision 19/2019. (VI. 18.) AB, which was initiated based on a judicial initiative aimed at establishing and annulling its unconstitutionality.

29. Decision 10/2020. (V. 28.) AB – Changed Capacity

*Petra Lea Láncos**

The HCC may directly apply findings of the ECtHR's judgment, in case those were made in respect of the petitioner's case. Accordingly, where the ECtHR rules that Hungary violated the 1st Additional Protocol to the ECHR for failing to pay benefits giving rise to a period of social cover, this period mus also be taken into account for recalculating the insurance period.

Decision Changed Capacity sought to provide remedy in a situation where, notwithstanding the compatibility of the applicable legislation related to eligibility for benefits with the relevant international treaty, due to maladministration by certain national authorities, the fundamental rights of the applicant had been violated. While the ECtHR had found a breach of the ECHR, subsequent actions of the applicant before the national courts for the payment of benefits remained fruitless, owing to the fact that the relevant national legislation excluded those in the situation of the applicant from the scope of those eligible for benefits. In the face of a situation where the applicable national legislation is constitutional and compliant with the ECHR, in order to forego a situation where, having exhausted all available national remedies the applicant would have to turn yet again to the ECHR for not having received benefits owed to her, the HCC adopted the constitutional requirement regarding the application of the national provisions governing eligibility for benefits.

1. *Background*

The restructuring of the system for determining the ratio of total health deterioration which governed eligibility for disability pension under Act CXCI of 2011 on the benefits payable to persons with changed work capacity and the amendment of certain laws (Act CXCI of 2011) has given

* PhD, Associate professor, Pázmány Péter Catholic University Faculty of Law and Political Sciences (Budapest).

rise to numerous applications before the HCC. Typically, these applicants seek the annulment of court rulings confirming the decision of national authorities denying benefits to applicants based on a review of their health status[1] according to the new methodology introduced under the Act CXCI of 2011. Applicants generally pleaded that their right to a fair trial or their right to property guaranteed under the FL had been breached. While complaints alleging a violation of the right to a fair trial may be successful, the fundamental right to property under the FL could not be invoked, since this right does not preclude the State from restructuring benefits, allowances and assistance and international treaties guaranteeing the right to property cannot be invoked through the vehicle of individual constitutional complaint. Complaints were also submitted to the HCC alleging a breach of the right to social security, however, as the HCC consistently held, Article XIX of the FL only enshrines a constitutional right to old age pension, meanwhile, assistance in the event of maternity, illness, invalidity, disability, widowhood, orphanage and unemployment shall be subject to provisions provided for under the law.[2]

However, in the present case, the applicant's lack of eligibility for the disability benefit was not the result of her health assessment based on the new rules, but much rather the maladministration of national authorities. A key feature of the present case was that the combination of the maladministration in the concrete case and the application of the eligibility rules of Act CXCI of 2011 amounted to a situation that was in contravention with the judgment of the ECtHR in the applicant's case.

The applicant, Béláné Nagy had received disability pension since 2001 when in 2010 her health status was reviewed based on the new methodology. In 2010 she was found to be non-eligible for continued payment of the benefit; on 13 December 2011 upon appeal, the authority proceeding in the second instance ordered the implementation of the applicant's 'complex rehabilitation' as well as the payment of rehabilitation allowance for the period of 36 months, effective on 1 January 2012. These, however, were never implemented or paid by the competent authority, for on the very

1 For an overview of the social security systems' approaches to determining the degree of disability in different European states, see: Könczei (ed), *A fogyatékosság definíciói Európában* (2009), 90.

2 Cf. Juhász, 'Az alkotmányeszme mostohagyermeke: néhány gondolat a szociális jog természetéről és szabályozásáról' (1996), 29 (34); Rab, 'A szociális jogok alkotmányjogi megközelítése a hazai és nemzetközi környezetben' (2008), 12.

day the applicant's entitlement to the rehabilitation allowance opened,[3] this type of social security support was repealed by Act CXCI of 2011 with effect from 1 January 2012. The applicant was subsequently re-examined upon her request, qualifying based on her newly assessed health status for the payment of the disability benefit. By then, however, Act CXCI of 2011 introduced new eligibility criteria relating to the period of social cover, setting forth that those applying for a disability benefit must give evidence of at least 1095 days of social cover over the five years preceding the submission of the application for the benefit, or must have received a disability pension or a rehabilitation allowance at the time of the entry into force of the Act.[4] Since the applicant had not been paid the rehabilitation allowance, she fulfilled neither condition and was therefore denied by the national courts the benefit she would have been entitled to based on her degree of disability.

The applicant Béláné Nagy then turned to the ECtHR, whose Grand Chamber found that while the applicant's health had remained unchanged, the perceived change in her disability resulted solely from successive changes to the methodology of health assessment.[5] Nevertheless, following a subsequent review of her health status, she was found to have a changed work capacity and the authority proceeding on the second instance had awarded her a rehabilitation allowance. In addition, her social cover as a condition for eligibility for the benefit under the new act lacked solely as a result of the competent authority's failure to implement the complex rehabilitation of, and pay the rehabilitation allowance to the applicant. Meanwhile, the applicant had cooperated fully with the authorities in good faith, having earned disability care through payments into the social security system in the course of her two decades of employment preceding her disability. This 'purchased right' to disability pension falls under the scope of Article 1 of the 1st Additional Protocol and gives rise to legitimate expectations and proprietary interests regarding the payment of benefits, should a contingency occur.

The Grand Chamber confirmed that legitimate expectations and proprietary interests cannot be extinguished by a new methodology for health assessment or changed eligibility criteria. In fact, while the State has a margin of appreciation in regulating eligibility for such benefits, they cannot

---

3 For more on the system of rehabilitation allowance, see: Könczei (ed), *A foglalkozási rehabilitáció Magyarországon: A szabályozás múltja, jelene, jövője* (2009)

4 Article 2 (1) a) aa) ac) of the Act CXCI of 2011.

5 *Béláné Nagy v. Hungary*, no. 53080/13, judgment of 10 October 2015.

deprive the entitlement of its very essence. Although the State is entitled to protect the public purse and overhaul the scheme of disability benefits, in the present case, it failed to strike a fair balance between the interests at stake, depriving the applicant of her legitimate expectation to receive disability benefits. Namely, the applicant had purchased the right to the benefit through her years of employment, had cooperated in good faith with the authorities and her health status remained the same throughout. The sole reason she was completely left without payment was the change in the eligibility rules in the Act and the authority's maladministration. As a direct consequence, the applicant had been totally divested of her disability pension, and had to bear 'an excessive and disproportionate individual burden', amounting to a breach of the 1st Additional Protocol to the Convention by Hungary.

In order to balance the interest of the protection of the public purse and legitimate expectations and to ensure, that 'purchased rights' to benefits are backed up by sufficient social cover while at the same time widening the scope for legitimate applications, the Hungarian legislator yet again amended the rules governing eligibility in Act CXCI of 2011. According to the new rules, persons with a changed work capacity were now eligible for the disability benefit in case they had a social cover of alternatively, at least 1095 in the 5 years or 2555 days in the 10 years or 3650 days in the 15 years preceding the submission of the application for the benefit.[6]

It is important to note, that the ECtHR's judgment in case *Béláné Nagy* triggered the adoption of another, earlier constitutional requirement in Decision 21/2018. (XI. 14.) AB. The HCC was petitioned by the Supreme Court (Kúria) that it annul and order the disapplication of the Act's provision foreseesing that 'with the exception of health improvement', the benefit paid following the health review cannot be less than the amount originally paid.[7] While the HCC rejected the petition, it adopted the constitutional requirement that in the application of the Act CXCI of 2011, 'health improvement' shall mean not only an improvement in the meaning of the categories under the law in a legal sense, but also the improvement of the actual physical condition of the person under review. This constitutional requirement guaranteed that those whose health condition remained the same could not lose benefits for the sole reason that the rules governing health status categories and underlying methodologhies had changed, while at the same time sparing the relevant legislation.

---

6 Article 2 (1) aa) ac) of the Act CXCI of 2011.

7 Article 33/A (1) a) of the Act CXCI of 2011.

2. Petition

Following the judgment of the ECtHR, the applicant had launched new proceedings for the payment of disability benefit, but this time, under the new eligibility rules of Act CXCI of 2011. In the framework of review proceedings before it, the Kúria suspended its proceedings and petitioned the Constitutional Court that it review the compatibility with the ECHR, annul the provisions of Act CXCI of 2011 on eligibility for benefits and order the disapplication of the provisions in the concrete case. The petitioner claimed that the contested provisions violated Article 1 of the 1st Additional Protocol to the ECHR as well as Article Q) 2 of the FL, which reads: 'In order to comply with its obligations under international law, Hungary shall ensure that Hungarian law is in conformity with international law.'

3. Decision and its reasoning

The HCC rejected the Kúria's petition to annul and order the disapplication of the contested provisions of Act CXCI of 2011 on the grounds that they are compatible with the ECHR. At the same time, the HCC adopted the following constitutional requirement: 'where in a final judgment binding on Hungary, rendered in a concrete, individual case the ECtHR finds the infringement of Article 1 of the 1st Additional Protocol of the European Convention on Human Rights because a benefit, otherwise giving rise to social cover due to the applicant had not been paid, the social cover generated by the unpaid benefit must also be taken into account'.

3.1. Only the HCC can find that national law violates the ECHR [Article 24 (2) f) of the FL].

As a starting point, the HCC considered the powers of the ECtHR and those of its own, respectively. It underlined that 'the abstract review of signatory states' laws or whether the given law is compatible with the Convention is not the task of the ECtHR, instead, it assesses the effects of the application of national rules by courts and authorities on the situation of the individual applicants in a concrete case. By contrast, it is up to the HCC to conduct the abstract review of the compatibility of national law with an international treaty. '[B]ased on the provisions of the Fundamental Law and the Convention, this review lies in the exclusive competence of the Contitutional Court' (Resoning [21]).[8] The HCC recalled, that in the course of its review, in order to establish the international obligation of Hungary, not only does it take into consideration the text of the international treaty, but also the jurisprudence of the forum entitled to interpret that treaty, i.e. in this case, the case-law of the ECtHR.

With these introductory considerations the HCC laid the groundwork for the purpose and the scope of its review, including the sources it involves when conducting its assessment.

3.2. *The Constitutional Court may directly apply findings of the ECtHR's judgment, in case those were made in respect of the petitioner's case (Article Q of the FL).*

Having established that it shall consider the jurisprudence of the forum entitled to interpret the international treaty serving as the standard for its review, the HCC zooms in on the concrete case and establishes the relevance of the ECtHR's judgment in case *Béláné Nagy* for its proceeedings: 'the applicant in the case *Béláné Nagy v. Hungary*, as indicated in the petition, is the same person as the plaintiff in the lawsuits on which the judicial petition is based, due to which the Constitutional Court expressly built on the relevant findings of the Grand Chamber of the ECtHR, in particular, since these could also be taken directly into account in the proceedings underlying the judicial petitions' (Resoning [22]).

3.3. *Benefits are insurance-type benefits which fall under the scope of the 1st Additional Protocol.*

The HCC confirms the applicability of the international treaty, i.e. the ECHR to the case *Béláné Nagy* before the Kúria, declaring that the benefits regulated under Act CXCI of 2011 are 'income replacing' social security benefits, which can only be paid to those who have a level of social cover from earlier employment. The HCC recalls that it was indeed based on this 'purchased' nature and the requisite social cover that the ECtHR found, that benefits under Act CXCI of 2011 fell under the scope of Article 1 of the 1st Additional Protocol to the Convention.

8 3157/2018. (V. 16.) AB, Reasoning [21].

3.4. *Signatory states have a wide margin of appreciation in setting the conditions for paying the benefit.*

Owing to this 'purchased' nature and the requisite social cover recognized also by the ECHR, the requirement to give evidence of such social cover as a condition for eligibility for disability benefits is justified. Therefore, the provision of Act CXCI of 2011 establishing the eligibility for disability benefits by reference to levels of social cover is compatible with Article 1 of the 1st Additional Protocol to the Convention. The HCC recalled its first judgment on compatibility with the 1st Additional Protocol where it expressly underlined that 'the Convention and its additional protocols do not foresee an obligation for states to establish a social security system, or [...] to make available certain types of benefits of a certain amount'.[9]

The HCC also pointed out that if it were to annul the provisions of the Act CXCI of 2011 under scrutiny, then benefits would be available to applicants irrespective of social cover, stripping these benefits from the social security nature. This would fly in the face of the legitimate purpose of protecting the public purse, as recognized also by the ECtHR. Therefore, the HCC declared, it follows from Article 1 of the 1st Additional Protocol to the Convention that Signatory States have a wide margin of appreciation in determining the conditions for paying benefits falling under the Protocol's scope. As such, an elibility system requiring that the applicant give evidence for social cover spanning at least two-thirds of the period (at least 1095 in 5 years or 2555 days in 10 years or 3650 days in 15 years) preceding their application for the benefit is clearly within the margin of appreciation of the State. Based on these considerations, the HCC rejected the petition for the annulment and the ordering of the disapplication of the provisions under scrutiny.

3.5. *Even if the law appied in the concrete case does not violate the international agreement, its application may exceptionally result in a situation that is contrary to the ECHR as an international agreement [Article 24 (2) (f) of the FL, Article 32 (2) of the HCC Act]*

The HCC went on to state that although the provisions under scrutiny are compatible with the Convention, should they be applied to the specific case *Béláné Nagy*, these would lead to a decision which, in essence, would

9 21/2018. (XI. 14.) AB, Reasoning [18].

be the same as the one with respect to which the ECtHR had found Hungary in violation for breach of the Convention. Namely, the application of the provision to the concrete case, owing to its specific circumstances, leads to a situation that is in contravention with the international treaty. Since Article Q) (2) prescribes that 'in order to comply with its obligations under international law, Hungary shall ensure that Hungarian law is in conformity with international law', and Article 46 (3) of the HCC Act empowers this court to adopt constitutional requirements to enforce the FL through legislative interpretation, the HCC investigated, whether there was an interpretation of the specific provisions under scrutiny that was in line with Article Q) of the FL, more precisely, in the present case, with the Convention as an international treaty.

3.6. The period of the payment of the benefit must be taken into consideration when calculating the insurance period for eligibility [Article Q (2) of the FL].

Examining the provisions under scrutiny, the HCC arrived at the conclusion that where the applicant eligible for social care receives one of the benefits under Act CXCI of 2011 (with the exception of extraordinary disability benefits), this period shall be considered insurance period in the meaning of the Act. The HCC then goes on to declare the constitutional requirement adopted: 'where the European Court of Human Rights rules in an individual case that Hungary had violated the 1st Additional Protocol to the European Convention on Human Rights for failure of having paid benefits otherwise giving rise to a period of social cover for the beneficiary, the period generated by the unpaid benefit must also be taken into account for the purposes of recalculating the insurance period'.

This way, the applicant's eligibility is ensured through the inclusion of the social cover that would have arisen with the payment of the benefit they had not received.

4. Doctrinal analysis

4.1. Leeway of the HCC to resolve the situation in contravention with the judgment of the ECtHR

An important aspect of the case before the HCC concerns the petitioner and the legal basis the petition was based on. Namely, the petition was submitted by the Kúria in the applicant's case. Based on Article 25 (1) of the HCC Act, judges petition the HCC to declare a provision unconstitutional and/or order the disapplication of the same when, in the course of their proceedings in a concrete case they must apply the provision they consider contrary to the FL. Meanwhile, Article 32 (1) (2) of the HCC Act provide the legal basis for requesting the review of the compatibility of legal provisions with an international treaty. It was these two legal bases under the HCC Act that allowed the petitioning court to request both the review of the compatibility of the provisions under scrutiny with an international treaty as well as their annulment and the ordering of their disapplication in the concrete case.

While judges may refer to Article Q of the FL in their petition, claiming that the provision they are bound to apply contravenes international law and is therefore unconstitutional, the same avenue is not open to petitioners in the context of the individual constitutional complaint. According to Article 26 (1) of the HCC Act, persons or organizations affected by a concrete case may petition the HCC in case the application of a provision in their case violates their rights enshrined in the FL. Since Article Q) does not contain a 'right enshrined in the Fundamental Law', petitioners cannot invoke it in their individual constitutional complaints. As discussed above, in cases concerning benefits (as opposed to old age pensions) references to the right to property guaranteed under the FL cannot succeed, since such benefits, allowances and assistance are provided for not by the constitution itself, but an Act CXCI of 2011.[10]

Therefore, the HCC only had the opportunity to resolve the situation arising from the combination of the provision of Act CXCI of 2011 governing eligibility for benefits and the maladministration by authorities in the applicant's case, because it was the Kúria that petitioned the HCC. Had

10 See Article XIX (1) of the FL. Article XIX of the FL is considered to enshrine a state aim to ensure social security, without giving rise to subjective rights under the constitution. For an overview, see: Drinóczi, 'Szociális jogok' in Jakab, Könczöl, Menyhárd, and Sulyok (eds), *Internetes Jogtudományi Enciklopédia* (2019), [15]–[21].

the applicant submitted an individual constitutional complaint in her case, the HCC would have been bound to dismiss it and the applicant would have had to yet again turn to the ECtHR to receive remedy. However, this 'second round' application to the ECtHR would have only meant that the applicant would have been awarded damages on the same grounds for the period dating from the last judgment of the Court in case Béláné Nagy. Next, the applicant would have been forced to yet again bring action before the national courts for payment of benefits, which would have rejected her claim for failure to meet eligibility conditions and so on, possibly leading to a neverending cycle of actions before the national and then the European fora.

4.2. Adoption of a constitutional requirement instead of annulment of the contested provision

The petitioning Kúria sought that the HCC annul the applicable elgibility provisions of Act CXCI of 2011 and order their disapplication in the case for violation of Article Q) of the FL. However, the HCC rejected this petition, since the contested provisions of the Act were fully compliant with the ECHR. Indeed, the HCC confirmed that 'in itself, regulation which requires as a condition for the payment of a benefit that the applicant be able to give evidence for social cover extending to two-thirds of the period preceeding the submission of the application [...] cannot be considered an unreasonable rule exceeding the scope of discretion' (Reasoning [27]), in particular, since this 'purchased' nature of the benefits is what differentiates them from other forms of social care for which applicants have a subjective right.

In case *Béláné Nagy*, the ECtHR expressly declared that 'the margin of appreciation available to the legislature in implementing social and economic policies should be a wide one and will respect the legislature's judgment as to what is »in the public interest« unless that judgment is manifestly without reasonable foundation', and the States are free to introduce systems with the aim of protecting the public purse, an aim that also underlay Act CXCI of 2011. As such, the contested provisions of the Act were not in contravention of an international treaty.

4.3. *Casuistic nature of the constitutional requirement adopted by the HCC*

It is the specific legal and factual setting of the case that explains the extremely specific wording of the constitutional requirement adopted in the decision. In fact, the purpose of the constitutional requirement is to spare existing legislation by reorienting those applying the law towards an alternative, constitutional interpretation of contested provisions. While the relevant legal basis does not preclude the adoption of single case constitutional requirements,[11] these are typically formulated in a more abstract way in order to serve as an interpretation aid in cases where the contested provisions apply. Such single cases are typically managed through the individual constitutional complaint, in this case however, owing to the reasons detailed above, this remedy would not have solved the situation.

At the same time, while the constitutional requirement was formulated in this casuistic way, it is nevertheless theoretically possible that there will be further applicants who find themselves in the same situation of being entitled to benefits, but are not eligible to receive them based on the provisions of Act CXCI of 2011, having the ECtHR find in their favour, and pursuing a renewed claim before the national courts.

In his concurring opinion, Judge Dienes-Oehm confirmed that judgments of the ECtHR that do not breach the national constitution, must be implemented by the signatory states. However, he underlined, he agreed with the majority decision 'in the firm hope and expectation that there are no further similar cases, in which the constitutional requirement [...] adopted in this decision may be applied, and it will not become a precedent for other cases'.

4.4. *Violations through continuous infringements following the decision of an international judicial forum*

An important aspect of the case is that it seems to provide authority for dealing with cases where continuous infringements following the decision of an international judicial forum prevail. In fact, not all cases may be closed following a judgment of an international judicial forum awarding damages to the applicant. As exemplified by case *Béláné Nagy*, the national social security system continued to owe disability benefits to the applicant, even following the damages award spanning the period between the point

11 Article 46 (3) of the HCC Act.

in time where her entitlement to the benefits was established and her case was disposed of by the ECtHR. Since she was denied benefits even after her success before the international forum, the infringement continued and had the HCC not been petitioned by the Kúria, it would have potentially put her yet again before the ECtHR.

The spirit of Decision Changed Capacity means that where an international forum makes a finding, and the infringement continues, the legislator and/or the authorities must take action to stop the infringement.

In his dissenting opinion, Judge Pokol referred to the principle of pacta sunt servanda, explaining that this principle only requires that signatory states adhere to the treaties they had ratified, yet when the court established to interpret this treaty engages in extensive interpretation to introduce additional obligations for signatory states, this shall be ultra vires, which the signatory states may reject as a decision undermining their national sovereignty. As a criticism of the dissenting opinion it may be pointed out that the ECtHR actually confirmed that the Hungarian legislator acted within its margin of appreciation in designing the national social security system and eligibility for benefits, what violated Article 1 of the 1st Additional Protocol was the specific application of these rules to the concrete case *Béláné Nagy* under its given circumstances.

4.5. An alternative to the HCC's 'bell rope' practice?

From Decision Changed Capacity it is clear that the Constitutional Court only examined the petition from the perspective of Article 32 (1) (2) on the HCC Act, namely, the compatibility of the provisions under scrutiny with an international treaty, namely, the ECHR. Since in the framework of this review the HCC arrived at the conclusion that the provisions of Act CXCI of 2011 were compatible with the ECHR and adopted a constitutional requirement, it did not conduct a review based on Article 25 (1) of the HCC Act to assess the conformity of the provisions with the FL in light of its Article Q).

In fact, according to the so-called 'bell rope' practice of the HCC, once it has annulled a provision for violation of the FL, it shall not assess further legal bases invoked in the petition. Thus, in an effort at judicial economy, the HCC only elaborates on the review in light of the provision of the FL, upon which the annulment is based. This however, does not mean, that the provision under scrutiny could not have been found unconstitutional on the basis of further legal bases in the FL. Nor does it help understand why the provision under scrutiny is not incompatible with other constitutional legal bases invoked.

The fact that in Decision Changed Capacity the HCC did not conduct a review based on Article 25 (1) of the HCC Act seems to echo this 'bell rope' practice. However, while the 'bell rope' practice only emerges in annulment cases, where, in the framework of a single procedure, the petitioner invokes multiple legal bases of the FL, in this decision, the HCC was instead faced with a petition initiating two distinct procedures, but invoking the very same Article Q) of the FL.

The procedural Article 32 (1) (2) of the HCC Act is meant to ensure national laws' compatibility with international treaties, meanwhile, Article 25 (1) is meant to ensure constitutionality of the law with the FL. In Decision Changed Capacity, the HCC proceeds under Article 32 (1) (2) to review the compatibility with the ECHR as an international treaty, nevertheless, it adopts a constitutional requirement on the basis of Article Q) of the FL. This shows that where cases involving compatibility with international treaties are concerned the distinction between procedures under Articles 25 (1) and 32 (1) (2) have the common aim of enforcing Article Q) of the FL: ensuring that Hungarian law is in conformity with international law.

4.6. *Factual and temporal intricacies of the case*

A crucial aspect of Decision Changed Capacity was that it was made in the case of an applicant whose specific entitlement to disability benefit had been confirmed by judgment of the ECtHR. Had anyone else petitioned the HCC upon the backdrop of the same facts but without a judgment of the ECtHR in his case, the HCC would have most likely dismissed the case, citing its consistent jurisprudence that it is not meant to act as 'a fourth instance court' 'overruling' the ordinary courts. However, this particular context forced the HCC to resolve the continuous infringement and the situation of Béláné Nagy. The HCC had to either annul the provisions under scrutiny *pro futuro*, or declare unconstitutionality by omission and instruct the legislator to adopt new legislation, or adopt a constitutional requirement.

This brings us to the question of why the case could only be solved through the vehicle of the constitutional requirement. The main issue here are the changes successively made to the eligibility rules enshrined in Act CXCI of 2011 and the effects these had on the case. As it emerged from the facts of the case, Béláné Nagy had originally been denied payment of rehabilitation benefits, since eligibility rules changed on the day her entitlement opened. Following the judgment of the ECtHR in her case, the legislator yet again changed the eligibility rules, expanding them to encompass a minimum social cover for 5, 10 and 15 years, respectively. Meanwhile, Béláné Nagy was pursuing and being denied disability benefits under these new rules as well. Thus, by the time the case made itself before the HCC, it reviewed different eligibility rules than those that the ECtHR had assessed in its judgment. Had the provision under scrutiny remained the same as in the ECtHR's case, foreseeing 1095 days of coverage over the 5 years preceding the submission of the application, the outcome of the HCC's decision would have been different. This is because no constitutional requirement of interpretation could make Béláné Nagy, whose case the HCC was bound to resolve owing to the ECtHR's judgment, objectively satisfy the 1095 days of social cover foreseen by the applicable rule.

Therefore, had the eligibility criteria not been expanded, the HCC could not have relied on the legislation sparing instrument of constitutional requirement. Instead, bound to resolve the case, it would have had to either annul the provision and/or instruct the legislator to adopt appropriate legislation. Yet the new, expanded eligibility conditions struck a balance between the competing interests of the public purse and those of the applicants' legitimate expectations, and, importantly, allowed for an interpretation which enabled Béláné Nagy to claim disability benefits. At the same time, the compatibility with international law of the new eligibility rules excluded the possibility of their annulment. Thus, the sole route to resolving the situation was through the adoption of the highly specific constitutional requirement.

5. *Aftermath of the Decision*

While Decision Changed Capacity resolved a highly interesting constitutional conundrum, with potentially far-reaching effects, it has not yet been discovered by legal scholarship. A search in the database of Hungarian courts' decisions (*Bírósági határozatok gyűjteménye*) yielded only the Kúria's specific judgment in case *Béláné Nagy*; no further references have been made to the decision by other courts. Since decisions of authorities are not searcheable in open, online databases, there is no data available on whether the ruling of the HCC has made its way into the decisions of authorities proceeding in benefits cases.

Bibliography

Timea Drinóczi, 'Szociális jogok' [Social Rights] in András Jakab, Miklós Könczöl, Attila Menyhárd, and Gábor Sulyok (eds), *Internetes Jogtudományi Enciklopédia* [Internet Encyclopedia of Legal Scholarship] (2019), http://ijoten.hu/szocikk/szocialis-jogok

Gábor Juhász, 'Az alkotmányeszme mostohagyermeke: néhány gondolat a szociális jog természetéről és szabályozásáról' [Some Thoughts on the Nature and the Regulation of the Social Law] (1996) 3 *Esély*, 29.

György Könczei (ed), *A fogyatékosság definíciói Európában, összehasonlító elemzés* [The Definition of Disablility in Europe – a Comparative Study] (ELTE BGGYK, Budapest 2009)

György Könczei (ed), *A foglalkozási rehabilitáció Magyarországon: A szabályozás múltja, jelene, jövőve* [Occupational Rehabilitation in Hungary: the Past, Present and Future of the regulation] (ELTE BGGYK, Budapest 2009)

Henriett Rab, 'A szociális jogok alkotmányjogi megközelítése a hazai és nemzetközi környezetben' [The Constitutional Approach to Social Rights in the Domestic and International Environment] (2008) 4 *Debreceni Jogi Műhely*, 12.

30. Decision 15/2020. (VII. 8.) AB – Fear-mongering II.

Fruzsina Gárdos-Orosz[*] *– István Ambrus*[**]

It is not contrary to the freedom of expression or the principle of *nullum crimen sine lege* for the State to punish a person who, in a special legal order, publicly alleges or spreads untrue facts or distorted facts in such a way that their disclosure is likely to hinder or frustrate the effectiveness of defence.

The HCC accepted the petition against the offence of spreading rumours defined in 2020, in the context of the coronavirus epidemic, by Act XII of on the Containment of the Coronavirus (Authorization Act) on Article 337 (2) of the Criminal Code, which entered into force on 31 March 2020, and examined its merits. Decision Fear-mongering II., as the only substantive decision of the HCC in the first term of the pandemic, declared that the criminal offence in question does not violate freedom of expression and the principle of *nullum crimen sine lege*, because it does not contain elements that are inherently uninterpretable and inapplicable in the light of the practice of criminal courts, and the norm is sufficiently defined and constitutes a necessary and proportionate restriction of freedom of expression.

1. Background

With regard to the legislative predecessors of fear-mongering, it may, at the outset, be noted that legislation was typically heterogeneous and not uniform up to the entry into force of Act V of 1961 on the Criminal Code of the People's Republic of Hungary (1961 Criminal Code); thus

* PhD, Senior research fellow, Centre for Social Sciences Institute for Legal Studies (Budapest), and Associate professor, Eötvös Loránd University Faculty of Law (Budapest).

** PhD, Research fellow, Centre for Social Sciences Institute for Legal Studies (Budapest), and Associate professor, Eötvös Loránd University Faculty of Law (Budapest).

the coexistence of several statutory definitions in this context, often under different laws, was not uncommon during the different time periods. Already specifically referring to the act as fear-mongering, Article 218 of the 1961 Criminal Code ordered that 'a person who, in front of others, states or disseminates any untrue fact or any distorted true fact that is capable of disturbing public peace and being harmful to the economic situation'[1] could be imprisoned for up to two years.

The phrase relating to the economic situation was dropped from the cited statutory definition by Article 270 of the Act IV of 1978 on the Criminal Code (1978 Criminal Code); thus the offence could only be committed by stating or disseminating any untrue fact or any distorted true fact capable of disturbing the public peace.

The Act XXV of 1989 amending the provision at the time of the fall of socialism further narrowed the scope of the statutory definition, by criminalising only acts committed in front of a large audience. This statutory definition was examined by the HCC in Decision 18/2000. (VI. 6.) AB (Fear-mongering I.) and was annulled. The main reason for this was the requirement to ensure the right to freedom of expression, according to which an opinion must be protected, irrespective of its value and truth. Following a necessity-proportionality test by the HCC, it held that it is neither necessary nor proportionate to restrict freedom of expression to protect the public peace by declaring scare-mongering—in the version in force at that time—to be a criminal offence; therefore its simple form, contained in paragraph 1, was unconstitutional. However, the HCC did not annul the qualified cases that could be committed at a site of public danger or in a time of war, as during a state of national crisis, state of emergency or a state of danger, freedom of expression may be subject to greater restriction.

Subsequently, the legislature re-regulated the statutory definition by Act CXXV of 2000 on the amendment of the 1978 Criminal Code, so that the criminal offence could be committed at a site of public danger and in front of a large audience by stating or disseminating any untrue fact or any distorted true fact that is capable of causing disturbance or unrest in a larger group of persons. According to the related ministerial Reasoning 'the Decision of the Constitutional Court did not rule out the possibility to re-regulate scare-mongering as an immaterial criminal offence'. Moreover, the new wording was supported by the fact that 'the capability of causing disturbance or unrest in a larger group of persons is more precise and

1 See Lázár, *A közhangulat káros befolyásolásával elkövetett bűntettek* (1968), 263–283.

provides clearer guidance for those applying the law than the result set out in the annulled statutory definition'.[2]

Article 337 of the Act C of 2012 on the Criminal Code (Criminal Code) further narrowed this statutory definition insofar as the site of public danger was not only represented as a specific situational element but it was pointed out in particular—although slightly tending towards tautology—that the capability of causing disturbance or unrest in a larger group of persons shall also be realised at a site of public danger.

Although the HCC did not examine the later norm texts of the criminal law regulation of scare-mongering, it emphasized in other similar cases that maintaining restrictions on the expression of opinion on public affairs by criminal law instruments may only grant protection against those most serious cases in which the expressed opinion violates constitutional rights, or in which an immediate threat to the right is present.

In the spring of 2020, the coronavirus SARS-CoV-2 emerged in Hungary as well. Within the framework of legislative precautions the version of the offence that could be committed during a special legal order was introduced by the Parliament as Article 337 (2) of the 2012 Criminal Code by Authorization Act. The offence which can be committed in the mentioned period (i.e. during a state of danger according to section 53 of the FL) is to state or disseminate any untrue fact or any distorted true fact that is capable of hindering or frustrating the efficiency of protection in front of a large audience.

The HCC had already pointed out, in the early 1990s, that the decriminalisation of the expression of an opinion involving an impairment of an individual right or one which has an adverse effect on constitutional values—such as the public peace—is a long-standing tendency in European countries (ABH 1994, 219, 224.). In the meantime, this effort remained unchanged: as regards the expression of opinion on public affairs, criminal protection—as an *ultima ratio*—is limited to sanctioning extremist behaviours.

A similar view is expressed by the ECtHR in Strasbourg on the criminal sanctions that emerged in conjunction with the interpretation of the article enshrining the freedom of expression. In the case of *Pussy Riot*, the ECtHR held that peaceful and non-violent forms of expression may

---

2 The wording of the latter part of the Explanatory Memorandum is inaccurate, since, as it also pointed out, scare-mongering is an immaterial criminal offence, thus the result is not regulated in the statutory definition. See Gellér and Ambrus, *A magyar büntetőjog általános tanai I.* (2019), 215. We follow here Koltay, 'A rémhírterjesztés büntethetőségének alkotmányosságáról' (2020), 332–338.

not be punished by imprisonment, and it shall be borne in mind for all restrictions that criminal legal intervention in the freedom of expression may have a chilling effect on the exercise of this right. This shall be taken into account when determining the proportionality of a restriction.[3]

2. *Petition*

The petitioner filed a constitutional complaint under Article 26 (2) of the HCC Act, in which he challenged the provisions Article 337 (2) of the Criminal Code, because, in his view, it is contrary to Article B (1) (the principle of the rule of law, in particular the principle of the universality of norms), Article I (3) (the principle of proportionality), Article IX (1) (freedom of expression) and Article XXVIII (4) (*nullum crimen sine lege certa*) of the FL.

The petitioner's involvement and the direct effect of the challenged rule—with reference to Decision 3/2019 (III. 7.) AB of the HCC—were justified by the fact that he considered himself to be a person who regularly posts on social networking sites, and who regularly expresses himself on public affairs, and that there was therefore a risk that his comments, which reach hundreds or even thousands of people, if they relate to the epidemic, might constitute the grounds of the new offence.

The applicant submitted that the new provision of the law is contrary to the freedom of expression enshrined in Article IX of the FL and also infringes the legal certainty deriving from the rule of law enshrined in Article B of the FL, because, first, it leaves the persons concerned in total uncertainty, since it is not possible to know in advance what kind of speech is to be punished and, second, the provision is interpreted in a way which is contrary to Article IX of the FL, and constitutes an unnecessary and disproportionate restriction on the freedom of expression. As an example, the petitioner mentions that under the new provision, a person may be held liable if, for example, he/she puts forward as an undisputed professional position a view on which there is in fact still a debate in the scientific community, and in the course of defending it the Government adopts a position contrary to his own. The legal requirement that an act be

---

3 *Jersild v. Denmark*, Series A no. 298, judgment of 23 September 1994, para. 35; *Brasilier v. France*, no. 71343/01, Judgment of 11 April 2006, para. 43; *Morice v. France [NK]*, no. 29369/10, para. 176, ECHR 2015; *Reichman v. France*, no. 50147/11, judgment of 12 July 2016, para. 73; *Mariya Alekhina and Others v. Russia*, no. 38004/12, judgment of 17 July 2018, para. 227.

capable of hindering or frustrating a defence is inconceivable. According to the petitioner, this also infringes the principle of *nullum crimen sine lege* enshrined in Article XVIII (4) of the FL, since a person becomes liable to prosecution for an act the unlawfulness of which he could not foresee. He, therefore, asked the HCC to declare the provision unconstitutional and annul it.

3. *Decision and its reasoning*

Fear-mongering as a crime defined by Criminal Code. Article 337 (2) is in conformity with the provisions of the FL, and therefore does not violate the freedom of expression or the principle of *nullum crimen sine lege* (and ultimately the principle of the rule of law). At the same time, it is a constitutional requirement that a statement of facts should only be punishable by criminal penalties if it involves the disclosure of a fact which the perpetrator must have known at the time of the offence to be false or distorted and which is capable of hindering or defeating protection under a special legal order.

3.1. *The cases of special legal order constitute a special constitutional situation where certain fundamental rights, such as the freedom of expression, may be restricted to a greater extent than is generally permissible in accordance with the FL [Article 54 (1) of the FL].*

The special legal order is a special part of the constitutional arrangements; it is the right to deal with periods of time other than peaceful ones, and, more generally, an extended range of instruments for periods in which the general rules of the functioning of the State are suspended (Reasoning [47]). According to the concept's scheme of objectives, it is both a state-level dimension of the category of 'necessity of the last resort' and a kind of deterrent toolkit to ensure the stability of a constitutionally based system. In times of a special legal order, the defence against impacts giving rise to such a situation is based on the Constitution. According to the HCC, it cannot be considered unnecessary to prevent communications which are capable of hindering or frustrating that defence. The rule of the Criminal Code under examination applies to all special legal orders, not only to emergency situations. Article 337 (2) of the Criminal Code does not cover all published statements of fact relating to the incident in general, nor does it cover statements of fact which are disputed at the time of communication or which are discovered to be untrue even after the communication, or in cases where the untruth of the statement of fact is not known to the perpetrator,

In the area of freedom of expression, the HCC, referring to Decision 13/2014. (IV. 18.) AB, explained that the difference between facts and value judgments is that the truth of the latter cannot be verified or justified. Factual statements, on the other hand, can be verified by means of an examination of reality. Freedom of expression is unlimited in relation to public affairs, but in the case of a statement (or rumour) of a false fact, the person making the statement is entitled to make it only if he or she did not know that it was false and did not fail to exercise the care required by his or her profession (Reasoning [50]).

Article 337 (2) of the Criminal Code does not in itself prohibit the expression of an opinion on the specific legal order or on the individual assessment of the measures taken. Rather, it penalises the expression of opinions based on knowingly false (or distorted) facts which may hinder the defence by their effect on the listener. The HCC stated that the justification for the restriction of speech in the special legal order is the public interest in the defence, the treatment of the cause giving rise to the special legal order and the effectiveness of that treatment by the State (Reasoning [52]).

Decision Fear-mongering I. annulled the contemporary facts of the offence because the public display of the offence was sufficient for its realisation, which unnecessarily and disproportionately restricted freedom of expression, and the element of the offence of being capable of disturbing public peace was, from the point of view of legal certainty, worryingly indefinite. No such concerns were raised in relation to the new crime.

Also in relation to the new offence of spreading rumours, it is an essential constitutional requirement that only the publication of a fact which the perpetrator must have known at the time of the offence to be false (distorted) and which is capable of hindering or defeating some form of defence in a special legal order should be punishable.

3.2. It is not a breach of the principle of nullum crimen sine lege if a new criminal offence does not contain elements that are inherently unintelligible and therefore inapplicable, so that the lawmaker can discover the immanent meaning of the norm on the basis of previous practice. The restrictive interpretation of criminal law provisions is also an obligation for the courts in the case of offences committed under a special legal regime [Article XXVIII (4) of the FL].

The HCC states that the constitutional principles of *nullum crimen* and *nulla poena sine lege* are one of the longest-standing guarantees of the rule of law, which guarantee predictability to citizens and limit the exercise of the criminal power of the State. The principles apply not only to the specific part of criminal law but to all relevant rules of criminal liability.

Referring to Decision 3106/2013. (V. 17.) AB, the HCC states that the difficulties arising from the drafting of a rule only give rise to a breach of legal certainty and make the annulment of the rule unavoidable where the rule is inherently uninterpretable, and this makes its application unpredictable and unforeseeable for the addressees of the rule. An indeterminate disposition is incompatible with the principle of *nullum crimen sine lege*, because in such a case the addressees of the legal rule cannot decide what conduct they must refrain from or what conduct the law may impose a penalty for.

As regards the new statutory definition of the offence of spreading rumours, there is no basis for concluding that certain definitions contained therein—fact, statement of fact, statement of untrue fact, distortion of a true fact, distinction between statement and rumour, special legal order, high publicity, etc.—are inherently unintelligible and therefore inapplicable. Other provisions of the Criminal Code contain elements identical or similar to these. The related case-law may provide guidance in assessing which acts may be contrary to the provisions Article 337 (2) of the Criminal Code (Reasoning [43]).

Therefore, the perpetrator must be aware that he or she is committing this act under a special legal regime; that the fact he or she alleges is untrue or that he or she has materially distorted the true fact; and that the communication of the allegation is (objectively) likely to hinder or frustrate the effectiveness of protection. Moreover, the intent of the offender must include the intent to knowingly make the above-mentioned communication publicly. If the knowledge or intent does not include any of these elements, or if the statement is not objectively likely to hinder or frustrate the effectiveness of the defence, the offence is not committed.

4. Doctrinal analysis

4.1. Restrictions on expression during special legal regimes

In its Decision 7/2014. (III. 7.) AB, the HCC compared the provisions of the Constitution and the FL on freedom of expression and freedom of the press. The HCC found that the FL confirmed the interpretation established in the practice of the HCC, according to which 'freedom of expression and freedom of the press has a dual justification, i.e. it is crucial for both individual expression and the democratic functioning of the political community. The dual justification confirmed by the Constitution means that the interpretation of the pre-eminent place of freedom of expression among fundamental rights remains unchanged'.[4]

Restrictions on freedom of expression in order to avoid disturbing public peace are therefore possible, but only in exceptional and narrow circumstances. Two doctrinal tools for defining this narrow scope are available in the toolbox of the constitutional practice of freedom of expression, while maintaining the principle of content neutrality: the distinction between the statement of facts and the expression of opinion, and the consideration of the consequences of the expression.[5] In Decision Fear-mongering II., the HCC examined the constitutionality of a criminal offence which, unlike many other decisions since the birth of the FL,[6] is a crime against public order, and therefore does not constitute a restriction on freedom of expression within the meaning of Article I (3) of the FL in order to protect 'another constitutional value'. Although it is true that the protection of individual rights is ultimately behind the formulation of any constitutional value, constitutional doctrine distinguishes between the protection of rights under the FL and the protection of other constitutional values, and in the case of the latter, the restriction of rights is necessary in a narrower context and the proportionality of the restriction of rights is different from that which exists when the restriction is imposed in direct defence of another fundamental right. It is therefore significant that the new situation examined by Decision Fear-mongering II. is not directly

---

4 Decision 7/2014. (III. 7.) AB, Reasoning [23].

5 Török, *Szabadon szólni, demokráciában* (2018), 114; Koltay, *A szólásszabadság alapvonalai – magyar, angol, amerikai és európai összehasonlításban* (2009), 488–494; Halmai, 'Túl kevés és túl sok szólásszabadság – egy utilitarista megközelítés' (2005), 186 (190); Molnár, 'Uszítás vagy gyalázkodás?' (2001), 110 (114); Molnár, 'Az alkotmányos mérce világosabb értelmezése felé' (2004), 141 (144).

6 Decision 13/2014. (V. 13.) AB; Decision 7/2014. (III. 7.) AB.

aimed at protecting individual rights, but at preserving public peace in order to ensure the effectiveness and efficiency of the State's protection in the special legal order, in this case the epidemic. The legitimate legislative aim was therefore acceptable as interpreted by the HCC in the light of the legislative reasoning, and we do not disagree with this.

After justifying the legitimate legislative purpose, Decision Fear-mongering II. sought to establish whether there was an interpretation of the norm that constituted a necessary and proportionate restriction on freedom of expression in order to protect public order. The HCC stated that the 'prohibition thus only applies to knowingly untrue (or distorted) statements of fact, not to critical opinions. There is well-established case-law to show that these should be included within the scope of protected opinions and, since epidemics are currently among the most important public affairs, the most stringent protection must be afforded to public debates on the subject within the framework of the substantive law.' (Reasoning [49]).

Although the HCC has laid down this very important principle, it has not formulated clear guidelines on any of the relevant fundamental doctrinal issues mentioned above. With regard to the distinction between statement of fact and expression of opinion, Decision Fear-mongering II. provides the following information (Reasoning [50]–[51]): the statement of fact is based on an objectively intelligible and verifiable element of reality, the falsity of which is therefore provable at the time of communication and of which the perpetrator was aware. However, the assertion of a false fact, together with its refutation, contributes to democratic public debate. It would therefore seem that the statement of a false fact does not contribute to the public debate which is the basis of the democratic organisation of the State, but that its refutation does. We also learn that the expression of opinion is, by contrast, any other communication. In practice, much of the legal debate on freedom of expression revolves around the question of the distinction between factual statements and expressions of opinion, and the HCC has made little contribution to clarifying this extremely complex—if at all clarifiable—issue in the context of the interpretation of the facts in the present case.

The HCC has sought to apply the other classic doctrinal test, after the communication of facts test, to the assessment of the constitutionality of the facts, namely the consideration of the consequences of prohibited speech. However, even in this case the HCC's position does not seem entirely clear.

The HCC has also maintained the importance of the doctrine of 'clear and present danger', albeit always with slightly varying content,[7] simplifying it on the basis of the argument that the legitimate legislative justification for restricting the expression of opinion can only be that the result of the expression of opinion constitutes a clear and present danger to society, a group or a member of society, i.e. that the communication disturbs public peace to such an extent that it may lead, even if indirectly, to a violation of individual rights.[8]

The preliminary question in the decision on the dissemination of fear-mongering was what effect the special legal order—the situation of danger—has on the assessment of the limits to the expression of opinion, since Article 54 (1) of the FL states, among the general rules of the special legal order, that the exercise of fundamental rights may be restricted beyond the limits laid down in Article I (3) of the FL, i.e. beyond the general constitutional limitation on fundamental rights.

The HCC, although this was a constitutional complaint procedure, had to carry out its assessment of the potential creation of a clear and present danger in the case of the legitimacy of the restrictive norm in an abstract manner, in fact in the form of an abstract *ex post* norm review. It had to examine what the circumstances of the emergency meant for the assessment of the clear and present danger, i.e. whether the assessment of the potential occurrence of a clear and present danger was fundamentally different in view of the fact that the legislation was applicable to a period of special legal order. In line with Decision 18/2000. (VI. 6.) AB, the HCC answered in the affirmative (even if it refrained from expressly applying the doctrine) when it held that false statements of fact are in any event dangerous in the special legal order, and that no further examination is required. Although the special legal order allows for a departure from the general rules as to the extent of the limitation of the fundamental right, the special legal order is not an extra-constitutional but an intra-constitutional legal order. Therefore, the discretionary considerations that require individual assessment and that derive from the principles of necessity and proportionality cannot be abandoned, even if the assessment of necessity and proportionality in a special legal order is different.[9] The test of clear and present danger is closely linked to the requirements of necessity and

7 Koltay, 'A rémhírterjesztés büntethetőségének alkotmányosságáról' (2020), 322.
8 Balogh, 'A véleménynyilvánítási szabadság értelmezésének a kezdetei Magyarországon" (2015), 7.
9 Koltay, 'A rémhírterjesztés büntethetőségének alkotmányosságáról' (2020), 322.

proportionality, and we cannot therefore accept an approach which would make the assessment of that danger in this situation unnecessary and take it for granted.[10]

If we take it as given that, in a situation of danger, the false statement of facts is capable of creating a clear and present danger, the HCC's examination would only have to determine, in order to assess the constitutionality of the legislation, when that false statement of facts, in addition to creating a situation of danger, has the effect of 'preventing or frustrating the effectiveness of protection'. However, the HCC says that this is something that will be determined by judicial practice. Judicial practice, however, can only develop rapidly in this matter if in many cases—almost automatically—the case reaches the stage of prosecution because of deliberately false statements of facts, until it is outlined in judicial practice when the false statement of facts hinders or impedes the state's defence against the epidemic at the time of the decision. However, this is certainly not consistent with either the declared legislative purpose or the principled considerations of freedom of expression. The dilemmas of interpretation of the norm under examination can therefore hardly be reduced to this element, and if the questions of assessment were to be reduced to this element, the work of the legislator should have been assisted by constitutional standards.

We can identify an even bigger problem in the reasoning of Decision Fear-mongering II. justifying the restriction of freedom of expression. Contrary to the wording of the contested law, the HCC formulates the constitutional requirement in such a way that anyone who knew or should have known of the falsity of the false statement of fact is punishable. The latter is not contained in the text of the norm, and the wording of the HCC fundamentally widens the scope of the restriction of freedom of expression, since not only those who deliberately state or report a false fact can be held liable, but also those who commit the act negligently, because they should have known of the falsity of the statement of fact. Since the reasoning of the decision no longer treats the issue in this way, and even refers explicitly to the content of the text of the norm, it is likely that the wording of the constitutional requirement is merely imprecise, which will be a matter for the judiciary to remedy.

In conclusion, the HCC has not departed from the standards of freedom of expression previously set out in its assessment of the issue, but has made them vague on three points. The first point is that it indicated that, under a special legal order, the communication of a false statement of fact is

10 Török, *Szabadon szólni, demokráciában* (2018), 100–101.

always capable of causing a clear and present danger; the second is that it left the criterion of hindering or preventing the defence of danger to future ordinary judicial practice; and the third is that it questioned the intentionality of the statement of false fact, presumably out of inadvertence. All this said, the decision did not represent a step backwards in principle in terms of the freedom of expression, because it emphasised, at a doctrinal level, the findings of previous case-law on the question of limitability.

4.2. *The new statutory definition of fear-mongering, the principle of nullum crimen sine lege and legal certainty*

In addition to the HCC's procedural arguments set out previously and those examining the implementation of the freedom of expression, and also apart from them, for the purpose of the enforcement of the principle of *nullum crimen sine lege* the following assessment may be provided.

At the national level, the principle of *nullum crimen* (and of *nulla poena*) *sine lege* was already introduced in Article 1 of the Csemegi Codex, Hungary's first Criminal Code (Act V of 1878), and after the state socialist legislation that consciously neglected it, the principle was included again in the criminal law by the entry into force of the Criminal Code in 2013.[11] Under section 1 (1) of the Criminal Code 'the criminal liability of the offender shall be established only for an act which was punishable under an Act at the time of commission'. However, even in the absence of an explicit criminal legislation it was present in Article 57 (4) of the Constitution under the Act XXXI of 1989, the text of which, having been amended in view of the EU accession, was transferred to Article XXVIII (4) of the FL.

The purpose of predictability is to fix the uncertain future regarding human behaviour[12] and, as such, is the most important requirement that a criminal norm must meet.[13] The subjective side of the requirement is the so-called intellectual accessibility, which is considered to be established in respect of a legal provision, if it is drafted in such a precise way that the meaning of the rule can be clearly ascertained by the average person (or at least by the average lawyer).[14] Among the sub-principles of *nullum crimen*

11 For an overview see Nagy, 'A nullum crimen/nulla poena sine lege alapelvről' (1995), 257–270.

12 Gellér and Ambrus, *A magyar büntetőjog általános tanai I.* (2019), 68.

13 Gellér and Ambrus, *A magyar büntetőjog általános tanai I.* (2019), 82.

14 Gellér and Ambrus, *A magyar büntetőjog általános tanai I.* (2019), 84.

derived from German criminal law, the aforementioned expectation can be associated with the sub-principle *certa,* which means that the wording of a statute shall be precisely determined and the imprecise formulation of a legal provision shall be prohibited.[15]

With regard to Article 337 (2) of the Criminal Code on fear-mongering, the argument of the HCC can be accepted, since either under statutory definitions or the earlier case-law the meaning of all statutory elements can be determined.[16]

The cases of a special legal order are laid down in the FL. According to the settled case law, the commission of the offence in front of a large audience can be established if a greater number of persons are present at the place of commission; furthermore, if there is a real possibility that a greater, *a priori* indeterminable, number of persons become aware of the criminal offence.[17]

The phrase 'efficiency of protection' in the statutory definition seemed *in concreto* clear at the beginning of the coronavirus epidemic; thus it is apparent from the ministerial Reasoning added to Article 10 of the Authorization Act that the aim of the legislature was 'to clearly define the legal status of the coronavirus epidemic, threatening to cause mass disease, in the legislation', as 'coronavirus threatens to cause potentially mass harm throughout the country'. According to Article 28 of the FL, with effect from 1 January 2019 in its present form due to the Seventh Amendment, 'in the course of the application of law, courts shall interpret the text of laws primarily in accordance with their objectives and with the FL. In the course of ascertaining the objective of a law, consideration shall be given primarily to [...] the justification of the proposal for, or for amending, the law.' Therefore, in so far as the court, in compliance with its constitutional obligation, reads Article 337 (2) of the Criminal Code in conjunction with the justification of the Act which gave rise to the statutory definition, it can be clearly established that ontologically and in the concrete case the legislature was driven by the need to provide criminal protection for the efficient containment of the virus. However, it could be raised as an

---

15 Gellér and Ambrus, *A magyar büntetőjog általános tanai I.* (2019), 75.

16 See Ambrus, 'The COVID-19 pandemic and Hungarian substantive criminal law' (2021), 462. Although, from a legal sociological point of view, it is problematic that, as the petitioner has pointed out, in the midst of the viral situation in people, doubts and uncertainties have prompted the emergence of a prohibition norm. See Bencze and Ficsor, 'A rémhírterjesztés tényállásának jogalkalmazási kérdései' (2020).

17 BH 1981. 223.

issue with implications beyond the COVID-19 crisis, what content the 'efficiency of protection' may have during a different sort of special legal order, for example during a state of emergency under Article 50 of the FL. However, the current legislature is expected to adopt a position thereon, depending on the nature of the concrete situation.

Hindrance, as a statutory element, also appears, for example, in the statutory definition of violence against a public officer. 'Frustration' as a criminal law category is known from the doctrine of interference with the proceedings of an authority or of accessory after the fact; thus, their content can be clearly established based on the results of prior jurisprudence. It is also a common solution in the Criminal Code to apply the wording 'capable of', by which—realising the elements following this phrase—the legislature does not demand that the abstract possibility of their occurrence is sufficient (an immaterial, abstract endangerment offence). However, it could be argued that to include frustration separately, in addition to hindrance, is unnecessary, as frustration is conceptually inconceivable without hindrance. Having said that, including such cumulative statutory elements in the Criminal Code was not previously unknown; it appeared, for example, in the case of the phrases 'damage and destruction' that can be read in the statutory definition of vandalism (Article 371 of the Criminal Code). Therefore, it can be assumed that if the conduct is not only capable of hindering protection but also of directly frustrating it, that latter situation can be assessed as an aggravating circumstance in the context of sentencing.

According to the necessity test, restriction of a fundamental right shall only be possible if the restriction is necessary to protect another fundamental right or freedom, the applied measure is adequate to reach the objective, the importance of the objective is proportionate to the degree of harm caused by the restriction, and furthermore, the applied restriction leads to the least possible harm.[18] In this regard, we can also share the HCC's view, because addressing the root cause of a special legal order, and the efficiency thereof, in order to return without delay to the normal practice of the constitutional exercise of power is an essential social interest. Therefore, to impose an imprisonment of 1 to 5 years is proportionate with this, as it enables the use of even the most imposing tool of criminal law, that is, imprisonment. However, the implementation can be suspended in minor cases (in the case of the imposition of a penalty of up to 2 years). Furthermore, if according to the circumstances of the case an

18 Gellér and Ambrus, *A magyar büntetőjog általános tanai I.* (2019), 89–90.

imprisonment of 1 year would also have been excessive, a shorter period of imprisonment or even a more lenient penalty may also be imposed (Article 82 of the Criminal Code).

Finally, the third aspect of predictability,—i.e. substantive justness—requires, among other circumstances, the principle of criminal liability based on individual guilt.[19] The statutory definition is in line with this requirement as the offence can only be committed intentionally. It is important to point out that all statutory elements at issue must be covered by at least indirect intent. Therefore, as a minimum, anticipation on the cognitive side and acquiescence on the volitional-emotional side are required to constitute a criminal offence. Otherwise, for example if the perpetrator was negligent in learning the truth, and that is why he or she shared the 'ominous report', his or her criminal liability may not be established.

5. *The aftermath of the Decision*

The offence of scare-mongering was not actually a matter of judicial practice prior to the coronavirus epidemic. However, the significance of that crime grew rapidly in 2020. Thus, according to statistical information published by the police on 15 July 2020, 134 prosecutions for spreading rumours were opened in connection with the epidemic between March 2020 and 14 July 2020.[20] However, on more than one occasion, despite the police's suspicion of scare-mongering, the prosecution upheld complaints made on the grounds that the accused had only expressed their opinion and not stated an untrue (or distorted) fact.[21] In several cases, convictions have already been reported where the perpetrator has edited and published false news about the spread of the coronavirus on the Internet.[22] Considering that in a significant number of cases the allegation was still a case of scare-mongering, while the conviction was a case of a threat to public safe-

19 Gellér and Ambrus, *A magyar büntetőjog általános tanai I.* (2019), 81.

20 Statistics on the criminal cases connected to the coronavirus-situation are available at: https://bit.ly/3xenJ3x

21 E.g. Nem követett el bűncselekményt a rémhírterjesztésért előállított 64 éves férf [A 64-year-old man arrested for scare-mongering was not charged with a criminal offence] (13 May 2020), https://bit.ly/3glhzHS

22 Elítéltek két rémhírterjesztőt, egy másik ellen vádat emeltek [Two scare-mongerers have been sentenced, and a third one has been charged] (22 May 2020), https://bit.ly/3ixc8sg; Elítéltek egy férfit álhírterjesztés miatt [A man was sentenced for scare-mongering] (2 September 2020), https://bit.ly/3xkOOSN

ty, the problem of distinguishing between these two offences will certainly require further study by both legal scholars and practitioners.

However, an even more important aspect for the present analysis is that, should a special legal regime be introduced at any time, whether for reasons of COVID-19 or the spread of other viruses, etc., the Criminal Code should be even more restrictive. Article 337 (2) should only be applied in the case of a statement or rumour of a fact (and not a mere expression of opinion) which is untrue or distorted to such an extent that, despite a true starting point, it is considered to be the same as the untrue fact, and the intention of the perpetrator covers all the elements of the offence.

Bibliography

István Ambrus, 'A Covid-19-világjárvány és a magyar anyagi büntetőjog egyes kérdései' [Covid19-pandemic and Some Issues of Hungarian Substantive Criminal Law'] in Fruzsina Gárdos-Orosz Fruzsina and Viktor Olivér Lőrincz (eds), *Jogi diagnózisok. A Covid-19-világjárvány hatásai a jogrendszerre* [Legal Diagnoses. Impact of the Covid19-pandemic on the Legal System] (L'Harmattan, Budapest 2020) 67.

István Ambrus, 'The COVID-19 pandemic and Hungarian substantive criminal law' (2021) 7–8 *Zeitschrift für Internationale Strafrechtsdogmatik*, 462.

Pál Angyal, *A veszélyes hírkeltés* [The Fear-Mongering] (Attila-Nyomda, Budapest 1942)

Balázs Gellér – István Ambrus, *A magyar büntetőjog általános tanai I.* [The General Part of Hungarian Criminal Law I.] (2nd ed., ELTE Eötvös, Budapest 2019)

Zsolt Balogh, 'A véleménynyilvánítási szabadság értelmezésének a kezdetei Magyarországon' [The Beginnings of the Interpretation of Freedom of Expression in Hungary] (2015) 6 *Acta Humana*, 7.

Mátyás Bencze – Krisztina Ficsor, 'A rémhírterjesztés tényállásának jogalkalmazási kérdései' [Issues of Criminal Practice on Fear-mongering] (2020) *JTI Blog*, https://bit.ly/3vfKfl2

Gábor Halmai: 'Túl kevés és túl sok szólásszabadság – egy utilitarista megközelítés' [Too Little and Too Much Freedom of Speech – a Utilitarian Approach] (2005) 3 *Fundamentum*, 186.

András Koltay: *A szólásszabadság alapvonalai – magyar, angol, amerikai és európai összehasonlításban* [Basics Issues of Free Speech – in Hungarian, English, American and European comparison] (Századvég, Budapest 2009)

András Koltay, 'A rémhírterjesztés büntethetőségének alkotmányosságáról' [On the Constitutionality of Criminalising Fear-mongering] (2020) *Medias Res*, 322.

Miklós Lázár, *A közhangulat káros befolyásolásával elkövetett bűntettek* [Crimes Committed with Detrimental Effects on Public Mood] (KJK, Budapest 1968)

Péter Molnár, 'Uszítás vagy gyalázkodás?' [Insult or Incitement?] (2001) 4 *Fundamentum,* 110.

Péter Molnár, 'Az alkotmányos mérce világosabb értelmezése felé' [Towards a Clearer Interpretation of the Constitutional Standard] (2004) 1 *Fundamentum,* 141.

Ferenc Nagy: 'A nullum crimen/nulla poena sine lege alapelvről' [About Principles of nullum crimen sine lege and nulla poena sine lege] (1995) 5 *Magyar Jog,* 257.

Bernát Török: *Szabadon szólni, demokráciában* [Free to Speak in Democracy] (Budapest: HVG-ORAC 2018)

Statistical Account*

The workload of the Constitutional Court 1990-2011

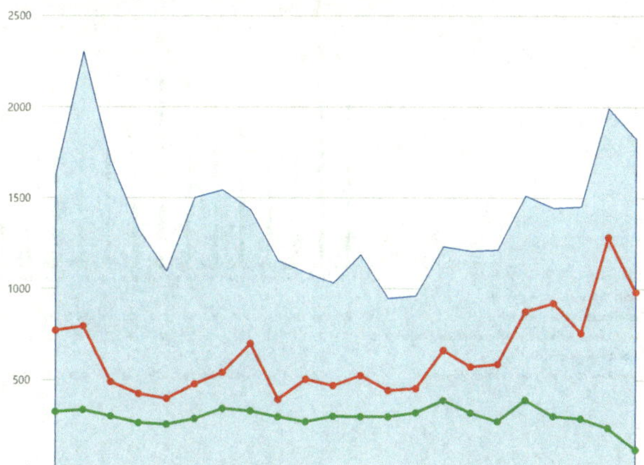

	1990	1991	1992	1993	1994	1995	1996	1997	1998	1999	2000	2001	2002	2003	2004	2005	2006	2007	2008	2009	2010	2011
Number of applications submitted	1625	2302	1700	1323	1098	1501	1543	1434	1155	1091	1031	1188	947	960	1233	1208	1214	1511	1444	1452	1994	1825
New cases assigned to judge rapporteurs	771	795	489	425	398	478	541	699	394	504	469	524	442	453	662	572	587	875	921	757	1284	983
Cases concluded with a decision by the Plenary Session	326	337	301	265	257	288	343	331	298	271	301	299	299	321	388	320	273	390	301	289	238	117

* Botond Bitskey, Secretary General of the Hungarian Constitutional Court

New cases assigned to judge rapporteurs 1990-2011

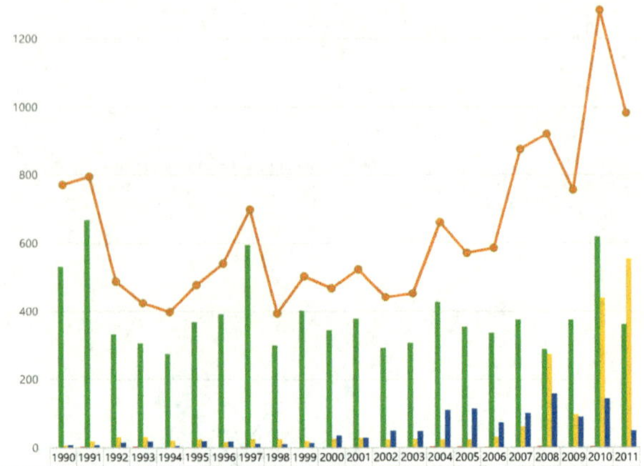

	1990	1991	1992	1993	1994	1995	1996	1997	1998	1999	2000	2001	2002	2003	2004	2005	2006	2007	2008	2009	2010	2011
Preliminary norm control		4	1	4	1		1	3		1	2	1		2	4	4	3	2	5	2	4	
Posterior norm control	532	668	333	306	275	368	391	595	300	402	345	379	293	307	427	355	337	375	290	375	620	362
Judicial initiation for norm control in concrete cases	7	20	31	32	22	25	17	26	26	21	27	30	25	26	25	25	32	63	275	98	440	556
Constitutional complaint	8	8	16	18	6	20	18	12	11	14	36	30	50	49	110	115	74	101	159	91	144	51
New cases assigned to judge rapporteurs	771	795	489	425	398	478	541	699	394	504	469	524	442	453	662	572	587	875	921	757	1284	983

Number of concluded cases 1990-2011

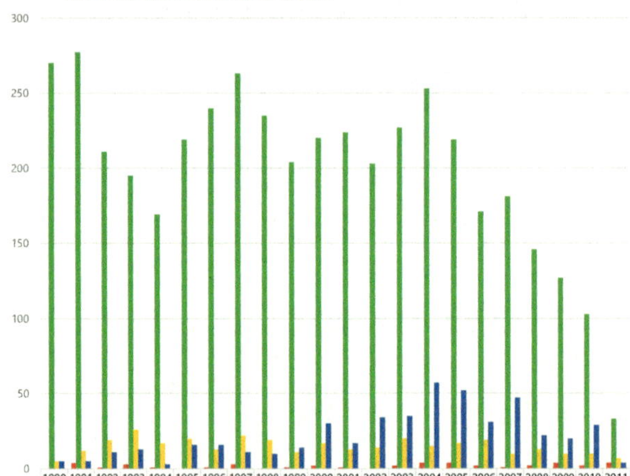

	1990	1991	1992	1993	1994	1995	1996	1997	1998	1999	2000	2001	2002	2003	2004	2005	2006	2007	2008	2009	2010	2011
Preliminary norm control		4	1	3	1		1	3		1	2	1		2	4	4	2	1	2	4	2	4
Posterior norm control	270	277	211	195	169	219	240	263	235	204	220	224	203	227	253	219	171	181	146	127	103	33
Judicial initiation for norm control in concrete cases	5	12	19	26	17	20	13	22	19	11	17	13	14	20	15	17	19	10	13	10	10	7
Constitutional complaint	5	5	11	13	3	16	16	11	10	14	30	17	34	35	57	52	31	47	22	20	29	4

Distribution of cases decided after examination in merits by content 1990-2011

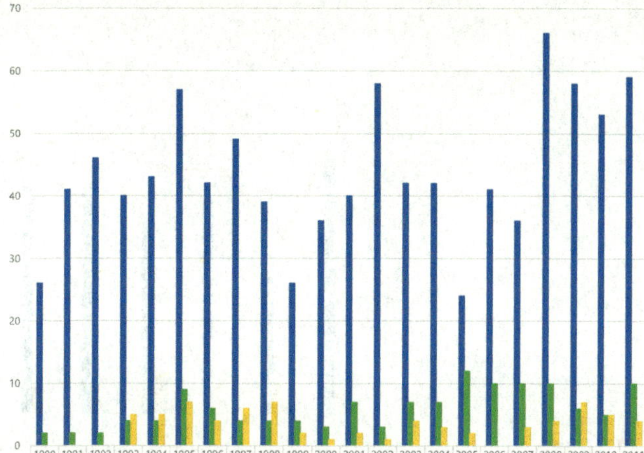

	1990	1991	1992	1993	1994	1995	1996	1997	1998	1999	2000	2001	2002	2003	2004	2005	2006	2007	2008	2009	2010	2011
Annulent of legal regulation/provision	26	41	46	40	43	57	42	49	39	26	36	40	58	42	42	24	41	36	66	58	53	59
Statement of omission	2	2	2	4	4	9	6	4	4	4	3	7	3	7	7	12	10	10	10	6	5	10
Statement of contitutional requirement	0	0	0	5	5	7	4	6	7	2	1	2	1	4	3	2	0	3	4	7	5	4

The workload of the Constitutional Court 2012-2020

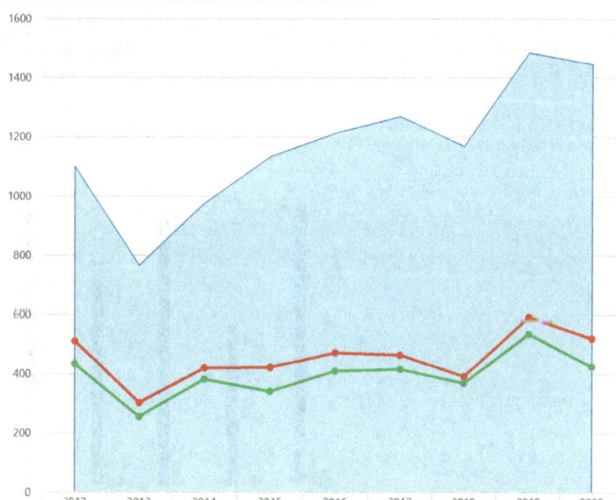

	2012	2013	2014	2015	2016	2017	2018	2019	2020
Number of applications submitted	1100	766	976	1133	1213	1269	1169	1486	1446
Number of new cases assigned to judge rapporteurs	511	302	419	421	471	464	391	592	520
Cases concluded with a decision by the corps	432	255	381	340	409	415	368	535	425

New cases assigned to judge rapporteurs 2012-2020

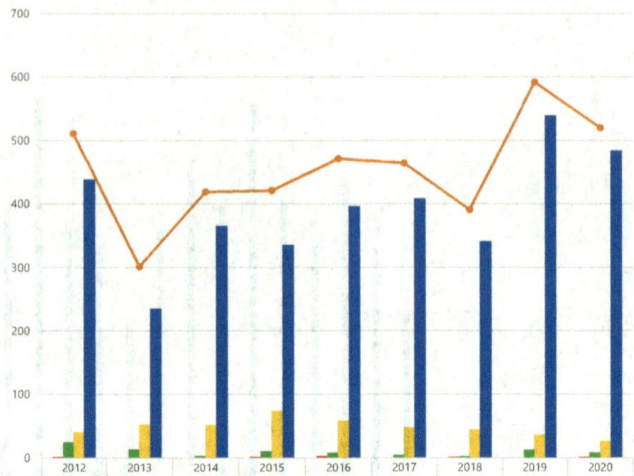

	2012	2013	2014	2015	2016	2017	2018	2019	2020
Preliminary norm control	1			1	3		1		1
Posterior norm control	24	13	3	10	8	4	2	12	8
Judicial initiation for norm control in concrete cases	40	52	51	73	58	47	44	36	26
Constitutional complaint	438	235	365	335	396	408	341	539	483
Number of new cases assigned to judge rapporteurs	511	302	419	421	471	464	391	592	520

Number of concluded cases 2012-2020

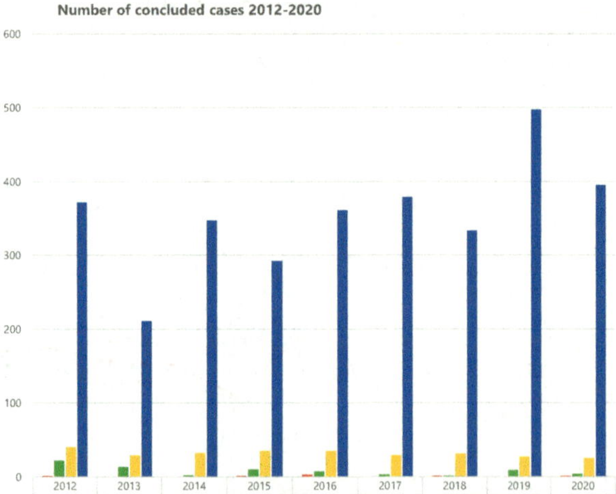

	2012	2013	2014	2015	2016	2017	2018	2019	2020
Preliminary norm control	1			1	3		1		1
Posterior norm control	22	13	2	10	7	3	1	9	4
Judicial initiation for norm control in concrete cases	40	29	32	35	35	29	31	27	25
Constitutional complaint	372	211	347	292	361	379	333	497	395

Number of constitutional complaints assigned to judge rapporteurs 2012-2020

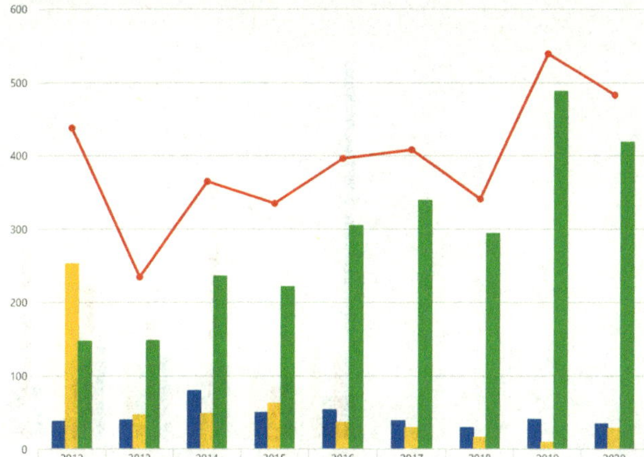

	2012	2013	2014	2015	2016	2017	2018	2019	2020
Based on ACC. Section 26. (1)	38	40	80	50	54	39	30	41	35
Based on ACC. Section 26. (2)	253	47	49	63	37	30	17	10	29
Based on ACC. Section 27.	147	148	236	222	305	339	294	488	419
Total number of constitutional complaints	438	235	365	335	396	408	341	539	483

Number of constitutional complaints 2012-2020

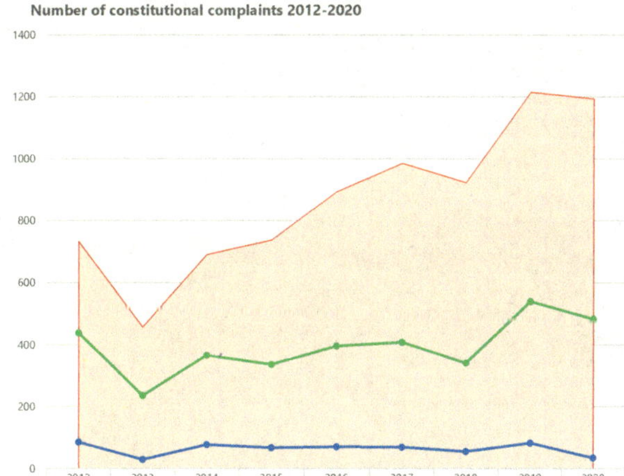

	2012	2013	2014	2015	2016	2017	2018	2019	2020
Constitutional complaints submitted	732	457	690	736	893	985	923	1214	1193
Number of constitutional complaints assigned to judge rapporteurs	438	235	365	335	396	408	341	539	483
Number of constitutional complaint cases decided after examination in merits	85	29	77	67	70	69	55	82	35

Distribution of cases decided after examination in merits by content 2012-2020

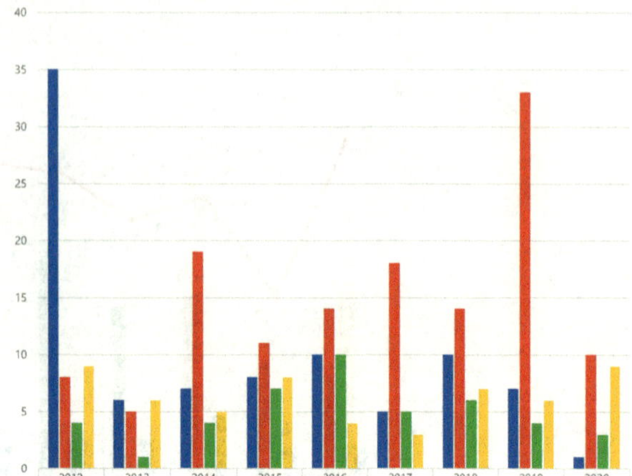

	2012	2013	2014	2015	2016	2017	2018	2019	2020
Annulent of legal regulation/provision	35	6	7	8	10	5	10	7	1
Annulment of judicial verdict or decisions of authorities	8	5	19	11	14	18	14	33	10
Statement of omission	4	1	4	7	10	5	6	4	3
Statement of contitutional requirement	9	6	5	8	4	3	7	6	9

List of Authors

Ádány, Tamás
PhD, Associate professor, Pázmány Péter Catholic University Faculty of Law and Political Sciences (Budapest)

Ambrus, István
PhD, Research fellow, Centre for Social Sciences Institute for Legal Studies (Budapest), and Associate professor, Eötvös Loránd University Faculty of Law (Budapest)

Bándi, Gyula
DSc, Professor, Pázmány Péter Catholic University Faculty of Law and Political Sciences (Budapest)

Békés, Ádám
PhD, Associate professor, Pázmány Péter Catholic University Faculty of Law and Political Sciences (Budapest)

Chronowski, Nóra
PhD, Senior research fellow, Centre for Social Sciences Institute for Legal Studies (Budapest), and University of Public Service Faculty of Law Enforcement (Budapest)

Csink, Lóránt
PhD, Professor, Pázmány Péter Catholic University Faculty of Law and Political Sciences (Budapest)

Deli, Gergely
PhD, Professor, National University of Public Service Faculty of Law Enforcement (Budapest)

Drinóczi, Tímea
DSc, Visiting professor, Federal University of Minas Gerais (Brazil)

Filó, Mihály
PhD, Assistant professor, Eötvös Loránd University Faculty of Law (Budapest)

Gárdos, Péter
PhD, Assistant professor, Eötvös Loránd University Faculty of Law (Budapest)

Gárdos-Orosz, Fruzsina
PhD, Senior research fellow, Centre for Social Sciences Institute for Legal Studies (Budapest), and Associate professor, Eötvös Loránd University Faculty of Law (Budapest)

Tóth J., Zoltán
PhD, Professor, Károli Gáspár University of the Reformed Church in Hungary, Faculty of Law (Budapest)

Jakab, András
DSc, Professor, University of Salzburg; honorary researcher, Pázmány Péter Catholic University Faculty of Law and Political Sciences (Budapest); external researcher, Centre for Social Sciences Institute for Legal Studies (Budapest)

Kiss, Máté Jenő
Doctoral student, Eötvös Loránd University Faculty of Law (Budapest), and Assistant Judge at the Pest District Court (Budapest)

Koltay, András
PhD, Professor, University of Public Service (Budapest), and Pázmány Péter Catholic University Faculty of Law and Political Sciences (Budapest)

Könczöl, Miklós
PhD, Research fellow, Centre for Social Sciences Institute for Legal Studies (Budapest), and Associate professor, Pázmány Péter Catholic University Faculty of Law and Political Sciences (Budapest)

Láncos, Petra Lea
PhD, Associate professor, Pázmány Péter Catholic University Faculty of Law and Political Sciences (Budapest)

Lápossy, Attila
Assistant professor, Eötvös Loránd University Faculty of Law (Budapest)

Osztovits, András
PhD, Professor, Károli Gáspár University of the Reformed Church in Hungary Faculty of Legal Sciences (Budapest)

Pap, András László
DSc, Research professor, Centre for Social Sciences Institute for Legal Studies (Budapest); Professor, Eötvös Loránd University and University of Public Service (Budapest)

Polyák, Gábor
PhD, Senior research fellow, Centre for Social Sciences Institute for Legal Studies (Budapest)

Pozsár-Szentmiklósy, Zoltán
PhD, Associate professor, Eötvös Loránd University Faculty of Law (Budapest)

Schweitzer, Gábor
PhD, Senior research fellow, Centre for Social Sciences, Institute for Legal Studies (Budapest), and Associate professor, National University of Public Service Faculty of Political Science and International Studies (Budapest)

Somody, Bernadette
PhD, Assistant professor, Eötvös Loránd University Faculty of Law (Budapest)

Sulyok, Márton
PhD, Assistant professor, University of Szeged Institute of Public Law

Szeibert, Orsolya
PhD, Professor, Eötvös Loránd University Faculty of Law (Budapest)

Szentgáli-Tóth, Boldizsár
PhD, Research fellow, Centre for Social Sciences Institute for Legal Studies (Budapest)

Török, Bernát
PhD, Associate professor, University of Public Service Faculty of Public Governance and International Studies (Budapest)

Varga, Réka
PhD, Associate professor, Pázmány Péter Catholic University Faculty of Law and Political Sciences (Budapest)

Varju, Márton
PhD, Research professor, Centre for Social Sciences, Institute for Legal Studies (Budapest)

Vincze, Attila
PhD, Senior lecturer, Masaryk University Brno Judicial Studies Institute (Brno)

Vókó†, György
PhD, Director, National Institute of Criminology (Budapest)

Zakariás, Kinga
PhD, Associate professor, Pázmány Péter Catholic University Faculty of Law and Political Sciences (Budapest)